Contemporary Authors®

ISSN 0010-7468

Contemporary Authors®

A Bio-Bibliographical Guide to Current Writers in Fiction, General Nonfiction, Poetry, Journalism, Drama, Motion Pictures, Television, and Other Fields

volume **417**

GALE
A Cengage Company

Farmington Hills, Mich • San Francisco • New York • Waterville, Maine
Meriden, Conn • Mason, Ohio • Chicago

Contemporary Authors, Vol. 417

Project Editor: Catherine C. DiMercurio

Composition and Electronic Capture:
  Charlie Montney

Manufacturing: Keith Helmling

For product information and technology assistance, contact us at
Gale Customer Support, 1-800-877-4253.
For permission to use material from this text or product,
submit all requests online at **www.cengage.com/permissions.**
Further permissions questions can be emailed to
permissionrequest@cengage.com

Gale
27500 Drake Rd.
Farmington Hills, MI, 48331-3535

LIBRARY OF CONGRESS CATALOG CARD NUMBER 81-640179

ISBN-13: 978-1-4103-8699-1

ISSN 0010-7468

This title is also available as an e-book.
ISBN-13: 978-1-4103-8713-4
Contact your Gale sales representative for ordering information.

Printed in Mexico
1 2 3 4 5 6 7 22 21 20 19 18

Contents

CONTENTS

CONTENTS

Preface

Contemporary Authors (*CA*) provides information on approximately 162,000 writers in a wide range of media, including:

- Current writers of fiction, nonfiction, poetry, and drama whose works have been issued by commercial publishers, risk publishers, or university presses. Authors whose books have been published only by known vanity or author-subsidized firms are ordinarily not included.

- Prominent print and broadcast journalists, editors, photojournalists, syndicated cartoonists, graphic novelists, screenwriters, television scriptwriters, and other media people.

- Notable international authors.

- Literary greats of the early twentieth century whose works are popular in today's high school and college curriculums and continue to elicit critical attention.

A *CA* listing entails no charge or obligation. Authors are included on the basis of the above criteria and their interest to *CA* users. Sources of potential listees include trade periodicals, publishers' catalogs, librarians, and other users.

How to Get the Most out of *CA*: Use the Gale Literary Index

The key to locating an author's most recent entry is the Gale Literary Index, which covers all entries in *CA* and *Contemporary Authors New Revision Series* (*CANR*) and can be accessed online at http://www.cengage.com/.

For the convenience of users, the Gale Literary Index also includes references to entries in these Gale literary series: *African-American Writers, African Writers, American Nature Writers, American Writers, American Writers: The Classics, American Writers Retrospective Supplement, American Writers Supplement, Ancient Writers, Asian American Literature, Authors and Artists for Young Adults, Authors in the News, Beacham's Encyclopedia of Popular Fiction: Analyses, Beacham's Encyclopedia of Popular Fiction: Biography and Resources, Beacham's Guide to Literature for Young Adults, Beat Generation: A Gale Critical Companion, Bestsellers, Black Literature Criticism, Black Literature Criticism Supplement, Black Writers, British Writers, British Writers: The Classics, British Writers Retrospective Supplement, British Writers Supplement, Children's Literature Review, Classical and Medieval Literature Criticism, Concise Dictionary of American Literary Biography, Concise Dictionary of American Literary Biography Supplement, Concise Dictionary of British Literary Biography, Concise Dictionary of World Literary Biography, Contemporary American Dramatists, Contemporary Authors Autobiography Series, Contemporary Authors Bibliographical Series, Contemporary British Dramatists, Contemporary Canadian Authors, Contemporary Dramatists, Contemporary Literary Criticism, Contemporary Novelists, Contemporary Poets, Contemporary Popular Writers, Contemporary Southern Writers, Contemporary Women Dramatists, Contemporary Women Poets, Contemporary World Writers, Dictionary of Literary Biography, Dictionary of Literary Biography Documentary Series, Dictionary of Literary Biography Yearbook, DISCovering Authors, DISCovering Authors 3.0, DISCovering Authors: British Edition, DISCovering Authors: Canadian Edition, DISCovering Authors Modules, Drama Criticism, Drama for Students, Encyclopedia of World Literature in the 20th Century, Epics for Students, European Writers, Exploring Novels, Exploring Poetry, Exploring Short Stories, Feminism in Literature, Feminist Writers, Gay & Lesbian Literature, Guide to French Literature, Harlem Renaissance: A Gale Critical Companion, Hispanic Literature Criticism, Hispanic Literature Criticism Supplement, Hispanic Writers, International Dictionary of Films and Filmmakers: Writers and Production Artists, International Dictionary of Theatre: Playwrights, Junior DISCovering Authors, Latin American Writers, Latin American Writers Supplement, Latino and Latina Writers, Literature and Its Times, Literature and Its Times Supplement, Literature Criticism from 1400-1820, Literature of Developing Nations for Students, Major Authors and Illustrators for Children and Young Adults, Major Authors and Illustrators for Children and Young Adults Supplement, Major 21st Century Writers* (eBook version), *Major 20th-Century Writers, Modern American Women Writers, Modern Arts Criticism, Modern Japanese Writers, Mystery and Suspense Writers, Native North American Literature, Nineteenth-Century Literature Criticism, Nonfiction Classics for Students, Novels for Students, Poetry Criticism, Poetry for Students, Poets: American and British, Reference Guide to American Literature, Reference Guide to English Literature, Reference Guide to Short Fiction, Reference Guide to World Literature, Science Fiction Writers, Shakespearean Criticism, Shakespeare for Students, Shakespeare's Characters for Students, Short Stories for Students, Short Story Criticism, Something About the Author, Something About the Author Autobiography Series, St. James Guide to Children's Writers, St. James Guide to Crime & Mystery Writers, St. James Guide to Fantasy Writers, St. James Guide to Horror, Ghost & Gothic Writers, St. James Guide to Science Fiction Writers, St. James Guide to Young Adult Writers, Supernatural Fiction Writers, Twayne Companion to Contemporary Literature in English, Twayne's English Authors, Twayne's United States Authors, Twayne's*

World Authors, Twentieth-Century Literary Criticism, Twentieth-Century Romance and Historical Writers, Twentieth-Century Western Writers, William Shakespeare, World Literature and Its Times, World Literature Criticism, World Literature Criticism Supplement, World Poets, World Writing in English, Writers for Children, Writers for Young Adults, and *Yesterday's Authors of Books for Children.*

How Are Entries Compiled?

The editors compile entries from biographical and bibliographical sources, including the Library of Congress and other national library catalogs, book reviews, author Web sites, and published interviews and feature stories. Each entry is sent to the listee for review, and the author is invited to add personal comments for the Sidelights section.

An asterisk (*) at the end of a sketch indicates that the listing has not been personally verified for this edition by the author.

What Kinds of Information Does An Entry Provide?

Sketches in *CA* contain the following biographical and bibliographical information:

- **Entry heading:** the most common form of author's name, plus any pseudonyms or name variations used for writing.

- **Personal information:** author's date and place of birth, family data, ethnicity, educational background, political and religious affiliations, and hobbies and leisure interests.

- **Addresses:** author's home, office, agent, and email addresses, as available.

- **Career summary:** name of employer, position, and dates held for each career post; résumé of other vocational achievements; military service.

- **Membership information:** professional, civic, and other association memberships and any official posts held.

- **Awards and honors:** military and civic citations, major prizes and nominations, fellowships, grants, and honorary degrees.

- **Writings:** a comprehensive list of titles, publishers, and dates of original publication for books, as well as production information for plays, television scripts, and screenplays.

- **Adaptations:** a list of films or other media that have been adapted from the author's work.

- **Sidelights:** a biographical portrait of the author's development; information about the critical reception of the author's works; revealing comments, often by the author, on personal interests, aspirations, motivations, and thoughts on writing.

- **Autobiographical essay:** odd-numbered CA volumes contain one original essay written by a listee about his or her life and work. The essay is generally accompanied by personal photographs.

- **Biographical and critical sources:** a list of books, periodicals, and Web sites used in compiling the entry or in which additional information on an author's life and/or writings appears.

Available in Electronic Formats

Literature Resource Center. *CA* is available on a subscription basis through Literature Resource Center, a comprehensive online database that features an easy-to-use interface, powerful search capabilities, and ease of access. For more information, call 1-800-877-GALE.

Suggestions Are Welcome

The editors welcome comments and suggestions from users on any aspect of the *CA* series. If readers would like to recommend authors for inclusion in future volumes of the series, they are cordially invited to write the Editors at *Contemporary Authors*, Gale, 27500 Drake Rd., Farmington Hills, MI 48331-3535 or call at 1-248-699-4253.

Indexing note: All *Contemporary Authors* entries are indexed in the Gale Literary Index, which can be accessed online at http://www.cengage.com/ and is the user's guide to the location of an individual author's listing.

CA Numbering System and Volume Update Chart

Occasionally questions arise about the *CA* numbering system and which volumes, if any, can be discarded. Despite numbers such as "29-32R," "97-100" and "417," the entire *CA* print series consists of 684 physical volumes with the publication of *CA* Volume 417. The following charts note changes in the numbering system and cover design, and indicate which volumes are essential for the most complete, up-to-date coverage.

***CA* First Revision**	• 1-4R through 41-44R (11 books) *Cover:* Brown with black and gold trim. There will be no further First Revision volumes as revised entries are now published in the *CA New Revision Series.*
***CA* Original Volumes**	• 45-48 through 97-100 (14 books) *Cover:* Brown with black and gold trim. 101 through 417 (317 books) *Cover:* Blue and black with orange bands. The same as previous *CA* original volumes but with a simplified numbering system and cover design.
***CA* Permanent Series**	• *CAP*-1 and *CAP*-2 (2 books) *Cover:* Brown with red and gold trim. There will be no further Permanent Series volumes as revised entries are now published in the *CA New Revision Series.*
***CA* New Revision Series**	• CANR-1 through CANR-340 (340 books) *Cover:* Blue and black with green bands. Includes only sketches requiring significant changes from any previously published CA, CAP, or CANR volume.

If You Have:	You May Discard:
CA First Revision Volumes 1-4R through 41-44R and *CA Permanent Series* Volumes 1 and 2	*CA* Original Volumes 1, 2, 3, 4 and Volumes 5-6 through 41-44
CA Original Volumes 45-48 through 97-100 and 101 through 417	**NONE:** These volumes will not be superseded by corresponding revised volumes. Individual entries from these and all other volumes appearing in the left column of this chart may be revised and included in the various volumes of the *New Revision Series.*
CA New Revision Series Volumes *CANR*-1 through *CANR*-340	**NONE:** The *New Revision Series* does not replace any single volume of *CA.* Instead, volumes of *CANR* include entries from many previous *CA* series volumes. All *New Revision Series* volumes must be retained for full coverage.

A Sampling of Authors and Media People
Featured in This Volume

Fred Aceves

Aceves has traveled the world, but the setting of his first novel is the place he most wanted to escape when he was young. Born in New York to a Mexican father and a mother of Dominican heritage, the Latino youth was raised in poor working-class neighborhoods from coast to coast. He spent several years in a poverty-stricken section of Tampa, Florida. The teenage Aceves spent so much time hustling spare cash at odd jobs that he ended up dropping out of high school. His discovery of reading at age nineteen helped him escape the cycle of poverty. Aceves attended college and then traveled around the United States, Europe, and South and Central America. Eventually Aceves settled permanently in Mexico, but it was his adolescence in Tampa that inspired his first novel, *The Closest I've Come,* the story of Marcos Rivas, a teenager stuck in a hopeless situation in inner-city Tampa. Marcos resigns himself to failure until a teacher notices the potential behind his poor grades and prankster facade.

Tianxia Bachang

Bachang is a Chinese writer whose real name is Zhang Muye. He holds a degree from the Nanjing Academy of Fine arts, has worked in the finance industry, and is also a popular gamer under his pseudonym. Bachang has written several novels in Chinese, some of which have been adapted for films. Bachang's first novels to be translated to English, *The City of Sand* and its sequel, *The Dragon Ridge Tombs,* were published in 2017 and 2018 and blend ancient Chinese history with modern-day adventure. The books' protagonist is Hu Tianyi, a seventeen-year-old boy who is a gifted practitioner of feng shui. He plans to use his abilities for gold hunting, or finding treasure in the tombs of aristocrats. Tianyi's best friend, Kai, is in on the plan. Their search leads them through difficult terrain, including the Talimakan Desert, where they are tormented by flesh-eating insects, killer sloths, reanimated corpses, and sandstorms.

Kaushik Barua

Barua has worked in international development and public policy for various organizations, including the United Nations. His work has taken him from South Asia to West Africa and Rome, Italy, where he is currently based. Barua holds a degree from St. Stephen's College in New Delhi, India, and has attended the London School of Economics. He is also the author of the novels *Windhorse* and *No Direction Rome.* A fictionalized history of Tibet, *Windhorse* won the Sahitya Academy Yuva Puraskar award and tells the story of a privileged young Indian man named Norbu whose life connects with Lhasang, a refugee from Tibet. Together they fight for Tibetan liberation. An Indian man named Krantik is the protagonist of Barua's 2017 novel *No Direction Rome.* In the novel, described by Barua as a commentary on contemporary rootlessness, the jaded Krantik is living in Rome, where he discourses on his meaningless work, his romantic relationships, and the social media proclivities of his peers.

Zinzi Clemmons

Clemmons's career trajectory as an aspiring novelist was suddenly disrupted when she learned that her mother had late-stage breast cancer. Clemmons had just completed an M.F.A. at Columbia University and had begun work on a traditionally structured novel about HIV/AIDS. Moving back to Philadelphia to care for her mother, she put this novel aside. Though she kept writing during the months that she tended to her dying mother, she could only manage fragmentary notes; eventually, she decided to abandon the novel and focus on weaving her notes into a fictional narrative. The result was *What We Lose,* hailed as an extraordinarily powerful debut novel about identity and the sometimes difficult relationship between a mother and daughter. Like the author, the book's protagonist, Thandi, is the daughter of a mixed-race South African mother and an African American father and was raised in an upscale suburban Philadelphia neighborhood. Thandi shares the challenges that the author faced having been raised by an immigrant mother who never felt fully comfortable in her adopted country. When Thandi is in college, her mother dies of cancer, and Clemmons tells her story in an unconventional, collage-like structure of sentence fragments, short paragraphs, diagrams, and lyrics.

Jessica Fellowes

Fellowes is a self-educated expert on the social history of the United Kingdom between the two world wars. Since childhood she has shared this interest with her uncle Julian Fellowes, who had acquired a substantial collection of anecdotes and first-person stories from their older family members. Julian went on to write and produce the hit television series *Downton Abbey,* a period drama set in England during and after World War I, and Jessica became the author of colorful companion volumes to the series, such as *The World of Downton Abbey* and *Downton Abbey: A Celebration.* After the series ended in 2016, Fellowes penned a crime novel, the first in a projected series set in the 1920s about the six sisters in the unconventional Mitford family. *The Mitford Murders* is a fictional exploration of the actual murder of the granddaughter of Civil War nurse Florence Nightingale on Christmas Eve, 1919—a murder that Fellowes connects to the eccentric Mitfords.

Keely Hutton

A former schoolteacher turned journalist, Hutton is the author of *Soldier Boy,* a novel based on the wartime experiences of Ricky Richard Anywar. In 1989, at the age of fourteen, Anywar was forced to become a soldier in the guerrilla army of Ugandan warlord Joseph Kony. Anywar was trained, armed, and then forced to fight alongside his rebel kidnappers. Ten years later, while the civil war was still raging and international organizations were unable to safely provide assistance, he founded Friends of Orphans to help former child soldiers like himself. *Soldier Boy* begins by relating the true story of Anywar as a child soldier and then moves forward twenty years to tell the story of the fictionalized character of Samuel, whose experiences as a boy soldier lead to an overriding fear and distrust of everyone around him, and who serves as a composite of the many children that Anywar helped through Friends of Orphans.

Aja Monet

Monet won the prestigious Nuyorican Poets Café Grand Slam Champion title when she was only nineteen years old, and she has since gone on to win the Andrea Klein Willison Prize for Poetry and the New York City YWCA "One to Watch Award." Monet's first collection, *The Black Unicorn Sings,* was published in 2010, and she next teamed with Saul Williams and Dufflyn Lammers to edit the poetry collection *Chorus: A Literary Mixtape* in 2012. Monet's second poetry collection, *My Mother Was a Freedom Fighter,* followed in 2017. With *My Mother Was a Freedom Fighter,* Monet intermingles verses concerned with coming-of-age with those about female power. Several poems celebrate black womanhood, the power of resistance, and the violence of racism. From her childhood in Brooklyn to her school days in Chicago, Monet covers the many metamorphoses that take place on the journey from childhood to adulthood. In this manner, Monet seeks to explore the nature of womanhood, both in herself and in her role models.

Wesley Snipes

Snipes is a well-known actor, film producer, and action film star who has appeared in more than seventy films, including *Passenger 57, Demolition Man, New Jack City, Jungle Fever, White Men Can't Jump,* and *Waiting to Exhale.* He also played the title character of Blade in a trilogy of movies featuring that Marvel Comics character. Blade is a half-vampire, half-human who becomes a vampire hunter and protects the human race against these creatures of the night. As an entrepreneur, Snipes cofounded Amen-Ra Films, its subsidiary Black Dot Media, and the Royal Guard of Amen-Ra, a security and bodyguard company for high-end clients. With *Talon of God,* Snipes adds novelist to his list of accomplishments. The novel, written with Ray Norman, is an action-based thriller very much in line with Snipes's roles in *Blade* and other high-energy films. It is also a very spiritual story, boosted by a war between literal angels and demons unfolding on the streets of Chicago and featuring the mysterious Talon Hunter, a sword-wielding superpowered protector who is a messenger of God.

Fred Aceves

■ Personal

Born in NY; married.

■ Addresses

Agent—Louise Fury, Bent Agency, 19 W. 21st St., Ste. 201, New York, NY 10010.

■ Career

Writer. Worked as teacher of English as a second language and as freelance translator and editor.

■ Writings

The Closest I've Come, HarperTeen (New York, NY), 2017.

■ Sidelights

Fred Aceves has traveled the world, but the setting of his first novel is the place he most wanted to escape when he was young. Born in New York to a Mexican father and a mother of Dominican heritage, the Latino youth was raised in poor working-class neighborhoods from coast to coast. He spent several years in a poverty-stricken section of Tampa, Florida. The teenage Aceves spent so much time hustling spare cash at odd jobs that he ended up dropping out of high school. "Too much happened . . . to summarize here," he wrote at his website, "but bits of that time tend to creep into my writing." When he discovered reading at age nineteen, escape from his cycle of poverty became a reality.

Aceves attended college and found work wherever he could, as a cook and food server, a car salesman, or a delivery person. He worked sometimes as an editor or translator, and often as a teacher of English as a second language. Aceves traveled around the United States, then ventured abroad to live in Europe—from France to the Czech Republic—and Latin America. In Buenos Aires, Argentina, he joined a group of expatriate North American writers with the notion of becoming an author himself. Eventually Aceves settled permanently in Mexico, but it was his adolescence in Tampa that inspired his first novel—"that difficult period . . . of first experiences and profound transformations," he explained at his website.

The Closest I've Come is the story of Marcos Rivas, a teenager stuck in a hopeless situation in inner-city Tampa. His home life is miserable, shared with an indifferent mother and her abusive boyfriend. His scattered menial jobs prevent him from striking out on his own or even finding a girlfriend. His flawed Spanish marks him as an outsider in the greater Latino community, and he is the product of a harsh environment that discourages him from expressing his true feelings in any language. School offers no haven from the racism and violence of the streets—and no hope for a better life. Marcos resigns himself to failure until a teacher notices the potential behind his poor grades and prankster facade.

Marcos is enrolled, unwillingly at first, in an after-school mentorship program for underachieving students like himself. Slowly he begins to recognize that he is no longer alone in the world. He might not end up delivering drugs for a living like his best friend Obie. He might even catch the eye of Amy, that resilient punk-music fan with the blue streaks in her hair. With the support of his new-found, nontraditional "family," Marcos can finally envision a goal that is worthy of his effort.

The Closest I've Come is "a remarkable debut novel," reported Charla Hollingsworth in *Voice of Youth Advocates*. Melissa Williams noted in *School Library Journal* that "the theme of finding family in unexpected places is valuable." Williams especially appreciated the "nuanced character development" that Marcos experiences as he comes of age, and she commended the author for balancing the "heavy subject material" with "ample doses of comedy." A *Kirkus Reviews* contributor observed: "Aceves infuses the narrative with insight about class, ethnicity, and the intricacies of power" in a story that is "heart-wrenching, funny, hopeful, and not-to-be-missed." A *Publishers Weekly* contributor recommended *The Closest I've Come* in a starred review as "a memorable, hard-hitting portrait of a teenager trying to shape his own destiny." It is an "inspirational" novel, according to Kristina Pino's assessment in *Booklist*, "about that kid readers all know . . . who deserves to have a shot at life." At the same time, Hollingsworth noted, Aceves conveys the message "that being true to yourself can be the option that requires the most courage."

■ **Biographical and Critical Sources**

PERIODICALS

Booklist, October 15, 2017, Kristina Pino, review of *The Closest I've Come*, p. 50.
Kirkus Reviews, September 1, 2017, review of *The Closest I've Come*.
Publishers Weekly, October 9, 2017, review of *The Closest I've Come*, p. 69.
School Library Journal, October, 2017, Melissa Williams, review of *The Closest I've Come*, p. 102.
Voice of Youth Advocates, August, 2017, Charla Hollingsworth, review of *The Closest I've Come*, p. 52.

ONLINE

Fred Aceves Website, https://fredaceves.com (March 9, 2018).*

Melissa Albert

■ **Personal**

Married. *Education:* Attended University of Iowa, c. 2001-03; Columbia College, Chicago, IL, B.J., 2006.

■ **Addresses**

Home—Brooklyn, NY. *Agent*—Faye Bender, Book Group, 20 W. 20th St., Ste. 601, New York, NY 20011.

■ **Career**

Powell's Books, Chicago, IL, bookseller, 2003-05; *Encyclopaedia Britannica*, Chicago, copy editor, 2006-08, research editor, 2008-10; Brooklyn Museum, Brooklyn, NY, associate editor and web editor, 2010-13; Barnes & Noble, Inc., New York, NY, editor of *B&N Reads*, 2013-16, founding editor of *Barnes & Noble Teen Blog*, beginning 2013, and managing editor of *BN.com* website. Also worked as freelance research editor, copy editor, and proofreader. Reckless Records, record seller, 2004-05; Madwell, copywriter, 2013.

■ **Writings**

The Hazel Wood, Flatiron Books (New York, NY), 2018.

Contributor to periodicals, including *Chicago Journal, Hairpin, Hollywood Crush, McSweeney's, SparkLife,* and *Time Out Chicago.*

■ **Sidelights**

When Melissa Albert published her first teen novel, she had already spent several years in the book business. The Illinois native began her career in Chicago in 2006 as a copy editor for *Encyclopaedia Britannica.* A year later she was supplementing her income as a freelance writer for local periodicals. Albert moved to New York City in 2010 to work for the Brooklyn Museum as an associate editor and web editor. She also worked as a copy editor of fiction for young readers. In 2013 Albert joined publisher Barnes & Noble as a blogger and editor of *B&N Teen Blog* and *B&N Reads.* Wherever she lived and worked, Albert brought with her a lifelong love of fairytales and fantasy novels, and not just the "happy ending" variety. She told an interviewer at *Book Wars* that her debut novel is "informed by all the stories and books I've loved since I was a kid."

The Hazel Wood was described in *Kirkus Reviews* as a "pitch-black fantasy." It features three generations of women toughened by lifetimes of flight from bad luck bordering on terror. The youngest is Alice Proserpine, who—at age seventeen—is endowed by her creator with the ambience of "a world-weary noir detective . . . resourceful, whip-smart, and incredibly impulsive," according to Emma Carbone's assessment in *School Library Journal.* Alice has spent her entire life on the road or in hiding. Until now she has been protected by her mother Ella, but Ella is missing, kidnapped perhaps by interlopers from the Hinterland first exposed by Alice's grandmother Althea many years ago.

Readers learn that Althea achieved cult status in the 1980s when she published *Tales from the Hinterland,* stories described in *Kirkus Reviews* as "simultaneously wondrous and horrific, dreamlike and bloody, lyrical and creepy, . . . brutally cruel." Then Althea retreated to her Hazel Wood estate to spend the rest of her life in seclusion. Alice never met her or read the book, which is now almost impossible to find. When news of Althea's death reaches the fugitives, they believe the family curse has died with her. Then Ella disappears, leaving Alice with a warning to stay away from the Hazel Wood.

Alice cannot stay away. Furious that otherworldly visitors have the power to draw her into their evil world, she resolves to track them to their source and destroy their hold over her family. Their source seems to be the Hazel Wood, a mysterious location that had never been revealed to the teenager. Alice recruits classmate and obsessive Hinterland fanatic Ellery Finch to help her find the elusive estate. He is only too happy to help, until the darkness descends upon their journey. "The ruthless citizens of the Hinterland creep further and further into reality," explained Caitlyn Paxson in her interview at *NPR.org*. When Alice arrives at the portal that Althea called the Hazel Wood, she realizes that the answers to her questions lie on the other side. She must decide whether the truth is worth the price she may have to pay for it.

"Some fairy tales ask to be lived in," Maggie Reagan observed in her *Booklist* review. *The Hazel Wood* is not one of them, she pointed out, "yet it is a dark story that readers will have trouble leaving behind." "The smoke-and-mirrors world of the Hazel Wood is deliciously creepy," noted Elizabeth Norton in *Voice of Youth Advocates*, and "Alice is a likeable, slightly jaded heroine" with a secret identity unknown even to her. A *Publishers Weekly* contributor highlighted "Alice's sharp-edged narration" and her determination "to be in charge of her own story."

Multiple reviewers recognized the affinity of Albert's work to classic fairytale literature. She has been credited with reworking parts of familiar stories into original and unsettling tales of her own. Albert filled the volume with references that reveal an intimate knowledge of children's literary classics. She peppered the narrative with snippets of frightening tales attributed to Althea's original collection, mimicking the traditional structure and foreboding tone of the darkest of the world's classics.

Paxson offered a mixed review of *The Hazel Wood*: "I enjoyed this book very much. But it also made me melancholy." She explained: "There is never a moment where we are allowed to look around the Hinterland and enjoy it." She would have preferred a story that could "show us how to win against the dark." Albert may not offer readers a typical happy ending, but Carbone informed readers of *School Library Journal*: "An aggressive lack of romance and characters transcending their plots make this story an empowering read."

For readers who might, like Paxson, wish for a chance to explore the Hinterland in greater detail, Kaley Connell—who on her website called *The Hazel Wood* "beautiful, and dark, and twisted"— offered hope. She learned from the author at a book signing that Albert has two more books in progress. One is expected to be another novel set in the world of *The Hazel Wood*. The other is a collection of the full-length Hinterland stories referenced in Albert's debut.

■ Biographical and Critical Sources

PERIODICALS

Booklist, November 15, 2017, Maggie Reagan, review of *The Hazel Wood*, p. 52.

Kirkus Reviews, October 15, 2017, review of *The Hazel Wood*.

Publishers Weekly, November 13, 2017, review of *The Hazel Wood*, p. 65.

School Library Journal, October, 2017, Emma Carbone, review of *The Hazel Wood*, p. 102.

Voice of Youth Advocates, December, 2017, Elizabeth Norton, review of *The Hazel Wood*, p. 64.

ONLINE

Book Wars, http://thebookwars.ca/ (January 21, 2018), author interview.

Kaley Connell Website, https://kaleyconnell. wordpress.com/ (February 2, 2018), review of *The Hazel Wood*.

NPR.org, https://www.npr.org/ (January 30, 2018), Caitlyn Paxson, review of *The Hazel Wood*.*

Stephen Alford

1970-

■ **Also Known As**

Stephen Anthony Alford

■ **Personal**

Born 1970, in Telford, England; married; children: Matilda. *Education:* Attended University of St. Andrews.

■ **Addresses**

Agent—George Lucas, InkWell Management, 521 5th Ave., New York, NY 10175.

■ **Career**

Cambridge University, Cambridge, England, British Academy postdoctoral research fellow and junior research fellow of Fitzwilliam College, 1997-99, Ehrman senior research fellow in history at King's College, 1999-2012, became assistant lecturer, lecturer, and senior lecturer in history; University of Leeds, Leeds, England, professor of early modern British history, 2012—, and department chair.

■ **Member**

Royal Historical Society (fellow).

■ **Writings**

The Early Elizabethan Polity: William Cecil and the British Succession Crisis, 1558-1569, Cambridge University Press (New York, NY), 1998.

Kingship and Politics in the Reign of Edward VI, Cambridge University Press (New York, NY), 2002.

Burghley: William Cecil at the Court of Elizabeth I, Yale University Press (New Haven, CT), 2008.

The Watchers: A Secret History of the Reign of Elizabeth I, Allen Lane (London, England), 2012.

Edward VI: The Last Boy King, Allen Lane (London, England), 2014.

London's Triumph: Merchant Adventurers and the Tudor City, Allen Lane (London, England), 2017.

■ **Sidelights**

Stephen Alford has won a reputation as a meticulous yet highly readable historian. He focuses his expertise upon the complicated era of Shakespeare and Marlowe, Sir Francis Drake, Mary Queen of Scots, and Elizabeth the Virgin Queen. His subjects tend, however, to be the unheralded or underestimated powers behind the throne and the entrepreneurs whose accomplishments contributed to England's rise to global prominence.

Alford was born in the British Midlands and educated in Scotland. He spent fifteen years at Cambridge University before moving to Leeds in 2012. Alford teaches early modern British history, which spans roughly the time period from 1500 to 1750.

Kingship and Politics in the Reign of Edward VI

The boy-king Edward VI, son of Henry VIII, reigned for only five or six years, dying at age fifteen of an undetermined pulmonary illness. Alford paints him as the ruler-in-training who laid the groundwork for the spectacular reign of his half-sister Elizabeth I. In *Kingship and Politics in the Reign of Edward VI,* Alford deviates from the prevalent focus on Edward's role in the success of the English Protestant Reformation. Instead he explores the political maneuverings that shaped the youth's historical legacy. Robert Braddock noted in *Renaissance Quarterly* that Alford "studied how politics actually worked and discovered a surprising degree of continuity and stability."

The young king was by necessity subject to the guidance of councilors and other members of the royal court. This resulted in a shift from the concept of governance by royal prerogative to polity by "parliamentary consent," as Dale Hoak described it in his *Albion* review. In dozens of documents contemporaneous with Edward's reign, Alford sees "a maturing king beginning to assert himself," Braddock reported, as evidenced in part by the dying youth's determination to control his succession. Both Braddock and Hoak mentioned flaws in Alford's thesis, but they found the work to offer a valuable perspective on Edward's legacy. Alford also offers a more recent summary of Edward's life in *Edward VI: The Last Boy King,* intended for a general audience.

Burghley

Burghley: William Cecil at the Court of Elizabeth I is the story of a young man who rose from the shadows of Edward's court to become Lord High Treasurer to Elizabeth I. In his faculty profile at the University of Leeds website, Alford described him as "the most powerful man in Elizabethan England." Cecil was a complicated man. This defender of the Protestant cause at Edward's court served the business interests of the young king's primary counselors, then turned his back on them to save himself. The scourge of Catholicism tortured priests, destroyed churches, and eventually arranged the execution of Mary Stuart, Queen of Scots, but he briefly embraced Catholicism to gain influence over Edward's half-sister Mary Tudor. Cecil's relationship with Elizabeth was often contentious, as he urged her in directions that she opposed—and sometimes rejected, but there were times when he virtually ran the country. According to D.R. Bisson in an assessment for *Choice,* Alford "regards Cecil as a committed Protestant determined to defend his faith."

"Here," wrote Michael Questier in *Catholic Historical Review,* "is the master polemicist and ideologue who formulated some of the crucial theoretical and legal defenses of the Elizabethan regime." To Questier, *Burghley* is an "intensely readable biogra-

phy." Leanda de Lisle observed in the *Spectator:* "Alford's scholarly but pacey biography reads so fluently, and his subject's career is so rich, it felt over too quickly." She added that Cecil "really leaps from the page . . . as politician and propagandist, . . . dynamic, ruthless and with a long reach."

The Watchers

In *The Watchers: A Secret History of the Reign of Elizabeth I,* Alford emphasizes that Elizabethan England was in dire straits. English Protestants were quite literally terrified of a Catholic takeover of the monarchy and the entire country. The pope had declared the Protestant Elizabeth a heretic and a bastard. European priests and English expatriates schemed to infiltrate the country. Nearly 500 native priests plotted against her; political and religious radicals devised plans to murder her and replace her with her imprisoned cousin, the Catholic Mary Queen of Scots. The Spanish king Philip II was waiting in the wings; he had already attempted three invasions. The final danger: Elizabeth was childless and resolutely determined to remain that way. With no legitimate heir, the very House of Tudor was under threat of extinction.

Elizabeth's defenders schemed relentlessly to protect the realm by any means necessary. *The Watchers* is "a page-turning tale of assassination plots, torture, and espionage," reported a reviewer in *Publishers Weekly.* The queen's secret agents even concocted a phony plot to rescue Mary from prison in order to trick her into incriminating herself in the treason.

"Alford has written an exhilarating and well-researched history," observed Tessa Minchew in *Library Journal.* Patricia Treble commented in *Maclean's* that "Alford weaves an exciting tale of intrigue, mystery and danger from the spies' and traitors' points of view." Alan Judd summarized in the *Spectator:* "If you want to know the inside story of that struggle, . . . this is the book to read."

London's Triumph

Elizabethan England was an economic hinterland compared to the wealth and glamour of European trading cities like Antwerp, but times were changing. *London's Triumph: Merchant Adventurers and the Tudor City* is Alford's story of a place and a time when entrepreneurship and serendipity combined to bring a stagnant backwater to life. The city of London teemed with foreigners, who brought with them visions of the riches of China and the untapped treasures of the New World. Merchants and adventurers saw opportunities everywhere, and the destitute monarchy envisioned much-needed sources of income from expanded trade routes. Clever investors devised ways to bypass anti-usury laws and profit from money-lending ventures. Religious violence on the continent drove European traders to the safer harbors west of the English Channel.

Alford shines his spotlight on the men who made it happen. There was Anthony Jenkinson, an unknown seafaring merchant who accidentally ended up in medieval Russia at the table of Ivan the Terrible. There was the geographer and travel writer Richard Hakluyt, who made it possible to populate, then colonize, the future Commonwealth of Virginia. Countless others made contributions, and Alford shares their stories great and small. According to Jessie Childs, writing in the London *Guardian*, "he throws out long threads . . . and weaves them into an exceptionally rich and variegated fabric." His "stories bring the past to life in warmly human terms," observed a commentator in *Kirkus Reviews*, "as do [his] evocative descriptions of the city's changing landscape and architecture." "Alford's touch is sure," reported Lucy Wooding on the *Times Higher Education* website; "to read this book is to stand abashed at the achievements."

■ Biographical and Critical Sources

PERIODICALS

Albion, fall, 2003, Dale Hoak, review of *Kingship and Politics in the Reign of Edward VI*, p. 466.

Booklist, August 1, 2012, Gilbert Taylor, review of *The Watchers: A Secret History of the Reign of Elizabeth I*, p. 21; October 15, 2017, Bryce Christensen, review of *London's Triumph: Merchants, Adventurers, and Money in Shakespeare's City*, p. 10.

Catholic Historical Review, October, 2009, Michael Questier, review of *Burghley: William Cecil at the Court of Elizabeth I*, p. 837.

Choice, July, 2009, D.R. Bisson, review of *Burghley*, p. 2190.

Christian Science Monitor, December 18, 2012, Emily Cataneo, review of *The Watchers*.

Contemporary Review, September, 2002, review of *Kingship and Politics in the Reign of Edward VI*, p. 188.

English Historical Review, April, 2003, G.W. Bernard, review of *Kingship and Politics in the Reign of Edward VI*, 496.

Guardian (London, England), July 6, 2013, Keith Thomas, review of *The Watchers*, p. 18.

History Today, September, 2008, Derek Wilson, review of *Burghley*, p. 61.

Kirkus Reviews, September 15, 2012, review of *The Watchers*; October 1, 2017, review of *London's Triumph*.

Library Journal, September 15, 2012, Tessa Minchew, review of *The Watchers*, p. 78.

Maclean's, January 21, 2013, Patricia Treble, review of *The Watchers*, p. 57.

New Statesman, January 9, 2015, review of *Edward VI*, p. 41.

New Yorker, February 11, 2013, review of *The Watchers*, p. 109.

Publishers Weekly, July 2, 2012, review of *The Watchers*, p. 54. October 9, 2017, review of *London's Triumph*, p. 57.

Renaissance Quarterly, autumn, 2003, Robert C. Braddock, review of *Kingship and Politics in the Reign of Edward VI*, p. 879.

Spectator, July 5, 2008, Leanda de Lisle, review of *Burghley*, p. 40; September 8, 2012, Alan Judd, review of *The Watchers*, p. 35; April 22, 2017, Sinclair McKay, review of *London's Triumph*, p. 38.

ONLINE

Guardian Online, https://www.theguardian.com/ (April 20, 2017), Jessie Childs, review of *London's Triumph*.

Kirkus Reviews Online, https://www.kirkusreviews.com/ (September 12, 2017), review of *London's Triumph*.

Times Higher Education, https://www.timeshighereducation.com/ (April 27, 2017), Lucy Wooding, review of *London's Triumph* and author interview.

University of Leeds Website, http://www.leeds.ac.uk/ (March 11, 2018), author profile.

Washington Independent Review of Books, http://www.washingtonindependentreviewofbooks.com/ (December 16, 2017), Alice Padwe, review of *London's Triumph*.*

Mesu Andrews

1963-

■ Personal

Born December 12, 1963; married, 1984; husband's name Roy; children: two. *Religion:* Christian.

■ Addresses

Home—NC.

■ Career

Writer.

■ Writings

NOVELS

Love amid the Ashes, Revell (Grand Rapids, MI), 2011.
Love's Sacred Song, Revell (Grand Rapids, MI), 2012.
Love in a Broken Vessel, Revell (Grand Rapids, MI), 2013.
In the Shadow of Jezebel, Revell (Grand Rapids, MI), 2014.
The Pharaoh's Daughter, WaterBrook (Colorado Springs, CO), 2015.
Miriam, WaterBrook (Colorado Springs, CO), 2016.
Isaiah's Daughter, WaterBook (Colorado Springs, CO), 2018.

■ Sidelights

Mesu Andrews is a writer based in North Carolina. She writes novels based on stories found in the Bible. In an interview with Brock Eastman that ap-

peared on Eastman's self-titled website, Andrews asserted: "My ONLY genre is biblical fiction. My first love is the study of God's Word. Biblical novels give me an excuse to keep my nose buried in the Bible and research books! What a joy to share with others both the passion and pleasure of my heart. I am most blessed."

Love amid the Ashes and *Love's Sacred Song*

Love amid the Ashes is Andrews's first novel. This retelling of the story of Job finds God and Satan betting against one another on Job's ability to withstand tragedy without cursing God. The book received mixed reviews. "Andrews fails to breathe humanity into her characters, though she gives it a good effort. Her purpose here seems more didactic," wrote a critic on the *Historical Novel Society* website. Joanne Renaud, a reviewer on the *Dear Author* website, commented: "*Love amid the Ashes* is a fascinating and frustrating book." Renaud added: "As a debut novel, it's an impressive achievement, and a great example of what midrash can accomplish. But there are a lot of problems with it. I'm not sure if the problems originate from the heavily patriarchal nature of the Old Testament, and the evangelical desire to take the original text literally. Or perhaps the problems originate from the passive nature of the protagonist. Or maybe it's all of the above."

In *Love's Sacred Song,* Andrews takes on another section of the Old Testament, the Song of Solomon. She focuses on the transition of power from King David to King Solomon. Other characters include Jehoshaphat, his daughter Arielah, and David's concubine, Abishag. A contributor to the *Historical Novel Society* website remarked: "This novel is a beautiful, dangerous, and romantically fictional portrayal of the world around this love of all loves." Ruth Anderson, a writer on the *Booktalk & More* website, suggested: "Rich with atmosphere and historical detail, including fascinating glimpses into everything from wedding customs to court protocol and intrigue, *Love's Sacred Song* is sure to delight historical and biblical fiction lovers alike. With lead characters who send sparks flying from the page and a host of well-drawn supporting players, Mesu Andrews's second novel is a rich, meaty read that will not only entertain, but if you'll let it, challenge and grow your faith, inspiring a deeper appreciation for the texts from which *Song* draws its inspiration."

Love in a Broken Vessel and *In the Shadow of Jezebel*

Andrews retells the biblical story of Hosea and Gomer in *Love in a Broken Vessel*. The two were childhood friends, but they lost touch. After a message from God, Hosea finds Gomer in Samaria and marries her, despite the fact that she has been working as a prostitute. "The author provides an engrossing and believable take on the biblical story with its universal themes," suggested a reviewer on the *Historical Novel Society* website. A critic on the *Good Book Reviews* website remarked: "This is one of the best examples of modern Christian fiction written primarily for women."

A young woman named Jehosheba prepares to take the throne as Queen of Destiny in the novel *In the Shadow of Jezebel*. According to a writer on the *Historical Novel Society* website: "Andrews' latest novel is packed with political intrigue and the clash of two religions." Amanda Geaney, a contributor to the *Christian Shelf-Esteem* website, commented: "This intriguing novel never slows but continues to draw the reader in through it's entirety. Prepare to be transported back in time through vivid descriptions. . . . The well researched details are truly insightful and enrich the storyline without becoming arduous."

The Pharaoh's Daughter and *Miriam*

The Pharaoh's Daughter tells the story of the title character, tracing her life from childhood until the fateful day when she discovers a baby in a basket floating in the Nile. In her interview with Eastman, Andrews discussed the theme of the book. She stated: "Each of my books has had an overarching theme. Job's story (*Love amid the Ashes*) spoke to those who suffer. Gomer and Hosea's story (*Love in a Broken Vessel*) challenged readers to God-sized forgiveness and the promise of God's grace. *The Pharaoh's Daughter* tackles that nagging—sometimes debilitating—emotion of fear. On September 11, 2001, our entire nation experienced fear, but fear was daily reality for the Hebrews in ancient Egypt. Personally, I have grown up afraid—why? I have no idea." Andrews continued: "I remember being afraid of the dark. Afraid a fire would burn down our house. Afraid of dogs. Afraid of . . . you name it. As I'm writing this, I'm afraid I'll run out of coffee creamer. We're all afraid of something. When the Pharaoh's Daughter pulled a Hebrew baby from the Nile, I believe she was motivated by fear. This book explores the choices that grew out of her fear and leads the reader through the consequences and victories, the joys and sorrows of those choices—and the faith that frees her from fear's prison." In a review of the book on the *Historical Novel Society* website, a contributor remarked: "Andrews grounds her story in the Biblical tradition and in the historical record and creates well-drawn, interesting characters."

Moses's sister is the star of Andrews's next Bible-based novel, *Miriam.* "This novel is biblical fiction at its finest," asserted a *Publishers Weekly* reviewer. A writer on the *Historical Novel Society* website commented: "This book propels the reader along to its climactic ending." The same writer described the book as "a thoroughly delightful read."

Isaiah's Daughter

In *Isaiah's Daughter*, Andrews retells the story of Ishma. Born a slave, she is ultimately adopted by Isaiah and marries Prince Hezekiah.

A *Publishers Weekly* critic offered a favorable assessment of *Isaiah's Daughter*, commenting: "Andrews's excellent tale invites readers to have a new appreciation for the time of the prophets." "Andrews, known for providing voice to women typically in the margins of biblical stories, paints a beautiful tale with heartfelt characters," asserted a contributor to the *Historical Novel Society* website. The same contributor described the book as "a very well-researched and deeply felt novel. Recommended."

■ Biographical and Critical Sources

PERIODICALS

Publishers Weekly, February 8, 2016, review of *Miriam*, p. 56; October 30, 2017, review of *Isaiah's Daughter*, p. 65.

ONLINE

Booktalk & More, http://booktalkandmore.blogspot.
com/ (March 20, 2012), Ruth Anderson, review of
Love's Sacred Song.

Brock Eastman Website, https://www.brockeastman.
com/ (February 23, 2017), Brock Eastman, author
interview.

Christian Shelf-Esteem, https://christianshelfesteem.
wordpress.com/ (May 21, 2014), Amanda Geaney,
review of *In the Shadow of Jezebel.*

Dear Author, http://dearauthor.com/ (May 5, 2015),
Joanne Renaud, review of *Love amid the Ashes.*

Good Book Reviews, http://www.goodbookreviews.
org.uk/ (September 3, 2014), review of *Love in a
Broken Vessel.*

Historical Novel Society, https://historicalnovel
society.org/ (August 1, 2011), review of *Love amid
the Ashes;* (May 1, 2012), review of *Love's Sacred
Song;* (August 1, 2013), review of *Love in a Broken
Vessel;* (May 1, 2014), review of *In the Shadow of Jezebel;* (August 1, 2015), review of *The Pharaoh's
Daughter;* (May 1, 2016), review of *Miriam;* (February 1, 2018), review of *Isaiah's Daughter.*

Mesu Andrews Website, http://mesuandrews.com
(March 21, 2018).

Novel Reviews, http://novelreviews.blogspot.com/
(March 1, 2016), Sarah Meyers, review of *The
Pharaoh's Daughter.**

Alys Arden

■ Also Known As

Lauren Alys
Lauren Alys Puglia

■ Personal

Born in New Orleans, LA. *Education:* University of New Orleans, B.S.B.A., 2003; RMIT University, Melbourne, Australia, M.A., 2008.

■ Addresses

Agent—Alexandra Machinist, ICM Partners, 730 5th Ave., New York, NY 10019.

■ Writings

The Casquette Girls, Skyscape (New York, NY), 2015.
The Romeo Catchers, Skyscape (New York, NY), 2017.

■ Sidelights

Alys Arden's work has taken her around the world, but absence from her hometown of New Orleans has only intensified her attachment to the French Quarter, where her life began. One winter day, in a city on the other side of the world, Arden began to weave those memories into a "slow-burning dark fantasy" of "magic and mystery," according to a starred review in *Publishers Weekly*.

The Casquette Girls

The Casquette Girls is a paranormal romance set in a city well known for its otherworldly population. Adele Le Moyne is sixteen years old when she and her father flee their New Orleans home to escape the fury of the massive no-name hurricane they call "The Storm." They return to a postapocalyptic cityscape, but Adele is relieved to be home in the city she loves. The city has changed, however, and so will Adele. She finds a corpse, one of many that will follow. She is clawed by an aggressive crow and then pelted with shards when an attic window in an old convent suddenly explodes above her head. She discovers that she has an eerie talent for controlling metal objects with her mind.

Adele explores the ruined streets in search of old friends and meets odd new ones, including the enigmatic young Isaac, who can take the form of a crow, and the darkly seductive Nicco Medici. Both of them will vie for her affection, each in his own way. Then she finds the 300-year-old diary of Adeline Saint-Germaine and learns that Nicco was once known to Adeline, too.

Adeline came to New Orleans in the early 1700s with "the casquette girls," who were selected from French orphanages and convents for their virtue and piety, then sent by order of the king to marry Creole settlers in the New World. The moniker came from the wooden *casquettes,* or chests, that were said to contain the orphaned girls' wedding finery and royal dowry. Legend has it that the chests were stored in the attic of the convent, untouched for years. When they were finally opened, the chests were empty, giving rise to rumors that the orphans had, wittingly or not, introduced a clan of vampires to the Louisiana territory of New France. The purported residents of the coffin-shaped chests have been sealed off in the attic for centuries, until Adele's presence accidentally sets them free to suck the blood of their victims, leaving the clawed bodies to rot in the storm-ravaged streets.

Adele gathers a coven of modern-day practitioners in the hope of subduing the thirsty monsters. Her goal is to stop the carnage and restore a sense of normalcy to her beloved city. Then Adeline's diary reveals another mysterious and unsettling family connection—one that could threaten her lofty goal.

Critics were enchanted by *The Casquette Girls*. The fantasy is anchored by the "weight of history," explained the reviewer in *Publishers Weekly*. The author "offers readers a full plate of Southern gothic atmospherics and sparkling teen romance," reported a contributor to *Kirkus Reviews*, and "Arden's insights regarding her fragile city color the narrative with tragic realism." Her love for the city "shines through her prose," observed the author of the *Nicolette Andrews* website, who complimented Arden for her "lush writing style and tangible descriptions."

The Romeo Catchers

Adele's adventures continue in *The Romeo Catchers*. She and her coven have used their magic to trap the vampires in the attic of the convent. Adele has a secret that she has not even shared with Isaac: one of the vampires is her own mother. Adele must balance the compulsion to free her mother against the potential repercussions for her mission to protect her city. The mission draws Adele toward the magnetic Nicco, whose dreams of ancient Florence might offer valuable guidance, if she can resist his charismatic allure. Isaac senses a danger even greater than Nicco's hold over the girl he is learning to love: a secret from his own past that could destroy everything.

Reviewers were generous with their praise. To a *Kirkus Reviews* commentator, *The Romeo Catchers* represents "a meticulous blend of witchery, New Orleans lore, and teen angst." *School Library Journal* contributor Amanda Raklovits found this installment to be "every bit as engrossing as the first, with deftly drawn character arcs and a captivating setting." Kerry Sutherland predicted in *RT Book Reviews* that "readers will be enchanted and horrified in turn."

■ Biographical and Critical Sources

PERIODICALS

Kirkus Reviews, February 1, 2014, review of *The Casquette Girls*; March 15, 2017, review of *The Romeo Catchers*.

Publishers Weekly, May 26, 2014, review of *The Casquette Girls*, p. S24.

School Library Journal, May, 2017, Amanda Raklovits, review of *The Romeo Catchers*, p. 100.

ONLINE

Advocate Online, http://www.theadvocate.com/ (February 7, 2015), Phil McCausland, author interview.

Alys Arden Website, http://www.alysarden.com (January 31, 2018).

Book Country, http://blog.bookcountry.com/ (September 23, 2013), Nevena Georgieva, author interview.

Casquette Girls Website, http://www.thecasquettegirls.com/ (January 31, 2018), author profile.

Fairy Dust Book Blog, https://thefairydustbookblog.wordpress.com/ (June 10, 2017), review of *The Romeo Catchers*.

Nicolette Andrews Website, https://www.fantasyauthornicoletteandrews.com/ (April 24, 2015), Nicolette Andrews, review of *The Casquette Girls*.

RT Book Reviews, https://www.rtbookreviews.com/ (February 4, 2018), Kerry Sutherland, review of *The Romeo Catchers*.

Times-Picayune Online, http://www.nola.com/ (April 15, 2015), Chris Waddington, author interview.

Tor.com, https://www.tor.com/ (September 17, 2014), author interview.

Two Chicks on Books, http://www.twochicksonbooks.com/ (May 23, 2017), review of *The Romeo Catchers*.

Tianxia Bachang

1978-

Also Known As

Zhang Muye

Personal

Born September 25, 1978. *Education:* Nanjing Academy of Fine Arts (China), graduated. *Hobbies and other interests:* Gaming.

Career

Writer. Has worked in finance.

Writings

The City of Sand, translated by Jeremy Tiang, Delacorte Press (New York, NY), 2017.
The Dragon Ridge Tombs (sequel to *The City of Sand*), translated by Jeremy Tiang, Delacorte Press (New York, NY), 2018.

Author of books in Chinese.

Adaptations

Books in Chinese have been adapted for films in China.

Sidelights

Tianxia Bachang is a Chinese writer whose real name is Zhang Muye. He holds a degree from the Nanjing Academy of Fine Arts and has worked in the finance industry. Bachang is a popular gamer whose online avatar is also called Tianxia Bachang. He has written several novels in Chinese, some of which have been adapted for films.

The City of Sand

In 2017, Bachang released his first novel to be translated to English, *The City of Sand.* The book's protagonist a Hu Tianyi, a seventeen-year-old boy who is a gifted practitioner of feng shui. He plans to use his abilities for gold hunting, or finding treasure in the tombs of aristocrats. Tianyi's best friend, Kai, is in on the plan. However, Tianyi's father becomes furious when he hears of Tianyi's plans. He had expected Tianyi to go to college instead. Disappointed in his son, Tianyi's father tells Tianyi that he must move out, so Tianyi decides to go to Beijing with Kai. There, they become acquainted with Julia Yang, a wealthy American, and Professor Chen, a respected archaeologist. The two ask Tianyi to assist them in their search for Jingjue, a lost city where a powerful queen is said to have been buried. Their search leads them through difficult terrain, including the Talimakan Desert, where they are tormented by flesh-eating insects, killer sloths, reanimated corpses, and sandstorms. Their luck does not improve when they arrive in Jingjue. They must find an ancient medallion that will allow them to access the valuable treasure there. As they search, they must protect themselves from further dangers, including becoming buried with the dead they seek to rob.

Booklist reviewer Stacey Comfort asserted: "Filled to the brim with ancient and modern Chinese history, this translation is a fun and spooky ride." A contributor to *Kirkus Reviews* suggested: "The audience is unclear: older readers may not tolerate the immature feel of the story, but younger readers will struggle with the reading level." "More able readers who enjoy constant action will be swept along with the explorers as they seek the lost kingdom and their own agendas," commented Sherrie Williams, a contributor to *Voice of Youth Advocates.* A *Publishers Weekly* critic remarked: "Tianxia's English-language debut is a richly imagined and artfully translated tale of history, adventure, and magic." Referring to Tianyi, Nancy Nadig, a reviewer in *School Library Journal,* stated: "He is an engaging narrator. However, the frenetic pacing makes it difficult to keep track of the plot."

The Dragon Ridge Tombs

The Dragon Ridge Tombs is another volume in English by Bachang. It is the sequel to *The City of Sand.* Tianyi and Kai return in this book. At the beginning of the story, the two are back in Beijing. There, they meet Gold Tooth, an antiques dealer with a questionable reputation. Gold Tooth asks Tianyi and Kai to accompany him to the far-flung city of Gulan, where ancient tombs are said to exist. He hopes that Tianyi can use his skills with feng shui to find the treasure in the tombs.

Gold Tooth assures Tianyi and Kai that the expedition will be quick and easy. However, the two boys soon realize that it will be much more difficult than they thought. The tombs are somewhere within an underground labyrinth in Gulan. The tunnels contain many traps and obstacles that put their lives in danger, and frightening creatures live inside them. It seems to Tianyi and Kai that they are unable to move forward or to escape. When Julie Yang arrives, they discover that the items in the underground labyrinth may have a connection to her family's history.

■ **Biographical and Critical Sources**

PERIODICALS

Booklist, November 1, 2017, Stacey Comfort, review of *The City of Sand,* p. 45.
Kirkus Reviews, October 15, 2017, review of *The City of Sand.*
Publishers Weekly, October 9, 2017, review of *The City of Sand,* p. 67.
School Library Journal, October, 2017, Nancy Nadig, review of *The City of Sand,* p. 99.
Voice of Youth Advocates, December, 2017, Sherrie Williams, review of *The City of Sand,* p. 65.

ONLINE

Encyclopedia of Science Fiction, http://www.sf-encyclopedia.com/ (March 19, 2018), author profile.
Penguin Random House Website, https://www.penguinrandomhouse.com/ (March 19, 2018), author profile.
TeenReads, https://www.teenreads.com/ (March 19, 2018), author profile.*

Johnny Ball

1938-

■ **Also Known As**

Graham Ball

■ **Personal**

Born May 23, 1938; married; wife's name Di; children: Zoe, Nick, Dan.

■ **Addresses**

Home—Buckinghamshire, England.

■ **Career**

Writer, educator, producer, and television personality. Glasgow University, Scotland, lord rector, 1993-96. Has written and hosted twenty television series; has appeared in educational stage musicals. Previously worked in the aircraft industry, as a standup comic, and as a Butlin's Redcoat (children's entertainer). Ambassador for British Engineering, 1995—. *Military service:* British Royal Air Force, 1957-59.

■ **Awards, Honors**

BAFTA award, for *Think of a Number*; World TV Awards (two), 1978, for *Think Again* (television show); ITVA Craft Award as Presenter of the Year, 1986.

■ **Writings**

Go Figure!, Dorling Kindersley (New York, NY), 2005.

Think of a Number, Dorling Kindersley (London, England), 2005.
Why Pi?, Dorling Kindersley (New York, NY), 2009.
Mathmagicians, Dorling Kindersley (London, England), 2009.
Wonders beyond Numbers: A Brief History of All Things Mathematical, Bloomsbury Sigma (London, England), 2017.

Also writer of educational stage musicals.

■ **Sidelights**

Johnny Ball is a British writer, educator, producer, and television personality. He is the host of numerous educational television series, many of which he has written, as well. Ball also served as the lord rector at Scotland's Glasgow University. He has worked variously as a performer in stage musicals, in the aircraft industry, as a standup comic, and as a Butlin's Redcoat—a type of children's entertainer. Ball has served as the Ambassador for British Engineering since 1995.

Go Figure!

In 2005, Ball released his first book, *Go Figure!* The volume is geared toward young readers and is divided into four sections. The first offers historical information on numbers and counting. Other sections include information on the importance of the number zero, the discovery of *pi*, and aspects of number theory. Ball also discusses fractals and logic. He cites the work of celebrated thinkers and mathematicians, including Albert Einstein and Ahmose. The book includes diagrams, puzzles, photos, and word problems. Answers to the problems appear at the end of the volume.

Though Jennifer Mattson, a critic in *Booklist*, highlighted the difficulty of some of the material in the book, Mattson suggested: "Some discussions and exercises . . . are spot-on for inquisitive kids who like to fiddle and ponder." "*Go Figure!* takes an adventurous approach to stimulating young minds and exploring mathematical mysteries," noted a *Children's Bookwatch* writer. Erlene Bishop Killeen, a reviewer in *School Library Journal*, described *Go Figure!* as "a dynamic book" and "a fun romp for number and puzzle lovers."

Wonders beyond Numbers

Ball again discusses math in his 2017 book, *Wonders beyond Numbers: A Brief History of All Things Mathematical*. The first section in his volume is devoted to early examples of mathematics discovered in excavations of sites in the ancient world. Papyri from ancient Egypt demonstrate mathematical calculations used in the construction of the great pyramids. Other ancient examples of mathematical equations come from Sumer, Greece, Central America, India, China, and Babylon. Ball profiles important mathematicians from the ancient world, including Pythagoras and Archimedes, and goes on to highlight key mathematical discoveries throughout history from other thinkers, including Tycho Brahe, Leonardo da Vinci, Isaac Newton, Robert Hooke, Albert Einstein, Florence Nightingale, and Ada Augusta Byron. In an interview with Nick Smith for the *E&T* website, Ball explained why he decided to release another book about mathematics: "Without maths we simply can't understand the world around us. It is the language of the physical world. . . . Galileo said that everything in the universe is written in the language of mathematics." In the interview, Ball noted that *The Ascent of Man*, a documentary series created by Jacob Bronowski, was an inspiration for *Wonders beyond Numbers*. He explained: "This is because he discussed the whole of the history of mankind and its development. I have done the same thing, only with maths. But I have illustrated this with examples from architecture, Renaissance art and all those things. And what you find is that if you get an understanding of the mathematics and are not scared of it, little bits of it will illuminate the situation for you and will help you understand it better."

A *Publishers Weekly* reviewer asserted: "Excellent as an introduction to the field, this is a brisk, well-rounded history of mathematics and its practitioners." Referring to Ball, Louise Jones, a critic on the *Bookbag* website, remarked: "His latest book proves that he has lost none of his passion and enthusiasm for his subject." Jones added: "Throughout the book, Johnny keeps his trademark enthusiasm, which shines through on each page. . . . This is an author who is truly excited and inspired by his specialist subject, and it rubs off on his readers."

■ Biographical and Critical Sources

PERIODICALS

Booklist, October 15, 2005, Jennifer Mattson, review of *Go Figure!*, p. 44.
Children's Bookwatch, October, 2005, review of *Go Figure!*
Publishers Weekly, October 23, 2017, review of *Wonders beyond Numbers: A Brief History of All Things Mathematical*, p. 77.
School Library Journal, January, 2006, Erlene Bishop Killeen, review of *Go Figure!*, p. 147.

ONLINE

Bookbag, http://www.thebookbag.co.uk/ (August 1, 2017), Louise Jones, review of *Wonders beyond Numbers*.
E&T, https://eandt.theiet.org/ (January 22, 2018), Nick Smith, author interview.
Johnny Ball Website, http://www.johnnyball.co.uk (March 19, 2018).*

Josiah Bancroft

■ Personal

Married; wife's name Sharon. *Hobbies and other interests:* Cooking, playing music, drawing.

■ Addresses

Home—Philadelphia, PA.

■ Career

Writer and educator. Has taught at college level. Member of the band Dirt Dirt.

■ Writings

Senlin Ascends, self-published, 2013, Orbit (New York, NY), 2018.
Arm of the Sphinx, Orbit (New York, NY), 2018.

■ Sidelights

Josiah Bancroft is a writer and educator based in Philadelphia, Pennsylvania. He has worked as an instructor teaching college courses. Bancroft is also a musician in a band called Dirt Dirt.

Senlin Ascends

Senlin Ascends is Bancroft's debut novel and the first in his "Books of Babel" series. The book's protagonist is Thomas Senlin, a school headmaster who lives in a small town and has recently married a woman named Marya. For their honeymoon, Thomas and Marya have decided to travel to the Tower of Babel. The Tower is a massive structure that is impossibly tall. It is surrounded with colossal walls and is teeming with people. Those with knowledge of the outside world understand that visiting the Tower can be risky, but the naive Thomas and Marya set off on their journey without worry. However, Marya disappears before she and Thomas even enter the city. Thomas is desperate to be reunited with his new bride. He must navigate the complex society of the Tower, its political turmoil, crime, and drug abuse along the way. Thomas becomes a target of the group that runs the Tower, but he also meets quirky supporters who offer to help him find Marya.

"Bancroft succeeds in creating a baffling world . . . in which pursuit of instinct and love, dedication, and shared sacrifice can overcome barriers," commented a *Publishers Weekly* contributor. Another writer in *Publishers Weekly* asserted: "This novel goes off like a firework and suggests even greater things in the author's future." Regina Schroeder, a reviewer in *Booklist*, remarked: "The pacing seems slow . . . but it allows for in-depth development of the setting." A *Kirkus Reviews* critic suggested: "The lush setting holds the reader through a slow start, but once the plot gets going, it ticks along with the tight precision and artistry of a well-wound watch."

Arm of the Sphinx

Thomas returns in *Arm of the Sphinx*. Now calling himself Captain Tom Mudd, he still has yet to be reunited with Marya. He has been working with his friends Edith, Iren, Adam, and Voleta to find a way to access the place where Marya is being held. Thomas and each of his four friends take turns narrating sections of the novel. Their crew has been disappointed in their attempts to enter part of the Tower. However, a new opportunity arises that may allow them to finally gain access. This opportunity may prove to be dangerous, but Thomas soldiers on regardless. Along the way, he meets a slave organizer who may be able to topple the corrupt leadership of the Tower.

Writing on a self-titled website, Dorian Hart praised multiple aspects of *Arm of the Sphinx*. Hart commented: "First, the sentence-crafting is every bit as good as in Senlin Ascends. Bancroft's sublime artistry with imagery and metaphors is on full display, making the story a joy to read on its lowest level." Hart added: "Where *Senlin Ascends* was a single sparkling jewel, *Arm of the Sphinx* is more like a high-end jewelry store. It feels sprawling, its narrative expanding in unexpected directions but never quite flying out of control." Dan Smyth, a critic on the *Elitist Book Reviews* website, suggested that the book features "rich description that doesn't get in the way of the story and enhances every aspect of it to the fullest extent; constant movement in the plot and pacing, development of our several characters in the best ways possible. The author is one that just understands how to relay character and emotion." Smyth described *Arm of the Sphinx* as "a fun, engaging story that continues the story of Tom Senlin while

he seeks to be reunited with his wife; a good entry, suffering only from what one might call some very simple newbie mistakes."

■ **Biographical and Critical Sources**

PERIODICALS

Booklist, November 15, 2017, Regina Schroeder, review of *Senlin Ascends*, p. 35.

Kirkus Reviews, December 1, 2017, review of *Senlin Ascends*.

Publishers Weekly, November 18, 2013, review of *Senlin Ascends*, p. S24; October 30, 2017, review of *Senlin Ascends*, p. 63.

ONLINE

Books of Babel Website, http://www.thebooksofbabel.com/ (March 19, 2018), author profile.

Dorian Hart Website, https://dorianhart.com (September 10, 2017), Dorian Hart, review of *Arm of the Sphinx*.

Elitist Book Reviews, https://elitistbookreviews.com/ (June 15, 2017), Dan Smyth, review of *Arm of the Sphinx*.

Casey Barrett

1975-

■ **Personal**

Born February 16, 1975. *Education:* Attended the University of Southern California and graduated from Southern Methodist University.

■ **Career**

Writer, sports commentator, and swimming instructor. Imagine Swimming, New York, NY, cofounder, co-CEO. Prime-time writer on NBC for the Olympic Games. Former member of the Canadian Olympic swim team.

■ **Awards, Honors**

Emmy Award (three); Peabody Award.

■ **Writings**

Under Water (novel), Kensington Books (New York, NY), 2017.

Maintains the blog *Cap & Goggles*.

■ **Sidelights**

Casey Barrett is a former member of the Canadian Olympic swim team. In an interview with Eli Rallo for the *Michigan Daily* website, he explained how he came to be an Olympic swimmer. Barrett recalled showing promise after taking swimming lessons as a child and told Rallo: "I liked working hard; became hooked on improving; success &

ambition fed on themselves . . . until it became my entire identity." After ending his competitive swimming career, Barrett has become a published author, cofounder of a swimming instruction company, and television sports commentator. Barrett's swimming instruction company, Imagine Swimming, is based in New York City, and Barrett serves as the organization's co-CEO. He has appeared as a commentator for NBC during that network's coverage of the Olympic Games and has won a Peabody Award and three Emmy awards for his coverage of the Games. Barrett attended the University of Southern California, where he took courses in journalism, and graduated from Southern Methodist University with a degree in journalism.

In 2017, Barrett released his first novel, a thriller called *Under Water*. In his interview with Rallo, Barrett discussed his preparation for writing the book. He stated: "I read as much as I possibly could in the genre, knowing that was where I was headed. Then, at some point around 2012 or so, I realized that the reading could (and would) go on forever, and that I was ready to write confidently in my chosen 'field'." In the book, Barrett tells the story of a former Olympic swimmer named Lawrence "Duck" Darley, who has fallen into crime and alcoholism after his swimming career ended. Duck is now a private eye, and his latest case involves a missing teenage swimmer named Madeline. The case becomes complicated when Duck discovers connections to the sex industry and the Russian mob. He relies on Cass Kimball, a dominatrix and colleague, for help.

According to a reviewer in *Publishers Weekly*, "Barrett relies on familiar genre tropes . . . but dials them up for high shock value." "Barrett's first-person narrative has a music of its own, and his alcoholic hero, just two drinks away from seeking his next fix, is appealingly vulnerable," asserted a critic on the *Kirkus Reviews* website. A writer on the *Bibliophile Book Club* website commented: "At times violent and gritty, *Under Water* has an almost hard-boiled crime kind of feel to it. It's noir-ish and quite old school but it's quite pacy." The same writer added: "There is a seedy undertone throughout the narrative, but it lends itself well to the investigative work Darley has to do."

■ Biographical and Critical Sources

PERIODICALS

Publishers Weekly, October 2, 2017, review of *Under Water,* p. 116.

ONLINE

Bibliophile Book Club, https://bibliophilebookclub. com/ (November 28, 2017), review of *Under Water.*

Casey Barrett Website, http://www.caseybarrett books.com (March 19, 2018).

Kirkus Reviews Online, https://www.kirkusreviews. com/ (September 1, 2016), review of *Under Water.*

Michigan Daily Online, https://www.michigandaily. com/ (January 8, 2018), Eli Rallo, author interview.

Kaushik Barua

1981(?)-

■ **Personal**

Born c. 1981. *Education:* St. Stephen's College (New Delhi, India), graduated; attended the London School of Economics.

■ **Addresses**

Home—Rome, Italy.

■ **Career**

Writer and businessperson. United Nations, Rome, Italy, employee. Has worked in international development and public policy.

■ **Awards, Honors**

Sahitya Akademi Yuva Puraskar award, for *Windhorse.*

■ **Writings**

Windhorse, HarperCollins Publishers India (Noida, India), 2013.
No Direction Rome, Permanent Press (Sag Harbor, NY), 2017.

■ **Sidelights**

Kaushik Barua has worked in international development and public policy for organizations including the United Nations. His work has taken him from South Asia, to West Africa, to Rome, Italy, where he is currently based. Barua holds a degree from St. Stephen's College in New Delhi, India and has attended the London School of Economics. He is the author of novels, including *Windhorse* and *No Direction Rome.*

Windhorse

Windhorse, released in 2013, is the winner of the Sahitya Academy Yuva Puraskar award. It tells the story of a privileged young Indian man named Norbu, whose life connects with Lhasang, a refugee from Tibet. They join together to fight for Tibetan liberation. In an interview with a contributor to the *Good Book Corner* website, Barua discussed the inspiration for his first novel, stating: "In the case of *Windhorse,* clearly it was the suffering and the struggle of the Tibetan community. Though the story wasn't mine, it moved me in ways I couldn't understand. But then, empathy and inspiration are whimsical beasts and you never know what might move you beyond comprehension."

Critics offered praise for *Windhorse.* A writer on the *Modern Gypsy* website suggested: "While it is a fictionalized history of Tibet, it is also a story about human beings and their search and struggle for purpose and freedom. All-in-all, it is a story that must be read. Highly, highly recommended!" A contributor to the *Good Book Corner* website commented: "The story moves fast and is gripping till the very end. The historical research is impeccable and the story is strong enough to reach out and create widespread awareness towards the Tibetan cause."

No Direction Rome

An Indian man named Krantik is the protagonist of Barua's 2017 novel *No Direction Rome.* Now living in Rome, the jaded Krantik comments on his meaningless work, his romantic relationships, and the social media proclivities of his peers. In the same interview with the contributor to the *Good Book Corner* website, Barua discussed the ideas behind *No Direction Rome*. He stated: "You could say it's inspired by . . . the rootlessness of our generation (especially the urban, social-media soaked generation), the fact that we don't have a struggle, not even a losing cause that we believe in."

The reviews of *No Direction Rome* were less than favorable. A *Publishers Weekly* critic remarked: "While the novel is occasionally sharp and even insightful in its cultural critique, its caustic, bitter voice grates." Shougat Dasgupta, a contributor to the *Hindu Business Live* website, commented: "Krantik is vividly drawn, an appropriately shallow example of a particularly shallow class of persons, the 'overpaid expat'. It's unfortunate that Barua felt it necessary to fill the rest of the novel with so much contrived 'zaniness'." Dasgupta added: "Some of the slapstick comedy, a prolonged scene with sleeping gas, for instance, is out of kilter with the blacker comedy, the social satire *No Direction Rome* gestures towards without fully committing to. Rome itself, where Barua works for an international aid agency, is an inspired setting, mouldering and falling apart albeit with far more grace than poor Krantik can muster." Writing on the *Indian Express* website, Amrita Dutta suggested: "While you coast along in the first half, following Krantik and his caustic stream of thoughts, his encounters with a crowd of other drifters like him blur into sameness. It's all very well to think of Sisyphus as a tragic hero, but not the wisest move to consign readers to the boredom of his life." Dutta continued: "Before the end, is there love? Or a sense of direction? Krantik is not the most likeable of characters but . . . he is impervious to happy makeovers. There is a sliver of a silver lining at the end of this novel, but even that could well be a pose." "Barua's prose in *No Direction Rome* is laboured, and the only relief, for those who must complete a book that they've started reading, is that at 190 pages, it ends sooner than most novels," asserted Elizabeth Kuruvilla, a reviewer on the *Live Mint* website. Kuruvilla also stated: "No guilty or acquiescing laughter emerges from us at Ba-

rua's dark humour. And the use of a fragmented narrative style appears a tired means to a familiar tale in Barua's hands." Kavya Kushnoor, a critic on the *Coldnoon* website, noted: "The novel has no coherent structure. Still, it retains the reader's attention with witty prose at every turn." However, Kushnoor added: "*No Direction Rome* is a successful experiment in its genre. It is an exposition into the protagonist's inner world and his shallow, yet courageously honest conscious thoughts. In contrast to Barua's previous novel which is about revolutionaries living and dying for a cause, NDR is about the reckless ways of a privileged millennial. In the narrator's crudeness, it is easy to miss the ideas that he presents. This book can easily provoke hearty laughter, but if we dig deeper, Krantik's ramblings could also be a doorway to important conversations and profound realizations."

■ Biographical and Critical Sources

PERIODICALS

Publishers Weekly, September 11, 2017, review of *No Direction Rome*, p. 40.

ONLINE

Coldnoon, https://coldnoon.com/ (December 30, 2017), Kavya Kushnoor, review of *No Direction Rome*; (March 19, 2018), author profile.
Good Book Corner, https://thegoodbookcorner.com/ (July 5, 2015), review of *Windhorse*; (March 19, 2018), author interview.
Guardian Online, https://www.theguardian.com/ (March 19, 2018), author profile.
Hindu Business Line, https://www.thehindubusinessline.com/ (May 15, 2015), Shougat Dasgupta, review of *No Direction Rome*.
Indian Express Online, http://indianexpress.com/ (November 14, 2015), Amrita Dutta, review of *No Direction Rome*.
Live Mint, http://www.livemint.com/ (February 2, 2016), Elizabeth Kuruvilla, review of *No Direction Rome*.
Modern Gypsy, https://moderngypsy.in/ (August 5, 2015), review of *Windhorse*.*

Ezgi Basaran

1981-

■ **Personal**

Born 1981. *Education:* Oxford University, M.Phil.

■ **Addresses**

Home—UK.

■ **Career**

Journalist. *Radikal,* Turkey, editor; St. Anthony's College, Oxford University, England, coordinator of Programme on Contemporary Turkey at South East European Centre.

■ **Awards, Honors**

Dulverton Scholarship, 2017.

■ **Writings**

Bars: bir varms bir yokmus: Kürt sorununun çözüm süreci (2010-2015), Dogan Kitap (Istanbul, Turkey), 2015.

Frontline Turkey: The Conflict at the Heart of the Middle East, I.B. Tauris (London, England), 2018.

■ **Sidelights**

Ezgi Basaran is a journalist based in the United Kingdom. A Turkish citizen, she began her career as the first female editor of the Turkish publication *Radikal.* Basaran left that publication when the Turkish government put in place strict censorship laws. Basaran moved to the UK to attend Oxford University, where she earned an M.Phil. degree. She also works at the school, serving as the coordinator of the Programme on Contemporary Turkey at the South East European Centre at St. Anthony's College.

In 2018, Basaran released her first book in English, *Frontline Turkey: The Conflict at the Heart of the Middle East.* In an interview with William Armstrong, a contributor to the *Hurriyet Daily News* website, Basaran explained: "The main aim of writing this book was to tell the truth about a period that has been so crucial for Turkey. It's about setting the record straight on how Turkey's deepest conflict has gotten deeper, despite there being a time when a solution possibility had emerged. It's about how the collapse of peace talks with the Kurds brought Turkey's democratic institutions to collapse." Basaran added: "I also wanted to offer an alternative way to look at the Middle East for a non-Turkish audience. Because a solution to what is happening in the Middle East is directly related to Turkey's forty-year-old Kurdish problem and how the government has chosen to deal with it." Basaran also told Armstrong: "In the book I track events from the emergence of the AKP to the start of the Turkish-Kurdish peace process. The consequences of the collapse of the peace process are very closely related to the Syrian war. When the war in Syria first erupted, Turkey's leadership was adamant that it would only be a matter of months before Bashar al-Assad was ousted. That obviously didn't happen."

In *Frontline Turkey,* Basaran chronicles the history of the tense relationship between the Turkish government and the Kurdish minority based in the country. The two have been at odds with one another for over four decades. Basaran also discusses the ways in which the Turkish government has evolved of the years. For a time, it was considered to be more progressive relative to its neighbors in the Middle East. However, in recent years, it has become increasingly conservative and authoritarian. It has also begun to embrace more Islamist views. Basaran profiles President Recep Tayyip Erdogan, whom she believes has been instrumental in making Turkey more authoritarian. She also closely examines the peace talks that occurred in 2015. Those talks became strained and ultimately failed to come to a resolution. Basaran identifies factors that complicated the talks, including the Kurds' decision to take part in the Syrian civil war, violence against the Kurds committed by the Turkey security forces, and tensions among the Kurds themselves. Also, Turkey was being considered for membership in the European Union around that time. Basaran laments the failure of the talks and hopes for fruitful negotiations between the Kurds and the Turkish government in the future.

In a review of *Frontline Turkey* in *Publishers Weekly*, a critic suggested: "Basaran's survey covers a huge amount of material and will be of interest to readers already well versed in the subject." Writing on the *New York Journal of Books* website, Thomas McClung commented: "This is neither a pleasure read nor an easy read. It should be realized that this volume is primarily only for those whose interest lies in Middle Eastern conflict and politics and, specifically, the relations between the Turks and Kurds." McClung concluded: "If one has an interest in Turkish-Kurdish history, relations and politics, this is an insightful book, providing a closeup look at a conflict that has bedeviled the Middle East and only added fuel to the ongoing fires in that region."

■ **Biographical and Critical Sources**

PERIODICALS

Publishers Weekly, November 20, 2017, review of *Frontline Turkey: The Conflict at the Heart of the Middle East*, p. 83.

ONLINE

Frontline Turkey Website, https://frontlineturkey. com/ (March 20, 2018), author profile.
Hurriyet Daily News Online, http://www. hurriyetdailynews.com/ (December 23, 2017), William Armstrong, author interview.
New York Journal of Books, https://www. nyjournalofbooks.com/ (January 9, 2018), Thomas McClung, review of *Frontline Turkey*.*

Tom Basile

1975-

■ Personal

Born 1975; married; wife's name Carrie; children: three. *Education:* Hofstra University, bachelor's degree; attended Georgetown University; Fordham University, J.D. *Politics:* Republican.

■ Addresses

Home—Stony Point, NY.

■ Career

Communications executive and educator. Environmental Protection Agency, Washington, DC, director of communications, 2001-03; Coalition Provisional Authority, Baghdad, Iraq, senior press advisor, 2003-04; Empire Solutions, principal, 2004—; Middleberg Communications, New York, NY, managing director, 2006-13.

Fordham University, New York, NY, adjunct professor, 2008—; press secretary of Joint Congressional Committee on Inaugural Ceremonies, 2004-05; councilman, then deputy town supervisor, of Stony Point, NY, 2014—; executive director of NY State Republican Party, 2009-11; member of advisory board of Hofstra University.

■ Member

National Italian-American Foundation (member of leadership council), New York Bar Association.

■ Awards, Honors

Joint Civilian Service Commendation Medal, Department of Defense; Young Alumnus Award, Hofstra University, 2007; Order of the Holy Sepulchre of Jerusalem, 2008.

■ Writings

Tough Sell: Fighting the Media War in Iraq, Potomac Books (Lincoln, NE), 2017.

Opinion contributor to *Forbes* and SiriusXM Radio.

■ Sidelights

Tom Basile is a communications executive and educator and is an active member of the Republican Party. He earned a bachelor's degree from Hofstra University and went on to study at Georgetown University and Fordham University, where he earned a J.D. Basile worked as an attorney for a time, becoming a member of the state bar of New York. However, he soon shifted his focus to communications and journalism. Basile was chosen to head up the communications department of the Environmental Protection Agency during the George W. Bush administration. He went on to serve as the senior press advisor for the Coalition Provisional Authority in Baghdad at the beginning of the Iraq War. After returning to the United States, Basile was awarded the Joint Civilian Service Commendation Medal by the Department of Defense. In 2007, he joined Middleberg Communications as its managing director. Later, Basile became an adjunct professor at Fordham University. He was the New York State Republican Party's executive director from 2009 to 2011. Basile has also been involved in the government of Stony Point, New York, serving as a councilman and, later, as the deputy town supervisor. He has contributed to the opinion sections of *Forbes* and SiriusXM Radio.

In 2017, Basile released his first book, *Tough Sell: Fighting the Media War in Iraq,* in which he recounts his time as the senior press advisor for the Coalition Provisional Authority. He also defends the George W. Bush administration's decision to send troops to the country in the first place. Basile shares the mission of the Coalition Provisional Authority, which he claims was harmed by the perceptions of the invasion created by the media. He blames the media for portraying the war in a bad light, suggesting that it has caused terrorist groups to become stronger. Basile also criticizes Barack Obama's handling of the conflict.

Referring to Basile, a *Kirkus Reviews* critic suggested: "His personal account of his experiences reporting the war is gripping." The same critic described *Tough Sell* as "an engrossing account of the author's own experiences written to justify questionable foreign policy that many readers will question." Similarly, Benjamin Welton, contributor to the *Foreword Reviews* website, commented: "Basile's politics are sure to turn off some readers. That being said, *Tough Sell* provides not only an excellent discussion about the nature of media during wartime, but also information about the war that is often ignored." Welton described the book as an "excellent addition" to the group of books on the subject of the Iraq War.

■ Biographical and Critical Sources

PERIODICALS

Kirkus Reviews, April 1, 2017, review of *Tough Sell: Fighting the Media War in Iraq*.

ONLINE

Forbes Online, https://www.forbes.com/ (February 13, 2018), author profile.

Foreword Reviews Online, https://www.forewordreviews.com/ (May 1, 2017), Benjamin Welton, review of *Tough Sell*.

New York Daily News Online, http://www.nydailynews.com/ (June 24, 2011), Celeste Katz, article about author.

Tom Basile Website, https://www.tombasile.com/ (February 13, 2018).*

Barret Baumgart

■ **Personal**

Male. *Education:* Attended the University of California, Berkeley; University of Iowa, M.F.A.

■ **Addresses**

Home—Los Angeles, CA.

■ **Career**

Writer and musician. Plays drums in a band called Wreche.

■ **Awards, Honors**

Iowa Prize in Literary Nonfiction, 2016, for *China Lake.*

■ **Writings**

China Lake: A Journey into the Contradicted Heart of a Global Climate Catastrophe, University of Iowa Press (Iowa City, IA), 2017.

Contributor to periodicals and websites, including *Vice, Literary Review, Seneca Review, Guernica, Iowa Review, Gettysburg Review,* and *Camera Obscura.*

■ **Sidelights**

Barret Baumgart is a writer and musician based in Los Angeles, California. He attended the University of California, Berkeley and obtained a master's degree from the University of Iowa. Baumgart has contributed articles to numerous periodicals and websites, including *Vice, Literary Review, Seneca Review, Guernica, Iowa Review, Gettysburg Review,* and *Camera Obscura.*

In 2017, Baumgart released his first book, a nonfiction volume called *China Lake: A Journey into the Contradicted Heart of a Global Climate Catastrophe.* He describes taking his climate change-denying mother to China Lake, an area in California occupied by the military, which has been devastated by climate change. Baumgart comments on other examples of climate changes and provides more information on his family dynamics.

In an interview with Landon Bates, a contributor to the *Los Angeles Review of Books* blog, Baumgart explained how he came to write about climate change: "I was at my computer reading about the floods sweeping Colorado in September 2013 when I clicked across this conspiracy site that tried to blame cloud seeding. I thought: 'What the hell's cloud seeding?' So I started reading about the history and this led me to China Lake. China Lake had been on my radar from backpacking in the Sierras and working for the Forest Service." Baumgart continued: "I'd also written a little about the Coso Range petroglyphs in an essay I submitted to John D'Agata's workshop in Iowa. There was a paragraph about the irony of Native American rock art being preserved on a government weapons test facility, which made it into the book. . . . Most people read that and were unimpressed. . . . They said: 'Go further.' But there was a seed there." Baumgart also told Bates: "I called it a 'journey' in the subtitle, because that's what it is. It's not a book exclusively about climate change—climate, and more specifically the China Lake base, serves as a prism that unlocks all these tangled and previously hidden threads. It's a journey into all these contradictions and into despair and yet hopefully for the reader it's also a positive immersive experience." In the same interview with Bates, Baumgart remarked: "The drama is in the information, in the factual reveals and reversals—in setting up readers' expectations, then undercutting or re-tuning them. I feel at times it's a movement akin to long poetry. While the book is obviously not a poem, it kind of has the logic of one. There's a poetic logic running throughout the book that ties the disparate threads, all the imagery, the research, and memoir into an ever-expanding web of meaning."

Again commenting on the writing process with Breene Murphy, contributor to the *Citizens Climate Lobby* website, Baumgart stated: "The writing of the book was in some ways like documentary filmmaking—you let someone go on talking for a while and then, as the writer or director, you don't have to refute them, you just cut and observe an image or fact in conflict with what they're saying. You don't have to explicitly tell the reader that you think so-and-so is wrong."

Christine Mi, reviewer on the *Brooklyn Rail* website, commented: "Equal parts memoir, investigative reporting, and bizarre dreamscape, *China Lake* . . . is an arresting inquiry into the accelerating decay of our planet." Mi concluded: "In today's political climate, *China Lake* is frighteningly timely. Reality is not enough. As our leadership abandons rational discourse on climate change and environmental disaster, maybe Baumgart's dose of bizarre, surreal storytelling is just what we need to incept our darkening fate."

Writing on the *Los Angeles Review of Books* website, Kevin Zambrano suggested: "In the fashion of the New Journalists, Baumgart weaves shoe-leather reportage—interviewing scientists and military personnel and drawing on a mélange of academic texts and US government records—with narratives of his personal experience. . . . But *China Lake*'s narrative scenes are more fluid and readable than its relaying of facts. The narrative can move abruptly between discrete pieces of information without an immediate semantic link, giving them a spliced-together feel akin to cinematic montage." Zambrano added: "The kind of literary nonfiction in which voice and sensibility stand in for an overarching thesis can yield powerful results; so *China Lake* often does, especially in its depiction of Baumgart's family life. But it is a delicate line to walk. So much wit, depth of research, observational prowess, as well as activist bona fides are on display throughout the book."

Anna Call, a critic on the *Foreword Reviews* website, asserted: "*China Lake* presents in literary form what science has thus far been unable to communicate: climate change may be survivable—maybe—but there's no telling whether it will be worth the cost. A devastating artistic achievement." A *Kirkus Reviews* contributor described the book as "a unique, alarming portrayal of the American military-industrial complex." The same contributor concluded: "Nearly indescribable and utterly engrossing, this book is an urgent and terrifying cultural reflection, a startling look in the mirror."

■ **Biographical and Critical Sources**

PERIODICALS

Kirkus Reviews, March 15, 2017, review of *China Lake: A Journey into the Contradicted Heart of a Global Climate Catastrophe*.

ONLINE

Barret Baumgart Website, http://barretbaumgart. com/ (February 12, 2018).
Brooklyn Rail Online, https://brooklynrail.org/ (July 14, 2017), Christine Mi, review of *China Lake*.
Citizens Climate Lobby, https://citizensclimatelobby. org/ (February 12, 2018), Breene Murphy, author interview.
Foreword Reviews Online, https://www. forewordreviews.com/ (January 10, 2018), Anna Call, review of *China Lake*.
Los Angeles Review of Books Online, https:// lareviewofbooks.org/ (May 10, 2017), Kevin Zambrano, review of *China Lake*; (June 24, 2017), Landon Bates, author interview.*

Christine Bell

1951-

■ Personal

Born January 12, 1951, in Yonkers, NY; married J.F. Freedman (a writer). *Education:* Mercy College New York, graduated (magna cum laude).

■ Career

Writer. Worked variously as a nurse's aide, an electrocardiogram technician, and a cardiovascular technologist.

■ Awards, Honors

Citations for notable adult fiction of the year, American Library Association and New York Public Library, and citation for notable book of the year, *Philadelphia Inquirer,* all for *The Pérez Family.*

■ Writings

Saint, Pineapple Press (Englewood, FL), 1985.
The Pérez Family, W.W. Norton (New York, NY), 1990.
The Seven-Year Atomic Make-over Guide: And Other Stories, W.W. Norton and Co. (New York, NY), 1996.
Grievance, Lake Union Publishing, 2017.

■ Adaptations

The Pérez Family was adapted by Robin Swicord as a film of the same title, directed by Mira Nair, starring Marisa Tomei, Anjelica Huston, and Alfred Molina, released by the Samuel Goldwyn Company in 1995.

■ Sidelights

Christine Bell grew up in a suburb of New York City with the youthful goal of becoming a poet. She worked at various jobs in the health-care field until it became clear that her road to success would not be paved with poems. Fiction offered a potential outlet for her imagination and her sense of humor. Bell lived and worked in Miami and Nashville before moving to the West Coast, and her time in those cities is reflected in her settings.

Saint

Saint is the story of Rubia, a free-spirited American who traded life in New York City for the sprawling hacienda in Argentina that the charismatic Federico promised her when he persuaded her to marry him. Fifteen years have passed, and Rubia feels increasingly smothered by the oppressive heat of the jungle and the weight of her husband's family. By day she manages her lingerie shop in town; the rest of the time she attempts to impose some sort of control over her extended household. Federico's mother, la señora, is dying of cancer, but death is in no hurry to claim her. Rubia's daughters complain, and her in-laws quarrel. Life in this traditional multigenerational family is a perpetual challenge for the transplant from the big city.

Saint "is a rollicking farce," offered a commentator in *Kirkus Reviews,* "a gem of satire and wit, debauchery and poignancy." A reviewer in *Publishers Weekly* noted that "Bell effectively conveys the feeling of being an outsider in a close-knit foreign clan." It is not clear if Bell ever lived at an Argentine hacienda, but according to a online posting at *WJEC,* she did once work as a lingerie saleswoman.

The Pérez Family

Life at Federico's hacienda pales in comparison to the wacky adventures of *The Pérez Family*. The story begins with the historical Marisel boat lift of 1980, when Fidel Castro salted convoys of Cuban refugees with inmates from mental hospitals and prisons and loosed them upon America. In the novel, one of the liberated convicts is Juan Raul Pérez, suddenly released after twenty years as a political prisoner. Time has not been kind. Juan is bald, emaciated, and nearly toothless, but he clings to the dream that his wife, Carmela, will welcome him with open arms when he reaches Miami.

In the meantime, Juan stumbles in a daze from one colossal mishap to another. Fate and an inattentive immigration official match him to an enterprising ex-prostitute who shares the same last name. Dorita "Dottie" Pérez is convinced that families will receive preferential treatment in resettlement, so she and Juan pretend to be husband and wife. They acquire a senile old "papa" and a bogus adult "son" named Felipe, who complicate the confusion and elevate the familial chaos to new heights.

In Little Havana, Carmela is, in fact, anxiously awaiting the arrival of her beloved husband. She sends her brother, Angel, to meet every boat, but nowhere can they find an unmarried man named Juan Pérez. Juan actually finds his way to Carmela's house one day, but she does not recognize the downtrodden stranger who accidentally triggers her burglar alarm. The star-crossed lovers are finally reunited, in a way, and Dottie manages to find her version of the American dream. Happy endings are hard to find in the exile community, but hope abounds. The story "is often wise, warm, affecting, but never sentimental," a *Kirkus Reviews* contributor wrote.

The Pérez Family received favorable notice from both the American Library Association and the New York Public Library. It was later adapted as a feature film starring Marisa Tomei as Dottie, Alfred Molina as Juan, and Anjelica Huston as Carmela. "Humor seasons the pathos of these characters," noted Elena Brunet in the *Los Angeles Times*, reflecting "the difficulty that assimilated Cubans had in accepting the new immigrants." "The characters, the Cuban life in exile, and Miami itself are all there," according to the commentator in *Kirkus Reviews*. Brunet concluded: "Bell's novel successfully combines historical verity and a subtle seriousness with the humor and laughs that are her trademark."

Grievance

More than twenty-five years would elapse before Bell's next novel appeared, and *Grievance* reveals a marked change of direction. Gone are the Latin ambience, the flaky humor, the undercurrent of hope amidst chaos. *Grievance* is set in Nashville, Tennessee, where Desmond Declan worked in the music business until his death from cancer. His widow, Lily, has been immersed in her grief for a year. She goes through the routine motions of daily living for the sake of her young sons, but her depression is deepening, and Lily fears she is losing touch with reality.

Then Lily receives condolences from a stranger—a woman who seems to have had an intimate connection to her husband. On the anniversary of her wedding, Lily receives a gift of intimate lingerie, and this is only the beginning of a series of untoward events. She reports her growing concerns to the police, but given her erratic touch with reality, they seem reluctant to investigate. Lily fears that she and her sons could be in danger, and only she can solve the mystery. The author of the *Clues and Reviews* blog found merit in "the aspect of grief and the psychology of grief that was core to the plot." According to a reviewer in *Publishers Weekly*, "this absorbing tale of loss unfurls like a rippling bolt of silk."

The Seven-Year Atomic Make-over Guide

Bell has also dabbled in short fiction, including the tales collected in *The Seven-Year Atomic Make-over Guide: And Other Stories*. One story sees a jewel thief forced to pay society back by serving in a group home for the mentally challenged. In another, a midwife takes one of a set of twins.

Although various critics mentioned the uneven quality of the entries, John Kennedy reported in the *Antioch Review* that the best of the stories "show Bell's talent for the zany and sometimes destructive circumstances encountered in contemporary life." Joanne Wilkinson informed readers of *Booklist*: "It's a real pleasure to be taken into her richly imagined if skewed scenarios."

■ Biographical and Critical Sources

PERIODICALS

Antioch Review, spring, 1997, John Kennedy, review of *The Seven-Year Atomic Make-over Guide: And Other Stories*, p. 245.

Booklist, June 1, 1996, Joanne Wilkinson, review of *The Seven-Year Atomic Make-over Guide*, p. 1673.

Kirkus Reviews, November 1, 1985, review of *Saint*.

Los Angeles Times, September 23, 1990, Elena Brunet, review of *The Pérez Family*.

Publishers Weekly, November 1, 1985, review of *Saint*; June 29, 1990, Sybil Steinberg, review of *The Pérez Family*, p. 85; April 22, 1996, review of *The Seven-Year Atomic Make-over Guide*, p. 59; May 22, 2017, review of *Grievance*, p. 74.

ONLINE

Christine Bell Website, https://www.christinesaintbell.com (February 1, 2018).

Clues and Reviews, https://cluesandreviews.wordpress.com/ (August 4, 2017), review of *Grievance*.

Kirkus Reviews Online, https://www.kirkusreviews.com/ (January 13, 2018), review of *The Pérez Family*.

WJEC Website, http://www.wjec.co.uk/ (February 4, 2018), author profile.*

Chloe Benjamin

- ## Personal

Born in San Francisco, CA; married. *Education:* Vassar College, graduated; University of Wisconsin, M.F.A.

- ## Addresses

Home—Madison, WI.

- ## Career

Writer.

- ## Awards, Honors

Edna Ferber Fiction Book Award, for *The Anatomy of Dreams.*

- ## Writings

The Anatomy of Dreams, Atria Paperback (New York, NY), 2014.
The Immortalists, G.P. Putnam's Sons (New York, NY), 2018.

- ## Sidelights

Chloe Benjamin is a writer based in Madison, Wisconsin. She holds degrees from Vassar College and the University of Wisconsin.

The Anatomy of Dreams

In 2014, Benjamin released her first book, *The Anatomy of Dreams.* The volume's protagonist and narrator is Sylvie. When she is close to finishing college, she has an unexpected visit from her high-school boyfriend, Gabe, who persuades her to take part in an experiment on lucid dreaming. Gabe is assisting Adrian Keller in conducting the experiment. Gabe and Sylvie get back together, but the lucid dreams Sylvie continues to have complicate their lives and friendships.

Benjamin's *The Anatomy of Dreams* received mixed reviews. Writing on the *Washington Independent Review of Books* website, Nick Wolven remarked: "Her writing, certainly, is anything but lurid—brought to such a journalistic polish that some passages, especially those giving background on sleep research, have the cool clarity of a highbrow magazine article. Surely we can't complain too loudly if a writer avoids the cheap pleasures of suspense in favor of a literary interest in memory and regret. (And the final chapters here, for you *Paris Review* readers, are satisfyingly wistful.) Yet I sometimes longed for this novel about the study of dreams to have more of the chills and suspense." "The twist at the end is hardly shocking enough to excuse the slow buildup. Though Benjamin can turn a nice phrase, this is an uneven first novel," commented a *Kirkus Reviews* critic. However, Meredith Turits, a contributor to the *Bustle* website, asserted: "*The Anatomy of Dreams* is an ambitious novel that puts Benjamin on display as a writer with talent—and shows that she has plenty more in the tank. The novel itself is an easy read, yet not always simple to digest. A book like that is, in ways, a dream." "The plot works best when the thriller elements focus on the love story," noted a *Publishers Weekly* reviewer. The same reviewer described the book as "a sly, promising, and ambitious debut." Kristine Huntley, a critic in *Booklist*, predicted: "The mounting tension . . . will definitely keep the pages of this taut psychological exploration turning."

The Immortalists

In her second novel, *The Immortalists*, Benjamin tells the story of four siblings: Simon, Klara, Varya, and Daniel Gold. As children, a psychic predicts the dates of each of their deaths. The novel follows them through the following decades to determine how the predictions play out. Klara and Simon both settle in San Francisco, where Klara becomes a professional magician and Simon a ballet dancer. Daniel joins the army and serves as a doctor. He marries and moves to Kingston, New York. Varya becomes a scientist studying longevity. In 2006, Daniel discovers the truth about the psychic he and his siblings visited and determines to find her.

Benjamin told *BookPage* writer Alice Cary: "*The Immortalists* felt like the book that I was always meant to write. . . . If I died now, at least I would have written this. I don't think I'll ever have a book like this again." In an interview with Mark Rubinstein, a contributor to the *Huffington Post* website, Benjamin stated: "It's fair to say the premise of the book derives from my own neuroses and anxieties. The uncertainty of life itself and our lack of control over much that awaits us, have gnawed at me for years. These preoccupations came together in this novel in the form of three children who encountered a fortune-teller, and each one's story slowly unfolds."

"Benjamin's . . . premise situates her novel in magical territory, but the spell doesn't quite work," remarked a writer on the *Kirkus Reviews* website. Other assessments of the book were more favorable. Bob Duffy, a critic on the *Washington Independent Review of Books* website, suggested: "In the siblings' tales, author Benjamin shines a subtle light on the bonds of kinship and familial love, counter-balanced by the freedom, or willingness, to choose one's own path. *The Immortalists* is a rich and rewarding novel, sure to rank among the very best of 2018's crop, and one to be re-read and savored for years to come." Reviewing the book at *NPR.org*, Jean Zimmerman commented: "The reader will likely be thoroughly taken by the world of the Gold siblings, in all its shades of brilliant color. It's not a totally comfortable realm, since we know all too well how this tale's going to end, but getting there is lovely." Referring to Benjamin, Constance Grady stated in a review for *Vox*: "At her best, she succeeds in infusing her scenes with a kind of worn-in depth that keeps the reader grounded and aware of they are as Benjamin

hurtles us from 1969 to the present." About the characters, a *Publishers Weekly* critic wrote: "In Benjamin's expert hands their story becomes a moving meditation on fate, faith, and the family ties that alternately hurt and heal." "Benjamin has created mesmerizing characters and richly suspenseful predicaments in this profound and glimmering novel," asserted Donna Seaman in *Booklist*.

■ Biographical and Critical Sources

PERIODICALS

Booklist, August 1, 2014, Kristine Huntley, review of *The Anatomy of Dreams*, p. 12; December 15, 2017, Donna Seaman, review of *The Immortalists*, p. 87.

BookPage, January, 2018, Alice Cary, "Only the Good Die Young," author interview, p. 11.

Kirkus Reviews, September 1, 2014, review of *The Anatomy of Dreams*.

Library Journal, June 15, 2017, review of *The Immortalists*, p. 11a.

Publishers Weekly, April 7, 2014, review of *The Anatomy of Dreams*, p. 38; October 23, 2017, review of *The Immortalists*, p. 61.

ONLINE

Bustle, https://www.bustle.com/ (September 17, 2014), Meredith Turits, review of *The Anatomy of Dreams*.

Chloe Benjamin Website, https://www.chloebenjaminbooks.com (March 20, 2018).

Huffington Post, https://www.huffingtonpost.com/ (January 9, 2018), Mark Rubinstein, author interview.

Kirkus Reviews Online, https://www.kirkusreviews.com/ (July 17, 2017), review of *The Immortalists*.

New York Times Online, https://www.nytimes.com/ (January 19, 2018), Tina Jordan, review of *The Immortalists*.

NPR.org, https://www.npr.org/ (January 9, 2018), Jean Zimmerman, review of *The Immortalists*.

Popsugar, https://www.popsugar.com/ (January 8, 2018), Chelsea Adelaine Hassler, author interview.

Vox, https://www.vox.com/ (January 24, 2018), Constance Grady, review of *The Immortalists*.

Washington Independent Review of Books, http://www.washingtonindependentreviewofbooks.com/ (August 21, 2014), Nick Wolven, review of *The Anatomy of Dreams*; (January 16, 2018), Bob Duffy, review of *The Immortalists*.*

Lauren Berry

■ **Also Known As**

Marie Berry

■ **Personal**

Born in London, England; children: one.

■ **Addresses**

Home—London, England.

■ **Career**

Writer. *KnockBack* (satirical feminist zine), founding editor.

■ **Writings**

Living the Dream, Holt Paperbacks (New York, NY), 2017.

Contributor to newspapers and magazines, including *Easy Living, Guardian, Observer,* and *Independent.*

■ **Sidelights**

Lauren Berry, who also uses the name Marie Berry, is a journalist and writer who is founding editor of the satirical feminist zine *KnockBack,* which has been described as an antidote to magazines such as *Cosmopolitan* that emphasize looks and glamorous wardrobes rather than meatier content. Berry told *Writers Bloc* interviewer Molly McLaughlin that she and two friends started *KnockBack* right after graduating from university, "motivated by anger and wanting an outlet for the kind of work that we were doing at the time." Each issue is organized according to a theme—such as fashion, sex, or money—with content that parodies the quizzes, tip columns, and other characteristic features of major women's magazines. Berry's other journalism has appeared in *Easy Living* and in the London newspapers *Guardian, Independent,* and *Observer.*

In the interview, McLaughlin described Berry's first novel, *Living the Dream,* as a book about two young Londoners "at the crossroads of creative success and mediocrity." Emma, a writer, is biding time at an advertising agency until she can figure out how to make her blog into a literary (and lucrative) sensation. Clementine, an aspiring screenwriter, has just returned to London from college in New York and is unhappily tending bar while trying to sell a movie script to producers. The friends experience the exhilarations and frustrations typical of young adulthood, including romances, financial debts, and career challenges. Emma contends with her mixed feelings for her DJ roommate, Paul, who is sexy but a bit crazy, and with her frenemy Yasmin, while Clementine seethes over the fact that her obnoxious ex-boyfriend has already become famous as an actor while her own career seems all but unlaunchable. Both women also commiserate about difficult bosses and other matters, often over several glasses of wine. Over the course of the narrative, the trajectory of Emma's life is reflected in her blog, which shifts from accounts of sexy dates and parties to gloomy reports of health scares and ruminations on ethics and morality.

A contributor to *Kirkus Reviews* found Berry's "enjoyable flair for drama" only partially successful in the novel, pointing out that the author brings up tensions that are then too easily resolved. Even so, the reviewer admired the novel's "relatable characters who can laugh at themselves even when they fall down hard." Cameron Woodhead, writing in the *Sydney Morning Herald*, expressed a similar view, pointing out that the author allows her characters to skirt their problems without fully facing them. As a result, said Woodhead, the novel's resolution feels "unearned." *Living the Dream* received a more favorable review in *Publishers Weekly*, however, where a contributor enjoyed its "snark-filled" observations and praised the book as a "witty and sardonic romp" that also contains "depth and relevance."

Noting that novels about flawed, unsettled young or adolescent female protagonists have become increasingly popular, *Culturefly* reviewer Rabeea Saleem felt that *Living the Dream* distinguishes itself by examining the "enduring friendships of grown women at the end of their twenties," an often stressful age when the support of old friends can be crucial. Saleem also observed that Berry nails the banalities of contemporary popular culture, from self-consciously hip and quirky journalism to the blandness of corporate branding. Berry's hilariously brutal honesty, Saleem concluded, "makes this razor-sharp debut a winner."

In her interview with McLaughlin, Berry stated that she had always been interested in the theme of friendships and group dynamics among friends.

Living the Dream, she acknowledged, is "definitely character driven" rather than focused on plot. "It's a slice of life," said the author. "I didn't write a plot piece because life isn't plot driven. Life is a series of events. . . . You don't get married and drive off into the sunset and then just die. You have to get on with life."

■ **Biographical and Critical Sources**

PERIODICALS

Kirkus Reviews, May 15, 2017, review of *Living the Dream*.

Publishers Weekly, May 22, 2017, review of *Living the Dream*, p. 66.

Sydney Morning Herald, July 21, 2017, Cameron Woodhead, review of *Living the Dream*.

ONLINE

Cosy Dragon, http://www.thecosydragon.com/ (February 19, 2018), review of *Living the Dream*.

Culturefly, http://culturefly.co.uk/ (February 19, 2018), Rabeea Saleem, review of *Living the Dream*.

KnockBack, https://knockback.co.uk/ (February 19, 2018), zine profile.

Writers Bloc, htttps://thewritersbloc.net/ (February 19, 2018), Molly McLaughlin, interview with Berry.*

Liora Blake

■ Personal

Married.

■ Addresses

Agent—Victoria Lowes, Bent Agency, 19 W. 21st St., Ste. 201, New York, NY 10010.

■ Career

Writer.

■ Writings

"TRUE" E-BOOK SERIES

True North, Pocket Star (New York, NY), 2015.
True Devotion, Pocket Star (New York, NY), 2015.
True Divide, Pocket Star (New York, NY), 2015.

"GRAND VALLEY" SERIES

First Step Forward, Pocket Books (New York, NY), 2016.
Second Chance Season, Pocket Books (New York, NY), 2017.
Ready for Wild, Pocket Books (New York, NY), 2017.

■ Sidelights

Liora Blake is a native of Colorado. She is especially fond of the fertile Grand Valley along the Colorado Western Slope of the Rocky Mountains, near the Utah border. She has found that to be an ideal setting for contemporary romances about handsome, hardworking country boys, the women who cross their paths, and the steamy sex that draws them together.

"True" Series

Blake launched her career somewhere north of Colorado. The "True" series of e-books begins and ends in Crowell, a small Montana town in the middle of nowhere. *True North* introduces local newspaper writer Kate Mosely, whose sole claim to fame is a best-selling novel. Lured to Hollywood for television interviews, she enters the magnetic orbit of a high-profile rap star called Trax. Kate resists his brash facade until she discovers the sweet Trevor Jenkins behind the public persona.

True Devotion follows Trevor's tough-girl, self-destructive sister, Devon, through her own journey to the brink of happiness. A hard life has turned Devon into her own worst enemy. It is Trevor's patient guitarist, Simon Cole, who leads her toward a better life—in spite of herself.

True Divide marks a return to Kate's hometown and her sister, Lacey. While Kate took a chance on a celebrity rock star with a "bad boy" image, prom queen Lacey stayed home to work at the local Beauty Barn. She put her secret fling with outcast Jake Holt behind her when he left town ten years ago without so much as a good-bye. Now he is back, having traded the lip ring and skateboard for the lifestyle of a globe-trotting private pilot. Lacey must decide if she has the courage for a second-chance romance.

"Grand Valley" Series

In the "Grand Valley" series, Blake brings readers down from the popular mountain resorts and out of the cities. *First Step Forward* introduces professional football player Cooper Lowry, who needs to step out of the limelight before his latest concussion threatens to end his career. At a local drugstore he meets Whitney Reed, who has come to Denver to save her rural apple farm from foreclosure. She goes home to Hotchkiss empty-handed but undeterred from her mission. Cooper shows up at her doorstep a few days later with a very different proposition in mind. He falls unexpectedly into the rhythm of country living, while Whitney gradually works her way into his heart.

Like some of Blake's other male protagonists, Cooper's chauvinistic attitudes and coarse language could intimidate a lesser woman, but Whitney's independent spirit cannot be quenched. Cooper develops increasing respect for this intrepid apple farmer, especially as her financial situation worsens and she continues to resist his monetary support. Cooper never met anyone like her. Whitney is not impressed by his celebrity or his athletic ability, and she doesn't want his money. She sees him for the man he is and the better man he can become.

"Cooper did grow on me," observed a correspondent to *Dear Author*: "I ended up liking him quite a bit." A *Harlequin Junkie* contributor noted of the unlikely couple: "Neither is looking for love, but it sneaks up on them." A *Book Binge* commentator appreciated a story of grownups whose "problems were real life problems," characters who "fumbled their way through each situation that came their way." She recommended *First Step Forward* as "a sweet romance that really dug its way into my head."

One of Cooper and Whitney's friends is Garrett Strickland, and *Second Chance Season* is his story. Garrett returned to the old family farm in Hotchkiss when his father died. He ended up losing the farm, moving into a trailer, dropping out of college, and taking a job with the local agricultural cooperative. He contents himself with solitary activities like hunting and fishing, but he always lends a hand when friends or neighbors need help. That is how he meets Cara Cavanaugh.

Cara has temporarily abandoned her comfortable life in Chicago for an experiment in independent living. She plans to write an article about the agricultural scene in rural Colorado, but her first step is to get lost on the way to Hotchkiss. Garrett is the one who stops to help and realizes that this city girl will need a lot more help than directions to the nearest town.

Garrett introduces Cara to local interview subjects. As they travel from farm to farm, he is impressed with her determination to succeed, and Cara is taken by his easygoing approach to living in the moment. Their growing friendship inevitably leads to "a slow simmering romance," commented a reviewer at *Book Binge*.

The critic added: "Blake did a great job of weaving a compelling romance that readers will connect with." According to a reviewer in *Publishers Weekly,* "the author's exuberant writing makes a stock story line fresh." A reviewer at *Harlequin Junkie* observed that "Blake balanced character development, romance, family, and friendships" in "a fun, sexy opposites attract romance" that features a "diverse and entertaining cast of characters." A commentator at *Smexy Books* hinted that "Garrett has a best friend that is a total curmudgeon" who deserves his own story.

Ready for Wild pits grumpy game warden Braden Montgomery against a celebrity hunter in pink camouflage. Amber Regan hosts a hunting show on the verge of cancellation. She hopes that a televised elk hunt near Hotchkiss, Colorado, will improve her ratings and save her show. Braden has no respect for people who hunt for fame and fortune, especially posers in short shorts, no matter how beautiful they are. It is inevitable that sparks will fly, but this is no case of spontaneous combustion.

During Amber's scouting visits, Braden is surprised to learn that she is an experienced hunter in her own right and she also shares his respect for the integrity of the hunt and his commitment to conservation. Braden resists the growing chemistry between them until the final scouting visit, when they finally yield to mutual desire.

Amber returns home to arrange the scheduled hunt, but separation only fuels their passion as "heat sizzles through every text message," according to a *Publishers Weekly* contributor, "and singes every look." Susan Andersen wrote in *BookPage* that Blake has created "characters and situations we can sink our teeth into and believe in." They have become one of the author's trademarks, and they have turned casual readers into loyal fans.

■ **Biographical and Critical Sources**

PERIODICALS

Kirkus Reviews, August 15, 2017, review of *Ready for Wild.*

Publishers Weekly, May 1, 2017, review of *Second Chance Season,* p. 45; September 11, 2017, review of *Ready for Wild,* p. 49.

ONLINE

Book Binge, http://bookbinge.com/ (December 23, 2016), review of *First Step Forward;* (July 10, 2017), review of *Second Chance Season.*

BookPage, https://bookpage.com/ (October 31, 2017), Susan Andersen, review of *Ready for Wild.*

Dear Author, http://dearauthor.com/ (December 14, 2016), review of *First Step Forward.*

Harlequin Junkie, http://harlequinjunkie.com/ (November 21, 2016), review of *First Step Forward;* (May 16, 2017), review of *Second Chance Season.*

Liora Blake Website, http://www.liorablake.com (February 1, 2018).

Smexy Books, http://smexybooks.com/ (December 8, 2016), review of *First Step Forward;* (June 20, 2017), review of *Second Chance Season;* (November 2, 2017), review of *Ready for Wild.*

That's Normal, https://thats-normal.com/ (June 26, 2017), author interview.*

Howard Bodenhorn

■ Personal

Male. *Education:* Virginia Tech, B.S., 1982; Rutgers University, M.A., 1987, M.Phil., 1990, Ph.D., 1990.

■ Addresses

Office—Clemson University College of Business, John E. Walker Department of Economics, 170 Sirrine Hall, Clemson, SC 29634.

■ Career

Economic historian. Rutgers University, New Brunswick, NJ, visiting instructor, 1988-89; St. Lawrence University, Canton, NY, visiting assistant professor, 1990-93; Lafayette College, Easton, PA, assistant professor, 1993-98, associate professor, 1998-2004, professor, 2004-09; Yale University, New Haven, CT, visiting professor, 2006-07; Clemson University, Clemson, SC, professor, 2008—.

Research associate, National Bureau of Economic Research.

■ Awards, Honors

Teaching Excellence award, Rutgers University, 1988; Arthur H. Cole Award for Best Article in *Journal of Economic History*, 1993; Otto Eckstein Prize for Best Article in *Eastern Economic Journal*, 1997-98; Student Government Superior Teaching Award, Lafayette College, 2003; Mary Louis Van-Artsdalen Prize for Scholarly Achievement, Lafayette College, 2003. Grants and fellowships from John Simon Guggenheim Memorial Foundation,

Dwing Marion Kauffman Foundation, National Science Foundation, Economic History Association, Richard King Mellow Foundation, and Earhart Foundation; John E. Rovensky Graduate Fellow, 1989-90; John M. Olin Junior Faculty Fellow, 1995-96; Laura O'Shaugnessy Fellow, 2001-02; Larry J. Hackman Residency Grant, 2015-16.

■ Writings

A History of Banking in Antebellum America: Financial Markets and Economic Development in an Era of Nation-Building, Cambridge University Press (New York, NY), 2000.

State Banking in Early America: A New Economic History, Oxford University Press (New York, NY), 2003.

The Color Factor: The Economics of African-American Well-Being in the Nineteenth-Century South, Oxford University Press (New York, NY), 2015.

Contributor to books, including *Strategic Factors in American Economic History: A Volume to Honor Robert W. Fogel*, edited by Claudia Goldin and Hugh Rockoff, Chicago University Press, 1992; *The Experience of Free Banking*, edited by Kevin Down, Routledge Press, 1992; *Anglo-American Financial Systems: Institutions and Markets in the Twentieth Century*, edited by Michael Bordon and Richard Sylla, Irwin, 1996; *Corruption and Reform: Lessons from America's History*, edited by Edward Glaeser and Claudia Goldin, University of Chicago Press, 2006; *Historic Statistics of the United States: Millennial Edition*, Volume 3, edited by Susan B. Carter, et al., Cambridge University Press, 2006; *Founding Choices: American Economic Policy in the 1790s*, edited by Douglas Irwin and Richard Sylla, University of Chicago Press, 2011; *Enterprising America:*

Financial Institutions, Firms, and Households in Historical Perspective, edited by William Collins and Robert A. Margo, University of Chicago Press, 2015; *Handbook of Finance and Growth,* edited by Thorsten Beck and Ross Levine, Edward Elgar, 2016; and *Research in Economic History,* 2018.

Contributor to reference works, including *American Civil War: A Handbook of Research and Literature,* edited by Steven Woodworth, Greenwood Press, 1996; *Oxford Companion to United States History,* edited by Paul Boyer, Oxford University Press, 2001; *Online Encyclopedia of Economic History,* edited by Robert Whaples, 2002; *Oxford Encyclopedia of Economic History,* edited by Joel Mokyr, Oxford University Press, 2003; and *Encyclopedia of American Business History,* edited by Charles Geisst, Facts on File Publishing, 2005.

Contributor to periodicals, including *Review of Economics and Statistics; Journal of Economic History; Journal of Money, Credit, and Banking; Journal des Économistes et des Études Humaines; Eastern Economic Journal; Business History Review; Business & Economic History; Explorations in Economic History; Financial History Review; Journal of Law & Economics; Research in Economic History; Journal of Urban Economics; Journal of Interdisciplinary History; American Economic Review; Advances in Agricultural Economic History; Journal of Population Economics; B.E. Journal of Economic Analysis & Policy; Policy Sciences; Journal of Economic Education; Economic Inquiry;* and *Economic & Human Biology.*

■ **Sidelights**

Howard Bodenhorn is an economic historian who teaches at Clemson University. His work focuses on banking and financial history in the United States; the economics of crime, as seen in sentencing disparities and correlations between crime rates and immigration; and the economics of race. A graduate of Virginia Tech, where he majored in business, Bodenhorn earned M.A., M.Phil., and Ph.D. degrees from Rutgers University. He joined the Clemson faculty after completing teaching appointments at Rutgers, St. Lawrence University, Lafayette College, and Yale University.

In addition to contributing to periodicals, books, and reference publications, Bodenhorn is the author of three books. In *A History of Banking in Antebellum America: Financial Markets and Economic Development in an Era of Nation-Building,* Bodenhorn argues that, by generating credit, American banks played a crucial role in promoting economic development in the years leading up to the Civil War. *State Banking in Early America: A New Economic History* is the author's analysis of how regional differences in banking structures across the country contributed to economic development that served the specific needs of various regions.

In *The Color Factor: The Economics of African-American Well-Being in the Nineteenth-Century South,* Bodenhorn examines economic data to determine whether lighter-skinned African Americans were more prosperous than those with darker skin in the late antebellum South. Studying qualitative information as well as statistical data, the author finds clear evidence that among both free blacks and slaves, those considered to be of mixed race fared better than those not identified as mixed. Slaves of mixed race were generally more skilled than darker slaves, for example, and were more likely to sue for their freedom because they had more hope of winning and more to gain economically as free persons. These advantages also made it more likely that mixed-race slaves would be successful if they attempted to escape from bondage.

Journal of Southern History reviewer J. Morgan Kousser pointed out that Bodenhorn's economic approach to the book's topic sheds new light on the popular postmodern view that slave owners routinely raped slave women or kept them as concubines. The author writes that this kind of exploitation would come with significant economic costs, such as work hours lost because of pregnancy and child-rearing, and would risk alienating slave communities. Bodenhorn also argues that, if white men were motivated to buy lighter-skinned female slaves primarily for sex, the price of such females would be higher than for darker women; data from New Orleans, however, do not demonstrate such a correlation. In Kousser's view, these data are "consistent with [the author's] theorizing."

Bodenhorn shows that mixed-race individuals tended to marry others of mixed race and that mixed-race men had distinct advantages compared with darker men regarding occupational status. Indeed, he cites data showing that, in 1860, this gap in occupational status was comparable to that between all African American men and all white men. In matters such as literacy, school enrollment, property ownership, and employment, mixed-race men fared significantly better than black men. Evidence from Virginia and Maryland also shows that mixed-race men were, on average, taller than black men; because height often correlates with good nutrition, it can be assumed that mixed-race men generally enjoyed better health than black men.

Writing in *Choice*, J.D. Smith observed that Bodenhorn's thesis confirms what many have long understood about race in America and recommended *The Color Factor* as book of great relevance to the topic of race and racial identity. Praising the author's thorough research and keen analysis, Kousser concluded: "This important book deepens and complicates the history of race relations and should remind historians of how useful the application of social scientific methods to historical issues can be."

■ Biographical and Critical Sources

PERIODICALS

Choice, December, 2015, J.D. Smith, review of *The Color Factor: The Economics of African-American Well-Being in the Nineteenth-Century South*, p. 618.

Journal of Southern History, August, 2017, J. Morgan Kousser, review of *The Color Factor*, p. 685.

ONLINE

Clemson University Department of Economics Website, http://economics.clemson.edu/ (February 20, 2018), author faculty profile.

EH.net, https://eh.net/ (February 20, 2018), Marianne Wanamaker, review of *The Color Factor*.

Howard Bodenhorn Website, https://sites.google.com/site/howardbodenhorn (February 20, 2018).*

Claire Booth

■ **Personal**

Female.

■ **Career**

Journalist and author. Work has been published in the *Miami Herald, San Jose Mercury News, Philadelphia Inquirer, Contra Costa Times*, and other newspapers.

■ **Writings**

The False Prophet: Conspiracy, Extortion, and Murder in the Name of God, Berkley Books (New York, NY), 2008.
The Branson Beauty, Minotaur Books (New York, NY), 2016.
Another Man's Ground, Minotaur Books (New York, NY), 2017.

■ **Sidelights**

Claire Booth is a former crime reporter for several major newspapers, including the *Miami Herald, San Jose Mercury News*, and *Miami Herald*. Her first book, *The False Prophet: Conspiracy, Extortion, and Murder in the Name of God*, is a true account of Glenn Taylor Helzer, who with his brother murdered five people in California in 2000 as part of a bizarre scheme to raise money to facilitate the Second Coming of Jesus Christ. The Helzers were convicted at trial in 2004 and sentenced to death. As of 2018, Glenn Taylor Helzer remains on death row; his brother, Justin Helzer, hanged himself in his prison cell in 2013.

The Branson Beauty

After the exhausting process of writing *The False Prophet*, Booth decided that she would prefer to write about fictional murders rather than real ones. Her debut novel, *The Branson Beauty*, is set in the Ozarks and begins when a showboat owned by a local businessman runs aground in a lake near Branson, Missouri. The town's sheriff, Hank Worth, must find the resources to rescue more than a hundred people from the foundering boat, while also trying to find out what had happened. The boat's captain, who appears to be in shock, can tell Hank nothing.

To make matters much worse, the body of a strangled college student, Mandy Bryson, is found locked inside one of the boat's cabins. Mandy had been a high school track star and prom queen, and had been on the boat to attend a birthday party for her boyfriend's grandmother. Who could have had a motive to kill this genuinely popular teenager? Hank and his team eventually discover that Mandy had been receiving letters from an anonymous stalker. As the investigation heats up, the boat explodes and is destroyed by fire, leading Hank to add arson to his list of suspicions.

Reviewers enjoyed the book's fast-paced plot and engaging characters. Hank, who had formerly served in the Kansas City Police Department, is not only a skilled detective but also a devoted family man who struggles to balance the demands of his job with those of his family: his wife, Maggie, a surgeon; their two young children; and Maggie's elderly father, who lives with them. Noting the book's "humor and humanity," *Booklist* contributor Michele Leber hailed *The Branson Beauty* as a "promising debut." A reviewer for *Publishers Weekly* expressed similar enthusiasm for the novel, calling it a "standout debut" with depth as well as "touches of sly humor."

Another Man's Ground

In *Another Man's Ground*, Hank is embroiled in a multiple-murder investigation while facing an election campaign to keep his job. Having been appointed sheriff of Branson County to fill a vacancy, Hank has never had to win an election before, and he has no appetite for the task. His opponent is a deputy with scant experience but powerful political and financial connections. With little time or interest to run a political campaign, Hank is happy to have his wife hire professional consultant Darcy Blakely to do this job. This gives him time to delve into a strange case involving the removal of bark from numerous slippery elm trees growing on land owned by Vern Miles and his family. Tempted at first to consider the case trivial, Hank learns that the bark is extremely valuable—a fact that sheds new light on the ongoing feud between the Miles family and the land's former owners, the Kinneys. When undocumented immigrant workers hired by the Miles family accidentally discover dead bodies on Kinney property, where slippery elms have also been stripped of bark, Hank realizes he will have to solve several cold cases. But he will also have to find a way to hide the fact that he had known that the undocumented immigrants were in the woods and had chosen not to look for them—which could mean certain defeat at the polls if his opponent uses this information against him. The murder investigation stokes the property feud to the boiling point, spelling grave danger not only for the immigrants but also for Hank, his team, and his family.

Meanwhile, the Taylor brothers have come to Hank's attention. They have a reputation for stealing pigs, but Hank suspects them of far more serious crimes after discovering more than one million dollars hidden beneath their trailer. With many of his staff secretly supporting his opponent in the upcoming sheriff's election, Hank must rely on two trusted deputies for help: young Sam, who is inexperienced but eager to learn; and veteran Sheila, who is the only woman and the only African American officer on the force.

A contributor to *Kirkus Reviews* found much to enjoy in *Another Man's Ground*, observing that the novel is "both an excellent police procedural and a surprisingly humorous look at politics and family feuds." Writing in *Publishers Weekly*, a reviewer observed that Booth's "affectionate treatment of the decent and shrewd people of Branson" and her nuanced insights into her protagonist make this novel worthwhile.

■ Biographical and Critical Sources

PERIODICALS

Booklist, May 1, 2016, Michele Leber, review of *The Branson Beauty*, p. 19.

Kirkus Reviews, June 1, 2017, review of *Another Man's Ground*.

Publishers Weekly, May 23, 2016, review of *The Branson Beauty*, p. 45; May 8, 2017, review of *Another Man's Ground*, p. 40.

ONLINE

Claire Booth Home Page, http://www.clairebooth.com (February 14, 2018).*

Dusti Bowling

■ **Personal**

Born in AZ; married; children: three.

■ **Addresses**

Home—Carefree, AZ. *Agent*—Shannon Hassan, Marsal Lyon Literary Agency, PMB 121, 665 San Rodolfo Dr. 124, Solana Beach, CA 92075.

■ **Career**

Author and novelist.

■ **Writings**

The Day We Met, Ketina Publishing House (Carefree, AZ), 2012.

The Boy Who Loved Me, Ketina Publishing House (Carefree, AZ), 2013.

Grace and Daisies, Ketina Publishing House (Carefree, AZ), 2013.

Insignificant Events in the Life of a Cactus, Sterling Children's Books (New York, NY), 2017.

■ **Sidelights**

Growing up in Scottsdale, Arizona, Dusti Bowling was an avid reader. "Books were my friends, my family, my entertainment, my therapy," Bowling noted in an interview with *School Library Journal Online* contributor Karen Yingling, referring to a difficult time during her childhood when her parents got divorced. Later in life, Bowling tried various careers before realizing that she wanted to be a writer. The author of several self-published books aimed at a teenage audience, Bowling made her middle-grade novel debut with *Insignificant Events in the Life of a Cactus,* about a teenager named Aven who was born without arms.

Bowling's interest in people without arms began after a cousin serving in Iraq lost an eye and was going to lose an arm as well. As a result, Bowling started to do research on people without limbs, but after her cousin died, Bowling discontinued her interest. A video of an armless bodybuilder viewed years later rekindled Bowling's desire to learn more about people without limbs. Commenting on the inspiration for her novel in her interview with Yingling, Bowling noted that she had seen a video of woman without arms "who did everything with her feet," from caring for her baby to driving to lifting weights. Bowling went on to tell Yingling: "I thought about her a long time afterward until Aven started to form in my mind. When I decided to finally write this story, I found there wasn't a whole lot written specifically about people without arms, but there were some really great videos online." A series of videos on YouTube by a woman who went by the name Tisha Unarmed especially impressed Bowling. "The more I watched Tisha's videos, the more I realized just how capable Aven would be," Bowling noted in the *School Library Journal Online* interview, adding that Tisha as well as the armless bodybuilder who lived near Bowling eventually reviewed a draft of the book to determine if Bowling had handled the character of Aven correctly. She received positive feedback from both.

In *Insignificant Events in the Life of a Cactus,* Aven Green has moved from Kansas to Arizona after her father lands a job as manager of a theme park called the Stagecoach Pass. Like most teenagers, Aven finds the move challenging, but she is facing the extra burden of explaining to her schoolmates her lack of arms, which is due to a rare genetic disorder. The stares and questions she faces make Aven miss her old home, but she fortunately is optimistic by nature and has a good sense of humor. These attributes keep "her looking for the silver linings in her new life," noted Evelyn Khoo Schwartz in *School Library Journal.*

Throughout the book Bowling not only highlights Aven's positive attitude but also addresses the stereotypes people with disabilities must endure. "Bowling hopes that they might feel validated by seeing an aspect of themselves represented," wrote a *Publishers Weekly* contributor. Bowling includes other characters with disabilities, including Aven's best friend, Connor, who has Tourette's syndrome. Bowling also researched this syndrome for the book and could relate to the character because her husband and children have similar disorders.

In the novel, Aven's "can-do" attitude is highlighted by the mysterious happenings at the rundown theme park her dad manages. Things keep going missing, from a photograph and a necklace to tarantulas. Aven decides that she is going to find out just exactly what is going on. The book's "portrayal of characters with rarely depicted disabilities is informative, funny, and supportive," wrote a *Kirkus Reviews* contributor. A reviewer writing for *Publishers Weekly* remarked that *Insig-*

nificant Events in the Life of a Cactus shows "how negotiating others' discomfort can be one of the most challenging aspects of having a physical difference."

■ Biographical and Critical Sources

PERIODICALS

Booklist, August 1, 2017, John Peters, review of *Insignificant Events in the Life of a Cactus*, p. 61.
Kirkus Reviews, July 1, 2017, review of *Insignificant Events in the Life of a Cactus.*
Publishers Weekly, May 15, 2017, "Dusti Bowling: *Insignificant Events in the Life of a Cactus*, Bowling's Middle Grade Novel about a Girl Born without Arms, Looks beyond Disability into the Complex Inner Life of a Teen Whose Life is Changing Rapidly," p. S89; June 19, 2017, review of *Insignificant Events in the Life of a Cactus*, p. 112.
School Library Journal, May, 2017, Evelyn Khoo Schwartz, review of *Insignificant Events in the Life of a Cactus*, p. 78.

ONLINE

Dusti Bowling Website, https://www.dustibowling.com (January 9, 2018).
School Library Journal Online, http://www.slj.com/ (September 20, 2017), Karen Yingling, "Chatting with Dusti Bowling, Author of *Insignificant Events in the Life of a Cactus*."*

Mary Lynn Bracht

■ **Personal**

Female. *Education:* Birkbeck College, London, M.A.

■ **Addresses**

Home—London, England.

■ **Career**

Author. *Military service:* Served in U.S. Air Force.

■ **Writings**

White Chrysanthemum, G.P. Putnam's Sons (New York, NY), 2017.

■ **Sidelights**

Novelist Mary Lynn Bracht's debut novel is *White Chrysanthemum,* based on stories she learned when she visited her mother's native Korean village in 2002. Bracht, who has a degree in anthropology and who served in the U.S. military, discovered the still largely unknown tale of the Korean "comfort women," who were kidnapped during World War II and forced into sexual slavery to occupying Japanese forces. Although the tale of the "comfort women" and their fate was well-known in Korea, the women themselves did not receive recognition as victims of war crimes until about half a century after the war. Many of them, in fact, had to live out their lives shunned by their communities for having been raped. "Masterfully crafted," wrote a *Publishers Weekly* reviewer, "Bracht's mesmerizing debut novel is rich with historical detail and depth of emotion."

The novel, the author noted in a *Library Journal* interview with Christine Barth, is not merely a recounting of an atrocity that occurred during what was perhaps the most atrocity-laden war in world history. It also speaks to the ongoing problem of human trafficking that continues to plague the world well into the twenty-first century. "My mother's friends all grew up in South Korea and married American soldiers before settling in Texas. Many of their stories revealed hardships with family, illness, poverty, and how they were let down by the patriarchal system at that time," Bracht said in her *Library Journal* interview. "When I first learned of the so-called 'comfort women' and their plight to be recognized as survivors of military war rape, I understood that [they wanted] . . . to declare their life stories in the words they chose." "When I heard about the 'comfort women', I was at a point when I was already researching Korean history," Bracht told Katherine Cowdrey in the *Bookseller.* "Probably over twelve years passed before I decided I would put this somewhere. I wrote a short story, which became my master's thesis, which became my novel." "I think it's a hole in our history," Bracht said in her interview with Cowdrey; "I would like to see it filled a bit more."

White Chrysanthemum begins in 1943, at a time when Japanese forces had already occupied the Korean peninsula for some time. "The novel introduces 16-year-old Hana who, while protecting her little sister Emi, is forcibly taken away by a Japanese soldier to become a 'comfort woman' for the Japanese army," explained Katherine Cowdrey in the *Bookseller.* Despite her situation, Hana refuses to be paralyzed by it and constantly tries to escape from her captors. For her part, Emi has to learn to cope with misplaced guilt over her sister's loss throughout her long life. "Coerced into a loveless marriage with a Korean policeman," stated a *Kirkus Reviews* contributor, "Emi is now an elderly widow with two adult children and horrific memories of what happened." Despite everything that has happened in her life—including the fate of her family in the Korean War less than a decade after Hana was taken away—Emi remains fiercely committed to seeing that her sister receives justice. "Reinforcing the book's feminist thread," Cowdrey continued, "the women are from a fiercely proud lineage of *haenyeo* (female divers who harvest marine life from the ocean floor) on Japanese-occupied Jeju Island, Korea, where, unusually for the broader patriarchal society, they are the breadwinners. Despite the atrocities each is forced to suffer in the other's absence during the war . . . their sense of self and sisterhood endures." Bracht's "captivating and heartbreaking debut novel," declared Bridget Thoreson in a *Booklist* review, "honors the many thousands of women who were enslaved through WWII."

■ Biographical and Critical Sources

PERIODICALS

Booklist, November 1, 2017, Bridget Thoreson, review of *White Chrysanthemum,* p. 33.

Bookseller, November 10, 2017, Katherine Cowdrey, "Mary Lynn Bracht: A Literary Historical Debut, the Redemptive Tale of Two Sisters Torn Apart by the Second World War, Breaks the long-held Silence on the Plight of Korea's 'Comfort Women.'" p. 16.

Kirkus Reviews, January 1, 2018, review of *White Chrysanthemum.*

Library Journal, June 15, 2017, review *of White Chrysanthemum,* p. 3A; February 15, 2018, Christine Barth, "Q&A: Mary Lynn Bracht," p. 53.

Publishers Weekly, November 13, 2017, review of *White Chrysanthemum,* p. 35.

ONLINE

James Grant, http://www.jamesgrant.com/ (March 21, 2018), author profile.

Mary Lynn Bracht Website, https://marybracht.com (March 21, 2018).*

Christopher Brown

■ Also Known As

Chris N. Brown
Chris Nakashima-Brown

■ Personal

Children.

■ Addresses

Home—Austin, TX. *Agent*—Mark Gottlieb, Trident Media Group, 41 Madison Ave., 36th Fl., New York, NY 10010.

■ Career

Writer, novelist, and lawyer. Also reported from war zones in Central America and cohosted a punk rock radio show.

■ Writings

(Editor, with Eduardo Jiménez Mayo) *Three Messages and a Warning: Contemporary Mexican Short Stories of the Fantastic*, Small Beer Press (Easthampton, MA), 2011.
Tropic of Kansas (novel), Harper Voyager (New York, NY), 2017.

Contributor of short stories to anthologies and periodicals.

■ Sidelights

Writer and lawyer Christopher Brown has taken companies public, worked on Supreme Court confirmations, negotiated hundreds of technology deals, investigated fraud, and protected whistle-blowers in his role as a lawyer. His short stories, some written under the name Chris Nakashima-Brown, have appeared in anthologies and periodicals. He is also the coeditor of *Three Messages and a Warning: Contemporary Mexican Short Stories of the Fantastic*, which was nominated for a World Fantasy Award.

In his first novel, *Tropic of Kansas*, Brown presents a dystopian future in which the United States no longer exists as a democratic nation, and a foster brother and sister find themselves on different sides of the law. "I set out to write an adventure story that began in the post-9/11 Middle East, and ended up starting an uprising in a dystopian America," Brown told Paul Semel in an interview at the *Paulsemel.com* website, adding: "I knew where I wanted to go, and I realized that to get there I needed to turn the world upside down, into a mirror America where 9/11 didn't happen, and all the dark energy of that event and its aftermath was focused on the domestic population."

In the novel, the United States has been broken up into warring territories. In the middle of these territories is an area known as the "Tropic of Kansas," a vast wasteland that serves as a demilitarized zone. In his interview with Semel, Brown noted that he chose to call the area the Tropic of Kansas because "the book is a dystopia of the American heartland, examining a very particular place to finder wider truths, an effort to pull off what my friend Bruce Sterling calls 'a regional novel of Planet Earth.'"

In the setup for the dystopian world of *Tropic of Kansas*, Brown informs readers that the end began when President Ronald Reagan died from the real-life assassination attempt in 1981 by John Hinckley. As a result, Alexander Haig went on to establish a militaristic presidency that went to war with Iran and the Soviet Union. Haig also oversaw efforts to take control of Central America's natural resources. By the twenty-first century, democracy in America has ended, and a dictator is in the White House. Thomas Mack is a narcissistic kleptocrat whose evil doings led a former vice president to try to assassinate him. Mack is so vain that he hires an actor to portray him at times. Writing for *NPR.org*, Jason Sheehan described the novel's setup as "not simple dystopia, but complicated by present reality and recognizable politics. Not nameless or alien, but very much named and very close to home."

The novel features eighteen-year-old Sig, who is an orphan of political dissidents. As the novel opens, Sig is being deported from Canada and sent back across the border wall to the United States. His foster sister, Tania, is a government investigator who has been ordered to hunt Sig following his escape from a midwestern Gitmo. It turns out that Sig is on his way to occupied New Orleans and a revolutionary stronghold that is operating there. Although he is a master of living off the grid, Sig still must navigate the dangerous terrain of the Tropic of Kansas, a barren land overseen by civilian militias and watched over with autonomous drones. One wrong move, and Sig will be captured or killed.

Tania does not want to hunt her foster brother, but she has agreed to do so for the promise by the government to free her mother. Working undercover in the underground to track down her brother, Tania is connected with Sig because her family briefly fostered him many years earlier, until Sig killed a police officer at the age of eleven during a riot. Tania ended up working as a lawyer in Washington, DC. However, after heckling President Mack on the White House lawn, she is detained and then offered the subsequent deal to find Sig, who authorities believe may be the key to breaking the resistance. The novel follows Sig and Tania in alternating chapters as they are on their respective "missions." Eventually, the two come together, along with a Texas billionaire who oversees pirate broadcasts and who is trying to find the deposed former vice president. It turns out that the vice president, with a National Guard colonel, helped to liberate Louisiana, but only temporarily.

Literary critic Jill Lepore's "insistence that dystopian literature 'used to be a fiction of resistance' and has now 'become a fiction of submission'

doesn't quite fit for Christopher Brown's timely and gritty debut novel," wrote *Los Angeles Review of Books* website contributor Christopher Urban. He went on to note later in the same review: "Brown's economical prose style ultimately fits this narrative, and the story essentially unfolds as a road novel." A *Publishers Weekly* contributor remarked that Brown does not allow his characters to "easily triumph . . . because he respects them too much to cheapen the costs that they must bear to succeed."

Brown told *CA*: "The music of language and the ability to create other worlds, or at least make this one more vivid, got me interested in writing.

"I have been most influenced by the example of writers who couple stylistic innovation with unflinching honesty, from science fiction writers like J.G. Ballard, William Gibson, and Joanna Russ to mainstream writers like Joan Didion, Cormac McCarthy, and Hunter S. Thompson.

"I try to write a kind of speculative realism, using the imaginative tools of fantastic literature to hold a fun-house mirror up to reality, while at the same time striving to have fidelity to the truth. The process involves working the material of the observed world through a weird mind-machine of language, invention, and feeling. It's hard!

"The most surprising thing I have learned as a writer is how writing teaches you to see.

"In addition to entertaining, I hope that my work can help people witness the world they live in with fresh eyes, by inverting it through a speculative prism that reveals truths hidden in plain sight."

■ **Biographical and Critical Sources**

PERIODICALS

Publishers Weekly, May 22, 2017, review of *Tropic of Kansas*, p. 76.

ONLINE

Boing Boing, https://boingboing.net/ (July 11, 2017), Cory Doctorow, "*Tropic of Kansas*: Making America Great Again Considered Harmful."
Christopher Brown Website, http://christopherbrown.com (January 9, 2018).
Civilian Reader, https://civilianreader.com/ (July 11, 2017), review of *Tropic of Kansas*.

Los Angeles Review of Books Online, https://lareviewofbooks.org/ (September 2, 2017), Christopher Urban, "Dystopian Resistance: Christopher Brown's *Tropic of Kansas.*"

NPR.org, https://www.npr.org/ (July 9, 2017), Jason Sheehan, "*Tropic of Kansas* Rips Dystopia from the Headlines."

Paulsemel.com, http://paulsemel.com/ (July 25, 2017), Paul Semel, "Exclusive Interview: *Tropic of Kansas* Author Christopher Brown."

RT Book Reviews, https://www.rtbookreviews.com/ (January 27, 2018), Leah Hansen, review of *Tropic of Kansas.*

SFF 180, http://sff180.com/ (January 27, 2018), review of *Tropic of Kansas.*

Carina Chocano

1968-

■ Personal

Born 1968. *Education:* Northwestern University, B.A., 1990; San Francisco State University, M.A., 1994.

■ Addresses

Home—Los Angeles, CA.

■ Career

Writer, film and television critic, and magazine journalist. *Los Angeles Times,* television critic, 2003-04, film critic, 2004-08; freelance writer, 2011—; *New York Times Magazine,* contributing writer, 2017—.

■ Writings

Do You Love Me, or Am I Just Paranoid? The Serial Monogamist's Guide to Love, Villard Books (New York, NY), 2003.
You Play the Girl: On Playboy Bunnies, Stepford Wives, Train Wrecks, and Other Mixed Messages, Mariner Books (Boston, MA), 2017.

Contributor to magazines and newspapers, including *New York, Elle, Vogue, Wired, Rolling Stone, Washington Post, Vulture, California Sunday, Texas Monthly, New Republic,* and *New Yorker.*

■ Sidelights

Carina Chocano is a writer, magazine journalist, cultural observer, and film and television critic. She was the TV critic for the *Los Angeles Times* from 2003 to 2004 and the film critic from 2004 to 2008. She is currently a contributing writer to *New York Times Magazine.* She has contributed to many prominent national magazines including *Vogue, Elle, Wired, Rolling Stone, New Yorker, Entertainment Weekly,* and *Bust.* She holds a B.A. in comparative literature and theory from Northwestern University and an M.A. from San Francisco State University in film production and theory. Chocano lives in Los Angeles, California.

Chocano's first book, *Do You Love Me, or Am I Just Paranoid? The Serial Monogamist's Guide to Love,* is a humorous look at the subject of love, dating, and monogamy. Basing the book on some of her own experiences in romance, Chocano offers amusing takes on some of the major elements of a relationship. She covers dating and what new couples can do on dates. She discusses the critical differences between living together and being married. She also helps women evaluate their dates and potential mates, and she eventually asks the critical question of whether one is in love or just insane. Chocano's tongue-in-cheek advice may well be considered bad advice by many, but it is through the irrationality of her suggestions that some important truths about romance and love are found.

You Play the Girl: On Playboy Bunnies, Stepford Wives, Train Wrecks, and Other Mixed Messages is based on the many films and television programs Chocano has viewed in her role as a television and movie critic. During these viewings, Chocano came to the realization that "despite the relative progress women made in the twentieth century, twenty-first century entertainment still completely fails to accurately and dynamically represent women," commented *Booklist* writer Courtney Eathorne. In response, Chocano wrote the book, which contains carefully considered essays on the frequently conflicting, sometimes completely negative images of women in American popular culture.

During her own childhood, Chocano notes, she and other girls were expected to identify with the image of the fairytale princess. She quickly realized that the princess archetype was unsatisfactory to her, and that it was more likely to be oppressive and limiting to the young girls who adopted it. The image of a frail and helpless princess waiting to be rescued by the stereotypical handsome prince was not an identity she could accept for herself, nor is it one that she considers useful for others.

Chocano observes that Hollywood has four female stereotypes that make up most of the female characters: the mother, the homemaker, the love interest, and the generic "girl." This last character is something of a contradiction: a female who can gain the admiration and camaraderie of men while still maintaining a highly feminine appearance and outlook. Perhaps more disturbing, this female character must maintain a position of being sexually appealing and desirable to males, even those males she sees as her friends but not potential partners.

Throughout the book, "Chocano finds much evidence that movies and TV send a message undermining girls' empowerment," observed a contributor to *Kirkus Reviews*. Films such as *Pretty Woman* send the wrong kind of message, while movies such as *Thelma and Louise* and *Private Benjamin* offer a narrative that resonates more thoroughly with feminist sensibilities. On television, she finds that hugely popular programs such as *Sex and the City* have succeeded only in creating objectionable stereotypes. Other shows, such as *Bewitched* and *I Dream of Jeannie*, create allegorical representatives of women who have the power to change, if not destroy, the world around them.

The *Kirkus Reviews* writer called *You Play the Girl* a "sharply perceptive look at the myths that constrain women." A reviewer in *Publishers Weekly* concluded: "These essays will appeal to anyone interested in how women's stories are told."

■ Biographical and Critical Sources

PERIODICALS

Booklist, July 1, 2017, Courtney Eathorne, review of *You Play the Girl: On Playboy Bunnies, Stepford Wives, Train Wrecks, and Other Mixed Messages*, p. 5.

Kirkus Reviews, June 15, 2017, review of *You Play the Girl*.

Publishers Weekly, May 8, 2017, review of *You Play the Girl*, p. 49.

ONLINE

Carina Chocano Website, http://www.carinachocano. com (February 9, 2018).*

John Clayton

1964-

■ Personal

Born 1964, in Greenfield, MA. *Education:* Graduated from Williams College, 1985.

■ Addresses

Home—MT.

■ Career

Writer and ghostwriter. Industrial Economics, Cambridge, MA, research assistant, 1985-90; Gateway Software, Fromberg, MT, product support writer, 1992-94; Information Engineering, Inc., Denver, CO, technical writer, 1994-97; Rocky Mountain College, Billings, MT, adjunct faculty member, 1995; Taliant Software, technical writer, 1997-2005; Metia Group, independent writer, 2005-12; Montana State University, Billings, visiting writer in residence, 2016; Grey Towers Heritage Association, Milford, PA, visiting scholar, 2018. Independent writer, 1992—.

■ Writings

Small Town Bound: Your Guide to Small-Town Living, from Determining If Life in the Slower Lane Is for You, to Choosing the Perfect Place to Set Roots, to Making Your Dreams Come True, Career Press (Franklin Lakes, NJ), 1996.

The Cowboy Girl: The Life of Caroline Lockhart, University of Nebraska Press (Lincoln, NE), 2007.

Red Lodge, Arcadia Publishers (Charleston, SC), 2008.

Stories from Montana's Enduring Frontier: Exploring an Untamed Legacy, History Press (Charleston, SC), 2013.

Wonderlandscape: Yellowstone National Park and the Evolution of an American Cultural Icon, Pegasus Books (New York, NY), 2017.

Contributor to periodicals, including *Montana Quarterly* and *Big Sky Journal.*

■ Sidelights

John Clayton is a freelance, technical, and business writer based in Montana. His essays and books focus on themes relating to the natural world. Born in western Massachusetts, Clayton attended Williams College and worked for several years in the Boston area before moving west in 1990. His experiences as a western transplant provide a personal perspective in his first book, *Small Town Bound: Your Guide to Small-Town Living, from Determining If Life in the Slower Lane Is for You, to Choosing the Perfect Place to Set Roots, to Making Your Dreams Come True,* which offers concrete advice on making the transition from the big city to a smaller town.

The Cowboy Girl

Clayton's *The Cowboy Girl: The Life of Carline Lockhart* was welcomed as an informative and engaging biography of a woman who has received relatively little scholarly attention. Caroline Lockhart (1871-1962) was a journalist, author, and editor who from 1926 to 1950 owned a ranch in Dryhead, Montana; after her death, it was listed with the National Register of Historic Places as the Caroline Lockhart Ranch. Lockhart had grown up in the Midwest and was educated in Pennsylvania. After a stint as a reporter for the *Boston Post*, she moved with a boyfriend to Cody, Wyoming, in 1904, and began writing pseudonymous local color stories for the *Philadelphia Press*. She developed a reputation for sometimes embellishing the truth in order to create what she considered an authentic representation of western life. Cody residents became the models for several of Lockhart's fictional characters; she attracted particular controversy for her harsh portrait of Francis Lane, a female physician, in the novel *Lady Doc*. Clayton writes that Lockhart and Lane had once been friends, but their relationship had ended after Lockhart published an article accusing the doctor of negligent care of immigrant workers in the area. A government investigation cleared Lane's name and damaged Lockhart's professional reputation. Nevertheless, Lockhart remained an active participant in the town's social life: Cody's annual rodeo, envisioned as an event that would preserve central elements of Old West culture, was her brainchild. Lockhart's years on her Montana ranch were also fraught with controversy as she battled neighbors over issues such as cattle rustling and water rights. She returned to Cody in 1950 and lived there until her death at age ninety-one.

Reviewing *The Cowboy Girl* in the *Oregon Historical Quarterly*, Laura Woodworth-Ney said that Clayton "unfolds Lockhart's life with little interpretation, though he draws conclusions from her actions and her words." About Lockhart's decision never to marry, for example, Clayton writes that she wanted to retain her independence and choose for herself "what she would work at, where she would live, and whom she could hate." Lockhart often comes across in her own writings as difficult, nasty, and homophobic, said Woodworth-Ney, but she also took up the cause for immigrant workers' rights, and she provided shelter and food for many in need. Observing that the book does not seek to resolve these contradictions about its subject, the reviewer described *The Cowboy Girl* as "an enjoyable and readable window" into Lockhart's world. With similar enthusiasm, *Booklist* contributor Colleen Mondor praised the book as both a biography of a fascinating woman and an exploration of the mystique of the American West.

Wonderlandscape

In *Wonderlandscape: Yellowstone National Park and the Evolution of an American Cultural Icon*, Clayton writes about the history and development of the country's first national park. Established in 1872, Yellowstone National Park covers almost 3,500 miles, mostly in Wyoming but also in part of Montana and Idaho. From its creation, the park has drawn tourists eager to witness its distinctive geological features, which include geysers, hot springs, and the Grand Canyon of Yellowstone. Early visitors, enthralled by the park's majestic landscapes, described their encounters with this landscape as sublime; these rapt accounts helped to foster increased interest tourism to the park. Visitors also enjoyed stories about surprise encounters with the park's grizzly bears. Yellowstone is also home to bison and, more recently, reintroduced wolves.

Living near Yellowstone for many years, Clayton has watched and pondered visitors' responses to the park. In *Wonderlandscape* he writes that Yellowstone is best understood through these stories, more as a cultural entity than a physical one. Indeed, he argues that the park's story is linked to the story of America itself. "The story of Yellowstone," he writes, "is the story of a place gifted with natural wonders and cultural force, and with powerful yet ever-changing ways to harness those gifts for the greater good. It is, in other words, the story of America."

Washington Post reviewer Dennis Drabelle considered Clayton's approach to his subject "energetic and insightful." Drabelle appreciated the author's argument that the creation of Yellowstone National Park had much to do with a desire to create a national identity based, in large part, on the exceptional features of the western landscape. Clayton discusses the role played by Cornelius Hedges, a well-connected lawyer who in 1870 hatched the idea among his wealthy associates of creating a means of protecting the Yellowstone wilderness from private ownership; by artists such as Thomas Moran, whose paintings of Yellowstone gave Congress an idea of the awe-inspiring landscape they had been asked to preserve from commercial development; and by entrepreneurs such as architect Robert Reamer, whose innovative design for the Old Faithful Inn ushered in a new style that came to be called National Park Service Rustic. By the mid-twentieth century, when photographer Ansel Adams received a federal commission to photograph the park, Yellowstone had become a frequent tourist destination. The photographer objected to this development, sensing that the park had become merely a vacation playground, and in his photographs he emphasized what he considered Yellowstone's spiritual essence. He also argued that the park's value lay in its wilderness, meant to be experienced without modern comforts and conveniences. An opposite view arose in the 1960s, when "The Yogi Bear Show," about a cartoon bear living in a park called Jellystone, sparked a huge increase in tourism and "secured [Yellowstone] for the masses."

Pointing out that *Wonderlandscape* does not do justice to the park's extraordinary features, particularly the Old Faithful geyser, Drabelle nevertheless admired the author's acknowledgment that there is more to Yellowstone than majestic scenery. In addition to its awe-inspiring peaks and geysers, write Clayton, Yellowstone also contains "vast quantities of empty backcountry, much of it monotonous lodgepole-pine forest," no less important to the park's ecology than its more picturesque attractions. The author ends the book with thoughts on the park's possible future, which might include destruction if its subterranean supervolcano erupts. A writer for *Kirkus Reviews* described *Wonderlandscape* as a "thoughtful study of a celebrated natural wonder," and in *Booklist*, contributor Dan Kaplan admired the way "Clayton enthusiastically tells the foundational stories of the magnificent park." "While not exhaustive," stated Sean Reichard in an online review for *Yellowstone Insider*, "*Wonderlandscape* is a great primer on Yellowstone history and a unique discussion of the park's place in America."

■ Biographical and Critical Sources

BOOKS

Clayton, John, *The Cowboy Girl: The Life of Caroline Lockhart*, University of Nebraska Press (Lincoln, NE), 2007.

Clayton, John, *Wonderlandscape: Yellowstone National Park and the Evolution of an American Cultural Icon*, Pegasus (New York, NY), 2017.

PERIODICALS

Booklist, April. 15, 2007, Colleen Mondor, review of *The Cowboy Girl*, p. 16; August 1, 2017, Dan Kaplan, review of *Wonderlandscape*, p. 19.

Kirkus Reviews, June 15, 2017, review of *Wonderlandscape*.

Oregon Historical Quarterly, spring, 2008, Laura Woodworth-Ney, review of *The Cowboy Girl*, p. 159.

Publishers Weekly, May 22, 2017, review of *Wonderlandscape*, p. 86.

Washington Post, August 25, 2017, Dennis Drabelle, review of *Wonderlandscape*.

ONLINE

John Clayton Website, http://www.johnclaytonbooks.com (February 5, 2018).

Yellowstone Insider, https://yellowstoneinsider.com/ (August 7, 2017), Sean Reichard, review of *Wonderlandscape*.*

Zinzi Clemmons

1985(?)-

■ **Personal**

Born c. 1985; daughter of Michael and Dorothy Clemmons; married André Naffis-Sahely (a poet and translator). *Education:* Brown University, B.A.; Columbia University, M.F.A.

■ **Addresses**

Home—Culver City, CA.

■ **Career**

Writer. Colburn Conservatory, Los Angeles, CA, faculty member; Occidental College, Los Angeles, faculty member.

■ **Awards, Honors**

Grants from MacDowell Colony, Bread Loaf, Provincetown Fine Arts Work Center, and Kimbilio Center for African American Fiction; 5 under 35 Honoree, National Book Awards, 2017.

■ **Writings**

What We Lose (novel), Viking (New York, NY), 2017.

Contributor to periodicals, including *Zoetrope: All Story, Transition,* and *Paris Review Daily.* Cofounder and editor, *Apogee Journal,* 2011; contributing editor, *Literary Hub;* associate editor, *Believer.*

■ **Sidelights**

Zinzi Clemmons's career trajectory as an aspiring novelist was suddenly disrupted when she learned that her mother had late-stage breast cancer. Clem-

mons had just completed an M.F.A. in fiction at Columbia University and had begun work on a traditionally structured novel about HIV/AIDS. Moving back to Philadelphia to care for her mother, she put this novel aside. Though she kept writing during the months that she tended to her dying mother, she could only manage fragmentary notes; eventually, she decided to abandon the novel and focus on "keeping those pieces and stitching them together . . . [into] a fictional narrative," as quoted in an *Atlantic* piece by Amy Weiss-Meyer. The result was *What We Lose,* hailed as an extraordinarily powerful debut novel about identity and the sometimes difficult relationship between a mother and daughter.

The novel is highly autobiographical. Like the author, the book's protagonist, Thandi, is the daughter of a mixed-race South African mother and an African American father and was raised in an upscale suburban Philadelphia neighborhood. Thandi shares the challenges that the author faced having been raised by an immigrant mother who never felt fully comfortable in her adopted country. As Clemmons explained to *Vogue* writer Megan O'Grady: "Mother-daughter relationships can be fraught anyway, and in our case, all of these different issues—race, gender, politics—were sort of wrapped up in her."

In the novel, Thandi is still in college when her mother dies of cancer. She is devastated with grief; undone, she rushes into a romantic relationship and soon becomes pregnant. But motherhood—and hasty marriage to the child's father, Peter—only worsens Thandi's emotional state, revealing the disastrous consequences of forming her own new family without having fully dealt with the loss of her mother. Clemmons uses an unconventional narrative structure to tell Thandi's story.

Rejecting chronology, the author creates a mix of single sentences, fragments, and short paragraphs as well as diagrams, photographs, charts, snippets of articles, blog entries, and song lyrics. These offer memories and associations that build on each other and cohere into a complex picture that illuminates the subject of grief while also making comments on issues such as racial identity, apartheid, wealth, class, abortion, and cultural attitudes toward cancer—a "privileged" disease that inspires rallies and political activism while other deadly diseases do not.

Many reviewers found the novel's collage-like structure fresh and exciting. But Anndee Hochman, writing in *Broad Street Review*, deemed some of the book's juxtapositions—a section on women who fall in love with serial killers, for example—merely "perplexing." Hochman also found the book's exploded chronology occasionally confusing. Others, however, expressed strong admiration for Clemmons's narrative technique. *What We Lose* is a "spectacular debut . . . written in bursts," said *Booklist* contributor Terry Hong, who added that the author "performs an exceptional sleight of hand that is both affecting and illuminating." In her *Vogue* article, O'Grady said that the novel is "as visceral as it is cerebral."

London *Guardian* reviewer F.T. Kola described the novel's associative form as "ambitious," but said that *What We Lose* "is at its best when it simply tells the story of Thandi's mother's struggle with cancer, and it is here that Clemmons's restrained prose reaches its full potential." The author writes matter-of-factly about Thandi's attempts to heal her mother by giving her only wholesome foods, and her frustration when well-meaning visitors bring rich, fatty comfort dishes to the house. Sitting by her mother's hospital bed, where her mother lies in a coma, Thandi forces herself not to turn away from the terrible smell of the disease "until I couldn't smell it anymore. The stench was nothing more than molecules moving in and out of my nostrils, the scene nothing more than light reflected off objects alive and inanimate, some dying." Also writing in the *Guardian*, Marta Bausells found that the "clear emotional insight with which [Clemmons] maps Thandi's grief is remarkable." The author told Bausells that she wanted the novel to confront some of the paradoxes that can complicate grief, among them sex. Grief can make it seem as if everything else in life just stops, said Clemmons, and sex "is one of the areas where you feel conflicted, because it's self-indulgent on a very basic level and you're giving yourself pleasure when someone has just gone through a lot of pain."

In a National Public Radio interview with Lulu Garcia-Navarro, posted at *NPR.org*, Clemmons said that her mother's death enabled her to see her mother from a different and more objective perspective. At the same time, she has mourned the fact that she has lost the opportunity to talk with her mother about the kinds of issues that Thandi deals with in the novel. "I do have to define myself much more strongly now," Clemmons told Garcia-Navarro, "because I don't have any other choice."

■ Biographical and Critical Sources

BOOKS

Clemmons, Zinzi, *What We Lose*, Viking (New York, NY), 2017.

PERIODICALS

Booklist, July 1, 2017, Terry Hong, review of *What We Lose*, p. 24.
Guardian, August 5, 2017, F.T. Kola, review of *What We Lose*; August 10, 2017, Marta Bausells, "Zinzi Clemmons on Her First Novel: 'I'm Proud of It, Because I Didn't Hold Anything Back.'"
Kirkus Reviews, May 1, 2017, review of *What We Lose*.
New York Times, May 25, 2017, John Williams, "A Novelist's Meditation on Loss and Identity."
Publishers Weekly, May 15, 2017, review of *What We Lose*, p. 32.
Vogue, June 20, 2017, Megan O'Grady, "Zinzi Clemmons Has Written the Debut Novel of the Year," interview with Clemmons.

ONLINE

Atlantic Online, https://www.theatlantic.com/ (August 1, 2017), Amy Weiss-Meyer, review of *What We Lose*.
Broad Street Review, http://www.broadstreetreview.com/ (July 18, 2017), Anndee Hochman, review of *What We Lose*.
Independent Online, http://www.independent.co.uk/ (July 12, 2017), Lucy Scholes, review of *What We Lose*.
NPR.org, https://www.npr.org/ (July 16, 2017), Lulu Garcia-Navarro, "New Novel Explores 'What We Lose' When We Lose a Parent," interview with Clemmons.
Washington Independent Review of Books, http://www.washingtonindependentreviewofbooks.com/ (August 4, 2017), Ellen Prentiss Campbell, review of *What We Lose*.
Zinzi Clemmons Website, http://www.zinziclemmons.com (February 6, 2018).*

Gwen Cole

■ Personal

Married; children: one daughter.

■ Addresses

Home—Richmond, VA.

■ Career

Writer. Worked variously as a pharmacy technician, ranch hand, meat clerk, and retail receiving specialist.

■ Writings

Cold Summer, Skyhorse Publishing (New York, NY), 2017.

■ Sidelights

Young adult author Gwen Cole is a native of New York. She has worked in a variety of jobs, including meat department clerk, ranch hand, pharmacy technician, and receiving specialist at a large national retail chain. At age eighteen, she played bass in a hardcore band, and she later married the band's lead guitarist. The couple currently lives with their daughter in Richmond, Virginia.

In her debut young adult novel, *Cold Summer,* Cole combines a time-travel theme with romance to tell the story of Harper Croft, a teenage girl whose involvement with an old friend will change both of their lives. As the novel begins, Harper's emotionally distant mother has apparently abandoned her, leaving her little choice but to return to the Iowa community where she grew up. There, she lives with her widower uncle, Jasper, and tries to make sense of what has happened to her.

To Harper's delight, she has been able to reunite with Kale Jackson, a friend she has known since they were next-door neighbors in childhood. Kale and Harper had many adventures together as children, and these happy memories give them a solid foundation from which to rekindle their friendship. It has been many years since they have seen each other, and in the meantime, they have both matured into teenagers. Soon, their old friendship has transformed into an intense teenage romantic relationship.

Gradually, Harper learns one of Kale's most carefully guarded secrets. Ever since he was a youngster, Kale has been inexplicably transported into the past. These unpredictable time hops, resulting in unexplained absences and mysterious injuries, have made his life difficult. As a result, he has dropped out of school and become detached from his family. Most recently, he has been traveling back and forth to a World War II battlefield, complete with all the dangers a full-scale war can impose on a terrified young man. Kale hopes his involvement with Harper will give him an anchor in the present that will keep him from returning to the war zone again. As he struggles with the PTSD his experiences have caused, Kale works to gain a measure of control over his time-travel abilities. Concurrently, Harper confronts her own slate of family problems while working to help Kale recover his stability. A chance discovery in a historical article suggests that Kale will become a casualty of war, adding even more desperation to the young couple's efforts.

Assessing *Cold Summer* in *Kirkus Reviews,* a writer commented, "This emotional journey for a time-traveling guy and his now-girl-next-door is better suited to romance readers than science-fiction aficionados." Readers "looking for a believable romance will be gratified by well-executed chapters that alternate between Kale's and Harper's perspectives," commented Blake Holman, writing in *School Library Journal.*

■ Biographical and Critical Sources

PERIODICALS

Kirkus Reviews, March 15, 2017, review of *Cold Summer.*
School Library Journal, April, 2017, Blake Holman, review of *Cold Summer,* p. 150.

ONLINE

Gwen Cole Website, http://www.gwenmcole.com (February 9, 2018).*

Kara Connolly

- **Personal**

Female.

- **Addresses**

Home—Arlington, TX.

- **Career**

Writer.

- **Writings**

No Good Deed, Delacorte Press (New York, NY), 2017.

- **Sidelights**

Kara Connolly is a writer of books for young adults. She is based in Arlington, Texas. In 2017, Connolly released her first novel, *No Good Deed*. In this volume, Connolly reimagines the legendary tale of Robin Hood. In contemporary times, a skilled female teen archer named Ellie Hudson has traveled to Nottingham, England, to take part in an important archery competition. Ellie sees a man in strange clothing from afar and begins following him. The man goes inside a nearby cave, and Ellie goes in after him. When she emerges, she finds herself in the Middle Ages. She dresses as a boy to avoid being bothered, but she is still forced to evade capture repeatedly. When the sheriff of Nottingham finally catches her, Ellie tricks him into

agreeing to set her free if she wins an archery competition. Meanwhile, a conspiracy unfolds involving usurping the power of the king. Ellie must find a way to punish the usurpers and protect the citizens of England.

In an interview with a contributor to the *Seeing Double in Neverland* website, Connolly explained how she developed the idea behind the story: "When we were kids (and maybe even after we were older) my brother and I loved the Disney *Robin Hood* movie. The one where Robin Hood is a fox and Little John is basically Baloo the bear. The legend of Robin Hood has so many variations and inconsistencies—and that's before Hollywood got a hold of it—that it's a natural story to twist into new shapes. It can be fun, or it can be serious, or somewhere in between. I figured if Robin Hood can be a talking fox, Robin Hood can be anything."

Reviews of *No Good Deed* were mixed. A contributor to *Kirkus Reviews* suggested that the volume features "an uneven plot and unconvincing premise." The same contributor concluded: "Even a gender-bending, butt-kicking, time-traveling heroine may not be enough to satisfy exacting readers." In a more favorable assessment in *Publishers Weekly*, a critic asserted: "Debut author Connolly's historic Nottingham is richly imagined and described." The same critic noted that the book offers a "fresh take on the Robin Hood mythology." "The protagonist is fully developed, and Connolly's attention to historical detail is strong," commented Meaghan Nichols in *School Library Journal*. Nichols also called the book a "page-turner." A writer on the *Book Smugglers* website remarked: "*No Good Deed* borrows from the 'Back to the Future' school of time meddling: Ellie needs to accomplish something in the past that changes the future in a personally positive way (and even, ultimately, involves a scrap of paper that is passed along over the centuries). While that may sound cynical, I'm all for it—Ellie's mission in the past, which isn't discovered until late in the book, is delightfully unexpected and well-executed, like one of Ellie's signature shots." The same writer continued: "Ultimately, that's the story of this particular Robin Hood retelling: delightfully unexpected and well-executed. Wholeheartedly recommended for those looking to escape from the present with a heroine of legend and her merry men." A reviewer on the website *Love Is Not a Triangle* declared: "*No Good Deed* was a lot of fun! This book has a classic world-time travel feel—like a Narnia or Alice in Wonderland, where the main character travels in time (or to a fantasy place) by going through a secret passage." A contributor to the *Vampire Book Club* website commented: "*No Good Deed* is a standalone, and as such, a pretty darn good one. It is refreshing to see a book that doesn't need to be part of . . . a series, and one that stands on its own as well as this one does. It's a perfect summer read."

■ Biographical and Critical Sources

PERIODICALS

Kirkus Reviews, May 15, 2017, review of *No Good Deed*.

Publishers Weekly, May 15, 2017, review of *No Good Deed*, p. 59.

School Library Journal, June 1, 2017, Meaghan Nichols, review of *No Good Deed*, p. 101.

ONLINE

Book Smugglers, https://www.thebooksmugglers. com/ (August 29, 2017), review of *No Good Deed*.

Kara Connolly Website, https://karaconnolly. wordpress.com/ (February 6, 2018).

Love Is Not a Triangle, http://www.loveisnota triangle.com/ (July 20, 2017), review of *No Good Deed*.

Penguin Random House Website, https://www. penguinrandomhouse.com/ (February 6, 2018), author profile.

Seeing Double in Neverland, http://seeingdoublein neverland.blogspot.com/ (July 1, 2017), author interview.

Vampire Book Club, http://vampirebookclub.net/ (August 14, 2017), review of *No Good Deed*.*

Ron Corbett

■ Personal

Married Julie Oliver (a photojournalist).

■ Addresses

Home—Manotick, Ontario, Canada.

■ Career

Journalist and writer. Bell Media Radio, CFRA (radio station), Ottawa, Ontario, Canada, talk show host.

■ Writings

The Last Guide: A Story of Fish and Love, Penguin Books Canada (Toronto, Ontario, Canada), 2001.

One Last River Run, General Store (Renfrew, Ontario, Canada), 2008.

A Grand Adventure: America's First Transcontinental Truck Run, General Store (Renfrew, Ontario, Canada), 2011.

First Soldiers Down: Canada's Friendly Fire Deaths in Afghanistan, Dundurn (Toronto, Ontario, Canada), 2012.

The Last Guide's Guide: To Family, Money, Fishing, and Everything Else That Matters, Ottawa Press and Publishing (Ottawa, Ontario, Canada), 2016.

(With Rick Smith) *Beyond Promises*, Big Fox (North Liberty, IA), 2017.

Ragged Lake (novel), ECW Press (Toronto, Ontario, Canada), 2017.

Author of columns with several Canadian periodicals.

■ Sidelights

Ron Corbett is a Canadian journalist and writer. He has worked at the CFRA radio station in Ottawa as a talk show host with Bell Media Radio and also as a columnist with several Canadian periodicals. Corbett has published several nonfiction books, including *One Last River Run, A Grand Adventure: America's First Transcontinental Truck Run, First Soldiers Down: Canada's Friendly Fire Deaths in Afghanistan,* and, with Rick Smith, *Beyond Promises.* He is also the author of *The Last Guide: A Story of Fish and Love,* a biography of Frank Kuiack, the last fishing guide in Algonquin Park in Ontario, and its sequel, *The Last Guide's Guide: To Family, Money, Fishing, and Everything Else That Matters.*

In 2017 Corbett published the novel *Ragged Lake.* Senior Detective Frank Yakabuski is accompanied by two Springfield Regional Police constables as they travel to Canada's Northern Divide to examine a remote cabin not on any maps. They find squatter Guillaume Roy and his wife, Lucy, and toddler daughter killed inside the cabin, marking the start of a series of murders in the tiny town of Ragged Lake. Yakabuski is returning to this homicide case after working for an extended period of time to bring down the Popeyes motorcycle gang leader. However, he is wary that this case is oddly similar to the murders committed by the Popeyes motorcycle gang. Yakabuski sequesters nine residents and visitors of the town to find out as much information as he can. After reading Lucy's journal, he learns that she had suspected someone may have wanted to kill her. Gangster Tommy Bangles, who had tormented Lucy before her ultimate death, enters town around the same time a bad blizzard complicates everyone's lives. Yakabuski, meanwhile, learns just how hard life in the North can be, particularly for the indigenous people when jobs are scarce.

In an article in the *Ottawa Citizen,* Corbett talked with Andrew Duffy about his move from nonfiction writing and journalism to penning a novel. Corbett admitted: "I wanted to do in fiction some of the stuff I've been doing in non-fiction. . . . I didn't want to all of a sudden start writing about vampires or something." Corbett recalled that he had visited a place called Ragged Lake on a four-day camping trip to Algonquin Park while writing an article in 2000. He confessed that *Ragged Lake* "is the same sort of geography and landscape as Algonquin Park. I wanted to have the novel set in the same location, and write about the same sort of people I've been writing about for years—but now as fiction."

A contributor to *Publishers Weekly* found the novel to be "well-crafted." The same reviewer admitted that "both the danger and the stark beauty of the place ring true on every level." A *Kirkus Reviews* contributor stated: "Familiar ingredients rarely combined—a starkly etched natural setting, a gungho cop, a series of soulful flashbacks, a violent climax—are expertly blended and brought to a full rolling boil." In a review in the *Reviewing the*

Evidence website, Sharon Mensing commented that while "Yakabuski is . . . well characterized . . . most of the villains are less thoroughly drawn." Mensing concluded that "this is a compelling start to a series set in an unusual location. I am very much looking forward to seeing where Yakabuski is sent next."

■ Biographical and Critical Sources

PERIODICALS

Kirkus Reviews, August 1, 2017, review of *Ragged Lake.*
Ottawa Citizen (Ottawa, Ontario, Canada), December 27, 2017, Andrew Duffy, "Former Columnist Ron Corbett Spins Old Notebook, Travels, into Crime Novel."
Publishers Weekly, August 28, 2017, review of *Ragged Lake,* p. 108.

ONLINE

Reviewing the Evidence, http://www.reviewingtheevidence.com/ (October 1, 2017), Sharon Mensing, review of *Ragged Lake.**

Victor P. Corona

■ Personal

Born in Mexico. *Education:* Yale University, B.A., 2003; Georgetown University, certificate of organizational performance management, 2007; Columbia University, Ph.D., 2009.

■ Addresses

Home—Los Angeles, CA.

■ Career

Sociologist, educator, and writer. Columbia University, New York, NY, instructor, 2009-11, 2015; Hofstra University, Hempstead, NY, instructor, 2012-15; Fashion Institute of Technology, New York, NY, instructor, 2013-14; Polytechnic Institute of New York University, NY, postdoctoral research fellow, 2014-18; California State University, Los Angeles, sociologist, instructor, 2018—.

■ Writings

Night Class: A Downtown Memoir, Soft Skull Press (New York, NY), 2017.

■ Sidelights

Victor P. Corona is a sociologist, educator, and writer based in Los Angeles, California. Currently an instructor and sociologist at California State University, Los Angeles, Corona has also taught at the Polytechnic Institute of New York University,

Fashion Institute of Technology, Hofstra University, and Columbia University, from which he obtained a Ph.D. He also earned a bachelor's degree from Yale University and a certificate of organizational performance management from Georgetown University.

In 2017, Corona released his first book, *Night Class: A Downtown Memoir.* In this volume, he recalls the years he spent in New York, studying at Columbia during the day and participating in the colorful downtown nightlife after hours. Corona also reveals his status as an undocumented immigrant from Mexico and tells of his interactions with members of the Club Kid scene, his friendship with Lady Gaga, and his exploits at clubs, including the Box.

In an interview with Nicole Bayiski for the website *Hamptons.com,* Corona discussed the book's evolution, explaining: "It started out as an academic research study and then the book became a much more personal story about why a sociology professor would dive into an outrageous world like New York nightlife. Although written by a sociologist, it's now a juicy set of tales about the downtown characters that make Manhattan such an interesting arena. And I talk about aspects of my own life that made me curious about them." He told Bayiski that the narrative of the book is "partly about my transformation from a bald, nerdy, plain researcher to someone with colored hair." Corona discussed reactions to the book in an interview with Tea Hacic on the *Stai Zitta* website, remarking: "Some people didn't like it. They didn't like how they were treated. But the book is very honest and in terms of this idea of 'spilling tea,' I also spilled plenty about myself! About my heartbreak, how I struggled to make my way through nightlife, how I was treated. I had never before revealed that I had been undocumented! Nobody knew that, not my students, not my friends, not people I dated." Corona continued: "I think that it's in the warts, it's in the honesty that we see our common humanity. So I understand that some people will never wanna talk to me again. But it's amazing to get messages from people like you or people around the world who enjoy the look I gave them into New York." In the same interview with Hacic, Corona was asked what message he hoped the book offered to readers. He responded: "That fame is a fascinating but dangerous thing. And that my journey through these different scenes in New York made me question why we want fame so desperately. Like, during my big book talk at Rizzoli, that was one of the first questions that came up. In light of all this, how do you make sense of who is in the White House now? And I'm like, the chickens came home to roost!" Corona added: "Fame is something that we understand so poorly and it's something that people end up regretting. You can't prepare for it! Nobody on this planet can prepare you for fame."

Reviewing *Night Class* in *Publishers Weekly*, a critic remarked: "Although Corona can be an engaging narrator, the personal material at the narrative core comes across as flat and rushed." However, a *Kirkus Reviews* writer described the book as "an engaging, if unlikely, memoir" and "sociology taken to the streets and basements, yielding a well-wrought introduction to a scene little known—and perhaps little imagined—to outsiders." "Readers interested in the glamorous . . . world of downtown New York will appreciate Corona's rich descriptions and deep research," asserted Laura Chanoux on the *Booklist* website.

■ Biographical and Critical Sources

PERIODICALS

Kirkus Reviews, May 15, 2017, review of *Night Class: A Downtown Memoir.*
Publishers Weekly, May 29, 2017, review of *Night Class*, p. 58.

ONLINE

Booklist Online, https://www.booklistonline.com/ (May 31, 2017), Laura Chanoux, review of *Night Class.*
Hamptons.com, http://www.hamptons.com/ (February 6, 2018), Nicole Bayiski, author interview.
New Inquiry, https://thenewinquiry.com/ (February 6, 2018), author profile.
Stai Zitta, http://staizitta.com/ (December 13, 2017), Tea Hacic, author interview.
Victor P. Corona Website, https://www.nightclass.nyc/ (February 6, 2018).*

Rebekah Crane

■ **Personal**

Married; children: two. *Education:* Attended Ohio University.

■ **Addresses**

Home—CO.

■ **Career**

Writer. Has also worked as a high school English teacher and yoga instructor.

■ **Writings**

YOUNG ADULT NOVELS

Playing Nice, In This Together Media (New York, NY), 2013.

Aspen, In This Together Media (New York, NY), 2014.

The Odds of Loving Grover Cleveland, Skyscape (New York, NY), 2016.

The Upside of Falling Down, Skyscape (New York, NY), 2018.

■ **Sidelights**

Rebekah Crane is a writer of young-adult novels. While studying to become an English teacher, she found her personal connection to young adult fiction and eventually turned her attention to writing. Crane has additionally worked as a high school English teacher and a yoga instructor.

Playing Nice

In 2013 Crane published the novel *Playing Nice*. High school junior Marty is not sure that the life her controlling mother and frenemy, Sarah, have ushered her into is the one she wants. While Marty had been involved in helping to decorate and plan for the school dances, volunteering with senior citizens, and working hard to get high grades, she finds in transfer student Lil Hartfield the opportunity to explore a new side of her personality. Lil smokes, lives in an odd trailer, and enjoys angry punk rock music, making her the object of gossipers at school. While the gossip and cyberbullying comes on thick in this small town suspicious of outsiders, Marty finds her new friend to be honest about who she is.

Reviewing the novel on the *YA Misfits* website, Dahlia Adler remarked that Marty's second love interest is "a sweet finishing touch to an interesting and varied cast of characters I greatly enjoyed spending a couple of hours with. I highly recommend *Playing Nice* to anyone who enjoys contemporary fiction on the darker side of light and/or a strong focus on friendship over romance." A contributor to the *Ella Bee Reads* blog noted: "As much as I really like the honesty, I'm not sure I totally loved all the sex—in thought or in conversation. I get it, they're teens, but I wish it was a little more subtle." The *Ella Bee Reads* blog reviewer found the plot "unpredictable," noting that it is "very much an attention grabber." The same reviewer commented that the character development throughout the novel is "the absolute best part of the book. All of the characters develop logically and do what someone in their position would do, even though it's not necessarily what a typical YA book would have them do." The *Ella Bee Reads* blog reviewer claimed that "this return to a more classic YA approach is truly refreshing and definitely worth your time."

Aspen

Crane published the novel *Aspen* in 2014. Aspen Yellow-Sunrise Taylor suffers from horrible nightmares and day dreams by reliving a tragic car accident that killed her friend Katelyn and left Aspen with a permanent scar on her face and a broken leg at the start of her senior year in high school. While the police believe that driver Katelyn was ultimately responsible for the accident, Aspen believes that it was indirectly her fault. Her attempts to suppress that belief leave her in torment as Katelyn's death hangs over her. While Aspen had been an outcast in school, she now finds that she has been included in social circles that she had been previously excluded from—particularly among Katelyn's friends. This even leads to her being voted homecoming queen. Additionally troublesome is her relationship with her mother and growing feelings for Katelyn's former boyfriend.

Writing in *School Library Journal*, Cary Frostick opined that "this is a tight, impeccably paced story with well-defined characters and intriguing relationships that will resonate with older teens." Frostick took notice of the "dry, often dark, humor" used to break up the more tense moments in the novel. A contributor reviewing the novel in the *Geeky Chiquitas* blog confessed: "I did not expect to like this book as much as I did, but wow, it was just phenomenal. Too beautiful for words. There are only few books that leave me speechless after reading it, and *Aspen* is one of them."

The Odds of Loving Grover Cleveland

In 2016 Crane published the novel *The Odds of Loving Grover Cleveland*. Sixteen-year-old Zander Osborne is haunted by her sister's death and feels pressured by her parents' unreasonable expectations for her life. Zander is sent to Camp Padua, a summer camp organized for at-risk teens. Zander cannot relate to any of the other teens, writing them off as being crazy. Zander eventually benefits from the "share-apy" approach to counseling and late-night rendezvous with other campers and opens up. She also meets Grover Cleveland, a teen who is paranoid about eventually becoming schizophrenic like his father. Together with rebel-lious and anorexic Cassie and also overweight, compulsive liar Bek, the four share secrets and form a close bond as they challenge authority at the camp. As the foursome develops over the course of the camp, they come to better understand their own vulnerability and the pleasures that can come from adult responsibilities.

Reviewing the novel in *Voice of Youth Advocates*, Lucy Schall observed that "engaging letters home . . . reveal characters' growth." Schall called the novel "*The Breakfast Club*-on-steroids" and concluded that "it is a great read for teens." Reviewing the novel in *RT Book Reviews*, Bridget Keown lauded that "the true beauty of Crane's [*The Odds of Loving Grover Cleveland*] lies in the way she handles the ugly, painful details of real life."

The Upside of Falling Down

Crane published the novel *The Upside of Falling Down* in 2018. After waking up in an Irish hospital, eighteen-year-old American Clementine Haas realizes that she cannot remember why she is there or anything else about her life. Her father travels to Ireland to meet her in the hospital, but she sees the disappointment on his face over her lack of memory. Unable to stand it any longer, Clementine runs away, unsure whether she is looking for who she is or if she will simply start over. Kieran helps her adjust, along with new friends Siobhan and Clive. Clementine falls in love with her perceived savior, Kieran, while coping with the freedom she has in her new life.

A contributor to *Kirkus Reviews* described the novel as "a light exploration of existential themes." The same reviewer insisted of Clementine that "readers will respond to her testing of new waters." A *Publishers Weekly* contributor observed that "much of the charm relies on the Irish setting" and Kieran's good looks. However, the reviewer conceded that "impulsive and spirited Teeny is equally enjoyable." In a review in *School Library Journal*, Sara Jurek suggested that "this quickly paced work will be enjoyed by teens interested in independence, love, self-discovery, and drama."

■ Biographical and Critical Sources

PERIODICALS

Kirkus Reviews, November 15, 2017, review of *The Upside of Falling Down*.

Publishers Weekly, November 13, 2017, review of *The Upside of Falling Down,* p. 66.

School Library Journal, June 1, 2014. Cary Frostick, review of *Aspen,* p. 116; December 1, 2017, Sara Jurek, review of *The Upside of Falling Down,* p. 106.

Voice of Youth Advocates, December 1, 2016, Lucy Schall, review of *The Odds of Loving Grover Cleveland,* p. 58.

ONLINE

Ella Bee Reads, http://ellabeereads.blogspot.com/ (January 24, 2013), review of *Playing Nice.*

Geeky Chiquitas, http://geekychiquitas.blogspot. com/ (January 1, 2015), Dahlia Adler, review of *Aspen.*

Rebekah Crane Website, http://www.rebekahcrane. com (March 18, 2018).

RT Book Reviews, https://www.rtbookreviews.com/ (December 1, 2016), Bridget Keown, review of *The Odds of Loving Grover Cleveland.*

YA Misfits, http://www.yamisfits.com/ (February 1, 2013), review of *Playing Nice.**

Laura Creedle

1962-

■ Personal

Born July 31, 1962; married; children: three.

■ Addresses

Home—Austin, TX.

■ Career

Writer. Also volunteers at a local kindergarten's preliteracy program.

■ Writings

The Love Letters of Abelard and Lily, Houghton Mifflin Harcourt (New York, NY), 2017.

Author of a blog.

■ Sidelights

Laura Creedle is a writer. She uses her experience with ADHD, dyslexia, and from being neurodivergent to add authenticity to her writing. She blogs on ADHD topics from her home in Austin, Texas. Creedle also volunteers at a local kindergarten's pre-literacy program.

Creedle published *The Love Letters of Abelard and Lily* in 2017. Sixteen-year-old Lily has a difficult time coping with her ADHD. Although she strongly dislikes being medicated all the time, living without her medicine can be quite difficult.

She must take it if she wants to be able to control her impulses and remain focused on her tasks. Her classmate, Abelard, has Asperger's syndrome. Coincidentally, both Lily and Abelard have read *The Love Letters of Abelard and Heloise,* a medieval account. They prefer to talk primarily through text messages, where they quote heavily from this work. Abelard sees the best in Lily, but his problems create tensions in their developing relationship, something that Lily fears will end in disaster. When Lily turns to destructive behavior for fear of losing him, though, she finds that may very well be her path to happiness.

A contributor to *Publishers Weekly* suggested that "readers will be moved by the sacrifices the teens make for each other." *Booklist* contributor Donna Scanlon claimed that "Creedle's debut novel is rich and thoughtful." Scanlon noted that Rosalind, Iris, and Lily's "mother are particularly realistic and effective foils to Lily's turmoil." Writing in *Voice of Youth Advocates,* Laura Woodruff stated that "funny, poignant, genuine Lily takes the reader into the brain of a neurodivergent young woman who has a great deal to offer." Woodruff branded *The Love Letters of Abelard and Lily* "amazing." A *Kirkus Reviews* contributor found the novel to be "entertaining, thought-provoking, and unsettling—in a good way." In a review in *School Library Journal,* Kate Reid described the novel as "a thought-provoking story to fill that empty space on YA shelves for tales of realistic fiction, romance, and humor."

■ Biographical and Critical Sources

PERIODICALS

Booklist, October 1, 2017, Donna Scanlon, review of *The Love Letters of Abelard and Lily*, p. 80.

Kirkus Reviews, September 15, 2017, review of *The Love Letters of Abelard and Lily*.

Publishers Weekly, October 9, 2017, review of *The Love Letters of Abelard and Lily*, p. 67.

Voice of Youth Advocates, October 1, 2017, Laura Woodruff, review of *The Love Letters of Abelard and Lily*, p. 56.

School Library Journal, January, 2018, Kate Reid, review of *The Love Letters of Abelard and Lily*, p. 86.

ONLINE

Laura Creedle Website, http://www.lauracreedle.com (March 18, 2018).*

Ian Crofton

■ Personal

Born in Edinburgh, Scotland.

■ Addresses

Home—London, England.

■ Career

Writer, editor, and publisher. Former publisher and editor for reference companies, including Macmillan, Collins, and Dorling Kindersley.

■ Writings

(Compiler, with Donald Fraser) *A Dictionary of Musical Quotations*, Schirmer Books (New York, NY), 1985.

(Compiler) *A Dictionary of Art Quotations*, Schirmer Books (New York, NY), 1988.

(Editor-in-chief) *The Guinness Encyclopedia*, Guinness Publishing (London, England), 1992.

(With Michael Allaby and Robert Anderson) *Deserts and Semideserts*, Raintree Steck-Vaughn (Austin, TX), 2002.

(With David Bradley) *Atoms and Elements*, Oxford University Press (New York, NY), 2002.

(Compiler) *Brewer's Curious Titles: The Fascinating Stories behind More Than 1500 Famous Titles*, Cassell (London, England), 2002.

Brewer's Britain & Ireland: The History, Culture, Folklore, and Etymology of 7500 Places in These Islands, Weidenfeld & Nicolson (London, England), 2006.

The Kings and Queens of England, Quercus (London, England), 2008.

Science without the Boring Bits: Cranks, Curiosities, Crazy Experiments, and Wild Speculation, Quercus (London, England), 2010.

(Editor, with John Ayto) *Brewer's Dictionary of Modern Phrase & Fable*, Weidenfeld and Nicolson (London, England), 2010.

A Dictionary of Scottish Phrase and Fable, Birlinn (Edinburgh, Scotland), 2012.

Big Ideas in Brief, Quercus (New York, NY), 2013.

World History: Fifty Ideas You Really Need to Know, Quercus (New York, NY), 2013.

History without the Boring Bits, Quercus (New York, NY), 2013.

Walking the Border: A Journey between Scotland and England, Birlinn (Edinburgh, Scotland), 2014.

A Curious History of Food and Drink, Quercus (New York, NY), 2014.

Scottish History without the Boring Bits, Birlinn (Edinburgh, Scotland), 2015.

(With Jeremy Black) *The Little Book of Big History: The Story of the Universe, Human Civilization, and Everything in Between*, Pegasus Books (Albany, CA), 2017.

■ Sidelights

Ian Crofton is a writer, editor, and publisher who has worked in the reference publishing business for decades. He has more than twenty years of experience as a publisher and has worked for reference publishers that include Macmillan, Collins, and Dorling Kindersley. He also served as the editor-in-chief of *The Guinness Encyclopedia*, a general reference work on science, politics, technology, and the arts. A freelance writer and editor, he is the author of well over a dozen books on history, science, art, and language.

Science Books

Crofton's books on science and technology include *Atoms and Elements, Deserts and Semideserts,* and *Science without the Boring Bits.*

In *Atoms and Elements,* Crofton and coauthor David Bradley cover basic atomic science in a style designed to inform and entertain young readers. Topics include subatomic particles, atoms as the basic building blocks of nature, the basic forms of matter, the elements and what they consist of, and more. The book also includes an introduction to the periodic table of elements.

Deserts and Semideserts covers basic concepts in earth science as it applies to deserts, semideserts, and related biomes. In collaboration with Michael Allaby and Robert Anderson, Crofton describes deserts such as the Gobi, the Sahara, and the Atacama. The book includes details on the people and creatures that live in these often harsh and inhospitable environments. *School Librarian* reviewer Gerry McSourley called the volume an "excellent book which conveys its information in straightforward fashion."

Science without the Boring Bits: Cranks, Curiosities, Crazy Experiments, and Wild Speculation offers a concise chronological account of the history of science, invention, and discovery. The book includes material on physics, botany, zoology, biology, medicine, and more.

History Books

In Crofton's writings on history, he continues with the theme of presenting subjects "without the boring bits" with *History without the Boring Bits* and *Scottish History without the Boring Bits.*

History without the Boring Bits includes multiple snippets and tidbits of historical facts and lore, all assembled with the intent of providing a lively look at history that may have been missing from its readers' formal educations. Crofton includes obscure facts, such as how an Egyptian caliph banned the making of women's shoes and how, for years, it was required of British citizens to assemble in church every November 5th to celebrate the foiling of the infamous Gunpowder Plot that planned to blow up Parliament. "At its best, this history lite gives to the historically challenged reader a path into history heavy," observed *Financial Times* contributor Jonathan Sale.

Scottish History without the Boring Bits similarly covers the history of Scotland, but with a focus on Scots-specific historical events and obscure facts.

Crofton covers Scottish royalty, the country's cultural history, religion, the supernatural, crime and punishment, and politics, such as the Jacobite Uprising. Jo Galloway, writing on the *Historical Novel Society* website, called the book a "well researched history from the Dark Ages through to modern times."

The Little Book of Big History: The Story of the Universe, Human Civilization, and Everything in Between, by Crofton and Jeremy Black, takes on the enormous task of summarizing the entirety of history. The authors start with the big bang, the event that started it all, and move at a rapid pace through evolution, prehistory, and modern civilization. The book "covers an enormous amount of material while trying to highlight all of the events, animals, concepts, and inventions" that make up the history of the universe and human civilization, commented Timothy Berge in *Xpress Reviews.* The volume "surprises with its distilled but generally comprehensive treatment of a vast subject," observed a *Kirkus Reviews* writer.

Language Books

In the field of language, Crofton is known as the editor of the popular reference book *Brewer's Dictionary of Modern Phrase and Fable,* in collaboration with John Ayto. The dictionary contains hundreds of definitions of terms, descriptions of characters, and other information on words, idioms, slogans, and events derived from television, literature, comic strips, music, and computer games. The material covers fictional characters, mythological beasts, and other imaginative subjects as represented in more than 8,000 phrases.

Brewer's Curious Titles: The Fascinating Stories behind More Than 1500 Famous Titles contains Crofton's survey of the titles of hundreds of novels, plays, paintings, works of art, and musical composition. He explains the stories behind the titles of these works, covering where they originated, what they mean, and how they were selected. For example, he explains that the title of T.S. Eliot's *The Waste Land* came from *Le Morte d'Arthur* by Sir Thomas Malory. Joseph Haydn's *Miracle Symphony* got its name after a chandelier crashed during its inaugural performance, "miraculously" missing the audience. James M. McCain's *The Postman Always Rings Twice* was derived from the mailman's habit of ringing the bell twice if bringing the writer a bill. *Library Journal* contributor Denise J. Stankovics called the book "informative and entertaining."

General Nonfiction

Walking the Border: A Journey between Scotland and England is a book outside of Crofton's usual areas of coverage. In this book, Crofton describes his adventures during a lengthy walk along the border between England and Scotland. His trip takes him "from the Lochmaben Stone near Gretna Green on the edge of the Solway Firth to the North Sea, and a precipitous cliff between Lamberton and the aptly named Conundrum," noted London *Guardian* reviewer Stuart Kelly. Crofton's trip was triggered by a political event, the Scottish referendum, a controversial vote taken in 2014 in which Scotland unsuccessfully sought independence from the United Kingdom.

Along the way, Crofton encounters numerous persons who define themselves as "borderers," who have lived their lives on the Scottish/English border and who identify strongly with that transitional area between countries. The walk gave him the opportunity to explore border culture in depth and find out what it was that influences the borderland population. He muses on the actual concept of a border itself and what it means, politically, socially, and culturally. Other concepts, such as immigration and independence, are threaded throughout the narrative. "There is a lot of excellent natural description in this book, alongside a number of comic encounters with humans and livestock," Kelly remarked.

■ Biographical and Critical Sources

PERIODICALS

Contemporary Review, October, 2005, review of *Brewer's Britain & Ireland: The History, Culture, Folklore, and Etymology of 7500 Places in These Islands,* p. 256; spring, 2011, review of *Brewer's Dictionary of Modern Phrase & Fable,* p. 393.

Financial Times, September 15, 2007, Jonathan Sale, review of *History without the Boring Bits.*

Guardian (London, England), January 11, 2003, John Mullan, review of *Brewer's Curious Titles: The Fascinating Stories behind More Than 1500 Famous Titles;* November 1, 2014, "*Walking the Border: A Journey between Scotland and England* by Ian Crofton: The Bleak Beauty of Dead Water and Hungry Law Transcends Politics in the Debatable Lands," p. 7.

Kirkus Reviews, June 1, 2017, review of *The Little Book of Big History: The Story of the Universe, Human Civilization, and Everything in Between.*

Library Journal, May 1, 2003, Denise J. Stankovics, review of *Brewer's Curious Titles,* p. 102.

Publishers Weekly, May 15, 2017, review of *The Little Book of Big History,* p. 49.

School Librarian, spring, 2011, Gerry McSourley, review of *Deserts and Semideserts,* p. 41.

Xpress Reviews, April 28, 2017, Timothy Berge, review of *The Little Book of Big History.*

ONLINE

Alex Roddie Website, http://www.alexroddie.com/ (May 21, 2015), review of *Walking the Border.*

Historical Honey, http://www.historicalhoney.com/ (February 9, 2018), biography of Ian Crofton.

Historical Novel Society, http://www.historicalnovelsociety.org/ (November 1, 2015), Jo Galloway, review of *Scottish History without the Boring Bits.*

Kitchen Frolic, https://www.kitchenfrolic.ca/ (March 31, 2016), review of *A Curious History of Food and Drink.**

Karen Crouse

■ **Personal**

Female. *Education:* Graduated from University of Southern California.

■ **Career**

Journalist and sportswriter. *Savannah News-Press,* Savannah, GA, sports reporter; *New York Times,* New York, NY, sports reporter, 2005—.

■ **Writings**

Norwich: One Tiny Vermont Town's Secret to Happiness and Excellence, Simon & Schuster (New York, NY), 2018.

■ **Sidelights**

Karen Crouse is a journalist and sportswriter. She graduated from the University of Southern California and served as the first female writer in the sports department at the *Savannah News-Press.* After working for a half dozen periodicals, Crouse began working as a sportswriter for the *New York Times* in 2005.

Crouse published *Norwich: One Tiny Vermont Town's Secret to Happiness and Excellence* in 2018. The account centers on the small town of Norwich, Vermont, which has produced eleven Olympic athletes from a population of 3,400 people. Crouse chronicles the lives of these athletes, showing how they came to be Olympic athletes and their post-Olympic careers. She also looks at the demograph-

ics and dynamics of the town to query how the "Norwich Way" can be used as a model for other towns. Among the athletes profiled are ski champion sisters Sunny and Betsy Snite, ski jumpers, Mike Holland and Jeff Hastings, mogul skier Hannah Kearney, runner Andrew Wheating, and snowboarder Kevin Pearce. Crouse pays particular attention to the roles of parents and the community at large on these athletes.

Writing in *Washington Post Book World,* Fred Bowen pointed out that "Crouse is a reporter, not a sociologist. While she cites studies and books to support the idea that the 'Norwich Way' is the best, she concentrates on the lives of Norwich's athletes. She's a good storyteller, and the stories make her point." Bowen concluded that "with her small but timely book, Crouse has given parents of young athletes a great gift—a glimpse at another way to raise accomplished and joyous competitors. Perhaps the more important question is: Will parents, dreaming of college scholarships and Olympic glory, bother to listen?" In a review in *Christian Science Monitor,* Kevin O'Kelly reasoned that "the lessons of *Norwich* are inspiring and compelling, but the book also includes occasional instances of truly awful writing. Most often, Crouse's style is competent and workmanlike. But she is enamored of cliches and sometimes remakes them in cringe-inducing ways." O'Kelly remarked that "Crouse seems so besotted with the town that it makes one automatically distrust her. Can any town be so perfect? One can't help but feel Crouse lacks perspective." A contributor to *Kirkus Reviews* claimed that *Norwich* "is a reminder that in an age that stresses winning at all costs, the true champions of the Olympic world are those who transition into lives as happy and productive adults." A *Publishers Weekly* contributor observed that "this important book highlights what's wrong with youth sports by focusing on a community that gets it right."

■ Biographical and Critical Sources

PERIODICALS

Christian Science Monitor, January 25, 2018, Kevin O'Kelly, "'Norwich' Is the Town That Grows Olympians."

Kirkus Reviews, November 15, 2017, review of *Norwich: One Tiny Vermont Town's Secret to Happiness and Excellence.*

Publishers Weekly, October 16, 2017, review of *Norwich,* p. 60.

Washington Post Book World, February 26, 2018, Fred Bowen, review of *Norwich.*

ONLINE

New York Times Online, https://www.nytimes.com/ (March 18, 2018), author profile.*

Emily Culliton

■ **Personal**

Born in Brooklyn, NY. *Education:* University of Massachusetts Amherst, M.F.A.; University of Denver, postgraduate studies.

■ **Career**

Writer.

■ **Writings**

The Misfortune of Marion Palm, Alfred A. Knopf (New York, NY), 2017.

■ **Sidelights**

Emily Culliton is a writer who was born and raised in Brooklyn, New York. She holds an M.F.A. degree from the University of Massachusetts Amherst and is a Ph.D. candidate in fiction at the University of Denver.

Culliton's first novel is *The Misfortune of Marion Palm.* The title character, Marion Palm, lives in Brooklyn Heights, an upscale section of the borough of Brooklyn. Her often oblivious husband, Nathan, lives off the proceeds of a trust fund and writes wretched poetry. Marion has long been accustomed to fancy vacations, a high-dollar home, and the best of electronics and other equipment. The money for these luxuries has come not from Nathan's trust fund, nor from her income as a worker in the development office at her daughter's private school. Unfortunately, it has come from a large sum of money that Marion has gradually embezzled from the school. When the school is scheduled for an audit and Marion is sure her theft will be discovered, she stuffs 40,000 dollars in cash into a knapsack and flees, leaving behind her husband, two daughters, and the life she knew—and, at the same time, a furious school board whose members desperately want to find her.

Marion doesn't get far in her flight from justice, not because she is caught but because she simply ends up in a sleazy section of Brooklyn not far from her former home. With Marion gone, the family she left behind must learn how to cope with her absence. Neither Nathan nor daughters Ginny and Jane know where she is or why she has left, and they see her disappearance as a tragic event. Clueless Nathan struggles to take care of his daughters while the two girls endure emotional distress over their mother's absence. Before the story is resolved, each of these characters will have to grapple with unaccustomed changes in their lives and in what they thought they knew about each other.

"Culliton aims to expose the lie of polite society, Brooklyn-based or otherwise, its barely suppressed derangements and contradictions. Locked within each character: an ugly secret self she tries feverishly to suppress, one fomented by her poisonous surroundings," observed Eugenia Williamson in a *Boston Globe* review. Williamson further remarked: "Culliton's narrative is fueled by the acid that drips quietly beneath every city sidewalk where white people gather to discuss community gardens and property taxes."

"Culliton's assured and clever novel reads more like that of a seasoned novelist than a debut," commented Kathy Sexton, writing in *Booklist.* A *Library Journal* writer called the book a "wildly entertaining debut."

■ **Biographical and Critical Sources**

PERIODICALS

Booklist, July 1, 2017, Kathy Sexton, review of *The Misfortune of Marion Palm*, p. 22.

Boston Globe, August 11, 2017, Eugenia Williamson, "One of the Best (and Hopefully the Last) of Brooklyn Novels," review of *The Misfortune of Marion Palm*.

Library Journal, June 15, 2017, review of *The Misfortune of Marion Palm*, p. 2A.

ONLINE

Blogcritics, http://www.blogcritics.org/ (September 28, 2017), Adriana Delgado, "Interview: Emily Culliton, Author of *The Misfortune of Marion Palm*."

Penguin Random House Website, http://www.penguinrandomhouse.com/ (February 9, 2018), biography of Emily Culliton.*

Peter Cunningham

1947-

■ **Also Known As**

Peter Benjamin
Peter Lauder

■ **Personal**

Born 1947; son of Redmond Cunningham; married; wife's name Carol; children: six.

■ **Addresses**

Home—Dublin, Ireland.

■ **Career**

Writer, journalist, newspaper columnist, and novelist. Worked variously in accounting, farming, commodities trading, and the sugar industry.

■ **Member**

Aosdana (the Irish academy of arts and letters).

■ **Awards, Honors**

Cecil Day-Lewis Bursary Award, 2011; Prix de l'Europe, 2013, and Prix Caillou, both for *The Sea and the Silence*.

■ **Writings**

NOVELS

(Under name Peter Lauder) *Noble Lord*, Stein and Day (New York, NY), 1986.

All Risks Mortality, Little, Brown (Boston, MA), 1988.
Who Trespass against Us, Arrow (London, England), 1994.
Tapes of the River Delta, St. Martin's Press (New York, NY), 1996, reprinted, Gemma (Boston, MA), 2012.
Consequences of the Heart, Harvill Press (London, England), 1998, GemmaMedia (Boston, MA), 2011.
(Under name Peter Benjamin) *Terms and Conditions*, Simon & Schuster/Townhouse (London, England), 2001.
The Taoiseach: Power, Whatever the Cost, Hodder & Stoughton (London, England), 2003.
The Sea and the Silence, New Island (Dublin, Ireland), 2008.
Capital Sins, New Island (Dublin, Ireland), 2010.
Love in One Edition, GemmaMedia (Boston, MA), 2012.
(Editor) *Sister Caravaggio*, Liberties (Dublin, Ireland), 2014.
Acts of Allegiance, Sandstone Press (Dingwall, Rossshire, England), 2017.
The Trout, Arcade Publishing (New York, NY), 2017.

Contributor to periodicals, including the *Irish Times*.

■ **Sidelights**

Peter Cunningham is an Irish writer, journalist, and novelist from Waterford, a seaport in southeastern Ireland and the country's oldest city. Early in his career, he worked as an accountant and a commodities trader. After his first novel, *Noble Lord*, was published in 1986, he devoted more and more of his time to writing thrillers. More thrillers followed, but in 1990, a family tragedy changed the direction of his writing. His eldest son, also named Peter, was killed in an automobile accident, which devastated Cunningham, his wife, Carol, and his other five children. From that point forward, "he began to write contemporary fiction, based on life in Waterford, which he fictionalized as Monument, a port town in Ireland's south east," noted a writer on Cunningham's website.

Tapes of the River Delta

The first of those contemporary novels, *Tapes of the River Delta*, explores the history of a family through almost one hundred years of Irish history during the twentieth century. At the beginning of the novel, narrator Theo Shortcourse is on the run after committing a murder and escaping from the psychiatric hospital where he was being held. While hiding in a river delta, he thinks back over his early childhood, when he was best friends with, and a frequent nemesis of, his nephew Bain Cross. He wonders why his mother has long preferred Bain to him and if there is an issue of parentage that he doesn't know about. He realizes that his mother also interfered in his first relationship and that her actions were probably deliberate.

As Theo grows older, he enters politics, as does Bain, and both men rise to prominent positions. They continue to encounter each other, bother personally and professionally, and the tension between them never fully dissipates. When Theo is seduced by a married British woman, he is warned that she intends to spy on him for Bain. Undeterred, Theo continues the relationship until the situation ends with the murder that started the book.

"This is a skillful production, written in prose that has a trace of Irish lilt," commented Mary Ellen Quinn in a *Booklist* review. With this novel, noted a *Publishers Weekly* writer, "Cunningham paints a dark and compelling canvas that writhes with incest, betrayal, spiritual and political bankruptcy—and the blasted hopes of 20th-century Ireland."

Consequences of the Heart

Chud Church, the protagonist of *Consequences of the Heart*, grows up in his maternal grandmother's care in Ireland. He is best friends with Jack Santry, the son of a prominent local family. The two young men are both romantically interested in Rosa Bensey, but only one can become her husband. A coin toss before Jack and Chud set out for their participation in the D-Day invasion grants Jack the privilege of marriage to Rosa, while Chud gives up his romantic aspirations and becomes a close

friend. In the years following the war, Jack is involved in a scandal, Chud murders a soldier who tries to blackmail Jack over an instance of battlefield cowardice, and Chud becomes involved in an intense and passionate affair with Rosa. Other forces are conspiring to affect Chud, including his own family history and Jack and Rosa's son Kevin, who seeks revenge against Chud.

A *Kirkus Reviews* writer called the novel a "lovingly detailed examination of twentieth-century Anglo-Irish culture as well as a dissection of personal relationships." Lucille Cormier, writing in *Historical Novels Review,* concluded: "*Consequences of the Heart* is much more than a love story; it is a finely woven and lyrical reflection on human nature."

Acts of Allegiance

Acts of Allegiance is a "masterful novel," commented Jane Casey in the *Irish Times,* the story of Marty Ransom, an Irish civil servant who becomes embroiled in spying for MI5 during the Troubles. As the story progresses, Marty finds that he has to choose where he allegiance lies, whether with Ireland or the British government. Making his decision even more difficult is his desire to know more about his father and what kind of person he was. His own memories of his father are dim and confused, and he can't even remember details about the man's death. Marty's decisions about his own identity are strongly bound to his father. As he searches for information on his father and the meaning he requires in his own life, the "revelations unfold like dark petals, with each sequential revealing the clues that lie hidden in Marty's memories," observed Maryam Madani on the *Totally Dublin* website.

Madani stated, "*Acts of Allegiance* is a rare find that manages to combine literary lyricism with a satisfyingly propulsive, airtight plot. It is a cracking tale of espionage, state secrets and betrayal." Assessing *Acts of Allegiance,* John Kilraine on the *RTE* website stated, "The crucial test for any book is whether it keeps you turning the pages to see what happens next, and the latest novel from Peter Cunningham certainly does that." Casey concluded, "The sign of a great writer is to take the personal and specific and draw out what is universal about it, and Peter Cunningham achieves this with tremendous skill."

The Trout

The Trout, Cunningham's 2017 novel, weaves a man's personal history into what appears to be a trap for him in the present. Narrator Alex Smyth is a successful Irish writer who has settled down with his wife in Bayport, Ontario, a rural Canadian community. When he receives a fishing lure in the mail, with no note, return address, or other identification, a series of disturbing childhood memories return. For most of his life, Alex has thought he killed someone when he was seven years old. He doesn't know who it might have been, and he has no solid memory of the events, just impressions. It is as if he has amnesia related to what would have been a traumatic event. The fishing lure—a specialized tool for catching trout—causes these troubling memories and feelings to resurface. It does not take long for these confusing memories to affect Alex and his marriage.

Alex believes that the answers to his questions have something to do with another boy he knew named Terence Deasy. Increasingly haunted and disturbed by his recollections, he returns to Ireland to find Terence, locate answers to his lifelong mystery, and put his troubled past to rest.

"Brief, cogent paragraphs about trout provide a connecting thread in this thoughtful, exquisitely told tale," commented a *Publishers Weekly* contributor. An *Internet Bookwatch* writer called *The Trout* a "masterfully written novel" and an "original and multilayered psychological thriller that will hold the reader's rapt attention from beginning to end." *Irish Times* contributor Tom Moriarty called the novel a "well-crafted, crisply written, gripping story."

■ **Biographical and Critical Sources**

PERIODICALS

Booklist, February 15, 1996, Mary Ellen Quinn, review of *Tapes of the River Delta*, p. 989.

Historical Novels Review, August, 2010, Patricia O'Sullivan, review of *The Sea and the Silence*; August, 2011, review of *Consequences of the Heart*.

Independent (London, England), January 27, 2018, Hilary A. White, "'No Day Goes By That I Don't Think of Peter Twenty Times'—Irish Writer on His Son's Death in Car Crash," profile of Peter Cunningham.

Internet Bookwatch, October, 2017, review of *The Trout*.

Irish Times, August 26, 2016, Tom Moriarty, review of *The Trout*; September 23, 2017, Jane Casey, "*Acts of Allegiance* by Peter Cunningham: Signs of a Great Writer," review of *Acts of Allegiance*.

Kirkus Reviews, May 1, 2011, review of *Consequences of the Heart*.

Publishers Weekly, February 19, 1996, review of *Tapes of the River Delta*, p. 205; December 13, 2010, review of *Capital Sins*, p. 38; May 15, 2017, review of *The Trout*, p. 41.

ONLINE

Million Kindle Books, http://www.amillionkindle books.com/ (July 9, 2013), P.S. Karr, review of *The Sea and the Silence*.

Peter Cunningham Website, http://www. petercunninghambooks.com (February 9, 2018).

RTE Website, https://www.rte.ie/ (October 25, 2017), John Kilraine, review of *Acts of Allegiance*.

Sandstone Press Website, http://www.sandstone press.com/ (January 9, 2018), biography of Peter Cunningham.

Totally Dublin, http://www.totallydublin.ie/ (February 9, 2018), Maryam Madani, review of *Acts of Allegiance*.

Undiscovered Scotland, https://www.undiscovered scotland.co.uk/ (February 9, 2018), review of *Acts of Allegiance*.*

Havilah Cunnington

■ **Personal**

Married; husband's name Ben; children: Judah, Hudson, Grayson, Beckham.

■ **Addresses**

Home—Redding, CA.

■ **Career**

Pastor. Rock of Roseville Church, Roseville, CA, church leader, worked for fifteen years; Moral Revolution, Redding, CA, former director; Truth to Table, a nonprofit online platform, coleader.

■ **Writings**

Stronger Than the Struggle: Uncomplicating Your Spiritual Battle, Nelson Books (Nashville, TN), 2018.

■ **Sidelights**

Havilah Cunnington is a pastor. On her website, she recalled the moment that she decided to turn her focus to religion. At the age of seventeen, Cunnington confessed one night: "God, I'm not much. I'm young, I'm a girl with no special gifting. But if You can use anyone, You can use me." Since then, she and her twin sister, Deborah, traveled around California, several other states, and into Mexico preaching their message. She and her husband, Ben, served as leaders at the Rock of Roseville Church for fifteen years before becoming directors of Christian values advocacy group Moral Revolution in Redding, California.

Cunnington published *Stronger Than the Struggle: Uncomplicating Your Spiritual Battle* in 2018. The account presents Cunnington's beliefs on the ways that Christians should deal with spiritual uncertainties and temptations. In the book, she reiterated a moment that was highly influential for her involving the demonic possession of a friend and the power of prayer by only those who truly believe to help. She equips her readers with tools to deal with Satan's agenda of stealing, killing, and destroying.

A contributor to *Publishers Weekly* suggested that "those with a literalist interpretation of the Bible looking for fortitude against sin will find much here." In a review in the Evangelical Church Library Association website, Aubree DeVisser reasoned that since "the book uses illustrations, anecdotes, examples, and stories, it is not preachy or stilted." DeVisser concluded that "these modern lessons are pragmatic, insightful, and nonthreatening." DeVisser remarked that *Stronger Than the Struggle* offers "clarity in understanding spiritual warfare."

■ **Biographical and Critical Sources**

PERIODICALS

Publishers Weekly, October 9, 2017, review of *Stronger Than the Struggle: Uncomplicating Your Spiritual Battle*, p. 60.

ONLINE

Evangelical Church Library Association Website, https://eclalibraries.org/ (February 10, 2018), Aubree DeVisser, review of *Stronger Than the Struggle*.
Havilah Cunnington Website, http://havilahcunnington.com (March 18, 2018).

Kevin Czap

1985-

■ Also Known As

Kevin Czapiewski

■ Personal

Born 1985, in Ann Arbor, MI. *Education:* Cleveland Institute of Art, B.F.A., 2008.

■ Addresses

Home—Providence, RI.

■ Career

Writer and visual artist. Comix Cube, cofounder; Czap Books, founder and publisher, 2012—. Genghis Con Cleveland, co-organizer, 2013-15; Center for Cartoon Studies fellow, 2017-18.

■ Awards, Honors

Best Webcomic SPACE Prize, 2011; CXC Emerging Talent Award, 2016.

■ Writings

Peace Signs: A Little Comic, Kevin Czap, 2011.

(As Kevin Czapiewski) *Velvet Ants: Purple + Beige + Black*, Dental Records, 2011.

(As Kevin Czapiewski) *Birthday Surprise: The TPB Version of the Last Twelve Minis*, Czap Books (Cleveland, OH), 2012.

(As Kevin Czapiewski) *Waffle: A Sexy Little Comic for Girls & Boys*, Czap Books (Cleveland, OH), 2012.

A Lesson in Survival, Czap Books (Cleveland, OH), 2013.

Fütchi Perf (graphic novel), Czap Books (Cleveland, OH), 2015, reprinted, Uncivilized Books (Minneapolis, MN), 2017.

Contributor to several anthologies.

■ Sidelights

Kevin Czap is an American writer and visual artist. Born in Ann Arbor, Michigan, in 1985, he completed a B.F.A. in visual arts and technology from the Cleveland Institute of Art in 2008. Czap is the recipient of numerous awards for his work, including the 2016 CXC Emerging Talent Award. He attended Providence, Rhode Island's Mothers News Residency and held the Center for Cartoon Studies Fellowship in 2017. He has contributed to several anthologies and self-published numerous comics. Czap cofounded Comix Cube in 2011 and served as co-organizer of Genghis Con Cleveland from 2013 until 2015. Czap has also served as founder and publisher of Czap Books since 2012.

Initially Czap self-published *Fütchi Perf* in 2015, and it was later published by Uncivilized Books in 2017. Set in a utopian Cleveland, the story centers on the think tank Kid Mind, which combines the collective power of children's minds to create societal harmony and inclusivity. There are no consequences for individuals sharing their creativity openly, the arts are well-funded, and infrastructure is designed to unite everyone equally. Czap uses short vignettes to illustrate not a fantasy but a possible future where utopian ideals are pursued without bias. The book employs illustrated street art with limited colors to present this new view for humanity.

Writing in *Xpress Reviews*, Douglas Rednour claimed that "this bold tour de force of illustrative, imaginative chutzpah will be enjoyed by a variety of readers." A contributor to *Publishers Weekly* found Czap's view of the future to be both "optimistic" and "loving." The same reviewer noted that Czap writes "with introspective ruminations on self-actualization and the beauty of radical love."

■ Biographical and Critical Sources

PERIODICALS

Publishers Weekly, October 30, 2017, review of *Fütchi Perf*, p. 66.

Xpress Reviews, October 13, 2017, Douglas Rednour, review of *Fütchi Perf*.

ONLINE

Kevin Czap Website, http://kevinczap.com (March 18, 2018).*

Barbara Davenport

1945-

■ **Also Known As**

Barbara Rosof

■ **Personal**

Born 1945; children: two daughters. *Education:* Graduated from Bennington College and Simmons College School of Social Work; Chicago Institute for Psychoanalysis, certificate in child psychotherapy.

■ **Addresses**

Home—San Diego, CA.

■ **Career**

Psychotherapist and author.

■ **Writings**

(Under pseudonym Barbara Rosof) *The Worst Loss: How Families Heal from the Death of a Child,* Henry Holt (New York, NY), 1995.

Grit and Hope: A Year with Five Latino Students and the Program That Helped Them Aim for College, University of California Press (Oakland, CA), 2016.

Contributor to professional journals and other periodicals, including *Christian Science Monitor, CityBeat, Reader, San Diego Union Tribune,* and *Stanford* magazine.

■ **Sidelights**

Barbara Davenport has been a psychotherapist for more than twenty years and has published two books on the problems faced by children and their families in modern America. In *The Worst Loss: How Families Heal from the Death of a Child,* which she wrote under the name Barbara Rosof, she examines the effect that the processes of grief and mourning have on families. "She explains the psychological tasks that parents and siblings face in coming to terms with their loss," explained a writer on the author's website.

In her second book, *Grit and Hope: A Year with Five Latino Students and the Program That Helped Them Aim for College,* Davenport looks at the successes and failures of Reality Changers, a program funded by a former University of California student named Christopher Yanov. Yanov used the money he won on the game show *Wheel of Fortune* to create a program for Hispanic students, giving them an opportunity to be the first members of their families to attend college. "Davenport furnishes a journalistically taut picture that unsentimentally presents the program's limitations as well as those of its founder," said a *Kirkus Reviews* contributor. "In addition, she expertly describes the legal and political horizons within which the students reside." "Told with deep affection and without sentimentality," according to a description of the book at the University of California Press website, "the students stories show that . . . the support of a strong program makes a critical difference."

■ Biographical and Critical Sources

PERIODICALS

Kirkus Reviews, March 15, 2017, review of *Grit and Hope: A Year with Five Latino Students and the Program That Helped Them Aim for College.*

ONLINE

Barbara Davenport Website, https://www.barbaradavenport.com (February 14, 2018).

University of California Press Website, https://www.ucpress.edu/ (February 14, 2018), synopsis of *Grit and Hope.**

Andy Davidson

1978-

■ **Personal**

Born 1978, in AR; married. *Education:* University of Mississippi, M.F.A., 2004.

■ **Addresses**

Home—GA.

■ **Career**

Writer and educator. Teaches English at a college in GA.

■ **Member**

Horror Writers Association, Mystery Writers of America.

■ **Writings**

In the Valley of the Sun, Skyhorse (New York, NY), 2017.

■ **Sidelights**

Andy Davidson is a writer and educator. Originally from Arkansas, he holds a master's degree from the University of Mississippi and has taught English at a college in Georgia.

In the Valley of the Sun is Davidson's first novel. Set in West Texas in the 1980s, the book tells the story of a serial killer named Travis, who, after a strange encounter with a female lover, experiences a dramatic change in his life. The lover, a vampire named Rue, has turned Travis into a vampire, too. He must control his urge to kill his employer and her son. Reader, a Texas Ranger, searches for Travis, hoping to charge him for his crimes.

In an interview with a contributor to the *Qwillery* website, Davison explained how he developed the idea for *In the Valley of the Sun.* He stated: "About five years ago, my wife and I decided to enclose our yard with a privacy fence. It turned out to be a massive fence, and when it came time to paint the sucker, I found myself outside for days on end. . . . I plugged into my iPod while I worked. One of the songs that kept cycling through was Dwight Yoakam's cover of Johnny Horton's 'Honkytonk Man.'" Davidson continued: "It struck me that the singer . . . is fessing up to a compulsion, a compulsion that leaves him a little broken when all's said and done. I thought it was kind of sinister, this song. At the time, I was learning scriptwriting by reading screenplays and books on writing, so I layered this idea—a psychotic cowboy who can't stop hooking up with women in jukejoints—over Horton Foote's *Tender Mercies,* which is one of my favorite films." Davidson added: "I wrote the script, then turned the script into a first draft of a novel. But what I had written just wasn't working. It had zero supernatural elements. It didn't spark my interest, as a reader. So I went back to my great childhood love of horror novels, and I'm reading *Salem's Lot* and it hits me: Travis is already a kind of metaphorical vampire, so why not make him a literal vampire?" Asked by Max Booth III, writer on the *Lit Reactor* website, if he would categorize *In the Valley of the Sun* as a vampire novel, Davidson responded: "I probably wouldn't use the word 'vampire.' Unfortunately, it's not a popular trope among mainstream readers anymore. Which is not to say there aren't great vampire books out there (Christopher Buehlman's *The Lesser Dead* springs to mind). But I've had very nice elderly ladies tell me, after hearing me read publicly from the book, that they probably won't read the book because they 'don't do vampires.' That's unfortunate (but also very funny)." Davidson continued: "So I consciously avoid using the word, even in the book itself, and the marketing has eschewed it, too, mostly. I'm convinced using it in my query letter got me rejected by a number of agencies, even though they claimed they were interested in horror. To answer your question: I'd probably tell people it's a book about what happens when evil walks into your life in the guise of everything you've ever wanted."

Reviews of *In the Valley of the Sun* were mostly favorable. William Grabowski, a critic on the *Horror Review* website, commented: "The author's frank descriptions of Reader's methods and feelings elevate the novel into literary naturalism. We're forced to endure the unfiltered ugliness of murder, its everydayness and emotional devastation." Grabowski added: "Davidson's unrelenting realism renders the supernatural—when it strikes—completely shocking, nearly inevitable." A reviewer on the *Lone Star Literary Life* website remarked: "Relentless momentum bounding toward the climactic scenes had me unconsciously holding my breath, consciously trying to stop my eyes from straying furtively to the next page. The payoff is satisfying and unexpectedly graceful. *In the Valley of the Sun* is a powerful, audacious debut." Writing on the *This Is Horror* website, Bob Pastorella suggested: "There's nothing typical at all about this novel, which is one of the reasons it's so good. Davidson has taken all his influences, wore them on his sleeve, and cobbled something distinctive and compelling, transcending his inspirations with a tale only he could conceive." Pastorella concluded: "*In the Valley of the Sun* could

very well be the debut horror novel of the year, and in a year that's already killing it with horror releases, that is something very special indeed. This one comes highly recommended, and Andy Davidson is one we should all keep our eyes on. We can't wait to see what horrors he'll unleash on us next." A contributor to *Publishers Weekly* described the novel as "bold, confident" and stated: "Davidson successfully makes the lines between genre and literary fiction bleed together in a complex novel." *Booklist* reviewer Becky Spratford called the book "hauntingly dark, yet oddly beautiful debut." Spratford also asserted: "This is one that readers won't easily forget after turning the final page."

■ Biographical and Critical Sources

PERIODICALS

Booklist, May 1, 2017, Becky Spratford, review of *In the Valley of the Sun*, p. 22.

Publishers Weekly, May 1, 2017, review of *In The Valley of the Sun*, p. 41.

ONLINE

Andy Davidson Website, http://theandydavidson. com (February 6, 2018).

Horror Review, https://www.horrorreview.com/ (June 26, 2017), William Grabowski, review of *In the Valley of the Sun*.

Lit Reactor, https://litreactor.com/ (July 26, 2017), Max Booth III, author interview.

Lone Star Literary Life, http://www.lonestarliterary. com/ (June 11, 2017), review of *In the Valley of the Sun*.

Qwillery, http://qwillery.blogspot.com/ (June 6, 2017), author interview.

This Is Horror, http://www.thisishorror.co.uk/ (June 26, 2017), Bob Pastorella, review of *In the Valley of the Sun*.*

Joshua Clark Davis

■ Personal

Male. *Education:* University of Pennsylvania, B.A.; University of North Carolina, Chapel Hill, M.A., Ph.D.

■ Career

Writer, historian, and educator. University of Baltimore, MD, assistant professor. Member of advisory board of Baltimore Uprising 2015 Archive Project; research associate for Radio Preservation Task Force, Library of Congress; codirector of Media and the Movement project.

■ Awards, Honors

Fellowships from organizations, including the Fulbright Scholar Program and the National Endowment for the Humanities.

■ Writings

From Head Shops to Whole Foods: The Rise and Fall of Activist Entrepreneurs, Columbia University Press (New York, NY), 2017.

Contributor to periodicals and websites, including *Black Perspectives, Jacobin, Slate,* and the *Washington Post.*

■ Sidelights

Joshua Clark Davis is a writer, historian, and educator. He holds a bachelor's degree from the University of Pennsylvania and both a master's degree and a Ph.D. from the University of North Carolina, Chapel Hill. Davis serves as an assistant professor at the University of Baltimore and is affiliated with public history projects, including the Baltimore Uprising 2015 Archive Project, the Radio Preservation Task Force, and the Media and the Movement project.

In 2017, Davis released his first book, a volume of nonfiction called *From Head Shops to Whole Foods: The Rise and Fall of Activist Entrepreneurs.* In this book, he focuses on activist activities by merchants of various types during the 1960s and 1970s in the United States. Davis notes that businesses supporting the counter culture were popping up throughout the country during those two decades. Among the businesses were head shops, health-food stores, African American bookstores, and businesses supporting feminism in various ways, including feminist credit unions. He offers explanations for why these activist entrepreneurs opened their respective businesses and what they hopes their businesses would achieve. Davis goes on to tell of what happened to the activist entrepreneurs and their businesses over the decades that followed. Larger banks bought up some of the feminist credit unions, while others ultimately failed. Larger companies, seeing an opportunity in the health-food sector, opened or invested in chain grocery stores, such as Whole Foods. When chain bookstores became popular, bookstores that supported the African American community began closing. Davis suggests that the rise of Amazon was the nail in the coffin of black bookstores. Activist owners of head shops moved on to focus their energies on advocating for drug legalization and/or decriminalization.

In an interview with Julie Hawks for the *Black Perspectives* website, Davis explained how he came to be interested in the subjects he discusses in *From*

Head Shops to Whole Foods. He stated that the book "had its origins in several different experiences of mine, some of them professional and others personal. I was in my second semester in grad school in spring 2004 when I first read Lizabeth Cohen's *A Consumer's Republic,* which had just recently been published. That book offered me an exciting model of a historic work that investigated consumption and business for explaining cultural and political change, and it made me want to write my own study of the politics of capitalism. Around the same time, I latched onto the idea of doing a project on the 1970s."

From Head Shops to Whole Foods received favorable assessments from critics. A *Kirkus Reviews* contributor described the volume as "scholarly in tone and approach but accessible and of interest to students of business history as well as to budding entrepreneurs." "This diligently researched, readable, but somewhat too narrowly focused study surveys the merchant activism of the 1960s and '70s," noted a writer in *Publishers Weekly.* A reviewer on the *Metropole* website commented: "If there are aspects of the book to critique, as there are with any work, one might point to the lack of any transnational perspective. Despite the fact black nationalists and feminists circulated ideas internationally, there is no real attention to this facet of any of the movements. Secondarily, in moments, it feels as if Davis jumps from example to example and that one unifying thread for each chapter does not always emerge. These are pretty minor quibbles." The same reviewer concluded: "In the end, Davis book makes a valuable contribution to the study of American capitalism and consumerism. It reveals some well-worn paths in American history but in new ways, while also establishing some of the ironic origins of today's corporate citizens."

■ Biographical and Critical Sources

PERIODICALS

Kirkus Reviews, June 1, 2017, review of *From Head Shops to Whole Foods: The Rise and Fall of Activist Entrepreneurs.*

Publishers Weekly, May 15, 2017, review of *From Head Shops to Whole Foods,* p. 48.

ONLINE

Black Perspectives, https://www.aaihs.org/ (December 18, 2017), Julie Hawks, author interview and review of *From Head Shops to Whole Foods.*

Joshua Clark Davis Website, https://www.joshuaclarkdavis.com (February 12, 2018).

Metropole, https://themetropole.blog/ (August 21, 2017), review of *From Head Shops to Whole Foods.*

University of Baltimore Website, http://www.ubalt.edu/ (February 12, 2018), author faculty profile.*

Mandy Davis

■ Personal

Female. *Education:* Hamline University, M.F.A. *Hobbies and other interests:* Photography, playing games, singing.

■ Addresses

Home—IN.

■ Career

Writer. Has worked as an elementary school teacher and record store clerk.

■ Awards, Honors

Thesis award, Hamline University.

■ Writings

Superstar, Harper (New York, NY), 2017.

■ Sidelights

Mandy Davis is a writer based in Indiana. She holds a master's degree from Hamline University. Before becoming a full-time writer, Davis worked as a record store clerk and elementary school teacher. In an interview with a contributor to the *Society of Young Inklings* website, Davis discussed the moment she determined to try to become a published author: "The year was 2008. I had been

an elementary school teacher for five years. While I loved the actual teaching, the mountain of papers always needing to be graded was wearing me down. One October evening, I was working late at school. It was 7:30 pm or so. I was tired. I was hungry. I was considering my options. Suddenly, a thought popped into my head. What if I wasn't a teacher anymore? . . . Without missing a beat, another thought popped in my head. I could write." In the same interview on the *Society of Young Inklings* website, Davis commented on her writing process and how it makes her feel. She remarked: "The act of writing is like walking into a giant, dark room. It's all unknown, and while some people find the unknown exciting, I happen to find it absolutely terrifying."

In 2017, Davis released her first novel, *Superstar.* The book is geared toward middle-grade readers. Its protagonist is Lester Musselbaum, who is ten years old. Lester's mother has been home-schooling him all of his life, but she has recently been hired at a library and no longer has the time. Lester must finally start going to public school, and he is not pleased. As a person on the autism spectrum, Lester tends to be upset by changes and new situations, so school is overwhelming to him at first. He does not like the loud noises in the lunchroom, and a change to his schedule causes him to panic, but he clings to a Superman figure his late father gave him for support. Lester also has embarrassing run-ins with students, including a bully named Ricky. Ricky destroys Lester's Superman figure, devastating him. However, a classmate, Michael Z, encourages Lester, who excels in the sciences and develops a particular interest in aerodynamics. It is revealed that Lester's late father was also a whiz at aerodynamics. While building a rocket, a deadly explosion occurred, and Lester's father was killed. Lester's mother is apprehensive about Lester's new interests, but she allows him to enter the science fair anyway. Lester's project proves to be excellent and pleases the judges. He wins the science fair. He also successfully plays sports with his classmates and develops a new friendship. Meanwhile, Ricky, the bully, has begun picking on Lester more and more. A classmate offers Lester advice on how to deal with the bullying. A member of the school administration sends a letter to Lester's mother about his autism spectrum disorder, and Lester intercepts it. He must deal with the implications of his diagnosis.

Reviews of *Superstar* were mostly favorable. A *Kirkus Reviews* critic praised Davis's creation of the character of Lester and stated: "The text never infantilizes or romanticizes him." The same critic described the book as "an intelligent and gently humorous story about an underdog who explores his place in a world." Anita Lock, contributor to *BookPage*, noted that the volume featured "a constantly moving plot that unfolds in short chapters, engaging dialogue and a well-defined cast." Of the book as a whole, Lock called it "an inimitable story." "There is plenty to enjoy in this story of friendship, bullying, education, and community," asserted Ed Spicer in the *Horn Book* magazine. A *Publishers Weekly* reviewer called *Superstar* "excellent" and suggested: "This unsentimental portrait of an endearing and memorable protagonist offers powerful insight into living with autism."

■ Biographical and Critical Sources

PERIODICALS

Booklist, November 1, 2017, Rob Reid, "Scientifically Minded Kids," review of *Superstar*, p. S40.

BookPage, July, 2017, Anita Lock, review of *Superstar*, p. 31.

Horn Book, July-August, 2017, Ed Spicer, review of *Superstar*, p. 130.

Kirkus Reviews, April 1, 2017, review of *Superstar*.

Publishers Weekly, May 1, 2017, review of *Superstar*, p. 59; December 4, 2017, review of *Superstar*, p. S75.

ONLINE

Mandy Davis Website, https://mandydavis.com (February 12, 2018).

Society of Young Inklings, http://www.younginklings.org/ (June 21, 2017), author interview.*

Lara Dearman

■ Personal

Born in Guernsey; children: three. *Education:* Attended University of Sussex and Richmond Adult Community College; Saint Mary's University, London, master's degree (with distinction), 2016.

■ Addresses

Home—Westchester, NY.

■ Career

Writer. Has worked in finance.

■ Writings

The Devil's Claw, Orion (London, England), 2017.

■ Sidelights

Lara Dearman is a writer. Born and raised on Guernsey, she studied international relations and French at the University of Sussex. Dearman worked in finance for a while before leaving her job to raise her three children. After taking a creative writing course at Richmond Adult Community College, she pursued a master's degree in creative writing at Saint Mary's University, London, graduating with distinction in 2016. Dearman has lived in the Channel Islands, Britain, France, Singapore, and in New York.

Dearman published *The Devil's Claw* in 2017. In the novel, news reporter Jennifer Dorey digs into the dark past of a series of murders in Guernsey after the discovery of a corpse on a local beach. Although eighteen-year-old Amanda Guile seems to have drowned accidentally, Dorey finds a pattern of woman with fair hair and blue eyes who also drowned at the beach in 1966, 1974, 1985, 1994, and 2002. Detective Chief Inspector Michael Gilbert agrees that Dorey's findings suggest that a serial killer may be responsible. Gilbert's interviews with the victims' surviving relatives give his investigation some momentum, while Dorey become increasingly paranoid over her findings.

A contributor to *Publishers Weekly* claimed that "well-developed characters ensure that readers will want to see more of Jennifer and company." A *Kirkus Reviews* contributor commented that "Dearman's debut is overwrought in its addiction to italicized flashbacks, highly competent in its use of serial-killer conventions, and appealingly heartfelt in its heroine's entirely believable dedication." Writing in *Xpress Reviews*, Lisa O'Hara opined that "there is a lot going on," pointing out that "the plot wanders" perhaps because of this. However, O'Hara conceded that "the end is satisfying."

■ Biographical and Critical Sources

PERIODICALS

Kirkus Reviews, November 1, 2017, review of *The Devil's Claw.*

Publishers Weekly, November 13, 2017, review of *The Devil's Claw*, p. 42.

Xpress Reviews, January 1, 2018, Lisa O'Hara, review of *The Devil's Claw.*

ONLINE

Lara Dearman Website, https://www.laradearman.com (March 18, 2018).*

Douglas Scott Delaney

■ **Personal**

Born in Brooklyn, NY.

■ **Addresses**

Home—Flint Hills, KS.

■ **Career**

Writer and tower climber. Has worked for film companies, including Columbia Pictures and Fox Searchlight. Has worked as a tower climber, 1991—.

■ **Writings**

Tower Dog: Life inside the Deadliest Job in America, Soft Skull Press (Berkeley, CA), 2017.

Has also written plays and screenplays. Contributor of short stories to publications, including *Western Humanities Review, Prism International*, and *Kansas Quarterly*.

■ **Sidelights**

Douglas Scott Delaney is a writer and tower climber for a cellular network. A native of Brooklyn, New York, he is based in Flint Hills, Kansas. Delaney has worked for film companies, including Columbia Pictures and Fox Searchlight. He has written plays and screenplays and has contributed short stories to publications, including *Western*

Humanities Review, Prism International, and *Kansas Quarterly*. Delaney has been working as a tower climber, or "tower dog," since 1991.

In 2017, Delaney released his first book, *Tower Dog: Life inside the Deadliest Job in America*, in which he discusses the dangers involved in his line of work. He describes his first ascent onto a tower in Kansas. The weather was very cold and felt even colder to Delaney as he climbed the 200 feet to the top of the tower. He recalls initially telling himself that the job would be bearable. However, as his eleven-hour shift passed, he became increasingly less able to deal with it. In addition to discussing his own experiences as a tower dog, Delaney also profiles his coworkers and tells stories of frightening incidents that he has seen or heard about involving tower dogs. A man named Joel Metz was decapitated by a cable on a tower, and his body remained in the air in his harness until coworkers could remove it. Other dangers to tower dogs include electrocution, lightning, wind, and falling debris. Despite the job's risks, Delaney notes that tower dogs typically make less than twenty dollars per hour.

In an interview with Josh Garner, a contributor to the *New York Post* website, Delaney explained why the job of a tower dog is so important. He stated: "A tower goes down, the cellphone companies start losing thousands of dollars per second and somebody has to fix it. . . . There's no waiting for a day when conditions are better and the work will be safer. . . . The cost of having a clear cell signal is blood and lives." In his interview, Delaney also discussed how he and his coworkers feel when they learn of the deaths of other tower dogs, stating: "When someone gets killed over something that [he] couldn't control—that is what puts gray hairs on our heads."

Reviewers offered favorable assessments of *Tower Dog*. Describing the writing style in the book, a *Kirkus Reviews* critic asserted: "Delaney is unfussy and workmanlike." The same critic described *Tower Dog* as "a vivid book guaranteed to make readers more aware of what it takes to get that cellphone signal into his or her hand, for better or worse."

■ Biographical and Critical Sources

PERIODICALS

Kirkus Reviews, March 1, 2017, review of *Tower Dog: Life inside the Deadliest Job in America*.

ONLINE

New York Post Online, https://nypost.com/ (April 22, 2017), Josh Garner, author interview and review of *Tower Dog*.

Soft Skull Press Website, https://softskull.com/ (February 12, 2018), author profile.*

Geoff Dembicki

1986-

■ Personal

Born 1986.

■ Addresses

Home—Vancouver, British Columbia, Canada.

■ Career

Journalist. The *Tyee*, Vancouver, British Columbia, Canada, staff reporter.

■ Awards, Honors

Media fellowship, Asia-Pacific Foundation of Canada, 2012-13; grant, Solutions Journalism Network; Dave Greber Freelance Writers Award, 2017, for *Are We Screwed?*

■ Writings

Are We Screwed? How a New Generation Is Fighting to Survive Climate Change, Bloomsbury (New York, NY), 2017.

Contributor to periodicals and websites, including the *Walrus, Toronto Star, Vice, Foreign Policy*, and *Salon.com*.

■ Sidelights

Geoff Dembicki is a Canadian journalist. He has worked as a staff reporter at the *Tyee*, a periodical based in Vancouver, British Columbia. Dembicki has also written articles that have appeared in publications and on websites, including the *Walrus, Toronto Star, Vice, Foreign Policy*, and *Salon.com*. He received a fellowship from the Asia-Pacific Foundation of Canada, a grant from the Solutions Journalism Network, and the 2017 Dave Greber Freelance Writers Award.

In his first book, *Are We Screwed? How a New Generation Is Fighting to Survive Climate Change*, Dembicki discusses what millennials might have to deal with if climate change is allowed to continue unchecked. The volume's origins lie in a series of the same name that Dembicki began publishing in the *Tyee*. In the book, he highlights the important work some millennials are undertaking to prevent disaster in the future. A group of college students brought attention to the Keystone XL pipeline and the dangers surrounding it; a Canadian activist organized young people to oust Prime Minister Stephen Harper; and a young man demonstrated how to live disconnected from the electrical grid.

Dembicki explained how he came to be interested in the topic of climate change in an interview with Jane van Koeverden, a writer on the *CBC* website. He remarked that his work at the *Tyee* had initially forced him to consider the issue, explaining: "One day, I realized that climate change is going to land harder on people my age, so maybe I should stop pretending I'm older and start looking at the issue from the perspective of myself and everyone else of my generation." Dembicki continued: "One thing in particular that changed my thinking was a climate change report from scientist James Hansen. I'm radically oversimplifying his paper, but what he suggested in the paper is that—worst case scenario—we don't do nearly enough at all to limit global warming and all the planet's coastal cities flood by the year 2065." In an interview with Breann Schossow for the *Wisconsin Public Radio* website, Dembicki commented: "You often think, you know, to deal with climate change, we have to change our light bulbs or ride our bicycles more or do whatever at the individual level, but so many of the people I met while researching this book were taking new and novel approaches to the issue and were creating a lot of interested and political and economic change in the process." Dembicki told Schossow that one of the most impactful things that can happen in terms of lessening climate change is "when people actually go out and vote for people, for politicians who are promising bold and aggressive action on climate change."

Are We Screwed? received mixed assessments from critics. A *Publishers Weekly* reviewer described the volume as "an unsatisfying work that doesn't feel representative of the generation as a whole, despite the author's insertion of general survey statistics." "Dembicki can be repetitious and sometimes comes across as self-righteous or smug; however, his profiles are wide-ranging and well-researched," asserted a critic in *Kirkus Reviews*. Roberta E. Winter, a contributor to the *New York Journal of Books* website, commented: "This book isn't the proverbial canary in the coal mine, it is a sharply written guide to getting enough oxygen to that lovely songbird." Winter concluded: "If you don't want your future to be in the hands of old white men, do read this evocative collection of stories about young people who are making a difference in environmental and political stewardship." Referring to Dembicki, Amos Lassen, writing on his *Reviews by Amos Lassen* website, remarked: "His book changes how we view the biggest existential challenge of our time and he helps to redefine the generation that is now battling against the odds to solve it."

■ **Biographical and Critical Sources**

PERIODICALS

Kirkus Reviews, June 1, 2017, review of *Are We Screwed? How a New Generation Is Fighting to Survive Climate Change.*
Publishers Weekly, May 22, 2017, review of *Are We Screwed?*, p. 84.

ONLINE

CBC Website, http://www.cbc.ca/ (August 29, 2017), Jane van Koeverden, author interview and review of *Are We Screwed?*
New York Journal of Books, https://www.nyjournalofbooks.com/ (February 12, 2018), Roberta E. Winter, review of *Are We Screwed?*
Reviews by Amos Lassen, http://reviewsbyamoslassen.com/ (August 16, 2017), Amos Lassen, review of *Are We Screwed?*
Transatlantic Agency Website, http://translatlanticagency.com/ (February 12, 2018), author profile.
Wisconsin Public Radio Online, https://www.wpr.org/ (August 28, 2017), Breann Schossow, author interview and review of *Are We Screwed?*
Writers Fest Website, http://writersfest.bc.ca/ (February 12, 2018), author profile.*

Victoria Denault

■ Personal

Born in Quebec, Canada; married. *Education:* Earned a B.A. and a graduate diploma; has studied at UCLA Extension School.

■ Addresses

Home—Los Angeles, CA.

■ Career

Writer. Has also worked as a journalist, actor, stand-up comic, editor, and in marketing and advertising.

■ Member

Romance Writers of America.

■ Writings

"HOMETOWN PLAYERS" SERIES; ROMANCE NOVELS

One More Shot, Forever Yours (New York, NY), 2015.
Making a Play, Forever Yours (New York, NY), 2015.
The Final Move, Forever Yours (New York, NY), 2015.
Winning It All, Forever Yours (New York, NY), 2016.
On the Line, Forever Yours (New York, NY), 2016.
Game On, Forever Yours (New York, NY), 2017.

"SAN FRANCISCO THUNDER" SERIES; ROMANCE NOVELS

Score, Forever (New York, NY), 2017.
Slammed, Forever (New York, NY), 2017.

■ Sidelights

Victoria Denault is a romance writer. She worked as a journalist, actor, stand-up comic, editor, and in marketing and advertising before turning her attention to writing romance novels. Denault uses her love of hockey and her experience of living around the United States to influence her writing.

One More Shot

One More Shot marks the start of the "Hometown Players" series. Jordan Garrison broke Jessie's heart when he left her for the NHL draft. Six years later, she is not sure if she still loves him or hates him. But Jordan is determined not to let her go this time.

A *Harlequin Junkie* website contributor mentioned: "I enjoyed *One More Shot* a lot, but it also frustrated me a lot, too. It wasn't a strong enough conflict." A contributor to the *Dear Author* website noted that "Jessie grew the most in the story. She had to put aside her pain and perceived betrayal. She had to trust Jordan and pursue him. . . . I felt that she was more vulnerable that Jordan and wished for a little more equality in the relationship. Overall, though, I enjoyed this angsty, sexy high school sweetheart story."

Making a Play

With *Making a Play*, sexy and scandalous hockey player Luc Richard is told by his team's manager to get out of the tabloids. He retreats to Silver Bay, Maine, where he reconnects with Rose Caplan. While Rose used to be shy, she shows Luc that the new Rose knows exactly what she wants.

A contributor to the *Fiction Fangirls* website stated: "I love the way [Rose and Luc's] relationship developed in this story. Clearly they have a past and the romantic feelings are already there, but once they both give validation to those feelings, it's full speed ahead and it's beautiful." A contributor to the *Badass Book Reviews* website commented: "Luc's interactions with the Garrison men in this book were a highlight for me; I loved the camaraderie. Their good-natured ribbing and determination to keep each other in line was so fun to read. As for Rose and her sisters, Rose is my favorite of the three. She is way more easygoing than the other two."

The Final Move

In *The Final Move*, hockey star Devin Garrison is dismayed as his marriage falls apart. Callie Caplan had a steamy affair with Devin, but she has avoided relationships. When the two reunite, they must sort out their feelings and priorities.

Writing in *Xpress Reviews*, Kellie Tilton suggested that readers who enjoyed "the first two titles will enjoy this denouement, while new readers won't get lost diving into this installment." A contributor reviewing the novel in *Harlequin Junkie* opined that "Callie is wonderful and real. I cared about her and her conflict, and I love her love and strength for all those around her." The reviewer also pointed out that the novel "can be read as a standalone."

Winning It All

With *Winning It All,* Shayne Beckford blames hockey for ruining her parents' marriage and her brother's dreams. She has a one-night stand with Sebastian Deveau, who she later finds out is a professional hockey player. While she moves to distance herself, he won't let her get away.

A *Harlequin Junkie* website contributor confessed that the novel "wasn't my favorite book of the series, mainly because of Shayne's blinding hatred of hockey players. . . . It left me frustrated with her at times. Still, it was a good book and I recommend it to anyone who enjoys hockey romances. If you've read the other books in the series, you'll want to read this one as well." A contributor to the *Book Briefs* website shared: "I really enjoyed *Winning It All.* I thought the writing was great, the romance was fantastic and the characters were fun. Overall, it is a book that I would recommend to others."

On the Line

In *On the Line*, hockey golden boy Avery Westwood tries to maintain a flawless image in the media. Stephanie Deveau is attracted to him but thinks their relationship would not go well. When he moves next door to her, though, they both break their life rules for potential happiness.

A contributor reviewing the novel in *Harlequin Junkie* reasoned that "Avery and Stephanie are a charming couple, and it is nice to read a romance that starts as a true friendship before developing into more. Their chemistry was electric and Ms. Denault built the sexual tension perfectly. My only complaint with the story is that I feel like Stephanie's addiction and sobriety was handled clumsily." A contributor to the *Book Starlets* website claimed that "this book is full of lust, passion, and some heartbreak," adding: "If you haven't read the 'Hometown Players' series I highly recommend reading them all! They are all fantastic for their own reasons, but Avery Westwood has officially skated away with my heart."

Game On

With *Game On,* hockey player Alex Larue is always the life of the party. Brie Bennett is suspicious of him when he volunteers at her charity. Both have secrets to hide but much to give each other.

A contributor to the *Ever After Book Reviews* blog confessed: "I loved every emotions-churning minute of this story." A contributor to the *Open Book Society* website admitted: "I really enjoyed all the couples from the previous books that I hadn't met since this is the first book I've read in the series! They were all engaging and fun." The same reviewer concluded: "The hockey itself took up very little of this book, as the main focus was really on the emotional side of things, specifically Alex's horrible childhood. And, of course I love a good emotional story, which made me love the book that much more. This book has impressed me enough that I feel I really need to go read the previous installments."

Score and Slammed

With *Score,* the first novel in the "San Francisco Thunder" series, Jude Braddock is a star hockey player who has a reputation for going through women quickly. Zoey is on the mend after a rough divorce. When these two former high school classmates reunite, each must trust that the other won't crush their heart. Writing in *RT Book Reviews,* Bridget Keown took note of "the consistent reinforcement of the female characters' strength and individuality." Keown also observed that "several genre-defying complications make the story feel unexpectedly fresh."

In *Slammed*, San Francisco Thunder hockey team publicist Dixie Braddock is enamored with the team's new goalie, Eli. If they get caught romancing, though, she will lose her job. Eli does not want to forfeit his place on the team, nor does he want to lose Dixie.

A contributor to *Publishers Weekly* claimed that "readers will appreciate that Denault knows her hockey and delivers a satisfying story." Again writing in *RT Book Reviews*, Keown found the novel to be "a bit slow to start." Nevertheless, Keown labeled the account a "spicy, emotional, and rewarding romance that will appeal to sports fans and hockey neophytes alike."

■ Biographical and Critical Sources

PERIODICALS

Publishers Weekly, October 23, 2017, review of *Slammed*, p. 69.
Xpress Reviews, December 11, 2015, Kellie Tilton, review of *The Final Move*, p. 1.

ONLINE

Badass Book Reviews, http://badassbookreviews.com/ (September 22, 2015), review of *Making a Play*.

Book Briefs, https://bookbriefs.net/ (September 6, 2016), review of *Winning It All*.

Book Starlets, http://bookstarlets.com/ (December 6, 2016), review of *On the Line*.

Cocktails & Books, http://www.cocktailsandbooks.com/ (April 2, 2017), review of *Score*.

Dear Author, http://dearauthor.com/ (June 20, 2015), review of *One More Shot*.

Ever After Book Reviews, https://everafterbookreviews.blogspot.com/ (November 25, 2017), review of *Game On*.

Fiction Fangirls, https://fictionfangirls.com/ (September 10, 2015), review of *Making a Play*.

Harlequin Junkie, http://harlequinjunkie.com/ (June 11, 2015), review of *One More Shot;* (December 21, 2015), review of *The Final Move;* (September 16, 2016), review of *Winning It All;* (November 23, 2016), review of *On the Line*.

Open Book Society Website, http://openbooksociety.com/ (October 10, 2017), review of *Game On*.

RT Book Reviews, https://www.rtbookreviews.com/ (March 4, 2018), Bridget Keown, reviews of *Score* and *Slammed*.

Victoria Denault Website, http://www.victoriadenault.com (March 18, 2018).*

Jayne Denker

■ Personal

Married; children: one son. *Hobbies and other interests:* Spending time on social media.

■ Addresses

Home—NY.

■ Career

Writer. Has worked formerly as an editor and proofreader.

■ Writings

NOVELS

By Design, Kensington Trade (New York, NY), 2013.
Down on Love, Kensington (New York, NY), 2013.
Unscripted, Kensington (New York, NY), 2013.
Picture This, Kensington Trade (New York, NY), 2014.
Lucky for You, Lyrical Shine (New York, NY), 2015.
Your New Best Friend, Gemma Halliday Publishing, 2017.

■ Sidelights

Jayne Denker is a New York-based writer. She has been a writer all of her life, both as a passion and as a career. She has worked as an editor, proofreader, and as a full-time writer. Wanting to focus on writing, Denker quit her last full-time job to raise her son and focus on writing romance novels. Denker joined NaNoWriMo (National Novel Writing Month) to motivate herself to write fiction. Her first book took three and a half years to complete. Denker lives in a small town in western New York. She is married and has a son. The family also has a cat. When Denker is not working on a novel, she enjoys spending time on social media.

By Design

Denker's *By Design* tells the story of Emmie Brewster, an interior designer living in a small town. Emmie's overbearing boss has unreachable expectations and treats Emmie like an unqualified receptionist. Emmie, highly talented, is lacking in confidence, and fails to speak up when her boss undermines or criticizes her.

Her personal life is not much better. Emmie's deadbeat boyfriend clearly seems to use her for sex, and she has caught him cheating. Her mother recently died, and her father is dating with success, something Emmie does not totally approve of. Despite these unpleasant aspects of her life, in the small town in which Emmie lives, she feels that she does not have any better options. That changes when she meets Graham Cooper, a new client of her company's. Graham, a recent widower and father of one, is an architect in need of an interior designer to help decorate the house he bought.

Emmie and Graham feel an immediate connection, and there is something about him that inspires Emmie to dream farther than the small town life she is currently living, but there is one problem. A woman from Graham's past, Juliette, does not seem to want to let go. Graham is also having difficulty fully leaving Juliette behind, despite his attraction to Emmie. With her heart full, Emmie has a newfound confidence, and is eager to win Graham over.

Samantha March at the *Chick Lit Plus* website described the book as "a fun contemporary romance with a cast of really likeable and fun characters that have lead really interesting lives." A contributor to the *Smexy Books* website wrote that protagonist Emmie is "funny and really engaged me with her internal dialogue," while also noting that some of the other characters' dispositions "felt too overdone and they exhausted me."

Down on Love

In *Down on Love,* Georgiana Down is a blogger and self-proclaimed man-hater. Following a series of disappointing attempts at romance in Boston, Georgiana writes off men altogether. This choice inspires her blog, "Down on Love," in which she writes wittily about her disastrous dates and rallies for other women to dump their boyfriends. The story takes a turn when financial difficulties force Georgiana to return to her hometown in Marsden in the Catskills of New York to help her sister care for her new baby.

Georgiana enjoys helping with the baby, but she looks forward to returning to Boston. That changes when she runs into Casey Bowen, her high-school crush. To Georgiana's surprise, her attraction to Casey has not dissipated. When she drunkenly publishes a blog post about Casey, everyone in Marsden reads it. And, just as in the gossipy days of high school, everyone seems to have an opinion about the two.

A *Fab Fan Fiction* website contributor wrote that the book is a "highly enjoyable read and Denker's humor was fabulous." Heather Andrews in *A Crazy Vermonter's Book Reviews* website wrote that *Down on Love* "did have funny moments, and cute and sweet moments but I felt like it was missing something."

■ Biographical and Critical Sources

PERIODICALS

Publishers Weekly, December 18, 2017, review of *Your New Best Friend,* p. 113.

ONLINE

A Crazy Vermonter's Book Reviews, http://heather-andrews.blogspot.mk/ (September 22, 2013), Heather Andrews, review of *Down on Love.*
Chick Lit Plus, http://chicklitplus.com/ (June 27, 2013), Samantha March, review of *By Design.*
Dear Author, http://dearauthor.com/ (May 6, 2013), review of *By Design.*
Fab Fan Fiction, http://www.fabfantasyfiction.com/ (October 24, 2013), review of *Down on Love.*
Harlequin Junkie, http://harlequinjunkie.com/ (August 11, 2014), review of *Picture This.*
Sandra's Book Club, http://sandrasbookclub.blogspot.com/ (September 14, 2016), review of *Down on Love.*
Smexy Books, http://smexybooks.com/ (May 29, 2013), review of *By Design.**

Heather Derr-Smith

1971-

■ **Personal**

Born 1971, in Dallas, TX. *Education:* University of Virginia, B.A.; University of Iowa, M.F.A.

■ **Career**

Writer.

■ **Awards, Honors**

Lexi Rudnitsky Prize, 2016, for *Thrust.*

■ **Writings**

POETRY COLLECTIONS

Each End of the World, Main Street Rag (Mint Hill, NC), 2005.
The Bride Minaret, University of Akron Press (Akron, OH), 2008.
Tongue Screw, Spark Wheel Press (Omaha, NE), 2016.
Thrust, Persea (New York, NY), 2017.

■ **Sidelights**

Poet Heather Derr-Smith earned a bachelor of arts degree from the University of Virginia, and she went on to complete her master of fine arts degree at the prestigious Iowa Writers' Workshop. Her first collection, *Each End of the World,* was released in 2005, and it was followed three years later by *The Bride Minaret.* Derr-Smith's next two collections, *Tongue Screw* and *Thrust,* came out in 2016

and 2017, respectively. The latter collection is a linked series of poems that follow a female speaker as she charts a world filled with violence and sex. The speaker watches a man beat her mother and then goes out in search of sex herself. Tales of hard partying and fights dominate, but moments of natural beauty seep through. The collection, which is set in the American South, is also haunted by echoes of the Civil War. Ultimately, the collection portrays a dark coming-of-age-tale, one in which the speaker reenacts the violent love she has grown up with.

Derr-Smith shared her hope for the poems in *Thrust* in an online *Cleaver* interview with Brian Burmeister. "I would like people to feel their own strength and resilience," she stated. "I hope that people can tap into the possibility of facing suffering and pain honestly, not pushing it away or denying its existence or impact or effect. But also, that each and every one of us is strong and gifted with a right to fight back and say NO to malevolence, wherever it comes from. This is a delicate message I'm trying so hard to communicate. The hurt is real, the pain is real, suffering is right here all around us and don't turn away from it. Your trauma is important and real. So is your power. You may not win or overcome, but just in standing firm you have done an incredibly powerful thing. I think I want them to feel that power of resistance."

Several reviewers praised *Thrust,* and the book received the 2016 Lexi Rudnitsky Prize. Despite its success, a *Publishers Weekly* critic called the collection "uneven," explaining: "While there is much to admire in this collection, the poems oscillate between innovation and convention." Barbara Hoffert, writing in *Library Journal,* was far more positive, and she announced that "there's uneasy satisfaction in watching the speaker turn her mean world around."

■ Biographical and Critical Sources

PERIODICALS

Library Journal, August 1, 2017, Barbara Hoffert, review of *Thrust.*

Publishers Weekly, October 16, 2017, review of *Thrust.*

ONLINE

Cleaver, https://www.cleavermagazine.com/ (March 15, 2018), Brian Burmeister, author interview.

Heather Derr-Smith Website, https://heatherderrsmith.com (March 15, 2018).*

Chess Desalls

■ **Personal**

Female.

■ **Career**

Writer.

■ **Awards, Honors**

Two IAN Outstanding Young Adult citations, both 2016, for *Travel Glasses* and *Insight Kindling;* Moonbeam Children's Book Awards Gold in YA Fiction—E-book, 2017, for *Beacon;* Literary Classics Gold in Best YA Series, 2017, for *The Call to Search Everywhen;* Literary Classics Gold in High School Mystery/Thriller, and Literary Classics Gold in High School Fantasy, both 2017, both for *Travel Glasses.*

■ **Writings**

NOVELS; EXCEPT WHERE NOTED

Insight Kindling, Czidor Lore (Silicon Valley, CA), 2015.

Lantern, Czidor Lore (Silicon Valley, CA), 2016.

Time for the Lost, Czidor Lore (Silicon Valley, CA), 2016.

Wrapped in the Past, Czidor Lore (Silicon Valley, CA), 2016.

Glistens, Czidor Lore (Silicon Valley, CA), 2016.

Travel Glasses, Czidor Lore (Silicon Valley, CA), 2017.

Flash Tales: A Collection of Short Stories for Children, Czidor Lore (Silicon Valley, CA), 2017.

Darker Stars, Czidor Lore (Silicon Valley, CA), 2017.

Glistens Part Two, Czidor Lore (Silicon Valley, CA), 2018.

Also author of the e-book *Beacon,* and author of *The Call to Search Everywhen.*

■ **Sidelights**

Chess Desalls is a prolific novelist who has released an average of three books a year since 2015. Her first book, *Insight Kindling,* received an IAN Outstanding Young Adult citation. Desalls's second book, the 2016 title *Lantern,* also earned the same award. Desalls released an additional three novels in 2016 as well, *Time for the Lost, Wrapped in the Past,* and *Glistens.* Next, in 2017, Desalls published *Travel Glasses.* The latter title was commended with a Literary Classics Gold in High School Mystery/Thriller and a Literary Classics Gold in High School Fantasy. The same year, Desalls published the novel *Darker Stars,* and she also wrote *Flash Tales: A Collection of Short Stories for Children.* The novel *Glistens Part Two* followed in 2018. Other e-books credited to Desalls include *Beacon* (winner of the Moonbeam Children's Book Awards Gold in YA Fiction—E-book), and *The Call to Search Everywhen* (winner of the Literary Classics Gold in Best YA Series).

One of Desall's most widely reviewed books is *Lantern,* a novel built of three linked novellas. The first tale follows sixteen-year-old Tori. The protagonist finds a haunted lantern on her grandmother's property, and the lantern is inhabited by a boy named Jared. Jared was working for his master, the lantern maker Machin, when he was cursed and trapped. He has been inside the lamp for centuries. When Tori and Jared fall for each other, Tori must find a way to free her true love from his curse. Teenager Serah Kettel is the protagonist of the next tale, and she is also one of Machin's apprentices. Machine asks the girl to open a sealed globe, and Serah becomes trapped inside. Centuries later, a boy opens the globe and Serah is released, but she struggles to cope in modern society. The third tale begins as Machin creates a lantern for Graham, and though the boy remains unharmed, a girl named Evelyn is sucked into the lantern and transported back in time.

A somewhat ambivalent assessment of the novel was proffered by *Buried under Books* website correspondent Lelia Taylor, who stated that the story is "sort of a modern-day fairy tale, sort of a romance (although a light one)." Taylor added: "*Lantern* is a sweet story, I might say even sugary." A *Kirkus Reviews* critic announced that each of the three "stories effectively stands alone." In fact, the critic explained, "Desalls casts a different slant on each telling . . . and among these . . . a shared tale emerges of how lives may develop and love may burgeon."

■ Biographical and Critical Sources

PERIODICALS

Kirkus Reviews, November 15, 2017, review of *Lantern*.

ONLINE

Buried under Books, https://cncbooksblog.wordpress.com/ (June 2, 2016), Lelia Taylor, review of *Lantern*.

Chess Desalls Website, http://www.chessdesalls.com (March 15, 2018).

Sudden Insight, http://blog.suddeninsight publishing.com/ (May 13, 2016), review of *Wrapped in the Past.**

Diane DeSanders

■ **Personal**

Female. *Hobbies and other interests:* Singing, gardening, theater.

■ **Addresses**

Home—Brooklyn, NY.

■ **Career**

Has worked as history teacher, tutor, and antiques dealer.

■ **Writings**

Hap & Hazard and the End of the World, Bellevue Literary Press (New York, NY), 2018.

■ **Sidelights**

Diane DeSanders's debut novel, *Hap & Hazard and the End of the World,* tells the story of a Texas family's life in the years immediately after World War II, told from the viewpoint of the eldest daughter and structured as a series of vignettes. The girl, whose name is never revealed, is about four years old when her father returns to their household obviously traumatized by his combat experiences, and together they move to their suburban Dallas home about a year later. In addition to his psychic pain, he is in physical pain from his wounds, and he sometimes has violent outbursts. While she adjusts to having her father back in the household, the narrator must also adjust to having two sisters, born in quick succession after his return and causing her to feel neglected. She deals with changes in the world and she ponders some less existential questions, such as whether Santa Claus is real. The girl "struggles to understand what is really going on in the adult world, and the truth of how things work in the greater world, but since she hardly ever gets a straightforward answer about anything, begins to look outside in ways that aren't always safe," DeSanders told an interviewer on the *Powell's Books* website.

Several reviewers found *Hap & Hazard and the End of the World* an engaging, moving tale. DeSanders "paints a vivid picture of childhood in postwar America, replete with all of the joys and sorrows that are part of growing up," remarked Kristine Huntley in *Booklist.* A *Kirkus Reviews* contributor noted: "While it rings true, the novel's childlike narration may be off-putting to some readers. Readers who can look past that will find a time capsule of American awakening." A blogger at *Me, You, and Books,* however, thought the narration was a strength of the book, saying: "The genius of DeSanders' writing is the way in which she brings adult readers into the remembrance of childhood vulnerability that continues to haunt us all." Susan L. Jackson, writing online at *Shelf Awareness,* likewise praised the use of the child narrator. "Funny and nostalgic and occasionally unsettling, this child's view of her own small world also provides a picture of the wider world at that time," she commented. A *Publishers Weekly* critic observed that the character comes off as "curious and thoughtful," making the novel a "smart and subtle debut."

DeSanders told *CA:* "I had a wonderful grade school English teacher in whose class I realized I could write and wanted to write. Miss Coleman at Walnut Hill Grade School, she would read to us and cry, and she would have us write poems.

"What I most want to convey is the complication of human character and the subtle beauty of the world."

■ Biographical and Critical Sources

PERIODICALS

Booklist, November 1, 2017, Kristine Huntley, review of *Hap & Hazard and the End of the World*, p. 30.
Kirkus Reviews, October 15, 2017, review of *Hap & Hazard and the End of the World*.

Publishers Weekly, November 20, 2017, review of *Hap & Hazard and the End of the World*, p. 69.

ONLINE

Bellevue Literary Press Website, http://blpress.org/ (March 19, 2018), brief biography.
Me, You, and Books, https://mdbrady.wordpress.com/ (July 1, 2017), review of *Hap & Hazard and the End of the World*.
Powell's Books Website, http://www.powells.com/ (January 9, 2018), interview with Diane DeSanders.
Shelf Awareness, http://www.shelf-awareness.com/ (February 6, 2018), Susan L. Jackson, review of *Hap & Hazard and the End of the World*.

Delphine de Vigan

1966-

■ **Also Known As**

Lou Delvig

■ **Personal**

Born March, 1966; partner of François Busnel; children: one daughter, one son.

■ **Addresses**

Home—Paris, France.

■ **Career**

Writer.

■ **Awards, Honors**

Prix des Libraires, 2008, for *No and Me*; Prix du Roman FNAC, Prix Roman France Télévisions, and Prix Renault des Lycéens, all for *Nothing Holds Back the Night.*

■ **Writings**

No and Me, Bloomsbury (New York, NY), 2010.
Underground Time, Bloomsbury (New York, NY), 2011.
Nothing Holds Back the Night: A Novel, Bloomsbury (New York, NY), 2014.
Based on a True Story, Bloomsbury (New York, NY), 2018.

■ **Sidelights**

Delphine de Vigan is a French writer who is based in Paris. She has written books that have won French literary awards.

No and Me

No and Me is the first of de Vigan's novels to be translated into English. It received the Prix des Libraires in 2008. The volume tells the story of an unlikely friendship between two teens, Lou and No. No is homeless, and Lou is dealing with her mother's depression after having lost a child.

A contributor to *Kirkus Reviews* suggested: "In a realistic ending . . . this quiet yet gripping translation proves its merit." Sue Roe, a reviewer in *School Librarian,* commented: "It employs a light tone and an endearing narrator to consider dark issues of grief, loss, mental illness, homelessness . . . and barriers to change and to mingle tragedy and hope in a moving and thought provoking novel for young adults." "The book is well-written, instantly absorbing, sometimes funny, the characters are complex and engaging and the tension well sustained," asserted Joy Steward in *Reading Time.* *School Library Journal* writer Jennifer Rothschild noted: "The directness of Lou's narration . . . gives it a spare quality, resulting in a profound and haunting book." Daniel Hahn, a contributor to the London *Independent* website, stated: "Well-structured, with moments of tenderness and truth about family and home, inadequate parents and neglected children, *No and Me* is honest (as revealing and insightful about Lou and home life as it is about No and homelessness) but also at least partially reassuring." In a review of the novel on the *Bookbag* website, Jill Murphy suggested: "It never loses sight of the social and moral issues it explores and, as it juxtaposes a lonely home with homelessness, it lifts itself into one of those singular books that absolutely anybody can read and be touched by. A great deal of rot is talked about crossover fiction that can be read by child and adult alike, but this truly is a genuine example."

Underground Time

In *Underground Time*, de Vigan focuses on two characters' struggles with work and their personal lives. The characters are a single mother named Mathilde and an emergency doctor named Thibault.

"This masterly author . . . throws a curveball that all sophisticated readers will want to catch," asserted Beth E. Andersen in *Library Journal*. A *Kirkus Reviews* critic commented: "This is ultimately a corporate horror story—often claustrophobic to the point of oppressive, but undeniably disturbing." Carol Gladstein, a reviewer in *Booklist*, suggested: "Despite an unexpected conclusion that may throw some readers off, this is an engrossing, well-paced story." Writing in the London *Guardian*, Nicola Barr described *Underground Time* as an "elegantly constructed, sympathetic, compelling, enjoyable novel." Eileen Battersby, a contributor to the *Irish Times* website, noted: "de Vigan's view of backstabbing corporate politics will amuse and chill. Her boldly intuitive novel may not quite engage, but it does convince and often succeeds, most certainly when describing the helpless fury of Mathilde and the wary detachment of her gutless colleagues. It is too real for comfort." "*Underground Time* has the germ of a good novel in it, but unfortunately that germ didn't quite develop the way it might have. Read it for Mathilde's extraordinary poise under pressure; skip the rest," wrote Allison Slegenthaler on the *Postgraduate Contemporary Women's Writing Network* website.

Nothing Holds Back the Night

Nothing Holds Back the Night: A Novel is a fictionalized retelling of de Vigan's mother's life. The protagonist, Lucille, deals with mental illness throughout her life and ultimately commits suicide at age sixty-one.

A *Publishers Weekly* reviewer described *Nothing Holds Back the Night* as "a striking personal journey." Leah Strauss, a critic in *Booklist*, called it a "gripping exploration into her mother's troubled life." "Sympathy and sadness infuse this compel-

ling investigation in which the author herself plays a difficult role," commented a writer in *Kirkus Reviews*. Evelyn Beck, a contributor to *Library Journal*, asserted: "The author's deep love, rage, frustration, and grief are moving and palpable." Writing in the London *Guardian*, Ursula Le Guin, an award-winning novelist herself, remarked: "Whether or not De Vigan is identical with the author-character, her portrait of the mother, Lucile, as an elusive girl who becomes a deeply troubled woman, is compassionate and powerful." Le Guin added: "Her book is what her delicate and mysterious metaphor promises—a beautiful paper coffin, inscribed with words chosen with painful care and tenderness." Nancy Kline, reviewing the work on the *New York Times* website, asserted: "Although language must inevitably fail to capture her full complexity, de Vigan's mysterious mother does flash into life in this 'novel,' which, despite its darkness, is shot through with light. Perhaps what's most amazing is that, repeatedly, in the midst of tragedy, its author suddenly thrusts us into the noisy, crazy, generous heart of her mother's." A contributor to the Dublin Literary Award website opined: "This harrowing inquiry in to the heart of the familial memory reveals brighter memories as much as hidden secrets. Fascinating and very sensitive."

Based on a True Story

De Vigan uses her own first name for one of the protagonists of *Based on a True Story*. Delphine, a writer unnerved by her recent success, strikes up a friendship with a woman called L. As Delphine confides in L. about her family and her writer's block, L. become increasingly manipulative.

Strauss, writing in *Booklist*, called *Based on a True Story* "a haunting, provoking tale that grows in intensity as the truth Delphine seeks becomes harder to find." "The insidious nature of a complex mind game masquerading as friendship is chilling to watch unfold," asserted a *Publishers Weekly* writer. Reviewing the book on the London *Guardian* website, Joanna Briscoe noted that it features "a deeply personal voice with a narrow focus that feels all-consuming. Lou is the very real, flawed, sympathetic person who gets to tell this story, but No is always very much there. She may be in the background but her actions—both on and off-stage—are a huge presence in the novel." A contributor to the *Better Reading* website remarked: "This is an enchanting story that weaves itself in your mind, slowly at first, until you begin to feel just as trapped by L. as Delphine does. It is cerebral, claustrophobic, and rattling. Although on

the surface it's a novel about psychological obsession and loss, it is ultimately shrouded by a
mystery that shudders to the core."

■ Biographical and Critical Sources

PERIODICALS

Booklist, August 1, 2010, Gillian Engberg, review of
No and Me, p. 49; November 1, 2011, Carol Gladstein, review of *Underground Time*, p. 23; March 1,
2014, Leah Strauss, review of *Nothing Holds Back
the Night: A Novel*, p. 19; May 1, 2017, Leah
Strauss, review of *Based on a True Story*, p. 55.

Guardian, May 14, 2011, Nicola Barr, review of *Underground Time*, p. 14; November 23, 2013, Ursula
le Guin, review of *Nothing Holds Back the Night*, p.
11.

Horn Book Guide, spring, 2011, Hannah Rodgers
Barnaby, review of *No and Me*, p. 96.

Kirkus Reviews, July 1, 2010, review of *No and Me*;
November 1, 2011, review of *Underground Time*;
December 15, 2013, review of *Nothing Holds Back
the Night*.

Library Journal, August 1, 2011, Beth E. Andersen,
review of *Underground Time*, p. 89; January 1, 2014,
Evelyn Beck, review of *Nothing Holds Back the
Night*, p. 94.

Observer, March 14, 2010, Hermione Ho, review of
No and Me.

Publishers Weekly, September 19, 2011, review of
Underground Time, p. 33; November 4, 2013,
review of *Nothing Holds Back the Night*, p. 42;
March 27, 2017, review of *Based on a True Story*, p.
82.

Reading Time, August, 2010, Joy Steward, review of
No and Me, p. 34.

School Librarian, summer, 2010, Sue Roe, review of
No and Me, p. 109; spring, 2011, Anna Griffin,
review of *No and Me*, p. 50.

School Library Journal, July, 2010, Jennifer Rothschild,
review of *No and Me*, p. 86.

ONLINE

Abu Dhabi National Online, https://www.
thenational.ae/ (February 12, 2018), Matthew Adams, review of *Based on a True Story*.

Better Reading, http://www.betterreading.com.au/
(May 15, 2017), review of *Based on a True Story*.

Bloomsbury Website, https://www.bloomsbury.com/
(February 12, 2018), author profile.

Bookbag, http://www.thebookbag.co.uk/ (March 1,
2010), Jill Murphy, review of *No and Me*.

Criminal Element, https://www.criminalelement.
com/ (May 8, 2017), Deborah Lacy, review of
Based on a True Story.

Dublin Literary Award Website, http://www.
dublinliteraryaward.ie/ (February 12, 2018),
review of *Underground Time*; review of *Nothing
Holds Back the Night*.

Evening Standard Online, https://www.standard.co.
uk/ (March 23, 2017), Jane Shilling, review of
Based on a True Story.

Financial Times Online, https://www.ft.com/ (April
13, 2017), Barry Forshaw, review of *Based on a
True Story*.

Fresh Fiction, http://freshfiction.com/ (February 12,
2018), author profile.

Guardian Online, https://www.theguardian.com/
(April 15, 2017), Joanna Briscoe, review of *Based
on a True Story*.

Independent Online, http://www.independent.co.
uk/ (February 28, 2010), Daniel Hahn, review of
No and Me; (June 30, 2011), Emma Hagestadt,
review of *Underground Time*; (March 11, 2012),
David Evans, review of *Underground Time*; (March
29, 2017), Lucy Scholes, review of *Based on a True
Story*.

Irish Times Online, https://www.irishtimes.com/
(October 17, 2013), Eileen Battersby, review of
Underground Time.

New York Times Online, https://www.nytimes.com/
(May 11, 2014), Nancy Kline, review of *Nothing
Holds Back the Night*.

*Postgraduate Contemporary Women's Writing Network
Website*, https://pgcwwn.org/ (October 18, 2013),
Allison Slegenthaler, review of *Underground Time*.

Readventurer, http://www.thereadventurer.com/
(October 22, 2012), review of *No and Me*.

Rumpus, http://therumpus.net/ (June 1, 2017),
Rebecca Schuh, review of *Based on a True Story*.

Scotsman Online, https://www.scotsman.com/
(March 20, 2010), review of *No and Me*.

Scottish Daily Record, https://www.dailyrecord.co.
uk/ (November 11, 2013), Gregor White, review
of *No and Me*.

Telegraph Online, http://www.telegraph.co.uk/
(March 25, 2017), Celia Walden, author interview
and review of *Based on a True Story*.*

Ramón Díaz Eterovic

1956-

■ Personal

Born July 15, 1956, in Punta Arenas, Chile; married Sonia González Valdenegro; children: three. *Hobbies and other interests:* Reading.

■ Addresses

Home—Chile.

■ Career

Author.

■ Writings

El hombre que pregunta, Lom Editorial (Santiago, Chile), 2002.
Dark Echoes of the Past, AmazonCrossing (Seattle, WA), 2017.

Also author of *La ciudad está triste*.

■ Adaptations

Author's novels were adapted for television and broadcast as *Heredia & asociados*, 2005.

■ Sidelights

Ramón Díaz Enterovic is well known in Chile, where his work as a crime writer has earned national acclaim. In an interview featured on the *Big Thrill* website, Díaz Enterovic explained that he picked up his love for writing through a much earlier love for reading. By the age of fourteen, Díaz Enterovic began dabbling with writing himself. His skill grew as he reached adulthood. He began networking with others in the writing industry and entering his work into contests. Díaz Enterovic finally made his professional literary debut in the year 1980, and has been writing ever since. He is most famous for his series of novels starring the character Heredia. In his interview on the *Big Thrill* website, Díaz Enterovic expressed that his interest in crime fiction was born from the political strife plaguing Chile throughout the 1980s. It allowed him to communicate the experience of living under an ever-watchful authority, while also fueling his personal interest in adventure stories. His novels have been adapted for other printed mediums, including graphic novels, as well as for television.

Dark Echoes of the Past

Dark Echoes of the Past marks Díaz Enterovic's literary introduction to English-speaking audiences. The novel stars Heredia, whose exploits drive the plot. Heredia works as a detective in Santiago, the capital of Chile, and supplements his income by writing book reviews for the local newspaper. He spends his days in a dingy apartment with the company of Simenon, Heredia's pet cat, who seems to have the peculiar ability to speak. *Dark Echoes of the Past* starts with Heredia being pulled out of a business slump when a new client approaches him with a case. The client's name is Virginia Reyes. She seeks justice for her brother, a man by the name of German, who died under what Virginia is sure were malicious circumstances. In the days leading up to his death, German expressed paranoia over being followed by an unknown, unseen assailant. Heredia accepts the case and decides to start off his sleuthing by figuring out who could have been stalking German prior to his death.

What starts out as a merely intriguing case soon leads Heredia into the underground aftermath of Chilean president Augusto Pinochet and his hellish rule. The world of *Dark Echoes of the Past* is thirty years past Pinochet's time, but its effects remain, hidden but present. Only a few of the bit players within the horrors of that era faced any punishment; those with enough power were allowed to escape and pick back up as if nothing happened. Heredia soon learns that German was deeply involved in attempting to take down those who helped further Pinochet's crimes and managed to get away unscathed, as well as uncover the truth of that dark period. In fact, German may have been on the verge of a breakthrough, only to be snuffed out before the truth could be delivered. Other individuals with connections to German are also losing their lives. A bystander on the night German died also winds up dead, giving Heredia further evidence to believe there is a government conspiracy at play. However, by getting involved with the case, Heredia finds his own life is at risk. He must rely on his wits and help from his allies in order to survive this case and get to the bottom of it—once and for all. *Booklist* contributor Thomas Gaughan called the book "a fine discovery for followers of international crime." A reviewer in *Publishers Weekly* called *Dark Echoes of the Past* "Chandleresque." A writer for *Kirkus Reviews* stated: "The surprise is the extent to which, despite its lack of big surprises, the book nevertheless works: Eterovic constructs an intricate plot peopled with dozens of characters, and he unravels the snarls patiently and often stylishly." On the *New York Journal of Books* website, D.R. Meredith remarked: "Senor Diaz Eterovic is both an eloquent writer and a profound one, veiling his philosophical musing in humor which does nothing to disguise the sting of his observations." Meredith also said: "*Dark Echoes of the Past* is a literary treat for fans of noir, but not so much for those who appreciate a softer, gentler cozy mystery."

El hombre que pregunta

El hombre que pregunta is another novel starring Heredia as he embarks upon a new case. The story starts with Heredia learning of the demise of Francisco Ritter, a renowned critic of literature. Berta Zamudio, Heredia's ex-girlfriend, and Heredia himself do not believe the claims that Ritter's demise came about unintentionally; rather, some-

one sinister must have been behind it, and they both want to figure out the identity of the culprit. Berta gets in touch with Heredia personally to hire him to look into the truth of the case. Through conversations with those involved in the literary world, Heredia is able to gather information. Claudio Ramon, a man with close ties to Ritter, was also found dead under violent circumstances mere days before Ritter lost his life. As Heredia continues his sleuthing, he uncovers further information that suggests a sinister motive behind Ritter's demise. For starters, in addition to his careers as a professor and critic, he also performed ghostwriting work for a mysterious client. Heredia believes the shadowy client may have some involvement in Ritter's demise, but he has to uncover the identity of the client before he can figure out anything else.

He starts by continuing his conversations with various writers and other people involved in the literary world, using his own complex understanding of literature and publishing to wheedle what he needs out of his interviewees. Along the way, Heredia discovers a less than pristine side to literature and those he create it; some people are so driven to find the recognition they crave that they will do absolutely anything to obtain it, or get rid of those who might hurt their chances of success. Barbara Mujica, writing in the *Americas* magazine, commented: "Like Perez Reverte, Ramon Diaz Eterovic elevates sleuth fiction to an art." She added: "His writing is erudite, engaging, and fun, all at the same time."

■ Biographical and Critical Sources

PERIODICALS

Americas, March-April, 2003, Barbara Mujica, "Poetic Enigmas and Intrigue," review of *El hombre que pregunta*, p. 60.
Booklist, November 1, 2017, Thomas Gaughan, review of *Dark Echoes of the Past*, p. 19.
Publishers Weekly, October 9, 2017, review of *Dark Echoes of the Past*, p. 47.

ONLINE

Big Thrill, http://www.thebigthrill.org/ (November 30, 2017), Layton Green, "International Thrills: Ramón Díaz Eterovic," author interview.
Kirkus Reviews, https://www.kirkusreviews.com/ (September 20, 2017), review of *Dark Echoes of the Past*.
New York Journal of Books, https://www.nyjournalofbooks.com/ (March 22, 2018), D.R. Meredith, review of *Dark Echoes of the Past*.*

Dawn Eastman

■ Personal

Married; children: one daughter, one son.

■ Addresses

Home—IA.

■ Career

Author.

■ Writings

NOVELS

Pall in the Family, Berkley Prime Crime (New York, NY), 2013.

Be Careful What You Witch For, Berkley Prime Crime (New York, NY), 2014.

A Fright to the Death, Berkley Publishing Group (New York, NY), 2015.

An Unhappy Medium, Berkley Prime Crime (New York, NY), 2016.

Unnatural Causes, Crooked Lane Books (New York, NY), 2017.

Do No Harm, Crooked Lane Books (New York, NY), 2018.

■ Sidelights

Dawn Eastman has built a career for herself within the fiction publishing industry as a writer. On her personal website, she explained that she has long held an interest in mystery novels. She has published several mystery novels of her own, such as *An Unhappy Medium, Be Careful What You Witch For,* and *Pall in the Family.*

Unnatural Causes is the start of a series of novels written by Eastman. The novel stars the titular Katie LeClair, who finds herself in the middle of a horrifying mystery. Katie has recently made the move to Baxter, Michigan, a small town, following her decision to break free from her bustling medical career in the city. With her new home comes a position at the community's clinic. Katie is grateful for the move; her old life in the city had grown too turbulent to bear, and life in Baxter represents the sense of peace she craves. However, her arrival to the town proves to be anything but peaceful.

After mere months, Katie rushes into work on an emergency call. Ellen, a patient who has come under her care, has taken a sudden and sharp turn for the worst after ingesting a toxic amount of medication. Despite the clinic's best efforts, Ellen does not survive, and her passing is determined to be a suicide. While this is tragic enough, Katie soon learns of even more unsettling news: the medication Ellen used to supposedly end her life was supplied to her by Katie via prescription. However, Katie never filled out the order for Ellen—or if she did, she can't recall the date or the details of it happening. The only real evidence of Katie's involvement is her name, which is stamped onto the bottle of pills Ellen ingested. Katie is devastated by Ellen's death, as Ellen was one of the few people in Baxter whom she had begun getting to know on a more personal level.

As new details emerge, Katie finds her suspicions rapidly growing. When autopsy specialists conduct further investigation on Ellen's death, they realize that a completely different medication caused her demise, and it may have entered her system through nefarious means. The authorities soon begin to hunt for the real culprit. Katie becomes determined to get to the bottom of the circumstances of Ellen's death and decides to join Beth, the daughter of Ellen, in cracking the case. Katie also enlists help from Caleb, her brother, who is highly technologically skilled.

In the process of unveiling the truth surrounding Ellen's demise, Katie stumbles upon a myriad of discoveries. One of them involves one of her work colleagues, Nick, whose conduct at work seems to be following a dangerous and sinister pattern. It was Nick's turn to handle on-call duties around the time that Ellen passed away. Furthermore, many of the patients Nick cares for wind up with easy access to powerful drugs for seemingly no reason. On top of this, Katie finds herself in the midst of a burgeoning relationship with another coworker by the name of Dr. Gregor. Dr. Gregor seems to return Katie's feelings, but the wounds from Katie's past—and her old life in the city—are still too raw for her to accept any opportunities to revive her love life.

As Katie begins to gather more and more evidence and clues, she realizes her own life may be in danger as well. She will have to act fast to reveal the reality behind Ellen's death, or else she may meet the same terrible fate as her late patient. A *Publishers Weekly* reviewer stated: "Readers will look forward to seeing more of the appealing Katie." In a review for the *New York Journal of Books,* Michael Thomas Barry remarked: "A highly recommended read, *Unnatural Causes* will engage anyone wanting a simple straight forward mystery and in Dr. Katie LeClair, Dawn Eastman has created a strong and appealing new heroine to the thriller mystery genre." A contributor to *Kirkus Reviews* commented: "In a change from her psychic series . . . Eastman introduces a strong new heroine who has her hands full with a large cast of potential killers." A writer on the blog *That's What She's Reading* called *Unnatural Causes* "a fast-paced and engrossing start to a series that I will definitely be on the look out for as more books come out." On the website *My Reading Journeys,* Grantham Lynn wrote: "This was a great read." Lynn added: "The

character(s) are fun to get to know." A reviewer on the *Dru's Book Musings* blog said: "This is a great debut series and I can't wait to see what adventures await Katie and her circle of friends." A contributor to the *Books, Movies, Reviews. Oh My!* blog remarked: "The author does a great job of giving you information that can make you think one thing when it was something else," and a writer on the *Kittling: Books* blog said: "*Unnatural Causes* is well-written and does have an appealing main character, so don't be afraid to give it a try."

■ **Biographical and Critical Sources**

PERIODICALS

Publishers Weekly, October 2, 2017, review of *Unnatural Causes,* p. 118.

ONLINE

Books, Movies, Reviews. Oh My!, https://www.booksmoviesreviewsohmy.com/ (December 14, 2017), review of *Unnatural Causes.*

Dawn Eastman Website, http://dawneastman.com (March 14, 2018), author profile.

Dru's Book Musings, https://drusbookmusing.com/ (December 3, 2017), review of *Unnatural Causes.*

Kirkus Reviews, https://www.kirkusreviews.com/ (September 18, 2017), review of *Unnatural Causes.*

Kittling: Books, http://www.kittlingbooks.com/ (December 13, 2017), review of *Unnatural Causes.*

Michael Thomas Barry, https://www.michaelthomasbarry.com (December 12, 2017), review of *Unnatural Causes.*

My Reading Journeys, http://myreadingjourneys.blogspot.com/ (December 15, 2017), review of *Unnatural Causes.*

New York Journal of Books, https://www.nyjournalofbooks.com/ (March 22, 2018), Michael Thomas Barry, review of *Unnatural Causes.*

Penguin Random House Website, https://www.penguinrandomhouse.com/ (March 14, 2018), author profile.

That's What She's Reading, http://www.thatswhatshesreading.com/ (December 19, 2017), review of *Unnatural Causes.**

Bill Eddy

1948-

■ **Also Known As**

William A. Eddy

■ **Personal**

Born 1948. *Education:* Yo San University of Traditional Chinese Medicine, B.A., 1970; San Diego State University, M.S.W., 1981; University of San Diego School of Law, J.D., 1992.

■ **Addresses**

Home—San Diego, CA.

■ **Career**

Speaker, therapist, and author. Mediator and attorney, 1993-2009; High Conflict Institute, president, 2007—, training director and cofounder, 2008—; University of San Diego School of Law, professor; National Conflict Resolution Center, San Diego, CA, Senior Family Mediator.

Monash University Law Chambers, visiting lecturer; National Judicial College, faculty member; Pepperdine University School of Law, faculty member.

■ **Writings**

High Conflict Personalities: Understanding and Resolving Their Costly Disputes, William A. Eddy (San Diego, CA), 2003.

Managing High-Conflict People in Court, High Conflict Institute (San Diego, CA), 2008.

New Ways for Families Parent Workbook, High Conflict Institute Press (San Diego, CA), 2009.

New Ways for Families Collaborative Parent Workbook, High Conflict Institute Press (San Diego, CA), 2009.

New Ways for Families Professional Guidebook: For Therapists, Lawyers, Judicial Officers and Mediators, High-Conflict Institute Press (San Diego, CA), 2010.

BIFF: Quick Responses to High-Conflict People, Their Personal Attacks, Hostile Email and Social Media Meltdowns, High Conflict Institute (San Diego, CA), 2011.

(With Randi Kreger) *Splitting: Protecting Yourself While Divorcing Someone with Borderline or Narcissistic Personality Disorder,* New Harbinger Publications (Oakland, CA), 2011.

It's All Your Fault! 12 Tips for Managing People Who Blame Others for Everything, High Conflict Institute: Unhooked Books (San Diego, CA), 2012.

Don't Alienate the Kids! Raising Resilient Children While Avoiding High-Conflict Divorce, High Conflict Institute Press (San Diego, CA), 2012.

(With Don Saposnek) *Splitting America: How Politicians, Super PACs and the News Media Mirror High-Conflict Divorce,* HCI Press (San Diego, CA), 2012.

The Future of Family Court: Structure, Skills and Less Stress, HCI Press (San Diego, CA), 2012.

So, What's Your Proposal? Shifting High-Conflict People from Blaming to Problem-Solving in 30 Seconds, High Conflict Institute Press (San Diego, CA), 2014.

It's All Your Fault at Work! Managing Narcissists and Other High-Conflict People, High Conflict Institute Press (San Diego, CA), 2015.

New Ways for Work: Coaching Manual: Personal Skills for Productive Relationships, High Conflict Institute Press (San Diego, CA), 2015.

High-Conflict People in Legal Disputes, High Conflict Institute Press (San Diego, CA), 2016.

Trump Bubbles: The Dramatic Rise and Fall of High-Conflict Politicians, High Conflict Institute Press (San Diego, CA), 2016.

(With Megan Hunter) *Dating Radar: Why Your Brain Says Yes to "The One" Who Will Make Your Life Hell,* BookBaby (Pennsauken, NJ), 2017.

5 Types of People Who Can Ruin Your Life: Identifying and Dealing with Narcissists, Sociopaths, and Other High-Conflict Personalities, TarcherPerigee (New York, NY), 2018.

■ **Sidelights**

Bill Eddy has made a name for himself through his work in the mental health field. Prior to launching his career, Eddy studied at the Case Western Reserve University, San Diego State University, and the University of San Diego, where he earned his B.A., M.S.W., and J.D., respectively. Eddy focused several years' worth of his professional efforts within the field of social work. He held the title of licensed clinical social worker in the city of San Diego. He then moved on to work in law during the early 1990s, earning the title of certified family law specialist. Throughout his time in the social work field, Eddy counseled numerous families and individuals. He has also lent his expertise to students pursuing the same subject, leading courses under the University of San Diego School of Law. He has worked at the National Judicial College as well as the Pepperdine University School of Law, serving for both of these schools as a member of their adjunct faculty. Eddy combines both his experience in the law field and the social work field to offer guidance to individuals dealing with toxic colleagues and loved ones. He shares this knowledge in the form of several self-devised principles, known formally as "New Ways for Work," "New Ways for Families," and the "High-Conflict Personality." Eddy serves as the training director for the High Conflict Institute, which he cofounded, a school specially designed to impart Eddy's teachings. He has released many books, including *BIFF: Quick Responses to High-Conflict People, Their Personal Attacks, Hostile Email and Social Media Meltdowns* and *High-Conflict People in Legal Disputes.*

5 Types of People Who Can Ruin Your Life

5 Types of People Who Can Ruin Your Life: Identifying and Dealing with Narcissists, Sociopaths, and Other High-Conflict Personalities is another of Eddy's books with the purpose of educating others on his subject of expertise. In an interview featured on the *Surviving a Borderline Parent* website, Eddy explained that he draws much of the information he shares within the book from hands-on experiences he has had in dealing with clients who often showed signs of the "High-Conflict Personalities" he describes in the book. The subjects of the book tend to designate one individual as the sole source of the any and all problems they may be experiencing. The purpose of *5 Types of People Who Can Ruin Your Life* is to help readers figure out how to navigate this situation and even avoid it before it can develop. Eddy identifies high-conflict people as having one of five distinct, disordered personalities: histrionic personality disorder, borderline personality disorder, antisocial personality disorder, paranoid personality disorder, and narcissistic personality disorder. Each of these disorders manifests its own symptoms, which Eddy outlines to help readers know what to look for. He also provides examples of well-known, real-life individuals who were diagnosed with these disorders for a further reference point. Eddy clarifies that personality disorders and high-conflict personalities are not mutually exclusive; someone can have one personality and not the other, while someone else might possess both.

The main teaching Eddy showcases within *5 Types of People Who Can Ruin Your Life* is titled the "CARS method," a technique for working with those with high-conflict personalities. The CARS method involves treating the high-conflict individual politely and gently; figuring out some decisions the high-conflict individual (or the person working with them) can realistically make to face the current problem; treating any negative reactions with assertive but kind answers; and keeping one's attention aimed on the issue at hand rather than anything else. Above all else, readers should not inform the high-conflict individual of their flaws, as this will automatically escalate the situation.

In addition to the CARS method, Eddy also offers several other acronyms for readers to memorize and refer to during their interactions with a high-conflict person. Eddy encourages readers to always be mindful of their own behaviors while interacting with those with high-conflict personalities, and to pay attention to their instincts when it comes to identifying those who may be exhibiting toxic behaviors. A *Publishers Weekly* contributor called the book "thought-provoking." On the *Unhooked Media* website, Larry Gaughan remarked: "The book is clearly written, full of relevant categories and useful examples, and covers much more than the title might indicate."

It's All Your Fault at Work!

It's All Your Fault at Work! Managing Narcissists and Other High-Conflict People also seeks to educate readers on how to interact with high-conflict individuals, which are prevalent within work environments. The book is specifically aimed at professional leaders, who will have to know how to approach high-conflict people in order to keep harmony within the office. Eddy offers advice on how to behave responsibly but kindly with high-conflict individuals, as well as how to identify them based on the symptoms and behaviors they may manifest.

By knowing the best ways to interact with high-conflict personalities, business leaders can make more progress throughout each work day. In a review for *California Bookwatch,* one reviewer said: "No manager should be without this analysis."

■ Biographical and Critical Sources

PERIODICALS

California Bookwatch, June, 2015, review of *It's All Your Fault at Work! Managing Narcissists and Other High-Conflict People.*

Publishers Weekly, November 6, 2017, review of *5 Types of People Who Can Ruin Your Life: Identifying and Dealing with Narcissists, Sociopaths, and Other High-Conflict Personalities,* p. 69.

ONLINE

High Conflict Institute Website, https://www.highconflictinstitute.com/ (March 21, 2018), author profile.

Psychology Today, https://www.psychologytoday.com/ (March 21, 2018), author profile.

Surviving a Borderline Parent, https://www.survivingaborderlineparent.com/ (February 12, 2018), "Author Q&A: Bill Eddy, 5 Types of People Who Can Ruin Your Life," author interview.

Unhooked Media, https://www.unhookedmedia.com/ (February 21, 2018), Larry Gaughan, review of *5 Types of People Who Can Ruin Your Life.**

Natalie Eilbert

■ **Personal**

Female. *Hobbies and other interests:* Pancakes.

■ **Addresses**

Home—Brooklyn, NY.

■ **Career**

Writer.

■ **Awards, Honors**

Jay C. and Ruth Halls poetry fellow, 2016; Poetry Prize, Noemi Press, 2016, for *Indictus.*

■ **Writings**

And I Shall Again Be Virtuous, Big Lucks Books (Washington, DC), 2014.
Conversation with the Stone Wife, Bloof Books (NJ), 2014.
Swan Feast, Bloof Books (NJ), 2015.
Indictus, Noemi Press (Blacksburg, VA), 2018.

Founding editor of the *Atlas Review.* Contributor to periodicals, including the *Philadelphia Review of Books, Kenyon Review, Handsome, Tin House, West Branch, Guernica, Jubilat, Granta,* and the *New Yorker.*

■ **Sidelights**

Natalie Eilbert has built a name for herself as an editor and poet. She serves as the *Atlas Review*'s founding editor and has contributed writing to a number of other periodicals. She has also published several books, including *Conversation with the Stone Wife* and *And I Shall Again Be Virtuous,* among others. Eilbert leads creative writing courses in addition to her editing and writing work.

Swan Feast

Swan Feast is one of Eilbert's books of poetry, and each of its pieces forms one part of an overarching narrative. The focal character of the book is a young woman by the name of N who is grappling with the effects of an eating disorder. To deal with it, she seeks counsel from Venus—specifically, Venus of Willendorf—who appears to N as a helpful figment. N nicknames Venus "V," and together the two of them traverse N's attempt to conquer her eating disorder. While V proves helpful at different points throughout the book, she also presents a self-centered persona at times. Throughout the poems, Eilbert explores the various trappings and perceptions related to the human form and body.

A *Publishers Weekly* contributor remarked: "Eilbert's array of referents can be dizzying, but her intoxicating language is sure to keep readers under her spell." Julie Marie Wade, a writer on the *Rumpus* website, said: "*Swan Feast* is an appropriately enigmatic title for a book in which everything—rage, joy, grief, fear, pain, hope—will happen to you, and more than once, and in more than one way." On the *Entropy* website, Carrie Lorig commented: "*Swan Feast* is full of a poetry and a trajectory that moves between intense concentration and enumeration." *Avidly* contributor Leora Fridman said: "In her first poetry collection, *Swan Feast,* Natalie Eilbert does fascinating things with the embodied and re-bodied victim." On the *Sink Re-*

view website, Nina Puro commented: "Eilbert's poems, taken singly, have a relentless intensity, necessitating gasps to surface for air."

Indictus

Indictus, another of Eilbert's books of poetry, deals with a much more personal subject involving the body: rape and sexual assault. In an interview feature on the *Entropy* website, Eilbert explained that her intentions for the book were to craft a conversation that allows survivors of sexual assault to begin processing their trauma in a more constructive way. The poetry featured within the book reflects the ideas commonly displayed by survivors of such incidents, and is framed from the direct perspective of someone who has recently been forced to endure an attack. The tones of the poems vacillate between denial of the situation and attempts to come to terms with what has happened, with the latter mindset being Eilbert's overall goal for readers. Eilbert guides readers through this harrowing experience and the thoughts that develop as a result, with the aim of helping readers to process their own situations in a healthier and more healing manner.

In *Publishers Weekly,* a reviewer commented: "Equally wise and perplexing, Eilbert's poems reflect all the troubling ways 'we understand others by breaking them apart.'" Sarah V. Schweig, a writer on the *Tourniquet Review* website, said: "It is a book of clarity while also being a book of wild invention—this is deeply hard to balance and Eilbert should be praised for her deftness." She added: "And even where the book appears to get tangled up in itself, I don't feel as though I want to put it down but rather that I want to return to it, to understand the tangles by reentering them." *Chicago Review of Books* contributor Peter Myers wrote: "Whether or not the need to write toward an adequate truth can be sated, and whether or not a narrative of trauma can arrive at closure, are not questions *Indictus* claims to answer." He concluded: "But it is a moving and captivating example of how poetry can reveal a way toward one." Sarah Huener, another writer on the *Chicago Review of Books* website, remarked: "*Indictus* is a tour de force." She also said: "Its anger is unafraid; it owes us nothing and refuses to apologize; it is a chronicle and an agent." On the self-titled *Rob Mclennan's Blog,* Rob McLennan stated: "Eilbert writes with a barely-contained rage, one carefully and craftfully harnessed and directed before released at full force." He also expressed: "If you think these are poems of unravelling, you are read-ing it wrong." Luiza Flynn-Goodlett, writing on the *East Bay Review* website, said: "This is a book that returns the reader's gaze (whether they've suffered sexual violence, perpetrated it, or simply been forged by our misogynistic culture), so it can't help but be a deeply personal book to encounter." On the *FIVE:2:ONE* website, Stephen Furlong remarked: "That skill is one of Eilbert's best: just as you think you can't be hit more, the writing hits harder and more direct, reflecting the impact trauma has over victims and survivors."

■ Biographical and Critical Sources

PERIODICALS

Publishers Weekly, April 20, 2015, review of *Swan Feast,* p. 52; November 20, 2017, review of *Indictus,* p. 71.

ONLINE

Avidly, http://avidly.lareviewofbooks.org/ (November 6, 2015), Leora Fridman, "I Could Form Edges: A Review of Natalie Eilbert's *Swan Feast,*" review of *Swan Feast.*

Chicago Review of Books, https://chireviewofbooks.com/ (January 18, 2018), Peter Myers, "*Indictus* Take One: Unabashed Verbal Maximalism," review of *Indictus;* (January 18, 2018), Sarah Huener, "*Indictus* Take Two: Breaking Poetry Apart 'Like a Bloody Geode,'" review of *Indictus.*

East Bay Review, http://theeastbayreview.com/ (January 19, 2018), Luiza Flynn-Goodlett, review of *Indictus.*

Entropy, https://entropymag.org/ (June 3, 2015), Carrie Lorig, "Mud Woman: A Review of Natalie Eilbert's *Swan Feast*"; (January 8, 2018), Vi Khi Nao, "Natalie Eilbert in Conversation with Vi Khi Nao," author interview.

FIVE:2:ONE, http://five2onemagazine.com/ (March 2, 2018), Stephen Furlong, review of *Indictus.*

Natalie Eilbert Website, http://www.natalie-eilbert.com (March 21, 2018).

Rob Mclennan's Blog, http://robmclennan.blogspot.com/ (January 2, 2018), Rob McLennan, review of *Indictus.*

Rumpus, http://therumpus.net/ (September 19, 2015), Julie Marie Wade, review of *Swan Feast.*

Sink Review, http://sinkreview.org/ (March 21, 2018), Nina Puro, review of *Swan Feast.*

Tourniquet Review, https://tourniquetreview.com/ (January 29, 2018), Sarah V. Schweig, review of *Indictus.**

T.W. Emory

■ Personal

Born in Seattle, WA. *Hobbies and other interests:* Cartooning, history, vintage comic strips, reading, sociology, philosophy.

■ Addresses

Home—Seattle, WA.

■ Career

Drywall contractor and author.

■ Writings

Trouble in Rooster Paradise, Coffeetown Press (Seattle, WA), 2015.
Crazy Rhythm, Coffeetown Press (Seattle, WA), 2017.

■ Sidelights

T.W. Emory holds a wide variety of interests. His main profession is drywall contracting, but he also dabbles in cartooning, reading, social sciences, philosophy, and history. He is also a novelist, specializing in the mystery genre.

Trouble in Rooster Paradise

Trouble in Rooster Paradise serves as Emory's literary debut. The novel focuses on Gunnar Nilson—a man who, at the start of the narrative, is entering his twilight years. Nilson finds himself stuck at a nursing home after suffering a serious injury. His sojourn at the nursing home is meant to help him recuperate, and he decides to pass the time by chatting with the staff about his old exploits back during his time as a detective. One staff member by the name of Kirsti seems particularly interested in Nilson's stories, and she takes it upon herself to sit and record her conversations with him regarding his past. The novel teleports back in time to the 1950s, during Gunnar's youth. At this point, he is thriving in his career and suddenly finds the most peculiar case right in his lap. He is approached by a jeweler who has recently lost an employee by the name of Christine—not to firing or layoffs, but to murder. Clues currently point to Christine's beau, who may have been jealous over the flirting Christine had to put up with while on the job. The strangest element of the case is that a business card belonging to Nilson was found on Christine's body. With no other leads or resources to turn to, the jeweler who originally hired Christine wants Nilson to investigate as secretly as possible. The jeweler's reputation is on the line, since if the circumstances around the murder get out to the public, the business could be heavily impacted. It is up to Nilson to decipher the case, but what he uncovers may turn out to be a lot of grime underneath a polished surface.

A reviewer in *Publishers Weekly* stated: "Emory's first novel vividly evokes the ambiance of classic American hard-boiled crime writing." *ReviewingtheEvidence.com* contributor Meredith Frazier remarked: "Whatever happens, readers will want to follow this detective and his delightful supporting cast of friends." On the *NW Book Lovers* blog, Jim Harris said: "Not only is this a fine mystery, it is also a look into Seattle's mid-twentieth century lifestyle and history." He added: "I urge you to read this."

Crazy Rhythm

Crazy Rhythm is the follow-up book to *Trouble in Rooster Paradise.* It picks up with a similar framing device to the first, setting the stage for an entirely different mystery. After being hired by a client looking to make a deal, Nilson stumbles upon his client's dead body. The motive behind the murder becomes the real question. Originally, the client wanted to recoup their earnings from a game of pool that had yet to be properly paid. All the client received was a pocket watch, made out of solid gold. The watch itself has now vanished, but the clues make little sense to Nilson. He begins looking into what truly happened on his own. His first tip is the connections he has to this client beyond work: the fact the brother of the client and Nilson were members of the same army unit during their time in World War II.

In the midst of pursuing the case, Nilson is presented with another job from a very wealthy client, whose future bride has been on the receiving end of various threats. Nilson goes ahead with pursuing both cases, but soon finds he may be in for more trouble than he initially anticipated. When he meets with his new client's fiancée, she suddenly switches from being nothing but refined to everything but, throwing Nilson entirely off guard. What's more, the two cases Nilson seeks to solve may have more in common than just the detective getting to the bottom of them. Nilson regularly confides in his neighbors at the boarding house he resides in, all of whom have backstories that are just as colorful as Nilson's own. A *Publishers Weekly* contributor remarked: "Fans of throwback PI novels will find plenty to like." Vicki Weisfeld, a writer on the *Crime Fiction Lover* blog, said:

"Writing a pastiche of someone as revered as Chandler is brave, and Emory carries it off well, with a style that's aptly embodied in the novel's title." She went on to call the book "a perfect novel for a long airplane flight!" On *ReviewingtheEvidence. com,* Susan Hoover expressed that "readers will be looking forward to what happens to Gunnar, his friends and girlfriends, and where his job will take him next." A writer on the *Mysteries in Paradise* blog commented: "The novel is filled with interesting characters, particularly those who live in the boarding house where Gunnar resides."

■ Biographical and Critical Sources

PERIODICALS

Publishers Weekly, May 18, 2015, review of *Trouble in Rooster Paradise,* p. 67; November 20, 2017, review of *Crazy Rhythm,* p. 78.

ONLINE

Crime Fiction Lover, https://crimefictionlover.com/ (January 25, 2018), Vicki Weisfeld, review of *Crazy Rhythm.*

Mysteries in Paradise, http://paradise-mysteries. blogspot.com/ (January 23, 2017), review of *Trouble in Rooster Paradise.*

NW Book Lovers, https://nwbooklovers.org/ (August 19, 2016), Jim Harris, review of *Trouble in Rooster Paradise.*

ReviewingtheEvidence.com, http://www. reviewingtheevidence.com/ (July 1, 2015), Meredith Frazier, review of *Trouble in Rooster Paradise;* (November 1, 2017), Susan Hoover, review of *Crazy Rhythm.*

T.W. Emory Website, https://www.twemoryauthor. com (March 22, 2018).*

Maki Enjoji

■ **Also Known As**

Maki Enjouji

■ **Personal**

Born December 8, in Tokyo, Japan. *Hobbies and other interests:* Traveling, cats.

■ **Career**

Manga artist.

■ **Writings**

SP Baby, Volume 1, VIZ Media: Shojo Beat (San Francisco, CA), 2017.
SP Baby, Volume 2, VIZ Media: Shojo Beat (San Francisco, CA), 2018.

Also author of *Dear Brother!, Hapi Mari?Happy Marriage!??, Yoru Café—My Sweet Knights, Sekai wa Bokura no Tameni!, Private Prince, Koisuru Heart de Taihoshite, Tsuiteru Kanojo, Atashi wa Sore o Gaman Dekinai,* and *Fu Junai.* Contributor to *Petit Comic.* Author's works have been translated into English, French, Spanish, and German.

■ **Sidelights**

Maki Enjoji is well known for her work as a manga artist. In terms of genre, her works mainly classify as *josei,* which is meant to appeal to young women who are interested in more mature comic stories than what is typically found in *shoujo* manga. Enjoji's works can be found serialized in the *josei* magazine *Petit Comics,* and it also comes in book form. Some of her works include *Dear Brother!, Fu Junai, Private Prince,* and *Hapi Mari?Happy Marriage!??* Her works are also available for English-, French-, Spanish-, and German-speaking audiences.

SP Baby, Volume 1 tells the tale of a young woman named Tamaki Hasegawa. Tamaki has spent several years devoting herself to her family. Since her teenage years, she has moved from job to job, doing everything she can to keep her brother and herself afloat. Since the two are parentless, their ability to survive falls on her. Tamaki's responsibilities leave her at a disadvantage; without a college degree, her job options are severely limited. However, a chance meeting may change her luck and her prospects dramatically. When she witnesses Sugou Kagetora being pursued, she subdues his would-be attacker, who is actually one of his bodyguards. Kagetora is impressed by Tamaki's physical prowess, and he soon grants her a position as his new bodyguard. While Tamaki is initially reluctant, she accepts the job upon realizing how few other options she has for work. Through her new job, Tamaki learns just how privileged Kagetora is; he is the nephew of the Prime Minister, which puts him in a place of high esteem but also makes him highly vulnerable to malicious intent. Protecting Kagetora leads Tamaki down the road of several misadventures. Along the way, she has to deal with spontaneous advances from Kagetora, who may be interested in her in ways that go beyond a work relationship. Tamaki must figure out the ins and outs of her new line of work while also blocking Kagetora's attempts at flirting. A contributor to *Publishers Weekly* expressed that "the character art is superb."

On the *Comic Bastards* website, Thea Srinivasan remarked: "I'm looking forward to what scenarios the author has to offer for this pair and I hope she is able to balance it out with a few romantic tropes." She added: "This manga is for the person who wants a light comedy that will get them through the night and feel refreshed for the next day."

■ Biographical and Critical Sources

PERIODICALS

Publishers Weekly, November 13, 2017, review of *SP Baby*, Volume 1, p. 46.

ONLINE

Comic Bastards, https://comicbastards.com/ (February 23, 2018), Thea Srinivasan, review of *SP Baby*, Volume 1.

Fangirl Nation, http://fangirlnation.com/ (December 11, 2017), Toni Adams, review of *SP Baby*, Volume 1.*

Chelsea Fagan

■ **Personal**

Female.

■ **Addresses**

Home—Brooklyn, NY.

■ **Career**

Author. *Thought Catalog*, writer.

■ **Writings**

I'm Only Here for the WiFi: A Complete Guide to Reluctant Adulthood, Running Press Adult (Philadelphia, PA), 2013.
(With Lauren Ver Hage) *The Financial Diet: A Total Beginner's Guide to Getting Good with Money*, Henry Holt (New York, NY), 2018.

The Financial Diet, founder and editor. Also author of *Take Out Your Earrings before You Fight (And Other Things I Learned in Public School)*. Contributor to *NYMag.com*, *Huffington Post*, and *Thought Catalog*.

■ **Sidelights**

Chelsea Fagan works primarily as a writer and blogger. She is most easily recognized through her work with *The Financial Diet*, a blog she founded that has since become a resource for those looking to better their financial planning. She has also worked as a writer with *Thought Catalog*; her ef-

forts there culminated into two books: *Take Out Your Earrings before You Fight (And Other Things I Learned in Public School)* and *I'm Only Here for the Wi-Fi: A Complete Guide to Reluctant Adulthood*. In a review featured on the *Billfold* website, Fagan explained that her inspiration to create the site came about when she noticed her lack of written content involving finances and money, as well as a solid budget. The blog gained considerable traction, so Fagan decided to make the blog into her new career.

The Financial Diet: A Total Beginner's Guide to Getting Good with Money serves as a condensed version of the content Fagan offers on her website. The book is aimed at millennials who are trying to get the hang of managing their own finances, offering advice on how to save money: where to cut splurging, where to invest, and similar matters. Fagan touches upon ways readers can save in every area of daily life, from meals to commuting to work and so on. Fagan frames the tone of the book as if she's speaking to readers one on one. Along the way, Fagan demonstrates how one's financial choices come to affect them in every area of life, and how what may seem like an innocent splurge can come with consequences. Fagan also offers definitions and explanations of some of the largest and most commonly expounded upon elements of one's financial life, such as putting away money for retirement and building or repairing credit. The book also comes complete with a glossary, featured at the back of the book.

In dispensing her advice, Fagan offers several anecdotes of her experiences with the topics at hand. For instance, she mismanaged her credit card in her earlier years and, in the process, racked up a hefty amount of debt. Much of the information featured in the book also comes from conversations with financial experts, who offer their own viewpoint on how readers can manage their finances more effectively. Through these multiple viewpoints, readers are able to get a plethora of advice on how to better their finances as well as their lives. Fagan offers a myriad of points for readers to follow, including not overindulging themselves when it comes to the things they want, picking up another income source if they can, and making some of their monthly expenses automatic to encourage budget-related mindfulness. Fagan also offers advice in other areas as readers begin their budgeting journey. She encourages her audience to adopt the mindset that, while saving money is important, it is not good to take on a miserly attitude. It is okay to treat oneself every so often, but within reason. Additionally, Fagan also counsels readers to go easy on themselves if they slip up in the process of managing their finances, as this is something that happens to everyone and can be used as a learning tool.

BookPage contributor Julie Hale expressed that "this appealing book can help you make 2018 the year of spending—and saving—wisely." Courtney Jones, a *Booklist* reviewer, commented: "*The Financial Diet* dispenses timeless advice that goes above and beyond asking readers to give up their avocado toast." In *Publishers Weekly*, a writer remarked: "The breezy lifestyle-magazine-like writing style and easy-to-digest layout make this guide a useful and readable resource." On the *Bassocantor Reviews* blog, Chris Lawson said: "I found *The Financial Diet* to be a surprisingly fun read—as well as a practical book." He added: "The author is a witty and funny writer." *LowestRates.ca* contributor Jessica Mach felt that "its advice is refreshingly scaled for humans—by which I mean that it puts people, not money, first." *New York Times* reviewer Paul B. Brown wrote: "If you had to give her a grade, it would be a solid 'B' because of both her supportive tone and her ability to reduce what can be fairly complicated concepts—such as how you put together a comprehensive investment plan—to easily understood bite-size pieces." On the *Financial Success Book* website, Jacob Highley stated: "This book is an excellent addition to any library, and I know its value will surprise you!" Jocelynne Flor, a writer on the self-title *Jocelynne Flor* blog, commented: "It's a true guide for beginners but would be useful for anyone who wants a fresh point of view on their personal finance." Carol Early Cooney wrote on her blog: "If you are looking for a gift for a college grad or high school grad starting out, this might be a helpful gift for them."

■ Biographical and Critical Sources

PERIODICALS

Booklist, December 1, 2017, Courtney Jones, review of *The Financial Diet: A Total Beginner's Guide to Getting Good with Money*, p. 10.

BookPage, January, 2018, Julie Hale, "Warning: Work in progress," review of *The Financial Diet*, p. 15.

Publishers Weekly, November 20, 2017, review of *The Financial Diet*, p. 83.

ONLINE

Bassocantor Reviews, https://www.bassocantor.com/ (December 22, 2017), Chris Lawson, review of *The Financial Diet*.

Billfold, https://www.thebillfold.com/ (February 17, 2015), Jasmine Rose-Olesco, "How Chelsea Fagan, Founder of *The Financial Diet*, Does Money," author interview.

Carol Early Cooney, https://cecooney.com/ (January 31, 2018), Carol Early Cooney, review of *The Financial Diet*.

Financial Diet, http://thefinancialdiet.com (March 22, 2018).

Financial Success Book, https://financialsuccessbook.com/ (February 16, 2018), Jacob Highley, review of *The Financial Diet*.

Jocelynne Flor, https://jocelynneflor.com/ (January 29, 2018), Jocelynne Flor, "*The Financial Diet* Book Review + Cultivating Financial Wellness," review of *The Financial Diet*.

LowestRates.ca, https://www.lowestrates.ca/ (January 8, 2018), Jessica Mach, "Chelsea Fagan's New Book Gives an Anxious Generation the Money Advice It Needs," review of *The Financial Diet*.

New York Times, https://www.nytimes.com/ (January 12, 2018), Paul B. Brown, "Personal Finance for Those Who Don't Have a Clue," review of *The Financial Diet*.

RateHub Blog, https://www.ratehub.ca/ (February 1, 2018), Jane Switzer, "Money Hungry: A Q&A with Author Chelsea Fagan on *The Financial Diet* Book," author interview.*

Erin Falconer

■ Personal

Female. *Hobbies and other interests:* Meditation.

■ Addresses

Home—Venice, CA.

■ Career

Blogger, author, and entrepreneur. Worked variously as a political consultant, comedian, and screenwriter. Co-founder, LEAFtv; editor in chief and partner, Pickthebrain.com.

■ Awards, Honors

Top 25 Motivational Blogs, Wealthy Gorilla, 2015; Top 50 Productivity Blogs, Zen Habits.

■ Writings

Rock Star Productivity: Time Management Tips, Leadership Skills, and Other Keys to Self Improvement, Hyperink (San Francisco, CA), 2012.
How to Get Sh*t Done: Why Women Need to Stop Doing Everything So That They Can Achieve Anything, Gallery Books (New York, NY), 2018.

■ Sidelights

Erin Falconer has held several careers, including political consulting, comedy, and screenwriting. However, her work as a blogger has brought her the most acclaim. She is partly responsible for the creation of *LEAFtv,* a site that specializes in lifestyle content. In addition, she runs the website *Pick the Brain,* which specializes in self-improvement and self-development.

How to Get Sh*t Done: Why Women Need to Stop Doing Everything So That They Can Achieve Anything marks Falconer's debut within the book publishing world. In an interview featured on the *Forbes* website, Falconer stated that her inspiration for the book came from personal experiences that inspired her to refocus her life on building positive memories, rather than simply moving from one task to the next. *How to Get Sh*t Done* encourages its audience to follow the same path. The book is partly autobiographical, as Falconer peppers anecdotes about her own life and her decision to adjust her personal trajectory throughout her suggestions and advice. In offering her advice, Falconer also underlines a problem she has frequently observed within her own life as well as within the lives of other women she's known over the years: they all base their lives around staying occupied, rather than delving into their personal interests. Many women work for the sake of working, never carving out a definite goal or dream for themselves. Falconer seeks to change that attitude within her audience, starting by helping them to develop the confidence to go after their dreams.

Throughout *How to Get Sh*t Done,* Falconer encourages her audience to start treating themselves with more care, and to cut out any tendencies to put themselves down. Falconer offers and describes a specific motto she has devised that forms the main principles she tries to follow throughout her life: productivity, opportunity, and personality, also known as "POP." Falconer uses this motto to illustrate the common ways women undermine their own personal fulfillment, as well as better ways readers can make the most of their time to meet their goals.

A *Publishers Weekly* contributor remarked: "The book's peppy self-improvement zeal is energizing." On the *Blogging Owl* website, S.L. Prielipp-Falzone said: "Even though the target audience of this book is women, I believe women of all ages and men will find value in reading it." A writer on the *Hitha on the Go* blog commented: "It's the first productivity book that I felt understood me—as an entrepreneur, as a mother and wife, as a friend."

■ **Biographical and Critical Sources**

PERIODICALS

Publishers Weekly, November 20, 2017, review of *How to Get Sh*t Done: Why Women Need to Stop Doing Everything So That They Can Achieve Anything*, p. 84.

ONLINE

Blogging Owl, https://thebloggingowl.com/ (January 28, 2018), S.L. Prielipp-Falzone, review of *How to Get Sh*t Done*.

Forbes, https://www.forbes.com/ (January 2, 2018), Dan Schawbel, "Erin Falconer: How Women Can Accomplish More In Their Careers," author interview.

Hitha on the Go, https://www.hithaonthego.com/ (March 9, 2018), review of *How to Get Sh*t Done*.

Inspired Conversations, http://inspiredconversations.net/ (January 2, 2018), "347 Erin Falconer, Author of *How to Get Sh*t Done!*," author interview and profile.

Pick the Brain, https://www.pickthebrain.com (March 22, 2018), author profile.

Simon & Schuster Website, http://www.simonandschuster.com/ (March 22, 2018), author profile.

Emmy J. Favilla

■ Personal

Born March 14. *Education:* New York University, B.A, 2005; London College of Fashion, M.A., 2010. *Hobbies and other interests:* Animal welfare.

■ Addresses

Home—New York, NY.

■ Career

Editor and writer. *Seventeen,* associate copy editor, 2005-07; *Natural Health,* copy editor, 2007-08; Delias, copy editor and copywriter, 2008-09; *Teen Vogue,* copy chief, 2010-12; *Alloy,* copywriter and copy editor, 2011-12; MediaBistro Education, instructor, 2012—; BuzzFeed, global copy chief, 2012—, senior commerce editor, 2017—.

■ Writings

A World without "Whom": The Essential Guide to Language in the BuzzFeed Age, Bloomsbury USA (New York, NY), 2017.

Also contributor to periodicals, including *POZ, Natural Health,* and *Every Day with Rachael Ray.*

■ Sidelights

Emmy J. Favilla has served as an editor for several publications, including *Alloy, Teen Vogue,* and *Seventeen,* among others. In 2012 she began working with BuzzFeed, where she serves as the company's global copy chief and senior commerce editor. It is through her direction that BuzzFeed has developed its signature style.

A World without "Whom": The Essential Guide to Language in the BuzzFeed Age serves as a guide meant to explain how BuzzFeed came to its unique usage of words. The book not only shows the ways BuzzFeed uses language but creates a narrative of how BuzzFeed achieved its style in the first place. It starts off by describing the purpose of style guides. The main argument of the book is that language cannot be put into a box; rather, it should be allowed to grow and remold itself according to societal changes and the context under which language is being used. Favilla introduces both lighthearted terms and weightier, socially conscious ones. In the introduction of each term, Favilla takes the time to explain why certain terms gained more prevalence than others, and why some words should be eliminated from modern language. Favilla also treats readers to a glossary of some of the terms found in the book, should the readers be interested in adding BuzzFeed's manner of language to their own writing or daily speech.

Booklist contributor Emily Dziuban wrote that the book "grants permission to dismiss those hobgoblins disguised as 'rules.'" In *Library Journal,* Jesse A. Lambertson called *A World without "Whom"* "a smart and amusing work." A reviewer in *Kirkus Reviews* expressed that the book is "a lighthearted take on communicating in the digital age," and a *Publishers Weekly* contributor remarked: "Favilla's style is light and breezy, which only makes it easier to absorb the serious import of her advice." On the *New York Times* website, John Simpson wrote that the book "provides a fascinating examination of how a modern grammar guru handles the quandaries that arise out of the dialect of social media, at a time when we are afraid—or perhaps excited—that the way we communicate online may be re-engineering our language itself." Steve Lampiris, a writer on the *Spectrum Culture* website, remarked: "Her writing style allows this to be a breezy read."

■ Biographical and Critical Sources

PERIODICALS

Booklist, October 15, 2017, Emily Dziuban, review of *A World without "Whom": The Essential Guide to Language in the BuzzFeed Age,* p. 5.
Kirkus Reviews, September 1, 2017, review of *A World without "Whom."*
Library Journal, September 15, 2017, "Social sciences," Jesse A. Lambertson, review of *A World without "Whom,"* p. 83.

Publishers Weekly, August 28, 2017, review of *A World without "Whom,"* p. 123.

ONLINE

Boston Globe, https://www.bostonglobe.com/ (November 25, 2017), Mark Peters, "Should We Still Say 'Whom'? LOL, No," author interview.
New York Times Online, https://www.nytimes.com/ (December 7, 2017), John Simpson, "Language Rules for the Digital Age," review of *A World without "Whom."*
Politico Media, https://www.politico.com/ (March 4, 2017), "The 60-Second Interview: Emmy Favilla, Buzzfeed Copy Chief," author interview.
Spectrum Culture, http://spectrumculture.com/ (December 3, 2017), Steve Lampiris, review of *A World without "Whom."**

Katherine Faw

1983-

■ **Also Known As**

Katherine Faw Morris

■ **Personal**

Born July 17, 1983, in Wilkesboro, NC; married Donald Morris (a creative director), c. 2007. *Education:* New York University, graduated; Columbia University, M.F.A.

■ **Addresses**

Home—Brooklyn, NY. *Agent*—Chris Parris-Lamb, Gernert Co., 136 E. 57th St., 18th Fl., New York, NY 10022.

■ **Career**

Writer.

■ **Awards, Honors**

Book of the year citations from *Times Literary Supplement,* for *Young God,* and from *New Yorker,* for *Ultraluminous.*

■ **Writings**

Young God, Farrar, Straus & Giroux (New York, NY), 2014.

Ultraluminous, Farrar, Straus & Giroux (New York, NY), 2017.

■ **Sidelights**

Katherine Faw was born and raised in Wilkesboro, North Carolina, an economically challenged rural community of Appalachia. In an interview published in *Granta,* she told Yuka Igarashi that she has "a love-hate relationship with the place." Surrounded by the weight of many generations of ancestors, Faw left home as soon as she could get away, but her conversations reflect a certain amount of nostalgia. In an interview with Juliet Escoria at *Electric Literature,* she said: "I can be very defensive about Appalachia. . . . It's the place that raised me."

Faw avoids readings, book tours, and social media, leaving readers to infer the story of her life from her writing. She told Igarashi that her fiction "is emotionally, psychologically true, even if all the events are not." However, critics have pointed to a verisimilitude that would be hard to achieve without personal experience, or at least close personal observation, allusions that Faw does not deny.

Young God

The titular character of Faw's first novel, *Young God,* also grew up in rural North Carolina. At age thirteen, Nikki witnesses the suicide of her mother. Her response is to initiate sex with her mother's boyfriend. She ends up in a group home until she decides to reconnect with her father. He is an ex-convict, drug dealer, and pimp for whom no level of violence is out of bounds. Nikki is determined to surpass him, but on her own terms. She succeeds, in what *Guardian Online* contributor Eimear McBride called "a story blasted by violence, exploitation and the unrelenting bleakness of lives cannibalised [sic] by poverty and addiction."

In a novel rife with violence against women, Nikki is no victim, and she is no sissy. Nikki will offer a teen acquaintance to her dad for purposes of prostitution and help to remove all traces of the body when the girl ends up dead. She will corrupt the only seemingly blameless person in her life out of jealousy over his innocence. She will end the competition with her father in the most permanent possible way, and without remorse. Nikki is a "feral creature," Faw told Jeva Lange on the *Vice* website, and "the biggest threat to a teenage girl is the people who love her."

This is a powerful story, critics observed, amplified by the author's minimalist narrative construction. Sean Madigan Hoen observed on the *Brooklyn Rail* website: "*Young God* haunts you with stark, clipped, almost expressionist scenes that track one of the most memorable anti-heroines in recent literature." In Nikki's case, the device "works to show her numbness," Igarashi commented. Faw reportedly reduced a manuscript of 100,000 words to a mere 20,000. She told Kate Loftus O'Brien on the *Huck* website: "I ended up with something anorexic and cracked-out and full of rage, which is basically what I [wanted]."

Critics expressed various degrees of shock and astonishment at Faw's debut. Lange reported that the author's "gut-punch delivery and cinematic structure leave an ache under the skin . . . like a bruise." McBride called *Young God* "a powerful portrait of humanity in the face of everyday atrocity." A contributor to *Hobart* summarized: "I haven't been this steamrolled by a novel in a long time."

Ultraluminous

Faw continued to push boundaries and raise eyebrows in her second novel. *Ultraluminous* is the story of K, a high-priced prostitute for rich bankers with "special" tastes. K is a heroin addict recently returned to New York after several years in Dubai. She has five clients, one for each day of the work week, and each has his own special fetish. None of them has a name; she calls them by descriptive nicknames according to their jobs or unique aberrations. K is also nameless. Each client knows her by a Slavic-sounding nickname beginning with the letter K. The reader knows her only by her actions and by snippets of her past that never satisfy the curiosity they arouse.

In her business, K exerts control through submission to her clients' twisted and often painful demands. She charges extra for the pain. Choosing to submit for money grants her the illusion of control. She describes her encounters with unfiltered frankness in clinically graphic detail that is as far removed from erotica as sex acts can possibly be, especially within her chosen niche. They are, after all, part of the job.

Off the clock, K maintains a relentlessly patterned schedule. She eats drugstore sushi, has sex, and indulges in pedicures and cosmetic maintenance. She sleeps gently with the one man in her life who is not a paying client, uses heroin, eats more sushi, and repeats.

The intentional repetition enables the reader to notice the tiny variations that begin to appear in K's obsessive schedule: hints of cracks in her facade of self-control, described by Noah Sanders in the *East Bay Review Online* as "a pattern of self-abuse subtly altered over the course of the book as K. slowly comes apart at the seams." There is only one possible end to her story, and it is violent. Jordan Larson noted on the *Bookforum* website that K has "little to hope for, but plenty to fear"; she "was always meant to be sacrificed for an idea."

"A story that, at first, seems shapeless, comes into focus at the end," concluded a *Kirkus Reviews Online* contributor, summarizing *Ultraluminous* as both "artful and ruthless." A *Publishers Weekly* commentator acknowledged that "Faw's writing is raw and not for all tastes," but found it to be an "incisive character study, featuring an exceptionally clear and memorable prose style." Escoria wrote that Faw's trademark spare language and "fragmentary, kinetic" structure result in "something thrilling and wholly unique, deliciously trashy yet highbrow, cementing her place as one of the most visionary writer around."

■ Biographical and Critical Sources

PERIODICALS

Booklist, April 1, 2014, Amber Peckham, review of *Young God*, p. 24; November 15, 2017, Katharine Uhrich, review of *Ultraluminous*, p. 24.

Kirkus Reviews, March 15, 2014, review of *Young God*; September 15, 2017, review of *Ultraluminous*.

Publishers Weekly, February 10, 2014, review of *Young God*, p. 66; October 2, 2017, review of *Ultraluminous*, p. 114.

ONLINE

Bookforum, http://www.bookforum.com/ (January 25, 2018), Jordan Larson, review of *Ultraluminous*.

Brooklyn Rail, https://brooklynrail.org/ (December 13, 2017), Sean Madigan Hoen, author interview.

Charlotte Online, http://www.charlottemagazine.com/ (February 5, 2018), Adam Rhew, review of *Ultraluminous.*

Creative Independent, https://thecreativeindependent.com/ (March 13, 2018), Brandon Stosuy, author interview.

East Bay Review Online, http://theeastbayreview.com/ (December 14, 2017), Noah Sanders, review of *Ultraluminous.*

Electric Literature, https://electricliterature.com/ (December 12, 2017), Juliet Escoria, author interview.

Granta, https://granta.com/ (February 25, 2014), Yuka Igarashi, author interview.

Guardian Online, https://www.theguardian.com/ (July 16, 2014), Eimear McBride, review of *Young God.*

Hobart, http://www.hobartpulp.com/ (May 13, 2014), author interview.

Huck, http://www.huckmagazine.com/ (May 20, 2014), Kate Loftus-O'Brien, author interview.

Katherine Faw Website, https://katherinefaw.com (March 21, 2018).

Kirkus Reviews Online, https://wwww.kirkusreviews.com/ (September 7, 2017), review of *Ultraluminous.*

Macmillan Website, https://us.macmillan.com/ (March 21, 2018), book description.

New Yorker Online, https://www.newyorker.com/ (October 19, 2017), Alexandra Schwartz, review of *Ultraluminous.*

Vice, https://www.vice.com/ (June 30, 2014), Jeva Lange, author interview.*

Jessica Fellowes

1974-

■ Personal

Born 1974; daughter of Roderick Olivier and Georgina Katherine Fellowes; married; husband's name Simon; children: George; stepchildren: Louis, Beatrix.

■ Addresses

Home—Oxfordshire, England. *Agent*—Caroline Michel, Peters Fraser & Dunlop, Drury House, 34-43 Russell St., London WC2B 5HA, England.

■ Career

Writer. *Mail on Sunday*, celebrity interviewer and lifestyle editor; *Country Life*, worked as deputy editor. Public speaker; guest on media programs.

■ Writings

Mud and the City: Do's and Don'ts for Townies in the Country, Book Guild (Brighton, England), 2008.
(With Kerry Daynes) *The Devil You Know: Looking Out for the Psycho in Your Life*, Coronet (London, England), 2011, published as *Is There a Psycho in Your Life?*, Coronet (London, England), 2012.
(With Sophie Cornish and Holly Tucker) *Build a Business from Your Kitchen Table*, Simon & Schuster (London, England), 2014.
Shape Up Your Business: The Founders of Notonthehighstreet.com Share Their Story in a 30-Day Success Plan, Simon & Schuster (London, England), 2014.
The Mitford Murders (novel), Minotaur Books (New York, NY), 2018.

"DOWNTON ABBEY" COMPANION VOLUMES

The World of Downton Abbey, St. Martin's Press (New York, NY), 2011.
(With Matthew Sturgis) *The Chronicles of Downton Abbey*, St. Martin's Press (New York, NY), 2012.
A Year in the Life of Downton Abbey, St. Martin's Press (New York, NY), 2014.
The Wit and Wisdom of Downton Abbey, St. Martin's Griffin (New York, NY), 2015.
Downton Abbey: A Celebration, St. Martin's Press (New York, NY), 2015.

Author of "Town Mouse," a column in *Country Life*; former columnist, *London Paper*. Contributor to other periodicals, including *Daily Telegraph*, *Guardian*, *Lady*, and *Sunday Times*.

■ Sidelights

Jessica Fellowes is a self-educated expert on the social history of the United Kingdom between the two world wars. Beginning in childhood she shared this interest with her uncle Julian Fellowes, who had acquired a substantial collection of anecdotes and first-person stories from older family members. Julian went on to write and produce the hit television series *Downton Abbey*. After establishing herself as a magazine journalist and newspaper columnist, Jessica became the author of colorful companion volumes to the series, which aired in the United Kingdom and the United States from 2011 to 2016.

"Downton Abbey" Companion Volumes

Downton Abbey was a historical period drama that thrilled television audiences for six seasons. The series follows the trials and tribulations of the upper-class Crawley family and their domestic staff during a period of great historical and social change. Their story begins in the year 1912, with a world on the brink of war. The Crawleys resides at the rural country estate of Downton Abbey, but their lives are nonetheless tossed and turned by events beyond the gates. Great care was taken to portray the aristocracy with authenticity and sensitivity, and many American viewers were mesmerized by their introduction to both the historical events and the upper-class lifestyle. They were hungry for more, and Fellowes was ideally situated to provide it. Lois Alter Mark observed in her *Huffington Post* interview of the author: "She is a wealth of knowledge about the characters, the time period in which the show is set and its changing customs, culture and costumes."

Three of the companion volumes include season-by-season summaries of the series in the form of lavishly illustrated coffee table books, but Fellowes offers readers much more. She presents a social history of England in the early twentieth century and enables fans of the show to peek behind the scenes with the cast and production teams. *The World of Downton Abbey* is arranged in chapters on family life, society, life in domestic service, the house and surrounding estate, romance, war, and more. Andy Lewis described the volume in the *Hollywood Reporter* as nothing less than "a love letter."

The Chronicles of Downton Abbey shines a spotlight on individual characters and marital couples, with summaries of what they did, why they did it, and how they interacted with the rest of the family entourage. *A Year in the Life of Downton Abbey* follows a typical year on the estate. Each month focuses on a theme, such as children, farming, travel, the ubiquitous "London season," and Christmas. Each chapter alternates with special production spotlights on food, filming locations, costumes and makeup, music, and more. Fellowes also includes a selection of recipes popular among the aristocracy of the period, from cream of watercress soup to Christmas pudding with brandy butter.

The Wit and Wisdom of Downton Abbey contains the author's favorite quips and quotations, arranged by topic, such as love or work. Fellowes offers equal space to the mighty and the meek, from the sharp tongue of the Dowager Countess of Grantham to the humblest of the maidservants. Carol J. Binkowski commented in *Library Journal*: "Readers will find humor, wisdom, and memorably stinging barbs."

As the series moved toward a finale, Fellowes published *Downton Abbey: A Celebration*. She takes readers on a retrospective tour of the estate, replete with lush photographs, interviews of the primary cast members, and behind-the-scenes anecdotes. Fellowes begins in the great hall and moves from room to room, all the way up to the servants' attic. She then ushers fans outdoors to glimpse the farms and cottages, the village, and the world beyond. The volume also includes a complete episode guide.

Fellowes told her *Huffington Post* interviewer that the companion volumes were always meant "to explore the social history of the period, to explain the context in which it is set and to give viewers/readers a better idea of why the characters behave in the ways that they do." *A Year in the Life* offers even more. Fellowes told Mark that she wanted fans of cosplay to be able "to recreate some Downton for themselves—so that meant recipes, games, tips on how to curtsy and so on." The Downton Abbey volumes constituted Fellowes's primary claim to fame until she turned to fiction in the form of *The Mitford Murders*.

Historical Fiction

By 2016, when the gates of Downton Abbey closed for the last time, Fellowes was recognized as a social historian of some note. When she was approached about writing a crime novel set in the 1920s, she was intrigued. The subject of her first novel would be an author whose work she had enjoyed for several years: Nancy Mitford.

Nancy was one of six Mitford sisters, most of whom became household names in one way or another. The Mitfords were an aristocratic family of relatively modest means, but their social connections reached the stratosphere of government and politics in the years following World War I. Nancy became a novelist, and Jessica became a muckraking, communist-leaning journalist in America. Diana and Unity were linked indirectly to prominent German fascists, including Joseph Goebbels and Adolf Hitler. Pamela was the quiet one, and Deborah became the only sister to follow the family aristocratic tradition as the Duchess of Devonshire. Fellowes decided to create a six-part series of crime novels, each one dedicated to one of the sisters. She began with Nancy.

The Mitford Murders is a fictional exploration of the actual murder of the granddaughter of Civil War nurse Florence Nightingale on Christmas Eve, 1919. Florence Nightingale Shore was killed on a train to Brighton, and her killer was never found. In Fellowes's iteration, the murderer's getaway was witnessed by one Louisa Cannon, who is on her way to Asthall Manor to become a nanny to the Mitford family. First, however, she must escape the clutches of her evil uncle, who intends to sell her into prostitution. She is rescued by a shy young railroad police officer named Guy Sullivan, and the two of them become devoted to solving the case—and, eventually, to one another. Louisa shares her story with the sixteen-year-old Nancy Mitford, whose imagination runs wild with excitement to join the chase.

In an interview with Sara Weal at the *British Heritage* website, Fellowes hinted that she found "a plausible link between the Mitfords and this particular murder," and her novel proceeds from there. Not all reviewers were equally convinced of her conclusion, but several critics appreciated the story. They included *Library Journal* contributor Terry Lucas, who singled out "glimpses of post-World War I England . . . and the workings of the eccentric Mitfords" for special notice. A *Kirkus Reviews* contributor observed that "the heroine is appealingly plucky, and the reader sinks into the rich period detail." *Booklist* contributor Henrietta Verma called *The Mitford Murders* a "pitch-perfect mystery" which reflects "the genteel Edwardian social dystopia beloved by fans of Downton."

■ Biographical and Critical Sources

PERIODICALS

Booklist, November 15, 2017, Henrietta Verma, review of *The Mitford Murders*, p. 27.
California Bookwatch, February, 2013, review of *The Chronicles of Downton Abbey*.
Kirkus Reviews, November 1, 2017, review of *The Mitford Murders*.
Library Journal, November 15, 2015, Carol J. Binkowski, review of *The Wit and Wisdom of Downton Abbey*, p. 87; November 15, 2017, Terry Lucas, review of *The Mitford Murders*, p. 76.
Publishers Weekly, October 23, 2017, review of *The Mitford Murders*, p. 64; November 20, 2017, Lenny Picker, author interview.

ONLINE

Book Smugglers, https://www.thebooksmugglers.com/ (October 24, 2017), review of *The Mitford Murders*.
British Heritage Website, https://britishheritage.com/ (December 25, 2017), Sara Weal, author interview.
Christian Science Monitor Online, https://www.csmonitor.com/ (December 12, 2012), Molly Driscoll, author interview.
Globe & Mail Online, https://www.theglobeandmail.com/ (March 22, 2018), Margaret Cannon, review of *The Mitford Murders*.
Huffington Post, https://www.huffingtonpost.com/ (January 6, 2015), Lois Alter Mack, author interview.
Jessica Fellowes Website, https://jessicafellowes.wordpress.com (March 22, 2018).
Macmillan Speakers Bureau Website, http://www.macmillanspeakers.com/ (March 22, 2018), author profile.
Peters Fraser & Dunlop Website, https://www.petersfraserdunlop.com/ (March 22, 2018), author profile.
Publishers Weekly Online, https://www.publishersweekly.com/ (November 17, 2017), Lenny Picker, author interview.
Telegraph Online, https://www.telegraph.co.uk/ (September 16, 2013), Jessica Fellowes, "The Awful 'Madness' That Robbed Me of My Mum."*

A.J. Finn

■ Also Known As

Daniel Mallory

■ Personal

Male. *Education:* Duke University, B.A.; Oxford University, master's degree and Ph.D.

■ Addresses

Home—New York, NY. *Agent*—Jennifer Joel, ICM Partners, 730 5th Ave., New York, NY 10019.

■ Career

Book editor and publisher. Little, Brown UK, London, England, editor in commercial publishing; William Morrow, New York, NY, vice president and executive editor.

■ Writings

The Woman in the Window, William Morrow (New York, NY), 2018.

■ Sidelights

A.J. Finn is the pseudonym for Daniel Mallory, who worked in publishing in New York and London editing and acquiring books, and has published his own Hitchcock-esque psychological thriller, *The Woman in the Window,* to critical acclaim. Finn earned a Ph.D. in literature at Oxford University in England. After working at Little, Brown in the United Kingdom, he returned to the United States, where he served as vice president and executive editor of William Morrow.

The Woman in the Window follows the set-up of *Rear Window.* An agoraphobic woman, Anna Fox, once a respected child psychologist, experienced a traumatic event in her past and suffers in isolation in her New York City apartment. To pass the time, she watches old movies and likes to spy on the new Russell family that just moved in across the way with a long-lens camera. One day as she spies into their apartment, she thinks she has just seen a woman she knew get stabbed to death. Few people believe Anna because Anna also drinks a lot of wine that she mixes with her medication, causing her perception to get fuzzy. The reader, too, is not sure what to believe, because Anna is an unreliable narrator.

In a review in *Kirkus Reviews,* a writer said, "Crackling with tension, and the sound of pages turning, as twist after twist sweeps away each hypothesis you come up with about what happened in Anna's past." About the reason Anna was traumatized, Finn explained in an interview on *NPR.org* with Lynn Neary: "Whether you anticipate its details or parameters or not is sort of by the by. It's really incidental. It's not about surprise. It's not about a jack-in-the-box effect. It's about how such an event would impact someone, how they would cope with it."

"Mallory . . . clearly knows a lot about the more diabolical elements in Hitchcock movies. And he hasn't been shy, as Finn, about plugging them into his plot," said Janet Maslin in *New York Times.* Finn said he was inspired by Sherlock Holmes stories, the work of Patricia Highsmith, classic cinema, and his own struggles with agoraphobia and depression. Diagnosed with bipolar II disorder, Finn had secluded himself in his apartment for several weeks and transitioned to various medications. "While the language is at times too clever for its own good," readers will enjoy it, according to a *Publishers Weekly* reviewer. Patrick Anderson said in the *Washington Post:* "It's a beautifully written, brilliantly plotted, richly enjoyable tale of love, loss and madness."

■ Biographical and Critical Sources

PERIODICALS

Kirkus Reviews, November 1, 2017, review of *The Woman in the Window.*

Publishers Weekly, November 6, 2017, review of *The Woman in the Window*, p. 60.

New York Times, January 4, 2018, Janet Maslin, review of *The Woman in the Window*, p. C6(L).

Washington Post, December 18, 2017, Patrick Anderson, review of *The Woman in the Window.*

ONLINE

NPR.org, https://www.npr.org/ (January 20, 2018), Lynn Neary, author interview.*

Amanda Foody

■ **Personal**

Female. *Education:* College of William and Mary, B.A., 2015; Villanova University, M.A., 2017; also attended the American Business School Paris.

■ **Addresses**

Home—Philadelphia, PA. *Agent*—Brianne Johnson, bjohnson@writershouse.com.

■ **Career**

PricewaterhouseCoopers, tax accountant, 2017—.

■ **Writings**

Daughter of the Burning City, Harlequin Teen (Buffalo, NY), 2017.
Ace of Shades, Harlequin Teen (Buffalo, NY), 2018.

■ **Sidelights**

Amanda Foody is a young-adult fantasy fiction writer based in Philadelphia, Pennsylvania. By day she is a tax accountant who holds a master's degree in accountancy from Villanova University and a bachelor's degree in English literature from the College of William and Mary. A Harry Potter fan, Foody likes to write about immersive settings and characters grappling with insurmountable destinies.

In 2017, Foody published her debut book, *Daughter of the Burning City,* which is set in a magical traveling carnival. At age three, Sorina was rescued from slavery by a man who then adopted her as his daughter. She has no eyes, yet she can see by magical means. She can also create lifelike illusions for her father, owner of the Gomorrah Festival, which boasts that it caters to anyone's dreams and desires. Sorina's illusions populate the carnival's Freak Show: a fish man, a fire-breathing baby, trapeze artists, and a two-headed boy. She loves her creations as if they were her own family. One day, the fish man is murdered, but how can he be dead if he is just an illusion? To help her investigate who is murdering her illusions, Sorina enlists the gossip-worker Luca, a demisexual person whom Sorina is attracted to even though Luca is overly critical of her. They uncover political machinations involved in the murders, the brewing war between the Northern and Southern cities, and danger at play within the sinister carnival itself. Sorina also wants to understand the extent of her illusion magic. Soon a forbidden romance begins between Sorina and Luca.

Generating circus excitement, Foody employs color, exotic foods, and geography to tell the story, observed Katherine Noone in *Voice of Youth Advocates.* Noone added that "the freakishness of Sorina's crew disappears into the normal squabbling and teasing of family life among well-characterized individuals" and that teens will enjoy the slowly developing romance between Sorina and Luca and the magical illusions. A writer in *Publishers Weekly* praised the magic, political intrigue, and colorful setting but questioned the romance between Sorina and the cold Luca and thought the finale was too neat and tidy. Nevertheless, the writer said: "A few big twists clear up most of the early inconsistencies that arise."

"A book that aims high but attempts to cover too much territory" is how a *Kirkus Reviews* writer characterized the novel, adding that it tries to champion the outsider but also stigmatizes the "freak" and eliminates Sorina's disability by giving her magical sight. In *Booklist,* Cindy Welch explained that "Foody's mystery seems focused on the illusion-killer, but there is a darker story of political unrest," along with social themes of the haves and have-nots and commentary on people who believe that "different" is perverse. According to Sunnie Scarpa in *School Library Journal,* "The richly drawn backdrop and imaginative fantasy world allow the author to thoughtfully explore complex issues such as what makes someone real."

On the *Fantasy Book Review* website, a writer noted: "The impact of the final reveal feels muted in part because of this hold up in development, meaning it lacks the punch it should have." Nevertheless, the critic thought that the novelty of the book is its fresh setting and world creation and found the novel "unfailing in its message of acceptance and individuality, woven within an interesting, curious and vivid world." Calling the book enticing, mysterious and compelling, Fay Tannerr wrote online at *YA Books Central* that "Foody did an excellent job with an intricately written plot filled with murder, mystery and excitement." She went on to single out "all the details that were described in a mesmerizing way from the smell of licorice cherries to the smell of the smoke that is continuously in Gomorrah's air."

■ Biographical and Critical Sources

PERIODICALS

Booklist, June, 2017, Cindy Welch, review of *Daughter of the Burning City,* p. 91.

Kirkus Reviews, June 1, 2017, review of *Daughter of the Burning City.*

Publishers Weekly, May 8, 2017, review of *Daughter of the Burning City,* p. 62.

School Library Journal, July, 2017, Sunnie Scarpa, review of *Daughter of the Burning City,* p. 88.

Voice of Youth Advocates, October, 2017, Katherine Noone, review of *Daughter of the Burning City,* p. 73.

ONLINE

Amanda Foody Website, http://www.amandafoody.com (February 1, 2018).

Fantasy Book Review, http://www.fantasybookreview.co.uk/ (February 1, 2018), review of *Daughter of the Burning City.*

YA Books Central, http://www.yabookscentral.com/ (November 10, 2017), Fay Tannerr, review of *Daughter of the Burning City.**

Jenny Forrester

■ Personal

Female. *Education:* University of Colorado.

■ Addresses

Home—Portland, OR.

■ Career

Literary writer and editor. Unchaste Readers Series, Portland, OR, curator; *Hip Mama,* editor; *Literary Kitchen,* editor.

■ Awards, Honors

Richard Hugo House New Works Competition, 2011; Monkey Puzzle Press Flash Fiction Contest, 2012.

■ Writings

Narrow River, Wide Sky (memoir), Hawthorne (Portland, OR), 2017.

Contributor of fiction to anthologies, including *Listen to Your Mother,* Putnam, 2015, and to periodicals, including *Penduline Press, Unshod Quills, Seattle's City Arts, Nailed, Hip Mama, Literary Kitchen, Indiana Review,* and *Columbia Journal.*

■ Sidelights

Jenny Forrester writes literary fiction and has been published in various magazines, including *Seattle's City Arts, Nailed, Hip Mama, Literary Kitchen, Indiana Review,* and *Columbia Journal.* Her work has also appeared in the *Listen to Your Mother* anthology. She is curator of the Unchaste Readers literary series in Portland, Oregon, and edits for *Hip Mama* and *Literary Kitchen.* Explaining the term *unchaste,* Forrester told an interviewer on the *Literary Arts* website: "We're damned if we do and damned if we don't, so we may as well be ourselves. We are Unchaste by default because we're women. Let's be that then and embrace our many ways of navigating our wondrous and frightening and complex experiences and our many realities."

In 2017, Forrester published her memoir, *Narrow River, Wide Sky,* a look into her strict life growing up in poverty in a double-wide trailer in the conservative western Colorado town of Mancos. Her small rural town was populated by God-fearing Republicans, gun lovers, religious fundamentalists, rattlesnakes, ranchers, Mormons, and Native Americans. American flags flew proudly amid morally certain citizens, and schoolchildren learned by rote memorization without discussion. Forrester experienced sexual assault, abuse from her boyfriend, and condemnation from her sin-obsessed neighbors. When her mother died suddenly, as young adults she and her brother wondered where they could bury her when they didn't know where they truly belonged. Using her family's strained relationship as a microcosm of America's political tension, Forrester provides a look into her search for identity.

Successfully escaping her environment to attend the University of Colorado on a scholarship, Forrester was able to express her feminist views and become a writer. "Forrester doesn't gloss over the difficult parts of her life, but rather tells stories of how that adversity formed a stronger individual," declared Jeff Fleischer in *ForeWord.* Fleischer added that the book is a moving memoir about the ways family can still be an influence even after they move apart. Forrester also describes her sometimes contentious relationship with her brother, her experiences with drugs, the effects of religion on her community, and her political awakening. Fleischer added that the narrative reads like literary fiction and that Forrester's excellent sense of place makes the town into a character.

In an interview with Amy Wang online at *Oregon Live*, Forrester explained that she wrote the memoir so that her daughter would know her grandmother. She began the book in 1995 just after her mother had died. Forrester said, "It was just going to be a history. And then I started writing and met real writers and then I met poets and then I met a lot of political activists and the book just kept changing and changing until it became what it is now. It's still for my daughter, but it's also—I wanted it to become eventually a piece of art."

"The landscape and culture of west Colorado are vividly evoked in an accomplished literary debut," noted a writer in *Kirkus Reviews*. As Forrester reflects on the culture that shaped and oppressed her, she has created "a modest, thoughtful memoir that traces hard-won liberation from the past," said the writer. Describing her creative process in her memoir, Forrester told Ariel Gore in an interview online at *Literary Kitchen*: "I want to tell stories that matter, that could speak to power, that could tear down big men and bring up little women or show the truth that those men aren't big and those women aren't little and maybe gender is a fallacy, but patriarchy wants it not to be so it all seems to matter still."

■ Biographical and Critical Sources

PERIODICALS

ForeWord, April 27, 2017, Jeff Fleischer, review of *Narrow River, Wide Sky*.
Kirkus Reviews, March 1, 2017, review of *Narrow River, Wide Sky*.

ONLINE

Literary Arts, https://literary-arts.org/ (November 1, 2015), author interview.
Literary Kitchen, http://literarykitchen.com/ (July 27, 2017), Ariel Gore, author interview.
Oregon Live, http://www.oregonlive.com/ (June 8, 2017), Amy Wang, author interview.*

Rowan Moore Gerety

■ **Personal**

Male. *Education:* Columbia University, B.A. (cum laude), 2007.

■ **Addresses**

Home—Miami, FL. *Agent*—Valerie Borchardt, Georges Borchardt, Inc., 136 E. 57th St., 12th Fl., New York, NY 10022.

■ **Career**

Writer, journalist, and radio producer. Freelance reporter and producer, 2012—; *Medium.com,* collection editor, 2013; KAXU FM, Seaside, CA, news reporter, 2013-14; Northwest Public Radio, Yakima, WA, bilingual news reporter, 2014-16; Produced radio stories and documentaries for National Public Radio (NPR), the British Broadcasting Corporation (BBC), *Marketplace, Reveal,* and *Latino USA.* Former Fulbright Scholar in Mozambique, 2011-12, and member of the International Reporting Project (IRP).

■ **Writings**

Go Tell the Crocodiles: Chasing Prosperity in Mozambique, New Press (New York, NY), 2018.

Contributor to periodicals and websites, including the *Virginia Quarterly Review,* the *Miami Herald,* the *Atlantic, Slate, Foreign Policy,* and the *Common.*

■ **Sidelights**

A former Fulbright Scholar, Rowan Moore Gerety is a freelance journalist and radio producer who contributes to periodicals and websites. Gerety, who speaks French, Haitian, Creole, Portuguese, and Spanish, is also the author of *Go Tell the Crocodiles: Chasing Prosperity in Mozambique.* The book explores the lives of the people in Mozambique who live on the margins of Mozambique's rapidly growing economy, which has experienced economic growth since the late 1990s that nearly matches the economic growth in China. As a result, Mozambique's economy is considered among the fastest-growing economies in the world and, as a result, has earned the country the reputation as being an African success story.

Gerety, who has lived and worked in Mozambique, points out in his book that despite the country's economic boom, the vast majority of Mozambicans have not shared in the wealth. Gerety provides a historical look at Mozambique and an analysis of its economic situation. Then he focuses primarily on his time in Mozambique in 2011, revealing the lives of ordinary people who strive to provide for themselves while corruption throughout Mozambique society prevents them from sharing in the overall economic prosperity. Writing in the introduction to *Go Tell the Crocodiles,* Gerety notes: "I've tried to explore the lives of people in Mozambique to uncover broader challenges to twenty-first century development throughout Africa: Can you fix a refugee system that abets human trafficking? Can you move beyond the specter of violence when a warlord leads the political opposition."

Telling the stories of several Mozambicans, Gerety reveals a country still coming to grips with the legacy of colonialism and the aftermath of a long-running civil war that began following Mozambiques independence from Portugal in 1974 following the Mozambican War of Independence.

Another major issue has been the ongoing struggle between the country's two major political parties, Frelimo and Renamo. The real people Gerety profiles include a child who lives on the street making one and a half dollars a day selling muffins, in direct violation of Mozambique law, and a human trafficker and profiteer. "Crocodile attacks, the intersection of language and disease, feuds between subsistence and commercial farmers, and holdover colonialist mindsets round out Gerety's subjects," wrote a *Publishers Weekly* contributor. For example, Gerety discusses a community by a river that has lost numerous people to crocodile attacks. A *Kirkus Reviews* contributor remarked: "Gerety effectively illustrates Mozambique's complexities and how people navigate difficult circumstances. As the author shows, chasing prosperity is rather different from catching prosperity."

■ Biographical and Critical Sources

BOOKS

Gerety, Rowan Moore, *Go Tell the Crocodiles: Chasing Prosperity in Mozambique*, New Press (New York, NY), 2018.

PERIODICALS

Kirkus Reviews, December 1, 2017, review of *Go Tell the Crocodiles*.
Publishers Weekly, November 13, 2017, review of *Go Tell the Crocodiles*.

ONLINE

Guardian Online, https://www.theguardian.com/ (February 2, 2018), Rowan Moore Gerety, "The Long Read: In Pursuit of the Tortoise Smugglers."
Rowan Moore Gerety Website, http://www.rowanmg.com (March 26, 2018).

Victoria Gilbert

■ Personal

Married. *Education:* B.A.; M.A. (library science); M.A. (liberal studies). *Hobbies and other interests:* Watching films, gardening, traveling.

■ Addresses

Home—NC. *Agent*—Frances Black, Literary Counsel, 30 W. 21st St., New York, NY 10010.

■ Career

Writer, novelist, and librarian. Has worked as a reference librarian, research librarian, and library director.

■ Member

Sisters in Crime, International Thriller Writers, Mystery Writers of America.

■ Writings

A Murder for the Books, Crooked Lane Books (New York, NY), 2018.
Shelved under Murder, Crooked Lane Books (New York, NY), 2018.

■ Sidelights

Victoria Gilbert is a mystery writer who grew up near the Blue Ridge Mountains. Gilbert developed an early love of reading, which led her to a dual career as an author and librarian. Gilbert is the author of the "Blue Ridge Library Mystery" series. "My series is set in a historic small town at the foot of the Blue Ridge Mountains in northern Virginia," Gilbert noted in an interview with Mayor Sonni for the *Readeropolis* website, adding: "It just so happens that I grew up in a similar location—in fact, the town of Taylorsford is an amalgam of many of the small towns in the county where I was raised."

The series begins with the mystery *A Murder for the Books*, which a *Publishers Weekly* contributor called a "captivating first novel." *A Murder for the Books* features librarian Amy Weber, who becomes involved in an investigation to solve a decades-old murder and clear the person accused of the crime. Amy was a librarian at Clarion University when she discovered that her boyfriend was cheating, leading her to cause a scene at a university reception. Humiliated and distraught, Amy leaves her job and home and moves to the historical mountain town of Taylorsford in Virginia, which is her ancestral family home, to live with her aunt. Taylorsford is a small, quiet town where very little that is sensational happens. Amy gets a job running the local public library, which needs careful oversight due to a lack of funding. The reader, along with Amy, soon meets many of the library's eccentric patrons.

Then a new neighbor moves in next door to Amy and her aunt. Richard Muir is a classically trained dancer who now teaches dance in college. He inherited the farmhouse from Paul Dassin, who was his great uncle. The house, however, has a reputation in that many people in Taylorsford believe the original owner's wife, Eleanora Cooper, poisoned him, resulting in a 1925 murder trial. The wife was not from Taylorsford, which made her the prime suspect. However, Eleanora was acquitted of the crime and soon afterward disappeared from town. Richard becomes intent on proving Eleanora's innocence in honor of his beloved great uncle, who believed she was innocent and once wrote a book about the case. Richard also suspects that his great uncle was in love with Eleanora.

In his effort to prove once and for all that Eleanora was innocent, Richard ends up going to the library to do some research. Amy is not that interested in the case and is skeptical of Richard's efforts but nevertheless agrees to help him with his research. Eventually, the duo start to discover some disturbing things about some of Taylorsford's leading families, including Amy's own family. It turns out that Amy's grandmother, Rose Baker Litton, had claimed she witnessed Eleanora with recipes for herbal poisoning and, as a result, was a star witness for the prosecution. Meanwhile Doris Virts, who suffered from demential and is found shot to death in the library's archives. Doris's murder, which was probably the result of her being in the wrong place at the wrong time, send the townspeople into a state of fear nearing chaos.

Meanwhile, Amy finds the handsome Richard attractive but is wary because her former lover was also in the arts and had broken her heart. Over time, Amy becomes closer to Richard and her distrust dissipates as they try to solve both the decades-old murder and the new murder. Amy narrates the novel, which features "an intricate mystery, an interesting look at the past, and a clever and determined heroine," according to a *Kirkus Reviews* contributor. Sue O'Brien, working for *Booklist,* remarked: "The mystery is nicely framed by details of library work and research."

■ **Biographical and Critical Sources**

PERIODICALS

Booklist, November 15, 2017, Sue O'Brien, review of *A Murder for the Books.*

Kirkus Reviews, October 15, 2017, review of *A Murder for the Books.*

Publishers Weekly, October 23, 2017, review of *A Murder for the Books.*

ONLINE

Readeropolis, http://readeropolis.blogspot.com/ (March 26, 2018), Mayor Sonni, "Author Q&A . . . Victoria Gilbert: *A Murder for the Books* Book Tour," author interview.

Victoria Gilbert Website, http://victoriagilbert mysteries.com (March 26, 2018).*

Emma Glass

■ **Personal**

Born Swansea, Wales. *Education:* Attended University of Kent; Swansea University, nursing degree.

■ **Addresses**

Home—South London, England.

■ **Career**

Writer, novelist, and nurse. Evelina London Children's Hospital, London, England, research nurse specialist.

■ **Writings**

Peach, Bloomsbury USA (New York, NY), 2017.

■ **Sidelights**

Emma Glass is a novelist and research nurse specialist in Great Britain. Her debut novel, *Peach*, tells the story of a girl named Peach who is the victim of a sexual assault. The origins of the novel, published in 2018, started a decade earlier when Glass attended a creative writing class during which her fellow classmates were pitching "ideas for really high-concept novels," Glass noted in an interview with *Guardian Online* contributor Marta Bausells. Glass had different ideas about the kind of story she wanted to write, drawing from the novels of Gertrude Stein and James Joyce that she was reading at the time. Glass told Bausells that

she was "fascinated with how everyone's reading of those books is highly different, because the focus is on the language and not necessarily the story." Although she was struggling with her writing, one night she was listening to music while writing and told Bausells that the idea for *Peach* "literally started with a beat" and a subsequent "image in my mind of a frustrated or sad person and I identified that person as a young girl."

In the novel, Peach comes home one night injured and staggering. However, her parents essentially ignore her, far more interested in their oversexed lives and their new baby. Peach has been assaulted by a stranger named Lincoln, and she stitches herself up in the bathroom. She does not tell her parents or her boyfriend, Green, about the rape. Peach goes on to have nightmares and lives in fear, especially after she thinks that she sees Lincoln walking in the woods near her school. As Peach tries to deal with the psychological and physical aftereffects of the rape, she seeks comfort with Green. A *Publishers Weekly* contributor noted that "tender moments between Green and Peach offer respite from an otherwise challenging story."

Still, Peach is struggling as she views her body as deformed and growing abnormally, especially in the form of a distended belly. She is also viewing those around her differently, primarily as food, such as her baby brother whom she sees as a jelly baby, or gummy bear. Meanwhile, she keeps thinking she is seeing Lincoln but cannot be sure because of her psychological state of mind. However, eventually after those around suffer attacks, she is sure that Lincoln is stalking her. As a result, she decides that it is up to her alone to take action. "With paragraphs that read like poems, this is a memorably crafted entry into the canon of revenge narratives," wrote a *Kirkus Reviews* contributor.

Annie Bostrom, writing in *Booklist,* remarked: "Glass . . . aptly portrays Peach's real and mythical struggles . . . in this darkly arresting debut."

■ Biographical and Critical Sources

PERIODICALS

Booklist, November 1, 2017, Annie Bostrom, review of *Peach,* p. 33.
Publishers Weekly, October 30, 2017, review of *Peach,* p. 55.

New Statesman, January 12, 2018, review of *Peach.*

ONLINE

Guardian Online, https://www.theguardian.com/books/ (January 11, 2018), Marta Bausells, "Emma Glass: 'I Hope My Book Will Help People Find the Language of the Ordeal,'" author interview.
Sydney Morning Herald Online, https://www.smh.com.au/ (January 19, 2018), Melanie Kembrey, "Interview: Emma Glass on Her Debut Novel *Peach.*"*

Michele Gorman

■ Also Known As

Lilly Bartlett

■ Personal

Born in Pittsfield, MA; immigrated to England, 1998; naturalized British citizen, 2006; married. *Education:* University of Massachusetts at Amherst, bachelor's degree; University of Illinois at Chicago Circle, M.A.

■ Addresses

Home—London, England. *Agent*—Hardman & Swainson Literary Agency, S86 New Wing, Somerset House, Strand, London WC2R 1LA, England.

■ Career

Writer. Formerly worked as an auditor and market analyst, London, England.

■ Writings

NOVELS

Christmas Carol, Notting Hill Press (London, England), 2013.
Bella Summer Takes a Chance, Notting Hill Press (London, England), 2013.
Perfect Girl, Notting Hill Press (London, England), 2014.

Weightless, Notting Hill Press (London, England), 2014.
The Reluctant Elf, self-published, 2014.
The Curvy Girls Club, Avon (London, England), 2015.
The Curvy Girls Baby Club, Notting Hill Press (London, England), 2015.
Match Me If You Can, Avon (London, England), 2016.
Love Is a Four-Legged Word, Notting Hill Press (London, England), 2016.
Life Change, Notting Hill Press (London, England), 2018.

"THE EXPAT DIARIES; SINGLE IN THE CITY" SERIES

Single in the City, Penguin Books (London, England), 2010, revised edition, Notting Hill Press/Amazon Digital Services, 2011.
Misfortune Cookie, Notting Hill Press (London, England), 2012.
The Twelve Days to Christmas, Notting Hill Press (London, England), 2013.

UNDER PSEUDONYM LILLY BARTLETT

The Big Little Wedding in Carlton Square, HarperImpulse (London, England), 2017.
The Second Chance Café in Carlton Square, HarperImpulse (London, England), 2017.
The Big Dreams Beach Hotel, HarperImpulse (London, England), 2017.
Christmas at the Falling-Down Guesthouse, Notting Hill Press (London, England), 2017.

■ Sidelights

Michele Gorman was born in Massachusetts and educated in the United States. She intended to pursue a career in finance, but several lackluster years as an auditor convinced her to change direction. She earned a master's degree in sociology and found herself "highly qualified, and unemployed," according to the author profile at her website.

In 1998 Gorman relocated to England, where she finally found work as a market analyst. What she really wanted to do was stay at home and work as a writer. Her experiences as a hapless American in London provided the springboard for a career that produced more than a dozen novels in half as many years.

Gorman is a proud representative of the "chick lit" genre, which consists of "humour, a sharp female protagonist, a love story and a happy ending," as she explained to an interviewer at the *Chicklit Club* website. Although she has a British publisher, Gorman decided that her U.S. releases should be published independently. To aid her in that endeavor, she became a cofounder of Notting Hill Press. Along with her growing success, Gorman has expanded her writing into an area that she calls "literary fiction," she said in her interview, and in 2017 she began to publish romantic comedies under the pseudonym Lilly Bartlett. Her career began, however, with the adventures of a young American expatriate in the big city.

Single in the City

Single in the City introduces an impulsive twenty-something American from Connecticut. Hannah's response to losing her job is to flee the country altogether and forge a new life in London, with no job, no home, and no friends on the horizon. Her transition to an unfamiliar lifestyle begins with a small faux pas and accelerates rapidly. Hannah seeks comfort in a local pub, where her slightly lubricated gaffes continue to attract attention. She does, however, begin to make friends, move into an apartment with three male roommates, and find a job of sorts. Then she decides to look for a boyfriend, a search that results in its own share of social disasters.

"*Single in the City* is a fun and sardonic read" in which "humorous situations and witty repartee abound," reported a reviewer at *Read in a Single Sitting*. Some readers noted that Hannah's serial mishaps fall short of sustaining a cohesive plot but, like a reviewer from the *Chicklit Club* website, they enjoyed "a hilarious book, full of romance and laugh-out-loud situations that no woman would want to be in." A *Book Bag* contributor

acknowledged that "this book had the potential to be awful" but was instead "a funny, insightful, highly entertaining read."

The U.S. edition of *Single in the City* required substantial modification, Forman informed her *Chicklit Club* interviewer. For example, the footnotes she offered British readers—to explain American products and slang—had to be reversed for an American audience. Despite the challenges, Hannah's adventures inspired two sequels. In *Misfortune Cookie*, Hannah follows her boyfriend to Hong Kong, another impulsive move that backfires when Sam seems to be more interested in his job—and his new boss—than he is in Hannah. *The Twelve Days to Christmas* reveals a mended relationship, as she and Sam are planning a trip to America and, quite possibly, a marriage proposal. This time, however, Hannah seems to be more inclined to look before she leaps into a potential disaster.

The Big Little Wedding in Carlton Square and The Second Chance Café in Carlton Square

Gorman describes the novels she writes under the name Lilly Barnett as romantic comedies. *The Big Little Wedding in Carlton Square* introduces a young woman with a dilemma. Emma must plan an extravagant wedding to her unexpectedly wealthy boyfriend that will please his parents without bankrupting her working-class father, who insists on shouldering the cost.

The Second Chance Café in Carlton Square reveals Emma as a married mother of twins, who has opened a promising new business in a changing neighborhood. She is stretched to the limit at home and at work when her optimism is challenged by incidents of vandalism and theft. Additional incidents suggest that someone wants her business to fail, and it will take her entire diverse community of customers to identify the culprit and save the little café that holds it together.

The Big Dreams Beach Hotel and The Curvy Girls Club

The Big Dreams Beach Hotel introduces Rosie MacDonald, an expatriate American who fled a failed romance to manage a quaint Victorian boarding hotel on the North Yorkshire coast of England. Her peace and quiet are disrupted by development plans that threaten the ambience—and perhaps the very existence—of her remote haven. The plan pits long-distance American investors against the eccentric permanent residents who could lose their homes to the tourism trade.

Rosie faces additional issues with the remodeler, Rory, who reminds her all too much of the man who broke her heart. The story attracted the notice of a *Publishers Weekly* contributor, who found "plenty of sweet moments" in this "simple and happy" story.

Gorman's forays into literary fiction demonstrate a wide range of story arcs. In *The Curvy Girls Club*, four overweight friends abandon the weight-loss clinics and diet clubs to start a social club where weight doesn't matter—until it does. When Katie begins to lose weight, her partners begin to wonder if she is an appropriate spokesperson for their membership demographic. A *Publishers Weekly* contributor called *The Curvy Girls Club* "a laugh-out-loud, heartwarming tale . . . of friendship, acceptance, and belonging." Writing at *Female First* about *The Curvy Girls Club*, Lucy Moore said she "loved this book because it focuses on the importance of female friendship," sending the message that "with the right people around you—you can move mountains."

Love Is a Four-Legged Word and *Match Me If You Can*

In *Love Is a Four-Legged Word*, two childhood friends share a dog services business successfully until a failed marriage and a husband come between them. A reviewer of *Love Is a Four-Legged Word* at the *Chicklit Club* website wrote that Gorman "writes great characters you can easily relate to and care about with storylines that are so entertaining, you can get lost in the book for hours."

In *Match Me If You Can*, Catherine and her ex-husband operate a dating site called RecycLove. com. Members have the option to trade in their ex-partners for a chance to win an upgrade from the discards of other members. The business is successful until Catherine's ex decides to leave the business and recycle his discarded girlfriend by making her Catherine's new business partner. As in her other works, critics praised the characters and relationships in *Match Me If You Can*. A *Harlequin Junkie* contributor wrote: "The characters are humorous, realistic and refreshing . . . and readers get to watch them grow as individuals."

■ Biographical and Critical Sources

PERIODICALS

Publishers Weekly, September 1, 2014, review of *The Curvy Girls Club*; November 6, 2017, review of *The Big Dreams Beach Hotel*, p. 68.

ONLINE

Book Bag, http://www.thebookbag.co.uk/ (February 2, 2017), review of *Single in the City.*
Chicklit Club, http://www.chicklitclub.com/ (March 23, 2008), author interview and reviews of *Single in the City, Misfortune Cookie, Bella Summer Takes a Chance, Perfect Girl, The Curvy Girls Club, Love Is a Four-Legged Word,* and *Match Me If You Can.*
Female First, http://www.femalefirst.co.uk/ (July 25, 2016), Lucy Moore, review of *The Curvy Girls Club.*
Girl Tries Life, http://www.girltrieslife.com/ (October 24, 2014), Victoria Smith, author interview.
Harlequin Junkie, http://harlequinjunkie.com/ (February 28, 2016), review of *Match Me If You Can.*
Michele Gorman Website, http://michelegorman. co.uk (March 23, 2018).
Novelicious, http://www.novelicious.com/ (March 15, 2016), Jenny Banks, review of *Match Me If You Can.*
Read in a Single Sitting, http://www. readinasinglesitting.com/ (September 2, 2010) author interview and review of *Single in the City.**

Sam Graham-Felsen

■ **Personal**

Born Boston, MA. *Education:* Harvard University, graduated cum laude, 2004.

■ **Career**

Writer, novelist, educator, and public speaker. The *Nation*, Washington, DC, reporter, 2004-07; Blue State Digital, Washington, DC, content director, 2008-09; Columbia University, New York, NY, adjunct assistant professor of creative writing. Previously worked as the chief blogger on Barack Obama's presidential campaign, 2007-08; produced videos for Current TV; and was a featured speaker with the American Program Bureau.

■ **Writings**

Green (novel), Random House (New York, NY), 2018.

Contributor to periodicals, including the *New York Times* magazine, the *Nation,* and the *Washington Post;* and to websites, including *LitHub* and the *Jewish Book Council* website. Also a writer and columnist for the *Harvard Crimson* while attending college.

■ **Sidelights**

Sam Graham-Felsen grew up in the Jamaica Plain neighborhood of Boston, Massachusetts. He graduated from Harvard University with a degree in social studies and has worked for and contributed to periodicals and websites. Graham-Felsen was also a video producer for Current TV, reporting from Cambodia, France, and Pakistan and a blogger for Barack Obama's first presidential campaign. His debut novel, *Green,* is a coming-of-age story in which Graham-Felsen presents his take on the so-called "American dream."

In an interview with Lauren Frayer published on *NPR.org,* Graham-Felsen noted that he campaigned enthusiastically for Barack Obama with the hope of bringing about significant change but added: "I never thought we would turn into a post-racial country overnight, but when I saw the sort of enormity and swiftness of the backlash against Obama . . ., it really gave me pause." Graham-Felsen went on to tell Frayer that he was contemplating the idea for his novel back in 2007 and 2008 while campaigning for Obama, noting that following the campaign he found he "wanted to explore . . . why is racism such an intractable problem in this country? And I realized . . . I have this fairly unique experience as a white kid who went to mostly black schools growing up, and maybe if I dive . . . into my own past, I can kind of understand what happened to me better and maybe a little bit better about what happened to my city and even my country."

The novel takes place in 1992. Its protagonist, David Greenfield, attends Martin Luther King, Jr., Middle School. As one of the only white kids at the school, he is constantly made fun of by his black and Latino classmates and largely ignored by girls. His parents are hippies who refuse to buy him high-end tennis shoes and deny his request to be transferred to a private school. David's only hope is to perform well enough on aptitude tests to get into one of Boston's better public schools.

Black classmate Marlon "Mars" Wellings lives in the public housing project close to David's neighborhood, which is becoming gentrified. One day David is astounded when Mars defends him during an incident at the school cafeteria. The two form a friendship that changes how Dave sees his black schoolmates and black culture in general. It turns out that Mars does not fit the typical stereotype of a youngster living in "the hood" but is smart, kind of nerdy, and more than a little neurotic. The two spend a lot of time together at Dave's house watching their favorite team, the Boston Celtics, with Mars's favorite player being the white Larry Bird. They also study together in hopes of passing the entrance exam to the prestigious Boston Latin high school.

Dave and Mars stick together at school as well, as they face taunts, bullying, and other middle-school dramas. Eventually, however, their bond starts to fall apart as they compete for a girl and as Dave demonstrates the advantages of being white as he tries to get ahead, sometimes betraying Mars in the process. Meanwhile, Dave does not seem to want to acknowledge that as a black boy, Mars is facing a much harder time trying to achieve a better life due to discrimination and overall societal viewpoints concerning the black members of American society. Eventually, Dave, who serves as the novel's narrator, comes to perceive the real impact of racial discrimination, which he calls the Force. Nevertheless, the two friends' vastly different backgrounds seem to be a barrier to a true, lasting friendship.

"Dave tells his story in his own idiosyncratic, vaguely streetwise voice, with hip-hop overtones that perfectly capture the [tale's] mood and tone," wrote Michael Cart in *Booklist*. Writing for *Library Journal*, Joshua Finnell remarked that *Green* "poignantly captures the tumultuous feelings of adolescence against the historical backdrop of a racially segregated city and country."

■ **Biographical and Critical Sources**

PERIODICALS

Booklist, October 1, 2017, Michael Cart, review of *Green*, p. 25.

Kirkus Reviews, October 15, 2017, review of *Green*.

Library Journal, September 1, 2017, Joshua Finnell, "Fiction," includes review of *Green*, p. 101.

Publishers Weekly, October 16, 2017, review of *Green*, p. 46.

ONLINE

NPR.org, https://www.npr.org/ (December 31, 2017), Lauren Frayer, "In *Green*, a Pre-Teen Wisens Up to His Privilege," author interview.

Sam Graham-Felsen Website, http://www.samgf.com (March 27, 2018).*

Vanessa Grigoriadis

1973-

■ Personal

Born September 21, 1973. *Education:* Graduated from Wesleyan University; also attended Harvard University for one year.

■ Addresses

Home—NY.

■ Career

Journalist and writer. *New York* magazine, New York, NY, began as an editorial assistant and became a contributing editor; *New York Times,* style writer, 2003.

■ Awards, Honors

National Magazine Award, 2007, for a profile of fashion icon Karl Lagerfeld.

■ Writings

Blurred Lines: Rethinking Sex, Power, and Consent on Campus, Houghton Mifflin Harcourt (Boston, MA), 2017.

Contributor to books, including *The Fourth Sex: Adolescent Extremes,* Charta, 2003; *Best American Magazine Writing 2007,* Columbia University Press, 2007; *Best American Magazine Writing 2007,* Columbia University Press, 2008; *Seventeen Real Girls, Real-Life Stories: True Crime,* Hearst, 2007; *New York Stories,* Random House Trade Paperbacks, 2008; and *Best Music Writing 2009,* Da Capo Press, 2009. Contributor to periodicals, including *New York* magazine, the *New York Times,* and *Vanity Fair.*

■ Sidelights

Journalist Vanessa Grigoriadis grew up in New York City and played classical violin and danced when she was a youth. Since graduating from college she has been a generalist writer working for and contributing to several periodicals. In her first book, *Blurred Lines: Rethinking Sex, Power, and Consent on Campus,* Grigoriadis provides an inside look at the controversy surrounding sex on U.S. college campuses, from entrenched sexism and sexual assault to a growing willingness for women to own their own sexuality. The book's origins date back to a 2014 cover story Grigoriadis wrote about Emma Sulkowicz, a Columbia University student who became known as the Mattress Girl after she conducted a performance work for her senior thesis. The work involved Sulkowicz and some of her female classmates carrying a dorm-room-like mattress around campus, saying they would continue to do so until a student that Sulkowicz alleged raped her in their dorm room two years earlier was expelled from or left the university.

The performance Sulkowicz and her friends undertook gained both accolades and some criticism, especially after the student was found not responsible following a university inquiry, which Sulkowicz and others criticized. The case was somewhat complicated because Sulkowicz acknowledge that the two had consensual intercourse but that the male student then forced her to have anal intercourse without her consent. "I was inspired by Sulkowicz and her peers, but in these women's impressive march into the nation's consciousness, they've left questions in their wake," Grigoriadis writes in the introduction to *Blurred Lines.* Grigoriadis goes on to note that not only did Sulkowicz's tactics raise questions but that Grigoriadis also began to think of other issues, from what kinds of students are assaulted to what exactly constitutes sexual assault, how to gain further knowledge about students who engage in sexual assaults, and how to use this information to guide future efforts to fight the problem.

In *Blurred Lines,* Grigoriadis writes about how attitudes are changing concerning consent on college campuses in the United States. To write the book and closely examine these changing attitudes, Grigoriadis traveled to colleges throughout the United States and took part in social activities. She interviewed more than one hundred students, some of whom were accusers and others who were accused of sexual misconduct. She also talks with administrators, parents, and researchers to examine how the common views and rules of sex and power are changing. Grigoriadis "paints a dismal picture of college social life, where students feel pressured to hook up, where boys are confused about what constitutes consent, and where girls . . . acquiesce to sex that they don't really want," noted a *Kirkus Reviews* contributor.

Grigoriadis provides insight into the conflicting data concerning sexual assaults on campus and demystifies the data in the process. She delves into what makes a sexual encounter sexual assault and makes her case that not all encounters classified as sexual assaults are the same. Grigoriadis also discusses how campuses can be made safer by the schools, students, and the students' parents. In the process, Grigoriadis writes about how modern life

has impacted the entire issues of sexual assault. For example, she examines the profound effects of social media and the dangers involved concerning increasing the risk for sexual assaults. In essence, Grigoriadis states that social media allows people to think they know other people better than they really do, which could lead them to letting down their guard down and into potentially dangerous situations. *Blurred Lines* includes recommendations for further reading and research as well as notes and an index. "The breadth of her research. . . and her exploration of toxic gender roles and stereotypes . . . are reason enough to pick up this book," wrote a *Publishers Weekly* contributor.

■ Biographical and Critical Sources

BOOKS

Grigoriadis, Vanessa, *Blurred Lines: Rethinking Sex, Power, and Consent on Campus,* Houghton Mifflin Harcourt (Boston, MA), 2017.

PERIODICALS

Commentary, December, 2017, K.C. Johnson, "Whitewashing Campus Tribunals," review of *Blurred Lines,* p. 41.
Kirkus Reviews, August 1, 2017, review of *Blurred Lines.*
Publishers Weekly, August 7, 2017, review of *Blurred Lines,* p. 64.

ONLINE

Los Angeles Review of Books, https://lareviewofbooks. org/ (November 17, 2017), Eric Nelson, "The Instinct to Protect Each Other: An Interview with Vanessa Grigoriadis."
Vanessa Grigoriadis Website, http://www. vanessagrigoriadis.com (March 27, 2018).*

Robin Hanbury-Tenison

1936-

■ Personal

Born May 7, 1936; married Marika Hopkinson (a food writer; died, 1982); married Louella Edwards Williams, 1983; children: (first marriage) Lucy, Rupert; (second marriage) Merlin, stepsons Harry and Peter. *Education:* Magdalen College, Oxford University, M.A.

■ Addresses

Home—Cornwall, England.

■ Career

Explorer, conservationist, broadcaster, filmmaker, lecturer, author, campaigner, and farmer. Founding member, Farming & Wildlife Advisory Group (FWAG); Survival International, cofounder, 1969, chair, 1969-81, president, 1981—; South West Regional Panel, U.K. Ministry of Agriculture, Fisheries and Food, member, 1993-96; British Field Sports Society, chief executive, 1995-98; Westcountry Development Corporation, ambassador.

■ Member

Society of Authors, Rain Forest Club (president, 2001-05), Cornwall Red Squirrel Project (president, 2011), Invest in Britain (formerly Think British).

■ Awards, Honors

Explorers Club, International Fellow; Winston Churchill Memorial Fellow, 1971; Linnean Society Fellow; Royal Geographic Society Patron's Gold Medal, 1979, and Mungo Park Medal, 2001; Krug Award for Excellence, 1980; OBE, 1981; named "greatest explorer of the past 20 years" by London *Sunday Times*, 1982, and one of 1000 "Makers of the 20th Century," 1991; Farmers Club Cup, 1998; International Council for Game and Wildlife Conservation Personality of the Year, 1998; Pio Manzu medal, Italian Chamber of Deputies, and CLA Contribution to the Countryside Award, both 2000; Patron of the Countryside Alliance, 2003; named "the doyen of British Explorers" by *Spectator*, 2006; Best Large Scale Renewable Energy Scheme in Cornwall Award, 2012.

■ Writings

The Rough and the Smooth: The Story of Two Journeys across South America, Hale (London, England), 1969.

A Question of Survival for the Indians of Brazil, Scribner (New York, NY), 1973.

A Pattern of Peoples: A Journey among the Tribes of Indonesia's Outer Islands, Scribner (New York, NY), 1975.

Mulu: The Rain Forest, Weidenfeld and Nicolson (London, England), 1980.

Worlds Apart: An Explorer's Life, Little, Brown (Boston, MA), 1984.

White Horses over France: From the Camargue to Cornwall, Granada (New York, NY), 1985.

(Editor) *The Oxford Book of Exploration*, Oxford University Press (New York, NY), 1993, reprinted, 2nd edition, 2005.

Worlds Within: Reflections in the Sand, Long Riders' Guild Press, 2006.

The Seventy Great Journeys in History, Thames & Hudson (New York, NY), 2006.

Land of Eagles: Riding through Europe's Forgotten Country, I.B. Tauris/Palgrave Macmillan (New York, NY), 2010.

(Editor) *The Great Explorers,* Thames & Hudson (New York, NY), 2010.

(Editor, with Robert Twigger) *The Modern Explorers,* Thames & Hudson (New York, NY), 2013.

Finding Eden: A Journey into the Heart of Borneo, I.B. Tauris (London, England), 2017.

Author of introduction, *Southern Cross to Pole Star: Tschiffeley's Ride,* by Aime Tschiffeley, Head of Zeus, 2014; author of preface, *Crossing the Congo,* by Mike Martin, Chloe Baker, and Charlie Hatch-Barnwell, Hurst, 2016. Contributor to periodicals, including *Times Literary Supplement, Times, Telegraph, Mail, Express, Geographical, New Scientist, Field, Traveller, Spectator,* and *Country Life.*

■ Sidelights

An acclaimed explorer, broadcaster, and author, Robin Hanbury-Tenison has achieved many distinctions, having made the first documented east-west crossing of South America at its widest point (with companion Richard Mason) in 1958, and the first north-south river crossing of South American in 1964 and 1965. Hanbury-Tenison began his exploring career in 1957, when he drove from London to Sri Lanka and then worked in exchange for ships' passage around the world. He has made numerous journeys on every continent, often traveling in order to raise funds for Survival International, which seeks to protect the human rights of indigenous peoples around the world. Hanbury-Tenison cofounded the organization in 1969 after learning about the exploitation of Amazon Indians, who face possible extinction due to disease, illegal deforestation, and violence. In 1971 the Brazilian government invited him to lead a Survival International field expedition to visit isolated Indian peoples in the Amazon region. This expedition led to increased global awareness of the critical importance of protecting tropical rainforests.

Since then, Hanbury-Tenison has walked across the Kalahari Desert; ridden across France on horseback; ridden along the Great Wall of China; led a mission to investigate illegal logging in Malaysia; traveled the length of New Zealand; made the pilgrimage to Santiago de Compostela in Spain; and visited tribal people in Russia's Kamchatka and Ussuria regions. He has also traveled in northern India, Labrador, the Sahara, Australia, Central America, and Antarctica, and made a trip on horseback, with his wife, across the length of Albania.

At his home in Cornwall, Hanbury-Tenison practices sustainable farming on Bodmin Moor, where he raises sheep and cattle as well as angora goats, red deer, and wild boar. In recent years he has focused on producing energy from renewable sources including wind, solar water, and biomass. In addition to editing several anthologies about explorers and the history of exploration, he is the author of a several books recounting his personal expeditions.

The Oxford Book of Exploration

In 2005 Hanbury-Tenison modernized and updated *The Oxford Book of Exploration,* originally published in 1993, adding contributions from writers such as John Hemming, a Canadian who studied indigenous peoples in the Amazon basin, and cave explorer Andy Eavis. But he admits in the book's introduction that he has begun to doubt the purpose of exploration in the modern world, and to question the assumptions and practices of earlier explorers. "Few of the great explorers were the first people to get to where they were going," he writes, "although they often fail to mention those who showed them the way. Often they were perfidious, shooting the welcoming natives without warning."

Organized geographically according to continent, the book includes writings by early explorers such as Vasco da Gama, John Cabot, Ferdinand Magellan, and Sir Francis Drake, as well as by more modern figures such as Alexander Von Humboldt, Dr. David Livingstone, Mary Kingsley, Alexandra David-Neel, Thor Heyerdahl, and Edmund Hillary.

The Great Explorers, The Modern Explorers, and The Seventy Great Journeys in History

The Great Explorers, which contains contributions from thirty-two explorers and academics, covers seven general subjects: oceans, land, rivers, polar ice, deserts, life on earth, and new frontiers. The legacies of iconic explorers from the 1550s to the twenty-first century are also discussed, and editor Hanbury-Tenison provides what *Contemporary Review* contributor Mick described as "elegant essays linking the separate sections." *The Modern Explorers,* which Hanbury-Tenison edited with Robert Twigger, focuses on more recent figures such as Karen Darke, a wheelchair user who climbed Yosemite's El Capitan; Meg Lowman, an ethnobotanist conducting research in French Guiana; and Pen Hadow, who researched changes in the Arctic's sea ice.

In *The Seventy Great Journeys in History*, editor Hanbury-Tenison has chosen narratives and commentary on journeys that he considers to be of epic importance, from ancient times to the twenty-first century. Among these are the journeys of Genghis Khan; the forced migration of the Cherokee Nation away from their ancestral lands in North America (a journey known as the Trail of Tears); the journeys of American aviation pioneer Amelia Earhart; and the Apollo space missions.

Worlds Apart and *Worlds Within*

In his memoir *Worlds Apart: An Explorer's Life*, Hanbury-Tenison reflects on his own travels and on the larger theme of exploration, acknowledging that the first encounters between Western explorers and indigenous peoples have too frequently led to colonization and exploitation. He describes his first visits to the Yanomami people of Brazil, the Penan people of Malaysia, and the Tuareg people of Libya, and writes of how he came to admire their self-sufficiency. Though he deplores colonialists' and missionaries' efforts to make these people change their habits—for example, by wearing clothing and becoming Christians—the author does not romanticize the lives of hunter-gatherers, pointing out that some of their traditions are "unnecessarily crude and cruel." Even so, he argues firmly against the West's assumption of cultural superiority, pointing out that the Yanomami have flourished on their own lands for some 15,000 years without any interference from outsiders.

The book discusses the founding of Survival International, and the Brazilian government's decision in 1982 to provisionally set aside a protected area for the Yanomami. Observing that the Yanomami care nothing for material possessions, the author states that their survival is crucial "because some societies, through their viability and the hope they can give to a desperate world which sees its own extinction as dangerously imminent, deserve to survive so that the species may survive." Pointing out that a nonfiction book should ideally "get the reader thinking about a human problem in a new way," *Smithsonian* contributor Dennis Drabelle wrote that *Worlds Apart* "does exactly that."

In recounting the details of a forty-day expedition across the Sahara by camel in *Worlds Within: Reflections in the Sand*, Hanbury-Tenison also shares his emotional journey to free himself from the "chatter of the universe." Writing in *Geographical*, Frankie Mullin said that the book's mix of exotic setting, "grueling conditions," and exciting anecdotes from the author's earlier travels make it an example of

"great armchair traveling." Mullin particularly admired the author's "deep-rooted enthusiasm" for the people he has encountered during his career.

Land of Eagles

Land of Eagles: Riding through Europe's Forgotten Country is Hanbury-Tenison's account of the journey he and his wife made across Albania on horseback. Albania is a mountainous country without any natural north-south routes; this difficult terrain, along with the fact that the author's maps dated mainly from the 1950s, contributed to several misadventures. Relying on Albanian guides who spoke little English, the travelers often got lost and encountered hostility from local people.

The book did not favorably impress *Geographical* reviewer Robert Carver, who described the author as an "old-school, upper-crust pukka sahib" with no concern for the local people except to see them as potential employees or as "picturesque background" to his own adventure. The reviewer went on to say that the author's difficulties were mostly self-created because of his rigid "expedition mentality." According to Carver, travel in Albania is not particularly difficult; had Hanbury-Tenison heeded advice from local people, his journey would not have been the gritty ordeal that this book recounts.

Finding Eden

Hanbury-Tenison's most recent book is *Finding Eden: A Journey into the Heart*, in which he recalls his expedition forty years earlier to the Gunung Mulu National Park in Borneo's remote interior. For fifteen months, the author and his team lived in a virgin rainforest inhabited by indigenous peoples who had almost no contact with the modern world. His diary entries from that time express his sense of wonder and excitement, but the book includes also material about his later visits to Mulu, which showed him the horrifying toll of deforestation and westernized lifestyles.

Despite the book's melancholy message, the author also expresses hope that it is not too late to take actions that could save what is left of Mulu. He argues that management of the park should be returned to the local people, who would reinstate traditional forestry practices that could enable the environment to thrive once again. A writer for *Publishers Weekly* admired Hanbury-Tenison's evocative description of this land and its people, concluding that the author "captures some of the beauty before its almost certain disappearance."

■ **Biographical and Critical Sources**

BOOKS

Hanbury-Tenison, Robin, *The Oxford Book of Exploration*, 2nd edition, Oxford University Press (New York, NY), 2005.

Hanbury-Tenison, Robin, *Worlds Within: Reflections in the Sand*, Long Riders' Guild Press, 2006.

Hanbury-Tenison, Robin, *Worlds Apart: An Explorer's Life*, Little, Brown (Boston, MA), 1984.

PERIODICALS

California Bookwatch, March, 2016, review of *The Modern Explorers*.

Contemporary Review, June, 2011, review of *The Great Explorers*, p. 254.

Geographical, July, 2005, Nick Smith, review of *The Oxford Book of Exploration*, 2nd edition, p. 84; November, 2005, Frankie Mullin, review of *Worlds Within*, p. 80; July, 2009, Robert Carver, review of *Land of Eagles: Riding through Europe's Forgotten Country*, p. 63; October, 2010, Mick Herron, review of *The Great Explorers*, p. 66; September, 2013, Mick Herron, review of *The Modern Explorers*, p. 60.

Library Journal, January 1, 2007, Margaret Atwater-Singer, review of *The Seventy Great Journeys in History*, p. 125.

Midwest Book Review, March, 2016, Paul Vogel, review of *The Modern Explorers*.

Publishers Weekly, October 30, 2017, review of *Finding Eden: A Journey into the Heart of Borneo*, p. 69.

Smithsonian, November, 1984, Dennis Drabelle, review of *Worlds Apart*, p. 227.

Spectator, January 21, 2006, Jeremy Swift, review of *Worlds Within*, p. 49; April 26, 2009, Robin Hanbury-Tenison, "Wilful Destruction of a World Wonder," p. 35.

ONLINE

Robin Hanbury-Tenison Website, http://www.robinsbooks.co.uk (March 21, 2018).*

Myronn Hardy

■ Personal

Male. *Education:* Graduated from University of Michigan and Columbia University.

■ Addresses

Home—New York, NY; Morocco.

■ Career

Poet and novelist.

■ Awards, Honors

PEN/Oakland Josephine Miles Award, 2002, for *Approaching the Center;* Hurston/Wright Legacy Award, 2008, for *The Headless Saints;* Griot-Stadler Prize for Poetry, 2012, for *Catastrophic Bliss.*

■ Writings

POETRY

Approaching the Center, New Issues Poetry & Prose (Kalamazoo, MI), 2001.
The Headless Saints, New Issues/Western Michigan University (Kalamazoo, MI), 2008.
Catastrophic Bliss, Bucknell University Press (Lewisburg, PA), 2012.
Kingdom, New Issues Poetry & Prose (Kalamazoo, MI), 2015.
Radioactive Starlings: Poems, Princeton University Press (Princeton, NJ), 2017.

■ Sidelights

Myronn Hardy is an award-winning poet and novelist. Raised in Arkansas, he divides his time between New York City and Morocco. He holds degrees from the University of Michigan and Columbia University. For his first poetry collection, *Approaching the Center,* he received the 2002 PEN/Oakland Josephine Miles Award.

The Headless Saints

Winner of the Hurston/Wright Legacy Award, *The Headless Saints* ranges across continents and cities, and across themes of oppression, survival, and the redemptive potential of art. Many poems reflect on the determination of enslaved Africans in the Americas to triumph over the near-extermination of their history and culture. Others consider the subject of art, as in a poem about a meeting between Abel Meeropol, an American poet of Russian Jewish descent who wrote the words to the anti-lynching ballad "Strange Fruit," and Billie Holiday, the African American singer whose 1939 recording of the song made it iconic.

"Sometimes the poems stop short," said a *Publishers Weekly* reviewer; "at others, their terse vigor reinvents what they see." The book's best poems, said *Phoebe* contributor Joe Hall, "remind us of the alluvial nature of the present . . . [and] suggest the imprints of the larger, messy, tectonic historical forces which have informed them."

Catastrophic Bliss

The themes of connections and disconnections inform the collection *Catastrophic Bliss,* for which Hardy won the Griot-Stadler Prize for Poetry in

2012. In these poems, Hardy alludes to figures as disparate as Persephone, Dante, Fernando Pessoa, Marianne Moore, Stevie Wonder, and Barack Obama. The book's title poem evokes an overabundance of sweetness: as honey pours from the sky, ants are "intoxicated" by the sweetness, and cooking pots overflow. But the poet reminds the reader that sweetness must be earned, and that by summoning it "we / chanted / until our / throats tore / to ribbons."

The poem "Making Stars with Jacob Lawrence" describes an imagined visit with painter and collagist Jacob Lawrence, most noted for his works on the theme of the Great Migration of African Americans from the Deep South to Northern cities such as Chicago. White linens drying on garden clothesline evoke memories of a Lorca play in "Linens Near a Ghost Town." In "Habits," the poet muses on memories from a Catholic school classroom.

Kingdom

In *Kingdom*, his fourth collection, Hardy "uses a mix of silence and incantatory language to evoke subjugation and revolt," according to a writer for *Publishers Weekly*. The poems reflect on religion, violence, and redemption, exhorting the reader to look unflinchingly at what is frightening or shameful, rather than looking away. The poet alludes to the 9/11 attack on the twin towers in New York City, and refers to both government-kept secrets and to the private secrets of individuals, suggesting the toxic nature of unacknowledged sins.

Finding the book's language sometimes distracting, the *Publishers Weekly* contributor described *Kingdom* as a serious collection in which the poet calls for respectful attention and offers "gorgeous lament without melodrama." Though Hardy insists that people accept responsibility for what is wrong in the world, he also offers hope for positive change.

Radioactive Starlings

Hardy's 2017 collection, *Radioactive Starlings: Poems,* addresses themes of journeys, memory, injustice, and identity. The poet's time spent in North Africa and the Middle East are evident influences in the book. The poem "Walking Jerusalem," for example, alludes to the work of Palestinian poet Mahmoud Darwish; in several others, the Portuguese writer Fernando Pessoa appears as a starling. And in "The Silence in Sunlight," Hardy refers to both the police shooting of Alton Sterling in Baton Rouge, Louisiana in 2016 and to the image of activist Iesha Evans peacefully confronting riot police during a protest sparked by the killing.

"The transnational character of Hardy's verse enables the poet to empathize with the downtrodden across a broad spectrum of cultures, ranging from the Muslim . . . to the Christian. The universality of his vision brings the past into sharp relief in terms of the present, and, above all, his humanity is seen to permeate his awareness of present sorrows against a backdrop of age-old conflict," said *Virily* reviewer Lois Henderson. A contributor to *Publishers Weekly* described *Radioactive Starlings* as "an illuminating, if occasionally difficult, collection."

■ **Biographical and Critical Sources**

PERIODICALS

Publishers Weekly, March 3, 2008, review of *The Headless Saints;* September 1, 2015, review of *Kingdom;* October 16, 2017, review of *Radioactive Starlings: Poems*, p. 48.

ONLINE

Myronn Hardy Website, http://www.myronnhardy. com (March 23, 2018).

Phoebe, http://phoebejournal.com/ (March 23, 2018), Joe Hall, review of *The Headless Saints.*

Virily, https://virily.com/ (March 23, 2018), Lois Henderson, review of *Radioactive Starlings.**

Daniel L. Haulman

1949-

■ Personal

Born 1949; married Ellen Evans; children: Evan. *Education:* University of Southwestern Louisiana, B.A.; University of New Orleans, M.A.; Auburn University, Ph.D., 1983.

■ Addresses

Home—Montgomery, AL.

■ Career

Air Force Historical Research Agency, Montgomery, AL, chief of Organizational History Division, 1982—; former faculty member, Huntington College, Auburn University Montgomery, and Faulkner University; former high school teacher.

■ Awards, Honors

Milo B. Howard Award.

■ Writings

Wings of Hope: The U.S. Air Force and Humanitarian Airlift Operations, Air Force History and Museums Program (Washington, DC), 1997.

The United States Air Force and Humanitarian Airlift Operations, 1947-1994, Air Force History and Museums Program (Washington, DC), 1998.

One Hundred Years of Flight: USAF Chronology of Significant Air and Space Events, 1903-2002, Air Force History and Museums Program, in association with Air University Press (Maxwell Air Force Base, AL), 2003.

(With Joseph Caver and Jerome Ennels) *The Tuskegee Airmen: An Illustrated History, 1939-1949,* NewSouth Books (Montgomery, AL), 2011.

Eleven Myths about the Tuskegee Airmen, NewSouth Books (Montgomery, AL), 2012.

The Tuskegee Airmen Chronology: A Detailed Timeline of the Red Tails and Other Black Pilots of World War II, NewSouth Books (Montgomery, AL), 2017.

■ Sidelights

Daniel L. Haulman is a historian and writer who is chief of the Organizational History Division at the Air Force Historical Research Agency. He holds degrees from the University of Southwestern Louisiana, the University of New Orleans, and Auburn University, where he completed his Ph.D. in 1983. He is the author of several books about U.S. Air Force history.

Wings of Hope

Wings of Hope: The U.S. Air Force and Humanitarian Airlift Operations presents a history of U.S. humanitarian airlifts from 1945 through the early 1990s. Among these was the Berlin airlift, which began in 1948 after the Soviet Union blockaded the city in an attempt to force out legitimate occupation forces in the Western sectors of the city. The blockade cut off supplies of food, heating fuel, and other items crucial to Berlin residents. Instead of a military response, U.S. President Harry S. Truman ordered a humanitarian operation. American planes based in England and in West Germany flew over Berlin and dropped supplies of clothing, fuel, food, and medicines. The blockade lasted for almost a year, during which the Air Force dropped more than 1.5 million tons of materials to Berliners.

Airlift missions continued through the Korean War, the Vietnam War, the Gulf War, and subsequent crises. In 1992, the United States joined an international airlift organized by the United Nations High Commissioner for Refugees to drop food and medicine to residents of Sarajevo, the capital of Bosnia and Herzegovina, who were living under siege by Bosnian Serb Army. The airlift, with some interruptions, ran until 1996. The United States made more than 4,500 flights as a participant in this airlift.

The United States Air Force and Humanitarian Airlift Operations, 1947-1994

The United States Air Force and Humanitarian Airlift Operations, 1947-1994 supplements previous publications on the history of Air Force humanitarian airlifts. As Haulman notes in the book's introduction, humanitarian missions have been part of the U.S. military tradition since before the creation of an independent U.S. Air Force in 1947. Aircraft from the U.S. Army dropped food supplies to flooded areas in south Texas in 1919; in 1922 military planes rescued trapped miners in California. In subsequent years, military planes bombed ice jams on rivers to save crucial bridges and other infrastructure, and dropped food and other supplies to victims of floods and other natural disasters. Perhaps most dramatic among these interventions was the 1935 bombing of Hawaii's Mauna Loa volcano, in order to stop its lava from destroying the city of Hilo.

Military flights to provide aid to foreign nations also predated the creation of the Air Force. During the 1930s, the U.S. military planes dropped medical supplies to earthquake victims in Chile. During World War II, the army's 2nd Bombardment Wing dropped diphtheria vaccination supplies to a vessel escorting a British aircraft carrier. Also during and immediately after the war, U.S. military planes dropped food to starving people in France and in the Netherlands.

After 1947, the U.S. Air Force continued to conduct domestic airlifts while also expanding these operations to countries most affected by the consolidation of the Soviet bloc in Eastern Europe. The escalation of the Cold War required the United States to maintain a robust military presence in Europe during peacetime. The large cargo planes used to supply these troops were also capable of delivering substantial amounts of relief supplies.

Haulman writes that although airdrops were targeted at specific communities in extreme need, the benefits of this aid spread across the entire

economic and political life of recipient countries. What is more, such aid benefits the United States as a powerful diplomatic tool because it builds goodwill and also increases the opportunities for trade and other friendly interactions across the world. In addition, the experience of operating airlifts provides Air Force personnel with valuable training applicable to both military and humanitarian settings.

The Tuskegee Airmen and The Tuskegee Airmen Chronology

Several of Haulman's books focus on the Tuskegee Airmen, who were the first African American military pilots. African Americans were not allowed to serve as military pilots in World War I. But starting in 1940, they were accepted into pilot training at the Tuskegee Army Air Field and went on to form combat groups in the U.S. Army Air Force. These groups were deployed to North Africa, Sicily, and mainland Italy starting in 1943.

Written with Joseph Caver and Jerome Ennels, *The Tuskegee Airmen: An Illustrated History, 1939-1949* provides an overview of the subject, from how the airmen were trained to the specific missions they flew during World War II. The book also includes the stories of support personnel such as mechanics, parachute riggers, navigators, and others who were part of the Tuskegee units. Writing in *HistoryNet*, Philip Handelman said that this story, which concludes with the Tuskegee pilots' success in integrating the Air Force in 1949, is "powerfully told."

In *The Tuskegee Airmen Chronology: A Detailed Timeline of the Red Tails and Other Black Pilots of World War II*, Haulman offers a concise but comprehensive history of the Tuskegee Airmen. Though much of the book deals with World War II, the author also discusses events before and after that period. He notes significant first achievements for African American pilots, and discusses both combat and non-combat missions. In addition, he provides information on the airmen's post-military careers.

Eleven Myths about the Tuskegee Airmen

In *Eleven Myths about the Tuskegee Airmen*, Haulman discusses misconceptions that have arisen about the famous African American pilots. First was the belief that these pilots were inferior to white pilots, a belief that the author firmly sets right by pointing to the facts. Among other data, he cites air victory credits for the 332nd Fighter Group—one comprised of Tuskegee Airmen—that were higher than those for two of the white groups. Another misconception is that no bomber being escorted by the Tuskegee Airmen was shot down during the war; in fact, The Tuskegee Airmen lost at least seven bombers during 1944 and early 1945.

The author clarifies the truth such romantic claims that the Tuskegee Airmen sank a German destroyer and were the first U.S. military pilots to shoot down German jets, and about less dramatic beliefs, such as that all Tuskegee Airmen were fighter pilots: in reality, many airmen flew non-combat missions, and others were trained as support personnel. The book received praise for its thorough research and its documentation of key facts about the Tuskegee Airmen.

■ Biographical and Critical Sources

PERIODICALS

Publishers Weekly, November 6, 2017, review of *The Tuskegee Airmen Chronology: A Detailed Timeline of the Red Tails and Other Black Pilots of World War II.*

ONLINE

HistoryNet, http://www.historynet.com/ (March 25, 2018), review of *The Tuskegee Airmen: An Illustrated History: 1939-1949.**

L.V. Hay

■ **Also Known As**

Lucy V. Hay

■ **Personal**

Married; children: three.

■ **Addresses**

Home—Devon, England.

■ **Career**

Writer, novelist, script editor, script reader, and film producer. Associate producer of the British films *Deviation,* 2012, and *Assassin,* 2015; script editor and advisor on numerous other produced features and shorts. Founding organizer of London Screenwriters' Festival.

■ **Writings**

The Other Twin (novel), Orenda Books (London, England), 2017.

NONFICTION; AS LUCY V. HAY

Writing & Selling Thriller Screenplays, Oldcastle Books (Harpenden, England), 2013.
Writing & Selling Drama Screenplays, Oldcastle Books (Harpenden, England), 2015.
Writing Diverse Characters for Fiction, TV & Film, Kamera Books (Harpenden, England), 2017.

Also author of the blog *Bang2Write.*

■ **Sidelights**

L.V. Hay, also known as Lucy V. Hay, is a novelist, script editor, and blogger, whose blog, *Bang2Write,* is a consultancy to help writers learn and improve upon their craft. She has been an associate producer on British films and has read for indie production companies, screen agencies, investment initiatives, producers, filmmakers, and writers. In her debut crime novel, *The Other Twin,* Poppy Wade returns to her home in Brighton, England from London when her younger sister, India Rutledge, falls off a bridge over a railway and is killed. Even though Poppy had not talked to India in more than four years after Poppy went off to graduate school, she is not convinced that that official explanation that India committed suicide is what really happened. As a result, she sets out to conduct her own investigation. "Hay may not be a name you are familiar with but this may be about to change as with her debut psychological thriller," wrote a contributor to the *Last Word Book Review* website.

The main drivers of Poppy's investigation are India's laptop and her blog, on which India seems to have created an entirely new identity and life for herself. "Hay uses the anonymity of the internet as a launching pad for a mystery of hidden lives and personal secrets," wrote a contributor to the *Crime by the Book* website. *Nudge* website contributor James Pierson remarked that Hay "has crafted a tale of hidden lives and the perils of social media."

Poppy zeroes in on trying to figure out who the person is who goes by the code name "Jenny" because India's last post was addressed to Jenny.

Poppy also ventures into the party and club scene in Brighton to find out more and to a seaside cafe where India once worked after she had lost her job as an accountant. Along the way, Poppy reconnects with her estranged mother and with her old boyfriend, Matthew Temple, whom she abandoned years earlier. As Poppy delves deeper into her sister's death she starts to uncover some disturbing truths.

Poppy begins to suspect that Matthew may be involved, along with his powerful parents and his twin sister, Ana. Even though they have offered to help Poppy, she becomes suspicious of their motives as she becomes more and more convinced that the Temples' veneer of respectability is hiding something sinister. Poppy also believes that India may have discovered something about the mysterious Jenny that may have led to her sister's death. Meanwhile, Poppy starts to realize she must reevaluate her own life and face up to things from her past while also reexamining her relationships and taking an honest look at the people closest to her. Poppy's investigation leads her down numerous dead ends as she faces drama within her own family and questions herself about trying to rekindle her romance with Matthew.

Throughout the narrative, Hay includes snippets from India's blog. The novel is narrated by Jenny but also includes third-person chapters from a man enthralled by "She Who Must Be Obeyed." A *Crime by the Book* website contributor noted: "*The Other Twin* is engaging and relentlessly absorbing—it's no surprise that author Hay has a background in the film industry, considering how movie-worthy her debut psychological thriller is." A reviewer writing for the *Crime Review* website remarked on the diversity of characters in the novel and called *The Other Twin* "an atmospheric, well-paced and interesting read that blends psychological thriller with an old-fashioned whodunnit in a compelling way," and added later in the same review: "The other factor that is really impressive is the way that the atmosphere in Brighton is built up."

■ Biographical and Critical Sources

PERIODICALS

Publishers Weekly, October 2, 2017, review of *The Other Twin*, p. 120.

ONLINE

Bang2Write website, http://www.bang2write.com/about-me (March 27, 2018).
Crime by the Book, http://crimebythebook.com/ (July 2, 2017), review of *The Other Twin*.
Crime Review, https://thecrimereview.com/ (July 21, 2017), review of *The Other Twin*.
Last Word Book Review, https://thelastwordbookreview.wordpress.com/ (July 18, 2017), review of *The Other Twin*.
Lucy V. Hay Website, http://www.lucyvhayauthor.com (March 27, 2018).
Nudge, https://nudge-book.com/ (August 6, 2017), James Pierson, review of *The Other Twin*.*

Sharon Heath

■ Personal

Children: two. *Education:* University of California, Los Angeles; Immaculate Heart College, M.A., 1982. *Hobbies and other interests:* Anglophile and a film buff.

■ Addresses

Home—CA. *Office*—Los Angeles, CA.

■ Career

Writer, novelist, and psychoanalyst. C.G. Jung Institute of Los Angeles, Los Angeles, CA, faculty member, 1993—; Jungian analyst in private practice, Los Angeles, 1994—.

■ Writings

The History of My Body ("The Fleur Trilogy"), Thomas-Jacob Publishing (Dalton, FL), 2016.
Tizita ("The Fleur Trilogy"), Thomas-Jacob Publishing (Dalton, FL), 2017.

Contributor to journals and websites, including *Psychological Perspectives, Jung Journal, Journal of Jungian Theory and Practice, Huffington Post,* and *TerraSpheres.* Former associate editor of *Psychological Perspectives* and guest editor of the special issue "The Child Within/The Child Without."

■ Sidelights

A certified Jungian analyst in private practice, Sharon Heath also writes fiction and nonfiction. Her works primarily focus on the interplay of sci-ence and spirit, politics, and pop culture, and contemplation and community. Heath is also an educator and public speaker who has given talks in the United States and Canada on a wide range of topics, including soul in social media, belonging, envy, gossip, and secrecy. Heath is also the author of "The Fleur Trilogy."

The History of My Body

The trilogy begins with *The History of My Body,* which introduces readers to Fleur Robins, a young girl believed by those around her to be weird and possibly autistic but who may really be a genius. In an article on the *Huffington Post* website, Heath mentioned *The History of My Body* as an example of novels with youthful protagonists who remind older readers that their younger lives were not as easy as they recall. Heath writes in the *Huffington Post* that adult fiction featuring child protagonists undergoing a catharsis gives "us a chance to revisit our early years with imagination and wisdom and see the world and our own lives with new eyes."

In *The History of My Body,* Fleur lives with her eccentric family on her father's estate in Philadelphia, Pennsylvania. Fleur is largely ignored by her family. Her mother is an alcoholic, and her father is an activist out to stop the evil abortionists. Fleur is an odd child who likes to whirl around and seems preoccupied with God, what she calls "the void," and her devotion to her grandfather. Then Fleur gets a new tutor, Adam Manus, who sees that Fleur has a lot of potential. He introduces her to Stanley H. Fiske, a Nobel Prize winner who ends up bringing Fleur to the California Institute of Technology, where he mentors Fleur in quantum physics. Fleur quickly proves that her tutor was right in recognizing her genius as she begins making important discoveries that may help phase out the use of fossil fuels. Still, Fleur is very naive and ends up losing her virginity by no conscious choice of her own.

"In her wise, superbly crafted debut novel, author Sharon Heath connects a series of highly improbable events into a tightly knit story about a self-taught young girl who believes her coming of age is a wonderful example of the butterfly effect: or, as Fleur came to understand nonlinear systems, a personal development with a sensitive dependence on initial conditions," wrote Malcolm R. Campbell for the *Malcolm's Round Table* website. A *Literary Aficionado* website contributor remarked: "Heath must be commended—there is a thin, dangerous line for a novelist between such complexity being the beautiful quirk of main character and an indication of poor planning and execution by a writer unable to bring their broad worldview into manageable scope. It is clear that Heath has been purposeful and exacting."

Tizita

The next book in "The Fleur Trilogy," *Tizita*, finds that Fleur is now a recognized physics wunderkind who still has difficulty understanding people, especially when it comes to love and sex. Fleur is working on a project to address climate change when it suddenly stalls. Her fiancé, Assefa, born in Ethiopia, ends up taking off following Fleur's twenty-first birthday to try to find his father, who has disappeared during an investigation into the Ark of the Covenant's potential discovery in Ethiopia. Meanwhile, Fleur has turned her attention to contemplating the parallel worlds theory in physics.

Fleur ends up going to the Gombe Stream Chimpanzee Reserve to console herself after learning that Assefa, who has found his father, has decided to remain in Ethiopia for a while. The decision is made after he comes across Makeda Getey, his beautiful childhood friend who is helping to run an orphanage for children with AIDS. Subplots include Fleur trying help her best friend who is in an abusive relationship while also dealing with a new research assistant who seems to be falling in love with her. "Heath's adroit writing makes Fleur's remarkable life consistently captivating," wrote a *Publishers Weekly* contributor.

■ Biographical and Critical Sources

PERIODICALS

Publishers Weekly, October 23, 2017, review of *Tizita*, p. 62.

ONLINE

Huffington Post, https://www.huffingtonpost.com/ (April 3, 2012), Sharon Heath, "7 Child Protagonists That Adults Can Relate To."

Literary Aficionado, http://literaryaficionado.com/ (April 3, 2017), review of *The History of My Body*.

Malcolm's Round Table, https://malcolmsroundtable.com/ (February 5, 2012), Malcolm R. Campbell, review of *The History of My Body*.

Sharon Heath Website, http://www.sharonheath.com (March 28, 2018).*

Susan Henderson

1967-

■ Personal

Born March 25, 1967.

■ Addresses

Home—King's Park, NY.

■ Career

Writer; founder of blog and *LitPark* (a "literary playground for writers and artists"); former counselor.

■ Awards, Honors

Five Pushcard Prize nominations; Academy of American Poets Prize.

■ Writings

Up from the Blue, Harper (New York, NY), 2010.
The Flicker of Old Dreams, HarperPerennial (New York, NY), 2018.

■ Sidelights

Susan Henderson is a writer and former counselor whose work has received five Pushcart Prize nominations as well as an Academy of American Poets Prize. The author of two well-received novels, she is also the founder of the literary blog *LitPark.*

Up from the Blue

Dysfunctional family dynamics resurface painfully when Tillie, the protagonist of Henderson's debut novel, *Up from the Blue,* gives birth to her first child. With her husband overseas and her mother out of the picture, Tillie must turn to her estranged father for help when she goes into labor prematurely. Reconnecting with him brings back difficult memories. Tillie had been a feisty child who had dearly loved her eccentrically artistic mother, Mara, but saw little of her father, a military officer who was often away from home. All seemed well enough until the day that Mara had suddenly taken ill and refused to leave her bed. With their father away from home, eight-year-old Tillie and her older brother Phil had had to fend for themselves for several days. On his return, their father responded angrily to this troubling situation, eventually moving the family from New Mexico to a new home in Washington, DC, where, to the children's horror, their mother is nowhere to be found.

The birth of her own daughter forces Tillie to confront the complex emotions she has harbored since her mother's disappearance. She remembers the fun and affection and joy that had emanated from Mara, and that their father had been unable to provide them after Mara's crisis. She remembers her loneliness, her acting out in school, and the one friendship she developed—with an African American classmate who was bused to the school. Eventually, Tillie comes to understand better why her father had acted as he did, abandoning Mara at a time when her particular mental illness, which would later become known as bipolar disorder, had been stigmatized and little understood.

The sensitivity with which Henderson handles the novel's themes of loss, family dysfunction, and grief favorably impressed reviewers of *Up from the Blue.* A contributor to *Publishers Weekly* described Tillie's emotional journey as "beautiful, funny, sad, and complicated." Writing in *Library Journal,* Bette-Lee Fox hailed the book as "a triumphant debut."

In an interview for *Psychology Today* conducted by Jennifer Haupt, Henderson said that she drew from some of her own memories in creating the eight-year-old Tillie. Like her protagonist, Henderson had been a biter at school, wanting friends but lacking the skills to get along with other kids. Asked about Tillie's toughness, Henderson explained that although Tillie becomes self-reliant because she is forced to take care of herself, she has also inherited some inner strength from her parents. From her mother, she learns to embrace her emotional self; her father, on the other hand, provides her with stability and a sense of order.

The Flicker of Old Dreams

Set in the small town of Petroleum, Montana, *The Flicker of Old Dreams* is the story of a shy, withdrawn woman whose perspective on life is changed when a neighbor suddenly reappears after a long absence. Two decades earlier, a teenager had died a grain elevator accident, and the incident prompted lasting anger and resentment among the population. Petroleum's economy suffered, and many people moved away. Mary, a quiet woman who works in her father's mortuary, has resigned herself to a life in which it is easier for her to interact with the deceased than with the living. Though she is lonely and had once nurtured dreams of an artistic career, she takes comfort in the fact that her work provides the town with a necessary and compassionate service.

Robert, the brother of the teen who had been killed, surprises everyone in Petroleum when he suddenly returns to town. He had left soon after his brother's death, but now wants to spend as much time as possible with his dying mother. He and Mary are drawn to each other. Being with Robert enables Mary to see her town as it really is: a place of cruelty, pettiness, and intolerance. Also through her relationship with Robert, Mary begins to imagine a different future for herself. *Booklist* reviewer Melissa Norstedt admired the way the novel addresses Mary's struggles to balance duty toward others with her responsibility toward herself. A writer for *Publishers Weekly* deemed *The Flicker of Old Dreams* "a contemplative and memorable novel."

■ Biographical and Critical Sources

PERIODICALS

Booklist, September 1, 2010, Aleksandra Walker, review of *Up from the Blue,* p. 47; February 1, 2018, Melissa Norstedt, review of *The Flicker of Old Dreams,* p. 26.
Library Journal, August, 2010, Bette-Lee Fox, review of *Up from the Blue,* p. 69.
Publishers Weekly, August 23, 2010, review of *Up from the Blue,* p. 27; January 15, 2018, review of *The Flicker of Old Dreams,* p. 32.

ONLINE

Psychology Today Online, https://www.psychologytoday.com/ (March 19, 2018), Jennifer Haupt, interview with Henderson.
Susan Henderson's LitPark, http://www.litpark.com (March 19, 2018).*

Alexander Hertel-Fernandez

1986-

■ Personal

Born October 10, 1986; son of Adriela Fernandez and Thomas W. Hertel; married Nathaniel Fuller West (a lawyer), 2017. *Education:* Northwestern University, B.A., 2008; Harvard University, A.M., Ph.D., 2016.

■ Career

Columbia University School of International and Public Affairs, New York, NY, assistant professor, 2016—.

■ Member

National Academy of Social Insurance

■ Awards, Honors

Grants from National Science Foundation, Russel Sage Foundation, Dirksen Congressional Center, Columbia University, Harvard Center for American Political Studies, Harvard Weatherhead Center, and Harvard Kennedy School; Scholars Strategy Network Graduate Fellowship, 2012-13; Harvard Benjamin Bainbridge Tregoe Graduate Fellowship, 2015-16.

■ Writings

Politics at Work: How Employers Deploy Their Workers to Shape American Politics and Policy, Oxford University Press (New York, NY), 2018.

Contributor to books, including (with Theda Skopcol) *Congress and Policymaking in the 21st Century,* edited by Jeffrey Jenkins and Eric Patashnik, Cambridge University Press, 2016. Contributor to periodicals, including *Bulletin of the World Health Organization; Health Affairs; Social Service Review; Perspectives on Politics; Studies in American Political Development; Journal of Health Politics, Policy, and Law; PS: Political Science & Politics;* and *Journal of Politics.*

■ Sidelights

Political scientist Alexander Hertel-Fernandez, an assistant professor at Columbia University School of International and Public Affairs, studies the U.S. political economy. In particular, he examines how organized interests and wealthy donors shape national and state policy. Hertel-Fernandez graduated from Northwestern University in 2008 with a degree in political science, and earned a Ph.D. in government and social policy from Harvard University in 2016.

Hertel-Fernandez's first book, *Politics at Work: How Employers Deploy Their Workers to Shape American Politics and Policy,* looks at the ways in which employers in the United States have increasingly sought to control workers' political stances and voting behaviors. As the author explained in an interview with Matt Terry posted on the Columbia University School of International and Public Affairs website, business managers recruit employees into politics "to help company bottom lines." Using data from surveys and interviews, Hertel-Fernandez examines the how prevalent this practice is, how workers respond to it, and how it affects public policy and elections.

As Hertel-Fernandez explains in the book, it is legal for private employers to require their workers to volunteer for political campaigns on pain of losing their jobs. It is also legal for a company to inform its workers of which political candidates it supports and to suggest that these candidates' defeat could result in undefined negative consequences for company employees. Companies can also require workers to attend campaign rallies, without pay, or to lobby for policies that would benefit the employer. What is more, the author points out, "there are no federal legal protections for employees who are fired or retaliated against for refusing to participate in political activities."

While increasingly prevalent in the twenty-first century, employer meddling in workers' political activities dates back to the 1896 presidential race between populist William Jennings Bryan and pro-business candidate William McKinley, whose supporters told workers that companies could not stay in business unless McKinley were elected. While the practice continued into the 1900s, it abated until the 2000s when new technologies, increased unemployment, and political polarization sparked increased efforts to control the political agenda through the coercement of employees. Hertel-Fernandez discusses the actions of GE, Georgia Pacific, and pharmaceutical companies—one of which has created a points system by which employees can win free vacations by collecting points for each of their political activities. He also discusses the implications of the *Citizens United v. Federal Election Commission* decision, in which the U.S. Supreme Court ruled in 2010 that the government could not restrict the amount of money that corporations and unions could spend on ads and other campaign tools. In essence, the decision gives companies and unions the right to spend as much as they wish on materials intended to influence voting.

The author concedes that employer political recruitment can push more people to get out and vote. Even so, he argues that the practice presents real threats to the democratic system because workers are often pressured into political activity and are reluctant to object because of the economic power that their employers hold over them. He explains that, for their part, companies view this type of political mobilization as a more effective means of influencing politics than contributing money to political campaigns or buying election ads. Hertel-Fernandez ends the book with ideas for reform and a call to end the business behaviors that are "most coercive and troubling."

A writer for *Kirkus Reviews* found *Politics at Work* "often dry" but also "remarkably important." In *Publishers Weekly*, a reviewer considered the book's message "eye-opening and timely," and praised the author for having performed "a great public service with this accessible and rigorously documented study."

■ Biographical and Critical Sources

BOOKS

Hertel-Fernandez, Alexander, *Politics at Work: How Employers Deploy Their Workers to Shape American Politics and Policy*, Oxford University Press (New York, NY), 2018.

PERIODICALS

Kirkus Reviews, January 15, 2018, review of *Politics at Work*.

New York Times, April 16, 2017, "Weddings: Alexander Hertel-Fernandez, Nathaniel West."

Publishers Weekly, October 30, 2017, review of *Politics at Work*, p. 67.

ONLINE

Columbia University, School of International and Public Affairs Website, https://sipa.columbia.edu/ (March 20, 2018), Hertel-Fernandez faculty profile; Matt Terry, interview with Hertel-Fernandez.*

Catherine Hewitt

■ Personal

Female. *Education:* Royal Holloway, University of London, B.A. (with first-class honors); Courtauld Institute of Art, M.A.; Courtauld Institute and Royal Holloway, Ph.D., 2012. *Hobbies and other interests:* Reading, cooking, and taking walks with her cockerpoo.

■ Addresses

Home—Surrey, England.

■ Career

Writer, biographer, translator, independent scholar.

■ Writings

Buddhism, Thomson Learning (Stamford, CT), 1995.
The Mistress of Paris: The 19th-Century Courtesan Who Built an Empire on a Secret, Icon Books (London, England), 2015, Thomas Dunne Books (New York, NY), 2017.
Renoir's Dancer: The Secret Life of Suzanne Valadon, St. Martin's Press (New York, NY), 2018.

■ Sidelights

British author Catherine Hewitt holds a doctorate in French art and literature and also works as a French translator. Her dissertation, *The Formation of the Family in 19th-Century French Literature and Art*, established Hewitt as an expert in French his-

tory and culture of the nineteenth century, and she has gone on to use this background to inform lively popular biographies. She is the author of two well-received works, *The Mistress of Paris: The 19th-Century Courtesan Who Built an Empire on a Secret* and *Renoir's Dancer: The Secret Life of Suzanne Valadon*.

In an online *Trip Fiction* interview, Hewitt commented on how she manages to make biography both interesting and accessible to non-academic readers: "I ensure there is complete underlying academic integrity in the work, but I also try to humanise the story. I'll add colour through what may have been seen or smelt at the time, or what the prevailing weather was on a given day. But only if supported by research. It took me slightly longer than two years to complete my research for *Renoir's Dancer*."

The Mistress of Paris

Hewitt blends a biography of the Comtesse Valtesse de la Bigne with a history of mid- to late-nineteenth-century Paris in *The Mistress of Paris*. Valtesse was indeed the mistress or inspiration of many men. She was painted by Edouard Manet, informed the main character of Emile Zola's novel *Nana*, and had rumored affairs with the powerful and mighty, including Napoleon III and the future king of England, Edward VII. She assembled a fortune in her lifetime, with three mansions and carriages and artworks that were envied by all. Yet behind this glamorous and hedonistic existence was the secret of the book's subtitle. Valtesse was not a comtesse or any form of royalty. Instead she was born into poverty, living in the slums of Paris as a child and working as a street prostitute. Through grit and determination and the fortune of good looks, she raised herself out of such humble origins to take Paris by storm, becoming a celebrity of the time but always hiding her damning secret.

Reviewing *The Mistress of Paris* in *Library Journal,* Stacy Shaw termed it an "entertaining read . . . [that] will likely appeal to history buffs as well as those who enjoy a well-written biography." A *Kirkus Reviews* critic also had praise, noting: "A biographer debuts with the astonishing story of Comtesse Valtesse de la Bigne." The critic added: "Her intriguing portrait shines through. A thoroughly researched and clearly written account of a determined and talented woman and of an era." Similarly, *French Studies* reviewer Sara Phenix observed: "Hewitt's monograph is a valuable contribution to our understanding of the complex lives of the great nineteenth-century courtesans, and proves to be a textual encounter much like, according to the rapturous descriptions in Hewitt's book, an evening spent with Valtesse herself—both pleasurable and edifying." London *Observer Online* writer Alexander Larman also had a high assessment, calling *The Mistress of Paris* an "enthralling story, told with both conviction and sympathy," as did online *Bookbag* reviewer Luke Marlowe, who dubbed the work a "skillfully woven tapestry of a fascinating life" and "a hugely interesting and surprisingly involving read." *Irish Examiner Online* writer Liz Ryan termed it a "handsome boudoir book," while *Historical Novel Society* website reviewer Elicia Parkinson found it to be a "fascinating read about a woman who started with nothing but ended with everything, including respect."

Renoir's Dancer

With *Renoir's Dancer,* Hewitt again offers a biography of a famous French woman of the late nineteenth century who had a secret. Suzanne Valadon became a famed model of the Impressionists but came from humble origins. The illegitimate daughter of a linen maid from the provinces, she was originally named Marie and was brought to Montmartre by her mother, where she changed her name to Suzanne and as a teenager was attracting the attention of Impressionist painters as a fine model. At eighteen she gave birth to an illegitimate child who became a famous painter of Montmartre scenes, Maurice Utrillo. She had affairs with Toulouse Lautrec and the composer Eric Satie, neither of which went well. She was the model for the dancer in Renoir's famous *Dance at Bourgival,* and she had yet another secret: she was a fine painter in her own right. She studied with Edgar Degas and created vibrant still lifes and portraits, with her work accepted for exhibition in 1894 at the Salon de la Société Nationale des Beaux-Arts. "Her

talent was towering, her breakthrough simply inspiring and her life genuinely extraordinary," noted Glasgow's *Sunday Herald Online* reviewer Hugh MacDonald, who added: "She was also one of a kind. Valadon loved sex and drink and never denied herself either." MacDonald found this a "compelling book."

Reviewing *Renoir's Dancer* in *Booklist,* Donna Seaman felt that "Hewitt's straight-ahead telling of Valadon's dramatic, many-faceted story captures this artist . . . with precision, narrative drive, and low-key awe." A *Kirkus Reviews* critic similarly called the biography a "well-researched tribute to and resurrection of a master of fin de siècle art," while a *Publishers Weekly* contributor termed it a "book that reads like an opera libretto revolving around a pioneering spirit who bristled at the limiting label of 'woman artist.'" Online *Bookbag* writer John Lloyd also voiced praise, commenting: "You get a very clear picture . . . at the hands of this author, and throughout the story the woman's multiple changes in name, persona and status are just fragments of the multifarious things you can take on board. Certainly, . . . I think that if you are in the market for hefty books where biography and the history of art collide, you will find little to disappoint you here." Writing in the *Washington Post Online*, Reagan Upshaw observed that in this "entertaining book . . . Hewitt makes her subject's life an armature on which to hang a history of the Belle Époque, and she includes erudite digressions into the major events of the time." Still higher praise came from *Historical Novel Society* website reviewer Janice Derr, who noted: "Hewitt's Paris sparkles with life and energy. The rich layering of details along with the eccentric cast of characters reads like a highly engrossing novel." *Sydney Morning Herald Online* contributor Steven Carroll was also impressed, commenting that "Hewitt tells her story with the colourful immediacy of a Renoir." Likewise, *Library Journal Online* reviewer Barbara Hoffert concluded: "Hewitt here paints a remarkable life."

■ Biographical and Critical Sources

PERIODICALS

Booklist, September 1, 1995, Ilene Cooper, review of *Buddhism*, p. 56; January 1, 2018, Donna Seaman, review of *Renoir's Dancer: The Secret Life of Suzanne Valadon*, p. 30.

French Studies, January, 2017, Sara Phenix, review of *The Mistress of Paris: The 19th-Century Courtesan Who Built an Empire on a Secret*, p. 124.

Kirkus Reviews, November 1, 2016, review of *The Mistress of Paris;* November 15, 2017, review of *Renoir's Dancer.*

Library Journal, February 1, 2017, Stacy Shaw, review of *The Mistress of Paris,* p. 87.

Publishers Weekly, November 13, 2017, review of *Renoir's Dancer,* p. 51.

ONLINE

Andrew Lownie Agency Website, http://www.andrewlownie.co.uk/ (February 13, 2018), "Catherine Hewitt."

Biographers, https://www.biographers.club/ (February 13, 2018), "Catherine Hewitt."

Bookbag, http://www.thebookbag.co.uk/ (November 5, 2015), Luke Marlowe, review of *The Mistress of Paris;* (February 13, 2018), John Lloyd, review of *Renoir's Dancer.*

Bookpage Online, https://bookpage.com/ (March 19, 2018), "What They're Reading: Catherine Hewitt."

Catherine Hewitt Website, http://catherinehewitt.co.uk (February 13, 2018).

Historical Novel Society, https://historicalnovelsociety.org/ (February 1, 2017), Elicia Parkinson, review of *The Mistress of Paris;* Janice Derr, review of *Renoir's Dancer.*

Irish Examiner Online, https://www.irishexaminer.com/ (November 31, 2015), Liz Ryan, review of *The Mistress of Paris.*

Library Journal Online, https://reviews.libraryjournal.com/ (September 11, 2017), Barbara Hoffert, review of *Renoir's Dancer.*

Observer Online, https://www.theguardian.com/ (November 22, 2105), Alexander Larman, review of *The Mistress of Paris.*

Sunday Herald Online, http://www.heraldscotland.com/ (November 18, 2017), Hugh MacDonald, review of *Renoir's Dancer.*

Sydney Morning Herald Online, https://www.smh.com.au/ (December 14, 2017), Steven Carroll, review of *Renoir's Dancer.*

Trip Fiction, https://www.tripfiction.com/ (October 13, 2017), "Talking to Author Catherine Hewitt about *Renoir's Dancer.*"

Washington Post Online, https://www.washingtonpost.com/ (March 12, 2018), Reagan Upshaw, review of *Renoir's Dancer.**

Aimee Hix

1971-

■ **Personal**

Born 1971; married; children: one daughter.

■ **Addresses**

Home—VA.

■ **Career**

Mystery writer; formerly worked as defense contractor.

■ **Member**

Sisters in Crime.

■ **Writings**

What Doesn't Kill You, Midnight Ink (Woodbury, MN), 2018.

■ **Sidelights**

Aimee Hix's debut as a mystery writer is the novel *What Doesn't Kill You*, a work that is the culmination of a long-held dream. "Ever since I realized that books weren't things that just were, that people made them, I had in my mind that I would be a writer at some point," Hix revealed in an interview with Hank Phillippi Ryan in *Big Thrill*. "I figured it would be after my career as Nancy Drew/FBI agent was over. Mostly, because my mother repeatedly told me that 'writer is not a real job—you need a real job.' So after the Nancy Drew/FBI agent thing fell through because of my eyesight, I got a 'real job' at a federal contractor and did that for twenty years."

Hix's protagonist is Willa Pennington, a former police officer working on becoming a licensed private investigator. "Willa," Hix said in an interview with John Valeri appearing on the website *Criminalelement.com*, "is the young woman I wish I had been and the woman I want my daughter to grow up to be. She's tough and takes no bullshit, but she's also someone who is caring and kind-hearted. She's actively dealing with emotional pain and loss instead of shoving it down like many fictional 'tough guy' types. She's capable of admitting she's wrong, but she won't allow embarrassment to cause her to drop the pursuit of justice. She's someone who will do the right thing even if it's not the first thing to mind. She's loyal but not to a fault." "Willa Pennington is the woman I wish I could have been at her age," Hix told Ryan. Heck, she's the woman I wish I could be now. She lives the axiom that being afraid and going ahead and doing it anyway is the best approach to life. And she was thrown for a loop when the thing she never thought would happen happened—she lost her best friend." As a result, "Willa trades in the badge for private investigation in an emotional moment," Hix told Valeri. "It's a life-changing emotional moment, and it's the right choice. Police work wasn't really what she was supposed to do with her life, even if the pursuit of justice is. There are trade-offs in each career and how each allows Willa to investigate." "Outwardly she does seem very tough," the author continued in her *Big Thrill* interview. "She's more prone to action than reflection, which is not uncommon amongst police. Michael, her late best friend, was her decoder ring for the more reflective/emotional side of the world. Losing him leaves her at a great disadvantage. I love that their relationship bucks the stereotypes that women are more emotional and men are more stoic."

In *What Doesn't Kill You,* Willa is performing a family favor for the granddaughter of her neighbors. She "has agreed to help Violet move out," wrote a *Publishers Weekly* reviewer, "as a favor to her good friends David and Susan Horowitz." In the process, however, she finds that Violet has disappeared and that her abusive boyfriend has been murdered. As an ex-police officer, Willa is not officially permitted to investigate the death, but that does not stop her from trying. "The result is a debut that saddles tough-girl noir with the heart of a cozy," declared a *Kirkus Reviews* contributor. "Hix's heroine is appealing enough to warrant a second chance."

In general, critics enjoyed Hix's first book. The author "shows a lot of restraint in her writing," assessed Kate Malmon in the online *Crimespree.* "She doesn't drop the entire story in the reader's lap at the start of the book. There isn't a page of exposition that you can dog ear to refer to later." "*What Doesn't Kill You* is Aimee Hix's debut novel," stated Kathy Reel in the *Reading Room,* "but if you didn't know that, you'd be hard pressed to realize it. This novel reads as smooth and seasoned as the middle of a series, not the beginning." "I enjoyed this tightly woven, multi-plot drama that had my adrenaline pumping," declared a reviewer writing for *Dru's Book Musings.* "This book is a great beginning to what I hope will be a long-running series and I look forward to the next exploits."

■ Biographical and Critical Sources

PERIODICALS

Kirkus Reviews, October 15, 2017, review of *What Doesn't Kill You.*
Publishers Weekly, November 13, 2017, review of *What Doesn't Kill You,* p. 42.

ONLINE

Aimee Hix Website, https://www.aimeehix.com (March 28, 2018).
Big Thrill, http://www.thebigthrill.org/ (December 31, 2017), Hank Phillippi Ryan, "Debut Author Spotlight: Aimee Hix."
Crimespree, http://crimespreemag.com/ (January 8, 2018), Kate Malmon, review of *What Doesn't Kill You.*
Criminalelement.com, https://www.criminalelement.com/ (January 8, 2018), John Valeri, "Q&A with Aimee Hix, Author of *What Doesn't Kill You.*"
Dru's Book Musings, https://notesfromme.wordpress.com/ (December 31, 2017), review of *What Doesn't Kill You.*
El's Book Reviews, https://elsbookreviews.blogspot.com/ (July 15, 2017), review of *What Doesn't Kill You.*
Reading Room, http://www.readingroom-readmore.com/ (January 8, 2018), Kathy Reel, review of *What Doesn't Kill You.**

Keely Hutton

■ Personal

Female. *Hobbies and other interests:* Playing piano, reading.

■ Addresses

Agent—Soumeya Bendimerad Roberts, HSG Agency, 37 W. 28th St., New York, NY 10001.

■ Career

Writer, journalist, and novelist. Former schoolteacher.

■ Awards, Honors

Highlights Foundation Writers Workshop scholarship at Chautauqua.

■ Writings

Soldier Boy (novel), afterword by Ricky Richard Anywar, Farrar, Straus and Giroux (New York, NY), 2017.

■ Sidelights

A former schoolteacher turned journalist, Keely Hutton is the author of *Soldier Boy*, a novel based on the wartime experiences of Ricky Richard Anywar. In 1989, at the age of fourteen, Anywar was forced to become a soldier in the guerrilla army of Ugandan warlord Joseph Kony. He was trained, armed, and then forced to fight alongside his rebel kidnappers. Hutton was introduced to Anywar via a cousin who first met Anywar while working in Africa with nonprofit organizations. The cousin told Hutton that Anywar, who still lived in Uganda, was looking for someone to recount his experiences as a child soldier. Via Skype chats and e-mail, Hutton and Anywar discussed various ideas for the book. Then, over the next several years, Hutton began writing *Soldier Boy* with Anywar via Skype giving feedback and clarifying details of the story.

According to Hutton, *Soldier Boy* was written with a thirteen- to eighteen-year-old audience in mind. In an interview with Kate Olson for the *Nerdy Book Club* website, Hutton noted: "As an 8th grade English teacher, I knew if my students were mature enough to handle the Civil War and Holocaust units taught at the 7th and 8th grade levels, they could handle reading about the Ugandan civil war and the LRA [Lord's Resistance Army]. In 2013, I created a compare-and-contrast curriculum to supplement my school's existing Civil War unit. Ricky's story proved an effective vehicle to show the similarities and differences between the U.S. Civil War and modern civil wars."

Soldier Boy begins by relating the true story of Anywar as a child soldier and then moves forward twenty years to tell the story of the fictionalized character of Samuel, whose experiences as a boy soldier lead to an overriding fear and distrust of everyone around him. In her interview with *Nerdy Book Club* website contributor Olson, Hutton discussed the reason for choosing the story's format, noting that Anywar "didn't want the story to be a series of shocking, graphically violent scenes." She added: "He wanted the message of his story to be one of hope and inspiration. I looked at my notes from our conversations and knew I had to find a way to give readers time to breathe."

Hutton eventually came up with the proposal to write alternating story lines focusing on Anywar's and Samuel's stories. The chapters focusing on Anywar reflect real-life events, while Samuel serves as a composite of many children that Anywar would later in life help via his organization Friends of Orphans, which he started in 1999 while the civil war was still raging and international organizations were unable to safely provide assistance. Hutton told Olson that she sees Samuel's story, which takes place twenty years later, "as a thread of light woven between the darkness of the Ricky chapters."

In Samuel's story, Anywar meets Samuel when the boy ends up at Friends of Orphans. It is 2006, and eleven-year-old Samuel is recuperating from serious injuries incurred in battle after being shot and then left behind by his fellow soldiers. Samuel is so traumatized by his experiences as a boy soldier that he does not trust his caregivers after he arrives at Friends of Orphans or the man who keeps trying to get him to tell his story. As a result, Samuel initially tries to escape, believing that he is being held captive. The novel switches back and forth in time to tell both Anywar's and Samuel's stories, via the two protagonists' points of view.

"The fictional interactions between every-child-soldier Samuel and Anywar at Friends of Orphans gives readers hope that recovery can happen," wrote Nicole Thompson in *Voice of Youth Advocates*. Noting that "Hutton doesn't shy from discussions of rape, torture, and abuse," a *Publishers Weekly* contributor went on to call *Soldier Boy* "eye-opening and relevant." Anywar writes an afterword for the novel, discussing how Friends of Orphans has helped 25,000 children impacted by the war through the organization's rehabilitation and vocational training center.

■ Biographical and Critical Sources

PERIODICALS

Booklist, April 15, 2017, Michael Cart, review of *Soldier Boy*, p. 60.

Kirkus Reviews, April 1, 2017, review of *Soldier Boy*.

Publishers Weekly, May 1, 2017, review of *Soldier Boy*, p. 62; December 4, 2017, review of *Soldier Boy*, p. S124.

School Library Journal, June 1, 2017, Monica Cabarcas, review of *Soldier Boy*, p. 108.

Voice of Youth Advocates, June, 2017, Nicole Thompson, review of *Soldier Boy*, p. 66.

ONLINE

Keely Hutton Website, http://keelyhutton.com/ (February 18, 2018).

Nerdy Book Club, https://nerdybookclub.wordpress.com/ (July 9, 2017), Kate Olson, "How *Soldier Boy* by Keely Hutton Came to Be," author interview.*

Rob Iliffe

■ **Personal**

Male.

■ **Addresses**

Office—University of Oxford, Linacre College, St. Cross Rd., Oxford OX1 3JA, England.

■ **Career**

Historian, educator, and writer. Oxford University, Oxford, England, professor of the history of science and codirector of the Oxford Centre for the History of Science, Medicine, and Technology, fellow of Linacre College, and general editor of the Newton Project. Previously taught at University of Sussex.

■ **Writings**

(General editor, with Milo Keynes and Rebekah Higgitt) *Early Biographies of Isaac Newton: 1660-1885*, Pickering & Chatto (Brookfield, VT), 2006.

Newton: A Very Short Introduction, Oxford University Press (New York, NY), 2007.

Priest of Nature: The Religious Worlds of Isaac Newton, Oxford University Press (New York, NY), 2014.

(Editor, with George E. Smith) *The Cambridge Companion to Newton*, Cambridge University Press (Cambridge, England), 2016.

Contributor to books, including *London and Beyond: Essays in Honour of Derek Keene*, Institute of Historical Research, 2012; *Newton and the Netherlands: How Isaac Newton Was Fashioned in the Dutch Republic*, Leiden University Press, 2013; and *The Uses of Humans in Experiment: Perspectives from the 17th to the 20th Century*, edited by E. Dyck and L. Stewart, Brill Rodopi, 2016. Editor of *History of Science*, 2001-08; coeditor of *Annals of Science*.

■ **Sidelights**

Rob Iliffe is a historian who has written about his primary research interests, including the history of early modern and Enlightenment science. Iliffe is particularly interested in historical interactions between science and religion, scientific voyages of discovery, the life and work of Isaac Newton, the development of ideas about scientific genius and scientific creativity, and the role of scientific instruments in scientific innovation. He is the author or editor of several books about Sir Isaac Newton, a British mathematician, astronomer, theologian, physicist, and author. In *Early Biographies of Isaac Newton: 1660-1885*, for which he served as general editor, Iliffe presents a collection of biographies that reveal how Newton's reputation continued to develop after his death.

Priest of Nature

In his book *Priest of Nature: The Religious Worlds of Isaac Newton*, Iliffe delves into the religious life of Newton. In the process, he shows the wide range and complexity of Newton's religious beliefs and writings. According to Iliffe, Newton's observations of and interests in Christianity and Christian history included theological discussions that covered topics from the Creation to the Apocalypse. "Recent publication of his religious, historical, and chronological papers has provided no support for the notion that there is some simple conceptual or methodological coherence to his work," Iliffe writes in the introduction to *Priest of Nature.* Iliffe went on to write later in the introduction that *Priest of Nature* "takes into account all the millions of his words on religious topics that have recently been published online, including his writings on natural theology, doctrine, prophecy, and church history. By taking seriously what he actually wrote and believed in these many domains, I aim to show that his religious studies were as expansive and technically demanding as any of his investigations in natural science."

Throughout the book, Iliffe examines how Newton's writing on religion related to his studies in mathematics and science, especially concerning the relationship between Newton's work in theology and natural philosophy. "We are all hugely in Rob Iliffe's debt," wrote *Spectator* contributor A.N. Wilson, who added: "Few of us would have the skill, in mathematics or philosophy or divinity, nor the patience, to do what he has done, which is read through the huge extent of Newton's obsessive theological writings." Iliffe, however, stresses that Newton's work in theology and religion was in many ways conducted in an entirely different sphere from that of his scientific pursuits. As a result, Iliffe also discusses Newton's religious thoughts and writing independently of his scientific accomplishments. Throughout the book, Iliffe also considers Newton's writings and beliefs within the institutional settings in which the famous scientists grew up, as well as the intellectual cultures that he experienced.

"Iliffe allows his readers to fully engage in the theological discussion that dominated Newton's age," wrote *MBR Bookwatch* contributor Able Greenspan. In the *Spectator* article, Wilson remarked: "This is a book which will take you several weeks to read, but the journey is worth it."

The Cambridge Companion to Newton

Iliffe is also the editor with George E. Smith of *The Cambridge Companion to Newton,* which features articles based on research into Newton's manuscripts. Many of the manuscripts concerning his religious beliefs had only recently been released at the time. Overall, fifteen authors contributed essays to the book. Contributors cover Newton's work from his scientific interests in physics and mathematics to his interest in alchemy, religion, and ancient chronology.

In addition to the introduction and preface written with Smith, Iliffe also wrote an essay titled "The Religion of Isaac Newton." Iliffe points out that Newton kept many of his religious writings secret for fear that, if the public gained knowledge about how Newton denied the Trinity in Christianity, he would likely have lost his position and standing in both science and society. Each chapter includes endnotes. *Choice: Current Reviews for Academic Libaries* contributor M. Dickinson called the book's introduction "excellent" and went on to recommend it to readers who have some familiarity with Newton's writings "and who have an understanding of basic physics."

■ Biographical and Critical Sources

BOOKS

Iliffe, Rob, *Priest of Nature: The Religious World of IsaacNewton*, Oxford University Press (New York, NY), 2014.

PERIODICALS

Choice: Current Reviews for Academic Libraries, March, 2017, M. Dickinson, review of *The Cambridge Companion to Newton*, p. 1051.
MBR Bookwatch, August, 2017, Able Greenspan, review of *Priest of Nature: The Religious Worlds of Isaac Newton.*
Publishers Weekly, May 8, 2017, review of *Priest of Nature*, p. 56.

ONLINE

Linacre College Website, http://www.linacre.ox.ac.uk/ (February 19, 2018), author faculty profile.
Spectator Online, https://www.spectator.co.uk/ (September 30, 2017), A.N. Wilson, "One of the Most Sensational Scoops of Recent Times: *Priest of Nature* Reviewed."
University of Oxford, Faculty of History Website, https://www.history.ox.ac.uk/ (February 19, 2018), author faculty profile.*

Elliott James

■ Personal

Male. *Hobbies and other interests:* Mythology, martial arts, live music, hiking, and used bookstores.

■ Addresses

Home—VA. *Agent*—Michelle Johnson, Inklings Literary Agency, 3419 Virginia Beach Blvd., Ste. 183, Virginia Beach, VA 23452.

■ Career

Writer.

■ Writings

"PAX ARCANA" SERIES

Charming, Orbit (New York, NY), 2013.
Charmed I'm Sure, Orbit (New York, NY), 2013.
Don't Go Chasing Waterfalls, Orbit (New York, NY), 2013.
Pushing Luck, Orbit (New York, NY), 2013.
Daring, Orbit (New York, NY), 2014.
Surreal Estate, Orbit (New York, NY), 2014.
Dog-Gone, Orbit (New York, NY), 2014.
Fearless, Orbit (New York, NY), 2015.
Talking Dirty, Orbit (New York, NY), 2015.
Bulls Rush In, Orbit (New York, NY), 2015.
In Shining Armor, Orbit (New York, NY), 2016.
Legend Has It, Orbit (New York, NY), 2017.

■ Sidelights

Elliot James is the author of the "Pax Arcana" urban fantasy series featuring former Knights Templar John Charming, a monster hunter who has become a werewolf. In an interview on the Orbit Books website, James remarked on what made him want to become an author: "The same things that make anyone want to become an author, really. A combination of crippling loneliness, habitual lying, greed, and delusions of grandeur. I mean, I could slather it on about how the imagination is the key to freeing the mind and all that, but let's face it, ultimately it all comes down to the wild parties, the women, and the limos full of cash. Speaking of which, when are those getting here anyway? Plus I like to read."

Charming and *Daring*

The first book in the "Pax Arcana" series, *Charming,* appeared in 2013. Since that time, James has produced several more novels in that world as well as a number of novellas. In this debut novel, James introduces his protagonist, John Charming, part werewolf and genetically inclined to maintain what is known as the Pax Arcana, the secret that keeps humans from becoming aware of supernatural beings all around them. This novel finds John much diminished from his line of dragon slayers and as a knight trained by a modern variant of the Knights Templar. He was one of the best-trained monster hunters until a curse turned him into one of these monsters that the modern Templars are sworn to hunt. But all this is in the past; now John tends bar in rural Virginia under an assumed name and tries to live quietly. Then he meets a six-foot blond who has the look of supernatural about her. It turns out that this woman, Sig, is a Valkyrie, and she is tracking vampires responsible for the disappearance of several young women. John's first instinct is to run, but then he decides to team up with Sig and her odd cohort—including Choo and Molly—instead. "Grab some snacks and settle back as splendid debut author James serves up a Prince Charming tale yanked sideways," noted *RT Book Reviews* website writer Jill M. Smith. *Booklist* reviewer Diana Tixier Herald termed this "masculine urban fantasy," adding: "In a saturated literary realm, James' tale stands out for the gritty, believable world he builds, and provides a reason for the genre's renewed strength." A *Publishers Weekly* contributor similarly termed this a "solid" tale, further commenting that though the plot "sometimes feels boilerplate . . . [it] eventually takes a darker, more personal twist."

The second novel in the series, *Daring*, finds John Charming enlisted to help the very Templars who have been hunting him. There is danger in the Pax Arcana as packs of werewolves are being united into an army of super soldiers by a mysterious figure. Any knight who attempts to challenge this new threat ends up dead. The Templars need someone who can infiltrate this new army, and John might be the one, though his own werewolf instincts are becoming stronger and stronger. But he strikes a bargain with the Templars in order to save Sig and her friends. Writing at the *RT Book Reviews* website, Smith noted: "If you like your supernatural chills and thrills with a hefty dose of humor, then James should be on your must-read list!" An online *All Things Urban Fantasy* writer was also impressed, commenting: "*Daring* was full of action and plot twists, just like *Charming*, and the plot was fast-paced and exciting for the most part. . . . With . . . the second book in the 'Pax Arcana' series, Elliott James becomes an urban fantasy author to watch."

Fearless and *In Shining Armor*

Fearless continues the action, with Charming, Sig, former priest Molly, and muscled Choo heading off to New York State to save a nineteen-year-old virgin college boy, Kevin Kichida, who is beset by threats from magical predators. As John and his team investigate, he begins to see that Kevin is not just a potential victim but is actually meant as a sacrifice. "What James's brash urban fantasy series lacks in depth, it makes up in rollicking action and pure fun," noted a *Publishers Weekly* reviewer. Writing at the *RT Book Reviews* website, Smith also had praise, commenting: "As always, when the situation gets dicey, you can expect John's wisecracks to rise in proportion. Sit back and enjoy this awesome ride!"

The fourth series installment, *In Shining Armor*, finds John Charming on the trail of whoever it was that kidnapped Constance, the baby who is the last descendant of the Grandmaster of the Knights Templar, and more importantly, John's goddaughter. Her kidnapping breaks the tenuous truce and alliance between the Templars and the werewolves, which is bad enough. But for John, getting Constance back is personal. Writing in the online *RT Book Reviews*, Smith lauded this series addition, noting: "James ups his game in both excellent character development and world expansion. If you love wisecracks in the face of ultimate danger, then John Charming is definitely your man!"

Legend Has It

In *Legend Has It*, citizens of New York City are suddenly being transformed into various monsters out of myths, fairy tales, and video games. The city is in chaos, and the Templars summon John and his team—Sig, his Valkyrie girlfriend, Molly, who specialize in arcane knowledge and exorcisms, and Choo the warrior. This team must find out who is responsible for these evil transformations, using a magical book for help. A *Kirkus Reviews* critic had a mixed assessment of this fifth series installment, terming it an "urban fantasy that features an irreverent, smart-mouthed hero and adventures that are entertaining, if not particularly thrilling."

Writing in the online *Reading Reality*, Marlene Harris had higher praise, observing: "The sheer amount of danger that John, his gang and the Templars are tipped into, while awesome and scary on so many levels, also brings out one of the inevitable twists of urban fantasy—that in order to keep the series interesting, the protagonist has to face and overcome more dangerous situations each outing, with bigger and badder villains, and hairier and scarier problems to solve. The hero becomes more powerful, and the villains get even more frightening and evil. The tone of the series gets darker the deeper you go. And so it proves with John Charming." Smith commented in the online *RT Book Reviews*: "Combining hair-raising peril and humor is a James trademark that works extremely well in taking readers on over-the-top UF adventures they won't soon forget!"

■ Biographical and Critical Sources

PERIODICALS

Booklist, September 1, 2013, Diana Tixier Herald, review of *Charming*, p. 52.

Kirkus Reviews, March 15, 2017, review of *Legend Has It.*

Publishers Weekly, July 1, 2013, review of *Charming,* p. 71; June 15, 2015, review of *Fearless,* p. 69.

ONLINE

All Things Urban Fantasy, http://allthingsuf.com/ (October 16, 2014), review of *Daring.*

Elitist Book Reviews, https://elitistbookreviews.com/ (June 13, 2017), Vanessa Christenson, review of *Legend Has It.*

Elliott James Website, https://elliottjamesauthor. wordpress.com (January 9 2018).

Orbit Books Website, https://www.orbitbooks.net/ (January 9, 2018), "Elliott James."

Reading Reality, https://www.readingreality.net/ (March 27, 2017), Marlene Harris, review of *In Shining Armor;* (April 17, 2017), Marlene Harris, review of *Legend Has It.*

RT Book Reviews, https://www.rtbookreviews.com/ (January 28, 2018), Jill M. Smith, review of *Legend Has It, In Shining Armor, Fearless, Daring,* and *Charming.**

Rachel McCarthy James

■ **Personal**

Daughter of Bill James; married; husband's name Jason. *Education:* Attended Hollins University.

■ **Addresses**

Home—Lawrence, KS.

■ **Career**

Writer.

■ **Writings**

(With father, Bill James) *The Man from the Train: The Solving of a Century-Old Serial Killer Mystery,* Scribner (New York, NY), 2017.

Contributor to periodicals, including *Bitch, Broadly,* and *New Inquiry.*

■ **Sidelights**

Rachel McCarthy James studied creative writing in college and is a contributor to periodicals. She is also author with her father, sportswriter Bill James, of *The Man from the Train: The Solving of a Century-Old Serial Killer Mystery.* The book focuses on an unsolved series of murders that the authors believe was the work of one of the deadliest serial killers in American history. Bill James has extensive expertise in statistics and analytics. "He has been called the 'Sultan of Stats,' Major League Baseball's

analytics pioneer," wrote *Kansas City Star Online* contributor Rick Montgomery. Montgomery added: "In researching ax murders of the early 1900s, however, James relied less on statistics and more on logic to conclude that a serial killer, riding the rails, invaded homes and unleashed mayhem on perhaps 100 victims."

Over the course of nearly a decade and a half, from 1898 to 1912, numerous families across the United States were found bludgeoned to death, usually from the blunt side of an ax. Most were killed in their sleep. Nothing of value was taken from the homes, and the murdered people were typically arranged together with their faces covered with cloth or, in one case, hay. Although a couple of the cases received national attention, no one thought that the many murders were connected. The authors were able to make connections among the murders only through the Internet. "Online newspaper archives and obscure true-crime accounts via Google Books allowed the Jameses to compare far-flung killings that authorities back then had little means of chasing down," wrote *Kansas City Star Online* contributor Montgomery. At the time of the murders, news did not spread rapidly, most homes still did not have telephones, and the federal government kept no national database of crimes. "The strength of the book hangs on [the authors'] diligent research and analysis connecting crimes into the closing years of the 19th century," wrote a *Publishers Weekly* contributor.

One of the things that the Jameses learned that seemed to connect the murders was that all of the victims lived within a short walking distance of a railroad line. Sifting through thousands of various local newspaper articles, court transcripts, and other public records, the authors believe they learned the true identity of the murderer. Meanwhile, the book points out that in several of the cases, people who were probably innocent were charged with murder. Often, those accused were African American, and at least two were lynched after being accused of murder.

To connect the murders, the authors point out the many commonalities among them, including the fact that axes were typically left at the scene alongside a lantern without its chimney. In addition, many of the female victims were arranged in sexually suggestive positions. Furthermore, the murders typically involved entire families, most in the Midwest, and often seemed to occur after dark when the family had gone to bed. Sometimes the bodies were burned. Overall, more than thirty commonalities are cited, although not all apply to every murder.

One murder that is especially highlighted in the book is the slaughter of a family in the summer of 1912 in Villisca in Montgomery County, Iowa. The murderer broke into the home of a businessman and his family, bludgeoning eight people with an ax's blunt side, including six children. The viciousness of the killings stood out, with all of the victims heads completely demolished. An investigation uncovered a number of suspects. One of them was tried twice, with one trial ending in a hung jury and the other in an acquittal. The crime was never solved. Jeremy Lybarger, writing for the *Millions* website, noted: "The idea that axe murders somehow represented America's id during a period of runaway modernization is one of the book's many fascinating theses" and went on to call the book "a riveting, evocative feat of reportage and historical sleuthing." A *Kirkus Reviews* contributor remarked: "The narrative becomes addictive, and it's easy to get caught up in the elaborate search and the authors' conclusions, which are plausible."

■ **Biographical and Critical Sources**

PERIODICALS

Publishers Weekly, May 22, 2017, review of *The Man from the Train: The Solving of a Century-Old Serial Killer Mystery*, p. 86.

ONLINE

Buffalo News Online, http://buffalonews.com/ (September 21, 2017), Gene Warner, review of *The Man from the Train*.

Kansas City Star Online, http://www.kansascity. com/ (September 14, 2017), Rick Montgomery, "What Do Baseball Stats and Century-Old Ax Murders Have in Common? This Guy."

Kirkus Reviews Online, https://www.kirkusreviews. com/ (May 15, 2017), review of *The Man from the Train*.

Millions, https://themillions.com/ (October 9, 2017), Jeremy Lybarger, review of *The Man from the Train*.

Star Tribune Online, http://www.startribune.com/ (October 27, 2017), Adam Morgan, review of *The Man from the Train*.*

Roy Johansen

1957-

■ **Personal**

Born 1957; son of Iris Johansen.

■ **Addresses**

Home—Los Angeles, CA. *Agent*—Andrea Cirillo, Jane Rotrosen Agency, 318 E. 51st St., New York, NY 10022.

■ **Career**

Screenwriter and novelist.

■ **Awards, Honors**

FOCUS Award, Films of College and University Students, and Edgar Allan Poe Award, best television miniseries or movie, Mystery Writers of America, both for *Murder 101*.

■ **Writings**

The Answer Man, Bantam Books (New York, NY), 1999.
Beyond Belief, Bantam Books (New York, NY), 2001.
Deadly Visions, Bantam Books (New York, NY), 2003.

WITH MOTHER, IRIS JOHANSEN

Silent Thunder, St. Martin's Press (New York, NY), 2008.
Storm Cycle, St. Martin's Press (New York, NY), 2009.

Shadow Zone, St. Martin's Press (New York, NY), 2010.

"KENDRA MICHAELS" SERIES; MYSTERIES; WITH IRIS JOHANSEN

Close Your Eyes, St. Martin's Press (New York, NY), 2012.
Sight Unseen, St. Martin's Press (New York, NY), 2014.
The Naked Eye, St. Martin's Press (New York, NY), 2015.
Night Watch, St. Martin's Press (New York, NY), 2016.
Look behind You, St. Martin's Press (New York, NY), 2017.
Double Blind, St. Martin's Press (New York, NY), 2018.

Coauthor of "With Open Eyes" (short story), with Iris Johansen, published by St. Martin's Press, 2012. Also author of script for *Back to Hannibal: The Return of Tom Sawyer and Huckleberry Finn* (television movie), 1990, and (with Bill Condon) of script for *Murder 101* (television movie), 1991.

■ **Sidelights**

Roy Johansen is best known for the suspense novels that he writes with his mother, the prolific author Iris Johansen. His career actually began earlier, when he was a college student and his mom was building her own portfolio as a romance novelist. Roy won a film award for his script *Murder 101* in a contest sponsored by film icons George Lucas, Martin Scorsese, and Steven Spielberg. He later collaborated on the television version that received a prestigious Edgar Award from the Mystery Writers of America. After a few years in the film industry, Johansen published his first novel.

Solo Novels

The Answer Man introduces Ken Parker, a lie detector operator whose life has spun into freefall. His marriage has failed, his car is repossessed, and he is about to be evicted from his office. When defense attorney Myth Daniels offers him a small fortune to teach her client how to cheat a polygraph test, Parker feels compelled to take the money. The client passes the test, only to die in an alley soon afterward. Other murders follow, and Parker becomes the primary person of interest. *Booklist* contributor George Cohen called *The Answer Man* "a thriller all lovers of the genre can sink their teeth into."

Johansen published two novels about Joe Bailey, a former magician and escape artist who joined the police force to unmask phony psychics. In *Beyond Belief*, a professor of parapsychology dies a gruesome death, and a child with the power of telekinesis is the primary suspect. In *Deadly Visions*, Joe chases an allegedly supernatural serial killer in order to save his own life and that of his daughter. Reviewers enjoyed the adventures of the so-called "Spirit Basher," but Bailey had solved his last case.

Novels with Iris Johansen

In 2008 Johansen was able to fulfill a longtime wish: to write a novel with his mother, Iris. *Silent Thunder* features marine architect Hannah Bryson, a Russian nuclear submarine in a Maine harbor, and a deadly secret that could bring the cold war back to life. The debut of the mother-son duo marked the beginning of a successful partnership. Hannah Bryson returns in *Shadow Zone*, as she investigates an archaeological site at the bottom of the sea. She discovers ancient metal panels full of coded symbols that could explain the sudden destruction of the ancient colony of Marinth. In the hands of the wrong person, the secret of the panels could destroy life on earth.

The Johansens also produced *Storm Cycle*, which "pits a supercomputer against hieroglyphics in an ancient Egyptian burial chamber," according to *Booklist* contributor Carol Haggas. Rachel Kirby hopes to find an ancient cure for her sister's rare illness, but first she must neutralize an international cabal willing to do anything to gain control of the secret. The Johansens were on their way to a promising future in espionage fiction. That was before Kendra Michaels made her appearance.

"Kendra Michaels" Series

Kendra Michaels spent the first twenty years of her life in darkness. Blindness forced her to hone her other senses to their maximum limits. When miraculous stem cell surgery gave her the power of sight, Kendra's extraordinary powers could operate at full throttle. When her ex-boyfriend, Jess, disappears in *Close Your Eyes*, she becomes a unique asset to the police department. Kendra is not the most collegial agent on the team, but investigator Adam Lynch has a special talent for engaging her interest. *Booklist* contributor Mary Frances Wilkens explained: "The scenes with Adam and Kendra ooze sexual tension." Kendra's talent for spotting clues that elude everyone else will lead her into a series of suspenseful, action-packed investigations.

In *Sight Unseen*, television viewers see footage of a deadly multiple-car accident on the Cabrillo Bridge in San Diego. Kendra sees a staged event salted with clues from her prior investigations. A copycat killer is at work, taunting her at every turn. Kendra must stop him before he can harm her loved ones. Haggas, a frequent reviewer of the series in *Booklist*, pointed to the Johansens' talent for "tying up all the loose ends . . ., but they always manage to leave one thread dangling," all but guaranteeing a loyal fan base.

In *The Naked Eye*, a series of ugly murders convinces Kendra that arch-villain Eric Colby was never executed at San Quentin, as reported. She shares her theory with reporter Sheila Hunter, whose body is found just hours after the interview. As the death toll rises around her, Kendra realizes that Colby is fulfilling his threat to murder everyone close to her before bringing her own life to an end. Her search for Colby is aided by a character from Iris Johansen's "Eve Duncan" series in what a *Publishers Weekly* contributor called "a thrilling race against time."

Night Watch reunites Kendra with the British surgeon who gave her the miracle of sight. She meets Dr. Waldridge for dinner in California and senses his unspoken anxiety. When he disappears soon afterward, Kendra immediately persuades her old ally Adam Lynch to join her search. The adrenaline flows as the danger rises, and so does the romantic attraction they first experienced in *Close Your Eyes*.

There is no shortage of serial killings in San Diego. In *Look behind You*, the murders have no obvious connections, but Kendra and her new co-investigator, Jessie Mercado, notice odd links to old murders committed all over the United States. The far-ranging crime locations draw a number of federal agents to San Diego to work with local agents Roland Metcalf and his partner, Gina Carson, who is skeptical of Kendra's exceptional skills. Kendra decides to strike out on her own in the search for a killer who seems able to follow her every move, until Adam Lynch arrives in town to protect the woman he has come to love. A *Publishers Weekly* commentator observed that "a long list of well-developed suspects makes this one of the more complex and satisfying" of Kendra's adventures.

Though some critics have mentioned a certain formulaic quality to Kendra's investigations, the Johansens continue to produce new installments, and readers continue to enjoy them. In *Double Blind*, Kendra is prepared to decline the latest investigation, until she learns that the body was found near her home, with an envelope addressed to her. One murder follows another, and each victim turns out to be connected to the conviction of a sadistic serial killer from Kendra's past. Jessie Mercado and Adam Lynch join the investigation to help her identify the killer before he (or she) strikes even closer to home.

■ Biographical and Critical Sources

PERIODICALS

Booklist, February 1, 1999, George Cohen, review of *The Answer Man*, p. 940; February 15, 2001, Connie Fletcher, review of *Beyond Belief*, p. 1119; March 1, 2008, Carol Haggas, review of *Silent Thunder*, p. 30; June 1, 2009, Carol Haggas, review of *Storm Cycle*, p. 6; May 15, 2010, Carol Haggas, review of *Shadow Zone*, p. 5; May 15, 2012, Mary Frances Wilkens, review of *Close Your Eyes*, p. 20; July 1, 2014, Carol Haggas, review of *Sight Unseen*, p. 43; June 1, 2015, Carol Haggas, review of *The Naked Eye*, p. 56; September 1, 2016, Carol Haggas, review of *Night Watch*, p. 58; June, 2017, Carol Haggas, review of *Look behind You*, p. 60.

Kirkus Reviews, July 15, 2012, review of *Close Your Eyes*; August 15, 2016, review of *Night Watch*; May 15, 2017, review of *Look behind You*.

Miami Herald, July 21, 2012, Connie Ogl, author interview.

Publishers Weekly, March 8, 1999, review of *The Answer Man*, p. 49; March 26, 2001, review of *Beyond Belief*, p. 65; May 12, 2008, review of *Silent Thunder*, p. 38; May 18, 2009, review of *Storm Cycle*, p, 32; May 31, 2010, review of *Shadow Zone*, p. 25; May 21, 2012, review of *Close Your Eyes*, p. 36; July 28, 2014, review of *Sight Unseen*; May 25, 2015, review of *The Naked Eye*, p. 35; August 29, 2016, review of *Night Watch*, p. 66; May 22, 2017, review of *Look behind You*, p. 73.

ONLINE

Always with a Book, http://alwayswithabook. blogspot.com/ (November 20, 2015), review of *The Naked Eye*.

Criminalelement.com, https://www.criminalelement. com/ (October 25, 2016), Kristen Houghton, review of *Night Watch*.

Just Talking Books, https://www.justtalkingbooks. com/ (July 23, 2014), review of *Sight Unseen*.

Kirkus Reviews Online, https://www.kirkusreviews. com/ (August 03, 2016), review of *Night Watch*; (May 2, 2017), review of *Look behind You*.

Linda McHenry Website, http://lindamchenry.com (August 5, 2014), review of *Sight Unseen*.

Mysterious Reviews, http://www.mysteriousreviews. com/ (January 11, 2018), review of *Silent Thunder*.

Roy Johansen Website, https://www.royjohansen.com (February 10, 2018).

Vic's Media Room, https://vicsmediaroom. wordpress.com/ (August 1, 2015), review of *Close Your Eyes*.*

Sheena Kamal

■ Personal

Born in Trinidad and Tobago. *Education:* University of Toronto, H.B.A.

■ Addresses

Home—Vancouver, British Columbia, Canada. *Agent*—Miriam Kriss, Irene Goodman Agency, 27 W. 24th St., Ste. 700B, New York, NY 10010.

■ Career

Writer, journalist, activist. Has also worked as a television and film researcher.

■ Awards, Honors

TD Trust Scholarship.

■ Writings

The Lost Ones, William Morrow (New York, NY), 2017, published as *Eyes Like Mine,* Zaffre (London, England), 2017.

■ Sidelights

Canadian author Sheena Kamal emigrated from Trinidad when she was six. She grew up in Toronto and attended the University of Toronto, studying political science. Thereafter she spent a number of years in the film industry. "I spent about a decade in the film and television industry trying to break into acting and screenwriting," Kamal noted in an *Irish Times Online* interview. "It's a journey that began after university when I realised I'd been hiding my light for far too long in a creaky old institution. I thought, Lord save me from strained eyesight! I've had enough of these sensible shoes! I'm going to be an actress, darling, and nobody can stop me. It wasn't smooth sailing. A tiny brown woman trying to make it as an actor? I was in for a rude awakening." She worked as a stand-in or stunt double and ended up auditioning for roles as maids or secretaries, all of which took a toll on her self-confidence, as she further noted in her interview: "I discovered that I'm 'ethnic'."

Those years spent around the film and television industry paid off, however, in unexpected ways. While working as a researcher for a television crime drama, she discovered that wanted to write a novel. "I've been involved in the film and TV world for many years; I tried to be a screenwriter, an actor, it really was the industry that provided me my bread and butter while I cut my teeth as a writer," Kamal told Désirée Zamorano at the *Los Angeles Review of Books* website. "For this particular job [as researcher for a crime drama] I had to pay attention to the criminal justice system. On a personal level, I was very affected by stories of gender violence. Then my imagination spawned this woman, who, when the daughter she'd given up for adoption many years ago goes missing, gets confronted by her past and her past trauma. My main character Nora Watts consumed me. Her story felt quite urgent."

Kamal decided to follow this inspiration, leaving the film industry and eastern Canada, and moving to Vancouver, British Columbia, where she set her first novel, *The Lost Ones* (published in England as

Eyes Like Mine). In a *Writing.ie* post, Kamal explained the background of her protagonist as a mixed-race woman. "Her mother was an immigrant and her father was an indigenous man who had been adopted and didn't know anything about his birth family. Nora is an outsider who has no connection to her cultural heritage on either side. But she looks like an indigenous woman, and that affects how people treat her. This is a minefield. I chose this back story for her because my story is centered on a missing girl and you cannot speak of the disappeared in Canada without talking about the extremely high rates of indigenous girls and women that go missing in my country."

Speaking with *Big Thrill* website contributor Sam Wiebe, Kamal remarked on a further benefit of her years spent in the film industry: "I've been told *The Lost Ones* is quite cinematic, which was entirely unintentional, but taking a step back I see that it is largely informed by my experiences in the screen arts. I'm also quite into outlining, which is the first step of screenwriting and where my research background comes in. I don't always stick to my outlines, but they help me find a direction. In addition to that, I've taken so many acting classes in the past decade that it certainly bleeds into how I approach character. I think that's why Nora's voice is so strong. I owe that to my performance training."

In a *Huffington Post* website interview with Mara White, Kamal commented on her choice of setting for this debut novel: "The Pacific Northwest is a rich setting. It's as atmospheric as anything you'd find in Scandinavian fiction, so-called Nordic Noir. And, on the one hand, Vancouver is one of the most beautiful cities in the world, surrounded by stunning natural landscapes. On the other, there is grinding poverty here. It is home to one of the worst high-risk drug areas in the region and is the epicenter of a serious opioid epidemic. The city itself is a bustling immigration center that lies on the unceded territory of three different First Nations. . . . It's a compelling place, one that I just knew I had to use for my book. I grew up on the east coast, in Toronto, but Vancouver called to me for this particular story."

Norah Watts is a woman with a troubled past in *The Lost Ones*. A research assistant for a private investigator, she meets with Lynn and Everett Walsh, discussing the disappearance of the their fifteen-year-old daughter, Bonnie. Norah figures they want to hire her PI boss, but in fact they have contacted Nora because she is Bonnie's birth mother who put her up for adoption as an infant. The Walshes believe Bonnie is trying to track her biological mother down. This brings up evil memories for Nora, as the birth of this baby was the result of a brutal rape. Finally, she decides that she needs to conduct her own search for this missing girl, an investigation that soon pits her against corporate interests that want the case quashed even if takes Nora's death to make it go away.

A *Publishers Weekly* reviewer was unimpressed with *The Lost Ones*, noting that the plot is "unconvincing and overly dependent on coincidence." The reviewer further observed, "Nora is too idiosyncratic to feel real, and none of her relationships ring true." Others, however, had a much higher assessment of the novel. A *Kirkus Reviews* critic commented: "Though comparisons to Stieg Larsson's Lisbeth Salander are inevitable, Nora blazes her own shining trail. A gritty, violent read with a tough, idiosyncratic, dryly witty heroine readers will root for even if they wouldn't want to invite her home." Similarly, *Booklist* writer Henrietta Verma felt that the author "has penned a believable survivor in Nora, a woman whose relentless struggles many readers will identify with." Further praise came from online *Washington Independent Review of Books* contributor Jesse Seigel, who noted: "Nora Watts is a noir antihero, a true female counterpart to the male of genre. She's tough, trusts no one, and will cut corners and break rules in order to get to the truth—whether that requires stealing cars, impersonating delivery people, hitting opponents with a tire iron, or taking advantage of people who may only be trying to help her."

■ Biographical and Critical Sources

PERIODICALS

Booklist, May 1, 2017, Henrietta Verma, review of *The Lost Ones*, p. 24.

Kirkus Reviews, May 15, 2017, review of *The Lost Ones*.

Publishers Weekly, May 8, 2017, review of *The Lost Ones*, p. 38.

ONLINE

Big Thrill, http://www.thebigthrill.org/ (May 31, 2017), Sam Wiebe, "Debut Author Spotlight: Sheena Kamal."

BooksPlease, https://booksplease.org/ (February 8, 2017), review of *Eyes Like Mine*.

Crime Pieces, https://crimepieces.com/ (January 26, 2017), review of *Eyes Like Mine.*

Criminal Element, https://www.criminalelement. com/ (July 24, 2017), Dirk Robertson, review of *The Lost Ones.*

Huffington Post, https://www.huffingtonpost.com/ (July 17, 2017), Mara White, author interview.

Irish Examiner, https://www.irishexaminer.com/ (June 3, 2017), Sue Leonard, review of *Eyes Like Mine.*

Irish Times Online, https://www.irishtimes.com/ (February 9, 2017), Sheena Kamal, "A Cautionary Tale about the Canadian Dream."

Los Angeles Review of Books, https://lareviewofbooks. org/ (August 7, 2017), Désirée Zamorano, author interview.

Sheena Kamal Website, https://www.sheenakamal. com (January 9, 2018).

Toronto Star Online, https://www.thestar.com/ (July 8, 2017), Jack Batten, review of *The Lost Ones.*

Vancouver Sun Online, http://vancouversun.com/ (July 25, 2017), Aleesha Harris, review of *The Lost Ones.*

Washington Independent Review of Books, http:// www.washingtonindependentreviewofbooks. com/ (August 13, 2017), Jessie Seigel, review of *The Lost Ones.*

Writing.ie, https://www.writing.ie/ (February 13, 2017), author interview.*

Lauren Karcz

■ **Personal**

Born in Atlanta, GA; married.

■ **Addresses**

Home—Atlanta, GA. *Agent*—Victoria Marini, Irene Goodman Literary Agency, 27 W. 24th St. Ste. 700B, New York, NY 10010.

■ **Career**

Writer. Has worked as an ESL teacher and a linguist.

■ **Writings**

The Gallery of Unfinished Girls, HarperTeen (New York, NY), 2017.

■ **Sidelights**

Lauren Karcz was born and grew up in Atlanta, Georgia, where she lives today with her family. She calls herself a "professional language nerd," having studied linguistics and been an ESL teacher. She has a job in the field of linguistics and writes in her spare time. She took to writing early in life, sitting on the sofa at home with her "blue binder and a mechanical pencil." As she put it at her eponymous website: "I loved sister stories, surrealist settings, and characters who get what they need instead of what they want." This was the genesis of her debut novel, *The Gallery of Unfinished Girls*.

The Gallery of Unfinished Girls follows the story of high schooler Mercedes Moreno, an artist. Mercedes finds herself suffering a creative block when her grandmother falls ill and lapses into a coma. At the same time, Mercedes falls in love with her best friend, Victoria. Her mother has left to care for her own mother in Puerto Rico, and Mercedes must look after her younger sister, Angela.

The tale soon becomes fantastical when a neighbor, Lilia Solis, tells Mercedes that she can come and paint at the Red Mangrove Estate. There she is in the company of other artists and finds herself able to create once more. She hopes to be able to match the award-winning work she created in her junior year. The oddity is that she cannot take her artwork off the Estate with her. The minute she leaves, she is cast back into her uncertain life. Elements of magical realism predominate, imparting a "dream-like quality" to Mercedes's life, according to Kristy Rademacher, writing in *Voice of Youth Advocates*. Rademacher found the story a "murky read" that was "unlikely to have broad appeal."

More favorably, Caitlin Kling, a critic in *Booklist*, called Karcz's debut novel "bold" in its mixing of magic realism and surrealism, with "expertly executed irony" that "propels the narrative." A contributor to *Kirkus Reviews* noted that while the narrative is "initially compelling, . . . this tribute to young artists ultimately underdelivers." On the other hand, a reviewer in *Publishers Weekly* applauded the "mix of self-discovery, art making, and the unknown." Faythe Arredondo, in *School Library Journal*, pronounced the novel a "great title that tackles death, love, creativity, growing up, and moving on." At *Teenreads*, a reviewer called *The Gallery of Unfinished Girls* "the discovery of a girl's self" and observed that Karcz's writing is "impeccable." The critic concluded: "Mercedes's life is about having faith and making choices. Gradually, she learns that sometimes all you need to do is to choose to believe in something impossible to learn how to make the unattainable a reality."

■ Biographical and Critical Sources

PERIODICALS

Booklist, June, 2017, Caitlin Kling, review of *The Gallery of Unfinished Girls*, p. 92.

Kirkus Reviews, June 1, 2017, review of *The Gallery of Unfinished Girls*.

Publishers Weekly, May 22, 2017, review of *The Gallery of Unfinished Girls*, p. 95.

School Library Journal, May, 2017, Faythe Arredondo, review of *The Gallery of Unfinished Girls*, p. 105.

Voice of Youth Advocates, August, 2017. Kristy Rademacher, review of *The Gallery of Unfinished Girls*, p. 73.

ONLINE

Lauren Karcz Website, https://www.laurenkarcz.com (February 1, 2018).

Teenreads, https://www.teenreads.com (July 28, 2017), review of *The Gallery of Unfinished Girls*.*

Daniel P. Keating

1949-

■ **Personal**

Born 1949. *Education:* Johns Hopkins University, Ph.D.

■ **Addresses**

Home—Ann Arbor, MI. *Office*—University of Michigan, Department of Psychology, 2008 East Hall, 530 Church St., Ann Arbor, MI 48109-1043.

■ **Career**

University of Michigan, Ann Arbor, professor of psychology, psychiatry, and pediatrics.

■ **Writings**

(Editor) *Mathematical Talent: Discovery, Description, and Development: Proceedings from the Hyman Blumberg Symposium on Research in Early Childhood Education,* Johns Hopkins University Press (Baltimore, MD), 1974.

(Editor) *Intellectual Talent, Research and Development: Proceedings of the Sixth Annual Hyman Blumberg Symposium on Research in Early Childhood Education,* Johns Hopkins University Press (Baltimore, MD), 1976.

(Editor, with Hugh Rosen) *Constructivist Perspectives on Developmental Psychopathology and Atypical Development,* L. Erlbaum Associates (Hillsdale, NJ), 1991.

(Editor, with Clyde Hertzman) *Developmental Health and the Wealth of Nations: Social, Biological, and Educational Dynamics,* Guilford Press (New York, NY), 1999.

(Editor) *Nature and Nurture in Early Child Development,* Cambridge University Press (New York, NY), 2011.

Born Anxious: The Lifelong Impact of Early Life Adversity—and How to Break the Cycle, St. Martin's Press (New York, NY), 2017.

Has contributed chapters to books, including *Equity and Justice in Developmental Science: Theoretical and Methodological Issues,* Academic Press (London, England), 2016, and *The Developmental Science of Adolescence: History through Autobiography,* Psychology Press (New York, NY), 2014. Has contributed articles to journals, including *Proceedings of the National Academy of Science, International Journal of Behavioral Development,* and *Child Development.*

■ **Sidelights**

Daniel P. Keating is a professor of psychology, psychiatry, and pediatrics at the University of Michigan in Ann Arbor. His profile at the university website notes that his "research focuses on integrating knowledge about developmental processes, population patterns in developmental health, and social factors affecting individual and population development." Before taking a position at the University of Michigan, Keating conducted research at various institutions, among them Berlin's Max Planck Institute and the Canadian Institute for Advanced Research, where he was a fellow and spearheaded the program in human development.

Over the course of his long career, Keating has contributed articles to professional journals and chapters to academic texts in the field of psychology. He also edited several books, both on his own and with colleagues, including *Nature and Nurture in Early Child Development*. The chapters in this book show that neither nature (genetic factors, that is, biological inheritance) nor nurture (a person's overall environment, along with life experiences and learning) alone control development. In interaction, both play a part in human development. As the book's introduction puts it, the offerings come from "developmental scientists" at the "cutting edge," working in areas "from neural mechanisms to population studies, and from basic laboratory science to clinical and community interventions." J. Mercer, reviewing *Nature and Nurture in Early Child Development* in *Choice*, found the book most useful for academics and singled out for praise the "handling of longitudinal and population studies and analytical methods and of practical concerns about parent-child psychotherapy and policy considerations."

In 2017, Keating released *Born Anxious: The Lifelong Impact of Early Life Adversity—and How to Break the Cycle*, which continues and fine-tunes the study of nature versus nurture. Keating looks closely at DNA research, specifically a factor called "epigenetic methylation." As the publisher's website describes it, "a key stress system has been welded into the 'on' position by the methylation process," leading to a predisposition to the production of stress hormones and, as a result, "lifelong, unrelenting stress and its consequences—from school failure to nerve-racking relationships." Thus, it looks more and more likely that what happens in utero sets up the human being to experience extreme responses to stress, which are the exacerbated by social and economic factors.

Claire Nana, critiquing the book at *Psych Central*, focused on the research underpinning this startling argument. In the year before birth, the stress a mother undergoes actually imprints on the unborn child's DNA. A child with the resulting "stress dysregulation" will exhibit behavioral problems and difficulty in learning. That, however, is not the entire story. Keating goes on to lay out a strategy to prevent or at least minimize the damage. Imposing routines and open communication can alleviate problems. In summary, Nana noted: "Keating has not just rewritten our understanding of stress, but the social mechanisms that drive it." A *Kirkus Reviews* critic observed that Keating "posits that the consequences of a growing 'stress epidemic' are myriad and profound," bleeding over into many parts of a person's life and health." Keating's insights into the possibilities for change, stated the critic, make *Born Anxious* an "empowering guide."

■ **Biographical and Critical Sources**

BOOKS

Keating, Daniel P., editor, *Nature and Nurture in Early Child Development*, Cambridge University Press (New York, NY), 2011.

PERIODICALS

Choice, July, 2011, J. Mercer, review of *Nature and Nurture in Early Child Development*, p. 2194.

Kirkus Reviews, March 1, 2017, review of *Born Anxious: The Lifelong Impact of Early Life Adversity—and How to Break the Cycle*.

ONLINE

Macmillan Website, https://us.macmillan.com/ (February 2, 2018), brief book description.

Psych Central, https://psychcentral.com/ (July 24, 2017), Claire Nana, review of *Born Anxious*.

University of Michigan Website, https://lsa.umich.edu/ (February 1, 2018), author faculty profile.*

Lucy Keating

■ Personal

Female. *Education:* Williams College, B.A., 2008; Columbia University Graduate School of Journalism, completed publishing course, 2008.

■ Addresses

Home—Cambridge, MA.

■ Career

Writer. *Departures,* editorial intern, 2008-09; Alloy Entertainment, editorial assistant, 2009-11; TV development assistant, 2011-14; Pocket Gems, manager of episode originals, 2015-17.

■ Writings

Dreamology, HarperTeen (New York, NY), 2016.
Literally, HarperTeen (New York, NY), 2017.

■ Sidelights

Lucy Keating writes young-adult novels from her home in Cambridge, Massachusetts. She attended Williams College, where she earned a bachelor's degree in art history, and then obtained a publishing degree from the Columbia University Graduate School of Journalism. Keating worked as an editorial intern and assistant for several years and in television development before deciding to focus on novels for the teen audience.

Dreamology

In 2016, Keating published her first young-adult novel, *Dreamology.* The main character of *Dreamology* is teenager Alice, who has an imaginary dream

friend, Max. Together they share adventures and find love. Max does not really exist, so Alice is startled when she moves with her family to Boston and finds him in class at her new school. Keating spoke about the genesis of the book with Katy Upperman: "I've always had crazy dreams. . . . I . . . would have dreams of people I had loved or dated, and always thought it was so weird that even though I hadn't seen them in months or years . . . they could feel so real in the dream. . . . I wanted to play around with that idea, of someone you saw while you slept, who seemed so real even though you didn't know them."

A *Kirkus Reviews* contributor was disappointed that "what begins as potentially intriguing, light sci-fi gradually devolves into preposterousness that doesn't even try to make sense." Kirsten Pickel, a critic in *Voice of Youth Advocates,* however, found the "characters . . . likable and the story . . . engaging" and pronounced *Dreamology* "a fun spin on contemporary romance." At *YA Books Central,* Amy Oliver found Keating's writing to be "hilarious, . . . quirky and fun." A critic at *Teenreads* termed this debut an "enchanting and whimsical story with lovable characters, along with a few facts about how brains and dreaming work."

Literally

Keating's second young-adult novel, *Literally,* offers an interesting mix of fantasy and reality as a premise. Annabelle, known as AB, seems to have tight control of her life. Then her parents decide to divorce, throwing her world into turmoil. At the same time, real-life author Lucy Keating pays a visit to AB's fiction-writing class and tells them the outline of her latest book. AB realizes that the plot describes her own life. How is this possible? Is Keating pulling the strings of her life? AB is torn between two boys—Will, who is clearly the perfect choice, and AB's friend Elliot, who is something of a ladykiller but with whom she is in love. As Lucy's "creation," AB feels trapped. Can she write her own story?

Christina C. Jones, critiquing the book in *Voice of Youth Advocates*, described *Literally* as a "whimsical novel" and a "light, satisfying read." Katie Ward Beim-Esche, writing in the *Christian Science Monitor*, remarked that *Literally* "will serve as a bubbly palate cleanser for some and skew saccharine for others" but also called it a "bouncy little summer read." A critic in *Kirkus Reviews* observed: "This festival of metafictive fun should particularly appeal to budding novelists."

■ Biographical and Critical Sources

PERIODICALS

Christian Science Monitor, May 5, 2017, Katie Ward Beim-Esche, "*Literally* Is a Bouncy Summer Read Built on a Sleight-of-Hand Trick," review of *Literally*.

Kirkus Reviews, March 1, 2017, review of *Literally*.

School Library Journal, January, 2016, Kathleen E. Gruver, review of *Dreamlogy*, p. 106.

Voice of Youth Advocates, April, 2016, Kirsten Pickel, review of *Dreamology*, p. 59; April, 2017, Christina C. Jones, review of *Literally*, p. 61.

ONLINE

Katy Upperman Website, https://katyupperman. com/ (April 21, 2016), author interview.

Kirkus Reviews, https://www.kirkusreviews.com/ (April 12, 2016), review of *Dreamology*.

Lucy Keating Website, http://www.lucykeating.com (February 2, 2018).

Teenreads, https://www.teenreads.com/ (April 11, 2016), review of *Dreamology*.

YA Books Central, http://www.yabookscentral.com/ (June 27, 2016), Amy Oliver, review of *Dreamology*.*

Amina Khan

■ Personal

Female. *Education:* University of California, Berkeley, B.A., 2007. *Hobbies and other interests:* Surfing and snowboarding.

■ Addresses

Home—Los Angeles, CA.

■ Career

Journalist. Classroom Matters, SAT instructor, 2004-07; *Los Angeles Times,* web assistant, 2007-08, reporter, 2009—; Right Is Wrong, editorial researcher, 2008; *Forbes,* reporter, 2008-09.

■ Writings

Adapt: How Humans Are Tapping into Nature's Secrets to Design and Build a Better Future, St. Martin's Press (New York, NY), 2017.

■ Sidelights

Amina Khan is a science writer and health blogger on the staff of the *Los Angeles Times.* She obtained her B.A. at the University of California, Berkeley, where she studied Spanish and linguistics. After graduation, she began working for Classroom Matters as an SAT instructor. She then became an editorial researcher and reporter, working first for the *Los Angeles Times* and then for *Forbes.* She returned to the *Los Angeles Times* in 2009 to focus on science reporting. Her articles have covered a wide range of topics, from the Mars rovers to bioengineering. To further her education, she attended the Kavli nanotechnology workshop at the

Massachusetts Institute of Technology and the HiPACC computational astrophysics bootcamp at the University of California, Santa Cruz.

In 2017, Khan released her first book, *Adapt: How Humans Are Tapping into Nature's Secrets to Design and Build a Better Future.* The Macmillan website describes Khan's premise, saying that she "presents fascinating examples of how nature effortlessly solves the problems that humans attempt to solve with decades worth of the latest and greatest technologies, time, and money." A critic in *Kirkus Reviews* pronounced the book "meticulous" and a "richly detailed account of biologically inspired engineering." Velcro, for example, was fashioned with the sticking power of a burr in mind. The critic concluded: "These well-crafted tales of bio-inspired innovation will entrance general readers and warrant the close attention of scientists and technologists." In *Booklist,* Carol Haggas noted that in her book Khan brings together a journalist's sensibility with a "storyteller's desire to enthrall an audience," going on to call it "hopeful and exciting reading for the future of personal and planetary challenges."

■ Biographical and Critical Sources

PERIODICALS

Booklist, March 1, 2017, Carol Haggas, review of *Adapt: How Humans Are Tapping into Nature's Secrets to Design and Build a Better Future,* p. 26.
Kirkus Reviews, March 15, 2017, review of *Adapt.*

ONLINE

Los Angeles Times, http://www.latimes.com/ (February 3, 2018), author staff profile.
Macmillan Website, https://us.macmillan.com/ (February 3, 2017), author profile and brief book description.*

Katie Khan

■ Personal

Female. *Education:* University of Manchester, Mus. B., 2004.

■ Addresses

Home—London, England. *Agent*—Juliet Mushens, Caskie Mushens, London, England; juliet@caskiemushens.com.

■ Career

Coca-Cola Company, senior digital writer, 2010-11; Abundant, head of social media, 2011-13; Paramount Pictures, head of digital, 2013-17; Warner Bros. Pictures, product liaison, 2017—.

■ Writings

Hold Back the Stars, Doubleday (London, England), 2017, Gallery Books (New York, NY), 2017.

■ Adaptations

Hold Back the Stars has been optioned for film by Dan Cohen and Shawn Levy.

■ Sidelights

Katie Khan has worked for nearly a decade as a digital writer and head of social media. She worked for Paramount Pictures for four years before moving to Warner Bros. Pictures as a product liaison in film production. Her debut novel, *Hold Back the Stars*, was released in 2017 and has already been translated into twenty-one languages. It is being adapted for film by producers Dan Cohen and Shawn Levy.

Hold Back the Stars is a sci-fi suspense tale set sometime in the future and in another world— Utopian Europia. The story follows protagonists Carys and Max, who meet and fall in love but cannot marry. Utopia Europia has a Couples Rule, which forbids marriage until couples have reached the age of thirty-five. They are so strict about it that they impose a Rotation system requiring people to move every three years and meant to "to prevent national and community attachment and competing loyalties," as Liz Bourke notes at *Tor.com.* As one of the characters in the novel describes it: "The biggest truth about Europia is that it's almost impossible to live here if you can't live by the utopian guidelines. . . . People who can't live by the rules of a utopia tend to find it's not really a utopia, for them. They are the ones who go looking for something else." Carys and Max sign on for a perilous space mission meant to be a "lab study on long-term romantic relationships" among twenty-somethings. After their space vessel is damaged and repairs prove ineffective, the two find themselves floating in space with no way home and just ninety minutes' worth of oxygen. Will they both live? Or die?

A critic writing in *Kirkus Reviews* termed this a "suspenseful novel" but complained that the "characters never fully come alive." Bourke, a reviewer at *Tor.com*, commented that *Hold Back the Stars* comes across as "science fictional soap opera." She went on to observe that the novel tries "too hard to say Deep Things about romantic love, and instead, manages to be more trite and less healthy than the sentiments on a Valentine's Day card." In the *Irish Times*, Sara Keating called this "essentially, an enjoyable space romance." A critic at *Little Hux Tales* found the "dialogue . . . biting, witty and completely honest" and the "world building . . . excellent."

Amy Martin, at *SciFi Now*, applauded the "great pace" and "real sense of intimacy." At *Utopia State of Mind*, a contributor described the utopian society as "fascinating," as well as the "technology of the new age and the concept of rotation." The critic concluded: "Khan expertly exposes us to little mysteries . . . all to illustrate the nature of fate: how we influence it and how it influences us."

■ Biographical and Critical Sources

PERIODICALS

Kirkus Reviews, March 15, 2017, review of *Hold Back the Stars*.

ONLINE

Irish Times, https://www.irishtimes.com/ (February 4, 2017), Sara Keating, review of *Hold Back the Stars*.

Katie Khan Website, https://katiekhan.com (February 3, 2018).

Little Hux Tales, https://huxtales.wordpress.com/ (January 25, 2017), review of *Hold Back the Stars*.

SciFi Now, https://www.scifinow.co.uk/ (March 1, 2017), Amy Martin, review of *Hold Back the Stars*.

Tor.com, https//www.tor.com/ (May 31, 2017), Liz Bourke, review of *Hold Back the Stars*.

Utopia State of Mind, https://utopia-state-of-mind. com/ (May 24, 2017), review of *Hold Back the Stars*.*

Ellen Kirschman

■ Personal

Born in New York, NY; married Steve Hollis Johnson (a photographer). *Education:* University of California, Berkeley, M.A.; Wright Institute, Ph.D.

■ Addresses

Home—Redwood City, CA. *Agent*—Cynthia Zigmund, Second City Publishing Services. Madison, WI.

■ Career

Psychologist, speaker, writer. Ellen Kirschman and Associates, licensed clinical psychologist specializing in police and public safety psychology, 1983—.

■ Member

Sisters-in-Crime, Mystery Writers of America (MWA), Public Safety Writers Association, International Thriller Writers (ITW), American Psychological Association, Society for the Study of Police and Criminal Psychology, International Association of Women Police, Association of Chiefs of Police.

■ Awards, Honors

Award for Distinguished Contribution to Psychology, 2014.

■ Writings

NONFICTION

I Love a Cop: What Police Families Need to Know, Guilford Press (New York, NY), 1997, 3rd edition, 2018.

I Love a Fire Fighter: What the Family Needs to Know, Guilford Press (New York, NY), 2004.

(With Mark Kamena and Joel Fay) *Counseling Cops: What Clinicians Need to Know,* Guilford Press (New York, NY), 2014.

"DOT MEYERHOFF MYSTERY" SERIES

Burying Ben, Oceanview Publishing (Longboat Key, FL), 2015.

The Right Wrong Thing, Oceanview Publishing (Longboat Key, FL), 2015.

The Fifth Reflection, Oceanview Publishing (Longboat Key, FL), 2017.

■ Sidelights

Ellen Kirschman is a San Francisco-based clinical psychologist who specializes in police and public safety psychology. Kirschman has employed these skills and experiences in nonfiction and fiction works alike. She is the author of *I Love a Cop: What Police Families Need to Know,* as well as the novels in the "Dot Meyerhoff Mystery" series, featuring this eponymous police psychologist. On her author website, Kirschman discussed her protagonist: "[Dot] gets to do things I wouldn't dream of, like impersonating a public official, breaking and entering, and assault with a deadly weapon. She is a spunky fifty-year-old who takes orders from no one, not even her chief, and persists in solving crimes when she should be counseling cops." Kirschman adds: "My hope is that readers will enjoy a good mystery at the same time learn something new about the hidden complexities and emotional challenges of police work."

I Love a Cop

Kirschman's *I Love a Cop* has gone through two revised editions since its original publication in 1997, reflecting the changing difficulties that the police face. Basically a coping guide for officers, the book looks at the challenges they face daily and also how families can help them deal with trauma. There are also chapters on domestic and alcohol abuse as well as a discussion of the particular problems female officers might have to deal with.

"The author maintains that police families can, in fact, thrive, and she's got the success stories to prove it," noted *Library Journal* reviewer Deborah Bigelow of *I Love a Cop*. Writing in the *FBI Law Enforcement Bulletin*, Linda S. Forst also had praise, commenting, "*I Love a Cop* provides such worthwhile information that police administrators should seriously consider making it required reading for promotional examinations." Likewise, an *Internet Bookwatch* writer concluded: "*I Love a Cop* is also highly recommended as supplemental reading for anyone considering a policing career, as there is also plenty of sage wisdom about what to expect on the job and how to balance demands of the job with those of family life."

Burying Ben, The Right Wrong Thing, and The Fifth Reflection

Kirschman's "Dot Meyerhoff Mystery" series was launched with *Burying Ben,* in which Dot is just getting started in her new position as psychologist for the Kenilworth Police Department in California when a rookie cop, Ben Gomez, commits suicide leaving behind a note that blames Dot. With her job at stake, Dot investigates this death, cutting through the shroud of secrecy Ben's widow and friends alike have thrown around the case. Finally, she is able to get to the truth of the suicide and bring those responsible to justice. Writing in *Reviewer's Bookwatch,* Margaret Lane had praise for this debut novel, noting: "A deftly crafted novel of compelling complexity, *Burying Ben* is an inherently absorbing read from beginning to end and marks author Ellen Kirschman as a novelist of exceptional storytelling talent."

Dot returns in *The Right Wrong Thing,* once again on the spot for certifying Randy Spelling for service on the Kenilworth department. Spelling's father and brothers have been cops, and she badly wants to join that family tradition. But disaster strikes early in the officer's career when she shoots and kills pregnant teenage Lakeisha Gibbs, who she mistakenly thinks is drawing a weapon. Dot is back in Spelling's life when the officer is diagnosed with PTSD, and again takes her job beyond the clinical mode, attempting to get to the bottom of things as regards this shooting. A *Publishers Weekly*

reviewer found this a "highly satisfying second novel . . . [that] treats complex racial, feminist, personal, and political issues while providing intimate knowledge of cops' shop procedure." Writing in the online *Corrections One: Harriet's Corner,* Harriet Fox noted: "Kirschman has proven yet again to be a brilliant author whose deadpan comedic delivery brightens the pages and her visionary detail paints a picture like you are right there with protagonist Dot, looking over her shoulder. I was engrossed by every word, at the edge of my seat for each chapter ahead, and impatiently awaited the big solution to the whodun-it. I was surprised all along the way." *Foreword Reviews* website contributor Laura Mahon similarly observed: "*The Right Wrong Thing* is brilliantly written with this dynamic in mind. Those looking for a meaningful story forged against the backdrop of a relevant social construct will enjoy going on this adventure with Randy and Meyerhoff. Not only is this a compelling read, but it is profoundly realistic."

The third series installment, *The Fifth Reflection,* offers a complex plot involving a missing child, a dedicated officer whose investigation is tearing his own family apart, and a provocative photographer whose nude photos of her own children put her in the investigative crosshairs. Once again Dot must go outside of her psychologist comfort zone to get to the truth. "Using her skills as a psychologist and then as amateur sleuth, Dot unmasks a surprising but unlikely team of bad guys," noted a *Publishers Weekly* reviewer of this series addition. An *Internet Bookwatch* contributor also had praise, commenting: "A deftly crafted and riveting read from beginning to end, *The Fifth Reflection* clearly reveals author Ellen Kirschman's genuine flair for originality and mastery of the genre."

■ Biographical and Critical Sources

PERIODICALS

FBI Law Enforcement Bulletin, April, 1998, Linda S. Forst, review of *I Love a Cop: What Police Families Need to Know,* p. 9.

Internet Bookwatch, April, 2007, review of *I Love a Cop;* August, 2017, review of *The Fifth Reflection.*

Library Journal, January 1, 2007, Deborah Bigelow, review of *I Love a Cop,* p. 129.

Publishers Weekly, August 17, 2015, review of *The Right Wrong Thing,* p. 54; May 1, 2017, review of *The Fifth Reflection,* p. 39.

Reviewer's Bookwatch, November, 2015, Margaret Lane, review of *Burying Ben.*

ONLINE

Corrections One: Harriet's Corner, https://www.correctionsone.com/ (January 28, 2018), Harriet Fox, review of *The Right Wrong Thing.*

Ellen Kirschman Website, http://ellenkirschman.com (January 9, 2018).

Foreword Reviews, https://www.forewordreviews.com/ (August 3, 2015), Laura Mahon, review of *The Right Wrong Thing.*

Psychology Today, https://www.psychologytoday.com/ (January 9, 2018), "Ellen Kirschman."

Quiet Fury Books, http://quietfurybooks.com/ (July 5, 2017), review of *The Fifth Reflection.**

Caroline Kitchener

■ Personal

Female. *Education:* Attended East China Normal University, 2013; Princeton University, B.A. (magna cum laude), 2014.

■ Addresses

Home—Washington, DC.

■ Career

Writer. Jiangxi Normal University, Nanchang, China, coach and Public Speaking Institute coordinator/founder, 2014.

■ Awards, Honors

All-American Witness Award, American Mock Trial Association, 2014; All American Attorney Award, American Mock Trial Association, 2014; Suzanne Huffman Thesis Prize, Gender and Sexuality Studies Department, Princeton University, 2014.

■ Writings

Post Grad: Five Women and Their First Year Out of College, Ecco (New York, NY), 2017.

Atlantic, associate editor, 2017—, and contributor.

■ Sidelights

Prior to launching her literary career, Caroline Kitchener studied at Princeton University, where she received her bachelor's degree. She has also studied and worked in China, having attended East China Normal University in the year 2013. In addition to her work as a writer, Kitchener has devoted her time to volunteering with various human and women's rights associations, such as WomanSpace and DC SAFE. Kitchener works with the *Atlantic* as an associate editor.

Post Grad: Five Women and Their First Year Out of College is Kitchener's debut book. As the title describes, Kitchener closely examines the lives of five individual women as they attempt to start their lives after graduating from college. Kitchener's experience is part of this documentation. The remaining women are fellow students she knew throughout her time in university. Like Kitchener, each of the other four women attended Princeton University, and they left school with an assortment of different degrees.

Kitchener finds herself facing considerable conflict after her graduation, as her romantic and familial relationships collide. Kitchener wants to be with her boyfriend, who is bound for Washington, DC, in pursuit of his own ambitions. However, Kitchener's mother disagrees with her decision, and their mother-daughter bond becomes rife with conflict as a result of their clashing ideals. In the meantime, Kitchener must also sketch out a trajectory for her own life.

Another woman, Denise, faces a more internal set of struggles. Denise dreams of heading to medical school. However, she is filled with uncertainty over her path. She spends her time after graduation developing her love life while also building her career experience by working in a hospital.

Michelle also finds her love life and professional life blossoming at once. Her interests lie in music, and this is what she studied during her time in

Princeton. Now she must figure out where this interest will take her, and what path will make her happiest. At the same time, she finds love with another, younger student. Life eventually leads Michelle into pursuing a career in jazz, which, while it won't provide her with the highest level of income, gives her the fulfillment she's been looking for.

Olivia is of Malaysian descent, but her ambitions and pursuits root her in the United States. She is from a family of successful businesspeople who have already secured work for her in Malaysia. However, Olivia's ultimate dream is to create a documentary following the lives of college students, just like she once was, who make a living by selling drugs. In order to give this film the funding it needs to get off the ground, Olivia takes up life of sugar dating.

Finally, Alex also finds herself trying to balance her career ambitions with romance. Alex fell out with her family long ago, after revealing to them that she is a lesbian. While there is still contention between her and her family, she and her brother remain close enough to try to enter the business world together using Alex's programming skills. At the same time, Alex is dating her girlfriend, who lives several miles away, and the distance is beginning to wear on them both.

Kitchener delves fully into the lives, dreams, and hopes of each woman profiled in her book to demonstrate the flurry of change and growth that comes with graduating college and entering a new phase of life. *Booklist* contributor Kristine Huntly remarked: "YAs curious about what life in the real world has to offer them might find Kitchener's narrative intriguing." Mary Jennings, a writer in *Library Journal*, commented that *Post Grad* "will strike a chord with young adults and those interested in future women of action." *School Library Journal* reviewer Mahnaz Dar said: "Teens curious about what the future will bring will appreciate this thought-provoking look at the first year out of college."

■ Biographical and Critical Sources

PERIODICALS

Booklist, March 15, 2017, Kristine Huntly, review of *Post Grad: Five Women and Their First Year Out of College*, p. 5.

Kirkus Reviews, March 1, 2017, review of *Post Grad*.

Library Journal, December 1, 2016, Mary Jennings, review of *Post Grad*, p. 110.

School Library Journal, June 1, 2017, Mahnaz Dar, review of *Post Grad*, p. 118.

ONLINE

Caroline Kitchener Website, https://www.carolinekitchener.com (February 6, 2018), author profile.*

Alexander Klimburg

1976-

■ **Personal**

Born 1976. *Education:* School of Oriental and African Studies, University of London, B.A., 2000; London School of Economics, M.S., 2003; University of Vienna, Ph.D., 2017.

■ **Addresses**

Home—Boston, MA.

■ **Career**

Cyber security expert, researcher, writer. Belfer Center, Harvard Kennedy School, Cambridge, MA, associate and research fellow, 2014-17; Hague Centre for Strategic Studies, Netherlands, program director, 2014—; Atlantic Council, nonresident senior fellow, 2015—. Former senior advisor, Austrian Institute of International Affairs, Vienna, for eight years. Has also acted as advisor to numerous other governments and international organizations on issues of cybersecurity strategy and internet governance.

■ **Writings**

(Editor, with Jan Pospisil) *Mediating Security: Comprehensive Approaches to an Ambiguous Subject: Festschrift for Otmar Holl,* Peter Lang Edition (Frankfurt am Main, German), 2013.

The Darkening Web: The War for Cyberspace, Penguin Press (New York, NY), 2017.

■ **Sidelights**

Alexander Klimburg is a program director at The Hague Centre for Strategic Studies as well as a nonresident senior fellow at the Atlantic Council, where he conducts research on "reconciling norms of state behavior in international cyber security with the ongoing dialogue within internet governance, in particular with the role of nonstate actors" according to his biography on the Atlantic Council website. His 2017 book *The Darkening Web: The War for Cyberspace* is an outgrowth of that research.

In *The Darkening Web,* according to *NPR.org* contributor Mary Louise Kelly, "Klimburg argues that to understand Russia's recent cyber intrusions into U.S. politics, not to mention other countries with aggressive cyber agendas—think China—[then] you have to understand this. The world divides into two broad factions on the basic question of how the Internet should run." On the one hand, countries of the West see the Internet as an opportunity, while on the other, countries like Russia and China see it as a threat to their power.

Klimburg remarked to Kelly in his interview: "Originally, Russia viewed cyber, which is an old term, as being helpful for government. They've been trying to build an Internet since the '50s. And they always construed it as being a means of control. That's actually also what cyber actually means. It means, a means of control in man and machine, and from that point of view, always was seen as being something beneficial. But the Western view of the Internet and cyberspace, which is larger than the Internet, has always been disconnected from governments per se. So these different visions did compete, and one side, if you will, did win. But this is not the war that was won. It was just a battle overall. And the old views of seeing cyber as a means of control are still very much there."

It is that war over cyberspace that Klimburg explores in *The Darkening Web.* The author provides an overview of the origins and the building of the Internet, and then proceeds to offer more in-depth coverage of the world's major cyber-warfare actors, including Russia, China, and the United States. Klimburg also looks into the future to describe how cyberspace is becoming a major battle ground for political conflict. He further describes how the "Wild West" days of the Internet are coming to an end, with both governments and corporations seeking to control and monitor it. He points out, for example, that China employs a vast number of Internet watchers to maintain its national firewall—an army larger in number than its actual standing army. Klimburg warns throughout that the West has largely underestimated the negative uses of cyberspace and the rise of covert influencing and information warfare are serious threats to democratic governments. For Klimburg, the battle for control of the Internet is as fraught with danger as was the danger presented by nuclear weapons in the Cold War. Ultimately, the author argues for an international/ intergovernmental approach to both keep the Internet open and also deal with bad actors.

"Klimburg delivers an urgent warning that civil libertarians and cybernauts alike will want to heed," noted a *Kirkus Reviews Online* critic of *The Darkening Web*. A *Publishers Weekly Online* reviewer also had praise, commenting: "The book serves as an excellent primer on cyberwarfare, especially useful in the context of the 2016 U.S. presidential election, as accusations of Russian interference continue to make headlines." Similarly, *Washington Post Book World* contributor Gordon M. Goldstein observed that this work "articulates a powerful central thesis: The Internet has arrived at a historical inflection point, the author asserts, and today has become an arena for a massive international security competition fought in an increasingly Hobbesian ecosystem of digital aggression and overt information warfare." Goldstein added: "As *The Darkening Web* demonstrates, explaining cyberspace and its acute geopolitical and geostrategic disruption is profoundly challenging; it is a history hurtling ahead at Internet speed." Likewise, *Nature Online* writer Steve Aftergood noted: "*The Darkening Web* provides a sweeping yet nuanced overview of how we got to where we are online, with ample backstory. provides a sweeping yet nuanced overview of how we got to where we are online, with ample backstory."

Writing in the *Christian Science Monitor*, Steve Donoghue focused on the "quietly horrifying" aspects of *The Darkening Web*: "With gut-clenching efficiency, Klimburg imagines plenty: power grids not only shut down but physically damaged, transportation networks disrupted or closed (eighty percent of Americans live in cities, dependent on food supplies that would only last a day if stopped), telecommunications warped or terminated, financial information deleted, and of course the stereotypical nightmare scenario, which involves nuclear weapons, tens of thousands of which have command-and-control sequences that are now 'cyber-enabled'—and therefore hackable." *New Scientist Online* reviewer Nina Jankowicz offered a less pessimistic summation: "Klimburg's warnings regarding Russian cyber-aspirations . . . are on the money. He does not think the US election was turned around solely by Russia's campaigns and incursions. Still, his recommendations might have helped the Obama administration retaliate while evading charges of partisanship. Klimburg argues that governments should be clear and transparent about what types of cyberattacks they face and what 'deterrence by cyber-means' should entail."

■ Biographical and Critical Sources

PERIODICALS

Christian Science Monitor, August 1, 2017, Steve Donoghue, review of *The Darkening Web: The War for Cyberspace*.
Library Journal, June 1, 2017, review of *The Darkening Web*, p. 125.
Washington Post Book World, August 4, 2017, Gordon M. Goldstein, review of *The Darkening Web*.

ONLINE

Atlantic Council, http://www.atlanticcouncil.org/ (January 9, 2018), "Alexander Klimburg."
Kirkus Reviews Online, https://www.kirkusreviews.com/ (May 2, 2017), review of *The Darkening Web*.
Nature Online, https://www.nature.com/ (July 5, 2017), Steven Aftergood, review of *The Darkening Web*.
New Scientist Online, https://www.newscientist.com/ (August 30, 2017), Nina Jankowicz, review of *The Darkening Web*.
NPR.org, https://www.npr.org/ (July 11, 2017), Mary Louise Kelly, "Author: Governments Seek to Dominate the 'Wild West' of Cyberspace."
Penguin Random House Website, https://www.penguinrandomhouse.com/ (January 9, 2018), "Alexander Klimburg."
Publishers Weekly Online, https://www.publishersweekly.com/ (May 22, 2017), review of *The Darkening Web*.
Wall Street Journal Online, https://www.wsj.com/ (July 14, 2017), Stephen Budiansky, review of *The Darkening Web*.*

Cheston Knapp

1982(?)-

■ **Personal**

Born c. 1982; married; children: one son. *Education:* Attended college.

■ **Addresses**

Home—Portland, OR. *Agent*—Bill Clegg, Clegg Agency, 156 5th Ave., Ste. 1210, New York, NY 10010.

■ **Career**

Writer, editor, and photographer. *Tin House,* Portland, OR, managing editor. Exhibitions: "Reclamation, Blue Moon Camera & Machine" (solo), Portland, 2017; "Reclamation" (group), Pacific Northwest Photography Viewing Drawers, Blue Sky Gallery, Portland, 2018.

■ **Writings**

Up Up, Down Down: Essays, Scribner (New York, NY), 2018.

■ **Sidelights**

Managing editor of the literary magazine *Tin House,* Cheston Knapp is also a writer and photographer. Knapp is the author of *Up Up, Down Down: Essays.* The collection features seven essays that "all circle questions of identity and authenticity," as Knapp told *Creative Nonfiction* website contributor Kaylee Ritchie. Knapp went on to tell

Ritchie: "Each essay sort of tilts at a previous iteration of myself, a former identity." Knapp revealed that, when writing the essays, he did not think about them being a book. However, Knapp continued, as he kept writing the essays: "All at once I was saddled with an inchoate collection of linked-ish essays." Knapp said he continued to write the subsequent essays with that idea in mind. Overall, the essays took six years to write.

As a whole, the essays in *Up Up, Down Down* chronicle the author's coming-of-age as Knapp addresses experiences from childhood to his marriage. In the opening essay, "Faces of Pain," Knapp writes about professional wresting promotion, segueing into an examination of pain and Knapp's relationship with his father. Another essay, "Mysteries We Live With," begins as a profile of a UFO enthusiast but eventually becomes a meditation on Knapp's own Christian upbringing and on various aspects of faith, including what limits, if any, there are to faith. The essay "Neighborhood Watch" revolves around the murder of a neighbor, leading Knapp to ponder community, gentrification, and how peoples' lives intersect.

Knapp examines his younger years in college in the essay "Beirut." A *Kirkus Reviews* contributor called the essay an "existential reflection on beer pong and the author's frat-house 20s." The collection's final essay, "Something Gotta Stick," is about Knapp attending a skateboarding camp for adults. His time at the camp leads him to analyze nostalgia while he ponders his relationship to the past and how to draw from it to move forward to the future.

"Knapp's roundhouse, fullmouthed style takes a firmly tongue-in-cheek approach to the existential crises of male maturity for the millennial generation," wrote a *Publishers Weekly* contributor. *New York Times Online* contributor Michael Ian Black remarked: "*Up Up, Down Down* truly soars when it relates life as it is actually lived, and not as it is weighed against the author's ideas about what a writer's life should be." Black especially pointed out the essays "Neighborhood Watch" and "Something Gotta Stick" within this context. Black went on to note that Knapp "has his own voice, an authentic voice worth developing and savoring."

■ Biographical and Critical Sources

PERIODICALS

Kirkus Reviews, December 1, 2017, review of *Up Up, Down Down: Essays.*

Publishers Weekly, October 9, 2017, review of *Up Up, Down Down*, p. 53.

ONLINE

Cheston Knapp Website, https://www.chestonknapp.com (March 19, 2018).

Creative Nonfiction, https://www.creativenonfiction.org/ (March 19, 2018), Kaylee Ritchie, "The Work Itself Is a Home: A Conversation with Cheston Knapp."

New York Times Online, https://www.nytimes.com/ (February 23, 2018), Michael Ian Black, "When It Comes to Writing, Cheston Knapp Is His Own Harshest Critic," review of *Up Up, Down Down*.*

Joseph Knox

■ Personal

Born in England. *Hobbies and other interests:* Running.

■ Addresses

Home—London, England.

■ Career

Writer and crime novelist. Worked in bars and bookshops.

■ Writings

Sirens, Crown (New York, NY), 2018.
The Smiling Man, Doubleday (New York, NY), 2018.

■ Sidelights

Born and raised in and around Stoke and Manchester, England, Joseph Knox is a crime novelist. Knox suffered from insomnia when he was young so his parents started giving him books and notebooks so he could occupy himself. "I was sketching out short stories, comedy routines and characters as soon as I could hold a pen," Knox noted in an interview for the *Fullybooked2017* website, adding that "it was a great early lesson in what writing really is: sitting alone for many hours, trying to reach that perfect moment where you forget you're a person, forget you're a boy in his bedroom writing, and begin to inhabit whatever world you're writing about."

Knox's debut novel, *Sirens,* is the first book in the "DC Aiden Watts" series. The series features a downtrodden detective constable in the city of Manchester, England, who is caught taking drugs from evidence. Although Aiden may have the makings of a good detective, he does not naturally fit in at work or anywhere else, for that matter. One of Aiden's major issues is his anger, which surprisingly sometimes helps in his investigation. In this opening book in the series, Aiden, who seems to be continuously high on cocaine as he narrates the story, is forced by a superior into going undercover as a bounced policeman in order to investigate a drug dealer named Zain Carver, who heads one of the most violent drug organizations in the country Aidan's boss, however, tells him that another goal is to gather information on a member of Parliament's daughter, Isabelle, who has apparently fallen in with Zain's nefarious circle of criminals.

Zain sells his drugs at bars and nightclubs that he owns. The money is collected by a group of beautiful women who works for Zain and are called the Sirens. Aiden eventually is able to infiltrate Zain's organization but soon hits a snag in his investigation when things turn up indicating that Isabelle has actually sought a form of safety with Zain, though Aiden is not sure what she was running from. When Isabelle overdoses on bad heroin, Aiden thinks that her death might be murder. Still, Aiden has other things to contend with as well, including a growing war among drug dealers.

"Hard-boiled fans will appreciate this debut's deep dive into the underworld and its well-concealed twists," wrote Christine Tran in *Booklist.* A *Kirkus Reviews* contributor called *Sirens* "a powerfully assured debut by a British novelist who has the potential to be a leading player in modern noir."

■ Biographical and Critical Sources

PERIODICALS

Booklist, November 15, 2017, Christine Tran, review of *Sirens*, p. 29.

Kirkus Reviews, February 1, 2018, review of *Sirens*.

Publishers Weekly, November 13, 2017, review of *Sirens*, p. 38.

ONLINE

Crime Fiction Lover, https://crimefictionlover.com/ (February 6, 2018), Catherine Turnbull, "Interview: Joseph Knox."

Dead Good Books, https://www.deadgoodbooks.co.uk/ (February 3, 2017), Karen Sullivan, review of *Sirens*.

Fullybooked2017 blog, https://fullybooked2017.wordpress.com/ (January 11, 2017), "Interview . . . Joseph Knox."

Guardian Online, https://www.theguardian.com/ (January 19, 2017), Barry Forshaw, "The Best Recent Thrillers—Review Roundup," includes review of *Sirens*.

Joseph Knox Website, http://www.josephknox.co.uk (March 19, 2018).

Lancashire Post Online, https://www.lep.co.uk/ (January 17, 2017), review of *Sirens*.

Yorkshire Post Online, https://www.yorkshirepost.co.uk/ (January 17, 2017), Kate Whiting, review of *Sirens*.*

Tadzio Koelb

■ Personal

Male. *Education:* Parsons School of Design, B.F.A., 1993; Winchester School of Art, M.A. (fine arts), 1997; University of East Anglia, M.A. (creative writing), 2008.

■ Addresses

Home—Brooklyn, NY. *Agent*—Anna Stein, ICM Partners, 65 E. 55th St., New York, NY 10022.

■ Career

Writer, journalist, editor, translator, and consultant. Freelance writer, editor, translator, and journalist, 2007—; freelance communications consultant, 2010—; Rutgers University, New Brunswick, NJ, lecturer in creative, business and technical writing, 2011—; Misty K. Snow for U.S. Senate, Utah, senior writer, 2016; New School, New York, NY, guest lecturer, October, 2017. Held residencies at the Corporation of Yaddo, Saratoga Springs, NY, 2010; Caldera Arts Center, Sisters, OR, 2011; and I-Park Foundation, East Hadden, CT, 2012. Moon Township for Obama, field organizer, 2008; NY Cares, GED adult education team leader, 2013-14; and Rutgers University Senate, senator, 2017—.

■ Member

American Association of University Professors, American Federation of Teachers (AFL-CIO), National Book Critics Circle.

■ Writings

(Translator) André Gide, *Morasses,* Calypso Press, 2015.

Trenton Makes, Doubleday (New York, NY), 2018.

Author of critical biography of Lawrence Durrell for *British Writers Retrospective Volume III,* edited by Jay Parini, Charles Scribners Sons, 2009. Translator and copyeditor of book-length publications, including *Persona,* a major exhibition catalogue for the Royal Museum for Central Africa, and *Keep on Running: The Story of Island Records* for Universal-Island Records. Contributor of reviews and features on books, literature, and art to periodicals, including the *Brooklyn Rail, New York Times Book Review, Times Literary Supplement, Guardian, Literary Review, New Statesman, Art in America,* and *Jewish Quarterly. Journal of Afrotropical Zoology* and *Africana Linguistica,* proofreader.

■ Sidelights

Tadzio Koelb is a writer whose work includes articles, reviews, and essays for a variety of publications. He also teaches creative writing and other writing courses. In terms of teaching, his primary areas of expertise include art criticism, creative nonfiction, literary criticism, literary translation, literature and creative writing, and technical editing and technical writing translation.

In his debut novel, *Trenton Makes,* Koelb tells the story of Abe Kunstler, whose life has become one of lies and deceptions. The novel takes place in Trenton, New Jersey, once a booming factory town after World War II but a place that is on a steady decline through the 1960s, when factories are closing and hippies and drugs are everywhere. Abe is not a happy man, primarily because he is keeping a deadly secret. Abe used to be a woman, but she killed her traumatized husband during an argument after he returned from World War II. Afterward she disguises herself as her husband with a haircut and tight bindings. Her deception is made slightly easier because of the physique she acquired working in a factory during the war.

Operating on the belief that only a man can truly make it the world, the woman now named Abe goes on to make a life, marrying a woman named Inez, an alcoholic and former dancehall girl. A son eventually comes on the scene, and Abe convinces Inez the boy is his. Abe sees the child as proof of his masculinity. The world, however, is changing rapidly. By the 1960s a generational divide is growing as America becomes mired in the Vietnam War, and a counterculture is rising. Meanwhile, Abe is still haunted by his past and the ruthless acts he has committed. Eventually, the life Abe has created is threatened, leading Abe to become desperate and unsure of what he willing to do keep his past a secret.

Koelb "deftly confronts gender, identity, and socioeconomic limits to create a piercing tragedy," wrote Terry Hong in *Booklist*, also pointing out in the review that the name Kunstler is significant because in German it means "both artist and performer." Calling *Trenton Makes* a "taut debut," a *Publishers Weekly* contributor went on to note: "Koelb is insightful, if not always subtle, about how short the era of triumphant white American manhood was." Patrick Sullivan, writing in *Library Journal*, noted that Abe's story explores the idea of gender and an individual's identity, especially in relation to the profound roles that they have in a person's life. Sullivan wrote that the tale reveals "how devastating it is for those who become strangers or impostors in their own lives."

■ Biographical and Critical Sources

PERIODICALS

Booklist, February 15, 2018, Terry Hong, review of *Trenton Makes*, p. 38.

Library Journal, February 15, 2018, Patrick Sullivan, "Fiction," includes review of *Trenton Makes* p. 51.

Publishers Weekly, November 20, 2017, review of *Trenton Makes*, p. 67.

ONLINE

Tadzio Koelb Website, https://tadziokoelb.com (March 19, 2018).*

Rafi Kohan

■ Personal

Male. *Hobbies and other interests:* Ivy grooming and basketball.

■ Addresses

Home—Brooklyn, NY.

■ Career

Editor and author. *New York Observer,* former deputy editor; *Atlantic,* head of editorial for branded content studio, 2018—.

■ Writings

The Arena: Inside the Tailgating, Ticket-Scalping, Mascot-Racing, Dubiously Funded, and Possibly Haunted Monuments of American Sport, Liveright Publishing Corporation (New York, NY), 2017.

Contributor to periodicals, including *Rolling Stone, GQ, Town & Country, Wall Street Journal,* and *Men's Journal.*

■ Sidelights

Rafi Kohan has built a career in the journalism industry. He has contributed writing to numerous periodicals, including *Rolling Stone, GQ, Wall Street Journal, Men's Journal,* and others. Kohan is affiliated with the *Atlantic,* where he is an editorial leader.

The Arena: Inside the Tailgating, Ticket-Scalping, Mascot-Racing, Dubiously Funded, and Possibly Haunted Monuments of American Sport focuses on one of Kohan's other interests: American stadiums. The book involves Kohan taking a national tour to some of the country's largest and most famous stadiums. Each visit brings Kohan in the midst of events or otherwise presents him with the opportunity to get to know the relationship between each stadium and its home city. In the process of traveling, Kohan uncovers each stadium's history and how deeply intertwined these edifices are with American culture, as well as information regarding some of the more unsavory elements surrounding these stadiums.

One of the first stadiums Kohan pays a visit to is Lambeau Field, which is situated in Green Bay, Wisconsin, and is home to the Green Bay Packers. It is there that Kohan recites the special Lambeau Oath and begins delving into stadium culture firsthand. Some of the stadiums Kohan visits have darker histories than others. For instance, the Superdome became a site of horror during the aftermath of Hurricane Katrina, when it was used to temporarily house tens of thousands of displaced residents. While the Superdome was unable to escape Katrina unscathed, it nonetheless eventually became a symbol of hope. Kohan takes the time to speak directly with New Orleans residents who took shelter in the Superdome during this period about what they witnessed and endured, while also recounting how the city's involvement in the football industry helped to rejuvenate morale. Other stadiums, such as those in Cleveland and Boston, were notorious for the presence of scalpers.

Kohan expounds upon the history and culture of ticket scalping alongside his discussion of stadiums and sports. Many areas witnessed an ebb and flow in this type of activity. Cleveland, in particular, witnessed an increase in scalping during Lebron James's career. Boston, however, saw their scalping activity fall to a standstill once the Red Sox won the World Series championship. Kohan also touches upon the impact of technology and the modern era upon the scalping world.

Kohan also discusses several other cultural and societal elements in relation to sporting stadiums, including governmental involvement in funding the creation of these structures. City governments actively use stadiums as leverage in order to evade their tax debts. Stadiums are built and renovated expressly because they cost more to create than they actually earn from year to year. At the same time, Kohan pays close attention to their mark on society not just through their architecture, but also in how they affect the citizens who visit and maintain them. Kohan speaks with an assortment of stadium staff for their opinion on their home arenas, from refreshment staff to groundskeepers to entertainers. *Booklist* reviewer Mark Levine remarked that Kohan's "account is comprehensive, accurate, and often quite funny." In *Kirkus Reviews*, a writer commented: "Kohan brings the modern sporting arena to life in this fine exploration of the 'corners of American stadiums that aren't necessarily hidden but are almost assuredly unseen.'" A *Publishers Weekly* contributor said: "[Kohan] has created an immersive, informative work that will delight and enlighten a wide range of readers." Richard Horan, writing in the *Christian Science Monitor*, stated: "You'll have to read those for yourself to understand why this book as a reflection of who we are 'as individuals, as cities, and as a society' really hits it out of the ballpark!"

Kohan told *CA*: "A ninth-grade teacher had us do some stream-of-conscious writing in class while listening to jazz music. I didn't produce anything worthwhile, of course, but I thought that was pretty cool. It showed me that writing wasn't just academic, but could also be a pursuit of adventure and art.

"Anytime I read a book or an article or anything, really, I look for lessons, stylistic, structural, or otherwise, that may help improve my work, if applied.

"My writing process is very structured and disciplined. I wake up early, write for four to five hours, go play basketball, and then spend the afternoon editing or outlining.

"The most surprising thing I have learned as a writer is it never really gets easier, unless you lean on your routine. It's all about muscle memory.

"My favorite book is *The Area*, because it's my only book. I hope people read and enjoy it. I have never worked so hard on anything in my life."

■ Biographical and Critical Sources

PERIODICALS

Booklist, July 1, 2017, Mark Levine, review of *The Arena: Inside the Tailgating, Ticket-Scalping, Mascot-Racing, Dubiously Funded, and Possibly Haunted Monuments of American Sport*, p. 10.

Christian Science Monitor, August 8, 2017, Richard Horan, "*The Arena* Explores America's Stadiums and Their Relation to the National Character."

Kirkus Reviews, June 1, 2017, review of *The Arena.*

Publishers Weekly, May 8, 2017, review of *The Arena*, p. 52.

ONLINE

Rafi Kohan Website, https://www.rafikohan.com (February 9, 2018), author profile.

Janel Kolby

1971-

■ Also Known As

Janel Kolby Cheng
Jane Kilby

■ Personal

Born May 21, 1971; children. *Education:* Hamline University, M.F.A.

■ Addresses

Home—Redmond, WA. *Agent*—Gallt & Zacker Literary Agency, 273 Charlton Ave., South Orange, NJ 07079.

■ Career

Writer, poet, and children's and young adult author.

■ Writings

Winterfolk, HarperTeen (New York, NY), 2018.

■ Sidelights

Janel Kolby has an M.F.A. in creative writing for children and young adults. In an interview for the *Storyteller's Inkpot* blog, Kolby remarked that she began writing poems and stories at a young age. She went on to note that she hid her writing aspirations from people except for her family. "As

I got older and grew confidence, I began to accept how much happiness I receive from writing, and that it's as much my future as it has been my past," Kolby said in the interview. Kilby went on to note she has primarily focused on writing middle-grade and young adult fiction, adding: "I tried out some picture books, and managed to create a passable one, but it's not a strength yet."

Kolby's first young adult novel, *Winterfolk,* revolves around a young girl named Rain, who serves as the novel's narrator. Rain is living in a homeless encampment outside of Seattle's Beacon Hill neighborhood. Those living there call themselves the Winterfolk. Rain has been homeless for as long as she can remember and has learned to remain hidden. Living in a tent with her father for the past five years, being "invisible" is important she is told by her father, who wants to keep her hidden from child welfare authorities who could take her away. Rain's life is so limited that the only entertainment she has is an old, stolen book of fairy tales. As Rain nears her sixteenth birthday, she learns through flyers distributed by the city that it plans on getting rid of the encampment and all the homeless people living there must disperse.

Rain's friend, a seventeen-year-old named King, offers to show Rain the city for her birthday. Once in the city, they encounter a small-time drug dealer named Cook, an old enemy of King. The meeting leads to a series of problems as Rain becomes separated from King and wanders the city alone. Rain finds the wide world of Seattle and the civilization it represents not to her liking. As a result, she is desperate to return home. In the process of trying to find her way back to the encampment, Rain encounters numerous dangerous situations, with many of the men she meets along the way representing the most serious danger in terms of potential abuse. It also becomes clear, however, that even the men who want to protect her, such as her father, also have made her life isolated and precarious

Rain's "journey leaves her changed, and more aware of who she truly is," wrote *NPR.org* contributor Caitlyn Paxson, adding: "It's rare to find a book that is so gentle and so brutal at once, but Rain will take your hand and show you the way through." A *Kirkus Reviews* contributor remarked: "Rain brings an outsider's perspective to every detail she encounters, allowing readers to see them that way too."

■ **Biographical and Critical Sources**

PERIODICALS

Booklist, November 1, 2017, Caitlin Kling, review of *Winterfolk*, p. 67.

Kirkus Reviews, November 15, 2017, review of *Winterfolk*.

Publishers Weekly, November 27, 2017, review of *Winterfolk*, p. 63.

Voice of Youth Advocates, February, 2018, Heather Christensen and Zara Roy, review of *Winterfolk*, p. 57.

ONLINE

Janel Kolby Website, http://janelkolby.com (March 19, 2018).

NPR.org, https://www.npr.org/ (February 10, 2018), Caitlyn Paxson, "*Winterfolk* Cloaks Harsh Reality in Fairy Tale Mist."

Seattle Book Review, https://seattlebookreview.com/ (February 11, 2018), review of *Winterfolk*.

Storyteller's Inkpot, http://thestorytellersinkpot.blogspot.com/ (January 5, 2015): "Meet the Grad: Janel Kolby."*

Josh Korda

■ Personal

Married Kathy Cherry. *Education:* Attended college.

■ Addresses

Home—New York, NY.

■ Career

Writer, Dharma teacher, lecturer, and radio broadcaster. Formerly worked in advertising. Dharma Punx NYC, New York, NY, guiding teacher, 2005—; New York Zen Center for Contemplative Care, New York, visiting teacher; also leads online and residential retreats for *Tricycle* and *Lion's Roar* magazines; conducts podcast. Weekly Dharma talks broadcast on WBAI radio in New York; has appeared on Viceland TV Channel's public-service announcements.

■ Writings

Unsubscribe: Opt Out of Delusion, Tune in to Truth, foreword by Noah Levine, Wisdom Publications (Somerville, MA), 2017.

Contributor to periodicals, including *Tricycle, Lion's Roar,* and *Buddhadharma,* and to websites, including the *Huffington Post.*

■ Sidelights

Josh Korda is a recovering addict who became a Dharma teacher in the Against the Stream lineage. Korda is also known for his podcasts, which have garnered more than 1.4 million downloads. He gives weekly Dharma talks on New York's WBAI radio and is a contributor to periodicals and websites. Korda is also the author of *Unsubscribe: Opt Out of Delusion, Tune in to Truth.* The book present's Korda's three-step guide to recovery from addiction. Korda, however, is not talking about addiction to drugs and alcohol but rather to consumerism, self-deception, and the life people think they have to live.

Writing in the book's introduction, Korda informs readers that he was relatively pleased with his own life in fast-paced New York City. However, riding on the subway to work one day he kept hearing talk about something happening in the city. When he got off the subway and up onto the street, he looked up to see black smoke billowing out of the Twin Towers and then witnessed them collapse. The 9/11 tragedy led Korda to reevaluate his life and purpose for living, ultimately suffering a nervous breakdown. "It was then that his lifelong fascination for Buddhism and Western psychology, which he had rediscovered some years prior, deepened, and he sought a community to further his study," wrote Salvador Pantoja in a profile of Korda for the *Asia Society* website. The seeking eventually led Korda to join the Buddhist community Dharma Punx.

Korda's three-step program as outlined in *Unsubscribe* begins with reprioritizing goals to focus on a fulfilling avocation instead of a materialist vocation. The second step is to gain an understanding of self and specific emotional needs. The final step is to form meaningful connections with others. Korda tells readers that taking these steps is not necessarily easy and can be highly uncomfortable. However, he writes that the rewards are worth it.

A major point is that people who gain a greater consciousness about their place in the world tend to find more meaning and purpose in their life. However, he stresses that society's prescribed roles should largely be left behind. As a result, he urges readers to questions many things about themselves, from the job to their relationships with a focus on how meaningful and fulfilling they are. He goes on to provide various Buddhist practices to help people reevaluate their lives, ultimately making them more meaningful. These practices focus on things such as being mindful of death and recognizing compulsive behaviors.

Korda has "developed a plan based around the Buddha's teachings that gives readers another option, one that can lead to happiness independent of possessions and circumstances," wrote Brent R. Oliver for the *Tattooed Buddha* website. A *Publishers Weekly* contributor called *Unsubscribe* "an intelligent, compassionate addition to popular Buddhist literature that doesn't shy away from the grim and sometimes bleak realities of life."

■ Biographical and Critical Sources

PERIODICALS

Publishers Weekly, September, 11, 2017, review of *Unsubscribe: Opt Out of Delusion, Tune in to Truth*, p. 62.

ONLINE

Asia Society Website, https://asiasociety.org/ (February 14, 2018) Salvador Pantoja, "How a 'Dharma Punk' Learned to Treat Addiction through Meditation."

Pregame, http://www.pregamemagazine.com/ (December 1, 2017), Ciara Pressler, review of *Unsubscribe.*

Spirituality & Health, https://spiritualityhealth.com/ (October 31, 2017), Sam Mowe, review of *Unsubscribe.*

Tattooed Buddha, http://thetattooedbuddha.com/ (March 20, 2018), Brent R. Oliver, review of *Unsubscribe.*

Tricycle Online, https://tricycle.org/ (March 20, 2018), Josh Korda, "Now What? Life as a Recovering Addict."*

Lee Daniel Kravetz

■ Personal

Married; children: two. *Education:* University of Missouri, Columbia, B.A., 2000; Santa Clara University, M.A., 2013; earned M.F.T.

■ Addresses

Home—San Mateo, CA.

■ Career

Psychologist. Public Broadcasting Service, Boston, MA, program writer, 2001-04; Stanford University Hospital and Clinics, psychology intern, 2010-14; VA Palo Alto, National Center for PTSD, Palo Alto, CA, psychology research, 2013-15; Reframe Counseling and Coaching, San Mateo, CA, counselor, 2013—. Founding board member of the Lit Camp Writers Conference; has appeared on National Public Radio's *Forum* and the Oprah Network.

■ Member

California Association of Marriage and Family Therapists.

■ Writings

(With David B. Feldman) *Supersurvivors: The Surprising Link between Suffering and Success,* HarperWave (New York, NY), 2014.
Strange Contagion: Inside the Surprising Science of Infectious Behaviors and Viral Emotions and What They Tell Us about Ourselves, HarperWave (New York, NY), 2017.

Contributor to periodicals and websites, including the *New York Times, Psychology Today,* the *San Francisco Chronicle,* and *PBS.org.*

■ Sidelights

Lee Daniel Kravetz is a psychologist, counselor, and writer. He studied journalism at the University of Missouri, Columbia and later pursued a master's degree in psychology at Santa Clara University followed by a postgraduate fellowship at Stanford University. He has contributed articles to a range of periodicals and websites, including the *New York Times, Psychology Today,* the *San Francisco Chronicle,* and *PBS.org.* Kravetz is a founding board member of the Lit Camp Writers Conference.

Kravetz's practice, Reframe Counseling and Coaching, is based in San Mateo, California. He specializes in counseling teens and adults and in executive coaching for Silicon Valley-based companies. With teens and adults, he focuses largely on mood disorders, suicidal thinking, stress, PTSD, and grief. With his executive coaching, the focus is on personal organization, career planning, public speaking, and media training in order to improve leadership abilities and aid in achieving professional goals. His counseling services have been recognized in *Time, Psychology Today,* and the *Harvard Business Review.* Kravetz has additionally appeared on National Public Radio's *Forum* and the Oprah Network.

Supersurvivors

With coauthor David B. Feldman, Kravetz published *Supersurvivors: The Surprising Link between Suffering and Success* in 2014. The account uses several case studies to show the difference between individuals who thrive and grow from great adversity compared to those who merely survive their traumatic incidents. The cases covered in the book range from breast cancer survivors to athletes who have had limbs amputated. By comparing the scenarios of how these individuals rose above their troubles, the authors aim to show a common thread that points to how everyone can take adversity and use it as a tool improve one's own lot in life or even that of others around the world. Emphasis is placed on the feeling that one has control over the path one takes in life and by acknowledging but also letting go of past traumas in order to focus on living in the present with an eye toward a positive future.

Reviewing the book in *MBR Bookwatch*, Able Greenspan lauded: "Informed, informative, thoughtful, thought-provoking, iconoclastic and exceptionally well written, organized and presented, *Supersurvivors* . . . is one of those 'life changing reads' that come along perhaps once in a generation." A contributor reviewing the book in *Publishers Weekly* recorded the authors as saying that while they originally intended to present a few miraculous cases of survivors of great trauma, instead, they "ended up writing about how every one of us can live more fully."

Strange Contagion

Kravetz published *Strange Contagion: Inside the Surprising Science of Infectious Behaviors and Viral Emotions and What They Tell Us about Ourselves* in 2017. The account looks into the notion that creating a common language for discussing conditions like bulimia or suicide can lead to an increase in the number of those cases. He posits that social media coverage and general sensationalizing of suicides can actually create cues for others to believe that doing likewise is an acceptable and even original idea on their behalf. In an article in *Publishers Weekly*, Marcie Geffner talked with Kravetz about his research behind writing this book. Kravetz recalled: "The book is a deep dive into something very scary, but at the end, it is also about how we can catch hope and resilience and we can spread that even in the darkest of times."

A critic reviewing the book in *Publishers Weekly* stated: "Though the subject of Kravetz's book may be emotionally disturbing for sensitive readers, the questions he asks are of vital importance." A *Kirkus Reviews* contributor found the book to be "too first-personal at too many turns." Nevertheless, the *Kirkus Reviews* contributor conceded that Kravetz "has covered the bases well, raising provocative questions on whether social contagion can be contained in the way that we ward off leprosy and smallpox."

■ Biographical and Critical Sources

PERIODICALS

Kirkus Reviews, May 1, 2017, review of *Strange Contagion: Inside the Surprising Science of Infectious Behaviors and Vital Emotions and What They Tell Us about Ourselves.*
MBR Bookwatch, June 1, 2015. Able Greenspan, review of *Supersurvivors: The Surprising Link between Suffering and Success.*
Publishers Weekly, May 5, 2014, review of *Supersurvivors*, p. 52; May 8, 2017, review of *Strange Contagion*, p. 51; June 19, 2017, Marcie Geffner, "Stopping Suicides," p. 104.

ONLINE

Lee Daniel Kravetz Website, http://leedanielkravetz.com (February 7, 2018).
Psychology Today, https://www.psychologytoday.com/ (February 7, 2018), author profile.*

Damon Krukowski

■ Personal

Married Naomi Yang. *Education:* Graduated from Harvard University, 1985.

■ Addresses

Home—Cambridge, MA.

■ Career

Musician, publisher, producer, and writer. Galaxie 500, musician, 1987-91; Exact Change, Chicago, IL, cofounder and publisher, 1989—; Damon & Naomi, musician, 1991—. Creative Capital/Andy Warhol Foundation fellow; Harvard University's Berkman-Klein Center for Internet and Society fellow; performer on music albums with Galaxie 500, including *Today,* 1988, *On Fire,* 1989, *This Is Our Music,* 1990, and with Damon & Naomi, including *More Sad Hits,* 1992, *Wondrous World of Damon & Naomi,* 1995, *Playback Singers,* 1998, *Damon & Naomi with Ghost,* 2000, *Song to the Siren,* 2002, *The Earth Is Blue,* 2005, *Within These Walls,* 2007, *The Sub Pop Years,* 2009, *False Beats and True Hearts,* 2011, and *Fortune,* 2015.

■ Writings

5000 Musical Terms, Burning Deck (Providence, RI), 1995.
Uncollected, Ryko (New York, NY), 2004.
The Memory Theater Burned, Turtle Point Press (New York, NY), 2005.
(With Marc Joseph) *Marc Joseph: New and Used,* Steidl (Gottingen, Germany), 2006.

Afterimage, Ugly Duckling Press (New York, NY), 2011.
The New Analog: Listening and Reconnecting in a Digital World, MIT Press (Cambridge, MA), 2018.

Contributor to *Pitchfork* and *Artforum.*

■ Sidelights

Damon Krukowski is a musician, publisher, producer, and writer. He performed in the rhythm section and occasionally on vocals with the band Galaxie 500. When it broke up, he and fellow band member Naomi Yang formed the duo Damon & Naomi and continued to release albums. The pair also cofounded the small press Exact Change, which publishes works on avant-garde literature and other artists' writings. Krukowski has contributed to *Pitchfork, Artforum,* and a number of periodicals and journals. He is the recipient of fellowships from both the Creative Capital/Andy Warhol Foundation and Harvard University's Berkman-Klein Center for Internet and Society.

In an article in the *New Yorker,* Sarah Larson wrote about Krukowski's six-episode podcast called *Ways of Hearing.* She recalled that it "begins with an exciting analog sound: that of a needle descending on a record," adding that the podcast series "makes us think about the act of listening itself, in ways that feel timely and vital." Larson reasoned that "*Ways of Hearing* makes you highly attuned to such shifts, and to the complexity and variety of aurally connecting." Larson concluded that "the act of listening, we realize—not just in conversation but in our headphones and in the world—is significant. How we control sound, how we use it to insulate ourselves, to transport ourselves, to educate ourselves, to provoke thoughts and to distract ourselves from thoughts, to connect, to escape, can have social, even political, ramifications," further explaining that "listening to podcasts—these intimate, sophisticated constructions of sound and ideas—can connect us intensely to other people and isolate us from our surroundings at the same time. Krukowski is especially convincing, even poetic, about the artistic and social value of noise—which headphone listening and digital audio often shut out."

In 2005 Krukowski published the poetry collection *The Memory Theater Burned*. The collection heavily employs the use of metaphors. Krukowski's poems also deal with memory and music. Writing in the *Antioch Review,* F.D. Reeve said that the author "has burst forth with his own poems, a sunny fistful of bright, brassy prose poems that gallop across the meadows and bridges of life."

Krukowski published *The New Analog: Listening and Reconnecting in a Digital World* in 2017. In line with his *Ways of Hearing* podcast, the account examines audio technology, the act of listening, and the social meanings behind it all. Krukowski insists that the development of audio technology has allowed for complacency and mediocrity to set into the music industry and listeners of recorded music. He posits that LPs from the 1960s have a higher sound quality than MP3s, which he believes are intentionally designed that way. In this Krukowski examines the interplay between the state of the consumer marketplace, artistic expression, and the march of technology to show how digital media represents a major step backward in quality since the days of analog.

Writing in *Stereophile,* Stephen Mejias suggested that "audiophiles will sympathize with what he calls 'thick listening'—perhaps especially because it does more to describe the differences between active listening (as an event unto itself) and casual listening (as a supplement to some other event) than it does to describe the differences between digital and analog media." Mejias opined that Kru-

kowski "writes with a poet's profundity and focus, a drummer's sense of rhythm: 'Analog is not simply old, and digital is not merely new'—a sentiment with which most audiophiles would quickly agree. Like many Stereophile readers, Krukowski is not interested in ranking various forms of media." *Booklist* contributor Raymond Pun believed that "readers who are interested in the history of technology, acoustics, and sound . . . will be engaged." A contributor to *Kirkus Reviews* observed that Krukowski discusses the subject matter "comfortably." The same reviewer remarked that "Krukowski's writing is witty and generally accessible, though his detours into recording minutiae and avant-garde ideas about sound and art may lose some readers."

■ Biographical and Critical Sources

PERIODICALS

Antioch Review, September 22, 2005, F.D. Reeve, review of *The Memory Theater Burned,* p. 798.

Artforum International, March 1, 2007, Damon Krukowski, "Notes from the Underground: Damon Krukowski on Cornelius Cardew," p. 81.

Billboard, December 8, 2012, Glenn Peoples, "The Myth of the Penny Pinchers," p. 10.

Booklist, March 15, 2017, Raymond Pun, review of *The New Analog: Listening and Reconnecting in a Digital World,* p. 12.

Kirkus Reviews, March 1, 2017, review of *The New Analog.*

New Yorker, August 9, 2017, Sarah Larson, "Damon Krukowski Will Change How You Listen."

Stereophile, August 1, 2017, Stephen Mejias, review of *The New Analog,* p. 41.

ONLINE

Damon & Naomi Website, https://www.damonandnaomi.com/ (February 7, 2018), author profile.*

Min Kym

1978-

■ **Also Known As**

Min-Jin Kym

■ **Personal**

Born 1978, in South Korea. *Education:* Studied at Purcell School of Music and Royal College of Music.

■ **Addresses**

Home—London, England.

■ **Career**

Violinist. Has performed with numerous orchestras, including the Philharmonia, the London Philharmonic Orchestra, the Royal Philharmonic Orchestra, the Royal Liverpool Philharmonic Orchestra, and the Dresden Staatskapelle. Recording artist; has served as a goodwill ambassador for the city of Seoul.

■ **Awards, Honors**

Premier Mozart competition winner, 1990; Heifetz Prize; International Jascha Heifetz Competition for Violinists winner, 2004.

■ **Writings**

Gone: A Girl, a Violin, a Life Unstrung, Crown (New York, NY), 2017.

■ **Sidelights**

Min Kym is a Korean-born violinist. A child prodigy, she won the Premier Mozart competition in 1990 and soloed with the Berlin Symphony Orchestra the following year. In 2004 she won the International Jascha Heifetz Competition for Violinists. Despite her many musical accomplishments, however, it was the theft of her violin that brought her to the attention of non-musicians.

Kym published the memoir *Gone: A Girl, a Violin, a Life Unstrung* in 2017. The personal account centers on the theft of Kym's rare Stradivarius violin at London's Euston Station in 2010. She relates the lead up to the theft by illustrating the centrality of music and that violin to her life. After its theft, Kym is able to reflect on other troubling aspects of her life after losing her passion for playing.

In an interview on National Public Radio's *All Things Considered,* Kym talked about the process of laying her life bare to the public in the form of this memoir. "One of the most important things that I learned throughout this whole process is that we have such little control over anything." Kym appended: "But one thing that we do control is how you deal with the next steps forward. Writing—actually finding this new voice—it helped unblock my musical life. And, you know, for the first time in seven years or so, I felt hopeful again."

A contributor to *Kirkus Reviews* observed that "the story at the heart of this memoir has a complexity with which the author still wrestles." The same reviewer called *Gone* "a pellucid memoir of letting go and coming to terms." In talking about the popularity of books that center on the "singularity of genius" in a review in the *Spectator*, Alexandra

Coghlan admitted that "while *Gone* goes some way towards feeding that, returning three times to the question of what it is to be a prodigy, delivering darker answers with each iteration . . . it is surprisingly light on music. We get the compulsion of playing, the ease of it, the urgency of it, but comparatively little about the repertoire that is generated by it. Kym could be a mathematician or a chess champion and the book would read much the same." Writing in the *Bookseller*, Caroline Sanderson revealed that "the title of Kym's memoir refers both to this dreadful moment and to its far-reaching consequences, not only for her career but for her state of mind and sense of identity." Sanderson explained that "the second half of *Gone* reveals both the fate of her Stradivarius and how its owner recovered from the trauma of losing her soulmate. The process was an immensely painful one, but with the hiatus in her career, Kym was able—for the first time ever—to properly reflect on her life to date: her strange, even dysfunctional childhood . . . her long-concealed eating disorder, and the nature of her former boyfriend's control over her." Sanderson insisted that Kym writes about how the violin served as a crutch for all the problems in her life "with devastating insight."

In an article in *Gramophone*, Charlotte Gardner pointed out that "*Gone* is not aimed primarily at specialist classical music lovers, but at a wider audience." Gardner remarked that "the more classically knowledgeable, and indeed anyone who prefers a more refined literary style, may find *Gone* rather irritating. But if you stick with it there are interesting nuggets." Gardner concluded: "Those familiar with *Gone Girl* will know that the final twist is that its narrators turn out to be unreliable. It would be wrong and I suspect inaccurate to accuse *Gone* and Kym of that, but certainly its conclusion leaves as many questions hanging as a suspense novel." Reviewing the memoir in the London *Guardian*, Ro Kwon noted that "Kym's achievement exceeds infelicities of prose. At one point in *Gone*, her mentor, Ruggiero Ricci, aged 85, has sold his violin of 50 years and retired to Palm Springs. 'Shall I tell you something, Min? I've had three wives but only one violin,' he says, and, thanks to Kym, we know what he means." Also reviewing the memoir in the London *Guardian*, Barbara Ellen remarked: "The loss of the violin represents the *Gone* of this remarkable and original memoir, though only in the context of all the other things that are taken-Kym's childhood, her future, her spirit, her trust in people, her sense of identity. How thrilling then that, eventually, Kym's agonising attempts to recover are rewarded with another violin (an Amati) to love, and, with it, a sense that the future could be hers to own again."

In a review in the *Financial Times*, Jonathan McAloon reasoned that "*Gone* communicates what it is like to 'be a natural and yet quite unnatural'; to perceive from inside this 'outside'. The strangeness of being told, for instance, that you will outgrow your adult teacher within the year as an eight-year-old, or of being given care of near-priceless violins as a teenager living on a Northolt council estate." Writing in the *Arts Desk*, Adam Sweeting stated: "In admirably lucid and uncluttered prose, she describes her intimacy with the instrument in almost scandalous detail." Sweeting recorded that "Kym artfully sweeps us up in her grand passion, using it like a magician's misdirection to lead us away from the yawning fault-lines in her life."

■ Biographical and Critical Sources

BOOKS

Kym, Min, *Gone: A Girl, a Violin, a Life Unstrung*, Crown (New York, NY), 2017.

PERIODICALS

ArtsBeat: The Culture at Large, December 24, 2010, Robin Pogrebin, "Stradivarius Violin Is Stolen from London Snack Shop."

Bookseller, February 10, 2017, Caroline Sanderson, "Min Kym," p. 22; May 4, 2017, Caroline Sanderson, "The Instrument Just Seemed to Complete My Life."

Financial Times, April 7, 2017, Jonathan McAloon, review of *Gone*.

Gramophone, September 15, 2013, Charlotte Smith, "At Long Last, a Violinist and Her Cherished Million-Pound Stradivarius Are Reunited," p. 13; June 1, 2017, Charlotte Gardner, review of *Gone: A Girl, a Violin, a Life Unstrung*, p. 100.

Guardian (London, England), July 31, 2013, James Meikle, "Violinist on 'Cloud Nine' at Stradivarius Find," p. 9; April 22, 2017, review of *Gone*.

Kirkus Reviews, March 1, 2017, review of *Gone*.

New York Times, April 24, 2017, John Williams, "Tell Us 5 Things about Your Book."

Poets & Writers, May 1, 2017, review of *Gone*, p. 14.

Spectator, April 8, 2017, Alexandra Coghlan, review of *Gone*, p. 34.

Straits Times, May 30, 2017, Olivia Ho, "Violinist Min-Jin Kym Discovers Her Voice Outside Music."

World Entertainment News Network, December 19, 2013, "Min-Jin Kym's Violin Sells for $2.1 Million."

ONLINE

All Things Considered, http://www.npr.org/ (May 7, 2017), Lakshmi Singh, "Her Violin Stolen, a Prodigy's World Became 'Unstrung'."

Arts Desk, http://www.theartsdesk.com/ (April 2, 2017), Adam Sweeting, review of *Gone.*

Gone the Album Website, https://www.gonethealbum.com/ (February 7, 2018), author profile.

Idle Woman, https://theidlewoman.net/ (April 30, 2017), review of *Gone.*

Min Kym Website, http://www.minkym.com (February 7, 2018).

Peters Fraser & Dunlop Website, https://www.petersfraserdunlop.com/ (February 7, 2018), author profile.*

Nicola Lagioia

1973-

■ **Personal**

Born 1973, in Bari, Italy.

■ **Addresses**

Home—Rome, Italy.

■ **Career**

Writer, editor, and literary critic. Turin International Book Fair, Turin, Italy, director, 2016—. Has served as one of the film selectors for the 2013 and 2014 Venice International Film Festival.

■ **Awards, Honors**

Viareggio Prize, 2010; Premio Strega, 2015, for *La ferocia*.

■ **Writings**

Babbo Natale: dove si racconta come la Coca-Cola ha plasmato il nostro immaginario, Fazi (Rome, Italy), 2005.
Riportando tutto a casa, Einaudi (Turin, Italy), 2009.
La ferocia, Einaudi (Milan, Italy), 2014, translation by Antony Shugaar published as *Ferocity*, Europa Editions (New York, NY), 2017.
Ferocity, Europa Editions (New York, NY), 2017.

Also author of the novels *Tre sistemi per sbarazzarsi di Tolstoj (senza risparmiare se stessi)*, 2001, and *Occidente per principianti*, 2004.

■ **Sidelights**

Nicola Lagioia is an Italian writer, editor, and literary critic. Born in Bari, Italy, in 1973, he published his first novel, *Tre sistemi per sbarazzarsi di Tolstoj*, in 2001. He was one of the film selectors for the 2013 and 2014 Venice International Film Festival. In 2016 Lagioia began directing the Turin International Book Fair.

Ferocity, the translation by Antony Shugaar of his 2015 Premio Strega-winning novel *La ferocia* was published in 2017. In *Ferocity*, Michele is not content with the police ruling that his half-sister Clara Salvemini's violent death is nothing more than a suicide. Being born to the mistress of the head of the Salvemini family, he has always been considered an outsider to the family except with Clara. His return to try to figure out what really happened to her brings up past conflict and creates new ones as Clara's life is exposed. Michele also learns just how corrupt his family's real estate empire is, and Clara's role in helping to keep it successful through illicit means.

Booklist contributor Annie Bostrom observed that "Lagioia's prose—in Shugaar's translation—depicts . . . a violently alive setting that plays off its characters." A contributor to *Publishers Weekly* commented that the "oblique kaleidoscopic" way that Lagioia shifts between multiple timelines permits "the mystery to slowly and captivatingly resolve while offering a layered portrait of contemporary Italian life and the abuses of power that money can excuse." Although a *Kirkus Reviews* contributor did not recommend the novel "for the casual reader," the reviewer insisted that readers "will be swept up in a rich and rewarding literary experience." The same reviewer called the novel "a mesmerizing exploration of failure, resilience, and profound, multifaceted loss." In a review in *Bomb*, Kristen Martin confessed: "I was disheartened to find that Lagioia never fully endows Clara with rich interiority or motivations that read as fully believable." Martin conceded, however: "As every other aspect of Lagioia's novel is intricately planned, I am willing to concede that perhaps the opacity of Clara's motives is purposeful. Michele reflects on this point before Clara's death: 'We're guided by forces of which we're unaware, we act without knowledge, we say things whose motive is unclear, crimes without guilt and deaths without any apparent cause.' *Ferocity* gives us plenty of these possibilities to consider."

Reviewing the novel in the *Financial Times*, Zoë Apostolides explained that "the story is one of extreme paradoxes—between wealth and poverty, duplicity and honesty, legitimate and illegitimate children—and though this can appear stark and hyperbolic, there's a sense throughout that the history of the Salveminis taps into a wider national consciousness about who has licence to ruin another person." Apostolides credited translator Shugaar, noting that the novel is "elegantly translated." Writing in the *Los Angeles Review of Books*, Deborah E. Kennedy mentioned that "the layers not only advance the story but also complicate our understanding of this world of men on the brink and women surrendering to despair." Kennedy remarked that since "Clara dies in the first chapter, very few pages are devoted to her point of view and the ones that are suffer from a frustrating brand of lyricism doing little to mask the fact that her actions are often contradictory to the point of absurdity." Kennedy appended: "As a somewhat creaking mechanism of plot and in-trigue, her erratic and self-destructive behavior doesn't have an explanation beyond grief over her estrangement from Michele; and it is in exploring Clara's affairs and the impact of her fidelity on her husband, Alberto, that Lagioia's hitherto artful critique of Italy's machismo culture veers off-course." Kennedy concluded: "Bleak though it may be in its view of humanity and the future we're facing, this novel offers many pleasures, not the least of which is Lagioia's rich approach to simile, his unique ability to bring together the terrifying and the beautiful."

■ Biographical and Critical Sources

PERIODICALS

Booklist, October 1, 2017, Annie Bostrom, review of *Ferocity*, p. 25.
Financial Times, October 6, 2017, Zoë Apostolides, review of *Ferocity*.
Kirkus Reviews, March 1, 2017, review of *Ferocity*.
Publishers Weekly, August 21, 2017, review of *Ferocity*, p. 82.

ONLINE

Bomb, https://bombmagazine.org/ (October 31, 2017), Kristen Martin, review of *Ferocity*.
Festivaletteratura, http://www.festivaletteratura.it/ (February 7, 2018), author profile.
Los Angeles Review of Books, https://lareviewofbooks.org/ (October 18, 2017), Deborah E. Kennedy, review of *Ferocity*.*

Alexander Langlands

1978-

■ **Personal**

Born 1978, Oxford, England; married; children: two. *Education:* Attended University College London; University of Winchester, doctorate.

■ **Addresses**

Home—Swansea, Wales. *Agent*—Sophie Laurimore, Factual Management, 14 Vernon St., London W14 0RJ, England.

■ **Career**

Archaeologist, historian, writer, broadcaster, and educator. Swansea University, Swansea, Wales, United Kingdom, teaches medieval history. Also regular presenter for the British Broadcasting Corporation (BBC), beginning c. 2003, including working for the broadcast media for BBC Two, BBC One, as well as Channel 4, History Channel, and the Discovery channel.

■ **Writings**

Craeft: An Inquiry into the Origins and True Meaning of Traditional Crafts, W.W. Norton & Company (New York, NY), 2018.

■ **Sidelights**

Alexander Langlands grew up in Sussex, a rural county in southwest England. A historian, archaeologist, writer, and broadcaster, Langlands also lectures college studies in Medieval history, archaeology, and issues connected with heritage and heritage crafts. His work as a research and commercial archaeologist has led him to work on excavating sites throughout Europe, ranging from sites connected with the prehistoric era to industrial age sites. He also has extensive experience working in British broadcast media and has appeared on historical reenactment shows.

In his first book, *Craeft: An Inquiry into the Origins and True Meaning of Traditional Crafts,* Langlands takes readers into the ancient world of traditional crafts. Langlands is primarily interested in what he says has been the transformation of society's understanding of craft following industrialization, proclaiming that modern understanding of craft is relatively simplistic. Langlands explains early on that the book's title word "cræft" appeared in Old English. It meant something very different from the modern concept of craft. Rather, craeft referred not to certain objects but rather to a hard-to-define type of knowledge wisdom, and resourcefulness.

After an initial chapter focusing on defining craeft, Langlands takes readers on a historical journey from his home in Wales through Europe and Iceland. In the process, he combines history, scientific analysis, and personal anecdotes to provide a deeper understanding of what craft is and represents. "For Langlands, the only way to understand it is through firsthand experience," wrote *New York Times Online* contributor Michael Bierut. As a result, Langlands recounts his personal experiences along the way, which include spending time herding sheep, keeping bees, spinning wool, and making a thatched roof. "Exploring this unfamiliar territory requires navigating a deliciously unfamiliar vocabulary: hafting (attaching an arrowhead to the tip of a spear); laying, pleaching and plashing (all required to nurture a hedge-row); carding, retting, scotching (for textile production); . . . flushing (for sheep farming); puddling (for cisterns); and pugging and wedging (for pottery)" wrote Bierut.

Langlands concludes his book with a postscript on the relationship between craeft and contemplation. "His idealism and his love of the natural world and what we can learn to make of it are contagious," wrote *Shelf Awareness* website contributor Sara Catterall, going on to call *Craeft* "an illuminating book on the pleasures of traditional work, and how we can rediscover that tactile world of skillful creation." Sarah Archer, writing for the *Atlantic Online,* remarked: "Langlands calls for living and working with awareness of our environments, materials, and challenges in real time."

■ **Biographical and Critical Sources**

PERIODICALS

Booklist, December 1, 2017, Andie Paloutzian, review of *Craeft: An Inquiry into the Origins and True Meaning of Traditional Crafts,* p. 14.

BookPage, January, 2018, Deborah Mason, review of *Craeft,* p. 23.

Publishers Weekly, October 30, 2017, review of *Craeft,* p. 69.

ONLINE

Alex Langlands Website, https://alexlanglands.wordpress.com (March 20, 2018).

Atlantic Online, https://www.theatlantic.com/ (February 25, 2018), Sarah Archer, "The Forgotten Everyday Origins of 'Craft.'"

Guardian Online, https://www.theguardian.com/ (November 19, 2017), Ben East, "*Craeft* Review—Not Just a Load of Old Corn Dollies."

New York Times Online, https://www.nytimes.com/ (January 8, 2018), Michael Beirut, "Before Glitter and Glue Sticks, *Craeft.*"

Shelf Awareness, http://www.shelf-awareness.com/ (January 2, 2018), Sara Catterall, review of *Craeft.**

Sara B. Larson

■ **Personal**

Married; three children.

■ **Addresses**

Home—UT. *Agent*—Josh Adams, Adams Literary, 7845 Colony Rd., C4 No. 215, Charlotte, NC 28226.

■ **Writings**

"DEFY" TRILOGY; FANTASY NOVELS; FOR YOUNG ADULTS

Defy, Scholastic (New York, NY), 2014.
Ignite, Scholastic (New York, NY), 2015.
Endure, Scholastic (New York, NY), 2016.

"DARK BREAKS THE DAWN" DUOLOGY; FAN-TASY NOVELS; FOR YOUNG ADULTS

Dark Breaks the Dawn, Scholastic (New York, NY), 2017.
Bright Burns the Night, Scholastic (New York, NY), 2018.

■ **Sidelights**

Sara B. Larson is an author of fantasy novels aimed at young adults. Her first published work, *Defy*, came out in 2014 as the first installment in a trilogy. "*Defy* actually came from a very difficult period in my life, when I lost someone I loved," Larson told an online interviewer at *Publishing Crawl*. "I was so upset by his death that I couldn't write any-thing, but a friend of mine told me to stop trying to write a book and just write what I was feeling. So that's exactly what I did. I sat down and wrote a scene, not intending for it to go anywhere . . . but then I got curious about the characters. This whole fascinating world unraveled itself."

Defy

The world of *Defy* is the tropical kingdom of An-tion, where young men serve as soldiers and young women are breeders, enslaved to produce more warriors. War seems to be endless in Antion, and magic is a fact of life. Twins Alexa and Marcel are orphaned when a sorcerer destroys their home, and Marcel helps his sister disguise herself as a boy, Alex, so she can escape becoming a breeder. Their skill at swordfighting earns them a place in the royal guard serving Prince Damian, the son of King Hector. Damian has secret ambitions to make Antion a more just and peaceful place, and he is not fooled by Alexa's disguise—he knows she is female, and they have a mutual attraction. Alexa has another love interest, however, in Rylan, a comrade in the guard who also realizes she is a woman. At one point all three are kidnapped.

Several reviewers found *Defy* an entertaining, action-filled fantasy. "Larson's debut is full of pas-sion and adventure, urging readers to cheer and weep simultaneously at Alexa's astounding cour-age," remarked Jamie-Lee Schombs in *School Library Journal*. In *Booklist*, Stacey Comfort noted that the novel offers "grand adventure, romance, and thrilling political intrigue." A *Kirkus Reviews* contributor, however, was not particularly im-pressed with *Defy*, saying that "Alexa's behavior is stereotypically—unpleasantly—'girly,'" as she has emotional outbursts and often needs to be rescued. The critic also deemed the secondary characters and the setting underdeveloped. *Voice of Youth Advocates* commentator Erin Wyatt, however, maintained that Alexa displays "competence as a fighter and quick thinking" and dubbed the book an "action-packed fantasy" with "much page-turning appeal."

Ignite

In the second entry in the trilogy, Damian has become king, and Alexa, although her true gender has been revealed, is his personal guard. She still loves him, but she believes she would not be an appropriate wife for him. Antion is enjoying a period of relative peace when it is visited by villains with mind-controlling powers. Alexa must use her fighting skills to defend the kingdom.

Some critics considered *Ignite* a worthy follow-up to *Defy*. "The characters in *Ignite* are what make this story for me, even more than the engaging plot," observed an online reviewer at *One Book Two*. "We are introduced to familiar faces and also meet a few new bad guys that provide trouble for Alexa, Damian, and the rest of the Antion realm." Wyatt, again writing in *Voice of Youth Advocates*, deemed it "not quite as strong as the first installment" but still "a quick, engaging read" full of "intrigue and action." A *Kirkus Reviews* contributor did not care for the book, finding Alexa's reasons for spurning Damian unconvincing and calling both Damian and Rylan "bland blank slates." The critic summed up *Ignite* as "adequate heroic fantasy only for those who must have every girl-with-a-sword." The novel received praise from *School Library Journal* commentator Schombs, however, as she predicted: "Readers who enjoy love stories that include multifaceted relationships and a suspenseful plot will be enthralled."

Endure

The trilogy's finale finds Alexa engaged to marry Damian but still bound to her duty as a warrior. Antion is under siege by evil forces, and Rylan is a prisoner in another country. Alexa journeys there to rescue him, at the same time trying to fight off an adversary bent on world domination.

"When I finished writing *Endure,* I was sobbing," Larson told Hikari Loftus, who interviewed her for Salt Lake City's *Deseret News*. "Part of it was in relief and part of it was just sadness—knowing that I was done with this world and these characters. I love them, and they have been such a big part of my life for so many years. It was very emotional to realize that I had done it . . . but also very emotional to write it. It's a very emotional book."

Several commentators thought *Endure* provided a compelling and satisfying conclusion to the series. It has "darker elements than the first two novels," related Alicia Abdul in *Voice of Youth Advocates*. She found that the love story "borders on saccharine" but added that on the whole the tale has "a charming arc." In *School Library Journal*, Bernice La Porta praised the characters, particularly the "independent and strong" Alexa, and predicted: "Fans will be very satisfied with this final journey." A *Children's Bookwatch* contributor pronounced *Endure* a "powerful finale."

Dark Breaks the Dawn

Larson begins a new saga with *Dark Breaks the Dawn*, inspired by the *Swan Lake* ballet. The protagonist is Princess Evelayn, who becomes queen of the Light Kingdom of Eadrolan upon the death of her mother, Queen Ilaria. Evelayn is just eighteen and developing magical powers that include the ability to take the form of various animals. She must learn to manage her powers while leading Eadrolan's armies in a war with the Dark Kingdom of Dorjhalan, ruled by the mad King Bain.

Dark Breaks the Dawn received several positive reviews. Larson "deftly weaves fantasy with the best parts of the *Swan Lake* ballet in this gripping first book of a duology," observed a *Publishers Weekly* critic. A contributor to the *Cracking the Cover* website added: "*Dark Breaks the Dawn* offers adventure, magic, love, fairy tale and fantasy all mixed into one. But all that wouldn't work if not for her well-developed characters, which make the novel worth reading." In *Voice of Youth Advocates*, Allison Babin noted that "universal themes flourish in Larson's fantastic setting," including "issues of morality and justice and the burdens of responsibility." *Booklist* commentator Maggie Reagan thought the novel had "a slow start and some incomplete world building" but was redeemed by "a plucky heroine, a sinister, surprise villain in the wings, and plenty of battle action." Readers, she predicted, will be eager for the sequel.

■ Biographical and Critical Sources

PERIODICALS

Booklist, December 15, 2013, Stacey Comfort, review of *Defy*, p. 45; April 15, 2017, Maggie Reagan, review of *Dark Breaks the Dawn*, p. 48.

Children's Bookwatch, August, 2016, review of *Endure*.

Deseret News (Salt Lake City, UT), December 27, 2015, Hikari Loftus, "Author Sara B. Larson Takes Readers on Emotional Journey in *Endure*"; May 24, 2017, Tara Creel, "*Dark Breaks the Dawn* Is Fantastical Swan Lake Retelling."

Horn Book Guide, fall, 2014, Jenn Matters, review of *Defy*, p. 116; fall, 2015, Jenn Matters, review of *Ignite*, p. 128; fall, 2016, Jenn Matters, review of *Endure*, p. 131.

Kirkus Reviews, November 15, 2013, review of *Defy*; October 15, 2014, review of *Ignite*; October 1, 2015, review of *Endure*; March 15, 2017, review of *Dark Breaks the Dawn*.

Publishers Weekly, March 27, 2017, review of *Dark Breaks the Dawn*, p. 99; December 4, 2017, review of *Dark Breaks the Dawn*, p. S105.

School Library Journal, February, 2014, Jamie-Lee Schombs, review of *Defy*, p. 108; November, 2014, Jamie-Lee Schombs, review of *Ignite*, p. 119; November, 2015, Bernice La Porta, review of *Endure*, p. 108; October, 2017, Sheila Acosta, review of *Dark Breaks the Dawn*, p. 57.

Voice of Youth Advocates, February, 2014, Erin Wyatt, review of *Defy*, p. 73; December, 2014, Erin Wyatt, review of *Ignite*, p. 81; December, 2015, Alicia Abdul, review of *Endure*, p. 71; Allison Babin, April, 2017, review of *Dark Breaks the Dawn*, p. 71.

ONLINE

Adventures in YA Publishing, http://www.adventuresinyapublishing.com/ (January 2, 2016), interview with Sara B. Larson.

Awesome Book Nuts, http://awesomebooknuts.blogspot.com/ (December 28, 2014), review of *Ignite*.

Cracking the Cover, https://www.crackingthecover.com/ (June 12, 2017), "Sara B. Larson's *Dark Breaks the Dawn* Is Nuanced YA Fantasy."

Cuddle Buggery, http://cuddlebuggery.com/ (January 22, 2014), Meg Morley, review of *Defy*.

New in Books, https://www.newinbooks.com/ (February 19, 2016), interview with Sara B. Larson.

One Book Two, https://onebooktwo.wordpress.com/ (April 6, 2017), review of *Ignite*.

Quite the Novel Idea, https://quitethenovelidea.com/ (December 7, 2017), review of *Dark Breaks the Dawn*.

Publishing Crawl, http://www.publishingcrawl.com/ (December 19, 2014), interview with Sara B. Larson.

Sara B. Larson Website, http://sarablarson.blogspot.com (February 21, 2018).

Story Sanctuary, http://thestorysanctuary.com/ (December 1, 2017), Gabrielle Nadig, review of *Dark Breaks the Dawn*.

YA Books Central, http://www.yabookscentral.com/ (January 25, 2014), C.J. Redwine, review of *Defy*.*

Jennifer Latson

■ **Personal**

Female. *Education:* Yale University, B.A., 2002; University of New Hampshire, M.F.A., 2013.

■ **Addresses**

Agent—Kneerim & Williams, 90 Canal St., Boston, MA 02114.

■ **Career**

Chronicle, Centralia, WA, reporter, 2002-04; *Olympian,* Olympia, WA, reporter, 2004-06; *Daily Press,* Newport News, VA, reporter, 2006-08; *Houston Chronicle,* Houston, TX, reporter, 2008-10; University of New Hampshire, Durham, NH, graduate instructor, 2010-13; *Rice,* Houston, TX, writer and editor, 2013-15; *Rice Business Wisdom,* Houston, TX, staff editor, 2017—.

■ **Writings**

The Boy Who Loved Too Much: A True Story of Pathological Friendliness, Simon & Schuster (New York, NY), 2017.

Contributor to periodicals, including *Boston Globe* and *Time.*

■ **Sidelights**

Jennifer Latson, a former newspaper reporter, is author of *The Boy Who Loved Too Much: A True Story of Pathological Friendliness,* about a boy with a rare disorder known as Williams syndrome. The syndrome, she writes, is a "genetic fluke that strip[s] one in every 10,000 people of the inherent wariness, skepticism, and inhibition . . . hardwired into the rest of us." People with Williams are loving and friendly to everyone they meet, and they tend to express affection effusively, not realizing that it is sometimes not welcome. They have difficulty with sustained conversations and relationships, however. They often have some degree of developmental delay and, sometimes, cardiovascular disorders; cardiologist J.C.P. Williams discovered the condition in 1961. It is caused by the absence of twenty-six genes out of the 20,000 that make up an individual's DNA.

Latson spent three years monitoring the boy of the title, Eli, and his single mother, Gayle. Both names are pseudonyms. The author met Eli in 2011, when he was twelve, and she saw him enter puberty, as the syndrome began to cause even more problems in his life. He already was the target of his schoolmates' ridicule, but it seemed not to bother him. He also had no awareness that strangers might mean him harm. As he became sexually mature, he developed a habit of hugging women he found attractive, even if he did not know them, and he had to be taught to avoid such displays of affection. His behavior eventually improved, but his mother has had to accept that Eli may never be able to live an independent life. Gayle has been a dedicated advocate for Eli, Latson reports, but she has had to modify her life for him. A lover of rock concerts and horror movies who once sported heavy makeup and tattoos, Gayle has opted for a more sedate lifestyle and appearance. The book closes with Eli entering high school.

Latson became interested in people with Williams syndrome after hearing a story on National Public Radio, she told Temple Grandin in an online interview at *Refinery 29*. "As an introvert, I wanted to learn from them, to study their social ease, because I kind of wanted to emulate them," Latson said. "But I also thought: 'How hard must it be to be that open to the world?' You know, to trust everyone, to really have this kind of unconditional love for everyone. To me that seems terrifying. They're so vulnerable." Gayle gave the author unlimited access in exchange for having her name and Eli's changed to protect their privacy, Latson told *Houston Chronicle* interviewer Alyson Ward. "They didn't censor themselves around me," Latson explained. "They didn't say 'leave the room' when they had a difficult conversation."

While Eli's condition makes him susceptible to abuse, Latson noted, many people have reacted positively to their encounters with him. "Most of the time, I feel like his kindness and joy brought out kindness and joy in other people," she told Ward. "There were times you could tell he had really affected someone, that he really made their day—and once in a while you could see they got something out of this meeting that was special. People were always giving him gifts or telling Gayle that he's such a blessing."

Several reviewers considered *The Boy Who Loved Too Much* a compelling story, told with empathy and respect. "The book could have been exploitative, but instead it's a moving portrait of a mother facing the fact that her child has a different future from the one she imagined," remarked Clare Wilson in *New Scientist*. She added: "Neatly interwoven with Eli's story are the reasons scientists are fascinated," such as the fact that research on Williams syndrome "has helped isolate genes for high blood sugar and hypertension." A *Publishers Weekly* contributor made a similar point, saying Latson "skillfully interweaves the science . . . with a powerful story line." In *Booklist*, Dane Carr noted that the author "blends life concerns and hard medical facts in this widely appealing chronicle."

Some critics focused on her narrative of those life concerns. Tucker Coombe related in the online magazine *Brevity*: "Latson does a delicate dance here, illustrating everyday moments that are often mortifying for Gayle, hilarious to the reader, and which would be embarrassing for most people—but not Eli. She depicts him in all his earnest awkwardness, with great affection and not a hint of condescension." A *Kirkus Reviews* commentator observed that the author "tells the story with great sympathy and eloquence, giving voice to the frustration, anguish, and despair a parent feels when their child struggles with a rare disorder."

Mike Snyder, writing in the *Houston Chronicle*, reported: "It would be a mistake to squeeze this book into the 'disease narrative' genre. It transcends that niche, partly through the author's reflections on what our reactions to people with Williams Syndrome have to say about the human condition." In the *New York Times Book Review*, Ruth Padawer concluded: "While Latson's storytelling is sometimes more dutiful than necessary, her book provides a thorough overview of Williams syndrome, and its thought-provoking paradox. No doubt life for people with Williams (and those who love them) has its difficulties. But given the state of the world today—the hate attacks, the divisiveness, the vitriol—it's hard not to wish that we all had more kindheartedness and openness, even if our embrace of other humans is only metaphorical."

■ Biographical and Critical Sources

PERIODICALS

Booklist, May 15, 2017, Dane Carr, review of *The Boy Who Loved Too Much: A True Story of Pathological Friendliness*, p. 4.

Boston Globe, June 27, 2017, Eric Liebetrau, "Saga of a Boy Who Was Genetically Nice."

Houston Chronicle, June 16, 2017, Alyson Ward, "Jennifer Latson Talks about Immersion Journalism and *The Boy Who Loved Too Much*"; Mike Snyder, "Debut Author Tells a True Story of 'Pathological Friendliness.'"

Houstonia, June, 2017, Jeanne Lyons Davis, "*The Boy Who Loved Too Much* Tells the Story of Pathological Friendliness."

Kirkus Reviews, May 1, 2017, review of *The Boy Who Loved Too Much*.

New Scientist, June 24, 2017, Clare Wilson, "Can Heightened Empathy Be a Bad Thing?"

New York Times Book Review, June 25, 2017, Ruth Padawer, "All His Loving," p. 17.

Pacific Standard, May/June, 2017, Peter C. Baker, "A Genetic Hunger for Connection and Friendship."

Publishers Weekly, May 1, 2017, review of *The Boy Who Loved Too Much*, p. 55.

ONLINE

Banner Website, https://www.thebanner.org/ (June 16, 2017), Kristy Quist, review of *The Boy Who Loved Too Much*.

Brevity, http://brevitymag.com/ (July 31, 2017), Tucker Coombe, review of *The Boy Who Loved Too Much*.

Jennifer Latson Website, http://www.jenniferlatson. net (February 19, 2018).

Refinery 29, http://www.refinery29.com/ (June 22, 2017), Temple Grandin, "What Williams Syndrome's 'Pathological Friendliness' Has to Do with Autism."

Simon & Schuster Website, http://www. simonandschuster.com/ (February 19, 2018), brief biography.

Utah Public Radio Website, http://upr.org/ (August 30, 2017), Tom Williams, "*The Boy Who Loved Too Much:* Williams Syndrome on Wednesday's *Access Utah,*" link to broadcast.*

Josh Lauer

■ Personal

Male. *Education:* Indiana University of Pennsylvania, B.A., 1992; University of Pittsburgh, M.L.I.S., 1997; University of Pennsylvania, M.A., 2005, Ph.D., 2008.

■ Addresses

Office—University of New Hampshire, Horton Social Science Center, Department of Communication, 20 Academic Way, Durham, NH 03824.

■ Career

University of New Hampshire, Durham, associate professor of communication. Previously taught at the University of Pennsylvania.

■ Writings

Creditworthy: A History of Consumer Surveillance and Financial Identity in America, Columbia University Press (New York, NY), 2017.

Contributor to books, including *The Rise of Marketing and Market Research*, Palgrave Macmillan, 2012, and *The Emergence of Routines: Entrepreneurship, Organization, and Business History*, Oxford University Press, 2017, and to periodicals, including *Technology & Culture*, *New Media & Society*, and *Enterprise & Society*.

■ Sidelights

Josh Lauer is associate professor of communication at the University of New Hampshire, teaching classes in media studies and media history. His research focuses on the history of communication technology, surveillance, and financial culture. Lauer earned his M.A. and Ph.D. at the University of Pennsylvania, where his dissertation won the Herman E. Krooss Prize for Best Dissertation in Business History at the Business History Conference. He has published articles in journals and contributed chapters to books in his fields. Lauer released his first book, *Creditworthy: A History of Consumer Surveillance and Financial Identity in America*, in 2017.

In *Creditworthy*, Lauer delves into the history of credit reporting in America, beginning with the infamous Panic of 1837, a financial crisis that produced a recession lasting well into the 1840s. Businesses and banks failed, and thousands of people were thrown out of work. Unemployment rose as high as twenty-five percent in areas of the United States, but no part of the country was entirely spared. Lewis Tappan and his brother Arthur saw their silk trade business in New York City wiped out in the panic, partly as the result of having extended credit to customers. In 1841 Lewis formed the Mercantile Agency, a precursor to today's credit-reporting agencies, as a way to assess customers' creditworthiness. The business boomed, and he soon opened branches in Boston, Philadelphia, and Baltimore. Lauer follows the history through to the formation of the leading credit bureaus Experian, Equifax and TransUnion. These powerful corporations track consumers' spending habits and other financial information, storing vast archives of personal data.

A *Publishers Weekly* reviewer noted that the "technological sophistication and scope" of credit agencies' information gathering has grown exponentially. In this light, Lauer's "top-down economic history is a thorough, enlightening, and long-overdue contribution." A correspondent at *UNH Today* called *Creditworthy* a "rigorous look at the intersection between creditworthiness and other measures of citizens' 'worth'" that is especially resonant in light of the Equifax security breach. Online at *We Make Money Not Art*, a critic noted Lauer's attention to "how U.S. citizens became objects of intensive surveillance." Specifically, the correspondent remarked: "He investigates how financial identity became a key marker of our personal trustworthiness and how increasingly centralised and invasive systems for monitoring an individual's behaviour and credits enabled the ascent of consumer capitalism in the U.S." In tracing the history, Lauer offers intriguing stories. Credit agencies even gathered tidbits from newspapers and court documents concerning bankruptcies, divorces, and lawsuits. The data was so extensive that the FBI and police departments would visit credit agencies to peruse the files to aid their own investigations. The reviewer at *We Make Money Not Art* concluded that *Creditworthy* "is impeccably researched and makes for a compelling read."

■ Biographical and Critical Sources

PERIODICALS

American Historical Review, April, 2018, Sarah E. Igo, review of *Creditworthy: A History of Consumer Surveillance and Financial Identity in America*, pp. 605-607.

Perspectives on History, September, 2017, Sarah Fentron, review of *Creditworthy*, pp. 29-34.

Publishers Weekly, May 15, 2017, review of *Creditworthy*, p. 49.

ONLINE

Josh Lauer Website, https://mypages.unh.edu/jlauer/bio (February 8, 2018).

UNH Today, https://www.unh.edu/unhtoday/ (November 28, 2017), review of *Creditworthy*.

University of New Hampshire Website, https://cola.unh.edu/ (February 8, 2018), author faculty profile.

We Make Money Not Art, http://we-make-money-not-art.com/ (August 28, 2017), review of *Creditworthy*.

Karissa Laurel

■ **Personal**

Married; children. *Hobbies and other interests:* Crafts, painting, and drawing.

■ **Addresses**

Home—NC.

■ **Career**

Writer and novelist.

■ **Writings**

"NORSE CHRONICLES" SERIES

Midnight Burning, Red Adept Publishing (Garner, NC), 2015.
Arctic Dawn, Red Adept Publishing (Garner, NC), 2016.
Molten Dusk, Red Adept Publishing (Garner, NC), 2017.

"STORMBOURNE CHRONICLES" SERIES

Heir of Thunder, Evolved Publishing (Cassville, MO), 2016.
Quest of Thunder, Evolved Publishing (Cassville, MO), 2018.

■ **Sidelights**

Karissa Laurel is a novelist and the author of two fantasy series that draw from the legends of the Norse gods. She lives in North Carolina with her husband and a child and is fond of motorcycles and flea markets. She is also a fan of sci-fi and fantasy and claims to be able to repeat the dialogue from the movie *The Princess Bride* verbatim.

"Norse Chronicles" Series

The "Norse Chronicles" series begins with *Midnight Burning*, which introduces readers to Solina Munday, who runs her family's bakery in a small North Carolina town. When she has a nightmare about her twin brother in Alaska being killed by a beast, she wakes the next day to find out that he has died. Shocked and disturbed by the dream, Karissa decides to go to Alaska to find out more. Before long, Solina discovers that she has paranormal powers and may also hold the key to the fate of the world. However, first she must be able to control her powers and protect her friends. "This story closely follows traditional themes of Norse mythology which the author then takes in a fresh and new directions" wrote a *Whispering Stories* website contributor, adding: "The respect shown to the original mythology is touching and makes it a lot easier for a mythology buff such as myself to follow without snorting 'well THAT never happened!'"

The next book in the series, *Arctic Dawn*, finds Solina returning to California after spending a month as a shooting star, part of her fiery powers associated with a Norse sun god. Her friend Skyla, however, is missing. A mysterious stranger and a weapon of mass destruction requires Solina to take action. First, she knows she needs Skyla's help and sets out to find him. "There were big surprises that kept the story fresh and moving," wrote an *I Smell Sheep* website contributor. *Molten Dusk* finds Solina working with Baldur Odinson, the current Allfather. Also helping are Valkyries and the thunder god Magni Thorin. Their enemies are led by Hela, goddess of the Underworld and controller of an army of stone golems. A *Publishers Weekly* contributor pointed out the "the character growth, the mystical elements, and the many battles of epic powers."

"Stormbourne Chronicles" Series

Laurel starts a new series, the "Stormbourne Chronicles," with *Heir of Thunder*. Eveyln (Evie) Stormbourne, who holds dominion over the sky, is faced with the task of defeating her kingdom's enemies following the death of her father, the Lord of Thunder. Evie is to ascend to the throne of Inxelgrau when her home is destroyed by revolutionaries. She escapes in disguise with the help of Gideon Faust, who was her father's horse master. Evie and Gideon are separated at sea when Evie is washed overboard and ends up with a band of nomads. As Evie tries to find her way back home, she has several adventures involving dark Magicians and a family who has laid claim to Evie's birthright. Laurel "creates a very in-depth story world and a cast of compelling characters," wrote a *Steampunk Cavaliers* website contributor.

The next book in the series, *Quest of Thunder,* finds Evie having claimed her birthright. However, she soon loses her powers and must be protected y her companion, Gideon Faust. Evie goes into hiding as she seeks to reclaim her power over the sky and lay rightful claim to the throne. A *Steampunk Cavaliers* website contributor "highly recommend both *Heir of Thunder* and *Quest of Thunder* for anyone who loves steampunk, fantasy, and adventure."

■ Biographical and Critical Sources

PERIODICALS

Publishers Weekly, November 6, 2017, review of *Molten Dusk,* p. 66.

ONLINE

Bull Spec, http://bullspec.com/ (September 16, 2015), "The Hardest Part: Karissa Laurel on *Midnight Burning*."

I Smell Sheep, http://www.ismellsheep.com/ (May 24, 2017), review of *Arctic Dawn;* (August 26, 2017), review of *Molten Dusk.*

Karissa Laurel Website, http://www.karissalaurel.com (March 20, 2018).

Steampunk Cavaliers, http://www.steampunkcavaliers.com/ (November 14, 2017), review of *Heir of Thunder;* (January 9, 2018), review of *Quest of Thunder.*

Whispering Stories, https://whisperingstories.com/ (April 18, 2016), "*Midnight Burning* by Karissa Laurel—Book Review & Interview."*

Richard Lawson

■ Personal

Born in Boston, MA.

■ Addresses

Home—New York, NY.

■ Career

Writer, film critic, columnist, and podcast cohost. *Vanity Fair*, New York, NY, film critic, entertainment news columnist, and cohost of *V.F.*'s *Little Gold Men* podcast.

■ Writings

All We Can Do Is Wait, Razorbill (New York, NY), 2018.

Contributor to periodicals, including the *Guardian* and *Out* magazine, and to websites, including the *Atlantic Wire* and *Gawker*. Contributed to the *Dinner Party Download* radio show.

■ Sidelights

A longtime film critic an entertainment news journalist, Richard Lawson is also a young adult (YA) novelist. His debut YA novel, *All We Can Do Is Wait*, tells the story of five Boston teenagers following a bridge collapse that rocks the city. In an interview with *Booklist Online* contributor Briana Shemroske, Lawson commented on why he de-

cided to write a novel, noting he had been wanting to write one since college when he began to focus on a career as a writer. "But it always seemed so daunting, to build this big thing from scratch," Lawson noted in the *Booklist Online* interview, adding: "I used to primarily write plays, and some bad poetry, and those seemed much more manageable in terms of scale. But the wish to write a novel—or, rather, to be done writing a novel—was always there, persistently lingering."

In *All We Can Do Is Wait,* Jason, Alexa, Scott, Skyler, and Morgan meet in the waiting room of Massachusetts General Hospital following the horrendous bridge collapse. Siblings Jason and Alexa are waiting to hear about the status of their parents while Scott's girlfriend was also on the bridge when it collapsed. Skyler's sister, who raised her, has also been injured. As for Morgan, she quickly learns that her father was not on the bridge after all but stays in the hospital to help her fellow teenagers, whom she has just met, cope with the disaster. The story is told through a third-person omniscient narrator who provides alternative views via the five teenagers' different perspectives. "Alternating viewpoints give multiple sides of the . . . story, while flashbacks give the important contexts of the characters' lives before the accident," wrote a *Kirkus Reviews* contributor.

Alexa is relying on Jason for emotional support, but as time passes and the conversation flows she learns about a secret that may place the siblings against each other. Scott's girlfriend, Aimee, was on a theater group bus. Scott is not only distressed about the accident but also is hoping to get to talk to Aimee at least one more time to patch up their rocky relationship and tell her he loves her. As for Skyler, her sister has been more like a mother than a sibling, and she cannot imagine life without her.

"Young readers . . . will be rewarded by this quiet yet powerful meditation on life and death," wrote Reinhardt Suarez in *Booklist*. Allie Kelley, writing for the *Blackbird Review* website, remarked: "Lawson did a good job of keeping the reader entertained, constantly throwing unexpected twists into the plot. It was an emotional journey, but it was one that will make readers think and not leave them disappointed."

■ Biographical and Critical Sources

PERIODICALS

Booklist, December 1, 2017, Reinhardt Suarez, review of *All We Can Do Is Wait*, p. 53.

Kirkus Reviews, December 1, 2017, review of *All We Can Do Is Wait*.

Publishers Weekly, November 27, 2017, review of *All We Can Do Is Wait*, p. 62.

ONLINE

Blackbird Review, http://blackbirdreview.org/ (November 9, 2017), Allie Kelley, review of *All We Can Do Is Wait*.

Booklist Online, https://www.booklistonline.com/ (January 18, 2018), Briana Shemroske, "An Interview with Richard Lawson."

RT Book Reviews Online, https://www.rtbookreviews.com/ (February 6, 2018), Daphne Gold, review of *All We Can Do Is Wait*.*

Ashton Lee

■ **Personal**

Born in Natchez, MS. *Education:* University of the South, B.A.

■ **Addresses**

Home—Oxford, MS.

■ **Career**

Writer, publisher's representative. Works as a publisher's representative/book vendor to public libraries in six southern states.

■ **Writings**

"CHERRY COLA BOOK CLUB" SERIES

The Cherry Cola Book Club, Kensington Books (New York, NY), 2013.

The Reading Circle, Kensington Books (New York, NY), 2014.

The Wedding Circle, Kensington Books (New York, NY), 2015.

A Cherry Cola Christmas, Kensington Books (New York, NY), 2015.

Queen of the Cookbooks, Kensington Books (New York, NY), 2016.

Book Club Babies, Kensington Books (New York, NY), 2017.

■ **Sidelights**

American writer Ashton Lee is the author of the "Cherry Cola Book Club" series, about a small-town Mississippi librarian who forms a town-wide book club in order to save the local library. Lee knows whereof he writes: he has been a publisher's representative and book vendor to public libraries in six southern states. "I've done it for decades and have learned just about everything about the inner workings of libraries," Lee noted in a *Traveling with T* website interview. "One of the biggest problems they often have is underfunding and dealing with budget cuts. Often, a library's budget will be cut first, restored last. An author should always write what he or she knows best. So I decided to write an entertaining series about the problems libraries have, hoping to become a national advocate for them as necessary, educational community resources."

Lee also has the benefit of growing up in a literary family. His father was a writer and editor, and his hometown, Natchez, Mississippi, is a "writing laboratory," as he further noted in his interview. "Growing up, I was immersed in the quirky, eccentric behavior of many members of my parents' and grandparents' generations. I listened, observed and remembered."

The Cherry Cola Book Club

Lee launched his series with the 2013 novel, *The Cherry Cola Book Club.* Set in the fictional town of Cherico, Mississippi, population 5,000, the novel details the efforts of young Maura Beth Mayhew, director of the Cherico Public Library, to save said library. She has been given an ultimatum by the town council to increase circulation and membership or the library will be closed in a matter of months. Thus she launches the Cherry Cola Book Club, encouraging local citizens to gather and discuss Southern literature and enjoy some tasty potluck dinners. These efforts are at first scoffed at by the pragmatic councilmen, but ultimately the small community rallies, and the library is saved for the time being.

Reviewing this first installment in *Booklist,* Carol Haggas commented: "Lee's buoyant David-versus-Goliath tale zestfully illuminates a real problem confronting libraries and cities of all sizes." Writing at the *RT Book Reviews* website, Lauren DuBois also had praise, calling this novel a "delightful read, written in a light and breezy style, with a cast of characters that is equal parts kooky and genuine, all set in a picturesque, quiet Southern town." Similarly, Lesa Holstine, writing at her *Lesa's Book Critiques* website, noted: "I don't know if Ashton Lee knows it or not, but his novel, *The Cherry Cola Book Club,* is a wonderful love letter to libraries, librarians, and all the people who love and support them. He took all the turmoil surrounding libraries in recent years, wrapped it up in one small Mississippi community library, and gave us a librarian heroine to cheer for."

The Reading Circle

The series continues with *The Reading Circle,* in which Maura must continue her struggles. The library has been given a one-year reprieve, but her major foe on the council, Sparks, desperately wants to use library funds to help build an industrial park named after him. To that end, he is planning on putting a mole in the regular book club meetings and disrupt the group. But Maura now discovers that she has her own spy in the Sparks camp when the councilman's former secretary joins the reading club.

Writing in *Booklist,* Haggas lauded this second installment, observing: "The challenges of keeping any library anywhere open and effectively serving its patrons is a problem facing most communities. Lee . . . brings these salient topics to light in an unpredictably entertaining series." Online *RT Book Reviews* writer DuBois also had a positive assessment, noting: "Lee enhances this installment by spicing the story up a bit more, adding even more opinions—and challenges—swirling around librarian Maura and her crowd of book lovers." Likewise, writing at *Lesa's Book Critiques,* Holstine concluded: "Whether you see *The Reading Circle* as a battle cry for libraries, a story of strained relationships, a novel featuring tasty recipes, or a charming story of the South, Ashton Lee's latest novel is entertaining and thought-provoking."

The Wedding Circle and A Cherry Cola Christmas

Twin challenges are presented in the third installment, *The Wedding Circle.* Things seem on the uptick for Maura and her circle, with a new library

being planned and Maura's wedding to English teacher Jeremy McShay in the offing. Then word leaks that a local politician is again trying to divert library funds and also Maura's socialite parents present sudden obstacles to her wedding. "Members of the Cherry Cola Book Club and citizens of Cherico, Miss., are back and as wonderful to read about as they ever were," noted DuBois in *RT Book Reviews.* Holstine similarly dubbed this a "charming wedding story," in a review for her *Lesa's Book Critiques* website.

Lee offers a holiday treat in the fourth installment, *A Cherry Cola Christmas,* "one of their most endearing and uplifting stories yet," according to *RT Book Reviews* writer DuBois. Maura is back from her honeymoon, but the mood in town is sour with some businesses closing and small-time crime on the rise. She calls a special holiday meeting of the book club to brace the town's spirits with good stories. Writing at *Lesa's Book Critiques,* Holstine noted: "When you have time to settle in for a Christmas comfort read, don't hesitate to reach for *A Cherry Cola Christmas.* It's a warm, comfortable visit with old friends."

Queen of the Cookbooks and Book Club Babies

Queen of the Cookbooks sees Maura relishing the opening of the new library on July 4. Her arch nemesis, Councilman Sparks, is scheduled to cut the opening ribbon—and why not, as the new library bears his name. Maura has arranged a cook-off to help the celebrations, but there are, of course, a few setbacks. The library furniture does not arrive in time and two competitive cooks start a fight at the cook-off, but Maura and her friends smooth things out. "Lee's feisty heroine makes light work of some tough problems in this small-town, small-stakes adventure," commented a *Kirkus Reviews* critic. *Booklist* reviewer Stephanie Turza also had praise, terming this series addition a "delightfully cozy novel that combines small-town politics and sky-high dreams."

The sixth and final series installment, *Book Club Babies,* sees Maura expecting her first baby, as are two of her good friends in town. Thus she forms the Expecting Great Things support group, intended to pass on tips on pregnancy and birthing. But there are unexpected results: with one friend to be a single mom and the other giving birth to a mixed-race child, the parents of both expectant mothers disapprove. "Lee's group of close-knit friends and her family handle serious issues of racism and repudiation, love and loyalty with their trademark homespun wisdom," noted Haggas in

Booklist. Writing at *Lesa's Book Critiques,* Holstine concluded: "Now that there is a new generation to attend story times, read books, use library computers, there's the promise of the future in *Book Club Babies.* This is the perfect way to end the series."

■ Biographical and Critical Sources

PERIODICALS

Booklist, March 1, 2013, Carol Haggas, review of *The Cherry Cola Book Club,* p. 17; February 1, 2014, Carol Haggas, review of *The Reading Circle,* p. 24; November 1, 2017, Carol Haggas, review of *Book Club Babies,* p. 13; December 1, 2016, Stephanie Turza, review of *Queen of the Cookbooks,* p. 26.

Kirkus Reviews, November 1, 2016, review of *Queen of the Cookbooks.*

Publishers Weekly, October 23, 2017, review of *Book Club Babies,* p. 62.

ONLINE

Book Series in Order, https://www.bookseriesinorder. com/ (February 13, 2018), "Ashton Lee."

Fantastic Fiction, https://www.fantasticfiction.com/ (February 13, 2018), "Ashton Lee."

Kensington Books Website, http://www. kensingtonbooks.com/ (February 13, 2018), "Ashton Lee."

Lesa's Book Critiques, https://lesasbookcritiques. blogspot.com/ (March 19, 2013), Lesa Holstine, review of *The Cherry Cola Book Club;* (March 27, 2014), Lesa Holstine, review of *The Reading Circle;* (March 26, 2015), Lesa Holstine, review of *The Wedding Circle;* (October 24, 2015), Lesa Holstine, review of *A Cherry Cola Christmas;* (December 9, 2016), Lesa Holstine, review of *Queen of the Cookbooks;* (November 25, 2017), Lesa Holstine, review of *Book Club Babies.*

RT Book Reviews, https://www.rtbookreviews.com/ (March 26, 2013), Lauren DuBois, review of *The Cherry Cola Book Club;* (March 25, 2014), Lauren DuBois, review of *The Reading Circle;* (March 31, 2015), Lauren DuBois, review of *The Wedding Circle;* (September 29, 2015), Lauren DuBois, review of *A Cherry Cola Christmas;* (November 29, 2016), Lauren DuBois, review of *Queen of the Cookbook;* (November 28, 2017), Lauren DuBois, review of *Book Club Babies.*

Times Record News Online, http://archive. timesrecordnews.com/ (November 22, 2015), Susan O'Bryan, review of *A Cherry Cola Christmas.*

Traveling with T, https://travelingwitht.com/ (August 5, 2013), "Interview with Ashton Lee—Author of *The Cherry Cola Book Club.*"*

Mira T. Lee

1970-

■ **Personal**

Born August 9, 1970; children. *Education:* Graduate of Stanford University. *Hobbies and other interests:* Salsa dancing.

■ **Addresses**

Home—Cambridge, MA. *Agent*—Susan Golomb, Writers House LLC, 21 W. 26th St., New York, NY 10010.

■ **Career**

Novelist. Worked as a graphic designer and a pop-country drummer.

■ **Awards, Honors**

Peden Prize, *Missouri Review;* recipient of an Artist's Fellowship from the Massachusetts Cultural Council.

■ **Writings**

Everything Here Is Beautiful, Pamela Dorman Books/ Viking (New York, NY), 2018.

Contributor of short fiction to periodicals, including the *Southern Review, Gettysburg Review, Missouri Review, Triquarterly, Harvard Review,* and *American Short Fiction.*

■ **Sidelights**

Novelist Mira T. Lee did not grow up wanting to be a writer and studied biology in graduate school. Nevertheless, a short story she wrote after her mother's death chronicled her mother's final weeks and was published in 2009 in the *Southern Review.* "It was my first published piece, and it was a story I wanted to tell," Lee noted in an interview with *Los Angeles Review of Books* website contributor Eleanor J. Bader, adding: "After that, I started to get more familiar with storytelling and found that I enjoyed seeing things branch out further and further from my actual life."

In her debut novel, *Everything Here Is Beautiful,* Lee tells the story of two Chinese-American sisters, one of whom begins to suffer from schizophrenia. In her interview with *Los Angeles Review of Books* contributor Bader, Lee noted that she writes about mental illness from experience because several people in her family have had schizophrenia. "I've dealt with doctors, hospitals, and social workers, and I am very familiar with the frustrations involved in trying to help someone with this kind of illness, so a lot of the emotions I include in the book are emotions I've felt," said Lee in the *Los Angeles Review of Books* interview.

In *Everything Here Is Beautiful,* Miranda is the older sister and has acted as Lucia's protector ever since they were young. Lucia has always been impulsive and unpredictable, unlike the steady, responsible Miranda. Although Lucia has become an accomplished journalist, her lapses into severe psychosis threatens both her career and her relationships, including her spouse and her relationship with Miranda. "To Lee's credit, Lucia, the more compellingly drawn of the two siblings, never seems like a psychological case study," wrote a *Kirkus Reviews* contributor.

Eventually, Lucia begins to hear voices and goes deeper into what psychiatrists have diagnosed as probable schizophrenia. Although Miranda is living in Switzerland, she frequently returns to the United States to see if she can save her sister as Lucia travels, fights the odds and develops a career, goes through marriages and relationships, and has a child. Meanwhile, Miranda begins to question just how far she is willing to go to honor family ties and her relationship with Lucia as a certain amount of bitterness arises over the demands Lucia has made on Miranda's life over several decades.

"This electrifying first novel is wistful, wise and utterly unforgettable," wrote Stephenie Harrison in *BookPage.* Noting that "Lee handles a sensitive subject with empathy and courage," a *Publishers Weekly* weekly contributor went on to remark: "Readers will find much to admire and ponder throughout."

■ Biographical and Critical Sources

PERIODICALS

Booklist, November 1, 2017, Margaret Quamme, review of *Everything Here Is Beautiful,* p. 29.

BookPage, January, 2018, Stephenie Harrison, review of *Everything Here Is Beautiful,* p. 16.

Kirkus Reviews, December 1, 2017, review of *Everything Here Is Beautiful.*

Library Journal, June 15, 2017, brief review of *Everything Here Is Beautiful,* p. 4A; September 1, 2017, Annalena McAfee, "Fiction," includes review of *Everything Here Is Beautiful,* p. 101.

Marie Claire, December, 2017, Samantha Irby, "What We're Reading," p. 122.

Publishers Weekly, October 23, 2017, review of *Everything Here Is Beautiful,* p. 61.

ONLINE

Asian American Writers' Workshop Website, http://aaww.org/ (February 7, 2018), Angie Kim, "Creating As You Go: An Interview with Mira T. Lee."

Boston Globe Online, https://www.bostonglobe.com/ (January 5, 2018), "Stories that Inhabit Gra Areas Attract Mira T. Lee," author interview; (February 2, 2018), Anna Parini, "A Shattering Debut about Mental Illness and the Bond between Sisters."

Los Angeles Review of Books, https://lareviewofbooks.org/ (January 16, 2018), Elanor J. Bader, "Multiculturalism and Mental Illness: An Interview with Mira T. Lee."

Masters Review, https://mastersreview.com/ (January 16, 2018), Katharine Coldiron, review of *Everything Here Is Beautiful.*

Mira T. Lee Website, http://www.miratlee.com (March 21, 2018).

San Francisco Book Review, https://sanfranciscobookreview.com/ (February 15, 2018), "Mira T. Lee, Author of *Everything Here Is Beautiful* Book.

Seattle Times Online, https://www.seattletimes.com/ (January 28, 2018), Ellen Emry Heltzel, "Mira Lee's *Everything Here Is Beautiful* Tells of Two Sisters and a Legacy of Mental Illness."

Shelf Awareness, http://www.shelf-awareness.com/ (January 16, 2018), review of *Everything Here Is Beautiful.*

USA Today Online, https://www.usatoday.com/ (Jan 16, 2018), Steph Cha, "Two Sisters, Bound by Love and Mental Illness, in 'Beautiful' Debut Novel."

Wall Street Journal Online, https://www.wsj.com/ (January 9, 2018), review of *Everything Here Is Beautiful.*

Washington Independent Review of Books, http://www.washingtonindependentreviewofbooks.com/ (January 9, 2018), Alice Stephens, review of *Everything Here Is Beautiful.**

Ruth Lehrer

1963-

■ Personal

Born January 2, 1963, in New York, NY; partner's name, Amy. *Education:* Attended Oberlin College.

■ Addresses

Home—Worthington, MA.

■ Career

Writer and sign language interpreter.

■ Writings

Tiger Laughs When You Push (poetry), Headmistress Press (Sequim, WA), 2016.
Being Fishkill (novel), Candlewick Press (Somerville, MA), 2017.

■ Sidelights

Ruth Lehrer is the author of the debut coming-of-age novel *Being Fishkill.* The story traces the relationship between a couple of preteens. "When Fishkill Carmel, born to a family of abuse and neglect, meets the eccentric, fearless optimist, Duck-Duck Farina, her life begins to change," Lehrer explained to Jonathan Rosen in a *Tuesday Writers* interview. Fishkill has been living alone in a run-down shack following the death of her abusive grandfather (who may, it is hinted, also be her father) and the disappearance of her drug-addicted mother. Fishkill greatly prefers life alone to living with her grandfather. At the age of twelve, starting the seventh grade, she has adopted a tough persona to cope with the pressures of her life. When Duck-Duck becomes her friend and initiates her into Duck-Duck's gang, however, she relaxes that persona. "But is it changing too much? Fishkill had forged an impenetrable, don't-mess-with-me identity to fight off poverty and bullies," Lehrer told Rosen. "If she lets that down how will she deal with the hard times ahead?"

Fishkill finds herself informally adopted by Duck-Duck and Duck-Duck's mother, who cheerfully admits Fishkill into her family circle. "A desperately sad story of profound abuse," stated a *Kirkus Reviews* contributor, "is softened somewhat by the highly intelligent Duck-Duck and her loving mother." Slowly, Fishkill begins to let her guard down—until she is surprised by the sudden reappearance of her mother, Keely. "The plot, as well as Duck-Duck and Fishkill's friendship, twists and turns," declared a *Publishers Weekly* reviewer, "as Keely reappears and disappears." As a result, stated Karen Jensen in *School Library Journal*, "this fragile new beginning is threatened by the reappearance of Fishkill's unstable mother—and by unfathomable tragedy."

Being Fishkill emerged, Lehrer has said, as a character study. "I got the first seed for the book several years ago . . . [driving] up and down the Taconic Parkway for months, passing the FISHKILL/CARMEL exit sign each time," Lehrer told Rosen. "'Doesn't that sound like girl's name?' I said. And so it began." "I didn't really build the plot. I was lucky enough to have the characters, Fishkill and Duck-Duck, knock loudly on my creative door," Lehrer said on the *Writer Writer Pants on Fire* website. On the other hand, she added, "the plot of *Being Fishkill* shifted in small ways during the process of writing and editing but my second book . . . seems to change every time I sit down to write." "Exploring themes of rebuilding one's identity," wrote Etienne Vallee in *Voice of Youth Advocates*, ". . . Fishkill and Duck-Duck will continue to haunt the reader long after the end of this emotionally intense book."

Critics celebrated Lehrer's fiction debut. "Poet Ruth Lehrer's young adult debut is a stunning, revelatory look at what defines and sustains 'family,'" Jensen declared. "And, just as it does for Fishkill, meeting Duck-Duck Farina and her mother will leave readers forever changed." "Lehrer," said *Booklist* contributor Courtney Gilfillian, "pulls at heartstrings in her thought-provoking debut, while leaving some questions unanswered." "I absolutely loved this novel," enthused a *Teen-Reads* website reviewer. "The achingly beautiful and heartbreaking story pulled me in without even trying. It was almost impossible not to be in enthralled in this book. Most importantly, it offered me a new perspective on a lot of things that I was taking for granted. I now look at my full fridge and pantry with more gratitude, appreciate my warm and Christmas tree-lit house much more, and hug my mom and dad." Lehrer's novel "will help readers understand the circumstances of those who are less fortunate than themselves," concluded Samantha Sheridan in the *Children's Book Review*, "as well as show them that it is important to help others who are in need."

■ Biographical and Critical Sources

PERIODICALS

Booklist, September 15, 2017, Courtney Gilfillian, review of *Being Fishkill*, p. 50.

Kirkus Reviews, August 15, 2017, review of *Being Fishkill*.

Publishers Weekly, September 18, 2017, review of *Being Fishkill*, p. 72.

School Library Journal, November 13, 2017, review of *Being Fishkill*.

Voice of Youth Advocates, October, 2017, Etienne Vallee, review of *Being Fishkill*, p. 59.

ONLINE

Children's Book Review, https://www.thechildrensbookreview.com/ (January 22, 2018), Samantha Sheridan, review of *Being Fishkill*.

Ruth Lehrer Website, http://ruthlehrer.com (March 28, 2018), author profile.

TeenReads, November 30, 2017, review of *Being Fishkill*.

Tuesday Writers, http://www.tuesdaywriters.com/ (October 10, 2016), Jonathan Rosen, "Interview with Ruth Lehrer, Debut Author of *Being Fishkill*!"

Writer Writer Pants on Fire, http://writerwriterpantsonfire.blogspot.com/ (January 16, 2018), "*Being Fishkill* Author Ruth Lehrer on Stumbling into Inspiration."*

David Leite

1960-

■ **Personal**

Born 1960, in Fall River, MA. *Education:* Rochester Institute of Technology, A.A.S., 1981; Hunter College, B.S., 1998. Studied theater at Carnegie Mellon University.

■ **Addresses**

Home—New York, NY; Roxbury, CT.

■ **Career**

Web publisher, food and travel writer, cookbook author, memoirist. Deutsch Advertising, copywriter, 1990-92; Merkley + Partners, senior copywriter, 1992-94; Ogilvy & Mather, Saatchi & Saachi, Y&R, and Wells, Rich, Greene, freelance advertising copywriter, 1995-2001; *Leite's Culinaria* website, founder, publisher, and writer, 1999—.

Has appeared as a guest on various television and radio programs; correspondent on public radio's food program *The Splendid Table;* moderator and speaker at panels for the Greenbrier. Member of advisory board, Community Culinary School of Northwest Connecticut.

■ **Awards, Honors**

Bert Greene Award for Food Journalism, 2006; James Beard Award for Best Internet Website for Food, 2006, 2007; Association of Food Journalists Award, 2006, 2007; James Beard Award for Best Newspaper Feature without Recipes, 2008; First Book/Julia Child Award, International Association of Culinary Professionals, 2010, for *The New Portuguese Table.*

■ **Writings**

The New Portuguese Table: Exciting Flavors from Europe's Western Coast, Clarkson Potter (New York, NY), 2009.
Notes on a Banana: A Memoir of Food, Love, and Manic Depression, Dey Street Books (New York, NY), 2017.

His work has been included in the *Best Food Writing* anthologies, 2001-15. Contributor to periodicals, including *New York Times, Martha Stewart Living, Bon Appétit, Saveur, Food & Wine, Gourmet, Food Arts, Men's Health, Los Angeles Times Magazine, Chicago Sun Times,* and *Washington Post.*

■ **Sidelights**

David Leite is a food and travel writer, cookbook author, memoirist, and website publisher. He began his career as an advertising copywriter, working both on staff and freelance for various organizations and corporations, including Deutsch Advertising, Merkley + Partners, Ogilvy & Mather, Saatchi & Saachi, Y&R, and Wells, Rich, Greene. In 1998, he turned his attention to food and travel writing, publishing articles in a host of magazines and newspapers, among them *New York Times, Martha Stewart Living, Bon Appétit, Saveur, Food & Wine, Gourmet, Food Arts, Men's Health, Los Angeles Times Magazine, Chicago Sun Times,* and *Washington Post.* He has also appeared as a guest on television shows, including for the Food Network and the

History Channel, and on the radio shows *All Thing Considered* and *Cooking Today*. Leite is a correspondent and guest host for National Public Radio's *The Splendid Table*. His articles on food have been anthologized in the series *Best Food Writing*. A correspondent at the Author's Guild website summarized the scope of Leite's articles, saying that he "has written about everything from Champagne and Welsh cuisine to living with bipolar disorder and the trials and tribulations of being a super taster."

The New Portuguese Table

In 1999, Leite set up a website called *Leite's Culinaria* where he featured food-related articles and columns, food facts and lore, and a database of recipes with a special focus on Portuguese specialties. In 2009 Leite released his first book, *The New Portuguese Table: Exciting Flavors from Europe's Western Coast*, in which he delves into the cuisine of his heritage. For the book, he won the 2010 International Association of Culinary Professionals First Book/Julia Child Award. In it, he outlines the regional cuisines of Portugal, following with recipes spanning appetizers to condiments.

Susan Hurst, writing in *Library Journal*, applauded the coverage, saying that *The New Portuguese Table* is "sure to appeal to adventurous cooks" and may "reinforce your urge to hit the sunny beaches of the Algarve." Critiquing the cookbook in *Booklist*, Mark Knoblauch found it unsurprising that the "Iberian Peninsula's other occupant should reinvent its cooking for a new generation" and offer it up to an "international audience." In *ForeWord*, Matt Sutherland commented that Leite "superbly" summarizes Portugal's thirteen regions with details of their food and wine. Many recipes, Sutherland advised, are "surprising in their Portuguese distinctness." Indeed, "Portugal brings something new to the table with an unpretentious satisfaction component sure to gain in popularity."

A critic in *Publishers Weekly* amusingly reported that Leite's book may be the "perfect cookbook for lovers of salt cod" before going on to say that it may be the perfect cookbook for those who hate the fish as well. The critic applauded the "extensive glossary" and the "delectable jumble of dishes that range from classic to contemporary." Writing online at *Kitchn*, Faith Durand called *The New Portuguese Kitchen* a "passionate yet lucid approach to Portuguese cooking" with "wonderful" photos. She summarized it as "gorgeous" and a "great introduction to Portuguese cooking."

Notes on a Banana

Leite next published *Notes on a Banana: A Memoir of Food, Love, and Manic Depression*. Shauna Sever spoke with Leite in an interview for *The Splendid Table*, where Leite described his childhood, growing up with extended family in what he called a "tenement"—a three-story building of three apartments. His parents were immigrants from the Azores. Everyone—as many as fifteen people—gathered for Sunday dinners, a vast spread of Portuguese foods. As a child, he found it alienating from American culture. He yearned for Spam and Velveeta, as well as Betty Crocker cake. When he met his partner, Alan, everything changed. Alan had a different relationship to food, which he imparted to Leite. Leite, who has suffered from manic depression, told Sever that "food, and specifically the act of cooking food, . . . calmed me." He continued: "I would get lost in those smells and the sights and the tastes of it. It'd be a diversion momentarily, and sometimes that's all it took to get through the day." Traveling back to his family's home in Portugal, he found his passion: "I say that if roots could have come out of my feet and burrowed their way into the volcanic soil of that island, they would have because I finally felt that I was where I belonged, and it was an extraordinarily powerful moment for me."

A *Kirkus Reviews* correspondent observed that in this memoir Leite "tells the story of his struggle to come to terms with his Portuguese heritage, bipolar disorder, and homosexuality." Of Leite's efforts, Jamie Schler wrote at *Huffington Post*: "Letting it go, exposing ourselves and our innermost secrets to the world is a tricky, delicate balance and it takes skill, tenderness, and humor. David Leite does it masterfully." The critic found the "chronicle of self-acceptance . . . brave and moving." Letie, said the critic, "impressively finds honesty and humor in the darkest of circumstances" in this debut. Karen Springen applauded this "warm, witty, sometimes heartbreaking" memoir, terming it a "candid and charming self-portrait" in *Booklist*. B. David Zarley, writing on the *Paste* website, called *Notes on a Banana*, "one of the finest portraits of bipolar disorder." On the *Same 24 Hours* website, a reviewer characterized the book as "poignant, astonishingly courageous, and unapologetically hilarious"—a "true tale that dazzles, touches the heart, and inspires."

■ **Biographical and Critical Sources**

BOOKS

Leite, David, *Notes on a Banana: A Memoir of Food, Love, and Manic Depression*, Dey Street Books (New York, NY), 2017.

PERIODICALS

Booklist, September 1, 2009, Mark Knoblauch review of *The New Portuguese Table: Exciting Flavors from Europe's Western Coast* p. 23; March 15, 2017, Karen Springen, review of *Notes on a Banana*, p. 13.

Library Journal, May 15, 2009, Susan Hurst, review of *The New Portuguese Table*, p. 93.

Publishers Weekly, April 20, 2009, review of *The New Portuguese Table*, p. 46.

ONLINE

ABC News, http://abcnews.go.com/ (April 19, 2017), Lauren Effron, review of *Notes on a Banana*.

Byrd's Books, http://byrdsbooks.com/ (April 10, 2017), review of *Notes on a Banana*.

ForeWord, http://www.forewordmagazine.com/ (July 1, 2009), Matt Sutherland, review of *The New Portuguese Table*.

Huffington Post, https://www.huffingtonpost.com/ (June 30, 2017), Jamie Schler, review of *Notes on a Banana*.

Kirkus Reviews, http://www.kirkusreviews.com/ (March 1, 2017), review of *Notes on a Banana*.

Kitchn, https://www.thekitchn.com/ (October 2, 2009), Faith Durand, review of *The New Portuguese Table*.

Paste, https://www.pastemagazine.com/ (April 12, 2017), B. David Zarley, review of *Notes on a Banana*.

Same 24 Hours, http://thesame24hours.podbean.com/ (May 22, 2017), review of *Notes on a Banana*.

Southern Kissed, https://www.southernkissed.com/ (May 17, 2017), review of *Notes on a Banana*.

Splendid Table, https://www.splendidtable.org/ (April 20, 2017), Shauna Sever, author interview.

Washington Times, https://www.washingtontimes.com/ (April 18, 2017), Tracee M. Herbaugh, review of *Notes on a Banana*.*

Amanda Lepore

1967-

■ **Also Known As**

Armand Lepore

■ **Personal**

Born November 21, 1967, in Cedar Grove, NJ.

■ **Addresses**

Home—New York, NY.

■ **Career**

Transgender model, singer, and performance artist. Has appeared in films and had cameos in music videos.

■ **Writings**

(With Thomas Flannery, Jr.) *Doll Parts: A Memoir,* Regan Arts (New York, NY), 2017.

Recorded a full-length album, *I . . . Amanda Lepore,* in 2011.

■ **Sidelights**

Amanda Lepore, born Armand, is a transgender model, singer, and performance artist. Lepore grew up in New Jersey in troubled circumstances. Her mother was schizophrenic and institutionalized for long periods, and her father abandoned the family

when Lepore was fourteen. Lepore, who was a raised as a boy but says she always knew she was female, rebelled early in life. She made transgender costumes for a friend in exchange for female hormones and ran off to marry a man at age seventeen. She underwent sex reassignment surgery at age eighteen (astonishingly, paid for by her father-in-law). Several years later she left her husband to move to New York City to establish herself as a model and singer.

In New York, she worked variously as a manicurist and dominatrix. In the 1980s, she was a member of the Club Kids, a group of dance club personalities on the underground nightlife scene who were best known for showy costumes and shocking behavior. Lepore has appeared in films and had cameos in the music videos of Elton John and Grace Jones, among others. Her debut full-length album, *I . . . Amanda Lepore,* came out in 2011. She has also released singles. Lepore was a part of the True Colors Tour 2007, a North American tour of fifteen cities to benefit the Human Rights Campaign, PFLAG, and the Matthew Shepard Foundation.

In 2017, Lepore released *Doll Parts: A Memoir,* written with Thomas Flannery, Jr. In this debut, she shares details of her difficult childhood and her gender transition. She also shares stories of her work as a dominatrix and her many cosmetic surgeries. Peter Davis reported in the *Observer* that the book "includes tip sheets on how to flirt with men, bleach your hair, do your nails and command a stage." A *Kirkus Reviews* contributor called *Doll Parts* a "wonderfully candid, unrushed text" paired with "impeccably styled, posed, and provocative photographs." The wealth of photographs were taken by such luminaries as David LaChapelle, Josef Jasso, Rob Lebow, and Joey

Falsetta. Writing in the *Cut,* Hyunjee Lee noted that Lepore "maintains an unapologetic sense of self."

In the *New York Times,* Jacob Bernstein commented that Lepore is famous largely for her extensive cosmetic surgery, so famous that "Swatch even put out a timepiece with Ms. Lepore's face and blowfish red lips emblazoned across the dial." In her quest for beauty, she has had silicone injections to fill out her breasts and derriere and even had her ribs broken to enhance her hourglass shape. Bernstein remarked, "Ms. Lepore's outsize presence has not always been embraced by fellow travelers on the night life circuit, who sometimes wonder aloud how a person with no discernible talent has managed to remain in the public consciousness for so long." Even so, she "remains extremely popular with nightclub audiences." Writing in *W,* Emilia Petrarca observed that "by the end of the book, readers learn that Amanda Lepore is so much more than just an expensive body; rather, she's the embodiment of a life much lived."

■ Biographical and Critical Sources

BOOKS

Lepore, Amanda, and Thomas Flannery, Jr., *Doll Parts: A Memoir,* Regan Arts (New York, NY), 2017.

ONLINE

Amanda LePore Website, http://amandalepore.net (February 8, 2018).

Cut, https://www.thecut.com/ (April 19, 2017), Hyunjee Lee, "How Burlesque Dancer Amanda Lepore Became a Transgender Icon," review of *Doll Parts.*

Filthy Dreams, https://filthydreams.org/ (July 27, 2017) Emily Colucci, review of *Doll Parts.*

Gay Book Reviews, https://gaybook.reviews/ (June 23, 2017), review of *Doll Parts.*

Kirkus Reviews, http://www.kirkusreviews.com/ (March 15, 2017), review of *Doll Parts.*

New York Times, https://www.nytimes.com/ (July 19, 2017), Jacob Bernstein, review of *Doll Parts.*

Observer, http://observer.com/ (April 20, 2017), Peter Davis, "Amanda Lepore, Confessions from Loving Life as a Living Doll," author interview.

Out, https://www.out.com/ (March 27, 2017), Michael Musto, author interview.

Reviews by Amos Lassen, http://reviewsbyamos lassen.com/ (February 8, 2018), Amos Lassen, review of *Doll Parts.*

Windy City Media Group Website, http://www. windycitymediagroup.com/ (May 17, 2017), Owen Keehnen, author interview.

W, https://www.wmagazine.com/ (April 20, 2017), Emilia Petrarca, review of *Doll Parts.**

Keith Lesmeister

■ **Personal**

Born in NC. *Education:* Bennington College, M.F. A., 2014.

■ **Addresses**

Home—Decorah, IA.

■ **Career**

Northeast Iowa Community College, Calmar, instructor in communications.

■ **Writings**

We Could've Been Happy Here (short stories), MG Press (Des Plaines, IL), 2017.

Has published fiction in journals, including *Gettysburg Review, North American Review, Redivider,* and *Slice,* and in the anthology *American Short Fiction.* Has published nonfiction in *River Teeth, Sycamore Review, Good Men Project, Tin House Open Bar,* and *Water-Stone Review.*

■ **Sidelights**

Keith Lesmeister was born in North Carolina and grew up in Iowa, where he still lives. He left only long enough to attend Bennington College, where he earned an M.F.A. in 2014. He teaches at Northeast Iowa Community College. His fiction has appeared in the journals *Gettysburg Review, North*

American Review, Redivider, and *Slice,* among others, and in the anthology *American Short Fiction.* Lesmeister's nonfiction has appeared in *River Teeth, Sycamore Review, The Good Men Project, Tin House Open Bar, Water-Stone Review,* and elsewhere. Barrett Bowlin, writing in *Fiction Writers Review,* termed his fiction "stunning" and remarked that he is "an author whose impressive body of work creeps up on you like an early autumn frost."

In 2017, Lesmeister released his debut collection, *We Could've Been Happy Here,* comprising twelve stories that all take place in Iowa. A critic in *Kirkus Reviews* noted that Lesmeister's "heartland . . . is a downcast place, replete with meth shacks, mortality, and regret" and called the book "a gritty, emotionally sensitive clutch of stories." In one story, meth addict Vincent loses custody of his children. In another, young Alice passes the time of her father's deployment killing the rabbits invading the family's garden. In a third, a bored middle-aged couple plan a bank heist. Critiquing the book on the *Coil* website, Jen Corrigan emphasized that "Lesmeister does not construct stagnant images of the Iowa setting but instead uses landscape and location to further illustrate the themes contained within his stories."

Ray Barker, in *Heavy Feather Review,* also mentioned Lesmeister's focus on locale. Lesmeister, he said, "populated [his stories] with men stuck in the painful middle-distance of life, haunting the rural and lonely locales of the Midwest, the Iowa small towns serving as a microcosm of their weary worldview." He continued: "The parameters of the physical geography are clear: fading horizons at sunset, wide-open skies, Indian summers, distant farms, pastures, and backroads on the margins." Corrigan found this aspect appealing: "Readers who seek a collection with a strong connection to place and setting would do well to pick up *We Could've Been Happy Here.* Lesmeister's stories are all about balance between character and situation, with the Heartland environment reflecting the themes of each narrative seamlessly."

Lesmeister spoke about his method with Bowlin in *Fiction Writers Review,* saying, "I think there are lots of things connecting the stories, not least is the motivation for writing each story, which all have some element of twisting the commonly understood writing advice: write what you know. In all of these stories, I'm trying to write what I don't know. . . . Part of the joy in writing these stories was allowing the characters to take over and make decisions that were wholly their own." He added: "I always start with situations—complicated, messy, unwieldy—and wait for my character(s) to say or do something. Once that happens—that action or piece of dialogue—we're off to the races."

In *Atticus Review,* Barrett Warner asserted: "Lesmeister can spin a tale." By way of explanation, Warner stated: "Although he firmly roots life matters in front of 'issues,' Lesmeister uses images in series to suggest infinity. . . . There's a wonderful endlessness in these stories. Each story doesn't begin so much as take up where an untold story left off." Terry Melia, contributor to *Sabotage Reviews,* applauded the "lean concise style dealing with complex adult and coming of age issues that capture the characters in moments of decline." She called attention to his open-ended style: "Teasingly Lesmeister doesn't tell us how the stories end, leaving us with an essence of the characters strange and dark souls whose journey will take them to whatever destiny has in store."

■ Biographical and Critical Sources

ONLINE

Atticus Review, https://atticusreview.org/ (July 10, 2017), Barrett Warner, review of *We Could've Been Happy Here.*

Coil, https://medium.com/the-coil/ (May 16, 2017), Jen Corrigan, review of *We Could've Been Happy Here.*

Cutbank, http://www.cutbankonline.org/ (September 6, 2017), Denton Loving, author interview.

Fiction Writers Review, http://fictionwritersreview.com/ (May 17, 2017), Barrett Bowlin, author interview.

Gazette, http://www.thegazette.com/ (September 16, 2017), Rob Cline, review of *We Could've Been Happy Here.*

Heavy Feather Review, https://heavyfeatherreview.com/ (September 28, 2017), Ray Barker, review of *We Could've Been Happy Here.*

Keith Lesmeister Website, https://keithlesmeister.com (February 9, 2018).

Kirkus Reviews, http://www.kirkusreviews.com/ (March 15, 2017), review of *We Could've Been Happy Here.*

Michigan Quarterly Review, http://www.michiganquarterlyreview.com/ (May 25, 2017), Cameron Finch, author interview.

Sabatoge Reviews, http://sabotagereviews.com/ (May 17, 2017), Terry Melia, review of *We Could've Been Happy Here.*

Tack, https://bvtack.com/ (October 13, 2017), Sarah Nicholson, review of *We Could've Been Happy Here.**

Derrick Levasseur

1984-

■ Personal

Born February 3, 1984. *Education:* Mitchell College, associate's degree, 2004; Roger Williams University, B.A. 2010; Salve Regina University, master's degree in business management, 2012.

■ Addresses

Home—Cumberland, RI.

■ Career

Central Falls Police Department, RI, Central Falls, RI, 2004-17, began as patrolman, became sergeant. Winner of TV game show *Big Brother*, 2014.

■ Writings

The Undercover Edge: Redefine the Rules to Win Life's Game, Sourcebooks (Naperville, IL), 2018.

■ Sidelights

Derrick Levasseur is best known for his role in the CBS television series *Big Brother*—a reality show that pits residents of a single house against one another for a monetary prize. Levasseur ended up winning the competition in 2014. After winning he retired from his job as a police sergeant in Rhode Island and became a motivational speaker and writer. Levasseur stated in his *Big Brother* cast biography, found on the *CBS* website, that he intended to use the celebrity he earned on the show "to make some positive changes. I would like to give back to my family and help out the kids of Central Falls. Also, I'm a huge animal lover. Sign me up for anything I can do to help."

Levasseur's book *The Undercover Edge: Redefine the Rules to Win Life's Game* was inspired by his experiences on *Big Brother,* but it draws on lessons (and language) he used as a police officer. "After my season, I had a lot of people ask me what was my *Big Brother* strategy—how did I win the game?" Levasseur told Andy Dehnart in *Reality Blurred.* He continued: "To be honest with you, Andy, I didn't have an answer. I didn't have a *Big Brother* strategy. What I had was an approach that was derived from my personal, professional experience as an undercover detective." "Through his life experiences, both personal and professional," wrote the contributor of a biographical blurb to the author's website, "Derrick has developed an innovative approach to building stronger relationships and achieving personal goals."

Critics appreciated Levasseur's first book, with its homely yet extremely pertinent advice. *The Undercover Edge* "is definitely not the typical book by a reality TV star," stated Dehnart. "It's friendly yet earnest, and surprisingly vulnerable." In it, Levasseur presents life lessons he has learned, some while serving the Rhode Island public as a police officer, and others from his own family. "Derrick views it as a conversation with his (eventual) readers, gradually opening up until he's sharing details about the time he shot a man while on duty, and its emotional aftermath: anger, alcohol, and eventually therapy," Dehnart continued. "The book covers everything from his father leaving when he was a kid to the mistakes Derrick has made as a father." "Though the cop-talk conceit can seem hackneyed," stated a *Publishers Weekly* reviewer,

"Levasseur's fresh and candid perspective makes for an empowering self-help guide."

■ **Biographical and Critical Sources**

PERIODICALS

Publishers Weekly, October 2, 2017, review of *The Undercover Edge: Redefine the Rules to Win Life's Game,* p. 127.

ONLINE

CBS, https://www.cbs.com/ (March 28, 2018), author profile.

Derrick Levasseur Website, https://www.officialderrick.com (March 28, 2018).

Reality Blurred, https://www.realityblurred.com/ (January 8, 2018), Andy Dehnart, "Big Brother 16: An Interview with Derrick Levasseur about His New Book, and Changing Your Life."*

Elise Levine

1959-

■ Personal

Born 1959, in Toronto, Ontario, Canada; married. *Education:* Vermont College of Fine Arts, M.F.A.

■ Addresses

Home—Baltimore, MD. *Office*—Johns Hopkins University, Krieger School of Arts and Sciences, Advanced Academics Programs, 1717 Massachusetts Ave. NW, Washington, DC 20036.

■ Career

Johns Hopkins University, Washington, DC, director of writing and science writing programs. Previously taught at American University in Washington, DC, University of Baltimore, and Dickinson College in Carlisle, PA. Also has worked as a security guard and delivery van driver.

■ Awards, Honors

Canadian National Magazine Award for fiction; Canada Council for the Arts, Ontario Arts Council, Toronto Arts Council, MacDowell Colony, and Yaddo, all fellowships.

■ Writings

Driving Men Mad (short stories), Porcupine's Quill (Erin, Ontario, Canada), 1995.

Requests and Dedications (novel), M&S (Toronto, Ontario, Canada), 2003.

Blue Field (novel), Biblioasis (Windsor, Ontario, Canada), 2016.

Has contributed to the anthologies *Best Canadian Stories* and *The Journey Prize Anthology*, and has published fiction and nonfiction in *Ploughshares, Gettysburg Review, Blackbird, Prairie Schooner*, and *Gargoyle*, among others.

■ Sidelights

Canadian-born Elise Levine received her M.F.A. at Vermont College of Fine Arts and went on to teach writing at Dickinson College in Carlisle, Pennsylvania, the University of Baltimore, and American University in Washington, DC. She is now director of the writing and science writing programs at Johns Hopkins University. She has published her stories, poems, essays, and critical reviews in *Ploughshares, Gettysburg Review, Blackbird, Prairie Schooner*, and *Gargoyle*, among others, and in the collections *Best Canadian Stories* and *The Journey Prize Anthology*. Her debut collection, *Driving Men Mad*, came out in 1995. In an interview with Rob McLennan at the *12 or 20 Questions* website, Levine shared that with the publication of that first book, she began to consider herself a true writer.

Speaking of the underpinnings of her work, she told McLennan, "I think I've always written about various characters' sense of place—especially the sense of mis-placement, exile—as part of my interest in the psychology of those who see themselves as marginalized, estranged, self-estranged." She continued: "Race and gender (and class) are intrinsic to my writing, which is character-driven, concerned with the mutable ways in which we think of ourselves." She cited as a few of her inspirations the work of Virginia Woolf and Joseph Conrad as well as that of the more modern writers Don DeLillo, J.M. Coetzee, and Mavis Gallant.

Requests and Dedications

Requests and Dedications is Levine's first full-length novel. The story, noted Eliza Clark in the *Globe & Mail*, "throws us into the mid-life, mid-heartache and ruin" of five characters living on a ranch in Ontario. The owner of the farm, Walker, takes on horses to board and train. He has a twelve-year-old daughter, Jena, with developmental disabilities, and a girlfriend, Mimi. Rounding out the quintet are Walker's sister, Joy, and her teenage daughter, Tanis, who live in a flat at the back of the farmhouse.

Writing at *Quill and Quire*, Bronwyn Drainie remarked: "Levine's fictional family is decidedly non-nuclear and dysfunctional. Five people reside in a state of tense domestic warfare." The novel follows the characters—"sad, disconnected, embittered"—through separate chapters, told in the first person by three of them. Clark observed that "the changing points of view can be disorienting" but that the "writing is dynamic and compelling" as well as "brazen, . . . risky and gorgeous." Drainie concluded: "This is one tough cookie of a writer, with the talent to carry off her bleak vision with few stumbles."

Blue Field

In *Blue Field*, Levine examines the life of a woman, Marilyn Wolf, who is sinking under a burden of grief. Her parents have both died, one right after the other. The blue field of the title refers to the underwater world that Marilyn plumbs as a participant in what is termed "crunch diving"—the "exploration of torturously claustrophobic underwater spaces," as Hannah LeClair described it online at *Music and Literature*, where "diving takes on an almost religious significance, allowing her to slip from a grief-stricken present into a submarine dream-time." LeClair found that "reading the novel is a sensation akin to drifting weightlessly beneath the surface of the text." Then Marilyn's diving partner and best friend, Jane, dies in a diving accident, and her marriage to her diving instructor husband, Rand, begins to unravel.

Bret McCabe interviewed Levine in *Johns Hopkins Magazine*, where she commented: "I . . . saw tremendous possibilities in depicting this underwater underworld, hidden from view for most of us,

as a way of modeling the depths of various modes of consciousness, including the ecstatic, and grief. It made sense to set these in broken, remote worlds—abandoned shipwrecks, caves formed by fractures in solid rock—to echo our own currently damaged places and to get at the sense of overwhelming grief and psychic brokenness Marilyn experiences." In his review of the book, McCabe found this to be true, calling *Blue Field* a "taut novel [that] immerses its readers in grief's disorienting morass." Adam Naman, writing in *Quill and Quire*, asserted: "Some novels draw you in; *Blue Field* drags you under and keeps clamping down, an exercise in storytelling as centrifugal force." A critic in *Kirkus Reviews* applauded the "raw, hallucinatory prose" and called the novel a "transgressive, gut-wrenching portrayal of grief that asks what it's like to drown."

■ Biographical and Critical Sources

ONLINE

12 or 20 Questions, http://12or20questions.blogspot. com/ (February 22, 2008), Rob McLennan, author interview.

Globe & Mail (Toronto, Ontario, Canada), http:// www.globeandmail.com/ (April 26, 2003), review of *Requests and Dedications.*

Jewish Book Council Website, https://www. jewishbookcouncil.org/ (February 10, 2018), author profile and review of *Blue Field.*

JMWW, https://jmwwblog.wordpress.com/ (June 12, 2017), Marnie Silverman, review of *Blue Field.*

Johns Hopkins Magazine, https://hub.jhu.edu/ (March 4, 2018), Bret McCabe, "Q&A with Elise Levine, Author of *Blue Field,*" and review of *Blue Field.*

Johns Hopkins University Website, http://advanced. jhu.edu/ (February 10, 2018). author faculty profile.

Kirkus Reviews, http://www.kirkusreviews.com/ (March 15, 2017), review of *Blue Field.*

Music and Literature, http://www. musicandliterature.org/ (October 10, 2017), Hannah LeClair, review of *Blue Field.*

Numero Cinq, http://numerocinqmagazine.com/ (April 5, 2017), Benjamin Woodard, review of *Blue Field.*

Open Book, http://open-book.ca/ (May 4, 2017), author interview.

Quill and Quire, https://quillandquire.com/ (February 10, 2018), Bronwyn Drainie, review of *Requests and Dedications;* Adam Nayman, review of *Blue Field.**

Cherry Lewis

1947-

■ **Also Known As**

C.L.E. Lewis
Cherry L.E. Lewis

■ **Personal**

Born September 6, 1947. *Education:* University of Bristol, B.Sc., 1984; Open University, Ph.D., 1989.

■ **Addresses**

Home—Bristol, England. *Office*—University of Bristol, School of Earth Sciences, Wills Memorial Bldg., Queens Rd., Clifton BS8 1RJ, Bristol, England.

■ **Career**

Writer.

■ **Awards, Honors**

Honorary Research Fellow, University of Bristol.

■ **Writings**

(Compiler) Gertrude Jekyll, *The Making of a Garden: Gertrude Jekyll, an Anthology of Her Writings Illustrated with Her Own Photographs and Drawings, and Watercolours by Contemporary Artists*, Garden Art Press (Woodbridge, England), 1984, published as *The Making of a Garden: An Anthology*, Garden Art Press (Woodbridge, England), 2005.

(Editor, under name C.L.E. Lewis, with S.J. Knell) *The Age of the Earth: From 4004 BC to AD 2002*, Geographical Society (Bath, England), 2001.

The Dating Game: One Man's Search for the Age of the Earth, Cambridge University Press (Cambridge, England), 2002, reprinted, 2012.

The Enlightened Mr. Parkinson: The Pioneering Life of a Forgotten Surgeon and the Mysterious Disease That Bears His Name, Pegasus Books (New York, NY), 2017.

■ **Sidelights**

Cherry Lewis is well known for her contributions to the geosciences, especially in the field of geology. She is aligned with the University of Bristol, where she earned her bachelor of science degree and serves as a honorary research fellow. Lewis has penned several books, including *The Dating Game: One Man's Search for the Age of the Earth* and *The Enlightened Mr. Parkinson: The Pioneering Life of a Forgotten Surgeon and the Mysterious Disease That Bears His Name*.

The Dating Game

The Dating Game chronicles the life and career of Arthur Holmes, the geologist responsible for penning *Principles of Physical Geology*, a text that is still widely utilized throughout the field of geology. In creating this text, Holmes started a revolution that elevated geology into consideration as a serious science. Lewis tracks Holmes's life to the end, starting with his younger years. Holmes developed his interest in geology as a teenager. It was during this period of his life that he saw the rise of advancements within the field and decided to embark upon that career path himself. In his early twenties, Holmes began investigating the best and most efficient ways to assign an age to the planet Earth. Throughout his career, Holmes developed several theories as to how old Earth could be, starting at 1.6 billion and arriving 3.35 billion by the later years of his career.

Holmes went on from research and fieldwork to secure a teaching position at Edinburgh University. There he was able to devise a time line of Earth's aging process and assign periods according to the planet's development. All of Holmes's research went on to culminate in his famed *Principles of Physical Geology,* which contained all of the most significant findings of his career. Holmes's book contains such concepts as the drifting of Earth's continents over time, as well as several other ideas that went against widely accepted norms at the time. To further flesh out the biography, Lewis takes advantage of myriad different types of writing penned and published by Holmes throughout his lifetime. In doing so, she illustrates the human side of Holmes, who expresses doubt over his career choices and his future. Lewis also asserts that Holmes is a bigger pioneer within the field of geology than he is often credited.

In a review for *New Scientist,* Sue Bowler commented: "Lewis has an excellent eye for a clever turn of phrase, and a keen interest in the characters in this story." She added: "The passages she highlights reveal Holmes's playful approach." A *Publishers Weekly* contributor remarked: "Science fans will appreciate Lewis's fast-paced biography tracing the evolution of Holmes's genius."

The Enlightened Mr. Parkinson

The Enlightened Mr. Parkinson covers the life and discoveries of James Parkinson, the surgical professional whose claim to fame was his discovery of what is now called Parkinson's disease. In expounding upon the finer details of Parkinson's life, Lewis tries to uncover his biography as an individual and professional outside his monumental discovery. Lewis reveals that Parkinson indulged in many curious pursuits, such as social advocacy, searching for and collecting fossils, geological science, and much more. Parkinson embarked upon his medical career during the Enlightenment period, which was marked by a slew of scientific and medical discoveries. Parkinson delved into common symptoms he noticed developing within some of his patients—namely, bodily tremors. Parkinson tried several experimental treatments to cure his patients, and with each trial he recorded his findings. This led to the publication of "An Essay on the Shaking Palsy," a study he released to the public in the year 1817.

Lewis highlights several other breakthroughs Parkinson either contributed to or was directly responsible for. One was his decision to administer the vaccine for smallpox to London citizens—he was among the earliest doctors to do so. Parkinson also assisted in creating the Geological Society of London. He was vocal about the need for several forms of sociopolitical change within society at the time and promulgated an assortment of academic advances and social contributions to the world throughout his life.

Lewis devotes much of the contents of the book to the areas of Parkinson's life that do not receive as much attention as his discovery of Parkinson's disease. She also delves into many details involving Parkinson's personal life, such as his relationship with his family and his viewpoint on religion and various other "hot button" issues of the period. All in all, Lewis seeks to profile Parkinson as someone who, despite being best known for just one facet of his professional life and endeavors, actually gave much more to the world through his many pursuits. A *Kirkus Reviews* contributor remarked: "Lewis delivers an appealing, often gruesome account of the life of a workaholic, highly respected physician from a far-off time." In *Publishers Weekly,* a reviewer called the book a "lively, captivating biography." *Washington Post* writer Vanessa Grubbs recommended the book to "anyone interested in the history of medicine, politics and geology." She also commented: "I finished it in awe of Parkinson's many accomplishments and contributions to politics, health and science, despite having a large family and a very busy medical practice." On *The Scotsman* website, Rob Ewing wrote: "Lewis's book shines a light on Parkinson, and gives something of the name back to the person: a man whose interests ranged far beyond medicine, and whose social engagement, and engagement with his time, sings from the page." *Prospect* reviewer Manjit Kumar stated that the book "is a fine, informative read."

■ Biographical and Critical Sources

PERIODICALS

Booklist, August 1, 2017, Tony Miksanek, review of *The Enlightened Mr. Parkinson: The Pioneering Life of a Forgotten Surgeon and the Mysterious Disease That Bears His Name,* p. 10.

Geoscience Canada, March, 2004, S. George Pemberton, review of *The Age of the Earth: From 4004 BC to AD 2002,* p. 46.

Kirkus Reviews, May 15, 2017, review of *The Enlightened Mr. Parkinson.*

New Scientist, October 14, 2000, Sue Bowler, "A Very Very Old Planet," review of *The Dating Game: One Man's Search for the Age of the Earth,* p. 50.

Publishers Weekly, November 13, 2000, review of *The Dating Game,* p. 97; May 29, 2017, review of *The Enlightened Mr. Parkinson,* p. 56.

Washington Post, September 4, 2017, Vanessa Grubbs, "Book World: Doctor's Legacy of Social Justice, Fossils and a Namesake Disease," review of *The Enlightened Mr. Parkinson.*

ONLINE

Conversation, https://theconversation.com/ (February 19, 2018), author profile.

Creation, https://creation.com/ (February 19, 2018), Tas Walker, "Western Culture and the Age of the Earth," review of *The Dating Game.*

Falmouth Public Library Website, http://www.falmouthpubliclibrary.org/ (February 19, 2018), Donna Burgess, review of *The Enlightened Mr. Parkinson.*

Prospect, https://www.prospectmagazine.co.uk/ (April 13, 2017), Manjit Kumar, review of *The Enlightened Mr. Parkinson.*

Science of Parkinson's Disease, https://scienceofparkinsons.com/ (April 8, 2017), author interview.

Scotsman, https://www.scotsman.com/ (May 3, 2017), Rob Ewing, review of *The Enlightened Mr. Parkinson.*

University of Bristol Website, http://www.bris.ac.uk/ (February 19, 2018), author profile.

Washington Post, https://www.washingtonpost.com/ (September 1, 2017), Vanessa Grubbs, "Tracing Parkinson's Other Passions Besides the Disease That Bears His Name," review of *The Enlightened Mr. Parkinson.**

Hallie Lieberman

■ **Personal**

Female. *Education:* University of Texas at Austin, M.A.; University of Wisconsin, Madison, Ph.D., 2014.

■ **Addresses**

Home—Atlanta, GA.

■ **Career**

Author and academic. Smithsonian, fellow, 2012; University of Wisconsin, Whitewater, instructor, 2014-15; Lebanon Valley College, teaching fellow in English, 2015-16; Georgia Institute of Technology, instructor, 2017—. Visiting scholar, Max Planck Institute for the History of Science, Berlin, Germany.

■ **Writings**

Buzz: A Stimulating History of the Sex Toy, Pegasus Books (Seattle, WA), 2017.

■ **Sidelights**

Georgia Institute of Technology communications instructor Hallie Lieberman is the author of the rather unique monograph *Buzz: A Stimulating History of the Sex Toy.* "As a graduate student in advertising at the University of Texas at Austin in the early 2000s, Lieberman became a sales rep for a company that threw Tupperware-like parties at customers' homes," explained Vicky Hallett in the *Washington Post Book World.* "Except instead of selling nifty plasticware, they hawked sex toys. But there was one big problem: Selling these items in Texas was illegal. To avoid arrest and fines, Lieberman had to stick with code lingo and say that the products were sold strictly for 'artistic, educational and scientific purposes.'" In order to try to understand how sex toys could be artistic or scientific, Lieberman began researching the history of their production. In 2014 she "wrote her dissertation on the history of sex toys—work that informed her new book," explained Katie Heaney in the *Cut* website. A *Publishers Weekly* reviewer called the study "a fascinating account of the way sex toys have touched feminists, queer communities, and American perceptions of sexuality."

Buzz begins its investigation with the earliest known development of sex toys. "Lieberman . . . [takes] us back some 30,000 years, when our ancestors carved penises out of siltstone; moving on to the ancient Greeks' creative use of olive oil; the buzzy medical devices of the 19th century . . . and the impact of early-20th-century obscenity laws," wrote Peggy Orenstein in the *New York Times Book Review,* ". . . before digging deeply into more contemporary influences." Heaney explained: "*Buzz* takes readers along for the long, hard journey (sorry, sorry) that led to the creation of the modern sex toy—from early newspaper ads claiming vibrators would help with 'indigestion,' to the partnership between a male disability activist and a queer female sex-toy shopowner which resulted in the cuter, purple-er dildos we see so often today." The author points out that, even in parts of twenty-first-century America, sex toys are still considered taboo. "The idea of female sexual pleasure and female sexuality unmoored from the male is still threatening and still freaks people out," Lieberman told Heaney. "We see stories about women being violated, sexually harassed, raped—we're okay with talking about women's sexuality when women are the victims of male sexual predation, because it fits into our idea of women as passive and men as active. But when we think of women as owning their sexuality and having sexual agency and being able to create their own pleasure, that threatens these deeply held beliefs." "Through its probing exploration," stated a *Kirkus Reviews* contributor, "the text . . . becomes a sharp commentary on contemporary society's ever changing sexual landscape and how sex is perceived, judged, accepted, and enjoyed with more variations than ever before."

■ Biographical and Critical Sources

PERIODICALS

Kirkus Reviews, September 1, 2017, review of *Buzz: A Stimulating History of the Sex Toy.*

New York Times Book Review, February 6, 2018, Peggy Orenstein, "The Sex Toy Shops That Switched On a Feminist Revolution."

Psychology Today, November 2, 2017, Ellen Airhart, "A Brief History of Good Vibrations."

Publishers Weekly, October 2, 2017, review of *Buzz*, p. 128.

Washington Post Book World, February 12, 2018, Vicky Hallett, review of *Buzz*.

ONLINE

Cut, https://www.thecut.com/ (November 17, 2017), Katie Heaney, "The 30,000-Year History of the Sex Toy."

Hallie Lieberman Website, https://www.hallielieberman.com (March 28, 2018).*

Phil Marcade

1954-

■ Also Known As

Philippe Marcadé
Philippe Pierre Marcadé

■ Personal

Born November, 1954, in Paris, France. *Hobbies and other interests:* Collecting and listening to vinyl records, singing, playing guitar.

■ Career

Painter, musician, and author. Lead singer of the Senders, 1976-2001; lead singer of the Backbones, 1983-87; lead singer of GangWar.

Singer and composer on albums, including *The Living End b/w No More Foolin'Me*, S.R.I, 1978, *Seven Song Super Single;* Max's Kansas City Records, 1980, Retour L'envoyeur, Skydog, 1981, *Various Artists: Live at the Continental Divide*, Divide Records, 1989, *Do the Sender Thing—Live at C.B.D. B.*, Midnight Records, 1989; *Various Artists: I Was Punk Begore You;* Skydog/P-Vine, 1998, *Various Artists: Lost Hits*, Skydog/P-Vine, 1998, *Back to Sender Revisited*, Skydog, 1998, *Goodbye Cruel World*, Action Records, 2000, and *Outrageous & Contagious, OUS*, Devils Jukebox, 2010.

■ Writings

Au-dela de l'Avenue D, Camion Blanc (Rosières-en-Haye, France), 2009.
Punk Avenue: Inside the New York City Underground, 1972-1982, Three Rooms Press (New York, NY), 2017.

■ Sidelights

Phil Marcade, also known as Philippe Marcadé, first came into prominence within American culture through his contributions as lead singer for the 1970s punk rock band the Senders. The band was active up until the early 2000s. In addition to his work with the Senders, Marcade has also participated in two other bands: the Backbones and GangWar. In addition to his musical endeavors, Marcade has also achieved recognition as an author and painter. His debut book, *Au-dela de l'Avenue D*, was published in France.

Punk Avenue: Inside the New York City Underground, 1972-1982 is Marcade's first English-language release, and it combines his interest in writing with his passion for music. The book is autobiographical and centers on the time Marcade first traveled to the United States as a young man. While Marcade first landed in Boston, he wound up traveling through the country until he decided to settle in New York. At the time, the city was entrenched in the rising wave of punk rock. Marcade fell in love with the genre and wound up starting his band, the Senders, as an expression of his interest in punk rock.

Marcade devotes much of the book to highlighting his escapades during this period, as well as his encounters with several notable people, some famous and some not. He recounts intimate conversations and moments with figures like Nancy Spungen, with whom he spoke prior to her decision to leave the country to live in London. He also received the opportunity to perform alongside the Clash, opening at one of their concerts. Marcade received additional opportunities to collaborate with Debbie Harry and jumpstart the career of the Ramones.

While Marcade delves into the fun and exciting elements of life within the 1970s punk rock scene, he also underlines some of the less pleasant aspects. Many of the people Marcade met and came to know fell victim to heroin and other substances. Marcade himself soon developed a heroin dependency, which he discusses within the book. The drug eventually tore the Senders apart, forcing them to go their separate ways. Nonetheless, Marcade pins the majority of his focus on the music industry at the time and the mark it made upon his life. In a review for *Midwest Book Reviews*, Able Greenspan remarked: "*Punk Avenue* . . . is a truly riveting read from cover to cover." He also called the book "very highly recommended for both community and academic library collections." A *Kirkus Reviews* contributor declared that *Punk Avenue* is a "must-read for those who love that era and want a fresh perspective on it." *Villager* reviewer Puma Perl wrote: "As I reached the end of Phil Marcade's upcoming memoir, *Punk Avenue* . . . I felt the urge to return to page one and start fresh, both literally and symbolically." On the *PopMatters* website, Christopher Laird commented: "*Punk Avenue* chronicles all of this from one human's perception, and it's worth reading for that reason." *Foreword Reviews* contributor Claire Foster said: "Marcade's memoir leaves no skirt unlifted and is peppered with familiar names, faces, and places." She added: "Even at their saddest, his stories surprise and delight, reviving an influential, exciting moment in American culture." A writer on the *I-94 Bar* website stated: "*Punk Avenue* "is lucid, grimly humorous and gripping." Elle Smith, a reviewer on the *Rock NYC* website, wrote: "I do not need to be part of the scene to feel a spirit of inclusion when I read *Punk Avenue*." She also said: "That is what the best books are, the ones where we are welcome into the story." *Punk Globe* writer Ginger Coyote commented: "It's a fun and dishy read!"

■ Biographical and Critical Sources

PERIODICALS

Kirkus Reviews, March 15, 2017, review of *Punk Avenue: Inside the New York City Underground, 1972-1982.*

Midwest Book Review, June, 2017, Able Greenspan, review of *Punk Avenue.*

ONLINE

Foreword Reviews, https://www.forewordreviews. com/ (May 1, 2017), Claire Foster, review of *Punk Avenue.*

I-94 Bar, http://www.i94bar.com/ (September 2, 2017), review of *Punk Avenue.*

Observer, http://observer.com/ (May 2, 2017), Justin Joffe, "Phil Marcade's '70s NY Punk Memoir Is the Stuff of Legend," author interview.

PopMatters, https://www.popmatters.com/ (May 3, 2017), Christopher Laird, review of *Punk Avenue.*

Punk Globe, http://www.punkglobe.com/ (February 13, 2017), Ginger Coyote, review of *Punk Avenue.*

Rock NYC, http://rocknycliveandrecorded.com/ (May 25, 2017), Elle Smith, review of *Punk Avenue.*

Senders, http://www.thesenders.us/ (February 13, 2018), author profile.

Stay Thirsty, https://staythirstymagazine.blogspot. com/ (February 13, 2018), "Five Questions for Punk Rock Author Phil Marcade," author interview.

Three Rooms Press Website, http://threeroomspress. com/ (February 28, 2017), "When Punk Was Fun: An Interview with *Punk Avenue* Author Phil Marcade."

Villager, http://thevillager.com/ (March 29, 2017), Puma Perl, review of *Punk Avenue.*

Volume 1 Brooklyn, http://www.vol1brooklyn.com/ (August 22, 2017), Tobias Carroll, "Phil Marcade on Revisiting New York's Musical Past in *Punk Avenue*," author interview.*

Lee Markham

■ Personal

Married; wife's name Becky. *Hobbies and other interests:* Shoes.

■ Addresses

Home—United Kingdom.

■ Career

Postman and author. No Man, founder; Chestnut Tree Tales, founder. Has also worked in brand development.

■ Writings

The Truants, Overlook Press (New York, NY), 2017.

Contributor of articles to *Brand Strategy* and *Admap*.

■ Sidelights

In order to release his first book, Lee Markham first left his career in marketing. In an interview featured on the *Book Bones & Buffy* blog, Markham explained that he had stopped enjoying his time in the marketing industry and saw the chance to publish a book as a means of forging a new and better career. He works as a postman alongside his contributions to the literary industry. Additionally, he is responsible for the creation of two publishing companies: No Man and Chestnut Tree Tales.

The Truants serves as Markham's literary debut. The novel centers on a vampire known only as the "Old One." He is mourning the loss of his lover, who suddenly committed suicide. However, the Old One's intentions of joining her in death quickly unravel beyond his control. The moment he steps out into the sun, he is attacked by a mysterious individual who slashes him with a knife. From there, the knife used to attack the Old One goes on a nefarious journey, slashing several other people in its wake. The Old One finds himself occupying the bodies of several former mortals, all of whom are children and have now acquired the Old One's vampirism. Because the Old One now inhabits these children's bodies, he can control them, and he does so for the sake of trying to track down the knife that was used to attack him, so he can piece his soul back together and complete his suicidal plans. However, someone else has their own plans for the Old One, and is set on keeping him from accomplishing his goal. In *Booklist*, Emily Compton-Dzak expressed that "[Markham's] thought-provoking consideration of social topics and the power of the subconscious create a unique vampire story." A *Publishers Weekly* contributor remarked: "Fans of vampire stories might enjoy the premise." A writer on the *Tattooed Book Geek* blog felt the book is "an informative and unique if somewhat disturbing look into the degradation and underbelly of modern society." *Cemetery Dance* writer Frank Michaels Errington said: "Overall, *The Truants* is decidedly different, in a good way." On the *Pile by the Bed* blog, a reviewer stated: "This is an original take on a long-running horror trope that is visceral, often poetic and sympathetic to many of its characters." Gavin Kendall, a contributor to the *Ginger Nuts of Horror* website, remarked: "*The Truants* is a remarkable piece of work that demands to be read." *Foreword Reviews* writer J.G. Stinson said: "Anyone interested in the varied tapestry that vampire fiction has become since Bram Stoker first popularized the genre should find much to enjoy—and ponder—in *The Truants*."

■ Biographical and Critical Sources

PERIODICALS

Booklist, June, 2017, Emily Compton-Dzak, review of *The Truants*, p. 72.
Publishers Weekly, May 15, 2017, review of *The Truants*, p. 43.

ONLINE

Books Bones & Buffy, http://booksbonesbuffy.com/ (August 17, 2017), "Interview & Giveaway: Lee Markham, Author of *The Truants*."

Cemetery Dance, http://www.cemeterydance.com/ (August 30, 2017), Frank Michaels Errington, review of *The Truants*.
Dread Central, http://www.dreadcentral.com/ (July 11, 2017), Debi Moore, "Guest Post: Author Lee Markham on Why *The Truants* Isn't 'Just' a Vampire Story."
Foreword Reviews, https://www.forewordreviews.com/ (July 1, 2017), J.G. Stinson, review of *The Truants*.
Ginger Nuts of Horror, http://gingernutsofhorror.com/ (August 15, 2017), Gavin Kendall, review of *The Truants*.
Overlook Press Website, http://www.overlookpress.com/ (February 13, 2018), author profile.
Pile by the Bed, http://pilebythebed.com/ (May 9, 2017), review of *The Truants*.
Tattooed Book Geek, https://thetattooedbookgeek.wordpress.com/ (May 25, 2017), review of *The Truants*.*

Tim Marshall

1959-

■ **Also Known As**

Timothy John Marshall

■ **Personal**

Born May 1, 1959.

■ **Career**

Author. LBC, Paris bureau correspondent; Independent Radio News, Paris correspondent; Sky Net, Middle East correspondent, foreign correspondent, diplomatic editor, and foreign affairs editor. Also worked for BBC Radio. Worked variously as a runner, painter, researcher, and decorator.

■ **Awards, Honors**

The New York TV Festival Prize; Royal Television Society Prize, 2004.

■ **Writings**

Man's Greatest Fear: The Final Phase of Human Evolution, Athena Books (West Chester, PA), 1995.

Shadowplay: The Overthrow of Slobodan Milosevic, BookBaby, 2002.

*"Dirty Northern B*st*rds!" and Other Tales from the Terraces: The Story of Britain's Football Chants*, Elliott & Thompson (London, England), 2014.

Prisoners of Geography: Ten Maps That Tell You Everything You Need to Know about Global Politics, Elliot and Thompson (London, England), 2015, published as *Prisoners of Geography: Ten Maps That Explain Everything about the World*, Scribner (New York, NY), 2016.

A Flag Worth Dying For: The Power and Politics of National Symbols, Scribner (New York, NY), 2017, published as *Worth Dying For: The Power and Politics of Flags*, Elliott and Thompson Limited (London, England), 2017.

Contributor of articles to *Daily Telegraph*, the *Times*, *Independent*, *Guardian*, and *Sunday Times*. Editor and founder of *The What and the Why*.

■ **Sidelights**

Tim Marshall has maintained a long career within the broadcast journalism industry. After failing to build an artistic career for himself, he found entry-level work at a news station. He has since worked in various foreign correspondence positions with Sky News, BBC Radio, and IRN. He has also served as Sky News's diplomatic editor. His work has garnered several awards, including a New York TV Festival Award and Royal Television Society Award. He now maintains his own independent blogs. One of them, *Foreign Matters*, landed on the 2010 shortlist for the Orwell Prize. His writing has also been featured in several periodicals, such as the *Sunday Times* and the *Guardian*. Additionally, Marshall has published several books.

A Flag Worth Dying For

A Flag Worth Dying For: The Power and Politics of National Symbols is known in England as *Worth Dying For: The Power and Politics of Flags*. In the book, Marshall delves into the history of the use of flags to represent organizations and countries throughout the world. According to Marshall's findings, the use of flags originated from the rise of the silk industry. Their regular usage, however, comes from history as well as the association of color with specific meanings. Each nation developed its flag according to which symbols best represented its overall goals and history, which is why certain elements are more common in some parts of the world than others. In his analysis of the meanings behind the symbolic choices used for different national flags, Marshall also unpacks their cultural significance and impact.

A *Kirkus Reviews* contributor called the book "a treasure vault for vexillologists, full of meaning beyond the hue and thread of the world's banners." In *Publishers Weekly*, a reviewer said: "Marshall presents an informative survey of these highly visible symbols of national or international pride." *Geographical* writer Chris Fitch commented that the book's contents are "deeply layered in meaning, and can stimulate powerful and wildly varying emotions." A *USA Today* reviewer wrote: "*A Flag Worth Dying For* is a fresh explanation of symbols we often take for granted and a keen meditation on what flags mean to those who embrace or recoil from them."

Prisoners of Geography

In *Prisoners of Geography: Ten Maps That Tell You Everything You Need to Know about Global Politics*, Marshall seeks to uncover the deep relationship between geography and a nation's political motives and goals. To help guide readers through his points, Marshall presents maps of each country profiled in every chapter. Marshall uses these visual aids to explain how the shape and border of each country or region came to define its aims as an independent government entity. For instance, certain elements of a country's geographical landscape present a stark disadvantage, forcing it to turn to outside sources to obtain resources. The locations of countries determine how they traverse the world and who they are most likely to come into immediate contact with, as well as why certain nations do not get along as well as others.

On the *Make Wealth History* website, Jeremy Williams stated: "*Prisoners of Geography* is a useful overview of geopolitics." He added: "If you haven't read anything like this before, it will be genuinely enlightening." *Prospect* reviewer Chris Tilbury remarked: "Marshall succeeds in making lucid a complex topic and the book is difficult to put down." A *Kirkus Reviews* contributor said:

"Marshall's broad survey of events in the light of geographical realities goes a long way to explaining Putin's concerns—and, for that matter, those of the CIA as well." Miles Rayner, writing on the *Words & Dirt* website, commented: "In the final analysis, *Prisoners of Geography* is an engaging and worthwhile read." He added: "Marshall doesn't have the power to settle our geopolitical problems, but he does bring us one step closer to understanding them."

*"Dirty Northern B*st*rds!" and Other Tales from the Terraces*

*"Dirty Northern B*st*rds!" and Other Tales from the Terraces: The Story of Britain's Football Chants* deals with cultural history on a smaller scale in comparison to Marshall's other books. In *"Dirty Northern B*st*ards!,"* Marshall addresses the close relationship Britain has with football, known as soccer in the United States. A large part of the culture surrounding British football is the use of chants, which vary by region and seem to be split between the southern and northern parts of the country. Several chants used in British football games come from nursery songs but have been repurposed for the sport. Marshall delves into how these chants originated as well as their status as representing a large part of British history. He profiles each popular chant individually, discussing where they originally came from and how they came to be used in football games in certain areas of the country.

London *Independent* contributor Simon Redfern called the book a "light-hearted but well-researched history." On the London *Telegraph* website, Jim White remarked: "Marshall's thesis is nicely researched, well considered and neatly paced."

■ Biographical and Critical Sources

PERIODICALS

Geographical, December, 2016, Chris Fitch, review of *Worth Dying For: The Power and Politics of Flags*, p. 64.

Kirkus Reviews, May 15, 2017, review of *A Flag Worth Dying For: The Power and Politics of National Symbols*.

Publishers Weekly, May 8, 2017, review of *A Flag Worth Dying For*, p. 50.

USA Today, July 3, 2017, "In Time for July 4, a Salute for *A Flag Worth Dying For*," p. 5D.

Washington Post, August 4, 2017, Moises Naim, "Book World: The History and Emotion Behind Our Reverence for National Flags," review of *A Flag Worth Dying For.*

ONLINE

Guardian, https://www.theguardian.com/ (April 16, 2007), Tim Marshall, "Every Newsroom Needs a Maverick."

Independent, http://www.independent.co.uk/ (September 13, 2014), Simon Redfern, review of *"Dirty Northern B*st*rds!" and Other Tales from the Terraces: the Story of Britain's Football Chants.*

Kirkus Reviews, https://www.kirkusreviews.com/ (September 30, 2015), review of *Prisoners of Geography: Ten Maps That Tell You Everything You Need to Know about Global Politics.*

London Speaker Bureau Website, https://londonspeakerbureau.com/ (February 13, 2018), author profile.

Make Wealth History, https://makewealthhistory.org/ (August 17, 2016), Jeremy Williams, review of *Prisoners of Geography.*

Prospect, https://www.prospectmagazine.co.uk/ (February 18, 2016), Chris Tilbury, review of *Prisoners of Geography.*

Speakers Corner, https://www.speakerscorner.co.uk/ (February 13, 2018), author profile.

Telegraph, http://www.telegraph.co.uk/ (August 9, 2014), Jim White, review of *"Dirty Northern B*st*rds!" and Other Tales from the Terraces.*

Washington Post Book World, https://www.washingtonpost.com/ (January 8, 2016), Colin Woodard, review of *Prisoners of Geography.*

What and the Why, http://www.thewhatandthewhy.com (February 13, 2018), author profile.

Words & Dirt, http://www.words-and-dirt.com/ (April 23, 2016), Miles Raymer, review of *Prisoners of Geography.**

Brendan Mathews

■ Personal

Born in NY; married; children: four. *Education:* University of North Carolina at Chapel Hill, B.A. (with highest honors), 1991; University of Virginia, M.F.A., 2005.

■ Addresses

Home—Lenox, MA. *Office*—Bard College at Simon's Rock, Hall College Ctr., 2nd Fl., 84 Alford Rd., Great Barrington, MA 01230.

■ Career

Writer and educator. *Bulletin of the Atomic Scientists,* associate editor, 1997-99; Britannica.com, News Division, story editor, 1999-2000; University of Chicago/Fathom, Inc., senior multimedia producer, 2001-03; University of Virginia, assistant director of media relations, 2005-07; Bard College at Simon's Rock, Great Barrington, MA, associate professor of creative writing and literature, 2007—, also division head of Languages & Literature. University College Cork, Ireland, Fulbright visiting professor, 2014.

■ Member

Phi Beta Kappa.

■ Awards, Honors

Fulbright Scholar to Ireland; recipient of grants and fellowships, including from the Massachusetts Cultural Council, Sustainable Arts Foundation, and Sewanee Writers Conference.

■ Writings

The World of Tomorrow (novel), Little, Brown and Company (New York, NY), 2017.

Work has appeared in *The Best American Short Stories 2010* and *The Best American Short Stories 2014.* Contributor to periodicals and websites, including *Glimmer Train, Virginia Quarterly Review, Salon,* and *Cincinnati Review.*

■ Sidelights

Brendan Mathews is a fiction writer, educator, and Fulbright Scholar who grew up in northern New York. He began his career writing short stories. At the time of an interview with Alice Chau for *Port Online,* Mathews was working on his debut novel, *The World of Tomorrow,* and told Chau: "I've been thinking a lot about the differences between short stories and novels because I've devoted most of the past two years to writing my first novel. This question of endings keeps coming up because when I'm writing a story I feel like the end is always in sight, however with the novel, there's so much territory to explore, even if I don't know where that exploration is ultimately going to lead."

The World of Tomorrow was called an "impressive, wide-ranging debut" by a *Kirkus Reviews* contributor. Writing for *NPR.org,* Jason Sheehan commented that *The World of Tomorrow* "is that rarest of historical novels, a book that catches a moment in a jar, holds it aloft and displays it for what it really is: Somebody else's day before tomorrow, the instant right before the future comes."

The novel takes place primarily over the course of one week in June during the 1939 New York World's Fair. *The World of Tomorrow* finds a roguish

Irishman, Francis Dempsey, sailing across the Atlantic in first class posing as a Scottish lord. Francis escaped from prison in Dublin, where he was incarcerated for selling supposed pornographic material, including the James Joyce novel *Ulysses.* He escaped prison to attend his father's funeral and is helped by their father's former friends in the Irish Republican Army. Along with his younger brother, Michael, who has left a Catholic seminary, Francis and the IRA members go to a remote safe house, where Francis accidentally sets off an explosive, leaving him and his shell-shocked brother the sole possessors of a large sum of money.

Once in America, Francis and his brother look up their older brother, a jazz musician named Martin living in the Bronx. However, Francis is being pursued by Tommy Cronin, an IRA member sent by his chief, Gavin, to get Francis and the money. As the story continues, Francis's infatuation with an heiress who is also an exquisite violinist leads to his getting caught by Tommy and directed by Gavin to assassinate the king of England, who is part of a British delegation scheduled to visit the World's Fair. If Francis refuses, Gavin notifies him that he will kill everyone in his family. As a result, he begins training under Tommy's tutelage.

Meanwhile, Michael, who was seriously impaired by the ill-fated bomb blast in Ireland and is now deaf and dumb, believes he can see the ghost of William Butler Yeats. "The schism in his identity is so acute that his mind conjures up a companion for him to 'speak' with," noted John Freeman Gill in a review for the *Washington Post Online.* After wandering around the city and getting lost, Michael meets a Czech photographer named Lily Block who is trying to delay returning to Prague, which has been occupied by the Nazis. Meanwhile, the older brother, Martin, is having difficulties with his uptight in-laws, who frown on his efforts to make a living as a musician. The novel follows the three brothers as they soon face major decisions as well as the prospect of an early demise.

"With the wit of a '30s screwball comedy and the depth of a thoroughly researched historical novel, this one grabs the reader from the beginning to its suspenseful climax," wrote a *Publishers Weekly*

contributor. Noting that "Mathews brilliantly creates characters who embody the esprit de corps of immigrants," Bill Kelly, writing in *Booklist,* went on to note that Mathews "movingly explores themes of class, society, race, and family."

■ Biographical and Critical Sources

PERIODICALS

Booklist, September 1, 2017, Bill Kelly, review of *The World of Tomorrow,* p. 56.

BookPage, September, 2017, Tom Deignan, "A Pulsating Prewar New York," review of *The World of Tomorrow,* p. 18.

Kirkus Reviews, June 15, 2017, review of *The World of Tomorrow.*

Publishers Weekly, May 15, 2017, review of *The World of Tomorrow,* p. 34.

ONLINE

Bard College at Simon's Rock Website, https://simons-rock.edu/ (February 18, 2018), author faculty profile.

Bookreporter.com, https://www.bookreporter.com/ (September 21, 2017), Amy Gwiazdowski, review of *The World of Tomorrow;* (February 18, 2018), author biography and synopsis of *The World of Tomorrow.*

Brendan Mathews Website, https://www.brendanmathews.com (February 18, 2018).

Chicago Tribune Online, http://www.chicagotribune.com/ (September 5, 2017), Michael Upchurch, review of *The World of Tomorrow.*

Fantastic Fiction, https://www.fantasticfiction.com/ (February 18, 2018), brief author biography.

New York Times Online, https://www.nytimes.com/ (September 13, 2017), Kevin Baker, review of *The World of Tomorrow.*

NPR.org, https://www.npr.org/ (September 6, 2017), Jason Sheehan, review of *The World of Tomorrow.*

Port Online, http://www.port-magazine.com/ (September 20, 2012), Alice Chau, "Author Interview: Brendan Mathews."

Washington Post Online, https://www.washingtonpost.com/ (September 3, 2017), John Freeman Gill, "*The World of Tomorrow* Captures Swirling New York in 1939."*

Frances Maynard

■ Personal

Married; children: a daughter.

■ Addresses

Home—Dorset, England.

■ Career

Writer, novelist, and educator. Teaches English part time to adults with learning difficulties.

■ Writings

The Seven Rules of Elvira Carr: A Novel, Sourcebooks Landmark (Naperville, IL), 2017, published as *The Seven Imperfect Rules of Elvira Carr*, Mantle (London, England), 2017.

■ Sidelights

Frances Maynard teaches English part time to adults with learning disabilities, including Asperger syndrome. In her debut novel, *The Seven Rules of Elvira Carr: A Novel*, published in England as *The Seven Imperfect Rules of Elvira Carr*, Maynard tells the story of a young woman who strongly believes in rules and who finds herself facing a wider world where the rules are not always ironclad. It turns out that twenty-seven-year-old Elvira Carr has not had to deal much with the outside world because her domineering mother has kept her safely at home after Elivra had several "incidents." However, when her seventy-two-year-old mother has a stroke and is sent to a nursing home, Elvira suddenly finds herself on her own, and the only help she receives from her mother is the repetition of the phrase "Not that way!"

To cope, Elvira develops seven basic rules, such as the idea that it is best not to look or sound different if you want to fit in and that people who are nice are not always your friend. Elvira is not at ease in the normal social world, but she receives help from her neighbor in navigating this world and the behavior of people referred to as "NormalTypicals." Elvira has volunteered at the nursing home where her mother resides and also at the local zoo. Her problems arise as she encounters the informal, unwritten rules of society and the people around her. Meanwhile, Evira finds herself struggling in society even with the rules she has placed on herself. A major issue is to convince those around her that she is actually capable of taking care of herself. As time passes, Elvira begins questioning what she really knows about her own family, especially her father. Her mother told her little about her deceased father and why he was absent for long stretches of time from home.

Maynard's "portrait of Elvira's inner life is nuanced," wrote a *Publishers Weekly* contributor, who also noted that Maynard "draws on her professional experience for her . . . debut." Online at the *Sydney Morning Herald*, Kerryn Goldsworthy also noted Maynard's use of her background in teaching educationally challenged adults to lend credibility to Elvira's narration of the story. Nevertheless, she remarked that "some . . . may feel discomfort at what can seem like appropriation of a neuro-atypical voice." Tracy Babiasz, writing for *Booklist*, observed that Elvira's "authentic voice offers a fresh perspective on being different."

■ **Biographical and Critical Sources**

PERIODICALS

Booklist, May 1, 2017, Tracy Babiasz, review of *The Seven Rules of Elvira Carr: A Novel*, p. 59.

Publishers Weekly, May 15, 2017, review of *The Seven Rules of Elvira Carr*, p. 32.

Xpress Reviews, June 23, 2017, Catherine Coyne, review of *The Seven Rules of Elvira Carr*.

ONLINE

Frances Maynard Website, http://francesmaynard. co.uk (February 20, 2018).

Sydney Morning Herald Online, http://www.smh. com.au (August 24, 2017), Kerryn Goldsworthy, *"Seven Imperfect Rules of Elvira Carr* Review: Frances Maynard's Question of Voice."*

John McCavitt

■ **Personal**

Male. *Education:* Queen's University Belfast, Ph.D., 1988.

■ **Addresses**

Home—Rostrevor, County Down, Northern Ireland.

■ **Career**

Historian, writer, and public speaker. Has given presentations at Folger Shakespeare Library, White House Historical Association, and U.S. Capitol Historical Society.

■ **Member**

Royal Historical Society (fellow).

■ **Writings**

Sir Arthur Chichester, Lord Deputy of Ireland, 1605-1616, Institute of Irish Studies, Queen's University of Belfast (Belfast, Northern Ireland), 1998.
The Flight of the Earls, Gill & Macmillan (Dublin, Ireland), 2002.
(With Christopher T. George) *The Man Who Captured Washington: Major General Robert Ross and the War of 1812,* University of Oklahoma Press (Norman, OK), 2016.

■ **Sidelights**

John McCavitt is a military historian who lectures widely. In addition to speaking engagements throughout Northern Ireland, he has given talks at Oxford University and the House of Lords, as well as in Lisbon, Rome, and Chicago. McCavitt has also lectured at several places in Washington, DC, and the surrounding area, including at the Folger Shakespeare Library, the White House Historical Association, the Navy Yard, and the Irish Embassy, along with the North Point Visitor Center near Baltimore, Maryland. His lecture to the U.S. Capitol Historical Society on the British capture of Washington in 1814 was broadcast on *American History* on C-SPAN in August 2012.

McCavitt is the author of books, including *The Man Who Captured Washington: Major General Robert Ross and the War of 1812,* written with Christopher T. George, founding editor of the *Journal of the War of 1812.* In an interview with Jeannette DiLouie for the *Innovative Editing* website, McCavitt noted that he first knew of Ross because there is a monument of the general erected in 1826 in Rostrevor, County Down, in Northern Ireland, Ross's hometown and where McCavitt lives. McCavitt told *Innovative Editor* contributor DiLouie that the monument "was allowed to become rather rundown until recent years." He added: "And even local knowledge about him was extremely limited." McCavitt went on to remark: "I simply wanted to know more about this man, and I had the historical skills to do so. His career was a remarkable one in so many ways and in so many theaters of war that it was obvious there was enough to fill a book."

In *The Man Who Captured Washington,* McCavitt and George provide an in-depth biography of Major General Robert Ross (1766-1814). Drawing from a wide range of both British and American sources, including memoirs of veterans, government records, newspaper accounts, and secondary sources, the historians detail Ross's life from his youth onward. Ross was educated in Dublin and joined the British Army in 1789. His military career was marked by a steady rise in the ranks as he became a commander and fought Napoléon's French army in several theaters, including Holland, southern Italy, Egypt, and the Iberian Peninsula. "McCavitt and George cast Ross as a popular leader who demonstrated efficiency and personal bravery in battle," wrote Jonathon Hooks in the *Journal of Southern History*. He went on: "They also argue that Ross fiercely protected the soldiers he commanded from censure whenever they stood accused of harassing or abusing civilians."

After nearly dying in battle following a serious wound, Ross was recovering when he received another assignment, namely, to lead a small army against U.S. troops in the War of 1812. Ross proved a capable leader in the war. His troops won the Battle of Bladensburgh and then moved on to Washington, DC. Although Ross spared individual homes, he became notorious for burning down public buildings, including the White House and the Capitol. According to McCavitt and George, Ross burned these buildings only because he had received orders to do so. McCavitt and George detail the major reasons that led to Ross's taking Washington, pointing primarily to the fact that the U.S. Army mistakenly believed that Ross and his troops were of little real threat. Ross and his troops were in Washington for just one day, and the general died only weeks later outside Baltimore,

Maryland, just before the September 12 Battle of North Point. According to McCavitt and George, the defeat of Washington almost led Congress to move the U.S. capital to another city.

The Man Who Captured Washington "accomplishes its goal of introducing readers to Ross's military skill and accomplishments," noted Hooks in the *Journal of Southern History*. *HistoryNet* website contributor Mike Oppenheim remarked: "This biography will . . . preserve the memory of the dynamic if largely forgotten general."

■ Biographical and Critical Sources

PERIODICALS

Journal of Southern History, August, 2017, Jonathon Hooks, review of *The Man Who Captured Washington: Major General Robert Ross and the War of 1812*, p. 670.

ONLINE

HistoryNet, http://www.historynet.com/ (October 27, 2016), Mike Oppenheim, review of *The Man Who Captured Washington*.

Innovative Editing, https://www.innovativeediting.com (May 1, 2017), Jeannette DiLouie, author interview.

Man Who Captured Washington Website, http://themanwhocapturedwashington.com (February 18, 2018).*

Ted McDermott

1982-

■ Personal

Born 1982; married; wife's name Shawn; children: Mae. *Education:* Graduated from the University of Michigan, 2004; University of Montana, Missoula, M.F.A., 2009.

■ Addresses

Home—Butte, MT.

■ Career

Writer. Has worked as a college instructor, an encyclopedist, a reporter, a baker, a mover, and a cook.

■ Writings

The Minor Outsider, ONE (London, England), 2016.

Contributor to periodicals and websites, including *VICE*, the *Believer*, *Portland Review*, and the *Minus Times*.

■ Sidelights

After earning his master's degree in creative writing, Ted McDermott started working as a baker. He was writing in his off hours and working to get an already-completed manuscript published. Then he crushed his hand at work, which led to several surgeries and an existential crisis. McDermott's first manuscript was not accepted anywhere,

and he had to start back at square one. He took a job as a reporter and then started what would become his debut novel, *The Minor Outsider*. McDermott noted in a *Montana Standard Online* interview with Susan Dunlap, "It was the first thing ever that I wrote purely out of personal motivation. . . . I was trying to be a writer and that wasn't working. Feeling desperate after I crushed my hand, I thought about what should I write and then why should I write." In a second interview, this time with Montana Public Radio correspondent Sarah Aronson, McDermott commented: "I wrote the book kind of gradually as a series of short stories. . . . It took me probably three years to write it. I didn't know I was writing it for most of that. I just started writing short stories that were semi-autobiographical and they started to kind of come together in a strange way. So then I put them together."

The Minor Outsider follows Ed, a Chicago-based editor who quits his job to get his master's degree in creative writing. Ed heads to the University of Montana, Missoula. Ed's brain tumor may have prompted his impulsive and sudden career change, but Ed refuses to acknowledge the time-bomb quietly ticking away inside his head. Ed approaches his life with a deadpan detachment, but then he meets Taylor and falls madly in love. Taylor is also in the creative writing program at Missoula, and the two move in together quickly. Complications immediately ensue, and the couple decides to make a last-ditch effort to salvage their relationship, with stunning results.

Reviews of *The Minor Outsider* were largely positive, and a *Publishers Weekly* critic praised "McDermott's droll observations and unique prose." The critic went on to advise: "This is a surprising, smart, and memorable novel." John Sunyer, writing in the *Financial Times Online*, was also positive, and he found that "McDermott is sharp on the indulgences of the creative set and, above all, portraying the life of many young men—drifting, hard to reach, doomed to try to make sense of a world that resists all explanation and interpretation." On the other hand, a *Nudge* website contributor stated: "I felt the ending was disappointing. The author leaves things very open to the imagination, hinting of what may happen rather than actually going ahead with it." *Guardian Online* columnist James Smart offered both pros and cons, and he remarked that "the self-absorbed and evasive Ed isn't the most sympathetic of narrators, but he anchors a hip, touching and thoroughly readable story." A far more laudatory assessment was proffered by Mara Panich-Crouch in the *Missoulian Online*, and she declared that, "with *The Minor Outsider*, McDermott has written a novel that is raw, yet refined. The characters are full of contradictions, absurdities, cynicism and affection. While flawed, the characters are relatable and engaging. Their stories and experiences drive the plot with a simple ease." According to Sarah Gilmartin in the *Irish Times Online*, "McDermott's novel is . . . impressive, focusing on life's contradictions and absurdities, with its title a nod to Camus's absurdist masterpiece." Gilmartin then added that "Ed's ability to pinpoint his own plight and that of those around him makes the novel sing."

■ Biographical and Critical Sources

PERIODICALS

Publishers Weekly, April 24, 2017, review of *The Minor Outsider*.

ONLINE

Financial Times Online, https://www.ft.com/ (May 27, 2016), John Sunyer, review of *The Minor Outsider*.

Guardian Online, https://www.theguardian.com/ (April 22, 2016), James Smart, review of *The Minor Outsider*.

Irish Times Online https://www.irishtimes.com/ (January 30, 2018), Sarah Gilmartin, review of *The Minor Outsider*.

Missoulian Online, http://missoulian.com/ (June 24, 2017), Mara Panich-Crouch, review of *The Minor Outsider*.

Montana Public Radio Website, http://mtpr.org/ (January 30, 2018), Sarah Aronson, author interview.

Montana Standard Online, http://mtstandard.com/ (January 30, 2018), Susan Dunlap, author interview.

Nudge, https://nudge-book.com/ (October 30, 2016), review of *The Minor Outsider*.

Ted McDermott Website, http://www.tedmcdermott.com (January 30, 2018).*

David Mealing

1982-

■ **Personal**

Born 1982, in Salt Lake City, UT; married August 14, 2005; wife's name Lindsay; children: three daughters. *Education:* Attended the University of California, Los Angeles, and the University of Oxford.

■ **Addresses**

Home—WA.

■ **Career**

Writer.

■ **Writings**

Soul of the World, Orbit (New York, NY), 2017.

■ **Sidelights**

David Mealing's family moved several times when Mealing was a child, and he found it easier to play games than make new friends in each new city. Mealing thus grew up playing video games, reading fantasies, and playing role-playing games (RPGs). Mealing continued playing RPGs in college, and he began writing fantasy plot lines and scenarios for his RPG characters. Mealing then started working on his own original fantasy novel, and his debut title, *Soul of the World* serves as the first installment of his "Ascension Cycle."

Commenting on his writing process in an online *Civilian Reader* interview, Mealing explained: "I've experimented with several different methods, and I find I do my best work in short bursts of one to two hours each, three to four times a day. I take breaks in between, preferably for physical stuff so my brain has a chance to soak and plan what I'm going to write next. I measure my wordcount output for every session, and have daily output goals of at least 2,000 words/day while I'm drafting."

Soul of the World switches between the points of view of Sarine, Erris, and Arak' Jur. Sarine is a street artist, but she is also a *binder,* which means she has the power to draw on ley lines. Sarine knows to keep her abilities secret, but then the commoners rebel in a manner akin to the French Revolution, and Sarine uses her power to aid them. Erris is far from the action, working as a cavalry commander in a distant colony. Erris is a loyal soldier, but the empire recalls its troops to deal with the revolt. Now, as Erris leaves the local tribesmen, he begins to question his loyalty to the crown. In the meantime, tribesman Arak' Jur prepares his own revolt, readying his people to face off with the empire's soldiers.

Mealing shared his inspiration for the story in an online *Qwillery* interview, and he stated that it "came about after my attempts to meticulously outline a fantasy western. As I mentioned above, that all went out the window as soon as I sat down to write the first scene. I was captivated by the idea of an artist sitting alone, sketching Louis XVI's court at Versailles. I wrote that, and the rest flowed from there. 100% pure discovery writing." The author went on to comment: "Epic fantasy in general is just an amazing genre to be working in. As epic fantasy writers we get the space to create lavish worlds and magic systems, and we can explore just about any facet of history or culture that catches our attention, real or imaginary. I want to take my readers all over my world, I want the stakes to be big, I want powerful heroes making life-changing decisions and villains who are just as convinced their decisions are right, even if it sets them against the heroes. Epics have always been my favorite books to read; I can't imagine writing anything else, at least for now."

Reviews of *Soul of the World* were somewhat mixed, and a *Publishers Weekly* critic offered both pros and cons: "Strong characters and rich world-building are undercut by the depiction of the tribes as primitive and sexualized." Elloise Hopkins, writing on the *British Fantasy Society* website, was also ambivalent, and she found that "the level of exposition . . . is not quite enough for the reader to fully connect, which is a great shame because in terms of concept, setting and initial promise it is rich and appealing." A far more positive assessment was proffered by Susannah Balch in the online *RT Book Reviews,* and she declared that "Mealing does a fabulous job with the intricate world-building and leaves the reader wanting to get their hands on the sequel."

■ Biographical and Critical Sources

PERIODICALS

Publishers Weekly, May 22, 2017, review of *Soul of the World.*

ONLINE

British Fantasy Society Website, http://www.britishfantasysociety.org/ (November 9, 2017), Elloise Hopkins, review of *Soul of the World.*

Civilian Reader, https://civilianreader.com/ (January 30, 2018), author interview.

David Mealing Website, https://www.davidmealing.com (January 30, 2018).

Qwillery, http://qwillery.blogspot.com/ (January 30, 2018), author interview.

RT Book Reviews, https://www.rtbookreviews.com/ (June 27, 2017), Susannah Balch, review of *Soul of the World.**

Jennie Melamed

■ Personal

Married. *Education:* University of Washington, doctoral studies.

■ Addresses

Home—Seattle, WA. *Agent*—Stephanie Delman, Greenburger Associates, 55 5th Ave., New York, NY 10003.

■ Career

Psychiatric nurse practitioner, writer, and novelist.

■ Writings

Gather the Daughters, Little, Brown and Company (New York, NY), 2017.

■ Sidelights

Jennie Melamed is a psychiatric nurse practitioner who works with traumatized children. During her doctoral work at the University of Washington, she investigated anthropological, biological, and cultural aspects of child abuse. In her debut novel, *Gather the Daughters*, Melamed presents a dystopian future where men on an island force girls into marriage when the girls reach puberty. In an interview for the *Qwillery* website, Melamed said she first got the basic idea for the novel when she was eighteen years old and realized many of her friends had suffered from child abuse, adding: "I

began wondering what it would mean for abuse to be encoded into a culture." Melamed also noted in the *Qwillery* interview: "When I was a child, I had post-apocalyptic daydreams all the time." She added: "To me, *Gather the Daughters* deals with types of violence that happen all the time, under our noses, and unless one has a way to be exposed to it, it happens hidden and unseen."

In *Gather the Daughters,* the descendants of ten families live on a tiny island just beyond the mainland United States, which is referred to as "the Wastelands." Writing for the London *Independent Online,* Lucy Scholes noted the story's similarity to Margaret Atwood's *The Handmaid's Tale* but went on to remark: "Unlike Atwood's tale, though, we're given barely any information regarding life beyond the island, Melamed cleverly keeping us as much in the dark, and thus just as frustrated, as her enquiring adolescent protagonists." Ruled by elite adult men who call themselves "the Wanderers," the island features no technology or money, with the people living on subsistence farming. The men sometimes take trips to the mainland to buy basic supplies. "Other men follow the kinds of trades one might find in a small medieval town: blacksmithing, weaving and carpentry," wrote London *Guardian Online* contributor Sarah Moss.

Also as in medieval times, the women are relegated to homelife and chores. They are strictly regulated by the men and are allowed to meet unchaperoned by men only when one of the women is giving birth. This typically occurs shortly after girls reach puberty, when they are forced to be married and bear children. Although the society is strictly regulated via male domination, the women do have a brief period of freedom when they are children. Each summer they are allowed to roam the island, building camps and sleeping on the beach. It is the only time that they are really free. The women, however, are starting to chafe at their role in society. For example, Janey starves herself to delay puberty and retain what freedom she has. It is during one of the summer excursions that a younger girl witnesses something that has been kept hidden from the women, terrifying her and marking the beginning of what could be the end of male domination.

"Fearsome, vivid, and raw: Melamed's work describes a world of indoctrination and revolt," wrote a *Kirkus Reviews* contributor. Rebecca Vnuk, writing in *Booklist,* remarked: "Melamed's gorgeous writing lets the details of this fundamentalist society drip out slowly," and she called *Gather the Daughters* a "quietly horrifying debut."

■ **Biographical and Critical Sources**

PERIODICALS

Booklist, July 1, 2017, Rebecca Vnuk, review of *Gather the Daughters,* p. 18.

Kirkus Reviews, May 15, 2017, review of *Gather the Daughters.*

Publishers Weekly, May 22, 2017, review of *Gather the Daughters,* p. 66.

ONLINE

All about Romance, https://allaboutromance.com/ (September 25, 2017), Dabney Grinnan, "An Interview with Jennie Melamed."

Early Bird Gets the Bookworm, http://earlybirdgetsthebookworm.com/ (October 11, 2017), "Author Interview with Jennie Melamed."

Guardian Online (London, England), https://www.theguardian.com/ (August 12, 2017), Sarah Moss, *"Gather the Daughters* by Jennie Melamed Review—a Misogynist Dystopia."

Independent Online (London, England), http://www.independent.co.uk/ (July 26, 2017), Lucy Scholes, *"Gather the Daughters* by Jennie Melamed, Book Review: I Doubt It Will Become a Cult Classic."

Jennie Melamed Website, http://www.jenniemelamed.com (February 20, 2018).

New York Times Online, https://www.nytimes.com/ (October 15, 2017), Claire Jarvis, "The Latest, Troubling Chapter in Feminist Dystopian Fiction," review of *Gather the Daughters.*

Qwillery, http://qwillery.blogspot.com/ (July 28, 2017), "Interview with Jennie Melamed, Author of *Gather the Daughters."*

Seattle Review of Books, http://www.seattlereviewofbooks.com/ (September 5, 2017), Conon Parks, review of *Gather the Daughters.*

Seattle Times Online, https://www.seattletimes.com/ (July 25, 2017), Ellen Emry Heltzel, *"Gather the Daughters* Review: A Grim Outlook for Women in a Fictional Dystopian World."

USA Today Online, https://www.usatoday.com/ (July 25, 2017), Zlati Meyer, "Debut Novel 'Daughters' Recycles 'Handmaid's Tale.'"*

Mark Alan Miller

1981-

■ **Personal**

Born December 29, 1981. *Education:* Chapman University, B.F.A., 2005.

■ **Addresses**

Home—Beverly Hills, CA.

■ **Career**

Writer. *OC Weekly*, columnist, 2008-10; Seraphim Inc., vice president, 2010—; BOOM! Studios, editor and writer, 2011—; Dark Horse Comics, writer, 2015—. Producer of animated shorts with the comedy troupe Superego for Nerdist Channel. Appears in podcasts, including *Nerdist, Bizarre States, Dork Forest, Nerdist Writers Panel,* and *Todd Glass Show.*

■ **Writings**

(With Clive Barker) *Hellraiser: The Toll,* Subterranean (Burton, MI), 2018.

Has written for the comics *Hellraiser, Hellraiser: Bestiary, Next Testament,* two volumes of *Hellraiser: Anthology,* and *The Steam Man of the Prairie and the Dark Rider Get Down.*

■ **Sidelights**

After obtaining a B.F.A. in film production from Chapman University, Mark Alan Miller went on to work as freelance writer at *OC Weekly,* a publica-

tion covering arts, entertainment, and news of Orange County and Long Beach, California. This job served as a launching site for his career in writing. He soon became the assistant editor to writer, film director, and visual artist Clive Barker for his horror novel *Abarat: Absolute Midnight.* He then worked on the director's cut of Barker's cult classic film *Nightbreed.*

In 2011, Miller began work for BOOM! Studios, where he is both editor and writer for Clive Barker's *Hellraiser* comic series. He has written for various comics, including *Hellraiser, Hellraiser: Bestiary, Next Testament,* two volumes of *Hellraiser: Anthology,* and *The Steam Man of the Prairie and the Dark Rider Get Down.* He has also produced a series of animated shorts with the comedy troupe Superego for the Nerdist Channel and can be heard on various Nerdist channel podcasts, including *The Nerdist, Bizarre States, The Dork Forest, The Nerdist Writers Panel,* and *The Todd Glass Show.* As vice president of Barker's production company Seraphim, Miller writes, produces, and directs original content.

In 2018 Miller released *Hellraiser: The Toll* in collaboration with Barker. The novella concerns an infamous character in the Barker horror *Hellraiser* canon—the Cold Man, or Pinhead (a Cenobite). His story plays out over the course of thirty years, beginning with *The Hellhound Heart* (1986) and ending in *The Scarlet Gospels* (2015). This novella follows the story of Kirsty Singer, who has been running and hiding from the Cenobites for three decades. She is persuaded by her former theology professor to go to a remote island, where she faces the Cold Man at last.

A *Publishers Weekly* reviewer praised the "vivid imagery," which "intensifies its atmosphere of dread." The critic went on to describe *Hellraiser* as a "mood piece whose infernal main character has grown Mephistophelian and tragic." Online at *Cemetery Dance,* Blu Gilliand noted that over the course of the tales in this canon, the "mythology has become something of a hash." Serving as a "bridge" between the first and last books, *Hellraiser* "could theoretically streamline the messy Hellraiser mythos." Gilliand found Miller's story an "entertaining piece of the Hellraiser puzzle" and Miller himself "as conscientious a steward of Barker's properties as we could ask for."

■ Biographical and Critical Sources

PERIODICALS

Publishers Weekly, October 9, 2017, review of *Hellraiser: The Toll,* p. 48.

ONLINE

Cedar Hollow Horror Reviews, http://www. cedarhollowhorrorreviews.com/ (November 4, 2017), review of *Hellraiser.*

Cemetery Dance, http://www.cemeterydance.com/ (February 5, 2018), Blu Gilliand, review of *Hellraiser.*

Clive Barker Podcast, http://www.clivebarkercast. com (October 3, 2017), José Armando Leitão, review of *Hellraiser.*

Dread Central, http://www.dreadcentral.com/ (October 6, 2017), Steve Dillon, review of *Hellraiser.*

Mark Alan Miller Website, http://www. markalanmiller.com (March 13, 2018).

Seraphim Inc. Website, http://www.seraphiminc. com/ (March 13, 2018), author profile.*

Sam J. Miller

1979-

■ **Personal**

Born February 7, 1979, in Hudson, NY; married. *Education:* Attended Rutgers University.

■ **Addresses**

Home—New York, NY.

■ **Career**

Writer and community organizer.

■ **Awards, Honors**

Shirley Jackson Award for short story, 2013.

■ **Writings**

(Editor, with Aviva Briefel) *Horror after 9/11: World of Fear, Cinema of Terror,* University of Texas Press (Austin, TX), 2011.
The Art of Starving, HarperTeen (New York, NY), 2017.
Blackfish City, Ecco Press (New York, NY), 2018.

Contributor to periodicals, including *Clarkesworld, Asimov's Science Fiction,* and *Lightspeed,*

■ **Sidelights**

Sam J. Miller began writing fiction in the early 2000s, and he won the coveted Shirley Jackson Award for one of his short stories in 2013. He

worked on several novels throughout this period, and two were published in 2017. Miller's young adult novel *The Art of Starving* was released first, while his adult novel, *Blackfish City,* followed months later. Commenting on his writing career in an online *AC Wise* interview, Miller stated: "I've been writing novels as long as I've been writing short stories, so there was no challenge transitioning. . . . I am similarly inept in both departments. . . . My process for novels and short stories is the same in that I have a whole bunch of ideas bubbling up in my brain all the time, and some will percolate for years without germinating, and then suddenly two or three of them will collide and I'll say AH-HA and the story will take shape, whether it's gonna be five pages long or 500."

With *The Art of Starving,* Miller presents high-school junior Matt. The protagonist is gay, and he has anorexia. Matt believes that hunger sharpens his senses, essentially giving him "superpowers." He draws on those superpowers to investigate senior soccer star Tariq. Matt suspects that Tariq sexually assaulted his sister, but it turns out that Tariq is also gay. The two then begin dating, but when Tariq learns of Matt's eating disorder, the relationship ends. In the meantime, Matt goes to work at the same slaughterhouse where his mother has worked for decades. Then she is let go during a company layoff, but Matt is offered a promotion. He decides to protest his mother's firing by letting all of the pigs in slaughterhouse free.

Miller, like his protagonist, is gay; and, like his protagonist, Miller suffered from an eating disorder as a teen. He told an online *Locus* magazine interviewer: "*The Art of Starving* is my debut novel, but it's also the seventh novel I've written. . . . I was trying to write a novel that would sell. I finally realized I should really not try to write the book I thought would sell—I should write the book that is my story, in the sense that it's my experience, and the thing that I've been frightened of talking about, and the thing that involves putting myself out there and discussing things that are tough to discuss, and that I couldn't have told without saying some things that many people prefer not to see on the page." Miller added: "When I decided to go there, that was the novel that came to life for me as a writer in a way my previous novels hadn't."

Reviews of *The Art of Starving* were largely positive, and a *Publishers Weekly* critic announced that "there is nothing romantic about debut novelist Miller's portrayal of anorexia; his descriptions are often graphic and disturbing." Sarah Weber, writing in *BookPage*, was also impressed, and she stated that "Matt's journey will feel familiar and hopeful to any reader who's experienced the precarious scramble for self-acceptance." In a rare negative assessment, *Voice of Youth Advocates* correspondent Suanne B. Roush warned that "the almost bloated nature of the prose is in direct opposition to the subject matter, and is the reason the novel will struggle to find a wide readership." On the other hand, a *Kirkus Reviews* critic felt that *The Art of Starving* is "a dark and lovely tale of supernatural vengeance and self-destruction." *Booklist* contributor Debbie Carton offered applause as well, and she declared that "Miller's heartfelt debut novel tackles difficult subjects with a bold mix of magical realism, tender empathy, and candor."

■ Biographical and Critical Sources

PERIODICALS

Booklist, May 15, 2017, Debbie Carton, review of *The Art of Starving*.

BookPage, July, 2017, Sarah Weber, review of *The Art of Starving*.

Kirkus Reviews, May 1, 2017, review of *The Art of Starving*.

Publishers Weekly, May 15, 2017, review of *The Art of Starving*; October 9, 2017, review of *Blackfish City*.

Voice of Youth Advocates, June, 2017, Suanne B. Roush, review of *The Art of Starving*.

ONLINE

AC Wise, http://www.acwise.net/ (January 31, 2018), author interview.

Fantasy Book Review, http://www. fantasybookreview.co.uk/ (January 31, 2018), review of *Blackfish City*.

Locus, http://locusmag.com/ (January 31, 2018), author interview.

RT Book Reviews, https://www.rtbookreviews.com/ (July 11, 2017), review of *The Art of Starving*.

Sam J. Miller Website, http://samjmiller.com (January 31, 2018).*

Joe Minihane

■ **Personal**

Male. *Education:* University of East Anglia, B.A., 2003; Cardiff University, M.A., 2005.

■ **Addresses**

Home—Brighton, England.

■ **Career**

Travel writer and journalist. BBC Worldwide, editorial junior, 2005-06; Lyceum Media, staff writer, 2006; *T3.com*, news writer, 2006-08.

■ **Writings**

Floating: A Life Regained, Overlook Press (New York, NY), 2017.

Contributor to the London *Guardian, Lonely Planet, CNN Travel, Escapism, Vacations and Travel, Emirates Open Skies, World Travel Guide*, and the London *Independent*.

■ **Sidelights**

Joe Minihane is a freelance journalist and travel writer, and his first book, the memoir *Floating: A Life Regained*, was published in 2017. The book is inspired by Roger Deakin's famed 1996 travel book, *Waterlog*. Deakin's account details his journeys as he swam his way across the United Kingdom, and Minihane followed in Deakin's

footsteps between 2012 and 2015. Where Deakin is an avid swimmer, Minihane is not. He admits to being fearful and hoping that swimming will relieve his anxiety. While Minihane eventually achieves his goal, he does so by adding therapy to his journey, and he discusses this aspect of his life in the memoir as well. Minihane also comments on the changes that have taken place across the United Kingdom since Deakin first traveled the same route. Thus, Minihane addresses issues of gentrification and urban expansion.

Reviews of *Floating* were mostly filled with praise, and critics commended Minihane's honesty and insight. According to a *Publishers Weekly* columnist, the book is "endlessly probing," and "Minihane's lyrical chronicle of swimming therapy is his own attack on worry and self-loathing." A *Kirkus Reviews* contributor was also impressed, asserting: "Detailed and searching, the book chronicles one man's search for inner peace while reaffirming the calming power of the natural world." The contributor went on to conclude that *Floating* is "a genuine and refreshing nature memoir."

Barney Bardsley in *On: Yorkshire Online* was more reserved, and he found that "the parts of the book where he explores difficulty and diversion—the breaking of his wrist during his journey, and the inevitable introspection that follows; the illuminating visits to a therapist when his mood begins to darken—are the liveliest by far. Sadly, the least compelling entries are the descriptions of the wild swims themselves, all of which start to blur, one into the other, as the writing accumulates and the quest comes close to completion." On the other hand, Gill Chedgey in the online *Nudge Book* remarked: "I loved the writer's honesty. In a world where so many are focused on creating identities of shallow veneer it was refreshing to read someone candidly admit they felt fear in certain situations and openly discussed their perceived shortcomings." Indeed, *Foreword Reviews* website correspondent Rebecca Foster stated: "The book is many things: a quest narrative, an atmospheric travel book ranging from the Yorkshire Dales to the Scilly Isles, and a record of psychic transformation."

■ Biographical and Critical Sources

BOOKS

Minihane, Joe, *Floating: A Life Regained*, Overlook Press (New York, NY), 2017.

PERIODICALS

Kirkus Reviews, May 15, 2017, review of *Floating*.
Publishers Weekly, May 8, 2017, review of *Floating*.

ONLINE

Foreword Reviews, https://www.forewordreviews. com/ (January 31, 2018), Rebecca Foster, review of *Floating*.
Joe Minihane Website, http://jmtravels.org (January 31, 2018).
Nudge Book, https://nudge-book.com/ (June 2, 2017), Gill Chedgey, review of *Floating*.
On: Yorkshire Online, https://www.on-magazine.co. uk/ (January 31, 2018), Barney Bardsley, review of *Floating*.*

A. Rafik Mohamed

■ **Personal**

Born in Washington, DC. *Education:* George Washington University, B.A.; University of California, Irvine, M.A., Ph.D.

■ **Addresses**

Office—CSUSB, College of Social and Behavioral Sciences, Office of the Dean, SB-207K, 5500 University Pkwy., San Bernardino, CA 92407.

■ **Career**

University of San Diego, San Diego, CA, associate professor, 1999-2009; Clayton State University, Morrow, GA, professor, chair of Department of Sociology, 2009-15; California State University, San Bernardino, dean of College of Social and Behavioral Sciences, 2015—.

■ **Writings**

(With Erik D. Fritsvold) *Dorm Room Dealers: Drugs and the Privileges of Race and Class,* Lynne Rienner Publishers (Boulder, CO), 2009.
Black Men on the Blacktop: Basketball and the Politics of Race, Lynne Rienner Publishers (Boulder, CO), 2017.

■ **Sidelights**

A. Rafik Mohamed did his undergraduate study at George Washington University and earned both a master's degree and a doctorate at the University of California, Irvine. He went on to teach at the University of San Diego and then at Clayton State University in Morrow, Georgia, before taking a position as dean of the College of Social and Behavioral Sciences at California State University, San Bernardino, which he has held since 2015. Mohamed has published two books: *Dorm Room Dealers: Drugs and the Privileges of Race and Class* and *Black Men on the Blacktop: Basketball and the Politics of Race.*

Dorm Room Dealers

Rafik teamed with sociologist Erik D. Fritsvold to write *Dorm Room Dealers,* a study of a group of upper-middle-class students who took part in a drug-dealing ring at college campuses across Southern California. On a black market network, the students sold marijuana, cocaine, Ecstasy, Ritalin, and Adderall. The social background of these students gave them cover from law enforcement. Even when these white, privileged college students sometimes get caught, they often are not held to account in the same fashion as those of the lower classes are. In their study, Fritsvold and Rafik observe: "When it comes to drug trafficking, there is substantial bias in the justice system based on, among other things, whether the offender is dealing in pharmaceuticals or street drugs. . . . This disparity is not based on any objective assessment of social harm or threats to public well being. Rather, it is more likely that the types of people who are apt to be abusing and trafficking in pharmaceuticals do not fit the stereotypical drug dealer profile that has come from the war on drugs and are, therefore, regarded quite differently by lawmakers and the criminal justice system."

At *Huffington Post,* Algernon Austin pointed out that drug use in this age group, contrary to what we may think, "is slightly lower among blacks." He noted: "Among 18-to-25 year olds, the 2009 National Survey of Drug Use and Health reports that thirty-nine percent of whites used an illicit drug in the past year. For blacks, the rate was thirty-four percent." Then, too, "because of the strong demand for drugs, dorm-room dealing is an easy, low-risk and profitable enterprise for white, middle-class youth."

Online at *StoptheDrugWar.org*, Phillip S. Smith explained: Mohamed and Fritsvold, "gained entrée into a network of drug sellers and users centered on a private college in San Diego and then spent six years interviewing and observing them as they partied hearty, gobbled and swapped pills, and peddled dope with reckless abandon." These young people are not the targets in the war on drugs. "They essentially get a free pass—from police, who ignore them; from college administrators, who don't want to upset their parents; from doctors, who are happy to prescribe them whatever pills they desire . . . because they are the children of 'good people,' i.e. white and wealthy people." In fact, some police officers were complicit in this story, taking bribes to look the other way. The students engaged in this activity simply because they could get away with it. Moreover, these students had career goals to achieve. They did not consider themselves to be in the same league as inner-city drug dealers. Smith concluded by calling *Dorm Room Dealers* a "valuable contribution to the ethnography of drug use and drug selling."

P.J. Venturelli, critiquing the book at *Choice*, called it an "informative, intriguing ethnography" and recommended it highly to "drug researchers, including practitioners, professionals, and anyone interested in social deviance." A critic writing in *Reference & Research Book News* found the study a "fascinating" take on "non-stereotypical drug dealers" as well as "highly readable." Austin, at *Huffington Post*, reported: "*Dorm Room Dealers* shows from a new angle that our illicit drug policy needs comprehensive reform to make it more just and more effective at protecting the public."

Black Men on the Blacktop

Black Men on the Blacktop looks at the cultural and political backdrop of basketball. Why does it seem to be a game for black men? As the publisher put it, Rafik "tells a story about race in its peculiarly American context, and about how the politics of race—and resistance—are mediated through

sports." In the book Rafik notes that "through their pose, language, and the attitude with which they play, young urban black males are repeatedly telling a counter-story to anyone deemed representative of the power structure and, just as important, to themselves."

Wes Lukowsky, writing in *Booklist*, found it a "revealing and well-researched study about an important form of resistance to a white-dominant culture." According to a *Publishers Weekly* reviewer, *Black Men on the Blacktop* is "written in a conversational tone . . . striking a balance between anecdote and scholarship" and "is an excellent study of the politics at play in everyday arenas."

■ Biographical and Critical Sources

BOOKS

Mohamed, A. Rafik, and Erik D. Fritsvold, *Dorm Room Dealers: Drugs and the Privileges of Race and Class*, Lynne Rienner Publishers (Boulder, CO), 2009.
Mohamed, A. Rafik, *Black Men on the Blacktop: Basketball and the Politics of Race*, Lynne Rienner Publishers (Boulder, CO), 2017.

PERIODICALS

Booklist, September 1, 2017, Wes Lukowsky, review of *Black Men on the Blacktop*, p. 38.
Choice, July, 2010, P.J. Venturelli, review of *Dorm Room Dealers*, p. 2204.
Publishers Weekly, September 11, 2017, review of *Black Men on the Blacktop*, p. 53.
Reference & Research Book News, February, 2010, review of *Dorm Room Dealers*.

ONLINE

Huffington Post, https://www.huffingtonpost.com/ (January 4, 2017), Algernon Austin, review of *Dorm Room Dealers*.
Inside CSUSB, https://inside.csusb.edu/ (May 31, 2017), author profile.
Lynne Rienner Publishers Website, https://www.rienner.com/ (March 14, 2018), brief book description.
StoptheDrugWar.org, https://stopthedrugwar.org/ (January 8, 2010), Phillip S. Smith, review of *Dorm Room Dealers*.*

Aja Monet

1987-

■ **Also Known As**

Aja Monet Bacquie

■ **Personal**

Born August 21, 1987.

■ **Addresses**

Home—Little Haiti, Miami, FL.

■ **Career**

Writer and activist. Smoke Signals Studio, cofounder.

■ **Awards, Honors**

Nuyorican Poets Café Grand Slam Champion, 2007; Andrea Klein Willison Prize for Poetry; New York City YWCA "One to Watch Award."

■ **Writings**

POETRY

The Black Unicorn Sings, Penmanship Books (New York, NY), 2010.

(Editor, with Saul Williams and Dufflyn Lammers) *Chorus: A Literary Mixtape*, Gallery Books (New York, NY), 2012.

My Mother Was a Freedom Fighter, Haymarket Books (Chicago, IL), 2017.

■ **Sidelights**

Poet Aja Monet won the prestigious Nuyorican Poets Café Grand Slam Champion title when she was only nineteen years old, and she has since gone on to win the Andrea Klein Willison Prize for Poetry and the New York City YWCA "One to Watch Award." Monet's first collection, *The Black Unicorn Sings*, was published in 2010, and she next teamed with Saul Williams and Dufflyn Lammers to edit the poetry collection *Chorus: A Literary Mixtape* in 2012. Monet's second poetry collection, *My Mother Was a Freedom Fighter*, followed in 2017.

With *My Mother Was a Freedom Fighter*, Monet mixes poems of coming-of-age with poems about female power. Several poems celebrate black womanhood, the power of resistance, and the violence of racism. From her childhood in Brooklyn to her school days in Chicago, Monet covers the many metamorphoses that take place on the journey from childhood to adulthood. In this manner, Monet seeks to explore the nature of womanhood, both in herself and in her role models. This rocky journey veers from ululation to desperation, and all of the girls and women portrayed strive to maintain their grace and power in the face of dehumanizing obstacles. In this manner, the poems' speakers and subjects become warriors, formed in the fires of white supremacy and patriarchy.

Reviews of *My Mother Was a Freedom Fighter* were largely positive, and a *Publishers Weekly* critic declared: "In stunning and evocative language,

Monet reveals the many ways that 'we exist between / a self for self and a self for others.'" Anna Ziering, writing on the *Warscapes* website, was also impressed, and she commented: "Situated firmly in the ongoing chaos of the present moment, [Monet] offers an extended meditation on what it means to be human in a brutal world. She asks this timeless question with urgency and a striking new voice." Ziering went on to note that "Monet carries readers on a journey from brittle rage to rooted resistance, using her poems to connect with her readers by sharing humanity and love, building a bridge that is also a well. Refreshed and with an army of readers united behind her, she closes the collection with a battle hymn for these 'daughters of a new day,' back on 'the streets, picket signs in our blood, our ancestors / marching through a nightmare, we rise toward freedom.'"

In the words of online *Los Angeles Review* correspondent John W.W. Zeiser, "Monet's poetry, like her activism, is one of resistance and reimagining. It resists simplicity, instead opening up new vistas for the reader and new points of entry into perspectives that are largely ignored." *Frontier Poetry* website reviewer Josh Roark offered both pros and cons, asserting that "Monet could have likely left out a few pieces without sacrificing the overall effect. . . . However, *My Mother Was a Freedom Fighter*'s music trumps any hesitations, and these issues are minor in comparison to the overwhelmingly generous scope of what Monet gifts to the reader." Roark concluded: "Hers is a voice pressing against injustice wherever it can, singing out accusations, threats—laying bare the realities of the oppressed and declaring their existences unjust. She's not afraid of any one or any system, and this book is a torch in the dark, a raucous and defiant singing on the horizon." Offering further praise in her online *Booked for Review* assessment, Claudia Rojas stated: "The zest in this book feels like debut instead of Monet's second poetry book. . . . *My Mother Was a Freedom Fighter* reminds us that women matter. These poems come to us from an activist's core, her ache to be."

■ Biographical and Critical Sources

PERIODICALS

Publishers Weekly, May 15, 2017, review of *My Mother Was a Freedom Fighter.*
This, November-December, 2012. Ryan B. Patrick, review of *Chorus: A Literary Mixtape.*

ONLINE

Booked for Review, http://bookedforreview.com/ (November 29, 2017), Claudia Rojas, review of *My Mother Was a Freedom Fighter.*
Frontier Poetry, https://www.frontierpoetry.com/ (May 24, 2017), Josh Roark, review of *My Mother Was a Freedom Fighter.*
Los Angeles Review, http://losangelesreview.org/ (February 1, 2018), John W.W. Zeiser, review of *My Mother Was a Freedom Fighter.*
Warscapes, http://www.warscapes.com/ (September 29, 2017), Anna Ziering, review of *My Mother Was a Freedom Fighter.**

N. West Moss

■ Personal

Married; husband's name Craig. *Education:* Sarah Lawrence College, B.A.; Mercy College, M.Ed.; William Paterson University, M.F.A.

■ Career

Writer. Visiting scholar, University of Virginia School of Medicine. Has taught at the Gotham Writers' Workshop, Passaic County Community College, William Paterson University, and Montclair State University.

■ Writings

The Subway Stops at Bryant Park (short stories), Leapfrog (Fredonia, NY), 2017.

Contributor to periodicals and websites, including the *New York Times, Lunch Ticket, Blotter,* the *Saturday Evening Post, McSweeney's, Salon, Brevity,* and *Hospital Drive.*

■ Sidelights

N. West Moss's debut short story collection, *The Subway Stops at Bryant Park,* was heavily influenced by her father's death. The author noted in an online *At One Sitting* interview with C.J. Arlotta, "Good writing comes from a place I call 'radical self-acceptance' in that we have to embrace who we are and what we obsess over, or our writing becomes flaccid. By the same token, at a certain point, we must consider our readers, if only to edit for clarity. So it's a balancing act." In the case

of *The Subway Stops at Bryant Park,* this balancing act features eleven tales that not only consider the loss of a parent, but also consider the changing nature of place. All of the stories in the collection are set in New York City's Bryant Park, both before and after gentrification. An Iranian doorman in "Omeer's Mangoes" watches gentrification unfold from his post, while a college student comes to Bryant Park to meet up with her beautiful but distant mother in "Beautiful Mom." The latter story portrays a young woman who aches for withheld parental love, while "Next Time" portrays a woman navigating the grief and challenges of settling her father's estate. In "Dubonnet," Moss follows and elderly widow who rejects her loving adult son and his family, deeming their good intentions to be overwhelming and suffocating. Yet, as the woman comes to terms with her husband's death, she eventually learns to accept her son's attentions.

Moss shared the story behind her book in a lengthy *American Micro Reviews and Interviews* website conversation with Elizabeth Martin, and she explained: "By the time my father was dying in about 2010, Bryant Park had been dramatically altered, and my father, unable to get around easily, spent more and more there because of its proximity. Unable to easily navigate the bicycle he used to use to get around the city, or even taxi cabs, he and I would slowly cross the street and sit in the park, quietly watching the world together for hours, just being together. We made up stories about the people we saw, and I came to understand that even mid-town Manhattan is made up of neighborhoods." Moss went on to state: "This park had, in addition to tourists, regular people living nearby. There were older people, street sweepers, doormen, people who lived in the shelters and came to the park during the day, the homeless. It was a microcosm of city life that I was only able to recognize because I sat there quietly, hour upon hour, with my dying father."

Indeed, as Maureen McCarthy put it in her *Star Tribune Online* assessment, "the pleasures of people watching infuse *The Subway Stops at Bryant Park,* a captivating collection of short stories set in and around a Midtown Manhattan park." A *Kirkus Reviews* critic was also impressed, asserting: "Moss' ability to probe the rich, complicated depths of those the city views as ordinary . . . and capture the profound currents of emotion found in the everyday animates this collection and makes it uniquely illuminating." Martha Witt, writing in the online *Literary Review* proffered praise as well, and she found that "each story in this collection shines an unrelenting light into the darkest corners of its characters' lives. . . . Moss's unerring ear allows her to tackle big thematic questions while never breaking away from her characters' voices." In the words of *Best New Fiction* website correspondent Clifford Garstang, the collection offers a "nuanced exploration of the many facets of loss." Garstang added: "The stories themselves are mostly quiet, without melodramatic conflict. They are about inner demons, rather than external villains, and because of this they are highly relatable. On the whole, the collection is an intimate portrait of real people, characters bound by the park."

■ Biographical and Critical Sources

PERIODICALS

Kirkus Reviews, March 15, 2017, review of *The Subway Stops at Bryant Park.*

ONLINE

American Micro Reviews and Interviews, http://www.americanmicroreviews.com/ (February 1, 2018), Elizabeth Martin, author interview.

At One Sitting, https://www.atonesitting.com/ (February 1, 2018), C.J. Arlotta, author interview.

Best New Fiction, https://bestnewfiction.wordpress.com/ (April 18, 2017), Clifford Garstang, review of *The Subway Stops at Bryant Park.*

Gotham Writers Website, https://www.writingclasses.com/ (February 1, 2018), author profile.

Literary Review, http://www.theliteraryreview.org/ (February 1, 2018), Martha Witt, review of *The Subway Stops at Bryant Park.*

N. West Moss Website, https://nwestmoss.wordpress.com (February 1, 2018).

Star Tribune Online, http://www.startribune.com/ (July 7, 2017), Maureen McCarthy, review of *The Subway Stops at Bryant Park.**

Eric L. Motley

1972-

■ **Also Known As**

Eric Lamar Motley

■ **Personal**

Born December 17, 1972, in AL. *Education:* Samford University, B.A., 1996; University of St. Andrews, M.Litt., Ph.D., 2000. *Religion:* Christian. *Hobbies and other interests:* Collecting first editions and rare books.

■ **Addresses**

Office—Aspen Institute, 2300 N St. NW, Ste. 700, Washington, DC 20037.

■ **Career**

Nonprofit executive. White House, Washington, DC, special assistant to the president, 2001-05; U.S. Department of State, Office of International Visitors, director, 2005-07; Aspen Institute, Commission to Reform Federal Appointments Process, executive director, 2009-12, Henry Crown Fellowship Program, vice president and managing director, 2007-13, National Programs, executive director, 2012-15, executive vice president and corporate secretary, 2016—.

Member of the board of directors of Barry-Wehmiller Companies, Library Cabinet for the Fred W. Smith National Library for the Study of George Washington, Smithsonian American Art Museum's National Council, and John F. Kennedy Centennial Memorial Task Force and sits on the National Advisory Board of Honored, Young Concert Artists, Advisory Board of Planet Word Museum, and Board of Overseers of Samford University.

■ **Awards, Honors**

Paul Harris Fellow of the Rotary International Foundation; Henry Crown Fellow of the Aspen Institute.

■ **Writings**

Madison Park: A Place of Hope, Zondervan (Grand Rapids, MI), 2017.

■ **Sidelights**

After attending Samford University, where he earned a B.A., and the University of St. Andrews, where he obtained both an M.Litt. and Ph.D., Eric L. Motley joined the administration of George W. Bush as special assistant to the president. He worked in the White House for four years and then briefly for the State Department before joining Aspen Institute, a nonpartisan think tank that acts as a forum—as its website describes it—for "values-based leadership and the exchange of ideas." At Aspen Institute, Motley is executive vice president and corporate secretary.

In 2017, Motley released his first book, *Madison Park: A Place of Hope,* a memoir. Motley was raised by his grandparents, Mamie and George Motley, after his mother—their own adopted daughter—gave birth to him and wanted to give him up. He grew up with them in Madison Park, a community near Montgomery founded by former slaves in 1880. Wil Haygood told readers of the *Washington Post:* "The outside world might not know much about it, but Madison Park has produced a scintillating array of black achievers: lawyers, doctors, educators, ministers." Motley is clearly one of them. *Madison Park,* Haygood commented, is "the tale of one man's journey through the labyrinth of racial expectations." The family was poor but proud and hardworking, and they attended the church George had helped build, Union Chapel AME Zion Church. Motley took jobs outside of school, always ready to help neighbors and teachers when needed. Haygood quoted one teacher: "'He was strange,' concedes Susan Mayes, one of Eric's seventh-grade teachers, who came to adore him. 'He was like a little old man'."

In high school, he began to form political views. Haygood quoted Motley: "I think it was also the first time I became truly illumined that I was expected to think a certain way, given my race. It was countering everything my grandparents taught me: Think for yourself. Use your own mind. Be your own person." He did just that, becoming what has long been considered a figure of controversy: a black conservative intellectual. A critic in *Christian Century* observed that his hometown gave Motley a foundation in the "unspoken social contracts that create community." In *Publishers Weekly,* a reviewer noted that *Madison Park* will give readers a sense of nostalgia for the kind of town "most have never visited and will intrigue those interested in how faith can strengthen community bonds." Anna Maria Polidori, writing at the blog *Articles and More,* called the book a "common and extraordinary story" and one that imparts

the "history of a harmonic community, of good people, where brotherhood, help, friendship the best values they knew and where negative sentiments closed out from their doors and unwanted."

■ **Biographical and Critical Sources**

BOOKS

Motley, Eric L., *Madison Park: A Place of Hope,* Zondervan (Grand Rapids, MI), 2017.

PERIODICALS

Christian Century, January 17, 2018, review of *Madison Park,* p. 35.
Publishers Weekly, October 9, 2017, review of *Madison Park,* p. 63.

ONLINE

Articles and More, https://alfemminile.blogspot.com/ (December 5, 2017), Anna Maria Polidori, review of *Madison Park.*
Aspen Institute Website, https://www.aspeninstitute.org/ (March 14, 2018), author profile.
Bible Gateway, https://www.biblegateway.com/ (November 14, 2017), Jonathan Petersen, author interview.
Days of My Life, https://kendraheatwole.wordpress.com/ (January 1, 2018), review of *Madison Park.*
Huffington Post, https://www.huffingtonpost.com/ (March 14, 2018), author profile.
NPR.org, https://www.npr.org/ (August 6, 2007), Farai Chideya, author interview.
Washington Post Online, https://www.washingtonpost.com/ (June 11, 2006), Wil Haygood, author profile.*

Tamsyn Murray

1984-

■ Personal

Born 1984, in Truro, Cornwall, England; married; children: one daughter, one son. *Education:* Attended university in London. *Hobbies and other interests:* Performing onstage.

■ Addresses

Home—Hertfordshire, England. *Agent*—Jo Williamson, Antony Harwood Ltd., 103 Walton St., Oxford OX2 6EB, England.

■ Career

Writer. Former teacher and IT support in schools. City University, London, Writing for Children course, current instructor.

■ Awards, Honors

Leeds Book Award, 11-14 category.

■ Writings

Snug as a Bug (picture book), illustrated by Judy Abbott, Simon & Schuster Children's (London, England), 2013.

Big Top Academy (picture book). illustrated by Adriana Puglisi, Oxford University Press (Oxford, England), 2017.

Instructions for a Secondhand Heart (young adult novel), Little, Brown and Company (New York, NY), 2017.

"STUNT BUNNY" SERIES; ILLUSTRATED BY LEE WILDISH

Stunt Bunny: Showbiz Sensation, Simon & Schuster Children's UK (London, England), 2010.

Stunt Bunny: Tour Troubles, Simon & Schuster Children's UK (London, England), 2011.

Stunt Bunny: Rabbit Racer, Simon & Schuster Children's UK (London, England), 2011.

Stunt Bunny: Medal Mayhem, Simon & Schuster Children's UK (London, England), 2012.

"AFTERLIFE" SERIES

My So-Called Afterlife, Piccadilly Press (London, England), 2010.

My So-Called Haunting, Piccadilly Press (London, England), 2010.

My So-Called Phantom Lovelife, Piccadilly Press (London, England), 2011.

My So-Called Christmas Carol (e-book) Amazon Digital Services, 2012.

"COMPLETELY CASSIDY" SERIES

Completely Cassidy Accidental Genius, Usborne Publishing (London, England), 2015.

Completely Cassidy Star Reporter, Usborne Publishing (London, England), 2015.

Completely Cassidy Drama Queen, Usborne Publishing (London, England), 2016.

"TANGLEWOOD ANIMAL PARK" SERIES

Baby Zebra Rescue, Usborne Publishing (London, England), 2016.

The Troublesome Tiger, Usborne Publishing (London, England), 2017.

Elephant Emergency, Usborne Publishing (London, England), 2017.

■ Sidelights

British children's author Tamsyn Murray got her start as a writer in 2008 when she bought a how-to book and decided she would like to try her hand at short stories. She sold her first short story that same year and also launched her popular "Afterlife" series for teens, and has gone on to write for younger readers in the "Stunt Bunny" series, for middle-grade readers in the "Completely Cassidy" series, and for young adults in her stand-alone novel *Instructions for a Secondhand Heart*.

In a *Words for Life* website interview, Murray remarked on whether or not her parents encouraged her writing: "On the surface, it doesn't seem like they did, much. But they did give me books from an early age—I clearly remember sitting outside our house when I must have been four, reading a *Ladybird Read It Yourself* story (Snow White and Rose Red if you're interested) on my own. And I think that my love of books grew and grew from there until I realised I could write my stories of my own. It would have been much harder to write if I hadn't absorbed so much knowledge from reading. So it was more about influence than encouragement."

My So-Called Afterlife

Murray launched her "Afterlife" series with *My So-Called Afterlife*, in which Lucy Shaw is a ghost, recently murdered when she walked home alone on New Year's against her parents' orders. Worse, she gets stuck in a men's room but is saved by a lighting engineer, Jeremy, who can actually see her. He introduces Lucy to a number of other ghosts at the Church of the Dearly Departed, including Hep, a suicide, who teaches Lucy some powers, and dishy Ryan. But her killer is still on the loose, and with Ryan's help she tracks the man down. Once her killer is captured, she and Ryan can move on.

"This is quite a deep book but on the surface funny and very readable," noted *School Librarian* contributor Janet Fisher, who added: "[Lucy] is a funny and touching character and this unusual story is worth a read for teens fourteen and up." A contributor in the online *Book Zone for Boys* was also impressed, commenting: "This book has everything a great story needs—it is well written,

it has realistic and memorable characters, sparkling dialogue, incredible humour and moments of nail-biting tension."

My So-Called Haunting and *My So-Called Phantom Lovelife*

The series continues with *My So-Called Haunting*, in which fourteen-year-old Skye is psychic and able to see ghosts, which complicates her early days at her new school. She does not want her communication with ghosts to come between her plans for good-looking Nico. Things become even more complicated when she tries to help a troubled teenage ghost, Dontay, but soon Dontay is taking more and more of Skye's time and attention. "This slightly light-hearted approach is a welcome relief to the copious amounts of blood and gore that ooze out of the pages of most of contemporary horror fiction," noted Anne-Marie Tarter in *School Librarian*.

The series concludes with *My So-Called Phantom Lovelife*, which again focuses on Skye who has now broken up with Nico, who she has discovered is actually a member of an ancient Romanian cult seeking to gain supernatural powers. Her attentions have been turned to Owen, a handsome youth she met at Hyde Park. The only trouble is, Owen is a ghost. "The novel blends recognisable elements of contemporary teenage life: school, relationships, social networking sites, with a matter-of-fact treatment of the supernatural, represented by psychic characters, a spiritualist church and arcane ritual," commented *School Librarian* contributor Sandra Bennett.

Star Reporter and *Drama Queen*

Murray writes for middle-grade readers in her "Completely Cassidy" series, set at St Jude's Secondary School and following the adventures of eleven-year-old Cassidy Bond as she searches for her special talent. She desperately wants to stand out from the rest of her family, and when she takes a test that labels her a genius, she asks no questions. Schools do not make mistakes, right? So she joins a school team headed for a regional Kids Quiz show with interesting results. This book "has loads of appeal and is destined for popularity," noted *School Librarian* reviewer Chris Routh. "Tamsyn Murray has a real talent for seeing the funny side of the everyday!" A student contributor to the London *Guardian* similarly termed it a "great read because it was exciting and funny."

In *Star Reporter*, Cassidy decides her special thing might be journalism. She petitions her school to let girls wear trousers. This gains more and more support and eventually thrusts her into the newspaper gang at school, but now she must learn to deal with a whole new set of problems. A *So Many Books, So Little Time* website contributor noted of this installment: "The sudden change in the way [Cassidy] had to act with information about her friends and classmates was sometimes hilarious, sometimes tense and other times heartbreaking. I really felt for her!"

Drama Queen completes the series. It is summer now, and Cassidy hopes that acting might be her thing so she tries out at the local drama academy. The only problem is, her best friend wants the same role Cassidy does, and now she must choose between friendship and stardom. "Completely Cassidy, totally enjoyable," noted Andrea Reece at the *Love Reading 4 Kids* website.

Instructions for a Secondhand Heart

Murray's young adult novel, *Instructions for a Secondhand Heart*, features teen Jonny, whose heart is giving out on him. He desperately needs a heart transplant but feels his life is slipping away. The potential organ donor has to have Jonny's rare blood type, which means his chances are even slimmer. Meanwhile, Neve Brody's twin brother Leo dies while the family is on vacation, and his organs are donated. Leo's life is saved, and now he sets out to find out who his donor was. Meeting Neve, he does not tell her who he really is, and then as their relationship blossoms he fears to do so, thinking he will lose her.

Reviewing *Instructions for a Secondhand Heart* in *Horn Book*, Rachel L. Smith commented: "Neve and Jonny are emotionally complex, vulnerable protagonists who help each other face realities they never dreamed they'd see." Further praise came from a *Publishers Weekly* contributor who noted: "Readers should find it easy to cheer on these two misfits who are figuring how they fit in and fit together." Similarly, *Booklist* writer Diane Colson felt this novel will "will appeal to readers drawn to romances featuring ill teenagers," while *Voice of Youth Advocates* reviewer Debbie Wenk concluded: "Family, friendship, trust, grief, and love are all topics that will capture readers' attention and hold it until the final page."

■ Biographical and Critical Sources

PERIODICALS

Booklist, October 1, 2017, Diane Colson, review of *Instructions for a Secondhand Heart*, p. 79.

Horn Book, November-December, 2017, Rachel L. Smith, review of *Instructions for a Secondhand Heart*, p. 111.

Publishers Weekly, October 2, 2017, review of *Instructions for a Secondhand Heart*, p. 143.

Voice of Youth Advocates, October, 2017, Debbie Wenk, review of *Instructions for a Secondhand Heart*, p. 62.

School Librarian, summer, 2010, Janet Fisher, review of *My So-Called Afterlife*, p. 118; spring, 2011, Anne-Marie Tarter, review of *My So-Called Haunting*, p. 54; autumn, 2011, review of *My So-Called Phantom Lovelife*, p. 182; summer, 2013, Angela Lepper, review of *Snug as a Bug*, p. 94; autumn, 2015, Chris Routh, review of *Accidental Genius*, p. 169; spring, 2017, Chris Routh, review of *Instructions for a Second-Hand Heart*, p. 56.

ONLINE

Book Zone For Boys, http://bookzone4boys.blogspot.com/ (February 15, 2010), review of *My So-Called Afterlife*.

Guardian Online, https://www.theguardian.com/ (September 20, 2011), review of *My So-Called Haunting*; (March 4, 2015), Tamsyn Murray, "How to Write about Your Own Family"; (July 8, 2015), review of *Completely Cassidy: Accidental Genius*

Love Reading 4 Kids, http://www.lovereading4kids.co.uk/ (January 1, 2016), Andrea Reece, review of *Drama Queen*.

Romantic Novelists Association Website, https://romanticnovelistsassociation.org/ (April 17, 2012), "Interview with Tamsyn Murray."

So Many Books, So Little Time, http://solittletimeforbooks.blogspot.com/ (July 13, 2015), review of *Star Reporter*.

Tamsyn Murray Website, http://www.tamsynmurray.co.uk (February 13, 2018).

Telegraph Online http://www.telegraph.co.uk/ (February 2, 2012), Martin Chilton, review of *Medal Mayhem*.

Words for Life, http://www.wordsforlife.org.uk/ (February 13, 2018), "Tamsyn Murray."*

Edoardo Nesi

1964-

■ **Personal**

Born November 9, 1964.

■ **Career**

Writer, filmmaker, translator, and business owner.

■ **Awards, Honors**

Bruno Cavallini Prize, for *L'eta dell'oro;* Strata Award, 2011, for *Story of My People.*

■ **Writings**

NOVELS; EXCEPT WHERE NOTED

Figli delle stelle, Bompiani (Milan, Italy), 2001.

L'eta dell'oro, Bompiani (Milan, Italy), 2004.

Story of My People (nonfiction; originally published as *Storia della mia gente*), translated by Antony Shugaar, Other Press (New York, NY), 2012.

L'estate infinita, Bompiano (Milan, Italy), 2015, translation by Alice Kilgarriff published as *Infinite Summer*, Other Press (New York, NY), 2017.

(With Guido Maria Brera) *Everything Is Broken Up and Dances: The Crushing of the Middle Class* (nonfiction; originally published as *Tutto e in frantumi e danza*), translated by Antony Shugaar, Other Press 2018.

Also writer and director of the film *Fughe da fermo*, Fandango, 2001; and translator of David Foster Wallace's *Infinite Jest.*

■ **Sidelights**

Edoardo Nesi is an Italian writer, filmmaker, and translator, though he has also owned and operated a large textile factory in Prato, Italy. Nesi recounts his experiences in the textile business in *Story of My People* (which was originally published as *Storia della mia gente*). While the volume begins as a memoir, it quickly becomes a more essayistic exploration of the impacts of globalization. Nesi explains that he inherited the textile factory from his father, and the business had been in the family for eighty years. Nesi was forced to shut it down in 2004, and his book describes how the shutdown affected the community. The author also explains that Italy's declining economy after China joined the World Trade Organization in the 1990s. This event created a major competitor country that offered cheaper labor and cheaper materials.

Story of My People

Story of My People was largely praised by critics, and the book won the Strata Award, Italy's most prestigious literary honor, in 2011. As a *New Yorker* reviewer put it, the book is a "blend of memoir, manifesto, and diatribe," as well as "an intimate account of a homespun world." While a *Publishers Weekly* contributor felt that the story is not without flaws, they nevertheless concluded that "much of the book is sad, honest, and biting; overall it is an important work." Meghan Dowell, writing in *Library Journal,* was also positive, and she advised that "this rich narrative should appeal to economists and social scientists researching globalization." A columnist in *Reference & Research Book News* echoed this sentiment, asserting that the book is "worth reading for anyone who likes good writing and wants a deeper understanding of either contemporary Europe or global business." The contributor also found that "the book is written with a literary richness of language and a deep love of culture."

In the words of a *Kirkus Reviews* correspondent, "the author mocks economist promoters of globalization as 'sorcerers and wizards and haruspices.'" Thus, the reviewer continued, *Story of My People* is "a tour de force that spares no one." Offering further applause in his *Finance & Development* assessment, Josh Felman remarked: "The story of Prato's demise is lyrically written and deeply moving. This is somewhat unusual for a book about business. But Nesi is not a typical businessman. Although he inherited his firm from his parents (and grandparents), he always wanted to be a writer." Felman concluded that this "is a book that spends more time exploring the impact of failure on people than describing the textile business."

Infinite Summer

Nesi again draws on his family's business for inspiration in his novel *Infinite Summer* (which was originally released as *L'estate infinita*). The story follows Ivo Barrocciai, Cesare Vezzosi, and Pasquale Citarella as they set out to build and open a textile factory in Florence. The tale is set during the 1970s; Ivo has just inherited his father's blanket factory, and he decides to modernize and expand the business. His partners, Cesare and Pasquale, are not natural businessmen. In fact, all three characters seem more interested in romantic conquest than financial success. While Cesare woos a new mistress, Ivo woos Cesare's wife.

Reviews of *Infinite Summer* were largely mixed, and a *Publishers Weekly* critic warned that "few women in the novel are fleshed out into full characters." A *Kirkus Reviews* contributor was even more negative, asserting: "Unfortunately, all these narrative threads fail to add up to anything." The result is "a bubbling but empty-headed tribute to manufacturing, production, and the wonders of capitalism." On the other hand, a writer on the *A Bookish Way of Life* website announced: "I enjoyed getting to know Ivo, Cesare, and Pasquale through their relationships with each other, but mainly through their relationships with their loved ones. It all made for quite a funny, captivating, and unputdownable read."

■ Biographical and Critical Sources

PERIODICALS

Finance & Development, June, 2013, Josh Felman, "Lament for a Textile Town."
Kirkus Reviews, June 1, 2013, review of *Story of My People*; May 15, 2017, review of *Infinite Summer*.
Library Journal, June 15, 2013, Meghan Dowell, review of *Story of My People*.
New Yorker, July 29, 2013, review of *Story of My People*.
Publishers Weekly, February 18, 2013, review of *Story of My People*; May 8, 2017, review of *Infinite Summer*.
Reference & Research Book News, December, 2013, review of *Story of My People*.

ONLINE

A Bookish Way of Life, http://abookishwayoflife. blogspot.com/ (July 13, 2017), review of *Infinite Summer*.
Kirkus Reviews Online, https://www.kirkusreviews. com/ (December 24, 2017), review of *Everything Is Broken Up and Dances: The Crushing of the Middle Class*.*

Vanessa Neumann

1972-

■ **Personal**

Born 1972, in Caracas, Venezuela; married Warren Cash (divorced, 2010). *Education:* Columbia University, B.A., 1994, M.A., 1998, M.Phil., 2000, Ph.D., 2004.

■ **Addresses**

Home—Washington, DC.

■ **Career**

Political theorist, journalist, and writer. *Daily Journal,* Caracas, Venezuela, journalist; Corimon, corporate planning and finance; Venezuelan embassy, Washington, DC, intern; Blue Channel Chemicals, purchasing agent; UNICEF, volunteer, 2001-04; Centre for Applied Philosophy and Public Ethics, Canberra, Australia, researcher, 2006; Hunter College, adjunct assistant professor; *Diplomat,* editor-at-large; Asymmetrica (strategic risk consultancy), president and consultant. Organisation for Economic Co-operation and Development, member of Advisory Group for the Task Force on Countering Illicit Trade; United Nations Security Council, member of Global Counter-Terrorism Research Network.

■ **Awards, Honors**

Fellowships from Yale University, Columbia University, and Foreign Policy Research Institute.

■ **Writings**

Blood Profits: How American Consumers Unwittingly Fund Terrorists, St. Martin's Press (New York, NY), 2017.

Contributor of articles to periodicals, including the *Wall Street Journal, Daily Beast,* London *Sunday Times, Guardian, Daily Telegraph, Weekly Standard,* and *Standpoint.*

■ **Sidelights**

As president of Asymmetrica, Venezuelan-American businesswoman Vanessa Neumann offers consulting on strategies for corporate clients and governments to dismantle illicit trade. In 2017, she published *Blood Profits: How American Consumers Unwittingly Fund Terrorists,* which explores how drug cartels, smugglers, and terrorist organizations use illicit trade for financial gain. Neumann is also on the Organisation for Economic Co-operation and Development's Advisory Group for the Task Force on Countering Illicit Trade. She is a consultant to United Nations Women on gender-based approaches to preventing and countering violent extremism. She lectures, publishes articles in the *Wall Street Journal* and *Guardian,* and appears on CNN and NTN24. She holds a Ph.D. in political philosophy from Columbia University.

In 2017, Neumann published *Blood Profits,* an examination of money raised by illicit trade of illegal goods that is funneled to terrorist groups around the world. She contends that the rise of illegal trade was born out of societal events such as the collapse of the Iron Curtain, out-of-work Soviet scientists and intelligence agents, regional trade pacts, and new-age technology that has made international organized crime and terrorists bolder and well-funded. Unsuspecting consumers may be purchasing fake products or goods obtained illegally that help these terrorist organizations.

Neumann describes specific illicit industries, such as cigarettes, oil, prostitution, fake drugs, and knock-off fashion, and how they benefit groups like Boko Haram and other terrorists, such as those responsible for the *Charlie Hebdo* attack and the Paris Bataclan and San Bernardino, California, shootings. Neumann uses examples from her own experience as a consultant and researcher with the United Nations. In addition to illicit trade, terrorists and drug cartels rely on money collected from corrupt government officials, gambling, slave labor, and human trafficking for control around the world. She gives examples from Central America to China's Silk Road market and a Hezbollah rally in Lebanon.

Acknowledging the serious nature of the subject matter, a reviewer in *Publishers Weekly* said: "Neumann rarely touches on how ordinary consumers can consciously opt out of supporting nefarious organizations." The reviewer noted that ordinary people may not care that they are buying counterfeit handbags and illicit drugs, but does give Neumann credit for bringing attention to the problem and offering solutions. In *Kirkus Reviews Online*, a contributor noted Neumann's alarming,

and sometimes alarmist, message, adding that "the needless repetition of her message and the hard-to-follow organization of the chapters make much of the narrative a slog. An uneven treatment of a topic that merits further study."

■ **Biographical and Critical Sources**

PERIODICALS

Publishers Weekly, October 2, 2017, review of *Blood Profits: How American Consumers Unwittingly Fund Terrorists*, p. 127.

ONLINE

Kirkus Reviews Online, https://www.kirkusreviews.com/ (September 14, 2017), review of *Blood Profits*.

Vanessa Neumann Website, http://vanessaneumann.com (April 1, 2018), author profile.*

Shiela Nevins

1939-

■ Personal

Born April 6, 1939, in New York, NY; daughter of Stella and Benjamin Nevins; married Sidney Koch (an investment banker), 1972; children: David Koch. *Education:* Barnard College, B.A., 1960; Yale University, M.F.A., 1963.

■ Career

Writer and producer. United States Information Agency, former actress; ABC News, former field producer, 1973; Time-Life Films, writer, 1973-75; Children's Television Workshop, former writer and producer, 1975; Scribner, former audiobook recorder; National Educational Television, former researcher and associate producer; CBS, producer, 1978-79; HBO, director of documentary programming, 1979-82, vice president of documentary programming, 1986, senior vice president of original programming, 1995, executive vice president of original programming, 1999-2003, president of documentary and family programming, 2004—. Also founder and owner of Spinning Reels production, 1983-85.

■ Awards, Honors

Lifetime Achievement Award, International Documentary Association, 1998; inducted into the Broadcasting & Cable Hall of Fame, 2000; News and Documentary Emmy for Lifetime Achievement, 2005; Directors Guild of America citation, 2011; Woman of Achievement Award, Women's Project Theater, 2013; Visionary Leadership Award, International Festival of Arts & Ideas, 2013. Documentaries and work produced under Nevins

have garnered thirty-five News and Documentary Emmy Awards, forty-two Peabody Awards, and twenty-six Academy Awards.

■ Writings

(Author of foreword) *Addiction: Why Can't They Just Stop? New Knowledge, New Treatments, New Hope,* Rodale (New York, NY), 2007.

You Don't Look Your Age . . . and Other Fairy Tales, Flatiron (New York, NY), 2017.

■ Sidelights

Shiela Nevins has produced over 500 documentaries while working for HBO, and she is also the author of *You Don't Look Your Age . . . and Other Fairy Tales.* Nevins's collection of personal essays was released when the author was already in her late seventies, and many section in the book comment on the challenges of aging. Nevins details her decision to get a face-lift and eye-lift in her late fifties, and she explains that her industry often put her in competition with young, beautiful women. While Nevins hoped the procedure would help her love her looks again, she found the opposite to be true. Instead, she became obsessed with every perceived flaw. Other essays in the book comment on Viagra, menopause, and conversations overheard on a train. The author additionally offers reflections on her relationship with her chronically ill mother. M. Bijman offered an ambivalent assessment of Nevins's efforts, remarking in her *Seven Circumstances* website review that, "as a woman who has worked most of my life in male-dominated industries . . . some of what [Nevins] wrote about the role of women in the workplace, and the glass ceiling, resonated with me. 'Advice to Women in a Male-Dominated Workplace' and 'From Cosmo to Ms.' were witty chapters, and I suppose, true to life." Bijman went on to state: "Even so, this is not a light version of Sheryl Sandberg's *Lean In*—or any other handbook for professional women, current or historical. It is the well-disguised, very select, very held-in thoughts and ideas of Sheila Nevins whose particular problem in her career has been that she is very beautiful and also extremely smart, educated and accomplished."

Nevins, as her comments in a *Vanity Fair Online* interview with Elize Taylor might indicate, was purposefully aiming for "well-disguised," and she explained: "I would call it a dark memoir, depending on what you think is me and what you think is not me. It's a mystery. It's a game. You have to figure out who all these women are. The only way you would know is to live with me, so you'd have to move in for how many years I have left . . . and follow my every move. Only I know the truth." The author added that the essays in *You Don't Look Your Age . . . and Other Fairy Tales* are "based on the truth of my experiences, whether they're my own or whether they're someone else's.

I think, in fact, there is perhaps imagining, but there's no real untruth." Thus, as a *Kirkus Reviews* critic put it, Nevins offers "a miscellany of musings about aging, love, work, and wisdom." The critic advised: "As in many collections, some of the pieces are disposable, but the best ones are honest, opinionated, and spirited."

■ Biographical and Critical Sources

PERIODICALS

Kirkus Reviews, March 15, 2017, review of *You Don't Look Your Age . . . and Other Fairy Tales.*

ONLINE

Internet Movie Database, http://www.imdb.com/ (February 5, 2018), author profile.

Seven Circumstances, https://sevencircumstances. com/ (May 5, 2017), M. Bijman, review of *You Don't Look Your Age . . . and Other Fairy Tales.*

Vanity Fair Online, https://www.vanityfair.com/ (May 2, 2017), Elise Taylor, author interview.*

Judith Newton

■ **Also Known As**

J.L. Newton

■ **Personal**

Female.

■ **Addresses**

Home—CA.

■ **Career**

University of California, Davis, professor emerita.

■ **Writings**

Oink: A Food for Thought Mystery, She Writes Press (Berkeley, CA), 2017.

■ **Sidelights**

Judith Newton writes mystery stories and tends garden in California. Her "Emily Addams Food for Thought" series begins with the 2017 *Oink: A Food for Thought Mystery.* Also going by the name Judith Newton, she is professor emerita at the University of California, Davis. Newton likes cooking for friends and family, and she incorporates that expertise into her story. *Oink* centers on foodie professor Emily Addams in the women's study department at Arbor State, a land grant university in Northern California. She is surprised to discover that she is a suspect in the poisoning of Professor Peter Elliott of the plant biology department. Elliott was developing a genetically modified corn plant that could be fed to pigs when he was suspiciously found in a coma in a pig pen holding a piece of Emily's cornbread.

Emily is especially hurt because she believes that food is an important element of community and culture. She gathers a group of colleagues to investigate and learns that their usually liberal-minded college has turned to profit-hungry corporate interests that want to defund the women's and ethnic studies programs. Meanwhile, Emily raises her daughter and dates the math teacher. Newton adds a recipe at the end of each chapter.

Able to adequately mix important subjects with an airy, fun tone, the book "is intriguing and full of twists, and it's hard to find fault with the author's theme of communal empowerment, her love of food, and her frequent instructional asides," according to a writer in *Kirkus Reviews*, who deemed the novel "a highly educated foodie's dream." On the other hand, Danielle Nielsen wrote in *Phi Kappa Phi Forum* that while the story's mystery and Emily's actions to find who poisoned Elliott are successful, "where Newton begins to lose this reader, at least, is in the simplistic and surface-level musings of campus politics that do not add to the mystery at hand."

Calling the new series promising, a *Publishers Weekly* contributor exalted: "The winning lead, superior prose, and clever plotting set this above the pack," adding that the recipes are a bonus. On the *Mystery Scene* website, Betty Webb observed: "*Oink* is an indictment of the ramifications felt whenever Big Business inserts itself into scientific research. Yet the book manages (mostly) to disguise itself as a cozy with recipes." Webb enjoyed the combination of gentle mystery with a strongly feminist theme that can be enjoyed by traditionalists. Webb also noted that the book is so deftly plotted that Newton proves to be an old hand despite this being her debut novel.

■ Biographical and Critical Sources

PERIODICALS

Kirkus Reviews, July 15, 2017, review of *Oink: A Food for Thought Mystery.*

Phi Kappa Phi Forum, fall, 2017, Danielle Nielsen, review of *Oink*, p. 31.

Publishers Weekly, November 13, 2017, review of *Oink*, p. 43.

ONLINE

Mystery Scene, https://mysteryscenemag.com/ (August 28, 2017), Betty Webb, review of *Oink*.*

Erin Nicholas

■ Personal

Married; children: a daughter, a son. *Education:* Attended college and graduate school. *Hobbies and other interests:* Travel, watching movies, watching college football.

■ Addresses

Home—Midwest.

■ Career

Writer. Also worked as a physical therapist.

■ Writings

"ANYTHING AND EVERYTHING" SERIES

Anything You Want, Samhain Publishing (Cincinnati, OH), 2012.
Everything You've Got, Samhain Publishing (Cincinnati, OH), 2013.

"COUNTING ON LOVE" SERIES

She's the One, Samhain Publishing (Cincinnati, OH), 2014.
It Takes Two, Samhain Publishing (Cincinnati, OH), 2014.
Best of Three, Samhain Publishing (Cincinnati, OH), 2014.
Going for Four, Samhain Publishing (Cincinnati, OH), 2015.

Up by Five, Samhain Publishing (Cincinnati, OH), 2015.

"BILLIONAIRE BARGAINS" SERIES

No Matter What, Samhain Publishing (Cincinnati, OH), 2010.
What Matters Most, Samhain Publishing (Cincinnati, OH), 2015.
All That Matters, Samhain Publishing (Cincinnati, OH), 2015.

"SAPPHIRE FALLS" SERIES

Getting Out of Hand, Self-published, 2014.
Getting Worked Up, Self-published, 2014.
Getting Dirty, Self-published, 2014.
Getting It All, Self-published, 2014.
Getting Lucky, Self-published, 2015.
Getting Over It, Self-published, 2015.
Getting His Way, Self-published, 2016.
After You, Self-published, 2017.

"TAKING CHANCES" SERIES

Twisted Up, Montlake Romance (Seattle, WA), 2016.
Tangled Up, Montlake Romance (Seattle, WA), 2017.
Turned Up, Montlake Romance (Seattle, WA), 2017.

"OPPOSITES ATTRACT" SERIES

Completely Yours, Forever (New York, NY), 2016.
Forever Mine, Hachette Book Group (New York, NY), 2016.
Totally His, Forever (New York, NY), 2016.

OTHER

Hotblooded, Samhain Publishing (Cincinnati, OH), 2012.

Going Down Easy, Montlake Romance (Seattle, WA), 2018.

■ Sidelights

Erin Nicholas is the author of more than thirty romance novels with a sexy edge to them. A former physical therapist, Nicholas only began publishing in 2010, but as she noted in an interview on the *Romance Junkies* website, she has been writing most of her life. "From the moment I first heard my first story I knew I had to be a writer," she remarked. "I don't remember one specific moment. I read avidly as a kid in a home of readers and full of books. Writing was just always something I did—poems, songs, short stories that gradually got longer and longer. I always preferred a book or a notebook and pen to any other activity. Still do! I wrote part-time even through college, grad school, working full-time with two little kids. It's just always been a part of my life."

Nicholas is the author of "Sapphire Falls" series, as well as a number of other popular romance series, including "Anything and Everything," "Taking Chances," and "Opposites Attract." In an interview with Melanie Shawn at Shawn's website, Nicholas pragmatically described her writing process: "Sit down, write words, get up and get more coffee, tell myself I need More Words, sit back down and write more words—or you know, check Facebook and email. Get more coffee. Tell myself I need MORE WORDS. Continue this process until the end. . . . Go back and fix everything I screwed up on the first draft that I learned about the characters by the end. Send to my beta readers. Revise. Send to my editor. Revise. Send back to my editor. Take a deep breath and have a cupcake. Start again on next book."

"Anything and Everything" Series

Nicholas launched her "Anything and Everything" series with *Anything You Want,* in which two people overcome mutual distrust to find real love. Sabrina Cassidy broke Luke Hamilton's heart when she left him to chase her musical dreams. Four years later, broke, she calls him for help, but she ends up talking to his business partner, Marc, who wants to protect Luke from more hurt. Marc has no time for Sabrina, and the feeling is mutual, but this pair ultimately makes an unlikely connection. "What an awesome ride," noted Taryn Elliott on her website. "I simply loved everything about this book," Elliott added.

In *Everything You've Got,* Luke Hamilton takes center stage and finds his own true love with Dr. Kat Dayton while stuck together in a three-day RV road trip. A contributor in the online *Dear Author* noted, "I did like the writing in the book. The sex scenes are pretty hot and parts of the novel are funny."

"Taking Chances" Series

Twisted Up is the first title in the "Taking Chances" series, set in the farming community of Chance, Nebraska, which has been hit by strong tornadoes two years running. Now, with former classmates returning to town for a high school reunion, the winds are up once more and once the winds hit, three different couples are trapped together in various locations around town. Forced to be in close contact, old passions and crushes are rekindled. The first installment features fire chief Avery Sparks and Jake Mitchell, her first love and one that was eager to get out of town after their graduation. A *Happily Ever Chapter* website contributor had praise for this first installment, noting: "The two of them had great chemistry together and couldn't keep their hands off of each other. When the secrets of what happened to Avery in the ten years since they saw each other last come out, I was happy to see Jake's protective instincts kick in." An online *Books of All Kinds* writer observed: "With lots of energy and action, a strong, independent heroine who knows what she wants, and a cheeky hero who you cannot help but like, this novel is a delightful read." And an *All about Romance* website reviewer concluded: "If you enjoy small town romances but are looking for one that stands out, *Twisted Up* provides a refreshing change."

Best friends Bree McDermott and Max Grady are at the center of *Tangled Up.* Max is a storm chaser, and he is happy to have Bree, a police officer, at his side. But now Bree wants to make their relationship more than best friends. A *Harlequin Junkie* website reviewer had praise for the second installment, commenting: "Overall, this was a fantastic second novel Ms. Nicholas has penned for her 'Taking Chances' series where the sex scenes were hot and illustrated just how right these two are for each other. The way this story ended with Bree confessing what ice cream flavors match their intimate moments together and how they can have everything they both want brought a smile to my face. I would recommend *Tangled Up* by Erin Nicholas, especially if you love the best friends to lovers trope or small town romances."

In *Turned Up,* former academic competitors Dillon Alexander and Kit Derby are thrown together, both medical professionals, but now their rivalry is transformed to romance when a blizzard traps them in Kit's grandmother's house. "I believe I would have enjoyed this more if I had read the first two books in the 'Taking Chances' series," noted a *Books of My Heart* website reviewer.

"Opposites Attract" Series

Completely Yours launched the "Opposites Attract" series. Kiera and Zach are opposites: she is a successful graphic designer more comfortable hanging out with people online, while Zach is an outgoing EMT first responder. Their paths cross when he is called to the scene of an accident involving Kiera. An online *Smut Matters* reviewer had a mixed assessment of this series launch, noting: "I really liked Kiera. And I liked that Zach was able to bring her out of her shell, though I didn't always love how he did it. But I was so annoyed with him for being such an awful EMT in the beginning that I could never completely come around on him. And I liked that Zach allowed himself to explore some of Kiera's world, too."

In *Forever Mine,* cop Maya Goodwin is the sort of person to step toward danger when others run away. Even after she is forced to retired following an injury, she is still a risk taker. Alex is her opposite, but Maya is there to help him deal with the arrival of a young daughter he never knew he had. A *Smart Bitches Trashy Books* website reviewer commented: "The best part of *Forever Mine* was that there's no real angst. Maya and Alex have to work some stuff out, but the obstacles that keep them apart aren't dire. And I loved how Maya helped him learn about the characters and worlds his daughter was passionate about in a genuine and enthusiastic way. Add some really hot sex scenes to the mix, and basically I was in heaven."

In *Totally His,* the third book in the series, sexy cop Finn, rescues actress Sophie when her theater catches fire. Sparks fly away from the inferno, as well in this "moving and inspiring" novel, according to a *Publishers Weekly* reviewer. Further praise was offered by *BookPage Online* contributor Billie B. Little, who observed: "In *Totally His,* Erin

Nicholas has woven a sweet and sexy tale set against the backdrop of a lively community theater and a noisy, rollicking Irish pub that readers won't want to leave behind."

■ Biographical and Critical Sources

PERIODICALS

Publishers Weekly, October 2, 2017, review of *Totally His,* p. 124.

ONLINE

All about Romance, https://allaboutromance.com/ (February 21, 2018), Maria Rose, review of *Twisted Up.*

BookPage Online, https://bookpage.com/ (October 31, 2017), Billie B. Little, review of *Totally Hi.*

Books of All Kinds, https://booksofallkinds.weebly.com/ (October 8, 2016), review of *Twisted Up.*

Books of My Heart, https://booksofmyheart.net/ (August 27, 2017), review of *Turned Up.*

Dear Author, http://dearauthor.com/ (April 6, 2012), review of *Everything You've Got.*

Erin Nicholas Website, https://erinnicholas.com (February 13, 2018).

Happily Ever Chapter, http://happilyeverchapter.blogspot.com/ (August 24, 2016), review of *Twisted Up.*

Harlequin Junkie, http://harlequinjunkie.com/ (January 30, 2017), review of *Tangled Up.*

Leigh Kramer, http://www.leighkramer.com/ (March 29, 2017), review of *Forever Mine.*

Melanie Shawn, http://melanieshawn.com/ (March 17, 2018), Melanie Shawn, author interview.

Romance Junkies, http://romancejunkies.com/ (August 23, 2016), author interview.

Romancing the Book, http://romancing-the-book.com/ (October 30, 2017), review of *Totally His.*

Smart Bitches Trashy Books, http://smartbitchestrashybooks.com/ (March 29, 2017), review of *Forever Mine.*

Smut Matters, http://smutmatters.com/ (January 5, 2017), review of *Completely Yours.*

Taryn Elliott, http://www.tarynelliott.com/ (January 23, 2012), Taryn Elliott, review of *Anything You Want.**

Ray Norman

■ Personal

Male. *Education:* University of Illinois, B.S.; Southern Illinois University, J.D. *Hobbies and other interests:* Reading, working out, movies, fine dining.

■ Career

Writer, ghostwriter, and playwright. Ghostwriter of books in genres that include health, nutrition, and spiritual self-help. Worked as an attorney recruiter and a corporate headhunter.

■ Writings

(With Wesley Snipes) *Talon of God,* Harper Voyager (New York, NY), 2017.

Also author of the play *And You Thought Your Family Was Crazy.*

■ Sidelights

Ray Norman is a novelist and ghostwriter who has written books for major clients on subjects such as health, nutrition, spirituality, and self-help. He is also a playwright. Norman previously worked as a corporate headhunter and a recruiter of attorneys and legal professionals. He holds an engineering degree from the University of Illinois and a law degree from Southern Illinois University.

Talon of God is Norman's first novel, written with well-known actor and action star Wesley Snipes. The book presents an action-based story very much in line with Snipes's roles in *Blade* and other high-energy films. It is also a spiritual story, boosted by a war between literal angels and demons unfolding on the streets of Chicago.

The novel's protagonist, Lauryn Jefferson, is the daughter of a minister. She has become a doctor and devoted her life to medicine rather than pursuing a religious life. When she is attacked in the emergency room one night, she realizes that the troubled veteran who assaulted her is under the influence of a drug that transforms humans into supernatural monsters. She is saved by the mysterious Talon Hunter, a sword-wielding superpowered protector who is a messenger of God. Teaming up with her ex-boyfriend, police officer Will Tannenbaum, Lauryn joins Talon in a search for those responsible for turning people into monsters in anticipation of a city-wide demon possession. At the same time, Lauryn seems to have a higher calling that she will ascend to, with Talon's help.

Wesley Baines, writing on the website *Beliefnet,* commented: "*Talon of God* is a fun, snappy read that doesn't shy away from the darkness. Snipes' story is one that effortlessly weaves spirituality into action and adventure that anyone can enjoy, regardless of belief. This isn't 'Christian fiction.' It's fiction that draws from Christianity to tell an awesome story, bringing readers face-to-face with terrifying evil."

In his *Beliefnet* interview with Baines, Norman remarked: "I think one of the interesting things about the book is that you're not only just seeing the human side of the drama, but we're able to kind of pull back the curtain, and you're able to see the activity taking place in the unseen spiritual world—the battles from the angelic and demonic forces, and the types of influences that unseen forces might have on our lives."

In *Kirkus Reviews*, a writer called *Talon of God* an "entertaining thriller with enough swordplay, religious prophecy, and demonic threats to entertain readers across lots of different genres." The authors "bring a cinematic flair to the proceedings," observed a *Publishers Weekly* writer. Brian Truitt, writing in *USA Today*, remarked: "Old-school fans of *Passenger 57* and *Demolition Man* will appreciate that Snipes has just as much punch with a keyboard as with his fists, and the realm of urban fantasy has an impressive new disciple."

■ Biographical and Critical Sources

PERIODICALS

Forbes, November 26, 2017, Dan Schwabel, "Ray Norman: How He's Adapting His Writing to Different Genres and Co-Authors," interview with Ray Norman.

Kirkus Reviews, May 15, 2017, review of *Talon of God*.

Publishers Weekly, May 8, 2017, review of *Talon of God*, p. 42.

USA Today, July 25, 2017, Brian Truitt, "Snipes Fights Evil with a Pen in *Talon of God*," review of *Talon of God*, p. 3D.

ONLINE

Beliefnet, http://www.beliefnet.com/ (February 19, 2018), "The Faith and Fiction of Wesley Snipes," interview with Wesley Snipes and Ray Norman.

HarperCollins Website, http://www.harpercollins.com/ (February 19, 2018), biography of Ray Norman.

Talon of God Website, http://www.talonofgod.com (February 19, 2018).*

Julian North

■ **Personal**

Male.

■ **Career**

Novelist.

■ **Awards, Honors**

Lyra Award Winner, Best Young Adult Novel, 2016, and Los Angeles Book Festival, Best Science Fiction Novel, 2017, both for *Age of Order.*

■ **Writings**

"AGE OF ORDER SAGA"

Age of Order, Plebeian Media (Pembroke Pines, FL), 2016.
State of Order, Plebeian Media (Pembroke Pines, FL), 2017.
Fate of Order, Plebeian Media (Pembroke Pines, FL), 2017.
Rise of Order, Plebeian Media (Pembroke Pines, FL), 2018.

■ **Sidelights**

A writer since childhood, Julian North now writes the young adult "Age of Order Saga" series of novels set in a dystopian future of manufactured inequality. North's 2016 *Age of Order* starts the series. In the near future, New York is now the capital of the United States. The Orderist movement runs a society in which those with merit, money, and genetic enhancements rule, while the poor are disenfranchised. Daniela Machado lives in the barrio in Bronx City, but because she is smart and athletic, she is allowed to attend Tuck School, usually reserved for children of Orderist families. When Daniela's brother comes close to death from a genetic disorder, Daniela begins to suspect there is an ulterior motive for her admittance.

Remarking on her life on the Upper East Side of Manhattan, North said in an interview online at *It's Write Now:* "*Age of Order* was inspired by my experiences trying to get my young children into school in our adopted home of New York City. As my frustrations grew, I would write my emotions down. . . . The reader will see a world that could easily be our own." While North's book is yet another young adult book that focuses on the divide between the haves and have nots, "what starts out as sort of a fish-out-of-water drama with sci-fi trappings becomes the story of a veritable clash of superbeings, but North maintains expert control over it," noted a writer in *Kirkus Reviews.* Writing in *Publishers Weekly,* a contributor commented: "Daniela is a pragmatic and compelling heroine whose voice will hold readers' attentions and linger long after the story is done."

Describing the range of the book, M. Corvid said online at *Chanticleer Book Reviews:* "The action is often thrilling, complete with high-tech rivalries, partisan politics, chase scenes, and class conflicts. While most of the major characters are teens, North's insights into their thoughts and feelings can apply to any age." In a review on the *Dutch Book Chick* website, Ellen Jansen said: "I liked the main character Daniela a lot, because she was a strong character and also because has a kind of sixth sense, which I was afraid might be a little too convenient for her, but instead of it being cheesy it was done very well."

The next book in saga, *State of Order,* follows events after the president and many of his supporters are killed. The elite vow to make the common people suffer to maintain order. Meanwhile, Daniela is still trying to save her brother as she navigates the nightmares perpetrated on society. Book three, *Fate of Order,* involves a new civil war, when freedom is all but gone.

■ **Biographical and Critical Sources**

PERIODICALS

Kirkus Reviews, March 1, 2017, review of *Age of Order.*

Publishers Weekly, October 30, 2017, review of *Age of Order,* p. 63.

ONLINE

Chanticleer Book Reviews, https://www. chantireviews.com/ (February 9, 2017), M. Corvid, review of *Age of Order.*

Dutch Book Chick, http://dutchbookchick.com/ (February 6, 2017), Ellen Jansen, review of *Age of Order.*

It's Write Now, https://itswritenow.com/ (February 9, 2017), author interview.*

Michael Nye

■ **Personal**

Born in Cincinnati, OH; married. *Education:* Ohio State University, B.A.; University of Missouri, St. Louis, M.F.A. *Hobbies and other interests:* Playing pickup basketball.

■ **Addresses**

Home—Columbus, OH. *Agent*—Mark Gottlieb, Trident Media Group, 41 Madison Ave., 36th Fl., New York, NY 10010.

■ **Career**

Writer. Former managing editor at *River Styx* and *Missouri Review;* current associate editor, *Boulevard.* Has also taught creative writing at several colleges.

■ **Writings**

Strategies against Extinction (short stories), Queen's Ferry Press (Plano, TX), 2012.
All the Castles Burned (novel), Turner Publishing Company (Nashville, TN), 2017.

Short fiction has appeared in *American Literary Review, Boulevard, Cincinnati Review, Crab Orchard Review, Kenyon Review, South Dakota Review, Sou'wester, Normal School, Epoch,* and *New South,* among others.

■ **Sidelights**

Ohio native Michael Nye is the author of the 2012 short-story collection *Strategies against Extinction* and the 2017 novel *All the Castles Burned.* An edi-

tor at literary journals including *Boulevard, Missouri Review,* and *River Styx,* Nye has also taught creative writing in colleges. In a *Lit Reactor* interview with Fred Venturini, Nye commented on how he has benefited from working as a magazine editor for a number of years: "Reading for a magazine has been the best and most valuable part of my training as a writer. I don't have a sophisticated guess as to how many stories I've read over the years, but it's well into the thousands, maybe over ten thousand now. So, even if I couldn't tell you exactly why, I have an immediate 'this is working' reaction to page one, or (and this is even better) a 'why is this working?' All the rookie mistakes are easy to avoid now, but I get to read and experience what my contemporaries are doing in real time: what other writers are working on right now. That's tremendously helpful as a writer, exciting as an editor, and fascinating as a reader."

Strategies against Extinction

Nye's story collection, *Strategies against Extinction,* offers nine tales of people who find themselves at turning points in their lives. "They are faced with hard choices, broken promises, and the fear of self-destruction," Nye explained in an interview on *Bill and Dave's Cocktail Hour* website. Among the characters are a 1940s war veteran who has become a radio broadcaster, a film projectionist who fears that her new boyfriend might be a terrorist, a comic-book store owner, a surgeon at a Boston hospital, an ex-baseball player who has now become a financial advisor, an American ambassador who has a judo match with Vladimir Putin, and a recently divorced woman who rents a room in her house out to an adulterous couple for their afternoons of love-making.

A *Publishers Weekly Online* contributor had praise for *Strategies against Extinction,* noting: "Nye holds his characters in sharp focus, and their emotional lives are rigorously yet sympathetically observed." Online *Journal* reviewer Nick Ripatrazone felt that this work "does not simply introduce the reader to roughly a dozen separate lives; it reaches emotional depths not often touched in the short form." Ripatrazone added: "A good short-story collection will leave a reader with a handful of narratives worth remembering; a great short-story collection, like Nye's, will leave a reader with lives worth remembering." Writing at the *Necessary Fiction* website, Ursula Villarreal-Moura also had praise, commenting: "Ultimately, what propels this collection is the urgency to survive every type of calamity: career uncertainty, loss of a home, physical combat, divorce, and death of a loved one. The strategies Nye's characters employ are as complex and varied as the wondrous species presently roaming the earth." Likewise, *Paste* website writer Laura Straub observed: "Nye's patience helps his stories keep their relevance. In *Strategies against Extinction,* he presents a collection of modest narratives, elegantly written, mostly in third person. He makes no effort to distract the reader with bewitching showmanship, bypassing overbearing voice and too-showy verbiage."

All the Castles Burned

Set in the 1990s, Nye's debut novel, *All the Castles Burned,* is a novel of male friendship at a prestigious private school between adolescents from vastly different backgrounds. Owen Webb is the product of a working-class family who wins a scholarship for Rockcastle Preparatory Academy. There he meets and is befriended by Carson Bly, an upperclassman from a wealthy family. Carson is a bit of a cipher, but a shared love of basketball unites the two, and Owen is desperate to keep this friendship as things at his family's home are beginning to fall apart. Owen is also starting to fall in love with Carson's sister. Then, when Owen's father is arrested for burglary, Carson begins to manipulate the younger student, playing on his anger and snaring him in a web of lies that threaten his future.

In an *Electric Literature* website interview with Adam Vitcavage, Nye remarked on the inspiration for this novel: "What struck me about these two characters and boys in general is that we don't often see that subtler type of friendship. It's rarely discussed unless there are these, like you said, extraordinary events. . . . I'm in my late 30s now and I've moved around a bit. I've noticed how men rarely make friends outside of school or work and we rarely discuss friendship. I'm surprised it isn't discussed more. There's nothing taboo about it and I think writers take it for granted. I wanted to explore it on a more personal level."

A *Publishers Weekly* reviewer lauded *All the Castles Burned,* terming it a "suspenseful and memorable novel." A *Kirkus Reviews* critic also had praise, noting, "Just as Nye's characters are glued to the O.J. Simpson trial, readers won't want to look away." *Columbus Dispatch Online* writer Margaret Quamme called it a "quietly brutal story, anchored in the everyday while hinting at dark paths there for the taking." Writing at the *Foreword Reviews* website, Angela Woltman commented: "A gripping bildungsroman that leaves many intriguing questions about trauma unanswered, *All the Castles Burned* is a powerful and poignant tale of human resilience."

■ Biographical and Critical Sources

PERIODICALS

Kirkus Reviews, November 15, 2017, review of *All the Castles Burned.*
Publishers Weekly, December 11, 2017, review of *All the Castles Burned,* p. 144.

ONLINE

Bill and Dave's Cocktail Hour, http://billanddavescocktailhour.com/ (February 13, 2018), "Guest Contributor: Michael Nye."
Columbus Dispatch Online, http://www.dispatch.com/ (February 11, 2018), Margaret Quamme, review of *All the Castles Burned.*
Electric Literature, https://electricliterature.com/ (January 29, 2018), Adam Vitcavage, author interview.
Foreword Reviews, https://www.forewordreviews.com/ (January 1, 2018), Angela Woltman, review of *All the Castles Burned.*
Journal, http://thejournalmag.org/ (January 7, 2013), Nick Ripatrazone, review of *Strategies against Extinction.*
Lit Reactor, https://litreactor.com/ (April 20, 2017), Fred Venturini, "Secrets of the Slush: An Interview with Editor and Author, Michael Nye."
Michael Nye Website, http://mpnye.com (February 13, 2018).
Necessary Fiction, http://necessaryfiction.com/ (March 28, 2018), Ursula Villarreal-Moura, review of *Strategies against Extinction.*
Paste, https://www.pastemagazine.com/ (November 29, 2012), Laura Straub, review of *Strategies against Extinction.*
Publishers Weekly Online, https://www.publishersweekly.com/ (August 20, 2012), review of *Strategies against Extinction.**

J.L. Oakley

■ Personal

Married; children: three sons.

■ Addresses

Home—Bellingham, WA.

■ Career

Novelist.

■ Awards, Honors

EPIC eBook Award, 2012, for *Tree Soldier;* Bellingham Mayor's Arts Award, 2013; Chanticleer Grand Prize, 2013; First Place Chaucer Award, 2014; WILLA Silver Award, 2015; Goethe Grand Prize, 2016.

■ Writings

NOVELS

Tree Soldier, CreateSpace Independent Publishing Platform, 2011.

Timber Rose, CreateSpace Independent Publishing Platform, 2013.

The Jøssing Affair, Fairchance Press (Oslo, Norway), 2016.

Mist-chi-mas: A Novel of Captivity, Fairchance Press (Oslo, Norway), 2017.

■ Sidelights

J.L. Oakley writes award-winning historical fiction of the nineteenth and twentieth centuries, as well as mystery novellas set in Hawaii. She grew up in Pittsburgh, Pennsylvania, listening to stories of how her grandmother's family settled the West, and inheriting a love of history from her family. She attended college, moved to Hawaii, and became a historian and award-winning author. She was a finalist twice at the Pacific Northwest Writers Association Literary Contest and has published fiction in various magazines, anthologies, and literary publications.

Tree Soldier and *Timber Rose*

In 2011, Oakley published *Tree Soldier,* set in the 1930s with the Civilian Conservation Corps in Washington State during the Depression. John "Park" Hardesty ostracized himself far away from his family after an argument with his brother led to an accident that caused his brother's disfigurement. Hardesty works with troubled teenagers planting trees and building bridges. Naturalist Kate Alford, barred from the Forest Service because of her gender, helps Hardesty deal with his past. "Oakley constructs this rugged romance with tremendous care, fully developing its characters," according to a *Publishers Weekly* writer.

In the 2013 *Timber Rose,* Oakley travels to 1907 to tell the story of Caroline Symington, a mountain climber who shocks her wealthy Portland, Oregon, family with her love of the wilderness. After her parents disown her, she elopes with forest ranger Bob Alford and dodges the intrusions of her malevolent uncle. Online at *Historical Novel Society,*

Laura Fahey observed: "Oakley does a skillful and confident job of weaving a good deal of historical material into her story."

The Jøssing Affair

The Jøssing Affair is Oakley's World War II thriller that follows a British-trained Norwegian intelligence agent named Tore Haugland. Operating in Norway where the Nazis still have a foothold, Haugland poses as a fisherman to help the Norwegian resistance intelligence service. His mission may be threatened by his attraction to German widow Anna Fromme, who was accused of betraying her husband. When his cover is blown, Haugland suspects Anna.

"Oakley effectively recreates a lesser-known chapter of WWII through well-developed characters and suspenseful situations," noted a reviewer in *Publishers Weekly*. On the *Chanticleer Book Reviews* website, Carrie Meehan called the book "a highly enriching experience, a fascinating and profound work of historical fiction penned by J.L. Oakley, one of the best in the business" and "a certain testimony to the underground heroes of WWII."

Writing online at *Historical Novel Society*, Laura Fahey commented that some of Oakley's characters can be melodramatic, but "her narrative is . . . sprawling and involving and intensely detailed."

■ Biographical and Critical Sources

PERIODICALS

Publishers Weekly, January 2, 2012, review of *Tree Soldier*, p. 47; August 7, 2017, review of *The Jøssing Affair*, p. 55.

ONLINE

Chanticleer Book Reviews, https://www.chantireviews.com/ (June 3, 2017), Carrie Meehan, review of *The Jøssing Affair*.

Historical Novel Society, https://historicalnovel society.org/ (April 1, 2018), Laura Fahey, reviews of *Timber Rose* and *The Jøssing Affair*.

J.L. Oakley Website, https://historyweaver. wordpress.com/ (April 1, 2018), author profile.*

Sarah Ockwell-Smith

1976-

■ Personal

Born 1976, in Bedfordshire, England; daughter of David and Lynda Ockwell; children: Sebastian, Flynn, Rafferty, Violet. *Education:* University of Greenwich, B.Sc. (with honors); also earned Dip. Hom. and H.B.C.E.

■ Addresses

Home—Saffron Walden, Essex, England. *Agent*— Eve White Literary Agency, 54 Gloucester St., London SW1V 4EG, England.

■ Career

Worked in pharmaceutical research and development; became therapist, doula, and hypno-birthing instructor; BabyCalm Ltd., founder and director, beginning 2007; *Gentle Parenting* (website), co-founder and operator. Also operator of Gentle Sleep Training (consultants); consultant to Tesco Baby Club and *Sky News;* guest on media programs.

■ Member

British Sleep Society.

■ Writings

Babycalm: A Guide for Calmer Babies and Happier Parents, Piatkus (London, England), 2012, published as *Babycalm: A Guide for Parents on Sleep Techniques, Feeding Schedules, and Bonding with Your New Baby,* Skyhorse Publishing (New York, NY), 2014.

ToddlerCalm: A Guide for Calmer Toddlers and Happier Parents, Piatkus (London, England), 2013.

The Gentle Sleep Book: A Guide for Calm Babies, Toddlers, and Pre-Schoolers, Little, Brown (Boston, MA), 2015.

The Gentle Parenting Book: How to Raise Calmer, Happier Children from Birth to Seven, Little, Brown (Boston, MA), 2016.

Why Your Baby's Sleep Matters, Pinter & Martin (London, England), 2016.

Gentle Discipline: Using Emotional Connection—Not Punishment—to Raise Confident, Capable Kids, TarcherPerigee (New York, NY), 2017, published as *The Gentle Discipline Book: How to Raise Co-operative, Polite, and Helpful Children,* Piatkus (London, England), 2017.

The Gentle Potty Training Book: The Calmer, Easier Approach to Toilet Training, Little, Brown (Boston, MA), 2017.

Ready, Set, Go! A Gentle Parenting Guide to Calmer, Quicker Potty Training, TarcherPerigee (New York, NY), 2018.

The Gentle Eating Book: The Easier, Calmer Approach to Feeding Your Child and Solving Common Eating Problems, Piatkus (London, England), 2018.

Contributor to magazines, newspapers, and websites.

Ockwell-Smith's books have been translated into several languages, including Chinese, Estonian, Romanian, Russian, and Turkish.

■ Sidelights

Sarah Ockwell-Smith began her career in pharmaceutical research, but parenthood inspired a major change of direction. She built upon her degree in child development by acquiring training in pre- and postnatal education, hypnotherapy, and developmental infant massage. Later Ockwell-Smith studied pediatric first aid, perinatal psychology, and birth trauma. The specialties that emerged from her ongoing research were in the areas of child sleep and attachment parenting, though she prefers a more intuitive and less restrictive version that she calls gentle parenting.

Ockwell-Smith became a popular writer, coach, and consultant in her native Britain. She founded the organization BabyCalm in 2007. The website *Gentle Parenting* and the consulting service Gentle Sleep Training were natural outgrowths of her primary objective: to provide parents with the science, common-sense advice, and self-confidence to raise healthy, happy children.

Ockwell-Smith published several books in England, and her writings are now widely available around the world. The first of these to appear in a U.S. version was *Babycalm: A Guide for Parents on Sleep Techniques, Feeding Schedules, and Bonding with Your New Baby.* In this volume, as in some of her later works, Ockwell-Smith shares her own early parenting experiences, along with stories contributed by other parents. Above all, according to a reviewer at the website *Aha! Parenting,* Ockwell-Smith reinforces her message that new parents need to "learn to trust themselves and their babies." In an interview with Karen Doherty posted at Doherty's website, the author observed that "so many parents over-intellectualise parenting," but if we can "slow down and just be present with our babies and children, the simpler it all becomes."

A recurring issue in parenting circles is that of discipline. In an interview with Bethany Braun-Silva for *NY Metro Parents,* Ockwell-Smith identifies three "misconceptions" that can derail the best intentions, the first among them that "too many parents expect children to act like adults." Also, she said, parents often believe erroneously that discipline fosters a motivation to improve, and that "punishing and shaming kids" provides that motivation. In *Gentle Discipline: Using Emotional Connection—Not Punishment—to Raise Confident, Capable Kids,* Ockwell-Smith offers "a primer on placing empathy and respect . . . at the center" of the conversation, wrote a *Publishers Weekly* contributor; she advocates the replacement of "authoritarian" methods with "authoritative" models. The book begins with the scientific underpinning of behavior and brain development, then deconstructs ineffective or harmful methods of discipline.

The chapters that follow are devoted to specific problems that frequently arise in children, including violent or destructive behavior, whining and sulking, failing to listen and follow directions, rudeness and swearing, sibling rivalry, and lying. The author then focuses on the parent: how to tame the parental demon within, and how to boost the child's self-esteem. According to Amy Scribner in *BookPage,* the author is "low on judgment and high on helpful insights." Ockwell-Smith continues her gentle parenting approach in additional works devoted respectively to gentle toilet training and gentle resolution of common eating problems.

■ **Biographical and Critical Sources**

BOOKS

Ockwell-Smith, Sarah, *Babycalm: A Guide for Calmer Babies and Happier Parents,* Piatkus (London, England), 2012, published as *Babycalm: A Guide for Parents on Sleep Techniques, Feeding Schedules, and Bonding with Your New Baby,* Skyhorse Publishing (New York, NY), 2014.
Ockwell-Smith, Sarah, *The Gentle Sleep Book: A Guide for Calm Babies, Toddlers, and Pre-Schoolers,* Little, Brown (Boston, MA), 2015.
Ockwell-Smith, Sarah, *Why Your Baby's Sleep Matters,* Pinter & Martin (London, England), 2016.

PERIODICALS

BookPage, August, 2017, Amy Scribner, review of *Gentle Discipline: Using Emotional Connection—Not Punishment—to Raise Confident, Capable Kids,* p. 20.
New York Times, August 13, 2017, Judith Newman, review of *Gentle Discipline,* p. BR27.
Publishers Weekly, May 15, 2017, review of *Gentle Discipline,* p. 52.

ONLINE

Aha! Parenting, http://www.ahaparenting.com/ (February 10, 2018), review of *Babycalm: A Guide for Parents on Sleep Techniques, Feeding Schedules, and Bonding with Your New Baby.*
Gentle Parenting Website, http://www.gentleparenting.co.uk (February 10, 2018).
Karen Doherty Website, http://www.karendoherty.com/ (July 10, 2013), Karen Doherty, author interview.
New York Times Online, https://www.nytimes.com/ (August 11, 2017), Judith Newman, review of *Gentle Discipline.*
NY Metro Parents, https://www.nymetroparents.com/ (August 31, 2017), Bethany Braun-Silva, author interview.
Sarah Ockwell-Smith Website, https://sarahockwell-smith.com (February 10, 2018).*

Lianne Oelke

■ **Personal**

Female. *Hobbies and other interests:* Camping, books, craft beer, cats.

■ **Addresses**

Home—Vancouver, British Columbia, Canada.

■ **Career**

Film staff member and author.

■ **Writings**

Nice Try, Jane Sinner, Clarion Books (New York, NY), 2018.

■ **Sidelights**

Lianne Oelke has made a primary career within the world of filmmaking. In an interview featured on the *Happy Ever After* website, Oelke explained that her literary debut came about as a result of an interim phase in her life. She was in her senior year of college when her debut book first began coming to fruition; at the time, Oelke found herself feeling disappointed at the lack of books for the young-adult demographic that focused on college-aged characters, as well as the various challenges that come with that stage of life.

Nice Try, Jane Sinner is Oelke's solution to that problem. The novel centers on the titular protagonist, Jane Sinner, who has hit something of a rut in

her life and has to recover as best she can, whether she wants to or not. At the start of the book, Jane is thrust into attending Elbow River Community College following her expulsion from her previous school. Going to Elbow River will allow her to wrap up the classes she needs to earn her high school diploma. However, Elbow River turns out to be able to help Jane with more areas of her life than just her grades. Jane's (deeply religious) parents are concerned about her downward spiral, and are attempting to help her through faith-based strategies that she finds suffocating. When Jane chances upon an advertisement at Elbow River for a reality show scouting for auditions, she sees it as a chance to get away from her parents and have some room to breathe. She likes the idea of immersing herself in a new setting, full of strangers and with absolutely no reminders of her past. Jane signs up for the show, titled *House of Orange,* and is soon given a spot on set with a full house of fellow cast members. Through her role in *House of Orange,* Jane embarks upon her own path of self-discovery and actualization as she navigates her past and who she is now.

A *Publishers Weekly* contributor remarked: "Debut novelist Oelke has created a complex and entertaining heroine in Jane." *Booklist* reviewer Maggie Reagan expressed that "this is an entertaining read for any teen." In *Kirkus Reviews,* a writer called the book "character-driven, humorous, and deceptively profound." *School Library Journal* contributor Susannah Goldstein wrote: "The protagonist is well developed." She added: "Readers will enjoy rooting for her on *House of Orange* and in life." On the *Globe and Mail Online,* Shannon Ozirny called *Nice Try, Jane Sinner* "a binge-read with hidden depths."

■ Biographical and Critical Sources

PERIODICALS

Booklist, November 1, 2017, Maggie Reagan, review of *Nice Try, Jane Sinner,* p. 65.

Kirkus Reviews, October 15, 2017, review of *Nice Try, Jane Sinner.*

Publishers Weekly, November 6, 2017, review of *Nice Try, Jane Sinner,* p. 83.

School Library Journal, October, 2017, Susannah Goldstein, review of *Nice Try, Jane Sinner,* p. 101.

ONLINE

Dana Mele, https://danamele.com/ (November 22, 2017), Dana Mele, "Author, I Never: An Interview with Lianne Oelke," author interview.

Globe and Mail, https://www.theglobeandmail.com/ (February 1, 2018), review of *Nice Try, Jane Sinner*

Happy Ever After, http://happyeverafter.usatoday. com/ (January 18, 2018), "Lianne Oelke and Becky Albertalli Discuss Lianne's New YA, *Nice Try, Jane Sinner,*" author interview.

Judi Lauren, http://judilauren.com/ (February 10, 2016), Judi Lauren, "Wednesday Writer Interview with Lianne Oelke," author interview.

Lianne Oelke Website, http://www.lianneoelke.com (March 28, 2018), author profile.*

Seamus O'Mahony

■ Personal

Male. *Education:* University College Cork, Ireland, graduated (with honors), 1983, M.D., 1991.

■ Career

Writer, editor, gastroenterologist, consultant physician, and patient advocate. Cork University Hospital, Cork, Ireland, consultant gastroenterologist, 1996—.

■ Member

Philosophical Society (auditor, 1980-81).

■ Awards, Honors

Blayney Prize in Medicine, 1983; RGG Barry Prize in Pediatrics; Honan Scholar; fellow of the Royal Colleges of Physicians of London and Edinburgh.

■ Writings

The Way We Die Now: The View from Medicine's Front Line, Thomas Dunne Books (New York, NY), 2016.

Contributor to medical journals and periodicals, including the *Dublin Review of Books.*

Journal of the Royal College of Physicians of Edinburgh, editor for medical humanities.

■ Sidelights

Writer and physician Seamus O'Mahony is a consultant gastroenterologist at Cork University Hospital in Cork, Ireland. He graduated with honors from University College Cork and obtained his M.D. in 1991. He received his medical training at institutions in Cork; Edinburgh, Scotland; and Leeds, England. O'Mahony writes frequently on medical subjects such as endoscopy, celiac disease, and inflammatory bowel disease, and conducts research in the area of medical humanities. O'Mahony is a fellow of the Royal Colleges of Physicians in London and Edinburgh.

In his role as a physician, O'Mahony is an advocate for patients' right to choose the way they die and for the availability of options that let them die with dignity. He urges the development of a respectful relationship between the patient, the patient's family, and the physician in charge of the case. In his book *The Way We Die Now: The View from Medicine's Front Line,* O'Mahony "addresses many aspects of this murky relationship and provides us with a rare glimpse into this world from the vantage point of a medical doctor," commented *Irish Times* contributor Paul D'Alton.

O'Mahony "makes the brave call for the demedicalization of death and dying, and argues for a halt to the madness that characterizes modern medicine's culture of excess," D'Alton stated. For example, he notes that modern medical practices generally involve keeping terminally ill patients uninformed about their impending deaths. Though some may believe this is a humane and compassionate approach, O'Mahony argues that patients facing the end of life should be fully aware of what is coming. The role of the doctor in this case is to be a source of support and comfort until the inevitable end.

The author also sees problems with letting patients die in general wards or even in intensive care units instead of in more peaceful surroundings, such as at home or in hospice care. The chaos of a hospital setting is unnecessary, he believes, when it is possible for patients to come to their end in an environment that is calming enough to ease their final passing.

O'Mahony also addresses issues such as overmedication and overintervention at the end of a patient's life, such as using too many procedures to extend life in a way that is often artificial. He endorses better use of living wills and similar orders addressing the end of life. He cautions that the use of assisted suicide may not be the best choice if it is a manifestation of excessive control rather than a means to allow patients to end their lives with dignity and on their own terms.

"O'Mahony's thorough exploration of an increasingly urgent topic should create solid demand" for his book, commented *Booklist* reviewer Dane Carr. A *Publishers Weekly* writer concluded, "O'Mahony's clear-eyed analysis is important, poignant, and immensely humane.

■ Biographical and Critical Sources

PERIODICALS

Booklist, June, 2017, Dane Carr, review of *The Way We Die Now: The View from Medicine's Front Line*, p. 32.

Irish Times, June 18, 2016, Paul D'Alton, review of *The Way We Die Now*.

Publishers Weekly, May 8, 2017, review of *The Way We Die Now*, p. 50.

ONLINE

APC Microbiome Ireland Website, http://apc.ucc.ie/ (February 19, 2018), biography of Seamus O'Mahony.

Macmillan Website, http://us.macmillan.com/ (February 19, 2018), biography of Seamus O'Mahony.*

Finbarr O'Reilly

1971-

■ Personal

Born 1971, in Swansea, Wales; immigrated to Canada, c. 1980; naturalized Canadian citizen. *Education:* Attended Ryerson University.

■ Addresses

Agent—Stuart Krichevsky Literary Agency, 6 E. 39th St., Ste. 500, New York, NY 10016.

■ Career

Photographer and writer. *Ottawa Citizen*, Ottawa, Ontario, Canada, intern, 1997; *Globe and Mail*, Toronto, Ontario, former arts correspondent, beginning 1998; *National Post*, Toronto, former writer; Reuters (news agency), correspondent in Kinshasa, Congo, 2001, Africa Great Lakes correspondent in Kigali, Rwanda, 2003-05, chief photographer for West and Central Africa in Dakar, Senegal, 2005-12, senior photographer for Israel and Palestinian Territories in Tel Aviv, Israel, 2014-15. Harvard University, Nieman fellow, 2012-13; Columbia University, Ochberg fellow at Dart Center for Journalism and Trauma, 2014; Yale world fellow, 2015; MacDowell Colony, fellow, 2016; Carey Institute for Global Good, writer in residence, 2016. Documentary film work includes coproducer of *The Ghosts of Lomako*, 2003; codirector of *The Digital Divide*, 2003; appearance in *Under Fire: Journalists in Combat*, 2011. *Exhibitions:* Work featured in the solo exhibition *Congo on the Wire*, Bayeux War Correspondent's Festival, 2008, then Carr Center for Human Rights, Harvard University, and in Canada; work included in the Italian exhibition *After A*, 2010.

■ Awards, Honors

World Press Photo of the Year Award, 2006, for photograph of a starving mother and child in Tahoua, Niger; first place award in multimedia category, Pictures of the Year International (POYi) program, Donald W. Reynolds Journalism Institute, Missouri School of Journalism, University of Missouri in Columbia, 2009; special judge's award, POYi, 2010; first place portrait award, National Press Photographers Association, 2010.

■ Writings

(With Thomas J. Brennan) *Shooting Ghosts: A U.S. Marine, a Combat Photographer, and Their Journey Back from War*, Viking (New York, NY), 2017.

Contributor to periodicals, including *Washington Post*.

■ Sidelights

Welsh-Canadian photojournalist Finbarr O'Reilly began his career as a print journalist with the *Ottawa Citizen* in 1997, but he is best known for his award-winning photographs from the world's conflict zones. O'Reilly joined the Reuters news agency in 2001 as a freelance correspondent in Congo. He began to illustrate his stories with modest photographs. Then, he explained at the *World Press Photo* website, "I noticed that my images were getting more play than my stories and that the message I was trying to convey had more immediate and emotional impact in the form of images." In 2005 he was hired by Reuters as the chief photographer for West and Central Africa.

O'Reilly spent ten years with camera in hand, except his time as a Nieman fellow at Harvard University. He won international acclaim for his photograph of an emaciated child with his mother in Niger, but his work took him all over the world, from conflict zones in Africa to combat zones in Afghanistan and elsewhere. As early as 2007 O'Reilly was beginning to feel the impact of his repeated exposure to trauma and his role as a documentarian of humans in distress. In fact, his Nieman fellowship was devoted to psychological research on traumatic experience in conflict situations.

By the time O'Reilly lost his Reuters job in 2014, he feared that he had lost his capacity for empathy. In an article at the *Washington Post Online,* he explained: "I grew increasingly uncomfortable with photographing people at their most vulnerable while being able to do little to help." He turned away from photography for a while, preferring to study and teach. He also reconnected with a man for whom his photography could actually make a tangible difference.

O'Reilly was embedded with a U.S. Marine Corps unit in Afghanistan in 2010. The squad leader at Outpost Kunjak was an American, Sergeant T.J. Brennan. O'Reilly's job was to stay out of the way and photograph the action. Brennan's job was to protect his men, even if it meant tossing a photographer off a hilltop. One fateful day in November, in a deserted village called Nabuaga, a rocket-propelled grenade exploded so close to Brennan that the shockwave triggered a traumatic brain injury. Brennan never saw it coming, but O'Reilly did. In an interview broadcast on *Fresh Air* and posted at the National Public Radio website, he said: "I have the whole sequence documented of [T.J.] running up the alleyway, . . . the explosion afterwards and the guys who went to recover T.J. and haul him back" to safety.

Both men lived to fight and film another day, but they returned to their respective homes changed forever. The two men stayed in touch, both haunted by what they saw, what they did, and what they didn't do. O'Reilly was able to find help for the depression that he brought home with him, but Brennan had to fight the military mindset, first to seek help, then to receive it. The memories and lessons learned come together in their memoir.

Shooting Ghosts: A U.S. Marine, a Combat Photographer, and Their Journey Back from War is a joint memoir, told in alternating first-person narratives. "We didn't want to write a book that glorifies war," O'Reilly explained in the *Washington Post Online.* He added: "*Shooting Ghosts* is about how and why war changes people, and what happened as we came to terms with the things we've seen and done."

A *Publishers Weekly* contributor reported that the authors "strip away any misplaced notions of glamour, bravery and stoicism to craft an affecting memoir of a deep friendship." Tim Perry wrote at the *CBS News* website that the writing process enabled both men to find a new purpose in life. A commentator in *Kirkus Reviews* called the shared volume "a courageous breaking of the code of silence."

With O'Reilly's help and encouragement, Brennan earned a journalism degree and became a writer. He founded an online newsroom called the *War Horse* and the charity Fog of War. O'Reilly gradually returned to photography, but not as a photographer of pain and anguish. He went to Senegal, for instance, to cover fashion week in Dakar. He told Joanne Laucius in an interview posted at the *Ottawa Citizen Online* that his work is now "about beauty and creativity rather than destruction."

■ Biographical and Critical Sources

BOOKS

O'Reilly, Finbarr, and Thomas J. Brennan, *Shooting Ghosts: A U.S. Marine, a Combat Photographer, and Their Journey Back from War,* Viking (New York, NY), 2017.

PERIODICALS

Kirkus Reviews, June 15, 2017, review of *Shooting Ghosts.*

Publishers Weekly, May 29, 2017, review of *Shooting Ghosts,* p. 55.

ONLINE

CBS News Website, https://www.cbsnews.com/ (August 30, 2017), Tim Perry, author interview.

Finbarr O'Reilly Website, http://www.finbarr-oreilly.com (February 10, 2018).

Kirkus Reviews Online, https://www.kirkusreviews.com/ (June 5, 2017), review of *Shooting Ghosts.*

National, https://www.thenational.ae/ (September 15, 2017), Kapil Komireddi, review of *Shooting Ghosts.*

National Public Radio Website, https://www.npr.org/ (August 24, 2017), Dave Davies, transcript of author interview broadcast on the program *Fresh Air*.

Ottawa Citizen Online, http://ottawacitizen.com/ (September 17, 2017), Joanne Laucius, author profile.

Reuters Website, https://widerimage.reuters.com/ (February 10, 2018), author profile.

Shooting Ghosts Website, https://www.shooting ghosts.com/ (February 10, 2018), author profile.

World Press Photo Website, https://www. worldpressphoto.org/ (February 10, 2018), author profile.*

Adam O'Riordan

1982-

■ Personal

Born 1982, in Manchester, England. *Education:* Graduated from Oxford University.

■ Addresses

Home—Manchester, England. *Agent*—Sarah Chalfant, Wylie Agency, 17 Bedford Sq., London WC1B 3JA, England.

■ Career

Author, poet, educator. Manchester, Writing School, Manchester Metropolitan University, Manchester, England, lecturer in poetry writing and director.

■ Awards, Honors

Somerset Maugham Award, 2011, for *In the Flesh.*

■ Writings

(Editor, with Maddy Paxman) Michael Donaghy, *The Shape of the Dance: Essays, Interviews and Digressions,* Picador (London, England), 2009.

In the Flesh (poetry), Chatto & Windus (London, England), 2010, W.W. Norton & Company (New York, NY), 2015.

The Burning Ground (short stories), W.W. Norton & Company (New York, NY), 2017.

A Herring Famine (poetry), Chatto & Windus (London, England), 2017.

■ Sidelights

Manchester-born Adam O'Riordan is a British poet and author. The winner of the Somerset Maugham Award in 2011 for his debut poetry collection, *In the Flesh,* O'Riordan was also the youngest poet-in-residence at the Wordsworth Trust. The academic director of the Writing School at Manchester Metropolitan University, O'Riordan is also the author of the story collection *The Burning Ground,* and a second book of poetry, *A Herring Famine.*

In an interview at the online *Story Prize,* O'Riordan commented on what influenced him to begin writing prose in addition to poetry: "Spending time in America—in New York and then Los Angeles—is what moved me from writing poetry, which is where I began, into writing prose. The plurality of the place, the patent sense of possibility, the promise of it and the way in which promises are broken there all conspired to make me into a writer of prose. And glad I am they did."

In the Flesh

O'Riordan's debut poetry collection, *In the Flesh,* contains some thirty poems dealing with a sense of place and moments in the past that can and cannot be recaptured. The centerpiece of the collection is the sonnet sequence "Home," which looks indirectly at the lives of William and Dorothy Wordsworth, and also includes more personal portraits. The collection opens with "Manchester," a poem that looks back to the heyday of the poet's hometown, when the city was an industrial giant. There are poems ranging from history—looking at the Derby of 1913—to the world of high technology and internet searches for lost lovers.

Guardian Online reviewer Sarah Crown had praise for *In the Flesh,* calling it a "bewitchingly recherché debut," and further noting: "There's a poise and precision to his writing, a gift for imagery and a willingness to venture far from home and explore multiple (frequently unsympathetic) voices that give his poems a preternatural maturity. Expect a great deal more from Adam O'Riordan in years to come." Writing in his blog, poet and critic Ben Wilkinson similarly commented: "On the strength of the collection taken as a whole, I'm even inclined—for once—to agree with the publisher's hype. . . . Adding to that list of superlatives, I'd also call his stuff jaunty, vibrant, and satisfyingly disorienting." Also writing in the *Guardian Online,* Kate Kellaway commented: "This collection does not read like a debut. It has an established feel—as if Adam O'Riordan, who is in his mid-20s, had been around for decades. Only that makes him sound dusty, and he isn't. The unfashionable beauty of this collection—shining, musical, aloof—is that it is intimate without being confessional."

The Burning Ground

O'Riordan turns to short fiction in *The Burning Ground,* eight tales set in on the West Coast of the United States and providing an outsider's keen observations on American life and loves. Most of the stories focus somehow on Los Angeles, and range from stories of lost love to the passage of time and absent figures. The characters are both travelers and residents. In "Wave-Riding Giants," a protagonist remembers a meal at his senior center; "The El Segundo Blue Butterfly" traces the connection between a teenager and the businessman he interviews for his school paper as their paths continue to cross throughout life. A hate crime is described in "Rambla Pacifico," while in another tale a lonely widower recalls the past and finally faces a long suppressed memory.

The Burning Ground earned praise from many reviewers. A *Kirkus Reviews* critic noted: "It's a work that feels fully lived-in. O'Riordan's attention to precise details helps make these stories memorable; at their best, they put familiar scenarios in a new light." Similarly, a *Publishers Weekly* contributor observed: "Lovers are lost and mourned in these sharp and sometimes violent stories, and characters suffer through turbulence both literal and metaphorical, haunted by questions they never asked." London *Guardian Online* writer Adam Foulds felt that "you are never in doubt that you are reading the work of an elegant and greatly accomplished writer whose future promises much." Also writing in the *Guardian Online,* Anita Sethi dubbed this a "lyrical debut short-story collection."

Further praise was offered by *Irish Times Online* reviewer Sarah Gilmartin, who noted: "The west coast of the United States is the backdrop for each of the eight stories in *The Burning Ground,* as immigrant Brits look for refuge and down-and-out locals seek to rebuild lives. This is an impressive range of stories that run from reflective to highly dramatic, and O'Riordan's verbal polish as a poet shines throughout." Likewise, Ross Jeffery, writing in the online *Storgy,* commented: "*The Burning Ground* has everything needed to burn up all the competition. O'Riordan's fuel for this are his delicately told short stories, the oxygen is his powerfully emotive and intelligently woven subjects of his stories; packing the heat and which completes our fire triangle is how 'you' as a reader are changed, warmed and feel completed by reading them. It's a tremendous accomplishment stepping out into a new genre and blowing up the competition, something truly brilliant exists within *The Burning Ground.*" And *Financial Times Online* critic Philip Womack concluded: "As a whole, this assured and elegant collection is interested not in answers but in questions, in ambivalence: passing moments, frozen in time as if by a photographer's keen eye, a lens catching light."

A Herring Famine

O'Riordan returns to poetry in his 2017 collection, *A Herring Famine,* a gathering that deals with many of the poet's earlier themes, from absence to new beginnings, and they also span time, from the herring famine of 1907 to the Strangeways Prison Riot of 1990.

Reviewing *A Herring Famine* in the *New Statesman,* Paul Batchelor found little to like in this second collection, noting that it "illustrates much of what is wrong with poetry in the UK." Batchelor added: "These poems are both unethical and boring, sadistic and genteel, unambitious and yet pretentious. Almost every one of them has been occasioned by a stranger's suffering and/or death. Like a ghoulish Forrest Gump, O'Riordan always seems to pop up in the right place at the right time to appropriate the misery." *Los Angeles Review of Books Online* contributor Declan Ryan, however, had a much higher assessment, observing: "*A Herring Famine* is a sleeper agent of sorts. The poems are refined, polished up like a cricket ball—and, like a cricket ball, much harder, denser, and more damaging than they initially appear. Their surface elegance suggests restraint, calm, and ease, but these are mostly poems of alarm, of panic and disappearance. Their craft and guile risk obscuring the talent that birthed them. . . . O'Riordan does indeed make hard work look easy; one potential consequence is the possibility of his being dismissed as a mere stylist, or fancy boy, when in fact he is fascinatingly terrified. What he exhibits here is less dandyish flair than the ability to cope under pressure." Likewise, *Guardian Online* writer Ben Wilkinson noted: "O'Riordan has a genuine gift, and for any talented writer it can be easy to slip into writing that asks and risks little. Where *A Herring Famine* excels is in poems that, alongside their craft and guile, wear their heart on their sleeve."

■ Biographical and Critical Sources

PERIODICALS

Kirkus Reviews, May 15, 2017, review of *The Burning Ground*.

New Statesman, July 14, 2017, Paul Batchelor, review of *A Herring Famine*, p. 47.

Publishers Weekly, May 8, 2017, review of *The Burning Ground*, p. 33.

ONLINE

Adam O'Riordan Website, http://www.adamoriordan.com (January 9, 2018).

Ben Wilkinson Blog, http://www.benwilkinson.org/ (June 6, 2010), "Adam O'Riordan, *In the Flesh*."

Book Forum, http://www.bookforum.com/ (June 2, 2017), Morten Høi Jensen, review of *The Burning Ground*.

Financial Times Online, https://www.ft.com/ (January 27, 2017), Philip Womack, review of *The Burning Ground*.

Guardian Online, https://www.theguardian.com/ (July 3, 2010), Kate Kellaway, review of *In the Flesh*; (September 3, 2010), Sarah Crown, review of *In the Flesh*; (January 25, 2017), Adam Foulds, review of *The Burning Ground*; (January 29, 2017), Anita Sethi, review of *The Burning Ground*; (February 18, 2017), Ben Wilkinson, review of *A Herring Famine*.

Irish Times Online, https://www.irishtimes.com/ (January 21, 2017), Sarah Gilmartin, review of *The Burning Ground*.

London Review of Books Online, https://www.lrb.co.uk/ (January 9, 2018), "Adam O'Riordan."

Los Angeles Review of Books, https://lareviewofbooks.org/ (April 16, 2017), Declan Ryan, review of *A Herring Famine* and *The Burning Ground*.

Star.com, https://www.thestar.com/ (August 4, 2017), Trevor Corkum, review of *The Burning Ground*.

Storgy, https://storgy.com/ (January 12, 2017), Ross Jeffery, review of *The Burning Ground*.

Story Prize, http://thestoryprize.blogspot.com/ (June 28, 2017), "Adam O'Riordan."

Varsity, https://www.varsity.co.uk/ (January 28, 2012), Charlotte Keith, review of *In the Flesh*.*

Lauren Doyle Owens

■ Personal

Female. *Education:* Florida International University, M.F.A.

■ Addresses

Home—FL.

■ Career

Writer.

■ Writings

The Other Side of Everything, Touchstone (New York, NY), 2018.

Contributor to periodicals, including *Concho River Review* and the *Seventh Wave.*

■ Sidelights

Lauren Doyle Owens has become well known for her writing. Prior to launching her career, she attended Florida International University, where she obtained her M.F.A. She has published work in several literary magazines, including *Concho River Review* and the *Seventh Wave.*

The Other Side of Everything is Owens's introductory novel. The narrative takes place in the state of Florida, following the lives of several residents of Seven Springs as they deal with the chaos within their own lives. All of the characters in the book find themselves affected by death and loss in one way or another. One such character is a young woman, Maddie, who meets a mysterious man through her job as a diner waitress. Maddie is dealing with the effects of an AWOL mother and the new responsibilities that have been thrust onto her plate. As a result, she is entirely focused on trying to support her family. However, her youth attracts endless advances from the male patrons of the diner, and it may turn out that the customer she finally chooses could have the worst possible motives. Another character is a woman named Amy, who has been afflicted with several intimate tragedies and attempts to cope by returning to her old passion of creating paintings. However, her artwork starts to become strangely prophetic, allowing her insight into the identity of a murderer who has been targeting the town's elderly community, as well as the events surrounding the demise of her neighbor. The final lead character is a man by the name of Bernard White, who claims he can hear Vera and Irene, two women Bernard deeply loved and lost, attempting to communicate with him. These three characters' lives intertwine in unimaginable ways in the face of a horrific string of crimes.

In *Kirkus Reviews,* a contributor called the book "a slow-burning thriller that explores the cost of love turned askew." *Booklist* reviewer Christine Tran expressed that the book possesses "fine writing, a flawlessly constructed story, and relatable characters providing plenty of questionable decisions rife for discussion." A writer in *Publishers Weekly* remarked: "Fans of crime fiction wanting literary flair and emotional depth will gladly follow this trio of complicated characters." On the *Out of the Bex* blog, a reviewer said: "With elegant, heartfelt writing, Owens has crafted a literary masterpiece hiding under the guise of a mystery." The reviewer added: "Perfect for readers who enjoy a sense of marrow in their mysteries, who love reading about characters that could be your own neighbor, not just a name in a book."

■ Biographical and Critical Sources

PERIODICALS

Booklist, November 15, 2017, Christine Tran, review of *The Other Side of Everything*, p. 27.

Kirkus Reviews, November 15, 2017, review of *The Other Side of Everything*.

Publishers Weekly, October 23, 2017, review of *The Other Side of Everything*, p. 60.

ONLINE

Lauren Doyle Owens Website, http://www.laurendoyleowens.com (March 28, 2018), author profile.

Out of the Bex, http://outofthebex.com/ (February 21, 2018), review of *The Other Side of Everything*.*

David Pedreira

■ Personal

Married; children: one daughter. *Education:* University of New Hampshire, B.A.; University of Maryland, M.A. *Hobbies and other interests:* Scuba diving, surfing, fishing, being outdoors, ice hockey.

■ Addresses

Home—Tampa, FL.

■ Career

Business owner and author. Worked previously as a reporter.

■ Writings

Gunpowder Moon, Harper Voyager (New York, NY), 2018.

Contributor to periodicals, including the *St. Petersburg Times* and the *Tampa Tribune*.

■ Sidelights

Prior to the release of his introductory novel, David Pedreira worked in the journalism field. He started down this career path after attending the University of New Hampshire and the University of Maryland, where he obtained his B.A. and M.A., respectively. His articles have appeared in such publications as the *St. Petersburg Times* and the *Tampa Tribune*, and they have garnered several awards from the American Society of Newspaper Editors, the Associated Press, the Maryland-Delaware-DC Press Association, and the Society of Professional Journalists. In his spare time, he participates in aquatic sports and ice hockey.

Gunpowder Moon falls under the sci-fi genre and follows the efforts of protagonist Caden Dechert as he attempts to rebuild his life. Caden has just broken free from a life of war. He served in the army back during his time on Earth and has grown tired of the various stressors that come with living in a wartime environment. Relocating to Earth's Moon, in one of its numerous settlements, represents the chance to start over and gain a long-desired sense of peace. However, Caden's idyllic life is not meant to last. On the planet Earth, those with political power are dealing with increasing turmoil that will soon affect the Moon. Caden himself is forced to witness a series of horrific events, and it ends up being up to him to try to quell the fighting before it escalates into another war.

A *Kirkus Reviews* contributor remarked: "Memorable visuals and well-executed action sequences mark this exciting foray into near-future hard sci-fi, which is at its best when framing the poignancy of the desire for peace." In *Publishers Weekly*, a writer said: "This is an exciting story with an unexpected depth—a solid winner." Ariel S. Winter, a writer on the *Washington Independent Review of Books* website, stated: "In the end, *Gunpowder Moon* succeeds as a hard-science fiction, military parable." She added: "The thrill of living on the moon is tangible, and as the plot kicks in, it becomes hard to put the book down." A reviewer on the *Bibliosanctum* website said: "No doubt, sci-fi fans seeking fast-paced action and clever intrigue would enjoy *Gunpowder Moon*." The reviewer later concluded that the book is "an entertaining read overall." On the *New York Journal of Books* website, Jerry Lenaburg commented: "Readers of hard science fiction, military science fiction, or just a good mystery will really enjoy this book."

■ Biographical and Critical Sources

PERIODICALS

Kirkus Reviews, February 1, 2018, review of *Gunpowder Moon.*

Publishers Weekly, November 6, 2017, review of *Gunpowder Moon*, p. 64.

ONLINE

Bibliosanctum, https://bibliosanctum.com/ (February 19, 2018), review of *Gunpowder Moon.*

David Pedreira Website, https://davidpedreira.com (March 28, 2018), author profile.

New York Journal of Books, https://www.nyjournalofbooks.com/ (February 21, 2018), Jerry Lenaburg, review of *Gunpowder Moon.*

My Life My Books My Escape, https://mylifemybooksmyescape.wordpress.com/ (February 13, 2018), "Author Interview: David Pedreira," author interview.

Washington Independent Review of Books, http://www.washingtonindependentreviewofbooks.com/ (February 19, 2018), Ariel S. Winter, review of *Gunpowder Moon.**

Daniel Pembrey

■ Personal

Born in England. *Education:* Attended Edinburgh University; INSEAD Business School, M.B.A.

■ Addresses

Home—London, England; Amsterdam, Netherlands.

■ Career

Writer, journalist. Worked in business for a decade in the United States and Luxembourg.

■ Writings

NOVELS; EXCEPT AS NOTED

The Candidate, CreateSpace Independent Publishing Platform, 2013.
The Woman Who Stopped Traffic, CreateSpace Independent Publishing Platform, 2014.
Simon Sixsmith, CreateSpace Independent Publishing Platform, 2014.

"HENK VAN DER POL" SERIES

The Harbour Master, No Exit Press (Harpenden, England), 2016.
Night Market, No Exit Press (Harpenden, England), 2017.
Initiation: Amsterdam, '83, Amazon Publishing, 2018.

Also the author of several self-published short novels and short stories. Contributor to periodicals, including *Condé Nast Traveller, Architectural Digest, Daily Telegraph, Financial Times,* and the *Times.*

■ Sidelights

Born in England, British author Daniel Pembrey grew up in Nottinghamshire in a village near Sherwood Forest. After studying history at Edinburgh University, he went to France, where he earned a M.B.A., and spent the next decade working both in the United States and in Luxembourg. Eventually, he made his way to Amsterdam, a city he fell in love with and he continues to divide his time between that city and London, writing for a number of periodicals and publishing novels in his "Henk van der Pol" detective series, set in Amsterdam.

In a *Liz Loves Books* website interview, Pembrey commented on his journalistic freelancing, writing on topics from Amsterdam nightlife to Dutch residential design, the Los Angeles of author Michael Connelly, and interviews with other writers and personalities. "I do [like writing features articles]," Pembrey noted. "Not just because they help pay the bills . . . even novellas take a long time to write and publish, whereas these features articles—written to deadline—are like timed essays by comparison. I find it refreshing. Plus I get to meet all these interesting people." In an article Pembrey published in the London *Guardian Online,* he further remarked on his decision to use Amsterdam as a setting for his series: "When I started visiting Amsterdam regularly a decade ago, I used to look for crime fiction novels set here and translated into English—but ended up writing my own! It involved doing research with the Dutch police force; I even went on an undercover operation with them in the Red Light District. Generally, it's a safe city, but any port as big as Amsterdam's attracts a good slice of criminality. My fictional detective, Henk van der Pol, has his own houseboat in the docklands area of the city."

The Harbour Master

Pembrey's "Henk van der Pol" series begins with the 2016 novel *The Harbour Master,* which was originally published as three Kindle e-book novellas and were then bought by No Exit Press, which republished them as this first novel in the series. This novel finds Amsterdam detective Hen van der Pol on the eve of retirement after serving with the force for almost thirty years. But plans for retirement are put on hold when a woman's body is found in Amsterdam Harbor. Warned off the investigation as it is out of his jurisdiction, van der Pol, a maverick among cops, trusts his instincts and investigates anyway. Soon he is involved in a mushrooming case that leads to police and government corruption, Hungarian human traffickers, and a growing threat to himself and his family. Ultimately the trail leads van der Pol through the Netherlands and Scandinavia.

A *Financial Times Online* reviewer had high praise for *The Harbour Master* and its author, calling Pembrey a novelist of "rare skill," and noting that this novel stands out from other crime books as the "real achievement is the characterisation of the ageing copper following a tangled, picaresque trail." Similarly, a contributor to the *Anne Bonny Book Reviews* website observed: "A murky case, straight out of the red light district, involving violent crime, drugs and branded prostitutes. With links to international diplomats, corrupt police alliances and the trafficking of people for sex. This is a novel not to be missed!" A critic at the *Daily Mail Online* also had praise, terming the novel "compelling and fast-moving," and further noting: "The exquisitely drawn Inspector van der Pol battles his way to the truth in a way that his fictional ancestor, Inspector Piet van der Valk, created by Nicolas Freeling, did in the Sixties." *Promoting Crime Fiction by Lizzie Hayes* website reviewer Hayes dubbed the novel "cleverly-crafted and unusual . . . dealing with real issues in a vividly-evoked setting." Online *Euro Crime* writer Ewa Sherman also had a high assessment of *The Harbour Master,* noting: "Daniel Pembrey is a master of concise stylish writing. It demonstrates not only his craftsmanship and discipline but also an intelligent ability to convey mood and atmosphere of the setting and

urgency of Henk's actions. . . . His vivid and mesmerising portrait of the city is not for the faint-hearted." An online *Crime Pieces* reviewer observed that "Van der Pol is clearly a maverick style policeman but this never stretches the limits of plausibility."

Night Market

Van der Pol returns in *Night Market,* in which the irascible and sometimes inconsistent cop is now commissioned by the Justice Minister and government officials in The Hague to look into child pornography by actually infiltrating the exploitation network. This is not a job he can turn down but once undercover, van der Pol discovers just how hard it is to stop the bad guys, and he pays for it with a very bad beating.

"The plot . . . is more and more unpredictable," noted a contributor in the online *Anne Bonny Book Reviews.* "It is written in such a style that you never know what will be revealed and discovered next. Obviously the theme is dark, dealing with issues of child abuse, exploitation of children in the system and child pornography within the novel. But I think this shows the obstacles that organisations/governments face in trying to bring down global, image sharing/creating, pedophile rings." A *Publishers Weekly* writer also had praise for this second installment, commenting: "Pembrey excels at revealing the psychological price police pay for investigating child pornography while sparing the reader the sordid details." Likewise, Paul Burke, writing at the *Nudge Book* website, observed: "The setting of Amsterdam was vividly brought to life in the first novel and *Night Market* rings with the same authenticity, both in the city and further afield. Pembrey is a keen observer and this gives a colour and texture to the book. *The Harbour Master* was an assured debut and *Night Market* is a fine sequel; intelligent, exciting and original."

■ Biographical and Critical Sources

PERIODICALS

Publishers Weekly, August 28, 2017, review of *Night Market,* p. 106.

ONLINE

Anne Bonny Book Reviews, https://annebonnybook reviews.com/ (April 10, 2017), review of *The Harbour Master* and *Night Market.*

Crime Pieces, https://crimepieces.com/ (January 5, 2015), review of *The Harbour Master.*

Crime Review, http://www.crimereview.co.uk/ (October 28, 2017), Chris Roberts, review of *Night Market.*

Daily Mail Online, http://www.dailymail.co.uk/ (November 3, 2016), review of *The Harbour Master.*

Daniel Pembrey Website, http://danielpembrey.co.uk (February 13, 2018).

Euro Crime, http://eurocrime.blogspot.com/ (November 11, 2015), Ewa Sherman, review of *The Harbour Master.*

Financial Times Online, https://www.ft.com/ (November 4, 2016), review of *The Harbour Master.*

Guardian Online, https://www.theguardian.com/ (December 29, 2017), Daniel Pembrey, "Amsterdam Holidays, Why I Love. . . ."

Liz Loves Books, http://lizlovesbooks.com/ (October 31, 2016), "When Crime Thriller Girl Interviewed Daniel Pembrey. . . ."

Nudge Book, http://nudge-book.com/ (April 3, 2017), review of *Night Market.*

Promoting Crime Fiction by Lizzie Hayes, http://promotingcrime.blogspot.com/ (February 17, 2017), Marsali Taylor, review of *The Harbour Master.**

Farrah Penn

■ **Personal**

Born in TX. *Hobbies and other interests:* YA books, her dog, pineapple pizza, hiking, Groupon browsing, Netflix binges.

■ **Addresses**

Home—Los Angeles, CA.

■ **Career**

Writer.

■ **Writings**

Twelve Steps to Normal (novel), foreword by James Patterson, Jimmy Patterson (New York, NY), 2018.

Contributor to *BuzzFeed*.

■ **Sidelights**

Farrah Penn works mainly as a writer. While the majority of her work can be found on *BuzzFeed*, Penn once stated on the *Author Mentor Match* website that she had a long-term interest in publishing her very own novel. In addition to creating her own work, she also seeks to help young authors as they write their own stories.

Twelve Steps to Normal is Penn's introductory work. The novel stars a girl by the name of Kira whose life has been shaken by circumstances beyond her control. Kira had moved away from her original home after her father's struggle with alcohol dependency became too severe for him to care for her. The move was a hard enough challenge for Kira to face, and it caused her to isolate herself from everyone she knew back home. After a year, her father has gotten sober, granting Kira the ability to come back to town and pick back up with her previous life. However, she soon finds she must contend with several new challenges. First, her friend circle has shifted, as a friend has suddenly taken up with the boy Kira used to date. Second, the house that used to belong to just her and her father has gained a swath of new residents—namely, some of the patients Kira's father met while seeking addiction treatment. Kira feels the sole individual she has to rely on is one of her few remaining old friends, but the realization that she may be developing an attraction to him throws her further off-kilter. As Kira tries to navigate her new life, she is forced to come to several revelations about her situation and the best way to proceed.

In *Kirkus Reviews*, a contributor called *Twelve Steps to Normal* "a smart recommendation for readers looking to escape into a substantive world of personal discovery." A *Publishers Weekly* reviewer felt that the book "emphasize[s] the importance of support and forgiveness." Lisa Ehrle, a writer in *School Library Journal*, commented: "This is a good choice for those seeking realism that isn't too disturbing." A contributor to the *Hedgehog Book Reviews* website said: "Farrah Penn represented the recovery process and community well and Kira's path to understanding her dad's illness was perfectly crafted." She added: "If you're interested in reading about the realities of having a loved one who struggles with alcoholism, please put *Twelve Steps to Normal* on your reading list."

■ **Biographical and Critical Sources**

PERIODICALS

Kirkus Reviews, January 15, 2018, review of *Twelve Steps to Normal.*

Publishers Weekly, December 18, 2017, review of *Twelve Steps to Normal,* p. 131.

School Library Journal, January, 2018, Lisa Ehrle, review of *Twelve Steps to Normal,* p. 82.

ONLINE

Author Mentor Match, http://authormentormatch. com/ (March 28, 2018), author profile.

Farrah Penn Website, http://farrahpenn.com (March 28, 2018), author profile.

Hedgehog Book Reviews, https://hedgehogbook reviews.com/ (February 11, 2018), review of *Twelve Steps to Normal.**

Jack Perconte

1954-

■ **Also Known As**

John Patrick Perconte

■ **Personal**

Born August 31, 1954, in Joliet, IL; children: three. *Hobbies and other interests:* Marathons.

■ **Career**

Baseball player, coach, and author. Los Angeles Dodgers, second baseman, 1980-81; Cleveland Indians, second baseman, 1982-83; Seattle Mariners, second baseman, 1984-85; Chicago White Sox, second baseman, 1986; Jack Perconte's Sports Academy, Naperville, IL, owner and coach; Velocity Sports Performance, Warrenville, IL, Director of Baseball Operations, 2009.

■ **Writings**

(And illustrator and editor) *60,000 Hitting Lessons: Hit It, Fix It, Coach It: A Hands-On Baseball Guide for Parents, Coaches and Players*, Second Base Publishing (Lisle, IL), 2007.

Raising an Athlete: How to Instill Confidence, Build Skills, and Inspire a Love of Sport, Second Base Publishing (Lisle, IL), 2009.

The Making of a Hitter: A Proven and Practical Step-by-Step Baseball Guide, Second Base Publishing (Lisle, IL), 2009.

Creating a Season to Remember: The New Youth-Sports-Coaching Leadership Handbook, Second Base Publishing (Lisle, IL), 2017.

Contributor to *Seamheads.com.*

■ **Sidelights**

Dan Perconte is known for his work in the world of professional baseball. He played for several Major League teams throughout the 1980s, including the Chicago White Sox, the Los Angeles Dodgers, the Seattle Mariners, and the Cleveland Indians. Prior to starting his professional career, he played minor league baseball with the Albuquerque Dukes. Perconte retired from baseball in 1987, but never lost his love for the game. Instead, he began devoting his time and effort to helping children learn the ins and outs of the game. He founded Jack Perconte's Sports Academy for this purpose. He later moved on to start teaching baseball privately. Perconte has written numerous books on the subject of coaching and baseball, including *The Making of a Hitter: A Proven and Practical Step-by-Step Baseball Guide* and *Raising an Athlete: How to Instill Confidence, Build Skills, and Inspire a Love of Sport.*

Creating a Season to Remember: The New Youth-Sports-Coaching Leadership Handbook is another of Perconte's books. The book is aimed at those who are interested in, or are currently embarking upon the job of, coaching children's sports teams. Perconte's own observations of the change in societal attitudes toward children's sports informs much of the book. He believes that coaches and spectators alike have become too preoccupied with achievement and being the best, and have lost sight of the true purpose of children's sports: enjoyment. As a result, Perconte devotes much of the book to trying to break readers out of this mindset so they can instead teach their team members how to revel in just playing their favorite sport. Perconte breaks his assertion down into bite-sized pieces to provide readers with a concrete method of learning how to coach more effectively. He peppers the book with reminders that the members of the team are the most significant part of coaching, and that coaches should remain as even-tempered as possible. Some of the suggestions Perconte offers to readers hearken back to the same strategies utilized by professional coaches throughout the history of sports. Overall, Perconte seeks to help coaches guide their players in the most effective and positive manner possible. A contributor to *Publishers Weekly* remarked: "This is a valuable resource for parents and coaches of youth sports." On the *Ask David* website, a reviewer stated: "This coaching handbook has the ability to change kids and their parents' attitudes and lives, and make coaching the enjoyable experience it should be."

■ Biographical and Critical Sources

PERIODICALS

Publishers Weekly, October 2, 2017, review of *Creating a Season to Remember: The New Youth-Sports-Coaching Leadership Handbook*, p. 129.

ONLINE

Ask David, http://askdavid.com/ (February 21, 2018), review of *Creating a Season to Remember*.
Hardball Times, https://www.fangraphs.com/ (September 14, 2011), Arne Christensen, "THT Talks with Jack Perconte," author interview.
Lookout Landing, https://www.lookoutlanding.com/ (March 26, 2010), Jeff Sullivan, "An Interview with Jack Perconte," author interview.*

Qiu Miaojin

1969-1995

■ Personal

Born May 29, 1969, in Taiwan; died June, 25, 1995, in Paris, France. *Education:* Graduate of National Taiwan University; attended University of Paris.

■ Career

Writer.

■ Awards, Honors

Central Daily News Short Story Prize, for "Prisoner"; United Literature Association Award, for novella *Lonely Crowds;* China Times Honorary Prize for Literature.

■ Writings

NOVELS

Ji mo de qun chung, Lian he wen xue chu ban she (Taipei, Taiwan), 1995.
Last Words from Montmartre, translated from the Chinese by Ari Larissa Heinrich, New York Review Books (New York, NY), 2014.
Notes of a Crocodile, translated from the Chinese by Bonnie Huie, New York Review Books (New York, NY), 2017.

Author of short stories, novella *Lonely Crowds,* and diaries.

■ Sidelights

Taiwanese novelist Qiu Miaojin's works are noted for their experimental qualities and their frank treatment of lesbian love; they were among the first novels from her country to deal with that subject. Qiu was born in 1969 in Taiwan and eventually immigrated to Paris for graduate studies in psychology. She committed suicide there in 1995, at age twenty-six, and since her death her writing has won acclaim from readers, critics, and scholars. "There's a reason Qiu's work earned her a cult following—a reason that her novels are so fiercely loved, by so many, as well as taught in high schools, produced as theater, and cited reverently by other novelists," observed Ari Larissa Heinrich, who translated Qiu's *Last Words from Montmartre* into English, in the online *Los Angeles Review of Books.* "All of Qiu's works contain a lush beauty, if you know where to look for it." Bonnie Huie, the translator of *Notes of a Crocodile,* wrote of Qiu's appeal in the *Kyoto Journal Online,* saying: "Qiu is what you'd call a writer's writer, usually someone you read because you love to follow the motions of his or her voice, Her prose reads like nonfiction, a genre which is, above all else, about cultivating a style."

Last Words from Montmartre

Last Words from Montmartre was Qiu's first novel to appear in English; it had been published in Chinese as *Mengmate Yishu* shortly after her death. It is written in the form of letters from a Taiwanese graduate student in Paris to her family, her friends, and the woman she has loved and lost, named Xu. The narrator, who is never named, discusses aspects of daily life, such as political events and the arts, but also her deepest emotions and desires, including her suicidal thoughts. Identities shift over the course of the novel; some of the letters appear to be written to the narrator by Xu. The chronology becomes blurry as well.

Last Words from Montmartre is unconventional but intriguing, according to several reviewers. "The exact facts of the narrative are unimportant," Dylan Suher remarked in the online journal *Asymptote*. "What drives the novel forward instead is passion—an obsessive, all-consuming passion." The author's voice, related a *Publishers Weekly* critic, "enchants even as she writes from the familiar perspective of a spurned lover." Josh Stenberg, however, writing in *World Literature Today*, thought that "the work's literary merits are a particular taste at best." The letters, he said, add up to "a meandering (very French) interior monologue," and "rather than experimentality, the general impression is of a young writer unable to tame her material." He added: "Its Parisian setting, its queer eroticism, its discovery of French loves and ideas must have been so much fresher in Chinese in 1995 than they are in English today." Suher, though, maintained that the novel had much to offer twenty-first-century audiences. "It is clear why it has mesmerized the Taiwanese queer community and a generation of Taiwanese rebels and outsiders, and thanks to this skillful translation, I expect it will enthrall a whole new community of readers," he concluded.

Notes of a Crocodile

Notes of a Crocodile, published in Chinese as *Eyu Shouji* in the early 1990s, focuses on a young woman figuring out her place in the world. Protagonist Lazi comes of age at a time of new freedoms in Taiwan, the years immediately following the end of martial law in 1987. The story follows her through high school, college, and her first job, and through various love affairs and friendships. The narrative takes the form of her letters and journals, but it alternates with scenes of crocodiles, dressed as humans and emulating human behavior. Lazi, as a lesbian, considers herself one of these crocodiles, an outsider trying to fit in.

The novel received substantial praise when it appeared in English. It "is an important work that explores the liberation of gender during a time when anything behind a façade of hetrosexuality in Taiwan was still considered taboo," commented T.F. Rhoden in the online *Asian Review of Books*. Rhoden pronounced it "candid and creative . . . a classic of Taiwanese contemporary literature that stirs the imagination as it confronts social inequities of gender and sexuality." A *Kirkus Reviews* contributor described *Notes of a Crocodile* as "a meandering, but moving, look at queer identity," further noting that "Qiu's willingness to show youth at its most self-absorbed and earnest is part

of the book's appeal." In the *New York Times Book Review*, Leopoldine Core observed: "It is refreshing to read a novel that so frankly examines patriarchy, misogyny, homophobia, gender normativity and capitalism—especially one that howls so freely with pain." On the whole, Core said, *Notes of a Crocodile* is a "thrillingly transgressive coming-of-age story," while "Bonnie Huie's translation is nothing short of remarkable—loving, even; one gets the sense that great pains have been taken to preserve the voice behind this lush, ontological masterwork."

■ Biographical and Critical Sources

PERIODICALS

Kirkus Reviews, March 1, 2017, review of *Notes of a Crocodile*.

New York Times Book Review, May 7, 2017, Leopoldine Core, "Risk and Reward," p. 25.

Publishers Weekly, April 14, 2014, review of *Last Words from Montmartre*, p. 31.

South China Morning Post, January 13, 2017, Enid Tsui, "Taiwanese Novelist Who Killed Herself in Paris at 26, Qiu Miaojin, Remembered and Reassessed in RTHK Film."

World Literature Today, September-October, 2015, Josh Stenberg, review of *Last Words from Montmartre*, p. 66.

ONLINE

Asian Review of Books, http://asianreviewofbooks.com/ (May 29, 2017), T.F. Rhoden, review of *Notes of a Crocodile*.

Asymptote, https://www.asymptotejournal.com/ (February 22, 2018), Dylan Suher, review of *Last Words from Montmartre*.

Full Stop, http://www.full-stop.net/ (July 3, 2014), Helen Stuhr-Rommereim, review of *Last Words from Montmartre*.

Kyoto Journal Online, http://www.kyotojournal.org/ (February 22, 2018), Bonnie Huie, "The Kids Are Too Straight: Translating Qiu Miaojin's *Notes of a Crocodile*."

Los Angeles Review of Books, https://lareviewofbooks.org/ (May 7, 2017), Ari Larissa Heinrich, "Consider the Crocodile: Qiu Miaojin's Lesbian Bestiary."

Paper Republic, https://paper-republic.org/ (February 22, 2018), brief biography.*

Richard Rothstein

1939-

■ Personal

Born 1939.

■ Addresses

Office—Historian. Chief Justice Earl Warren Institute on Law and Social Policy, University of California, Berkeley, School of Law, 2850 Telegraph Ave., Ste. 500, Berkeley, CA 94705-7220.

■ Career

Chief Justice Earl Warren Institute on Law and Social Policy at the University of California, Berkeley, School of Law, senior fellow; Economic Policy Institute, Washington, DC, research associate; Thurgood Marshall Institute of NAACP Legal Defense Fund, fellow; Haas Institute at University of California, Berkeley, fellow.

■ Writings

NONFICTION

The Way We Were? Myths and Realities of America's Student Achievement, Century Foundation (New York, NY), 1998.

(With Martin Carnoy and Luis Benveniste) *Can Public Schools Learn from Private Schools? Case Studies in the Public and Provate Nonprofit Sectors*, Economic Policy Institute (Washington, DC), 1999.

(With Martin Carnoy and Luis Benveniste) *All Else Equal: Are Public and Private Schools Different?*, Routledge (New York, NY), 2003.

Class and Schools: Using Social, Economic, and Educational Reform to Close the Black-White Achievement Gap, Economic Policy Institute (Washington, DC), 2004.

(With Martin Carnoy, Rebecca Jacobsen, and Lawrence Mishel) *The Charter School Dust-up: Examining the Evidence on Enrollment and Achievement*, Economic Policy Institute (Washington, DC), 2005.

(With Rebecca Jacobsen and Tamara Wilder) *Grading Education: Getting Accountability Right*, Economic Policy Institute (Washington, DC), 2008.

The Color of Law: A Forgotten History of How Our Government Segregated America, Liveright Publishing (New York, NY), 2017.

■ Sidelights

Richard Rothstein, a historian who often writes on race and class issues, examines how the federal, state, and local governments enabled segregated housing patterns in the United States in *The Color of Law: A Forgotten History of How Our Government Segregated America*. While private companies were behind many racially exclusionary policies, various levels of government gave their blessing to these arrangements, Rothstein writes. For instance, in numerous cities, white homeowners had to agree not to sell their properties to African Americans. These so-called covenants were private contracts, but courts usually upheld them. The federal government made low-interest loans available for home buyers in whites-only communities, such as the popular postwar suburban development of Levittown, New York. The Federal Housing Administration, the source of many such loans, refused to insure mortgages in areas near black neighborhoods. In examples of direct government action, municipal zoning laws helped enforce segregation, and these zoning regulations often allowed factories or waste disposal businesses to locate in black neighborhoods but not white ones, damaging the environment in the black areas. Rent control laws, such as New York City's, led white families to hold on to their apartments for generations. Even liberal icons such as President Franklin D. Roosevelt contributed to segregation, with his administration building separate public housing projects for blacks and whites—projects that were then designed to address a housing shortage among the middle class rather than subsidize homes for the poor. The federal Fair Housing Act was passed in 1968, finally prohibiting racial discrimination in housing, but integrated neighborhoods are still rare in the United States, Rothstein notes, and blacks of all income levels are more likely than whites to live in impoverished neighborhoods. He proposes several ways to integrate housing, some of which he admits are unlikely to find support, such as having the federal government buy up houses in all-white areas and sell them at a discount to African Americans, or offering government subsidies for middle-class blacks to buy properties in affluent white suburbs. He also suggests changes in zoning laws to allow families with moderate incomes into affluent communities, as racial diversity will accompany class diversity, and he notes that some cities are already adjusting zoning in this manner.

Housing segregation has high societal costs, Rothstein told Terry Gross on National Public Radio's *Fresh Air*, excerpted at *NPR.org*. "Today African American incomes on average are about sixty percent of average white incomes," he said. "But African American wealth is about five percent of white wealth. Most middle-class families in this country gain their wealth from the equity they have in their homes. So this enormous difference between a sixty percent income ratio and a five percent wealth ratio is almost entirely attributable to federal housing policy implemented through the 20th century." This phenomenon has contributed to other disparities, he continued. "The white families sent their children to college with their home equities; they were able to take care of their parents in old age and not depend on their children," he told Gross. "They're able to bequeath wealth to their children. None of those advantages accrued to African Americans, who for the most part were prohibited from buying homes in those suburbs."

On another National Public Radio program, *All Things Considered*, Rothstein told Ari Shapiro the motivations for racially exclusionary policies were complex. "One thing that should be remembered is that it can't be blamed simply on the standards of the time because there were people who dissented," he said. "People did know better, but they had other priorities. And they caved in to private prejudice and some of their constituents. They themselves were prejudiced. It was assumptions about racial superiority, but it also was cowardice in not confronting popular views about racial superiority." Some politicians denigrate government programs to end segregation as unnecessary "social engineering," but Rothstein said the policies that resulted in segregation were also social engineering. To reverse the pattern of segregation, "there will be prices to be paid, but those prices are small compared to the costs of the social engineering that was conducted in the first two-thirds of the 20th century by the federal government," he told Shapiro. "And that's a price that we have to pay to rectify a serious constitutional violation."

Several reviewers thought Rothstein makes important points. "He quite simply demolishes the notion that government played a minor role in creating the racial ghettos that plague our suburbs and inner cities," related David Oshinsky in the *New York Times Book Review*. "Going back to the late 19th century, he uncovers a policy of de jure segregation in virtually every presidential administration, including those we normally describe as liberal on domestic issues." The result, Oshinsky said, is "a powerful and disturbing history of residential segregation in America." In *Washington Monthly*, Richard D. Kahlenberg called *The Color of Law* "a searing indictment of racially segregating policies" and "a story particularly well told" that "should help educate a younger generation of Americans." *Booklist* contributor James Pekoll termed it "a timely work that should find a place in the current national discussion."

Some critics had a few quibbles. Rothstein "writes again and again about 'black' and 'white,' as if we had not seen a massive influx of Latino immigrants, who face their own discrimination in America," Kahlenberg remarked. Rothstein maintains that Latinos have not been subject to the same systemic housing segregation as blacks, an assertion that Kahlenberg found dismissive. Oshinsky took issue with this aspect of the book as well, saying: "While the history of African Americans is undoubtedly unique, ranking groups by the discrimination they endured may not be the most productive way to proceed." Kahlenberg also thought Rothstein should have paid more attention to segregation by economic class, although he noted that the author's proposed solutions do address class. Both commentators praised the work overall. "Rothstein's provocative book lays the moral groundwork for a strong government role in undoing the harm that government helped to create in the first place," Kahlenberg concluded. Oshinsky added that "there is no better history" of housing segregation than *The Color of Law*. A *Kirkus Reviews* contributor likewise offered a positive summation, dubbing the book "an informed, important expose of the nation's institutionalized racism."

■ Biographical and Critical Sources

PERIODICALS

Booklist, April 1, 2017, James Pekoll, review of *The Color of Law: A Forgotten History of How Our Government Segregated America,* p. 4.

City Limit s, September-October, 2004, review of *Class and Schools: Using Social, Economic and Educational Reform to Close the Black-White Achievement Gap,* p. 33.

Kirkus Reviews, March 1, 2017, review of *The Color of Law.*

New York Times Book Review, June 25, 2017, David Oshinsky, "Don't You Be My Neighbor," p. 15.

Washington Monthly, June-August, 2017, Richard D. Kahlenberg, "Why Segregated Neighborhoods Persist: The Long Historical Reach of Racial Housing Policy," p. 72.

ONLINE

Economic Policy Institute Website, http://www.epi.org/ (February 14, 2018), brief biography.

NPR.org, https://www.npr.org/ (May 3, 2017), "A 'Forgotten History' of How the U.S. Government Segregated America," excerpts from *Fresh Air* interview by Terry Gross; (May 17, 2017), "'The Color of Law' Details How U.S. Housing Policies Created Segregation," transcript of *All Things Considered* interview by Ari Shapiro.

University of California, Berkeley, School of Law Website. https://www.law.berkeley.edu/ (February 14, 2018), brief biography.*

Grant Rumley

■ Personal

Male. *Education:* Michigan State University, B.A.; Hebrew University of Jerusalem, M.A.; attended the University of Alexandria, Egypt.

■ Addresses

Office—Foundation for Defense of Democracies, P.O. Box 33249, Washington, DC 20033.

■ Career

Writer, editor, political scientist, and researcher. Foundation for Defense of Democracies, research fellow; consultant on Middle East issues in Washington, DC; Mitvim: The Israeli Institute for Regional Foreign Policies, visiting fellow.

■ Awards, Honors

Rotary Ambassadorial Scholar, 2012-13.

■ Writings

(With Amir Tibon) *The Last Palestinian: The Rise and Reign of Mahmoud Abbas,* Prometheus Books (Amherst, NY), 2017.

Contributor to magazines and newspapers, including *Foreign Affairs, Atlantic, Foreign Policy, Wall Street Journal, New York Times,* and *Newsweek.*

Jerusalem Review of Near East Affairs, founder and former editor.

■ Sidelights

Grant Rumley, a political scientist, is a research fellow at the Foundation for Defense of Democracies and specializes in Palestinian politics. His work has appeared in major publications such as the *Atlantic, Foreign Affairs,* and *Foreign Policy,* as well as the *New York Times* and *Newsweek.* He served as a visiting fellow at Mitvim: The Israeli Institute for Regional Foreign Policies. While living in Jerusalem, he founded and edited a journal, the *Jerusalem Review of Near East Affairs.* Rumley has also spent time as a consultant on Middle East politics and issues. Rumley holds a B.A. in international relations from Michigan State University and an M.A. in Middle East studies from the Hebrew University of Jerusalem.

The Last Palestinian: The Rise and Reign of Mahmoud Abbas, written by Rumley and Amir Tibon, an Israeli journalist, presents an in-depth political biography of Abbas, the president of the Palestinian Authority. In the online journal *Fathom,* Rumley explained the origins of the book to interviewer Samuel Nurding. "We decided to write the book after the 2014 peace talks, driven by the U.S. Secretary of State John Kerry, fell apart. It was clear that the White House was not going to reengage at the level they had in 2013-4, so there was a window for some deeper analysis. Amir and I were struck by the fact that there were no biographies of Abbas, who is as big a part of the equation as anyone, and we both believe that not enough attention is paid to Palestinian politics. We hope the book sheds new light and will improve the discourse about the peace process," Rumley told Nurding.

The authors base their account of Abbas's personal and political life on more than seventy interviews with people who know or worked with the man.

The interview subjects came from areas in Palestine, Israel, and the United States. Some of the interviews were conducted off the record. Abbas himself declined to be interviewed for the book. Many of the interview subjects are individuals who see Abbas as a man with whom they are "personally friendly and for whom most hold a great deal of respect, but whose rule they see as a disappointment," noted a *Publishers Weekly* reviewer.

Rumley and Tibon describe how Abbas emerged as the leader of the Palestinian Authority after the death of the charismatic and capable Yasser Arafat. He became the president of Palestine and worked to bring Palestine and Israel into negotiations, with the ultimate goal of peace between the two long-standing foes. Yet as the authors relate, Abbas was never able to completely bring into existence a cohesive vision for progress, despite demonstrated good intentions and some transformative successes. In many ways they see this as making him a tragic leader who could not fully put into effect the changes he believed would benefit his people. "Rumley and Tibon's book is a thoughtful biography of a man who, by a combination of circumstance and miscalculation, has struggled to fulfill the aspirations for which he spent his life preparing," commented J. Dana Stuster, writing on the website *Lawfare*.

"For the Western non-specialist who tries to stay abreast of the freighted layers of conflict between the state of Israel and the Palestinians, this briskly paced book succeeds in bringing a plausible portrait of an enigmatic man to life," commented Noah Kennedy, writing in the *Washington Independent Review of Books*. Kennedy further stated, "The book admirably covers a long, eventful life during a complicated crucible of history that is still central to global politics."

Karl Helicher, reviewing *The Last Palestinian* in *Foreword Reviews*, concluded, "Rumley and Tibon make the complexities of the Middle East accessible for those who have little background within this political cauldron. This is an excellent choice for public libraries and an important work for international relations specialists."

■ Biographical and Critical Sources

PERIODICALS

Foreword Reviews, July-August, 2017, Karl Helicher, review of *The Last Palestinian: The Rise and Reign of Mahmoud Abbas.*
Publishers Weekly, May 29, 2017, review of *The Last Palestinian*, p. 58.

ONLINE

Fathom, http://www.fathomjournal.org/ (February 19, 2018), Samuel Nurding, interview with Grant Rumley and Amir Tibon.
Foundation for the Defense of Democracies Website, http://www.defenddemocracy.org/ (February 19, 2018), biography of Grant Rumley.
Lawfare, http://www.lawfareblog.com/ (September 6, 2017), J. Dana Stuster, interview with Grant Rumley and Amir Tibon.
Washington Independent Review of Books, http://www.washingtonindependentreviewofbooks.com/ (July 30, 2017), Noah Kennedy, review of *The Last Palestinian.*
Washington Institute Website, http://www.washingtoninstitute.org/ (February 19, 2018), biography of Grant Rumley.*

Erika L. Sanchez

■ Personal

Female.

■ Addresses

Home—Chicago, IL.

■ Career

Poet, essayist, and fiction writer. *Cosmopolitan for Latinas,* advice columnist.

■ Awards, Honors

Ruth Lilly and Dorothy Sargent Rosenberg Poetry Fellowship, Poetry Foundation; Discovery/*Boston Review* Poetry Prize; CantoMundo Fellowship; Fulbright Scholarship to Madrid, Spain; Princeton Arts Fellow, 2017-19.

■ Writings

Lessons on Expulsion: Poems, Graywolf Press (Minneapolis, MN), 2017.

I Am Not Your Perfect Mexican Daughter (novel), Knopf Books for Young Readers (New York, NY), 2017.

Contributor of poetry, fiction, and nonfiction to periodicals and news outlets, including *Rolling Stone, Salon, Al Jazeera, Cosmopolitan, ESPN.com, Guardian,* NBC News, and the *Paris Review.*

■ Sidelights

The daughter of Mexican immigrants, Mexican-American poet, essayist, fiction writer, and feminist Erika L. Sanchez received the Discovery/*Boston Review* Poetry Prize and a Ruth Lilly and Dorothy Sargent Rosenberg Poetry Fellowship from the Poetry Foundation. She is a sex and love advice columnist for *Cosmopolitan for Latinas* and has contributed poetry, fiction, and nonfiction to *Rolling Stone, Salon,* the *Guardian,* and the *Paris Review.* She has received numerous fellowships, including the CantoMundo Fellowship, a Fulbright scholarship to Madrid, Spain, and a 2017-2019 Princeton Arts fellowship. She lives in Chicago, Illinois.

Lessons on Expulsion

In 2017, Sanchez published her debut poetry collection, *Lessons on Expulsion: Poems,* which describes her dual Mexican and American heritage, life on both sides of the border, disparity of language and culture, shame and race, American xenophobia, violence, and suspicion and suppression. She also writes with a view toward feminism, as well as the brutal 2014 massacre of Mexican students. Most of all, her poems uncover a portrait of survival as she tells the story of her own family, parents who were undocumented Mexican immigrants who imparted on their children faith, work, and expectations for a better life. Sanchez writes her poems in English with some Spanish phrases.

Covering numerous viewpoints from sex workers, farmers, hormonal adolescents, and churchgoers, Sanchez chronicles what it is like to live and love as an immigrant. "In her hallucinatory debut collection, Sánchez negotiates an imaginative space between oral history and journalistic reportage, overloading the senses," according to a *Publishers Weekly* contributor. Writing in *Library Journal*, Doris Lynch described Sanchez's collection as a mixture of harsh, vibrant, and superbly written poems and stated: "Brutal, raw, yet forgiving in the tradition of Walt Whitman, this work is not to be missed."

I Am Not Your Perfect Mexican Daughter

Sanchez next published a humorous young adult novel, *I Am Not Your Perfect Mexican Daughter*, which some reviewers saw as a mixture of *Jane the Virgin* with *The Absolutely True Diary of a Part-Time Indian*. In the story, set in Chicago, fifteen-year-old Julia Reyes is not the perfect Mexican daughter: she argues with her parents, wants to be a writer, and worst of all, wants to leave home to attend college. Her older sister Olga is perfect: she dresses conservatively and obeys her parents. After Olga dies in a tragic car accident at age twenty-two, Julia's parents put more restrictions on Julia, her mother pointing out her every flaw, stifling Julia to a breaking point. Julia finds solace in her first serious boyfriend, Connor, a white boy from an affluent family. But clues reveal that Olga was not as perfect as everyone thought, and Julia embarks on a journey to find the truth.

In an interview with M.J. Franklin online at *Mashable*, Sanchez explained her goals writing the book: "I feel like it's a classic American story, and a story that's not often told. . . . I wanted to create a story that documented the experiences of an immigrant family because that's the family that I belonged to. And I think it's really important to read different narratives about people so you can understand what it's like to be them."

A *New York Times* best seller, the book frustrated some reviewers. Julia is presented as "a sympathetic character, but Sanchez's often expository writing keeps her and her struggles at arm's length," noted a writer in *Publishers Weekly*. In *Kirkus Reviews*, a writer said: "This gritty contemporary novel about an unlikable first-generation Mexican-American teen fails to deliver as a coming-of-age journey." Other reviewers praised the book for weaving story elements along with "a tragic story of distant sisters to create an earnest and heartfelt tale," noted Reinhardt Suarez in *Booklist*. "This novel richly explores coming-of-age topics; a timely and must-have account of survival in a culturally contentious world," according to Alea Perez in *School Library Journal*.

■ Biographical and Critical Sources

PERIODICALS

Booklist, September 1, 2017, Reinhardt Suarez, review of *I Am Not Your Perfect Mexican Daughter*, p. 102.
Kirkus Reviews, August 15, 2017, review of *I Am Not Your Perfect Mexican Daughter*.
Library Journal, April 15, 2017, Doris Lynch, review of *Lessons on Expulsion: Poems*, p. 87.
Publishers Weekly, May 15, 2017, review of *Lessons on Expulsion*, p. 33; August 7, 2017, review of *I Am Not Your Perfect Mexican Daughter*, p. 74.
School Library Journal, September, 2017, Alea Perez, review of *I Am Not Your Perfect Mexican Daughter*, p. 150.

ONLINE

Erika L. Sanchez Website, https://erikalsanchez.com (February 1, 2018), author profile.
Mashable, https://mashable.com/ (November 15, 2017), M.J. Franklin, author interview.*

Sarah Schmidt

1979-

■ **Personal**

Born September 10, 1979, in Melbourne, Victoria, Australia. *Education:* Bachelor of Arts, a Master of Arts, and a Graduate Diploma of Information Management.

■ **Addresses**

Home—Melbourne, Victoria, Australia.

■ **Career**

Reading and literacy coordinator at a regional public library.

■ **Writings**

See What I Have Done, Atlantic Monthly Press (New York, NY), 2017.

■ **Sidelights**

Australian writer Sarah Schmidt is a reading and literacy coordinator at a regional public library. She holds a bachelor's degree in professional writing and editing, a master's degree in creative writing, and a graduate diploma of information management. She lives in Melbourne, Australia. Her 2017 debut novel, *See What I Have Done,* is a retelling of the infamous double axe murder that history has pinned on Lizzie Borden. While the historical Lizzie was arrested, tried, and acquitted by a jury that was sure a woman could not com-

mit such a heinous act, Schmidt also casts doubt on Lizzie's role by focusing on other suspects within the volatile Borden family. After dreaming of the famous murderess, Schmidt has said she immersed herself in Lizzie Borden lore, reading transcripts and flying the ten thousand miles from Australia to the Borden home in U.S. state of Massachusetts.

See What I Have Done is Schmidt's recounting of the events. On August 4, 1892, in Fall River, Massachusetts, thirty-two-year-old Lizzie tells her maid, Bridget, that someone has killed Father. It is soon discovered that Andrew Borden and his second wife, Abby, have been brutally killed with an axe. Schmidt reveals that the spinster sisters, Lizzie and the decade-older Emma, are desperate to leave the house run by strict Andrew and cold Abby. Irish-born Bridget is resentful that Mrs. Bordon is stealing her savings, thus making her unable to move out of the house. Another character, created by Schmidt, is Benjamin, a mysterious stranger and friend of an uncle, who becomes a fourth suspect. The summer's stifling heat, the setting, and tense emotions spur the dread of the terrible deed. According to a *Kirkus Reviews* contributor: "There are books about murder and there are books about imploding families; this is the rare novel that seamlessly weaves the two together, asking as many questions as it answers."

"Equally compelling as a whodunit, 'whydunit,' and historical novel, the book honors known facts yet fearlessly claims its own striking vision," commented a reviewer in *Publishers Weekly,* who described the Bordens' cruel claustrophobic lives and Schmidt's well-crafted and convincing fictional world. In *Booklist,* Jen Baker noted: "The elegant and evocative writing style, combined with a mesmerizing, subtly menacing thrum of psychological suspense." Baker also praised Schmidt's inventive and perceptive presentation of clues to the killing and revelation of each character's possible motive for killing. Baker likened *See What I Have Done* to Christobel Kent's *The Crooked House* and John Harwood's *The Asylum*.

Writing in *Library Journal*, Reba Leiding queried: "What better subject for a psychological thriller than one of the most notorious murders in U.S. history," adding that Schmidt's prose is filled with creepy physicality and imagery as readers are privy to the interior monologues of the four suspects. Leiding recommended the book to fans of mystery and true crime stories. Of the horrific family dynamics within the Bordon household, *Guardian* website reviewer Justine Jordan observed: "We get only glimpses into the particular hell of the Borden household; the fact that we can fill in the blanks from our own darkest places draws us closer, more uncomfortably, in. Schmidt's unusual combination of narrative suppression and splurge makes for a surprising, nastily effective debut."

Despite an unusual tendency to use nouns, like critter, as verbs and to give her characters a similar voice despite their different classes and levels of education, Schmidt focuses on Lizzie: "her protagonist comes more fully alive than almost any character in recent memory, and the final pages are a wild, mind-bending revelation. Maybe she was unhinged, or perfectly sane; maybe she was framed, or should have run away," according to Leah Greenblatt in *Entertainment Weekly*.

■ Biographical and Critical Sources

PERIODICALS

Booklist, May 1, 2017, Jen Baker, review of *See What I Have Done*, p. 29.

Entertainment Weekly, August 11, 2017, Leah Greenblatt, review of *See What I Have Done*, p. 60.

Kirkus Reviews, June 1, 2017, review of *See What I Have Done*.

Library Journal, May 1, 2017, Reba Leiding, review of *See What I Have Done*, p, 68.

Publishers Weekly, May 8, 2017, review of *See What I Have Done*, p. 33.

ONLINE

Guardian, https://www.theguardian.com/ (April 27, 2017), Justine Jordan, review of *See What I Have Done*.

Sarah Schmidt Website, https://sarahschmidt.org (February 1, 2018), author profile.*

Sarah Scoles

- ## Personal

Female. *Education:* Agnes Scott College, B.A.; Cornell University, M.F.A.

- ## Addresses

Home—Denver, CO.

- ## Career

Writer, editor, and science journalist. National Radio Astronomy Observatory, Green Bank, WV, former public education officer.

- ## Writings

Making Contact: Jill Tarter and the Search for Extraterrestrial Intelligence, Pegasus Books (New York, NY), 2017.

Contributor to magazines and newspapers, including the *Atlantic, Washington Post, Scientific American, Wired: Science, Motherboard,* and *Popular Science.*

Astronomy, former associate editor.

- ## Sidelights

Science journalist Sarah Scoles is a prolific contributor to major science publications such as *Scientific American* and *Popular Science* as well as general-interest periodicals, including the *Washington Post* and the *Atlantic.* Currently making her home in Denver, Colorado, Scoles was the public education officer at the National Radio Astronomy Observatory in Green Bank, West Virginia. She also served as the associate editor for *Astronomy* magazine. Scoles holds a B.A. in astrophysics from Agnes Scott College and an M.F.A. in fiction writing from Cornell University.

Scoles profiles a scientific pioneer in the field of astronomy in her book *Making Contact: Jill Tarter and the Search for Extraterrestrial Intelligence.* Jill Tarter is a prominent astronomer who is largely unknown outside the field, but whose presence and experience within the scientific community has made her a role model for many young scientists. Tarter was one of the cofounders of the SETI institute, a scientific organization dedicated to the search for life elsewhere in the universe. SETI stands for Search for Extraterrestrial Intelligence, and the institute bearing that name was started in 1984. Tarter, however, has been on the lookout for radio transmissions from space and other signs of off-Earth intelligence since the late 1960s.

In a book that is a combination of biography and history, Scoles gives an in-depth account of Tarter's professional career and her experiences both as a female scientist and as a researcher involved in an area considered controversial by some, foolish by others. The author relates that Tarter was the only woman in her class of 300, and that she was a prominent astronomer before she became interested in the radio emissions from space that had the potential to indicate intelligence. Over the years, Tarter experienced misogyny and sexual harassment from colleagues, skepticism from the general public and the scientific community, and indifference and budget cuts from government agencies and donors that funded her mission.

Undaunted, she has continued her search despite conditions and setbacks that would have defeated someone less dedicated to the cause.

Supplemental to Tarter's biographical information, Scoles also includes background on the history of the SETI Institute and the decades-long search for extraterrestrial life. More importantly, she charts astronomical discoveries that have greatly increased the odds that intelligent life lives somewhere in the vastness beyond our terrestrial awareness, along with the changes in technology that make discovering that intelligence more likely.

Scoles's book pulls "double duty as a history of the SETI Institute and the only adult biography of Tarter," commented a *Library Journal* writer. For this book, Scoles "has done her homework, so readers will both understand and sympathize with Tarter, who has become an icon and role model despite pursuing a goal she knows she will never achieve," remarked a writer in *Kirkus Reviews*.

■ **Biographical and Critical Sources**

PERIODICALS

Kirkus Reviews, June 1, 2017, review of *Making Contact: Jill Tarter and the Search for Extraterrestrial Intelligence.*

Library Journal, July 1, 2017, review of *Making Contact,* p. 95.

Publishers Weekly, May 1, 2017, review of *Making Contact,* p. 49.*

Jared Yates Sexton

1981-

■ **Also Known As**

Rowdy Yates

■ **Personal**

Born October 7, 1981, in IN. *Education:* Southern Illinois University, M.F.A., 2008.

■ **Addresses**

Office—Creative Writing Program, Georgia Southern University, 1332 Southern Dr., Statesboro, GA 30458.

■ **Career**

Writer, educator. Georgia Southern University, Stastesboro, assistant professor of creative writing. *BULL* literary magazine, editor-in-chief.

■ **Writings**

Amalgamation Schemes: Antiblackness and the Critique of Multiracialism, University of Minnesota Press (Minneapolis, MN), 2008.

(Editor) *Racial Theories in Context*, Cognella (San Diego, CA), 2010.

An End to All Things (short stories), Atticus Books (Kensington, MD), 2012.

(As Rowdy Yates) *Bring Me the Head of Yorkie Goodman* (novel), New Pulp Press (Key West, FL), 2015.

The Hook and the Haymaker, Split Lip Press (Richmond, VA), 2015.

I Am the Oil of the Engine of the World, Split Lip Press (Wyncote, PA), 2016.

The People Are Going to Rise Like the Waters upon Your Shore: A Story of American Rage, Counterpoint Press (Berkeley, CA), 2017.

Black Men, Black Feminism: Lucifer's Nocturne, Palgrave Pivot (New York, NY), 2018.

Blogger for *Atticus Review*. Contributor to periodicals, including *Salon, Southern Humanities Review, PANK, Hobart, New York Times*, and *New Republic*.

■ **Sidelights**

Jared Yates Sexton is an American writer, educator, and political correspondent. The author of several works of fiction and nonfiction, Sexton came to prominence during the 2016 presidential campaign for his coverage of then candidate Donald Trump. Taking to *Twitter*, Sexton attracted a large readership with his incisive tweets from Trump rallies—tweets that earned him death threats from Trump supporters. But they also earned him 142,000 followers. He additionally blogged for the literary review *Atticus Reviews*, and these efforts caught the eye of major media outlets, leading to Sexton writing for the *New York Times, New Republic, Salon*, and others, and becoming a regular guest on television, radio, and podcasts.

In an interview with James Figy in the online *Fear No Lit*, Sexton commented on his switch from fiction to political narratives: "In a way, I just wanted to be there as the campaign unfolded. I reached out to *Atticus Review*, and said I wanted somewhere I could write analysis and articles and [they] graciously let me do it. I never intended to end up in the middle of any controversies or gain any attention. I just wanted to try this out and engross myself in a cultural moment." Sexton added: "I think growing up in the Midwest gave me insight into a part of the country that has been pretty misunderstood, particularly in publishing and media. The current cultural crisis we're in has its roots in what's happened to my family and neighbors, and I think it's been more or less the problem that's really drug us into our situation now." Sexton's political reporting resulted in the 2017 nonfiction book *The People Are Going to Rise Like the Waters upon Your Shore: A Story of American Rage.*

An End to All Things and *Bring Me the Head of Yorkie Goodman*

Sexton has written several short-story collections. His debut, *An End to All Things,* features "characters frustrated by situations beyond their control," according to a *Publishers Weekly Online* reviewer. These tales were largely inspired by the author's return to his Indiana hometown, which was plagued by unemployment and uncertainty about a new direction. The subsequent tales highlight such turmoil. The *Publishers Weekly Online* contributor further noted: "Though some of his characters' voices blend together and lack nuance, Sexton is successful in earnestly capturing their futile grasps at agency." Writing in the online *Portland Book Review,* Gregory A. Young had higher praise, terming the stories "compelling" and adding that as this is the author's debut collection, it "suggests that he has a long literary career ahead of him, and readers should be excited for that."

Sexton's first novel, the 2015 *Bring Me the Head of Yorkie Goodman,* was written under the pseudonym of Rowdy Yates. A *Publishers Weekly Online* reviewer called it a "violent, darkly funny novel." At the heart of the tale is the efforts by enforcer Bill Wallace and hit man Carp to complete a mission for the drug lord who employs them, known only as the Boss. He wants them to collect an unpaid debt from some character in Indiana, Yorkie Goodman. Proof of the completion of their mission is the head of Goodman. But things quickly go awry in this "over-the-top tale whose infectious energy will prove irresistible to devotees of modern noir," according to the *Publishers Weekly Online* reviewer. Online *Foreword Reviews* contributor Anna Call was also impressed, concluding: "Sparse, clean prose recalls westerns, pulp and noir fiction, and the cadence of another age. An easy read, *Bring Me the Head of Yorkie Goodman* is an entertaining few hours that leaves a larger impression than a book its size has any right to do. A highly recommended treat for fans of crime fiction."

The People Are Going to Rise Like the Waters upon Your Shore

In *The People Are Going to Rise Like the Waters upon Your Shore,* Sexton recaps much of his reporting of the 2016 presidential campaign, looking at the appeal of a man like Donald Trump to a large part of the electorate. Sexton examines this appeal through the lens of his own blue-collar Indiana family, who would, in private, voice many of the inflammatory opinions of candidate Trump. On that level, Trump was able to connect with disaffected voters who amazingly took this New York plutocrat to heart as one of their own simply because of his rhetoric. Sexton also comments on why Hillary Clinton was unable to connect with that swath of voters—a minority in the nation, but still enough to swing the electoral college. Additionally, Sexton examines the appeal of Bernie Sanders, who appealed to the left with the same passion as Trump did to the Republican base. However, he also goes on to criticize the so-called purists of the left who declared there was no difference between Trump and Clinton and refused to vote. Throughout it all, however, Sexton, like much of the population, did not believe until election night that Trump could actually win.

Some reviewers found fault with *The People Are Going to Rise Like the Waters upon Your Shore.* The *Rumpus* website managing editor Lyz Lenz noted: "Begun with a series of tweets, *The People Are Going to Rise* fails to rise above surface-level observations, privileging white male rage over all other strains of anger that surge through America, including the anger we now see growing against the current administration. . . . To ignore this anger is the willful ignorance of white male privilege." Similarly, *Washington Post Online* writer Carlos Lozada complained that this book "was published quickly for a book on the 2016 campaign, though not so quickly as to excuse its typos and cliches." Lozada added: "Worse yet, Sexton, who teaches creative writing, delivers markedly uncreative prose, in which waters are always muddied, coffers are always lined, dealings are always shady, breath is always bated, memory lanes are always strolled and forests are always missed among trees."

Writing in the online *Los Angeles Review of Books,* award-winning journalist Blake Morlock had a more mixed assessment, observing: "[Sexton's] chapters are full of often keen, always judgmental personal observations available to a guy free from the pack. It mixes personal accounts with broad campaign context and the pages flip. I just wish he had tried to get to the story that no one really covered: what the hell happened to a country radicalize it so much in eight years and what are the terms of assuaging it? His book is entertaining in the manner of Hunter S. Thompson's *Fear and Loathing on the Campaign Trail '72*, in that it contains one man's quirky observations. But that becomes its biggest flaw: it is so full of fear and loathing that Sexton missed the real story of what fueled American rage."

A *Publishers Weekly* reviewer had much higher praise for *The People Are Going to Rise Like the Waters upon Your Shore*, noting of this "chilling" account: "Sexton's reporting provides a unique nuts-and-bolts look at the campaigns, and his eyewitness reports of the aggressive displays at Trump rallies are both terrifying and fascinating." Similarly, a *Kirkus Reviews* critic termed it a "useful snapshot of a tumultuous presidential race."

■ Biographical and Critical Sources

PERIODICALS

Kirkus Reviews, July 15, 2017, review of *The People Are Going to Rise Like the Waters upon Your Shore: A Story of American Rage*.

Publishers Weekly, May 15, 2017, review of *The People Are Going to Rise Like the Waters upon Your Shore*, p. 47.

ONLINE

Creative Sweet, https://southerncreativesweet. wordpress.com/ (February 3, 2018), "Creative Writing Faculty."

Daily Beast, https://www.thedailybeast.com/ (December 10, 2017), Jared Yates Sexton, "Fascism Runs in My American Family."

Fear No Lit, http://www.fearnolit.com/ (September 20, 2017), James Figy, "Fail Better," author interview.

Foreword Reviews, https://www.forewordreviews. com/ (August 27, 2015), Anna Call, review of *Bring Me the Head of Yorkie Goodman*.

Jared Yates Sexton Website, https://www.jysexton. com/ (February 4, 2018).

Los Angeles Review of Books, https://lareviewofbooks. org/ (October 20, 2017), Blake Morlock, review of *The People Are Going to Rise Like the Waters upon Your Shore*.

New York Times Online, https://www.nytimes.com/ (October 13, 2016), Jared Yates Sexton, "Donald Trump's Toxic Masculinity."

Portland Book Review, http://portlandbookreview. com/ (April 7, 2013), Gregory A. Young, review of *An End to All Things*.

Publishers Weekly Online, https://www.publishers weekly.com/ (January 14, 2013), review of *An End to All Things*; (March 25, 2015), review of *Bring Me the Head of Yorkie Goodman*.

Rumpus, http://therumpus.net/ (August 14, 2017), Lyz Lenz, review of *The People Are Going to Rise Like the Waters upon Your Shore*.

Washington Post Online, https://www.washington post.com/ (August 25, 2017), Carlos Lozada, review of *The People Are Going to Rise Like the Waters upon Your Shore*.*

Vivian Shaw

■ **Personal**

Born in Kenya; immigrated to the United States. *Education:* Holds B.A. and M.F.A. degrees. *Hobbies and other interests:* Writing fan fiction.

■ **Career**

Writer and novelist. Worked in academic publishing and development.

■ **Writings**

Strange Practice, Orbit (New York, NY), 2017.

■ **Sidelights**

Vivian Shaw is a Kenyan-born writer and novelist. She spent most of her early childhood in England before moving to the United States at the age of seven. In her professional life, she has worked in the field of academic publishing and development. She holds a B.A. in art history and an M.F.A. in creative writing.

In her debut novel, *Strange Practice,* Shaw introduces readers to Dr. Greta Helsing, a thirty-four-year-old physician in London with a highly specialized medical practice. Like her father before her, Greta treats the sick, the injured, and the infirm. She is not interested in the diseases and wounds that afflict mortals, however. Dr. Helsing is a physician for the supernatural creatures of the world, providing medical services to vampires, werewolves, ghouls, mummies, and demons. If a mummy is falling apart, she can fashion a new bone to set a loose limb. If a vampire needs blood, she can secure a supply through connections at local blood banks. "She grew up with vampires in the sitting room and demons in the parlor, and being able to help them to live their best lives through her work at her small, private clinic is all she has ever wanted to do," commented Jason Sheehan in a review at *NPR.org.*

Greta is a descendant of probably the most famous person to bear her family name, Abraham Van Helsing, who struggled against the most famous of vampires, Dracula, in the late 1800s. Though her family dropped the "Van" years ago, Greta is fully aware of her close ties to history. Throughout the book, Shaw's "affection for her characters is obvious, and Greta is a sensitive, genuinely nice person who loves her job, is unerringly discreet, and cares deeply about her patients, even ones that try to kill her."

In this first adventure, Greta finds herself helping a famous member of the vampire clan, Sir Francis Varney, who has shown up seriously wounded at the home of Edmund Ruthven. Varney, who is well known to readers of Victorian-era penny dreadfuls but proves to be nothing like he was depicted in them, has been attacked by what appeared to be a group of monks, chanting in a strange language and spraying garlic. When Greta herself is attacked, her throat nearly slit by a man hiding in the back seat of her car, she realizes the stakes are high. Together, she and her monstrous friends, along with human ally August Cranswell from the British Museum, search for answers to the mystery to discover who has the strength and the nerve to attack members of the supernatural community.

Sheehan called *Strange Practice* a "warm quilt of a thing that's made for curling up with." A *Publishers Weekly* contributor found it to be an "appealing, amusing collection of London's modern un-dead and the humans who care for them." The book is an "appropriately dark breath of fresh air in the arena of urban fantasy," remarked *Booklist* writer Dawn Kuczwara.

■ Biographical and Critical Sources

PERIODICALS

Booklist, June, 2017, Dawn Kuczwara, review of *Strange Practice,* p. 72.

Kirkus Reviews, June 1, 2017, review of *Strange Practice.*

Publishers Weekly, May 1, 2017, review of *Strange Practice,* p. 41.

ONLINE

NPR.org, http://www.npr.org/ (July 26, 2017), Jason Sheehan, "*Strange Practice:* The Doctor Is In," review of *Strange Practice.**

Ashley Shelby

1977-

■ Personal

Born 1977. *Education:* Indiana University, B.A.; Columbia University, M.F.A.

■ Career

Writer, novelist, editor, short-story writer, educator, and journalist. Former editor at Penguin; Gotham Writers Workshop, writing instructor; Loft Literary Center, teaching artist.

■ Awards, Honors

Third Coast Fiction Prize, for short story that was the basis for *South Pole Station;* Red Hen Press Short Story Award; Enizagam Short Story Award.

■ Writings

Red River Rising: The Anatomy of a Flood and the Survival of an American City, Borealis Books (St. Paul, MN), 2003.
South Pole Station (novel), Picador (New York, NY), 2017.

Contributor to periodicals, including the *Los Angeles Review, Nation, Post Road, Seattle Review, Sonora Review, Southeast Review,* and *Third Coast.*

■ Sidelights

Ashley Shelby is a writer, journalist, editor, and educator. She is a former editor for Penguin, where she acquired and edited narrative nonfiction and memoir, and she is an instructor at the Gotham Writers Workshop. Shelby holds a B.A. from Indiana University and an MFA in Nonfiction Writing from Columbia University.

Red River Rising

Shelby's first book, *Red River Rising: The Anatomy of a Flood and the Survival of an American City,* was a narrative nonfiction account of the catastrophic 1997 flood of the Red River and the devastation it caused to Grand Forks, North Dakota. The flood occurred on April 19, 1997, and was the result of a series of blizzards that occurred during the winter of 1996-97 and the resulting runoff from melting in April. The flood was not predicted by any of the usually reliable sources, particularly the National Weather Service (NWS) and the U.S. Army Corps of Engineers, nor could these agencies accurately determine when or at what level the river would crest. In total, some 50,000 families were displaced from their homes because of the flooding, and a major portion of Grand Forks's downtown was damaged by flooding and subsequent fires.

In the wake of the flood, the National Weather Service was harshly criticized for not being able to predict the disaster, though Shelby points out that such blame was most likely unfounded since the NWS had actually predicted major flooding of the river. *Library Journal* contributor Stephen L. Hupp called *Red River Rising* a "readable, thoughtful, and eye-opening account of a possibly unpreventable natural disaster" and its aftermath.

South Pole Station

In her first novel, *South Pole Station,* which a *Kirkus Reviews* contributor called "smart and inventive," Shelby writes about the troubles, triumphs, and relationships of a group of researchers, scientists, and artists who are assigned for a year to a remote research station at the South Pole. She begins the book with a series of psychological assessment questions that are used to determine if someone has the right mental state to live for an extended period in the inhospitable conditions of the South Pole. She then introduces her characters—not only the expected complement of scientific personnel and their support staff but also a group of artists, writers, and dancers who have been included as part of a National Science Foundation program encouraging creative work based on a polar adventure.

Main character Cooper Gosling is a painter who is part of the group of creatives qualified to join the mission. She is talented, but so far unsuccessful with her work. She is haunted by a family tragedy and is seeking escape, like many of her colleagues, in the frozen southern world. She derives comfort from the closeness of the team at the polar station, and finds herself attracted to Sal, a physicist. The arrival at the base of Dr. Frank Pavano throws the entire team into turmoil. Pavano is a climate change denier whose work and opinions are at odds with the scientists at the base. The mission is further jeopardized when Cooper helps Pavano with an unauthorized experiment and is injured in the process.

"This is a fascinating novel, loaded with interesting history of Antarctic exploration, current scientific operations, and the living and working condition" in a harsh and unforgiving environment where the sun shines only six months out of the year, noted a *Publishers Weekly* reviewer. Shelby "writes well about science and the peculiar, pressurized human ecosystem at the bottom of the world," observed the writer in *Kirkus Reviews*. The author "eschews easy choices and treats interpersonal relations, grief, science, art, and political controversy with the same deft, humorous hand," remarked Alene Moroni in a *Booklist* review. *BookPage* writer Chika Gujarathi concluded: "Shelby's exploration of the human spirit continuously digs deeper, ever in search of answers to all of life's important questions—scientific and otherwise."

■ Biographical and Critical Sources

PERIODICALS

Booklist, June, 2017, Alene Moroni, review of *South Pole Station*, p. 55.
BookPage, July, 2017, Chika Gujarathi, review of *South Pole Station*, p. 22.
Kirkus Reviews, June 15, 2017, review of *South Pole Station*.
Library Journal, April 15, 2004, Stephen L. Hupp, review of *Red River Rising: The Anatomy of a Flood and the Survival of an American City*, p. 101.
Publishers Weekly, May 1, 2017, review of *South Pole Station*, p. 34.

ONLINE

Gotham Writers Workshop Website, https://www.writingclasses.com/ (February 19, 2018), biography of Ashley Shelby.
New York Times Online, https://www.nytimes.com/ (August 8, 2017), review of *South Pole Station*.
Washington Post Online, https://www.washingtonpost.com/ (July 14, 2017), review of *South Pole Station*.

Craig Shirley

1956-

■ Personal

Born September 24, 1956, in Syracuse, NY; son of Edward and Barbara Shirley; married; wife's name Zorine; children: Matthew, Andrew, Taylor, Mitchell. *Education:* Springfield College, B.A., 1978. *Hobbies and other interests:* Sailing, waterskiing, sport shooting, renovating buildings, and scuba diving.

■ Addresses

Home—Lancaster, VA. *Office*—Shirley & Banister Public Affairs, 122 S. Patrick St., Alexandria, VA 22314.

■ Career

Author, lecturer, historian and public affairs consultant. Has consulted and helped run numerous political campaigns, 1978-84; Shirley & Banister Public Affairs, communications and public relations firm, Alexandria, VA, founder, chair, CEO, 1984—. Former contract agent for CIA. Member of the Board of Governors of the Reagan Ranch. Makes regular appearances on television and radio.

■ Member

Philadelphia Society, Fusionist Society, Lyn Nofziger Society.

■ Awards, Honors

Outstanding Alumnus, Springfield College, 2005.

■ Writings

Reagan's Revolution: The Untold Story of the Campaign That Started It All, Nelson Current (Nashville, TN), 2005.

(With others) *Secrets of Videoblogging,* Peachpit (Berkeley, CA), 2006.

Rendezvous with Destiny: Ronald Reagan and the Campaign That Changed America, ISI Books (Wilmington, DE), 2009.

December 1941: 31 Days That Changed America and Saved the World, Nelson Books (Nashville, TN), 2011.

Last Act: The Final Years and Emerging Legacy of Ronald Reagan, Nelson Books (Nashville, TN), 2015.

Reagan Rising: The Decisive Years, 1976-1980, Broadside Books (New York, NY), 2017.

Citizen Newt: The Making of a Reagan Conservative, Nelson Books (Nashville, TN), 2017.

Contributor to numerous periodicals, including *Washington Post, Washington Times, Los Angeles Times, Townhall, Weekly Standard, Washington Examiner, Newsmax, National Review, Reuters, Investors Business Daily, Politico, Breitbart,* and *Lifezette.*

■ Sidelights

Craig Shirley is an American author, lecturer, historian and public affairs consultant. He has been involved in conservative politics since he was a child, going door-to-door for the Barry Goldwater campaign at age eight. Shirley has gone on to work on other presidential campaigns and has become a major biographer of Ronald Reagan, penning four works on aspects of the Reagan presidency.

Reagan's Revolution

In his first book, *Reagan's Revolution: The Untold Story of the Campaign That Started It All*, Shirley details the largely forgotten story of the unsuccessful Reagan presidential campaign of 1975-76, running against incumbent Gerald Ford. Shirley interviewers journalists, campaign insiders, and politicos to demonstrate his major thesis: that this failed campaign actually succeeded in bringing the Republican Party's right wing to the ascendancy and paved the way for Reagan's 1980 election and the birth of the modern conservative movement.

Reviewing *Reagan's Revolution* in *PR Week*, Douglas Quenqua felt that this "tirelessly researched, well-written book by conservative public affairs maven Craig Shirley proves a satisfying first entry." Similarly, *National Review* contributor Michael Potemra noted: "Shirley is well known as a talented political operative; he shows himself in this suspenseful book to be, as well, a skillful and engaging writer."

Rendezvous with Destiny

Shirley provides an in-depth account of Reagan's 1980 presidential campaign in *Rendezvous with Destiny: Ronald Reagan and the Campaign That Changed America*. Interviewing more than 150 campaign insiders and advisors, and with access to campaign files, Shirley follows the path of Reagan from his 1976 defeat, his time in the political wilderness, his subsequent battle through the Republican primaries for the 1980 election, and the debates with then President Jimmy Carter, in which the Reagan team managed to get hold of the Carter debate team's briefing books. The subsequent election was a blowout, with Reagan securing the electoral vote at 489-49 and winning the popular vote by nine million. Through it all, Shirley shows how perilous and uncertain Reagan's path to victory actually was.

Writing in the *American Spectator*, Jason Emerson noted: "Shirley's *Rendezvous with Destiny*, just as in his previous book, *Reagan's Revolution*, is a paradigm of this period of Reagan scholarship. It is an exhaustive study that will be at the very core of the Reagan bibliography for future generations, and will not anytime soon—if ever—be surpassed." *National Review* contributor Jay Cost similarly noted: "*Rendezvous with Destiny* is an important, timely book that conservatives, Reagan admirers, and students of electoral politics will cherish and enjoy for years. Credit is due to Shirley for a monumental accomplishment." *American*

Spectator reviewer Artur Davis felt that this book "is proof that a 30-year campaign can unfold like a suspense novel if it has the right storyteller." Davis added: "This is the single best book on an American election since Teddy White laid down his notepad."

Last Act

Last Act: The Final Years and Emerging Legacy of Ronald Reagan tells the story of the final years of Reagan after departing the White House. This includes the opening of the Reagan Library and the discovery that the former president was suffering from Alzheimer's, a condition that led to his death in 2004. Shirley takes the reader into Reagan's final hours, surrounded by his family, and into the pageant of the funeral.

"The story Shirley unfolds . . . is detailed, colorful, and summons the emotions," according to *American Spectator Online* contributor Jeffrey Lord, who added: "By bringing together the details of Reagan's death and the funeral that followed, a portrait made possible by extensive interviews with the Reagan family, friends, and members of the Reagan administration, Craig Shirley has compiled a fascinating and—speaking as someone who worked for Ronald Reagan—a wonderfully poignant account of Ronald Reagan's 'last act.'" Reviewing *The Last Act* in *Washington Times Online*, John R. Coyne, Jr., also had praise for Shirley's "clean and forceful prose."

Reagan Rising

Shirley's fourth book on the former president, *Reagan Rising: The Decisive Years, 1976-1980*, is an examination of the years Reagan spent in the political wilderness following his defeat in the Republican primary of 1976. That was Reagan's second unsuccessful bid for the presidency, and many pundits counted him out for future attempts. However, just a year after the 1976 defeat he was, as Shirley shows, resurrecting his career speaking at the annual Conservative Political Action Conference, to present his vision for a new Republican Party that could capture the votes of the working class and not just the members of board rooms. Shirley details Reagan's rebirth, attracting young conservatives to the party and talking tough about Cold War dynamics.

Reviewing *Reagan Rising* in the *National Review*, Clark S. Judge noted: "Reading Craig Shirley has become essential for any Ronald Reagan student. Reagan Rising strengthens his already high standing among Reagan biographers." Writing in the *New York Times Online*, Romesh Ratnesar also had praise, commenting: "Shirley, the author of books on Reagan's 1976 and 1980 presidential campaigns, is a sure-footed and entertaining observer of the hurly-burly of national politics."

Citizen Newt

Shirley changes focus with his 2017 work, *Citizen Newt: The Making of a Reagan Conservative*, penning a biography of Republican conservative firebrand, Newt Gingrich, former Speaker of the House. The author takes the reader back to Gingrich's childhood in Pennsylvania, his years as a young history professor, and his early foray into politics as a congressman. Shirley follows Gingrich's growth as a major actor in the Reagan Revolution, battling more mainstream Republicans such as President George H.W. Bush from the right and proving to be a thorn in the side of President Bill Clinton as the Speaker developed what was known as the Gingrich Revolution and his Contract with America. Shirley leaves off the narrative at this high point in Gingrich's career. Hubris ultimately brought the overreaching Gingrich down, but he has continued to play behind-the-scenes as well as in-front-of-the-camera roles in Republican politics.

Reviewing *Citizen Newt* in the conservative-leaning *Washington Times Online*, Coyne, Jr., had praise, commenting: "At a time when our history books and biographies are being revised at warp speed by practitioners of identity politics and a generation of academics fearful of being accused of being politically incorrect and losing their jobs, Craig Shirley stands out as an honest and highly talented biographer who is also a man of conviction." Coyne, Jr., added: "In this deeply researched biography, written in strong clear prose with wit and understanding, while never glossing over missteps and mistakes, Craig Shirley has given us . . . [an] honest accounting." A *Publishers Weekly* contributor, however, was less impressed, pointing out that Shirley ends his narrative at "Gingrich's most triumphant moment," without mention of his final resignation from Congress. The contributor felt that this "goes against the author's stated purpose of complete honesty."

■ Biographical and Critical Sources

PERIODICALS

American Spectator, December, 2009, Jason Emerson, review of *Rendezvous with Destiny: Ronald Reagan and the Campaign That Changed America*, p. 86; December, 2012, Artur Davis, review of *Rendezvous with Destiny*, p. 44.

California Bookwatch, November, 2013, review of *Rendezvous with Destiny*.

National Review, April 11, 2005, Michael Potemra, review of *Reagan's Revolution: The Untold Story of the Campaign That Started It All*, p. 49; January 25, 2010, Jay Cost, review of *Rendezvous with Destiny*, p. 49; April 17, 2017, Clark S. Judge, review of *Reagan Rising: The Decisive Years, 1976-1980*, p. 40.

PR Week [US], April 4, 2005, Douglas Quenqua, review of *Reagan's Revolution*, p. 24.

Publishers Weekly, May 1, 2017, review of *Citizen Newt: The Making of a Reagan Conservative*, p. 47.

ONLINE

American Prospect, http://prospect.org/ (August 13, 2014), Adele M. Stan, "A Question of Character: Craig Shirley's Scurrilous Attack on Liberal Historian Rick Perlstein."

American Spectator Online, https://spectator.org/ (December 22, 2015), Jeffrey Lord, review of *Last Act: The Final Years and the Emerging Legacy of Ronald Reagan*.

Craig Shirley Website, http://www.craigshirley.com (January 9, 2018).

Huffington Post, https://www.huffingtonpost.com/ (January 9, 2018), "Craig Shirley."

National Review, https://www.nationalreview.com/ (April 17, 2017), Clark S. Judge, review of *Reagan Rising*.

New York Times Online, https://www.nytimes.com/ (March 31, 2017), Romesh Ratnesar, review of *Reagan Rising*.

U.S. News, https://www.usnews.com/ (January 9, 2018), "Craig Shirley."

Washington Examiner, http://www.washingtonexaminer.com/ (November 19, 2015), Myra Adams, "Reagan Biographer Craig Shirley: O'Reilly's *Killing Reagan* Is a 'Pile of Garbage'."

Washington Post Online, https://www.washingtonpost.com/ (July 21, 2013), Krissah Thompson, "Meet Craig Shirley and Diana Banister, the Right's Pitch-perfect Conservatives."

Washington Times Online, https://www.washingtontimes.com/ (October 26, 2015), John R. Coyne, Jr., review of *Last Act*; (September 11, 2017), John R. Coyne, Jr., review of *Citizen Newt*.*

Laura Silverman

1990-

■ **Personal**

Born December 15, 1990. *Education:* University of Georgia, B.A.; New School, M.F.A.

■ **Addresses**

Home—Atlanta, GA.

■ **Career**

Writer, novelist, editor, and publishing consultant.

■ **Writings**

Girl out of Water, Sourcebooks Fire (Naperville, IL), 2017.

Contributor to *BuzzFeed.*

■ **Sidelights**

Laura Silverman is a writer, editor, publishing consultant, and novelist living in Atlanta, Georgia. She is the owner of an editing service in Atlanta, where she works with unpublished writers and novelists to improve their manuscripts and shape their work into publishable form. She holds degrees in English and advertising from the University of Georgia and an M.F.A. in writing for children from the New School.

Silverman is also an advocate and supporter for individuals who suffer from the effects of chronic pain. As a person with an undiagnosed condition that causes her a debilitating level of chronic pain, Silverman knows the physical and mental trouble that can result. Her condition started right after her twenty-first birthday, while she was still a student at the University of Georgia. At first her doctors thought it was fibromyalgia, but as the condition worsened, that diagnoses was abandoned. After years of testing, hospitalizations, and medical examinations, her doctors still do not know what her condition is.

In an interview on the website *Adventures in YA Publishing,* Silverman stated: "I . . . have to write in short bursts because typing hurts my hands and sitting up hurts my back and chest. I used to be able to get seven or eight hours of writing done in a day. Now, on a 'good' pain day, I can maybe get two to three hours in if I dedicate my full day to writing" with frequent breaks. Despite her pain, Silverman persists as a writer and editorial consultant, determined to make the most of her talents and skills.

Girl out of Water is Silverman's debut novel, and concerns Anise, a seventeen-year-old surfer girl living in Santa Cruz, California. She has a pleasant and relatively stable life with her father and friends, especially long-term best friend Eric, who may be turning into something more serious than just a friend. As Anise and her friends look forward to their last summer before college, a family disaster disrupts everyone's plans. Anise's aunt has been seriously injured in a car accident, and she and her father must move to Nebraska to care for her aunt and her children. In landlocked Nebraska, there will be no surfing, and Anise will literally be a girl out of water. Family responsibilities must take precedence, and she leaves California.

In Nebraska, however, she meets skateboarder Lincoln, a young black man whose skateboarding skills aren't affected by the fact that he is missing an arm. Gradually, Anise and Lincoln become good friends, with Lincoln teaching her to skateboard. An increasing maturity also enfolds Anise as she recognizes her responsibility to her aunt and cousins and begins to feel compassion for both her father and her aunt. With Lincoln's patience and help, she begins to realize that she can make her home wherever she wants and adapt to situations as needed.

Silverman "realistically captures Anise's love for her surfing life and the terrible sacrifice she makes" when she has to leave it behind to tend to a greater responsibility, noted *Booklist* reviewer Diane Colson. A *Kirkus Reviews* writer called *Girl out of Water* a "quick summer read to reassure teens who worry about college or blooming where they're planted."

■ Biographical and Critical Sources

PERIODICALS

Booklist, April 15, 2017, Diane Colson, review of *Girl out of Water*, p. 50.

Kirkus Reviews, March 1, 2017, review of *Girl out of Water*.

ONLINE

Adventures in YA Publishing, http://www.adventuresinyapublishing.com/ (May 5, 2017), interview with Laura Silverman.

Laura Silverman Website, https://www.laurasilvermanwrites.com (February 19, 2018).*

Morgan Simon

1987-

■ **Personal**

Born 1987. *Education:* Swarthmore College, B.A. (with high honors).

■ **Addresses**

Home—CA.

■ **Career**

Financial executive. Responsible Endowments Coalition, founding executive director; Toniic, founding CEO, 2010-13; Transform Finance, chair and cofounder, 2013—; Pi Investments, managing director, 2015-17; Candide Group, managing director and coleader, 2017—. Middlebury College, adjunct professor. Also worked as a freelance consultant, 2013-15. SJF Institute, treasurer, 2008-12; Social Venture Network, board member, 2009-11; the Working World, board member, 2011—; Restaurant Opportunity Center, board cochair, 2013—; CARE Enterprises, board member, 2015—.

■ **Writings**

Real Impact: The New Economics of Social Change, Nation Books (New York, NY), 2017.

■ **Sidelights**

Morgan Simon has built a strong reputation within the financial industry. Before launching her professional career, she attended Swarthmore College and earned her bachelor's degree. Simon has served as the leader of several businesses in her field, including Transform Finance, Toniic, and Candide Group; she also founded Transform Finance and Toniic. In addition to her businesses, Simon is affiliated with Middlebury College as an adjunct professor. She devotes part of her time to helping with various social reform organizations, including CARE Enterprises, the Working World, and the Restaurant Opportunity Center. Simon is part of the board for all three of these organizations as well.

Real Impact: The New Economics of Social Change is Simon's debut book. It centers on her field of expertise and deals specifically with "impact investment," which Simon defines as the idea of using one's money for the good of society as well as for personal financial gain. In using money in this way, Simon asserts that people can bring positive change to the world. Simon draws some of her research from the theories of Muhammad Yunus, a financial professional who preaches similar ideas; however, Yunus's theories align more closely to developing nations and encourage young business people to follow through with their financial goals for the benefit of society.

Simon breaks her central argument into several key points, which also serve as suggestions for readers to follow if they are interested in taking on the task of impact investment for themselves. One of those suggestions is to cut ties with large banks and store money elsewhere; specifically, instead of relying on the likes of Wells Fargo and similar large financial institutions, readers should consider joining credit unions and smaller banks within their community. This will give them the support they need to grow while helping the community as a whole. Simon also recommends that readers consider creating better jobs for people throughout their community with much better wages and prospects for creating an actual career, provided that readers have the power and capability to do so. Simon aims her advice toward people of various socioeconomic levels, establishing the idea that we can all take part in reshaping our communities and economy. In building her argument, Simon posits that the current capitalistic system is currently doing society no favors in terms of socioeconomic advancement. Therefore, she encourages readers to dismantle some of the problems associated with capitalism through her suggestions for better and more constructive financial habits. Simon argues that by putting more money toward communities and less toward one's personal goals, readers can create a better local society, economy, and world. A *Kirkus Reviews* contributor remarked that *Real Impact* is "a clear-eyed case for socially conscious investment, of much interest to those who want their dollars to do good." In *Publishers Weekly*, a reviewer commented: "This is a clarion call that the world of well-meaning social-justice activists needs to hear." Melissa Plotsky and Kesha Cash, in a review for the *Stanford Social Innovation Review* website, said: "[Simon's] experience, knowledge, and passion in guiding wealthy families, foundations, and financial institutions coalesce powerfully." *Seeking Alpha* website reviewer Hazel Henderson commented that *Real Impact* "will be useful to adventurous asset allocators, trustees, high net worth owners, family offices and researchers, as well as international agencies

and the UN now driving the SDGs toward their goals in 2030." On the *Lunarmobiscuit* website, Michael "Luni" Libes declared: "The book is the best primer I've read on impact investing."

■ Biographical and Critical Sources

PERIODICALS

Kirkus Reviews, August 15, 2017, review of *Real Impact: The New Economics of Social Change*.
Publishers Weekly, May 22, 2017, review of *Real Impact*, p. 82.

ONLINE

Lunarmobiscuit, https://lunarmobiscuit.com/ (October 15, 2017), Michael "Luni" Libes, review of *Real Impact*.
Middlebury Institute of International Studies at Monterey, https://www.middlebury.edu/ (February 21, 2018), author profile.
Morgan Simon Website, http://morgansimon.com (February 21, 2018).
Seeking Alpha, https://seekingalpha.com/ (January 26, 2018), Hazel Henderson, review of *Real Impact*.
Stanford Social Innovation Review, https://ssir.org/ (February 21, 2018), Melissa Plotsky and Kesha Cash, "Keeping It Real," review of *Real Impact*.
Toniic, http://www.toniic.com/ (February 21, 2018), author profile.*

Yuri Slezkine

1956-

■ Personal

Born February 7, 1956, in Soviet Union; immigrated to United States, 1983. *Education:* University of Moscow, M.A.; University of Texas, Austin, Ph.D.

■ Addresses

Home—Berkeley, CA. *Office*—University of California, Berkeley, Department of History, 3229 Dwinelle Hall, Berkeley, CA 94720-2550.

■ Career

Historian, educator, writer. Former assistant professor, Wake Forest University; University of California, Berkeley, current Jane K. Sather Professor of History; Hoover Institution, Stanford University, W. Glenn Campbell and Rita Ricardo-Campbell National Fellow. Former fellow, National Endowment of Humanities, American Council of Learned Societies, National Council for Soviet and East European Research, John Simon Guggenheim Memorial Foundation, and Center for Advanced Study in the Behavioral Sciences.

■ Awards, Honors

National Jewish Book Award, Wayne S. Vucinich Prize (Best Book in Any Discipline), American Association for the Advancement of Slavic Studies), and Association of American Publishers' Best Scholarly Book in Religion Award, all for *The Jewish Century;* fellow, American Academy of Arts and

Sciences. Also worked as a translator in the Soviet Union, Mozambique, and Lisbon, Portugal, before immigrating to the United States.

■ Writings

(With Marisa Fushille and Lisa Little) *Speak Russian!*, University of Texas Press (Austin, TX), 1990.

(Editor, with Galya Diment) *Between Heaven and Hell: The Myth of Siberia in Russian Culture*, St. Martin's Press (New York, NY), 1993.

Arctic Mirrors: Russia and the Small Peoples of the North, Cornell University Press (Ithaca, NY), 1994.

(Translator; editor, with Sheila Fitzpatrick) *In the Shadow of Revolution: Life Stories of Russian Women from 1917 to the Second World War*, Princeton University Press (Princeton, NJ), 2000.

The Jewish Century, Princeton University Press (Princeton, NJ), 2004.

The House of Government: A Saga of the Russian Revolution, Princeton University Press (Princeton, NJ), 2017.

Contributor to books and to journals.

■ Sidelights

Russian-born American historian Yuri Slezkine is the Jane K. Sather Professor of History at the University of California, Berkeley. He is the author or editor of a number of books dealing with Russian history and with the history of the Jews. Among these are *Arctic Mirrors: Russia and the Small Peoples of the North*, from 1994, *In the Shadow of the Revolution: Life Stories of Russian Women from 1917 to the Second World War*, coedited with Sheila Fitzpatrick, *The Jewish Century*, winner of multiple awards, including the National Jewish Book Award, and the 2017 study *The House of Government: A Saga of the Russian Revolution.*

Arctic Mirrors and *In the Shadow of Revolution*

In *Arctic Mirrors,* Slezkine examines the complex relationship between the twenty-six indigenous groups that inhabit the Arctic tundra and subarctic regions with the people of Russia, who first entered and began colonizing the region in the eleventh century. Slezkine looks at how Russians view these peoples, who survive by fishing, hunting, trapping, and herding reindeer. To that end, he inspects both historical documents and popular fiction, and he closely examines their fate during the Stalinist era when many of what the Russians termed "savage" people were transformed into industrial laborers. Reviewing *Arctic Mirrors* in *Booklist,* Joe Collins felt that the author's "descriptions of the trials of the northern Russians help make this book an invaluable look at the people the totalitarian Soviets forgot."

In the Shadow of Revolution is a collection of life stories of Russian women in the first half of the twentieth century that gathers recollections and memoirs of women of all classes—from aristocrats to milkmaids. These narratives are organized chronologically around important events of the time, including the 1917 Revolution, the ensuing Civil War of 1918-20; the collectivization of the 1920s, and the Stalinist Great Terror of the 1930s. "These 36 accounts explore the schism that split Russian society for a century: Us and Them, Red and White, Bolshevik and Bourgeois," according to a *Russian Life* contributor.

The Jewish Century

In his award-winning study *The Jewish Century,* Slezkine argues that the Modern Age is really the Jewish Age, and that we are all metaphorically Jews. His central thesis is a division of the humanity into two groups: Apollonians, who are the food-producing majority, and Mercurians, the "service nomads," as anthropologist term them—free agents who specialize in the delivery of goods and services. The Mercurians—Jews and Armenians among others—became the entrepreneurial minorities, but by the modern age, their model of urban, literate, mobile, and occupationally flexible characteristics has become the standard, and Apollonians are now becoming Mercurians. The Jews, according to Slezkine, are the most successful of the Mercurians, and thus they are the model moderns. Slezkine looks at the fortunes of Russian Jews who have immigrated to America and Palestine and at those who remained in Russia. The author further argues that both Bolshevism and American capitalism and liberalism were deeply affected by the Jewish exodus.

Commentary reviewer Hillel Halkin had a varied assessment of *The Jewish Century,* observing: "This is the problem with Slezkine's categories. 'Apollonianism' and 'Mercurianism' may explain many things, but when used as all-purpose historical tools they turn out, like all tools when applied to tasks for which they are not precisely fitted, a very roughly finished product. . . . *The Jewish Century* is, on its own terms, a successfully provocative work, but only because Yuri Slezkine's visit to Jewish history has been a brief one. Had he stayed any longer, he would have rightly begun to feel confused himself." A similar nuanced evaluation came from *Books & Culture* writer Jonathan Kahn, who commented: "Trapped within Yuri Slezkine's *The Jewish Century,* struggling to free itself from Slezkine's ideological thesis, is a poignant history of Russia's Jews. It is a history of desire—of 19th-century Jews seeking to free themselves of the Jewishness of the Pale of Settlement by exulting in the Russia of Tolstoy and Chekov; of zealous Jewish commitment to and success within the early Soviet Revolution." However, in the end, Kahn felt that the author does not do the "hard and necessary work . . . [of] spend[ing] time in specific historic contexts, gathering and analyzing evidence of what worked and what didn't." Kahn added: "He gives us myth instead."

Higher praise was offered by *New Leader* reviewer Gene Sosin, who noted: "When Slezkine focuses on the transformation of Jewish life in pre-revolutionary Russia and the Soviet Union, where most of Europe's Jews lived, his book gains in interest and momentum. Although the subject is familiar, he gives it a fresh perspective." A *Publishers Weekly* contributor also had a positive assessment, noting: "Slezkine's work is one of the most innovative and intellectually stimulating books in Jewish studies in years."

The House of Government

In his narrative history *The House of Government,* Slezkine tells the story of the Russian Revolution in a new manner—through the true stories of the top Communist officials and their families who lived in a huge Moscow apartment building called the House of Government, located across the Moscow River from the Kremlin. This complex included over five hundred furnished apartments.

Additionally, there were a number of public spaces, including a library, movie theater, shooting range, and tennis court. The author employs accounts from diaries, letters, and interviews to tell the story of 800 of these roughly 2,700 residents who were ultimately evicted from the House of Government during Stalin's purges and led to prisons or to death.

Library Journal contributor Laurie Linger Skinner termed *The House of Government* a "comprehensive work of scholarship and storytelling," and further noted: "Throughout the book, first-person entries taken from diaries, letters and memoirs illuminate daily life and private thoughts." Similarly, a *Publishers Weekly* reviewer commented, "Slezkine aggregates mountains of detail for an enthralling account of the rise and fall of the revolutionary generation." Writing in *Foreign Affairs*, Robert Legvold also had praise, dubbing the work an "epic narrative" and adding: "The book's depth (not to mention its length) invites the reader to luxuriate in it, chapter by chapter, rather than simply plowing through." *New York Times Book Review* critic Marci Short likewise observed: "Slezkine's *The House of Government* is a history of the Soviet project as experienced by those who carried it out." Short added: "The chapters on the Stalinist Terror are the most vivid. Overall, Slezkine's writing is sharp, fresh, sometimes playful." *New York Review of Books Online* writer Benjamin Nathans was also impressed with the work, observing: "Constructed on what feels like a lifetime of research and reflection, *The House of Government* offers a virtuosic weaving of novelistic storytelling, social anthropology, intellectual history, and literary criticism. . . . Slezkine . . . has caught an extraordinary set of lives in this book. Few historians, dead or alive, have managed to combine so spectacularly the gifts of storyteller and scholar."

■ **Biographical and Critical Sources**

PERIODICALS

Booklist, October 15, 1994, Joe Collins, review of *Arctic Mirrors: Russia and the Small Peoples of the North*, p. 399.

Books & Culture, July-August, 2005, Jonathon Kahn, review of *The Jewish Century*, p. 40.

Commentary, December, 2005, Hillel Halkin, review of *The Jewish Century*, p. 73.

Foreign Affairs, November-December, 2017, Robert Legvold, review of *The House of Government: A Saga of the Russian Revolution*, p. 164.

Library Journal, July 1, 2017, Laurie Linger Skinner, review of *The House of Government*, p. 88.

New Leader, September-October, 2004, Gene Sosin, review of *The Jewish Century*, p. 24.

Publishers Weekly, June 21, 2004, review of *The Jewish Century*, p. 49; May 22, 2017, review of *The House of Government*, p. 82.

Reason, November, 2017, Matthew Harwood, "The Insatiable Utopia: The Soviet Elite Who Built a 'Dictatorship of the Proletariat' and Paid with Their Lives," p. 74.

Russian Life, March, 2001, review of *In the Shadow of Revolution: Life Stories of Russian Women from 1917 to the Second World War*, p. 60.

ONLINE

Commentary Online, https://www.commentary magazine.com/ (December 1, 2005), Hillel Halkin, review of *The Jewish Century*.

E and T, https://eandt.theiet.org/ (October 16, 2017), Vitali Vitaliev, review of *The House of Government*.

Financial Times Online, https://www.ft.com/ (August 11, 2017), David Priestland, review of *The House of Government*.

Guardian Online, https://www.theguardian.com/ (December 15, 2017), Owen Hatherley, review of *The House of Government*.

London Review of Books Online, https://www.lrb.co.uk/ (March 1, 2005), Sheila Fitzpatrick, review of *The Jewish Century*; (July 1, 2017), Sheila Fitzpatrick, review of *The House of Government*.

Los Angeles Review of Books, https://lareviewofbooks.org/ (January 9, 2018), "Yuri Slezkine."

New York Review of Books Online, http://www.nybooks.com/ (November 23, 2017), Benjamin Nathans, review of *The House of Government*.

New York Times Book Review Online, https://www.nytimes.com/ (August 18, 2017), Marci Shore, review of *The House of Government*.

Tablet, https://www.londonreviewbookshop.co.uk/ (October 10, 2017), David Mikics, review of *The House of Government*.

Times Literary Supplement Online, https://www.the-tls.co.uk/ (December 19, 2017), Stephen Lovell, review of *The House of Government*.

University of California, Berkeley, Department of History Website, http://history.berkeley.edu/ (January 9, 2018), "Yuri Slezkine."*

Mark Smith

- ## Personal

Male. *Hobbies and other interests:* Adventure nonfiction.

- ## Addresses

Home—Victoria, Australia.

- ## Career

Writer and outdoor educator.

- ## Writings

The Road to Winter, Text Publishing (Melbourne, Victoria, Australia), 2016.

- ## Sidelights

Before Mark Smith published his debut book, he worked in the field of outdoor education. He stated in an interview featured on the *My Best Friends Are Books* website that part of his inspiration for the book came from his career, which inspired an interest in nonfiction adventure stories. He has also had his fiction work featured in several publications.

The Road to Winter is set in a postapocalyptic version of Australia that has yet to recover from its devastation. The protagonist of the novel is a boy by the name of Finn. At just fifteen years of age, he has been forced to try to survive entirely alone.

Finn's only guardian, his father, perished prior to the events of the novel; now Finn must rely on his father's old tools and teachings in order to carve out any decent chance of making it in such a harsh environment. The world Finn lives in has been ravaged by a virus that has wiped out a sizeable percentage of the world's populace. Everyone Finn has ever known and loved is gone, wiped out either by illness or the aftermath of it.

However, Finn soon finds himself with much more to deal with than simply staying alive. He chances upon a young girl named Rose, who has been caught up in an even deadlier situation. She has just escaped being captured by a criminal group and must now rely on Finn to help her reunite with her sister. However, Rose is incapacitated, meaning Finn has to go solo in his quest and must avoid great dangers to assist Rose. A *Publishers Weekly* contributor remarked: "It's a solid debut . . . and future installments may yet find ways to further establish its identity." A writer in *Kirkus Reviews* called *The Road to Winter* "a breakout new series full of romance, danger, and a surprisingly engaging world." On the *Readings.com.au* website, Holly Harper commented: "That's what I liked best about this novel—where most post-apocalyptic YA skews towards the fantastical and pits heroes against zombies and the like, this scenario is terrifyingly real." A reviewer on *The-bookkat . . . breathing books* blog said: "Smith shows sympathy and concern for those who are marginalised—in this case asylum seekers and females in general—and I really like that." Simon McDonald, writing on the self-titled *Simon McDonald* blog, stated: "*The Road to Winter* is great." He went on to call it a "fast-paced, relentless, poignant" story.

■ Biographical and Critical Sources

PERIODICALS

Kirkus Reviews, March 15, 2017, review of *The Road to Winter.*

Publishers Weekly, May 1, 2017, review of *The Road to Winter,* p. 60.

ONLINE

My Best Friends Are Books, https://bestfriendsarebooks.com/ (July 11, 2016), "Interview with Mark Smith about *The Road to Winter.*"

Readings.com.au, https://www.readings.com.au/ (June 27, 2016), Holly Harper, review of *The Road to Winter.*

Simon McDonald, https://writtenbysime.com/ (May 25, 2016), Simon McDonald, review of *The Road to Winter.*

Thebookkat . . . breathing books, https://thebookkat.com/ (September 7, 2016), review of *The Road to Winter.**

Stephen Kennedy Smith

■ Personal

Son of Stephen Edward and Jean Kennedy Smith. *Education:* Harvard University, B.A., 1979; Columbia University, J.D., 1984; Harvard Graduate School of Education, Ed.M., 1991. *Politics:* Democrat.

■ Addresses

Home—New York, NY.

■ Career

Investor and entrepreneur. Principal, Park Agency—Joseph P. Kennedy Enterprises, New York, NY; member of board, John F. Kennedy Library and Joseph P Kennedy Foundation; partner, Kennedy Smith Sammaweera; partner, Emlink; U.S. CEO, Valcent Technology. Cofounder and vice president, World Leadership Alliance. Former staff member, Senate Judiciary and Foreign Relations committees; deputy campaign manager, Senator Edward Kennedy presidential and senatorial campaigns; youth coordinator, campaign of Mario Cuomo; member of New England steering committee, Obama presidential campaign. Lecturer, Sloan School of Management; fellow, Connection Science Group, MIT; member of advisory board, INCAE Business School. Consultant, Conflict Management Group, Organization of African Unity, World Bank, IDB, and others.

■ Awards, Honors

Danforth Award for excellence in teaching, Harvard University (three times).

■ Writings

(Editor, with Douglas Brinkley) *JFK: A Vision for America in Words and Pictures,* Harper (New York, NY), 2017.

■ Sidelights

Stephen Kennedy Smith is the older son of Jean Kennedy Smith, the youngest sibling of President John Fitzgerald Kennedy, Senator and Attorney General Robert F. Kennedy, and Senator Ted Kennedy. Smith's father, Stephen Edward Smith, was part of President Kennedy's staff and served as the business manager of the Kennedy fortune—a tradition that the younger Smith continues as a principal with the Park Agency—Joseph P. Kennedy Enterprises. "He has also served on the board of the John F. Kennedy Library, the Robert F. Kennedy Memorial, and the Congress on New Urbanism and the Northeastern University School of Public Policy," reported a contributor to the *Abana* website. "He has served on the staff of the Senate Judiciary and Foreign Relations Committees," noted a writer for the HarperCollins Speakers Bureau website, who added that "Smith was Deputy Campaign Manager for Senator Edward Kennedy during his Presidential and Senatorial campaigns, Youth Coordinator for the campaign of Mario Cuomo, served on the New England Steering Committee for the Obama presidential campaign, and continues to be active in Democratic politics." Currently, said a contributor to the ICV Group website, "Stephen is . . . a lecturer at the Sloan School of Management in the visionary investing program, as well as a fellow at the Connection Science Group."

Smith is the coeditor, along with Rice University professor of history Douglas Brinkley, of *JFK: A Vision for America in Words and Pictures*—a profusely illustrated collection of President Kennedy's speeches, combined with essays about his impact and his legacy from contemporary world leaders, released to commemorate the centennial of his birth. Kennedy, whose term in office was cut short by his assassination in November 1963, became a symbol of an expansive postwar America, in which the ideals of the founders of the republic could finally be realized. "JFK, with his expansive intellect and charm," stated Dan Kaplan in *Booklist*, "captured Americas imagination and portended the possibilities of a new era." His idealism and skill as a negotiator, expressed in diplomatic successes like the end of the Cuban Missile Crisis in 1962 and the 1963 Nuclear Test Ban Treaty that followed, helped reduce tensions during one of the most dangerous stages of the Cold War. "Ultimately, the collection illustrates Kennedy's wide-ranging knowledge and curiosity, sense of the importance of public service and international cooperation, belief in religious diversity, commitment to deliberate action and negotiation, respect for the position of the presidency, love of the country, and rich understanding and appreciation of its history," concluded Lily Geismer in the *Washington Post Book World*. "Thus, if anything, *JFK* reminds us to heed Kennedy's warning that 'if we don't know anything about our past, then we don't really have any base from which to move in the days ahead.'"

In some ways, critics stated, *JFK* serves as a celebration of Kennedy's life and work, which were cut short by his assassination. The "celebratory volume," wrote William D. Pederson in *Library Journal*, "is . . . a useful compendium and reference tool for anyone interested in learning more about his presidency." Smith and Brinkley's work "is a book to spend quality time digesting," said a reviewer for *Bluejayblog*. "For those of us who lived during the time of Kennedy, the book is more than a nostalgia trip; it's an important record of the times. For people born after the Kennedy years, *JFK* provides an in-depth history of the nation in the middle of the 20th century. This is a book to be treasured." "Amid the stream of JFK books," declared a *Kirkus Reviews* contributor, ". . . this work should emerge as one of the most complete and useful."

■ Biographical and Critical Sources

PERIODICALS

Booklist, April 15, 2017, Dan Kaplan, review of *JFK: A Vision for America in Words and Pictures*, p. 10.

Kirkus Reviews, March 15, 2017, review of *JFK*.

Library Journal, April 1, 2017, "JFK in Memory: Revisiting the 35th U.S. President, in Time for the Centennial of His Birth." p. 99.

Washington Post Book World, May 8, 2017, Lily Geismer, "Assessing the Substance of Kennedy's Presidency."

ONLINE

Abana, https://www.abana.co/ (February 21, 2018), author profile.

Bloomberg, https://www.bloomberg.com/ (February 21, 2018), "Company Overview of K.S.S. Realty Partners, Inc."

Bluejayblog, https://bluejayblog.wordpress.com/ (June 3, 2017), review of *JFK*.

HarperCollins Speakers Bureau Website, http://www.harpercollinsspeakersbureau.com/ (February 21, 2018), author profile.

ICV Group Website, http://www.icvgroup.org/ (February 21, 2018), author profile.*

Emma Smith-Stevens

1982-

■ Personal

Born May 10, 1982; married. *Education:* Bard College, B.A.; University of Florida, M.F.A.

■ Addresses

Home—NY.

■ Career

Author and educator. Teacher of fiction workshops, literature, and composition, University of Florida, and Santa Fe College, Gainesville, FL, and Bard College Prison Initiative. Also worked as server at pancake house in Delray Beach, FL, gift-wrapper in Boca Raton, FL, personal assistant in Los Angeles, CA, and scriptwriter for virtual patients used by nursing students.

■ Writings

The Australian, Dzanc Books (Ann Arbor, MI), 2017.

Also author of *Greyhounds* (short-story collection). Contributor to anthologies, including *Not That Bad: Dispatches from Rape Culture*, edited by Roxane Gay, HarperCollins (New York, NY), 2018; and *Against Death*, edited by Elee Kraljii Gardiner, Anvil Press. Contributor to periodicals, including *BOMB, Conjunctions, Day One, Hobart, Joyland, Literary Hub, Lucky Peach, Subtropics*, and *Wigleaf*.

■ Sidelights

Emma Smith-Stevens is the author of *The Australian*, a novel based a real character she encountered in New York City when she was a drug-addicted teenager. "The protagonist of my novel *The Australian*, who is only ever referred to as 'the Australian,' was inspired by a man I knew for one day—mid-30s, savagely handsome, verbose, and Australian, of course—when I was nineteen," Smith-Stevens stated in an interview appearing on the blog *Largehearted Boy*. "He talked, delivering a hyper-monologue—the details of his life like projectiles that, to this day, remain lodged in my mind. He'd put himself through university in Melbourne by dressing as Superman and posing for tourist photos. . . . At twenty-three he'd moved to New York to work on Wall Street as a day trader and was now a venture capitalist." Smith-Stevens left the Australian's apartment that afternoon and never saw the man again, but he left a strong impression on her. After reading the self-help book he gave her, she sought help for her addiction. "After that encounter he became a memory," the author declared in *Fiction Advocate*, "which years later became a brief character sketch, which was subsequently forgotten, and then found and read and built upon until it was a long Microsoft Word document, which was then edited and edited and copyedited—and now it's a novel! So, I owe that fellow—big time." "In retrospect and from a certain angle," Smith-Stevens concluded in *Largehearted Boy*, "that man—the real Australian, as I think of him now—saved my life."

The character in the novel *The Australian* is a man caught between the expectations he has had for his life and the realities of his situation. "Estranged from his mother in Melbourne and suffering from the absence of the adventurer father he never met," wrote a *Kirkus Reviews* contributor, "the Australian has always been unsure of himself." "On the streets of Melbourne, the Australian parades around dressed as Superman, paying his way through university by posing for photos," Smith-

Stevens explained in an excerpt from the novel appearing in *BOMB*. "He is smart—smart enough to know when effort is absolutely required and when he can fake it—and he is handsome, with chiseled abdominal muscles underneath the chiseled abdominal muscles of his costume. He smiles widely, his teeth luminous, his canines threatening. All his life, he has been indiscriminate with his enthusiasm, invincible within the hedonistic splendor of the present moment, like some kind of inverted Buddha." "After graduation, the Australian moves to New York to work on Wall Street," Smith-Stevens continued. "After six months of trying to reckon with his haughty overseer, he quits the brokerage firm and goes to work for himself. He takes the money he has recently inherited from his estranged father . . . and triples it within eight months through some risky and uncalculated investments. The Australian knows he has struck upon the kind of luck that can turn on you in a heartbeat." "Smith-Stevens proves that the picaresque will never die, not as long as there are characters like her titular, never-named fellow," said Bethanne Patrick in *Literary Hub*. "It's a bit like reading a loose biography of Jemaine from *Flight of the Conchords*, if Jemaine were Australian instead of from New Zealand and an aimless git instead of a musician git, but the tone is the same: Droll, quick, and occasionally cruel."

After making a small fortune in investments, the Australian enters into a marriage with an American woman, opens a club that enjoys a brief success, and becomes a father. When he learns that his mother is suffering from a fatal disease, however, he feels compelled to see her again. "As the Australian returns to his homeland seeking hope, redemption, and happiness," concluded a *Publishers Weekly* reviewer, "readers are treated to a captivating . . . journey."

■ Biographical and Critical Sources

PERIODICALS

Kirkus Reviews, March 15, 2017, review of *The Australian.*
Publishers Weekly, May 1, 2017, review of *The Australian.*

ONLINE

BOMB, https://bombmagazine.org/ (May 5, 2017), "From *The Australian* by Emma Smith-Stevens."
Emma Smith-Stevens Website, http://emmasmith stevens.com (February 21, 2018), author profile.
Fiction Advocate, http://fictionadvocate.com/ (May 16, 2017), author interview.
Largehearted Boy, http://www.largeheartedboy.com/ (May 24, 2017), author interview; review of *The Australian.*
Literary Hub, https://lithub.com/ (June 12, 2017), Bethanne Patrick, "5 Books You May Have Missed This May."*

Wesley Snipes

1962-

■ **Also Known As**

Wesley Trent Snipes

■ **Personal**

Born July 31, 1962, in Orlando, FL; son of Wesley Rudolph and Maryann Snipes; married April Dubois, 1985 (divorced, 1990), married Nakyung "Nikki" Park, 2003; children: five. *Education:* Attended State University of New York at Purchase and Southwest College, Los Angeles. *Hobbies and other interests:* Martial arts (holds a 5th dan black belt in Shotokan karate and a 2nd dan black belt in hapkido).

■ **Career**

Actor, film producer, entrepreneur, and writer. Amen-Ra Films (a film and television production company) and Black Dot Media (its subsidiary), founder. Royal Guard of Amen-Ra (a security and bodyguard company), cofounder, late 1990s.

Actor in more than seventy films, including *Wildcats*, 1986; *Streets of Gold*, 1987; *Mo' Better Blues*, 1990; *New Jack City*, 1991; *Jungle Fever*, 1991; *White Men Can't Jump*, 1992; *Waterdance*, 1992; *Passenger 57*, 1992; *Demolition Man*, 1993; *Sugar Hill*, 1994; *Waiting to Exhale*, 1995; *To Wong Foo, Thanks for Everything! Julie Newmar*, 1995; *Blade*, 1998; *Blade II*, 2002; *Blade: Trinity*, 2004; *Brooklyn's Finest*, 2009; *Gallowwalkers*, 2012; *The Expendables 3*, 2014; and *Armed Response*, 2017.

Actor in television shows, including *Miami Vice*, *Vietnam War Story*, *A Man Called Halk*, *The Days and Nights of Molly Dodd*, and *The Bernie Mac Show*.

■ **Awards, Honors**

Best Actor Volpi Cup, Venice Film Festival, 1997; Image Award, outstanding lead actor in a television movie or mini-series, for *America's Dream*; CableACE Award, best actor in a dramatic series, for *Vietnam War Story*; received a star on the Hollywood Walk of Fame.

■ **Writings**

(With Ray Norman) *Talon of God*, Harper Voyager (New York, NY), 2017.

■ **Sidelights**

Wesley Snipes is a well-known actor, film producer, and action film star. He has appeared in more than seventy films and had major or lead roles in films such as *Passenger 57*, *Demolition Man*, *New Jack City*, *Jungle Fever*, *White Men Can't Jump*, and *Waiting to Exhale*. In *To Wong Fu, Thanks for Everything! Julie Newmar*, Snipes played a character that was definitely against type: Noxeema Jackson, a drag queen.

Snipes played the title character of Blade in a trilogy of movies featuring that Marvel Comics character, a half-vampire, half-human who becomes a vampire hunter and protects the human race against these creatures of the night. In an interview with Dan Schawbel in *Forbes*, Snipes stated, "I truly enjoyed playing the character of Blade as I felt he was a complicated, passion-driven and deeply introspective individual caught between two worlds—one light, the other dark—who was on a mission for good, yet was consumed with finding the meaning of his own existence in a world fraught with danger, intrigue and uncertainty."

Snipes is an entrepreneur, the cofounder of the film and television production company Amen-Ra Films and its subsidiary Black Dot Media. He was also the cofounder of the Royal Guard of Amen-Ra, a security and bodyguard company that provided elite protection services for celebrities and other high-end clients.

In addition to his work in film, Snipes is also a noted martial artist who has trained in multiple fighting styles since the age of twelve, earning distinctions such as a fifth-degree black belt in Shotokan karate and a second-degree black belt in hapkido. Because of his experience in martial arts, he often serves as fight coordinator on films.

With *Talon of God*, Snipes adds novelist to his list of accomplishments. The novel, written with Ray Norman, is an action-based story very much in line with Snipes's roles in Blade and other high-energy films. It is also a very spiritual story, boosted by a war between literal angels and demons unfolding on the streets of Chicago.

The novel's protagonist, Lauryn Jefferson, is the daughter of a minister. She has become a doctor and devoted her life to medicine rather than pursuing a religious life. When she is attacked in the emergency room one night, she realizes that the troubled veteran who assaulted her is under the influence of a drug that transforms humans into supernatural monsters. She is saved by the mysterious Talon Hunter, a sword-wielding super-powered protector who is a messenger of God. Teaming up with her ex-boyfriend, police officer Will Tannenbaum, Lauryn joins Talon in a search for those responsible for turning people into monsters in anticipation of a city-wide demon possession. At the same time, Lauryn seems to have a higher calling that she will ascend to, with Talon's help.

Wesley Baines, writing on the website *Beliefnet*, commented: "*Talon of God* is a fun, snappy read that doesn't shy away from the darkness. Snipes' story is one that effortlessly weaves spirituality into action and adventure that anyone can enjoy, regardless of belief. This isn't 'Christian fiction.' It's fiction that draws from Christianity to tell an awesome story, bringing readers face-to-face with terrifying evil."

In *Kirkus Reviews*, a writer called *Talon of God* an "entertaining thriller with enough swordplay, religious prophecy, and demonic threats to entertain readers across lots of different genres." The authors "bring a cinematic flair to the proceedings," observed a *Publishers Weekly* writer. A reviewer in *USA Today* remarked, "Old-school fans of *Passenger 57* and *Demolition Man* will appreciate that Snipes has just as much punch with a keyboard as with his fists, and the realm of urban fantasy has an impressive new disciple."

■ Biographical and Critical Sources

PERIODICALS

Forbes, November 27, 2017, Dan Schawbel, "Wesley Snipes: How He Built a Career as an Actor, Entrepreneur, and Novelist," interview with Wesley Snipes.

Kirkus Reviews, May 15, 2017, review of *Talon of God*.

National Post, August 3, 2017, "Q&A: Wesley Snipes on How *Blade* Films Influenced His Debut Novel *Talon of God*."

Publishers Weekly, May 8, 2017, review of *Talon of God*, p. 42.

USA Today, July 25, 2017, "Snipes Fights Evil with a Pen in *Talon of God*," review of *Talon of God*, p. 3D.

ONLINE

Beliefnet, http://www.beliefnet.com/ (February 19, 2018), Wesley Baines, "The Faith and Fiction of Wesley Snipes," interview with Wesley Snipes and Ray Norman.

Christian Post, http://www.christianpost.com/ (July 27, 2017), Jeannie Law, "Wesley Snipes Writes Spiritual Thriller *Talon of God* on Demons Influencing People's Behavior."

Deadline, http://www.deadline.com/ (December 8, 2016), Greg Evans, "Wesley Snipes's Debut Novel Lands at HarperCollins Imprint for 2017," profile of Wesley Snipes.

Talon of God Website, http://www.talonofgod.com (February 19, 2018).

USA Today Online, https://www.usatoday.com (July 24, 2017), Brian Truitt, "Wesley Snipes Fights Evil with His Pen in *Talon of God*," review of *Talon of God*.*

Jimmy Soni

■ Personal

Born in Toulouse, France. *Education:* Graduated from Duke University, 2007.

■ Career

Writer, editor, public speaker. Managing editor, *Huffington Post,* 2012-14. Formerly worked as editor at *New York Observer* and *Washington Examiner,* as campaign aide to Missouri Governor Eric Greitens, strategy consultant, McKinsey and Company, and as speech writer, Office of the Mayor of the District of Columbia. Former member of steering committee, the Mission Continues. Featured TEDx speaker, Duke University, 2012.

■ Awards, Honors

Young Influentials list citation, *AdWeek,* 2012; People to Watch list citation, MinMedia, 2012; 30 under 30 Media list citation, *Forbes,* 2013; 40 under 40 list citation, Crain's Communications New York, 2013; Excellence in Online Media citation, Anokhi, 2013; Men of Vogue list citation, *Vogue India,* 2013; Most Poachable Tech Talent list citation, *Betabeat,* 2014; Lords of the Viral Internet citation, *Politico,* 2014.

■ Writings

(With Rob Goodman) *Rome's Last Citizen: The Life and Legacy of Cato, Mortal Enemy of Caesar,* Thomas Dunne Books (New York, NY), 2012.
(With Rob Goodman) *A Mind at Play: How Claude Shannon Invented the Information Age,* Simon & Schuster (New York, NY), 2017.

Contributor to periodicals and media outlets, including *AdWeek, Atlantic, Business Insider,* CNN, *Huffington Post, Politico,* and *Slate.*

■ Sidelights

Jimmy Soni was celebrated as one of the leading young technology gurus of the second decade of the twenty-first century following his graduation from Duke University in 2007. His career took off in 2012, when he was hired to be the new managing editor of the online magazine founded by Ariana Huffington, the *Huffington Post.* During his tenure there, Soni was cited by organizations ranging from Crain's to *Forbes* to *Vogue India* as a rising star. His varied interests were recognized by his books, cowritten with fellow Duke University graduate Rob Goodman: a biography of the influential Roman statesman and Stoic philosopher of the first-century BCE Cato the Younger, in *Rome's Last Citizen: The Life and Legacy of Cato, Mortal Enemy of Caesar,* and *A Mind at Play: How Claude Shannon Invented the Information Age.* Soni's reputation as a leader in electronic media led him to explore the life of Shannon, a professor at Massachusetts Institute of Technology whose "noteworthy discoveries," stated a *Publishers Weekly* reviewer, "include a way to rationally design circuits using Boolean algebra, and information theory, which understands communications as bits."

Soni's tenure at the *Huffington Post* was cut short by allegations that he had sexually harassed female colleagues. The women were known as fellows, but they were under his supervision and were essentially interns. "In early April [2014]," stated Danny Wicentowski in the *Riverfront Times,* "two fellows, who had not dated or slept with Soni (but were friends with fellows who had), approached their section editor about Soni's entreaties. He had created an atmosphere, they said, in which many felt that if they didn't flirt with Soni, their chances of landing a full-time position would suffer." "One month later, in May 2014, the *Huffington Post* announced that Soni was leaving his post" to take up a new position in his parents' native India, Wicentowski continued. "Announcing his appointment to the position," wrote Jeremy Barr in *Politico*, "Huffington said, 'In his 9 months with *HuffPost*, Jimmy has proven himself to be a man of many talents.'"

Following his exit from the *Huffington Post*, Soni moved on to work for the gubernatorial campaign of Eric Greitens, a former Navy SEAL who ran a successful campaign to become governor of Missouri. According to Wicentowski, Soni and Grietens had a professional relationship stretching back to 2011, and Soni had served on the steering committee of The Mission Continues, which provides recent veterans with the opportunity to use the skills they learned in the military to help local communities.

In 2012, the same year he was hired by the *Huffington Post*, Soni and Goodman released their biography of Cato, *Rome's Last Citizen*. Cato was best known for his opposition to Julius Caesar in the Roman Senate—he committed suicide rather than serve Caesar after the latter's victory in the Roman civil war—but he was also an influential proponent of the philosophy of Stoicism. The philosophy gained ground in first-century Rome and was later adopted by many more modern figures, like George Washington and Thomas Jefferson, who admired its principles. "Cato was my gateway drug into stoicism," Soni reported in an interview appearing in the *Daily Stoic*. The philosophy emphasizes the importance of living a balanced life, recognizing that fretting over the things one cannot control is counterproductive. "There's a scene from Homer's *The Odyssey* that is arguably the original 'life hack': the story of Odysseus lashing himself to his ship's mast to avoid the temptation of the Sirens' song," he explained in an interview with Andy Orin appearing on *LifeHacker*. "A whole body of research exists now that validates the story's underlying lesson, which is that our willpower is substantially more limited than we think it is—but that we can engineer circumstances that determine our behavior. I try to apply that concept—'lashing yourself to the mast'— whenever I can. Think about the binding structures you can build to force yourself to do the things you avoid."

Cato's example led Soni to begin practicing Stoicism himself. "I'd always been a fan of Roman history, particularly the history of the late Republic," Soni said in his *Daily Stoic* interview. "There's a lot of drama in that period, and a lot of fascinating figures. People, for instance, like Julius Caesar and Cicero, who were giants of their day. I had read a few biographies of figures from that time, and I went on Amazon to buy a biography of Cato, just assuming, because he was who he was, that there would be one on offer. When I didn't find one, I called up a friend of mine." Soni comes "from the world of journalism," declared Ann Pedtke in the *Historical Novel Society*, ". . . and thus write[s] with a verve not always found in academic biographies." "The authors succeed brilliantly," concluded a *Kirkus Reviews* contributor, "in bringing this fascinating statesman to life."

■ Biographical and Critical Sources

PERIODICALS

Financial Times, July 20, 2017, review of *A Mind at Play: How Claude Shannon Invented the Information Age.*

Journal of Social, Political and Economic Studies, fall, 2013, Dwight D. Murphey, review of *Rome's Last Citizen: The Life and Legacy of Cato, Mortal Enemy of Caesar*, p. 361.

Kirkus Reviews, September 1, 2012, review of *Rome's Last Citizen*; May 15, 2017, review of *A Mind at Play.*

Library Journal, September 1, 2012, Evan M. Anderson, review of *Rome's Last Citizen*, p. 108.

Publishers Weekly, July 9, 2012, review of *Rome's Last Citizen*, p. 50; May 1, 2017, review of *A Mind at Play*, p. 50.

Washington Times, July 16, 2017, Gary Anderson, "A Mind at Play: The Mathematical Prodigy Who Gave the World 'Bits.'"

ONLINE

Armchair General, http://www.armchairgeneral. com/ (January 7, 2013), Adam Koeth, review of *Rome's Last Citizen.*

Daily Stoic, https://dailystoic.com/ (February 14, 2018), "The Life and Legacy of Cato: An Interview with Author Jimmy Soni."

Historical Novel Society, https://historicalnovel society.org/ (November 1, 2012), Ann Pedtke, review of *Rome's Last Citizen.*

Jimmy Soni Website, http://jimmysoni.com (February 14, 2018), author profile.

Lifehacker, https://lifehacker.com/ (April 23, 2014), Andy Orin, "How I Work: Jimmy Soni, Managing Editor of the *Huffington Post.*"

New American, https://www.thenewamerican.com/ (October 18, 2012), Joe Wolverton II, review of *Rome's Last Citizen.*

Politico, https://www.politico.com/ (May 21, 2014), Jeremy Barr, "HuffPost M.E. Jimmy Soni Transfers to India."

Poynter, https://www.poynter.org/ (May 22, 2014), Andrew Beaujon, "HuffPost Names New Managing Editor as Jimmy Soni Moves to India."

Quantum Times, http://thequantumtimes.org/ (October 6, 2017), Ian Durham, review of *A Mind at Play.*

Riverfront Times, https://www.riverfronttimes.com/ (November 16, 2017), Danny Wicentowski, "Governor's Adviser Jimmy Soni Is Again Exhibit A in Bombshell Sex Harassment Report."*

Laura Spinney

◾ Personal

Female.

◾ Addresses

Home—Paris, France; London, England.

◾ Career

Author, science writer, and journalist.

◾ Writings

The Doctor, Methuen (London, England), 2001.
Pale Rider: The Spanish Flu of 1918 and How It Changed the World, Public Affairs (New York, NY), 2017.

◾ Sidelights

Science writer Laura Spinney is the author of the history *Pale Rider: The Spanish Flu of 1918 and How It Changed the World*, which tells the story of the first pandemic of the twentieth century. "Coolly, crisply and with a consistently sharp eye for the telling anecdote," reported John Preston, writing in the *Daily Mail*, "Spinney shows how flu has been around in one guise or another since the 16th century—the word 'influenza' was coined by the Italians who attributed the disease to the influence of the stars." "The estimated number of deaths resulting from [the 1918-20] . . . illness," stated *Booklist* reviewer Tony Miksanek, "ranges between fifty and one hundred million people." According

to Gavin Francis in the *London Review of Books*, "Laura Spinney's book attempts to collate what is known about the pandemic, and takes a stab at examining its legacy: 'The flu resculpted human populations more radically than anything since the Black Death,' she writes. 'It influenced the course of the First World War and, arguably, contributed to the second. It pushed India closer to independence, South Africa closer to apartheid, and Switzerland to the brink of civil war. It ushered in universal healthcare and alternative medicine, our love of fresh air and our passion for sport.'" "It is curious that an event that shaped the world as much as, perhaps arguably more, than the First World War, has been so neglected by history," stated a reviewer for *Librarian on Parade*. "This is a welcome addition to a thin field, and serves as a fine overview."

One of Spinney's major points in *Pale Rider* is that the Spanish flu has been largely ignored in the history of the early twentieth century. "Spinney believes the pandemic has been forgotten by most of us partly because so many deaths occurred outside Europe and North America," explained Peter Carty in a review in the *Spectator*. "Accordingly, she delves into the unfolding of the tragedy around the globe, looking at Brazil, China, Iran, India and Russia. There is fascinating detail of the behaviour of diverse populaces in extremis. In a desperate attempt to stem the disease's onslaughts, the residents of Odessa staged a 'black wedding'—the ancient Jewish *shvartze khasene* ritual." "During spring and summer, it behaved like the usual flu," explained a *Kirkus Reviews* contributor, "but in fall 1918, it turned deadly and spread across the world, killing 2.5 to 10 percent of victims." "Medical science helped only modestly," reported a *Publishers Weekly* reviewer, "as political considerations (including wartime censorship), tradition, and racism all trumped safeguards." "She also demonstrates," said Preston, "how Spanish flu cast a long, dark shadow over the 20th century. In its wake, the idea of quarantining people who were thought to pose a danger to society gained enormous popularity—thus paving the way, albeit indirectly, for the Nazi concentration camps. Even now the consequences are with us."

Although it appears that the first cases of the 1918 flu were reported in the United States, the virus may have had its origins in other parts of the world. Recently, Spinney reveals, disease investigators have collected and experimented with tissue samples taken from the bodies of well-preserved victims to try to sequence the DNA of the virus. "Researchers now believe that the 1918 virus originated in birds, but exactly when and where it made the leap to humans remains under debate," wrote Amanda Schaffer in the *New York Times Book Review*. "Spinney explores three possibilities: In March 1918, a mess cook at the United States Army's Camp Funston in Kansas contracted the disease, possibly from a nearby farm. Yet more than a year earlier, a flulike illness had ravaged a military camp, close to the Western Front in northern France. And in 1917 an unknown respiratory disease also swept communities in Northern China." By 1920 the devastation had spread even farther, and the consequences for vulnerable populations were dire. "In some Indian regions, six per cent of the population perished," wrote Jon Wright in *Geographical*; "in parts of South Africa this rose to ten per cent."

Even the common name of the virus reflected the geopolitics and racism of the early twentieth century, "The flu wasn't Spanish at all," said Francis. "The name stuck when in May 1918 the Spanish king, the prime minister and his entire cabinet all came down with it. In Madrid, it was known as the Naples Soldier after a catchy tune

then in circulation, while French military doctors called it Disease 11. In Senegal it was Brazilian flu; in Brazil it was German flu. Poles called it the Bolshevik Disease and the Persians thought the British were responsible (Spinney writes about its devastating effect on the city of Mashed, where it probably arrived with a Russian soldier from the north)." "In Europe and North America the first world war killed more than Spanish flu; everywhere else the reverse is true," said a reviewer for the *Economist*. "Yet most narratives focus on the West, and only partly because that is where the best records are. Ms Spinney's book goes some way to redress the balance."

■ Biographical and Critical Sources

PERIODICALS

Booklist, September 1, 2017, Tony Miksanek, review of *Pale Rider: The Spanish Flu of 1918 and How It Changed the World*, p. 23.

Daily Mail, June 1, 2017, John Preston, review of *Pale Rider*.

Economist, May 27, 2017, "One Hundred Million Dead; Disease in History," p. 75.

Geographical, September, 2017, Jon Wright, review of *Pale Rider*, p. 66.

Kirkus Reviews, July 1, 2017, review of *Pale Rider*.

London Review of Books, January 25, 2018, Gavin Francis, "The Untreatable," p. 3.

New York Times Book Review, December 31, 2017, Amanda Schaffer, "Disease," p. 26.

Publishers Weekly, May 15, 2017, review of *Pale Rider*, p. 47.

Spectator, May 27, 2017, Peter Carty, "The Last Great Pandemic," p. 61.

ONLINE

Librarian on Parade, http://librarianonparade.com/ (August 16, 2017), review of *Pale Rider*.*

Staci Sprout

■ Personal

Married. *Education:* B.A.; M.A.

■ Addresses

Home—WA. *Office*—1818 Westlake Ave. N., Ste. 118, Seattle, WA 98109.

■ Career

Licensed psychotherapist, Certified Sex Addiction Therapist, author, publisher, retreat and conference speaker, and sexual ethics for professionals trainer. Has worked in community mental health settings, hospitals, and a private clinical practice.

■ Writings

Naked in Public: A Memoir of Recovery from Sex Addiction and Other Temporary Insanities, Recontext Media (Seattle, WA), 2015.

■ Sidelights

Staci Sprout is a writer, licensed psychotherapist, and publisher. Sprout has worked as a therapist and social worker in community mental heath practices, hospitals, and in a private clinical practice. As a Certified Sex Addiction Therapist, the focus of her practice is to help individuals, groups, and couples in recovery from sex and relationship addictions. Sprout has spoken at retreats and conferences, and she conducts trainings on sexual ethics for professionals. Sprout lives near Seattle, Washington, with her husband.

Sprout's memoir, *Naked in Public: A Memoir of Recovery from Sex Addiction and Other Temporary Insanities*, documents her struggle with sex addiction and other various mental health illnesses. The book opens with a presentation of Sprout's childhood and family history. Sprout explains that her grandfather was a pedophile, though she herself was never a victim. She describes a childhood that included alcoholism and a strict dedication to religion. A damaged sense of self-worth began for Sprout at a young age, as she dealt with abusive comments from her father and her parents' failure to deal with dark family secrets in any sort of healthy way. Sprout was exposed to and interested in sex at a young age, exploring *Playboy* magazines and explicit late-night television in her home. She recalls the practice at an all-girls summer camp of secretly sharing 'dirty' books.

In college, away from her parents and with much more freedom, Sprout's addictive behaviors and unhealthy coping mechanisms began to emerge. She entered into a serious relationship with a man but quickly found herself unable to stay faithful. She began binge eating and binge drinking, and started developing an obsessive fascination with pornography. As Sprout's sexual addiction took hold, she found herself drawn to mental health issues. Despite struggling in private, she was able to graduate college, gain a master's degree in social work, and pursue a career in mental health counseling.

In adulthood, Sprout's compulsions changed but did not go away. She continued to delve into a pornography obsession and turned to abusing credit cards. During this time, Sprout began a long-term relationship with a jazz musician and self-proclaimed sex addict. This was the first time Sprout encountered the term sex addict, and she began to wonder if the same label could be applied to her. Sprout understood she had a problem, but it took her many years to be able to address her sexual addiction directly. She writes about seeking out help through any means possible. She went to therapy, took antidepressants, and addressed co-dependency and eating disorder issues. Unfortunately, the therapist she saw used unethical practices and developed an unprofessional attachment to Sprout's sister, causing Sprout to write off therapy altogether.

Having nowhere else to turn, Sprout decided to try a twelve-step program. Initially horrified by the group, in part because it was nearly entirely comprised of men, Sprout left the program, dejected and hopeless. Eventually she decided to give the twelve-step program another shot and found a group with more female participants. At this point, the book takes a turn. Sprout experiences her deepest low points, but recognizes that these dips were essential to bring her to ultimate recovery. Sprout writes about processing childhood trauma, leaving her long-term unhealthy relationship, and eventually, finding success and love.

Robert Weiss at the *Psychology Today* website wrote that the book offers a "much needed look at the pain and darkness of female sexual compulsivity, coupled with an equally real and necessary message of hope." A contributor to *Kirkus Reviews* wrote, "A curious reader who fears that he or she might be suffering from similar problems, or who knows someone else who is, couldn't expect to find a more welcoming place to begin their investigation than this memoir."

■ Biographical and Critical Sources

BOOKS

Sprout, Staci, *Naked in Public: A Memoir of Recovery from Sex Addiction and Other Temporary Insanities*, Recontext Media (Seattle, WA), 2015.

PERIODICALS

Kirkus Reviews, November 15, 2017, review of *Naked in Public*.

ONLINE

Psych Central, https://blogs.psychcentral.com/ (October 23, 2015), Robert Weiss, author interview.
Psychology Today, https://www.psychologytoday. com/ (October 29, 2015), Robert Weiss, review of *Naked in Public*.*

Vesper Stamper

■ **Personal**

Married; children: two. *Education:* Parsons School of Design, B.F.A. (with honors); School of Visual Arts, M.F.A. *Religion:* Jewish. *Hobbies and other interests:* Singing and playing guitar.

■ **Addresses**

Home—New York, NY.

■ **Career**

Writer and illustrator.

■ **Writings**

(And illustrator) *What the Night Sings,* Knopf Books for Young Readers (New York, NY), 2018.

■ **Sidelights**

Vesper Stamper is writer and illustrator. She grew up in New York and received a bachelor of fine arts degree in illustration with honors from Parsons School of Design in New York City and a master of fine arts degree in illustrations as visual essay from the School of Visual Arts. She lives near New York City with her husband and two children.

Vesper's first book, *What the Night Sings,* is an illustrated story about one girl's experience of the Holocaust. Aimed at readers aged twelve and up, the book is illustrated in tones of deep brown, with larger scenes divided by periodic spot images.

The story opens in 1945, with the British liberation of German concentration camps. The book opens with teenaged protagonist Gerta Rausch holding her dying bunkmate, Rivkah, in her arms as British troops arrive at Auschwitz to free the prisoners. The story details Gerta's life before the war, her experiences in the Nazi concentration camp, and how she adjusts to life outside of the prison camp. Briana Shemroske in *Booklist* described *What the Night Sings* as "a well-researched, elegant, and fittingly melodic exploration of reclaiming one's voice—and the many kinds of faith it can spark."

Prior to the war, Gerta did not even know she was Jewish. According to her Ahnenpass, a certificate of Aryan lineage, her name was Gerta Richter, not Gerta Rausch. Gerta was an aspiring musician, excelling in viola and singing. She and her father, a violist in the Wurzburg Orchestra, lived a sheltered life in Wurzburg, focusing on music and turning a blind eye to the realities of what was happening in Germany. She is preparing for her first performance when she and her father are captured by the Nazis and sent to Auschwitz. On the train to the concentration camp, her father reveals the truth about the family ancestry. Gerta has no personal connection to the faith, and relates judaism to abuse and extermination. Once at the camp, Gerta's familiarity with viola saves her and she is enrolled in the Women's Orchestra of Auschwitz. Unfortunately, she discovers later, her father did not survive the death camp.

With the British liberation of concentration camp, Gerta is free, or so it seems. She is placed in the Bergen-Belsen Displaced Persons Camp, a temporary camp for World War II refugees. Life at Bergen-Belsen is still far from what her world was life prior to the war, but her musical talent saves her once again. Gerta plays at the orchestra at

Bergen-Belsen, which grants her opportunities she would not otherwise have. Gerta experiences the difficulty of adjusting to the post-World War II world, and experiences the effects of lingering anti-semitism.

At the displaced persons camp Gerta meets Michah, Rivkah's son, and Lev, a devout teen survivor. Through Lev, Gerta discovers a sense of Jewish identity that she had never previously known. A sort of love triangle develops, but Gerta's true ambitions cannot be dampened by romance. She seeks to continue pursuing music, longing to sing again. Lev sees her passion and tries to help her find opportunities to pursue her passion. Gerta eventually takes the route of many Jewish refugees and flees to Palestine, hoping to find hope and safety there.

Carla Riemer in *School Library Journal* wrote: "The illustration style and muted color palette work beautifully with the text," adding that "the narrative is spare but powerful." Amos Lassen at the *Reviews by Amos Lassen* website wrote that Gerta is "one of those literary characters that stays with the reader long after the book is closed," adding

that the book left him "smiling and weeping on the same page."

■ Biographical and Critical Sources

PERIODICALS

Booklist, November 1, 2017, Briana Shemroske, review of *What the Night Sings*, p. 67.

Publishers Weekly, November 20, 2017, review of *What the Night Sings*, p. 94.

School Library Journal, February, 2018, Carla Riemer, review of *What the Night Sings*, p. 96.

Voice of Youth Advocates, December, 2017, Matthew Weaver, review of *What the Night Sings*, p. 63.

ONLINE

BookPage, https://bookpage.com/ (February 20, 2018), Jill Ratzan, author interview.

Reviews by Amos Lassen, http://reviewsbyamoslassen.com/ (March 4, 2018), Amos Lassen, review of *What the Night Sings*.*

Nate Staniforth

■ **Personal**

Married.

■ **Addresses**

Agent—Stephen Barr, Writers House 21 W. 26th St., New York, NY 10010; Brian Schwartz, 7S Management, 925 W. 7th Ave., Denver, CO 80204.

■ **Career**

Writer, magician, lecturer. *Breaking Magic*, Discovery Channel, host. TEDx lecturer.

■ **Writings**

Here Is Real Magic: A Magician's Search for Wonder in the Modern World, Bloomsbury USA (New York, NY), 2018.

■ **Sidelights**

Nate Staniforth is a magician, lecturer, and writer. He is the host of Discovery Channel's *Breaking Magic* and has toured the United States for over a decade, performing at colleges. He has lectured about magic at Oxford Union and has given a TEDx talk on the subject.

Staniforth grew up in Ames, Iowa. After seeing David Copperfield perform, Staniforth was intent on becoming a magician. He studied the magic of such magicians as Blackstone, Houdini, David Ber-

glas, Paul Harris, and David Blaine and would practice tricks at home for hours. Staniforth would perform his tricks for his classmates on the playground and loved the feeling of inspiring awe.

In adulthood, Staniforth pursued a career as a magician, hitting the road and performing around the country. However, after five exhausting years, he was burned out and disheartened. Seeking inspiration, he traveled to India to explore the magic there. The trip inspired his memoir and first book, *Here Is Real Magic: A Magician's Search for Wonder in the Modern World*.

Described by a contributor to *Kirkus Reviews* as an "amiable and engaging memoir," the book documents Staniforth's relationship with magic, starting in childhood. He began learning tricks at age nine, and by age ten had mastered some small-scale magic. He recalls being the new kid at school and inspiring awe and fascination on the playground by performing a disappearing coin trick. His new classmates were mesmerized and terrified, leading to a school teacher coming outside to breakup the commotion. Staniforth then performed the trick for teacher, who was impressed, and Staniforth highlights this memory as the moment at which he recognized the transformative power that magic can have.

Yet, as he pursued a life in magic, he found the world he hoped he would inspire to be unwilling to see magic. Additionally, the culture of magic had morphed into a very showy, Las Vegas-style of performance that drained the excitement out of the craft for Staniforth. He found himself losing passion for magic and began to look elsewhere for inspiration. While on tour in Milwaukee, he came across a book about the magicians of India and the three-thousand-year-old traditions of magic there.

He read about cobras, fire breathing, levitation, and fantastical tricks with blood, guts, and resurrections. Finding the spark that had been missing from his life for so long, he decided to go for a trip.

Staniforth writes about being chased by an enraged cobra and meeting a one-armed monkey in India. More memorable, though, are the people he meets there. Most notable was a meeting with a magician and teacher in Rishikesh, India. The man told Staniforth that his skill was solid, but he was lacking a sense of depth in his practice. He encouraged Staniforth to perform magic for something deep within himself, rather than for a quick dollar on stage. Staniforth took the advice to heart, and in returning to the U.S. and a life as a magician, he dedicated himself to reject the trend of flashy, shallow magic.

While on his trip, Staniforth took a flight to England to visit world-famous illusionist David Berglas. When Staniforth arrived, Berglas welcomed him and asked him to name his wife's favorite flower. When Staniforth stated, "Peonies," Berglas pointed to the garden, where peonies suddenly appeared. Staniforth admits that to this day he does not know how the illusionist pulled off the trick. In a way, he notes, he enjoys the fact that even he can still be awed and perplexed by magic.

A contributor to *Publishers Weekly* wrote that Staniforth "wonderfully captures the joys and struggles of becoming a working magician and what happened to him when his fascination with his craft faded," while Poornima Apte in *Booklist* described the book as "a passionate and eloquent call to seek to renew one's purpose in life."

■ **Biographical and Critical Sources**

PERIODICALS

Booklist, December 1, 2017, Poornima Apte, review of *Here Is Real Magic: A Magician's Search for Wonder in the Modern World*, p. 14.

Kirkus Reviews, October 15, 2017, review of *Here Is Real Magic*.

Publishers Weekly, October 30, 2017, review of *Here Is Real Magic*, p. 70.

ONLINE

Chicago Now, http://www.chicagonow.com/ (February 13, 2018), Teme Ring, author interview.

Little Village, http://littlevillagemag.com/ (January 16, 2018), Genevieve Trainor, review of *Here Is Real Magic*.

Renton Reporter Online, http://www.rentonreporter.com/ (January 25, 2018), Terri Schlichenmeyer, review of *Here Is Real Magic*.*

James G. Stavridis

1955-

■ **Personal**

Born February 15, 1955, in West Palm Beach, FL; son of Paul George and Shirley Anne Stavridis; married Laura Hall. *Education:* Graduated from U.S. Naval Academy, 1976, and United States National War College, 1992; Tufts University, M.A., 1983, Ph.D., 1984.

■ **Career**

Admiral; dean, Fletcher School of Law and Diplomacy, Tufts University, 2013—. U.S. Navy, operations officer, USS *Valley Forge;* commander, USS *Barry,* 1993-95; commander, Destroyer Squadron 21 in Persian Gulf, 1998; commander, Enterprise Carrier Strike Group, 2002-04, senior military assistant, United States Secretary of Defense; commander, U.S. Southern Command, 2006-09, commander, U.S. European Command and NATO Supreme Allied Commander Europe, 2009-13, retired, 2013. Public speaker and commentator, CNN, Fox News, BBC, and Bloomberg. Chief international security and diplomacy analyst, NBC News, 2016—. Associate fellow, Geneva Centre for Security Policy; member, Inter-American Dialogue.

■ **Awards, Honors**

Gullion Prize, Tufts University; John Paul Jones Award for inspirational leadership, Navy League; Distinguished Graduate Leadership Award, Naval War College, 2003; Intrepid Freedom Award, Intrepid Sea, Air & Space Museum, 2011; David Sarnoff Award, Armed Forces Communications and Electronics Association, 2011; Athenagoras Human Rights Award, Archons of the Ecumenical Patriarchate Order of St. Andrew the Apostle, 2011; Alfred Thayer Mahan Award for Literary Achievement, Navy League of the United States, 2011; Henry M. Jackson Distinguished Service Award, Jewish Institute for National Security Affairs (JINSA), 2011; Distinguished Military Leadership Award, Atlantic Council, 2011; Eisenhower Award, Business Executives for National Security, 2012; 33rd Annual Homeric Award, Chian Federation, 2012; Distinguished Ally of the Israel Defense Forces Award, 2013; Pragmatist + Idealist Award, Stimson Center, 2013; Lifetime Achievement Award, Alpha Omega Council, 2015; Distinguished Sea Service Award, Naval Order of the United States, 2015; Building Bridges Award, Truce Foundation of the USA, 2016; Scholar-Statesman Award, Washington Institute, 2016; Dr. Jean Mayer Global Citizenship Award, Institute for Global Leadership, Tufts University, 2017; Ellis Island Medal of Honor, 2017; Andrew Goodpaster Prize, American Veterans Center, 2017; Award for Leadership in Development, Society for International Development, 2017; "Archbishop Iakovos Leadership 100 Award for Excellence," Leadership 100 Conference, 2018.Received awards for service from U.S. Navy, including Surface Warfare Officer badge, Navy Distinguished Service Medal, Defense Superior Service Medal, Legion of Merit with four gold award stars, Meritorious Service Medal with two gold award stars, Joint Service Commendation Medal, Navy Commendation Medal with three gold award stars, Navy Achievement Medal, Joint Meritorious Unit Award with one oak leaf cluster, Navy Unit Commendation, Navy Meritorious Unit Commendation with 2 bronze service stars, Navy Expeditionary Medal, National Defense Service Medal with two bronze service stars, Armed Forces Expeditionary Medal with one bronze service stars, Southwest Asia Service Medal with one bronze service star, Global War on Terrorism Expeditionary Medal, Global War on Terrorism Service Medal, Armed Forces Service Medal with two bronze service stars, Navy Sea Service Deployment Ribbon with one silver and two bronze service stars, Navy & Marine Corps Overseas Service Ribbon with bronze service star, Navy Expert Rifleman Medal, and Navy Expert Pistol Shot Medal. Received awards from foreign governments, including Commander's degree, National Order of the Legion of Honour of France, Grand Cross Order of the Crown (Belgium), Grand Cross Order of the Phoenix (Greece), Commendation Ministry of Defense: "Cross of Merit and Honour First Class" (Greece), Estonian Order of the Cross of the Eagle First Class, Order of Merit of the Italian Republic Knight Grand Cross of the Republic, Order of Merit of the Federal Republic of Germany Grand Merit Cross with Star, Grand Officer of the Order of Merit of the Grand Duchy of Luxembourg, Commander's Cross with Star of the Order of Merit of the Republic of Hungary, Commander's Cross of the Order of Merit (Poland), Order of Duke Trpimir (Croatia), Cross of Commander of the Order for Merits to Lithuania, Investiture Medal of the Kingdom of the Netherlands, Order of Naval Merit (Argentina), Order of Naval Merit in the degree of Grand Officer (Brazil), Cruz de la Victoria (Chile), Order of Naval Merit Admiral Padilla (Colombia), Order of the Peruvian Cross of Naval Merit in the rank of Grand Cross along with a White Ribbon (Peru), Emblem of Honor of the General Staff of Romania, Medal of Honorary Recognition of Latvia, Military Merit Grand Cross Medal of the Portuguese Republic, Order of Vakhtang Gorgasali—I Rank (Georgia), Albanian Medal of Gratitude, Slovenian Medal for multinational cooperation 1st grade, Navy National Defense Cross (Guatemala), Grand Cross (Dominican Republic), NATO Meritorious Service Medal, NATO Medal for Former Yugoslavia, Kuwait Liberation Medal (Saudi Arabia), Kuwait Liberation Medal (Kuwait).

■ Writings

Division Officer's Guide, Naval Institute Press (Annapolis, MD), 9th edition (with John V. Noel, Jr.), 1989, 11th edition (with Robert Girrer), 2004, 12th edition (with Jeffrey Heames and Thomas Ogden), 2017.

Watch Officer's Guide: A Handbook for All Deck Watch Officers, Naval Institute Press (Annapolis, MD), 13th edition, 1992, 15th edition (with Robert Girrier), 2007.

Command at Sea, Naval Institute Press (Annapolis, MD), 5th edition (with William P. Mack), 1999, 6th edition (with Robert Girrier), 2010.

Destroyer Captain: Lessons of a First Command, Naval Institute Press (Annapolis, MD), 2008.

Whatever Happened to the "War on Drugs"?, Defense Technical Information Center (Fort Belvoir, VA), 2008.

Partnership for the Americas: Western Hemisphere Strategy and U.S. Southern Command, National Defense University Press (Washington, DC), 2010.

An Intelligent Theater, Defense Technical Information Center (Ft. Belvoir, VA), 2010.

(With Richard E. LeBron) *Taming the Outlaw Sea*, Defense Technical Information Center (Ft. Belvoir, VA), 2010.

The Accidental Admiral: A Sailor Takes Command at NATO, Naval Institute Press (Annapolis, MD), 2014.

Convergence: Illicit Networks and National Security in the Age of Globalization, United States Department of Defense (Pittsburgh, PA), 2015.

(With R. Manning Ancell) *The Leader's Bookshelf*, Naval Institute Press (Annapolis, MD), 2017.

Sea Power: The History and Geopolitics of the World's Oceans, Penguin Press (New York, NY), 2017.

Also author of *NATO Review: Making the Concept a Reality*, 2012. Contributor to periodicals, including *Foreign Policy, Huffington World Post, Nikkei Asian Review*, and *Time*.

■ Sidelights

James G. Stavridis is one of the most decorated American military officers of twenty-first century. A 1976 graduate of the U.S. Naval Academy, his career began after the Vietnam War but encompassed the global conflicts of the late twentieth and early twenty-first centuries. He commanded destroyers and destroyer squadrons, and he wrote about the experience in his 2008 book *Destroyer Captain: Lessons of a First Command*. "This window into the thoughts and feelings of one of the Navy's most successful officers of the era," wrote Robert E. Henstrand in *Joint Force Quarterly*, "makes this a captivating read and is one of the most valuable aspects of the book." In 2006, Stavridis was promoted to lead the U.S. Southern Command—the first Naval officer to fill the important post. Three years later he accepted the position of Supreme Allied Commander Europe (SACEUR), the head of NATO's Allied Command Operations in Belgium. He retired as SACEUR in 2013.

Stavridis also spent major portions of his career as a strategic analyst, serving at various stages of his career as an advisor to three different Chiefs of Naval Operations, to Secretary of the Navy John F.

Lehman, Jr., and to Chair of the Joint Chiefs of Staff General Colin Powell. He also served as the senior military assistant to the United States Secretary of Defense. Many of his publications, such as *Partnership for the Americas: Western Hemisphere Strategy and U.S. Southern Command, An Intelligent Theater, Taming the Outlaw Sea,* and *Convergence: Illicit Networks and National Security in the Age of Globalization,* reflect his thinking on global strategy. Stavridis's experience was reflected by the fact that Hillary Rodham Clinton's 2016 presidential campaign vetted him as a potential running mate and vice presidential candidate, while President Donald Trump's administration reportedly considered him as a candidate for the office of Secretary of State.

During his tenure as commander of the U.S. Southern Command, Stavridis launched significant changes to the focus of the military, "making the most of limited resources to create goodwill and mutual respect," explained a reviewer writing about *Partnership for the Americas* for *Joint Force Quarterly.* Stavridis suggested in the volume that the twenty-first-century military needs to be able to combat enemies, but also to subdue criminal networks and to respond to natural disasters throughout the hemisphere. In the story of his tenure as the head of NATO, *The Accidental Admiral: A Sailor Takes Command at NATO,* "Stavridis . . . offers two meditations on current realities that might assist civilian strategists," stated Heather Hurlburt in the *Washington Monthly.* "One could be summarized as 'When you're in a hole, stop digging.' Know when you've lost a fight, whether over personal ethics, strategic communications, or military offensive—and retire with grace. Recognize when time-honored strategies, such as badgering allies to make good on commitments to burden sharing that neither leaders nor publics have any intention of keeping, have become counterproductive. Invite the allies to do what they are good at—economic development, policing, legal system reform—instead."

Stavridis's *Sea Power* builds on the influential study by Alfred Thayer Mahan, whose 1890 study *The Influence of Sea Power upon History, 1660-1783* helped articulate American naval strategy for the twentieth century. The author's "strong conviction in 'Sea Power' isn't only that Mahan was right in crediting naval force with a key role—perhaps the key role—in geopolitics," stated Steve Donoghue in the *Christian Science Monitor,* "but also that there are many dimensions to that key role, sometimes surprising dimensions verging on the diplomatic and the humanitarian. Stavridis in his career

oversaw such humanitarian missions, and he's very convincing on their effectiveness." "The advantage the United States has, according to Admiral Stavridis, is that it can look at the oceans from a strategic sense by elaborating that 'while the essence of sea power is the connective power of the unity of the oceans into a single global commons, there are historical, cultural, political, economic, and military reasons to think about each from a strategic perspective,'" said Chad Pillai in the *Center for International Maritime Security.* "The United States grapples with an increasingly complex security environment described as contested norms and persistent disorder according to the Joint Operating Environment."

Even in the twenty-first century, the ability of the United States to leverage sea power, said Stavridis, maintains a crucial role. "First and foremost, it's international trade. Ninety-five percent of the world's trade moves across the oceans. Secondly, there are still nations contending. In fact, I'd point to two very hot spot parts of the world today," Stavridis told Steve Inskeep in an interview on *NPR.org.* "One is the eastern Mediterranean, where the United States and Russia are jostling. And the other, most obviously, is the South China Sea," where China is expanding its control by creating new islands from submerged reefs and claiming those islands as its own territory. "The Pacific remains a site of both ambition and communication," declared a *Publishers Weekly* reviewer, "with corresponding possibilities for 'an explosive war.'" "*Sea Power* is clear-eyed about the dangers of the modern nautical realities," Donoghue concluded, "but it doggedly retains this tone of hope throughout."

In many ways, said John R. Satterfield in a review for the *Naval Historical Foundation* website, *Sea Power* takes off from where the author left off in *The Accidental Admiral.* Stavridis "shifts his focus from continental concerns and prescriptions in the earlier book to the oceans surrounding the continents," Satterfield declared. "Stavridis' dual naval and scholarly career makes the author uniquely qualified to take on these topics. . . . Based on his experience in combined commands, Stavridis is a stellar proponent of complementary military and diplomatic means to security and peace, and few can claim clearer practical experience with global alliances to facilitate these methods." Stavridis "seeks to accomplish something . . . elusive, sophisticated, and significant: To show how service at sea in one of the world's great global navies simultaneously expands tactical, operational, strategic, and policy knowledge and skills in an officer and—most important—develops insights in him or her regarding myriad possible interconnections among those levels of conflict," explained Peter M. Swartz in the *U.S. Naval Institute*'s magazine *Proceedings*. "The result: Navy senior leaders such as Admiral Stavridis in his last several tours who can employ their unique backgrounds at sea in a highly nuanced fashion to deal with burning contemporary and future national military problems." "As I look at America in today's environment, we need to avoid that tendency to be overly impulsive," Stavridis told Inskeep. "We need to work with our allies and friends. The allies are the tugboats of this metaphor. You don't have to operate unilaterally in the world."

■ Biographical and Critical Sources

PERIODICALS

Christian Science Monitor, June 27, 2017, Steve Donoghue, "*Sea Power* Views the World's Oceans as Crucial Avenues of Hope and Danger."

Joint Force Quarterly, July, 2008, Robert E. Henstrand, "Off the Shelf," p. 140; January, 2011, review of *Partnership for the Americas: Western Hemisphere Strategy and U.S. Southern Command,* p. 1; July, 2013, review of *Convergence: Illicit Networks and National Security in the Age of Globalization,* p. 121; October, 2013, review of *Convergence,* p. 109.

Kirkus Reviews, April 1, 2017, review of *Sea Power: The History and Geopolitics of the World's Oceans.*

Publishers Weekly, April 10, 2017, review of *Sea Power,* p. 65.

Washington Monthly, January-February, 2015, Heather Hurlburt, "Is a Grand Strategy for America Even Possible?," p. 68.

ONLINE

Center for International Maritime Security, http://cimsec.org/ (September 26, 2017), Chad Pillai, review of *Sea Power.*

Naval Historical Foundation. https://www.navyhistory.org/ (September 21, 2017), John R. Satterfield, review of *Sea Power.*

NPR.org, https://www.npr.org/ (June 6, 2017), Steve Inskeep, "Stavridis' Book *Sea Power* Explains Why Oceans Matter in Global Politics."

U.S. Naval Institute, https://www.usni.org/ (June 1, 2017), Peter M. Swartz, review of *Sea Power;* author interview.*

Roger Steffens

1942-

■ Personal

Born June 17, 1942, in Brooklyn, NY.

■ Addresses

Home—Los Angeles, CA.

■ Career

Actor, writer, lecturer, editor, reggae archivist, photographer, and producer. Former cohost, *Reggae Beat*; founding editor, *The Beat*.

■ Writings

Light Benders, Goliards Press (Bellingham, WA), 1972.

(Author of text) Bruce W. Talamon, *Bob Marley: Spirit Dancer*, W.W. Norton (New York, NY), 1994.

(With Leroy Jodie Pierson) *Bob Marley and the Wailers: The Definitive Discography*, Rounder Books (Cambridge, MA), 2005.

(With Peter Simon) *The Reggae Scrapbook*, Insight Editions (San Raphael, CA), 2007.

The Family Acid Jamaica, Family Acid (Los Angeles, CA), 2016.

(And photographer) *So Much Things to Say: The Oral History of Bob Marley*, W.W. Norton (New York, NY), 2017.

Contributor to books, including *Bob Marley and the Golden Age of Reggae*, by Kim Gottieb-Walker, Titan Books.

■ Sidelights

Roger Steffens is known as the world's foremost authority on reggae music and the life of its best-known musician, Bob Marley. Steffens's works include the text of Bruce W. Talamon's *Bob Marley: Spirit Dancer*, the book (coauthored with Leroy Jodie Pierson) *Bob Marley and the Wailers: The Definitive Discography*, *The Family Acid Jamaica*, and *The Reggae Scrapbook*—"an excellent addition," wrote Bill Walker in *Library Journal*, "to any reggae history collection as well as a prize for fans." "While paying homage to 'reggae royalty' icons such as Bob Marley, Peter Tosh and Jimmy Cliff, the authors go to great lengths to explore lesser-known musicians in glossy photographs, essays, copies of advertisements and detachable postcards," stated a *Publishers Weekly* reviewer. "The editors successfully use the reggae aesthetic in a burst of bright primary colors and a flurry of marijuana leaves (with accompanying clouds of thick smoke)." Steffens also maintains a reggae archive from which much of the information and illustrations for these works is drawn.

Steffen's reggae archive provides the material behind the creation of *So Much Things to Say: The Oral History of Bob Marley*. "Marley is reggae: he remains an international celebrity, honoured with a waxwork at Madame Tussaud's," declared Ian Thomson in the *Spectator*, "and, as Roger Steffens reminds us, listed in *Forbes* magazine at Number Five among the 'highest-earning dead celebrities' for 2014. Steffens, a US-based music critic and longtime Marley fan, has spent years interviewing friends, associates and admirers of the Jamaican superstar. *So Much Things to Say*, an 'oral' account of Marley's life and times, amounts to an absorbing alternative biography." Steffans, wrote a *Publishers Weekly* reviewer, "brings the singer to life through conversations with his bandmates, lovers, family members, and musical associates."

Even today, decades after his death from cancer, Marley remains an iconic figure in international music. "Marley introduced reggae and Rastafarianism to much of the globe, making him a crucial ambassador for those subcultures," declared *New York Times Book Review* contributor Touré, "and he is the face of Jamaica, by far its most famous son." "Steffens . . . offers a more grounded approach in this sprawling but absorbing 'oral history,' drawing on interviews with seventy-five assorted relatives, band members, fellow travellers and lovers; a lifetime's research," wrote Neil Spencer in the London *Guardian*. "Their accounts, not infrequently contradictory, are effectively marshalled by Steffens, who acts as a reliable narrator. Among the revelations is the extent of Marley's deprivation in his early years. Abandoned by his elderly white father, an itinerant government overseer who had gotten a local teenage girl pregnant, Marley grew up first in the rural parish of St Ann, later moving to . . . west Kingston." Steffens's book, critics agree, gives a clearer sense of how complicated Marley and his legacy are. "If he is a cultural senator, then that's part of his delivering for his constituents—he spread an image of Jamaica around the world, and now everyone has a soft spot in his or her heart for that magical island," Touré continued. "But at the same time Marley's politics were revolutionary. . . . He sent concert-goers home with the sound of him urging 'stand up for your rights' ringing in their ears. Marley was that rarity—a black revolutionary who didn't scare white people." "What emerges is a not a clear picture of Marley the man," explained a *Kirkus Reviews* contributor, "but rather a true sense of how complicated his life was."

Critics recognized the importance of Steffens's work. "Composed from interviews with more than seventy-five friends, family and confidants of Marley and amassed over several decades," declared Agatha French in the *Los Angeles Times*, "So Much Things to Say* is the biographical equivalent of a statistical mean: a way to compile a complete portrait of the musical legend from the sum experiences of the people who knew him best." Steffens's book, said *Paste* reviewer Jason Rhode, "reveals a Marley of flesh and blood who passed too young in a world that was never too old to learn. 'In the abundance of water, the fool is thirsty,' the singer said, and there is water aplenty here. Drink and be satisfied." "Devoted fans and all readers," concluded Michael Ruzicka in *Booklist*, ". . . will find this many-voiced, richly subjective chronicle dramatic and compelling."

■ Biographical and Critical Sources

PERIODICALS

Booklist, June, 2017, Michael Ruzicka, review of *So Much Things to Say: The Oral History of Bob Marley*, p. 34.

California Bookwatch, February, 2011, "Bob Marley and the Golden Age of Reggae."

Guardian (London, England), August 14, 2017, Neil Spencer, review of *So Much Things to Say*.

Kirkus Reviews, June 1, 2017, review of *So Much Things to Say*.

Library Journal, January 1, 2008, Bill Walker, review of *The Reggae Scrapbook*, p. 103.

Los Angeles Times, July 13, 2017, Agatha French, "Going behind the Scenes with Bob Marley in the New Book *So Much Things to Say*."

New York Times Book Review, July 30, 2017, Touré, "Bob Marley Comes Alive in This Collection of Interviews with the People Who Knew Him Best," p. 10.

Publishers Weekly, October 6, 2008, "Music Books Rock," p. 47; May 8, 2017, review of *So Much Things to Say*, p. 51.

Spectator, September 23, 2017, Ian Thomson, "The Cult of Holy Bob," p. 32.

ONLINE

Paste, https://www.pastemagazine.com/ (July 13, 2017), Jason Rhode, review of *So Much Things to Say*.*

Mike Steib

■ Personal

Married Kemp Webber (a business executive). *Education:* University of Pennsylvania, B.A.

■ Addresses

Home—New York, NY.

■ Career

Writer. XO Group, Inc., New York, NY, president, 2013-14, CEO, 2014—. Guest speaker on NBC's *Today,* CNBC, Bloomberg, and Fox Business. Inventor of three digital media patents. Formerly worked at Walker Digital; at McKinsey & Company; as vice president at NBC Corporate Development group; as general manager of Strategic Ventures at NBC Universal; at Google; as CEO of Vente-Privee USA, 2011-13. Played a supporting acting role in *The Mad Ones.* Board member of Ally Financial; cochair of Board of Literacy Partners.

■ Awards, Honors

GE Imagination Breakthrough Award; CEO World Award; Stevie International Business Award. Named a Crain's New York "40 under 40"; Multichannel News "40 under 40"; Folio's "100" honoree; TV Week's "Twelve to Watch"; and TV Week's "Hot List."

■ Writings

The Career Manifesto: Discover Your Calling and Create an Extraordinary Life, TarcherPerigee (New York, NY), 2018.

Contributor to numerous periodicals, including the *New York Times, Wall Street Journal, Fortune, Entrepreneur,* and *TechCrunch.*

■ Sidelights

Mike Steib is a writer and the CEO of XO Group, Inc., a company that helps individuals utilize industry-leading digital and media products, such as the Knot, the Bump, the Nest, and Gigmasters, to improve their quality of life. Steib began working for XO Group as president in July 2013. He was offered the position of CEO in 2014. Prior to working for XO Group, Steib was CEO of Vente-Privee USA between 2011 and 2013. He has also worked at Google, NBC Universal, NBC Corporate Development group, McKinsey & Company, and Walker Digital.

Steib attended college at the University of Pennsylvania, where he received bachelor's degrees in economics and international relations. Steib's work has appeared in the *New York Times, Wall Street Journal, Fortune, Entrepreneur,* and *TechCrunch,* and he has appeared as a guest on NBC's *Today,* CNBC, Bloomberg, and Fox Business. He is the inventor of three digital media patents. Steib has been named a Crain's New York "40 Under 40," Multichannel News "40 Under 40," Folio's "100" honorees, and TV Week's "Twelve to Watch," and "Hot List." He is a recipient of a CEO World Award and a Stevie International Business Award. Steib lives in New York with his wife Kemp Steib, the CFO of The Second Shift.

The Career Manifesto: Discover Your Calling and Create an Extraordinary Life is Steib's guide to help achievers find happiness and success when their career satisfaction falls short. The book started out as an online document—a Google Doc—he created to inspire and motivate his employees. Steib decided to expand the document into a book when he realized he was not satisfied in his career. As a straight-A student who ended up in a great job, he felt that he should feel a sense of success. However, at a career-day event in which he was speaking to a group of kindergartners, he was confronted with a question that made him reconsider his life choices. When a kindergartener asked him if his job is important, he realized that he did not believe it was. From that moment on he decided to seek out ways to reorganize his life to achieve his goals and experience a true sense of success.

"Steib covers several enormously important topics," wrote M.B. Roberts at the *Parade* website, "making a commitment to managing stress in and out of the workplace." Steib writes that there are five essential components of success. He divides the book into these five pillars: purpose, plan, productivity, people, and presence. He uses examples from his own career trajectory to elucidate on these pillars. While working at Google, he saw himself surrounded by many unhappy overachievers, working diligently but not feeling that their desire to lead was being met. To fill this void within himself, he began an internship program. This decision both gave him the opportunity to lead and allowed him to develop a reputation as a leader, catching the eye of individuals higher up in the organization.

Steib also emphasizes the importance of structuring time, pointing to the zero-basing business management method. He suggests that after a person meets their basic requirements, such as eating and sleeping and the demands of a full-time job, he or she should have five free hours a day. He details methods readers can use to approach those precious five hours with the most productivity and happiness. Jeff Haden at the *Inc.* website wrote that the book "provides an actionable blueprint to becoming more productive, more effective, more fulfilled . . . and better able to make a difference in the lives of the people around you," while a contributor to *Publishers Weekly* wrote that Steib "lays out a sound and logical approach, with easily applicable and customizable advice aplenty."

■ **Biographical and Critical Sources**

PERIODICALS

Publishers Weekly, November 20, 2017, review of *The Career Manifesto: Discover Your Calling and Create an Extraordinary Life,* p. 82.

ONLINE

Inc., https://www.inc.com/ (January 31, 2018), Jeff Haden, review of *The Career Manifesto.*
Monster, https://www.monster.com/ (March 5, 2018), Anne Fisher, review of *The Career Manifesto.*
Parade, https://parade.com/ (January 30, 2018), M.B. Roberts, review of *The Career Manifesto.**

Bill Steigerwald

■ Personal

Male. *Education:* Attended Villanova University, 1969.

■ Addresses

Home—Pittsburgh, PA.

■ Career

Journalist for newspapers, including *Los Angeles Times, Pittsburgh Post-Gazette,* and *Pittsburgh Tribune-Review;* full-time writer, 2009—.

■ Writings

Dogging Steinbeck: How I Went Looking for John Steinbeck's America, Found My Own America, and Exposed the Truth about "Travels with Charley," Fourth River Press (Pittsburgh, PA), 2012.

30 Days a Black Man: The Forgotten Story That Exposed the Jim Crow South, Lyons Press (Guilford, CT), 2017.

■ Sidelights

Bill Steigerwald retired from the *Pittsburgh Tribune-Review* in 2009 and began a new career as the author of nonfiction books that use his reporting skills to tell unremembered stories from twentieth and twenty-first-century America.

Dogging Steinbeck

In *Dogging Steinbeck: How I Went Looking for John Steinbeck's America, Found My Own America, and Exposed the Truth about "Travels with Charley,"* he tells the story behind a putative work of nonfiction by a great modern American writer. "In 1960," explained Lewis Jones in the *Spectator,* "John Steinbeck set off with his poodle Charley to drive around the United States in a truck equipped with a bed, a desk, a stove and a fridge. To renew his acquaintance with that 'monster of a land', he planned to cross the northern states from the east coast to the west, then drive down the Pacific and across the southern states. He was fifty-eight, and recovering from a mild stroke. . . . *Travels with Charley* was published in 1962. It was a great success, and his last major work. Four months later he won the Nobel Prize."

Steigerwald shows that, in fact, Steinbeck fabricated many of the stories he told. "In the book, Steigerwald points out that when Steinbeck was supposed to have been roughing it, camped out on a farm near Lancaster, N.H., he actually booked a room at a luxury hotel," wrote Bill Lucey in *NewspaperAlum.* "He also discovered that Steinbeck spent precious little time in campers, and was hardly alone, as he led readers to believe; but traveled with his wife Elaine on more than half of the trip; other times he stayed at the Steinbeck family cottage in Pacific Grove, Calif., and another week at a Texas cattle ranch for millionaires." "Apart from some surprised indignation at the brazenness of Steinbeck's fabulism," said Shawn Macomber in the *Weekly Standard,* "this friendliness is the primary motif of *Dogging Steinbeck,* offering a corrective to the original sin by beautifully detailing Steigerwald's own journey hopscotching across a nation which 'despite the Great Recession and national headlines dripping with gloom and doom' remained 'a big, beautiful, empty, healthy, rich, safe, clean, prosperous, and friendly country.'" "Anyone who's interested in John Steinbeck, the truth about *Travels with Charley* and how much

America has changed in the last half century America should read it," concluded a *Community Voices* contributor.

30 Days a Black Man

In *30 Days a Black Man: The Forgotten Story That Exposed the Jim Crow South*, Steigerwald "offers a valuable corrective," reported a *Kirkus Reviews* contributor, "in resurrecting Ray Sprigle (1886-1957), an old-school white Pittsburgh newspaperman who produced an expose after traveling the South disguised as a black man." "Sprigle traveled from Pittsburgh to Atlanta to rural Georgia, Alabama and Tennessee. He talked to sharecroppers and black doctors and families whose lives were torn apart by lynching. He visited desperately underfunded schools for black children and resort towns where only white people were allowed to bathe in the ocean," stated Lorraine Boissoneault at *Smithsonian.com*.

Boissoneault recounted: "In one of the most striking moments of his reporting trip, he met the Snipes family—a black family forced to flee their home after their son"—a combat veteran—"was killed voting in a Georgia election." The book, said Nick Gillespie in *Reason*, "does a masterful job of recreating an America in which de facto and de jure segregation was the rule not just in the former Confederacy but much of the North as well. It's a deeply disturbing and profoundly moving account."

■ Biographical and Critical Sources

PERIODICALS

Kirkus Reviews, March 1, 2017, review of *30 Days a Black Man: The Forgotten Story That Exposed the Jim Crow South*.

Spectator, January 3, 2015, Lewis Jones, "Three Men, Two Men, One Man and His Dog . . .," review of *Dogging Steinbeck: How I Went Looking for John Steinbeck's America, Found My Own America, and Exposed the Truth about "Travels with Charley*," p. 28.

Weekly Standard, January 21, 2013, Shawn Macomber, "Chicanery Row," review of *Dogging Steinbeck: How I Went Looking for John Steinbeck's America, Found My Own America, and Exposed the Truth about "Travels with Charley."*

ONLINE

Community Voices, http://communityvoices.post-gazette.com/ (November 14, 2012), "Travels without Charley."

NewspaperAlum, http://www.newspaperalum.com/ (April 17, 2013), Bill Lucey, "Bill Steigerwald Refused to Let Sleeping Dogs Lie: John Steinbeck Exposed."

Reason, http://reason.com/ (May 12, 2017), Nick Gillespie, author interview.

Smithsonian.com, https://www.smithsonianmag.com/ (February 14, 2017), Lorraine Boissoneault, "The Complicated Racial Politics of Going 'Undercover' to Report on the Jim Crow South."*

Abby Stern

■ **Personal**

Female.

■ **Addresses**

Home—Los Angeles, CA.

■ **Career**

Writer; freelance celebrity reporter.

■ **Writings**

According to a Source (novel), Thomas Dunne Books (New York, NY), 2017.

Contributor to periodicals, including *People* magazine.

■ **Sidelights**

Freelance celebrity reporter Abby Stern's debut novel is *According to a Source*, a work that draws its inspiration from her career in Hollywood. Its protagonist and narrator is Ella Warren, a celebrity reporter who hides her identity in order to score the best and juiciest stories about the comings and goings of Hollywood's upper crust. Her lifestyle is threatened, however, when a new editor takes over her workplace and threatens Ella with dismissal if she fails to meet arbitrary guidelines. "Fast-paced and charming," stated a *Kirkus Reviews* contributor, "the novel gives a glimpse into the secret world of celebrity—and celebrity reporting—that many readers will eat up like the latest tabloid or . . . television show."

Part of the fun of reading *According to a Source*, critics agree, is in identifying the real-world counterparts to Stern's fictional celebrities. "I wrote this book as a work [of] fiction so I would have the creative license to make the story as fun as possible!" Stern enthused in an interview with *Huffington Post* contributor Brandi Megan Granett. "With non-fiction, you're obviously married to the truth, which isn't always as interesting as we think. In choosing to make it fiction, I was able to create celebrity archetypes and use my imagination to craft scenarios that would both be exciting for the reader and would heighten the stakes for Ella." "Despite its glossy, bubble-gum-pink cover," explained Maureen Lenker in *LA Weekly*, "the book isn't afraid to dig deep and show some of the seedier aspects of fame and nightlife. Stern says part of the fun of writing this story was the chance to peek behind the velvet rope. 'Being on red carpets, it looks like so much fun and so glamorous, and being there, you're standing around, you're waiting forever, your feet hurt, it could be raining,' she says. 'It's kind of nice to take that peek behind the curtain and see a little bit of what really goes on in a fictitious way.'"

"Not only is it fun to do some detective work of your own, but it also paints a much more realistic picture in your head," asserted Meagan Portorreal on her eponymous website, "one where you feel completely attached to the story's L.A. setting." "Readers who relish celebrity gossip," opined Kristine Huntley in *Booklist*, "will have a blast trying to identify the various celebrities alluded to . . . in this fun, frothy read."

■ **Biographical and Critical Sources**

PERIODICALS

Booklist, April 1, 2017, Kristine Huntley, review of *According to a Source*, p. 28.

Kirkus Reviews, March 15, 2017, review of *According to a Source*.

ONLINE

Huffington Post, https://www.huffingtonpost.com/ (May 25, 2017), Brandi Megan Granett, "According to a Source: A Conversation with Abby Stern."

LA Weekly, http://www.laweekly.com/ (May 23, 2017), Maureen Lenker, "A Hollywood Insider Offers a Glimpse beyond the Red Carpet in Her New Book."

Meagan Portorreal, http://meganportorreal.com/ (October 11, 2017), Meagan Portorreal, review of *According to a Source*.*

Bianca Stone

1983-

■ **Personal**

Born 1983 in Burlington, VT; married Ben Pease (a poet); children: Odette. *Education:* New York University, M.F.A.

■ **Addresses**

Office—Ruth Stone Foundation, 788 Hathaway Rd., Goshen, VT 05733.

■ **Career**

Writer and visual artist. Ruth Stone Foundation, Goshen, VT, codirector; Monk Books, cofounder and editor.

■ **Writings**

(Illustrator) Sophocles, *Antigonick,* translated by Anne Carson, New Directions (New York, NY), 2012.
Someone Else's Wedding Vows, Tin House Books (Portland, OR), 2014.
The Mobius Strip Club of Grief, Tin House Books (Portland, OR), 2018.

Also author of chapbooks. Has published poems, poetry comics, and nonfiction in a variety of magazines, including *Poetry, Jubilat,* and *Tin House.*

■ **Sidelights**

Bianca Stone, a poet and artist, received her master of fine arts degree from New York University and then moved with her husband, poet Ben Pease, back to her native Vermont. There she and Pease took over the directorship of the Ruth Stone Foundation and founded Monk Books. Ruth Stone was a poet who lived in Vermont and published thirteen books of poetry. At the foundation's website, the mission statement states that the foundation "serves to fulfill Ruth Stone's wish that her physical and literary estate would be used for the furthering of poetry and the creative arts." Ruth was Bianca's grandmother. Through Monk Books, founded in 2009, Stone and Pease have developed the *Ruth Stone House Reader,* a yearly anthology of chapbook-length collections by four poets—all of whom are given residencies to conduct their work. Stone herself has illustrated or written several books, chapbooks, and "poetry comics."

Antigonick

Antigonick, the Sophocles play known more commonly as *Antigone,* was translated by Anne Carson and illustrated by Stone. The tragedy follows the main character, Antigone, who is the daughter of Oedipus—born through the incest of Oedipus with his mother, Jocasta. A critic in the *New Yorker* thought that Stone's "enigmatic illustrations" do not serve the "light, swift" poetry of the translation. Emily Stokes underscored this opinion in the London *Guardian,* remarking that the illustrations are a "surreal assortment of icy landscapes, domestic interiors, gothic houses, unravelling spools of thread, precarious staircases and drowning horses" that "relate only occasionally to what is happening in the play." A reviewer in *Books & Culture,* however, commented: "The drawings, on semi-transparent pages overlaying the text, depict bleak landscapes, mundane interiors, and hopeless figures, like panicking horses and three cheerleaders standing listlessly in a row, with cement blocks in place of heads. Colors are sparse, and in places almost random-looking. These illustrations . . . are impressive."

Rebecca Bates, in her critique in *Guernica,* found the entire book "an art object unto itself." Carson wrote the book by hand, largely in black ink interspersed with red portions. She also observed: "Stone's illustrations are devastating in their own right and are essential to completing the world of disarray in which Carson's nightmare interpretation of Antigone takes place." The blocks drawn in the place of heads, Bates claimed, lend the illustrations "magic . . . from the complete anonymity of the figures depicted." The "images' anonymity," she pointed out, "is central to Carson's text." In the *Globe & Mail,* Ewan Whyte noted that "at first appearance, it looks like a graphic novel of outsider art," with "illustrations [that] are immediate and visceral." Dan Kois, writing in *Slate,* called *Antigonick* a "beautiful, bewildering book, wondrous and a bit scary to behold, that gives a reader much to think about."

Someone Else's Wedding Vows and The Mobius Strip Club of Grief

Stone's next book is *Someone Else's Wedding Vows,* her first full-length poetry collection. In *Heavy Feather Review,* M. Forajter explained that this book "explores the self from a distance in order to construct a clearer view of its movements and position within the larger world," and the poems "flow as if from dream to dream" with "bits of the everyday . . . tangled up with the surreal logic of visions." Forajter concluded: "If you enjoy the trend of quietly surreal poems, soaked with tender reflections on the domestic, then these poems are for you. If you are looking for something more radical, something that will change the chemical make-up of your bones, you may have to turn somewhere else." According to Analicia Sotelo in *American Microreviews and Interviews,* the collection is one of "astronomically good poems . . . written with a straightforward, metered gravity that will immediately let you in."

Online at *Bookslut,* J.P. Poole called *Someone Else's Wedding Vows* "enviably good." The critic found a "kinship with Emily Dickinson." Stone is likewise "fascinated with domestic life, its quietness, and . . . sort of 'loaded gun' sexuality." Poole lamented the lack of illustration from this talented artist but recognized that the "danger of including illustrations in a book of poems is that they inform the work too much or not enough." Poole summarized: "She isn't accessible in a way that is

overly easy to understand, but she also isn't so out there than no one but a student of the classics can parse her—she's just the right amount of mystery and relatability; she's one to watch out for." In *Colorado Review,* Kent Shaw described the world of these poems: "A world emphasized by imaginative potential and explanation. An exaggerated world. A world on the verge of detonation." He concluded: "Big love, the kind of love continually appearing in Stone's *Someone Else's Wedding Vows,* is the kind of love that will be lived with for years, that will be analyzed and exploded and breathlessly evaded only to be breathlessly clutched at too tightly. How is the imagination not the natural part of a process like this?"

Stone next wrote *The Mobius Strip Club of Grief.* In this collection—whose title harks back to Ruth Stone's poem "The Möbius Strip of Grief"—Stone acts as a sort of guide through the land of the dead for those still living. In *Publishers Weekly* a critic described the book as an exploration of "grief, familial connection, and the small things that sustain life" using a "confessional voice with humor and portentous imagery." Lauren Kane reviewed the book at *Paris Review,* explaining that Stone "is our Virgilian guide through a wildly conceived purgatorial landscape."

■ Biographical and Critical Sources

PERIODICALS

Books & Culture, July-August, 2012, Sarah Ruden, review of *Antigonick,* p. 38.
Publishers Weekly, November 20, 2017, review of *The Mobius Strip Club of Grief,* p. 70; February 3, 2014, review of *Someone Else's Wedding Vows,* p. 35.
New Statesman, July 2, 2012, Olivia Laing, "Such a Devoted Sister," review of *Antigonick,* p. 52.

ONLINE

American Microreviews and Interviews, http://www.americanmicroreviews.com/ (March 5, 2018), Analicia Sotelo, review of *Someone Else's Wedding Vows.*
Bianca Stone Website, http://www.poetrycomics.org (March 22, 2018).
Bookslut, http://www.bookslut.com/ (May 1, 2014), J.P. Poole, review of *Someone Else's Wedding Vows.*
Cold Front, http://coldfrontmag.com/ (August 20, 2013), Timothy Liu, review of *Antigonick.*
Colorado Review, http://coloradoreview.colostate.edu/ (March 5, 2018), Kent Shaw, review of *Someone Else's Wedding Vows.*

Comics Journal, http://www.tcj.com/ (August 24, 2012), Alex Dueben, author interview.

Full Stop, http://www.full-stop.net/ (June 27, 2012), Amanda Shubert, review of *Antigonick.*

Globe & Mail (Toronto, Ontario, Canada), http://www.globeandmail.com/, (June 23, 2012), Ewan Whyte, review of *Antigonick.*

Guardian (London, England), https://www.theguardian.com/ (June 8, 2012), Emily Stokes, review of *Antigonick.*

Guernica, https://www.guernicamag.com/ (July 13, 2012), Rebecca Bates, review of *Antigonick.*

Heavy Feather Review, https://heavyfeatherreview.com/ (June 12, 2014), M. Forajter, review of *Someone Else's Wedding Vows.*

New Statesman, https://www.newstatesman.com/ (June 27, 2012), review of *Antigonick.*

New Yorker, https://www.newyorker.com/ (June 25, 2012), review of *Antigonick.*

Paris Review, https://www.theparisreview.org/ (December 1, 2017), Lauren Kane, review of *The Möbius Strip Club of Grief.*

Poetry Foundation, https://www.poetryfoundation.org/ (August 7, 2012), Harriet Staff, brief author profile.

Poet.org, https://www.poets.org/ (March 22, 2018), brief author profile.

Ruth Stone Foundation, http://ruthstonefoundation.org/ (March 23, 2018).

Slate, http://www.slate.com/ (September 7, 2012), Dan Kois, review of *Antigonick.*

Times Literary Supplement, https://www.the-tls.co.uk/ (August 1, 2012), George Steiner, review of *Antigonick.**

Sarah Stovell

1977-

■ **Personal**

Born 1977; has a partner; children: two.

■ **Addresses**

Home—Northumberland, England.

■ **Career**

Writer and educator. Lincoln University, Lincoln, England, lecturer.

■ **Writings**

Mothernight, Snowbooks (London, England), 2008.
Exquisite, Orenda Books (London, England), 2017.

■ **Sidelights**

Sarah Stovell is a British writer and educator. She works at Lincoln University, where she serves as a lecturer. In an interview with a contributor to the *WriteWords* website, Stovell discussed the beginnings of her interest in writing. She stated: "I was probably about six. I gave myself enough time to master letter formation, and then I was off. At the height of my infant school rebellion, I used to write stories while pretending to get on with my maths, and that pretty much set the tone for life."

Mothernight

In 2008, Stovell released her first book, *Mothernight.* It tells the story of a complicated friendship between boarding-school classmates Leila and Olivia.

Stovell discussed the writing process for *Mothernight* in an interview with a writer on the *Vulpes Libris* website. She stated: "I have always been interested in family relationships, particularly in those families that just seem so dysfunctional you wonder why they haven't all shot each other. One of my major bugbears in life is the issue of maternal guilt, and how blame is always placed with the mother if their children go off the rails, even if the children are now in their forties. I also think guilt is a part of motherhood in a way that— dare I say it—it isn't for fathers. So I initially wanted to explore all these issues." She told the same writer that she had planned to retell the biblical story of Eve: "Initially, I wanted to tell her story—how this woman felt to have been such a useless specimen that her own son killed his brother. But as I went along, I found more and more Genesis myths, particularly the one of Lilith, where Adam is said to have had a previous who died and who spawned evil children, and so that, in the end was where Leila came in. And maternal guilt was lost along the way somewhere."

Exquisite

Exquisite finds writers Alice and Bo in an intense mentor-mentee relationship that eventually becomes dangerous. In an interview with Lucia N. Davis on Davis's self-titled website, Stovell commented on the themes of the book: "I am very drawn to female relationships. Partly, this is because I am a woman, but also because the most significant (by which I mean complicated, not necessarily fulfilling) relationships in my life have been with women. I am interested in the deep bonds of friendship that women often forge. I also interested in mother-daughter relationships, which can be the most fraught relationships around."

John M. Murray, a reviewer in *ForeWord*, asserted: "Sarah Stovell's *Exquisite* is a dark, sensual, and twisted character study." Murray added: "*Exquisite* is an engrossing story about two troubled people who connect despite having every reason not to. Tensions mount, making it hard to put down." A *Publishers Weekly* critic described the book as a "dismal tale of obsession, cruelty, and betrayal" and noted: "Those expecting an unhappy ending won't be disappointed." A writer on the *Crime Review* website was particularly impress with the book's "language," explaining: "This is the aspect of the novel that makes you want it to continue on forever, if only to enjoy the lyrical, almost sensual way that Stovell describes the beautiful landscape around the village, the emotions of the characters, and the subtlety of the way she uses the language to actually manipulate you." "*Exquisite* is a very competent debut from Sarah Stovell that highlights some very strong themes—obsession, narcissism, and manipulation," asserted a contributor to the *Writing.ie* website. The contributor added: "It would work very successfully on the big screen. The sizzling chemistry between Alice and Bo is palpable off the pages with very astute descriptions and characterisations. . . . *Exquisite* will be a book that will be among the top recommendations for many this year."

■ Biographical and Critical Sources

PERIODICALS

ForeWord, August 27, 2017, John M. Murray, review of *Exquisite*.

Publishers Weekly, August 28, 2017, review of *Exquisite*, p. 106.

ONLINE

Crime Review, https://thecrimereview.com/ (April 4, 2017), review of *Exquisite*.

Lucia N. Davis Website, https://luciadavis.com/ (November 21, 2017), Lucia N. Davis, author interview.

Orenda Books Website, http://orendabooks.co.uk/ (March 25, 2018), author profile.

Vulpes Libris, https://vulpeslibris.wordpress.com/ (March 5, 2008), author interview.

Writes of Woman, https://thewritesofwoman.com/ (June 2, 2017), review of *Exquisite*.

WriteWords, http://writewords.org.uk/ (January 22, 2008), author interview.

Writing.ie, https://www.writing.ie/ (March 5, 2018), review of *Exquisite*.*

Corinne Sullivan

1990(?)-

■ Personal

Born c. 1990. *Education:* Boston College, B.A., 2014; Sarah Lawrence College, M.F.A., 2016.

■ Addresses

Home—Long Island City, NY. *Agent*—U.S. Agent: Stephen Barbara, stephen@inkwellmanagement. com; UK Agent: Juliet Mushens, juliet@caskiemushens.com.

■ Career

Writer, dancer, bookseller, and exercise instructor. InkWell Management, New York, NY, royalties and accounting assistant; Book Culture, New York, bookseller; DanceWorks, New York, performer. Also teaches spin classes.

■ Writings

Indecent, Wednesday Books (New York, NY), 2018.

Contributor of stories to periodicals, including *Knee-Jerk, Night Train,* and *Pithead Chapel.*

■ Sidelights

Corinne Sullivan is a writer, dancer, bookseller, and exercise instructor. She holds a bachelor's degree from Boston College and a master's degree from Sarah Lawrence College. Sullivan has worked as a royalties and accounting assistant at InkWell Management in New York City and has performed with the DanceWorks company, also in New York City. She has worked for the Book Culture bookstore and has served as an instructor for spin classes.

In 2018, Sullivan released her first book, *Indecent.* Its protagonist is a young woman named Imogene Abney. Imogene has recently earned a college degree and has obtained an apprenticeship with a prestigious boarding school called the Vandenberg School for Boys. She is set to spend the year in Scarsdale, New York, where the school is located. Imogene is thrilled for the opportunity to work at the school, a place she wishes she could have attended. However, as a female from a middle-class family, she wouldn't have had the chance to attend classes in the beautiful, ivy-covered buildings. Imogene gets to know the students and faculty at the school, and one particular student begins to stand out to her. The student is Adam "Kip" Kipling, and Imogene finds herself drawn to him because of his intelligence and confidence, which borders on arrogance. The insecure and anxious Imogene wishes she could be more like Kip. Eventually, Kip recognizes Imogene's attraction to him, and the two begin having an affair. The narrative includes vignettes that demonstrate the depth of Imogene's anxiety and depression. When she is in a depressed state, she finds it difficult to get out of bed, to bathe, or to eat. Imogene also has a habit of picking at her facial skin to the point that it begins bleeding. Meanwhile, the affair between Imogene and Kip becomes intense, and the two are in serious danger of being found out. Ultimately, Kip becomes increasingly distant, leaving Imogene confused and hurt.

Critics offered favorable assessments of *Indecent.* Courtney Eathorne, a contributor to *Booklist,* asserted: "Sullivan's debut is a smart and delicious page-turner." A *Publishers Weekly* reviewer described the book as a "tense and surprising debut." The same reviewer commented: "This is an affecting novel, examining self-doubt, self-sabotage, and the lasting impact of both." Writing on the *Library Journal* website, Erin Holt called *Indecent* "a steamy debut" and concluded: "Imogene's backstory adds a layer to the story that will have readers sympathizing with her."

■ Biographical and Critical Sources

PERIODICALS

Booklist, February 1, 2018, Courtney Eathorne, review of *Indecent,* p. 28.

Publishers Weekly, October 9, 2017, review of *Indecent,* p. 40.

ONLINE

Book Culture Website, http://www.bookculture.com/ (November 7, 2017), author interview.

Bookseller, https://www.thebookseller.com/ (August 25, 2017), Natasha Onwuemezi, review of *Indecent.*

Corrine Sullivan Website, https://www.corinnesullivanbooks.com (March 24, 2018).

Library Journal Online, https://reviews.libraryjournal.com/ (November 7, 2017), Erin Holt, review of *Indecent.*

Thought Catalog, https://thoughtcatalog.com/ (March 24, 2018), author profile.*

Emily Suvada

■ Personal

Born in Australia; married. *Education:* Graduated from college. *Hobbies and other interests:* Reading, writing, cooking, coding, hiking, powerlifting, art, watching Star Trek.

■ Addresses

Home—Portland, OR.

■ Career

Writer. Former data scientist in the finance industry.

■ Writings

This Mortal Coil, Simon Pulse (New York, NY), 2017.

■ Sidelights

Originally from Australia, Emily Suvada now lives in Portland, Oregon, and writes fantasy novels. She holds degrees in mathematics and astrophysics and has worked as a data scientist. Suvada told a contributor to the *Wanderlust Reader* website: "I studied astrophysics because I've always loved thinking about how the universe works, and that's what has had the biggest impact on my writing—thinking about how things work, which is a skill I learned and honed through studying science." Suvada continued: "My characters are constantly on a quest to understand themselves and the world they live in, and they generally pursue the answers to these questions through a scientific lens. That style of thinking definitely comes from my studies. I also love coding, which gives me a sense of creation—the same feeling I get from writing! All those interests make their way into . . . my writing and give it color and texture."

Suvada's first novel is *This Mortal Coil*. She discussed the plot of the book in an interview with Dorine White, a contributor to the *Write Path* website. Suvada stated: "*This Mortal Coil* is set two years after the outbreak of a plague that kills its victims by detonating their bodies into towering plumes of infectious mist that spread through the air, infecting everyone in a mile-wide radius. The majority of the population died in the outbreak, and most survivors now live in underground bunkers run by a shady organization called Cartaxus." Suvada continued: "Our heroine, Catarina, has been told by her father to stay away from Cartaxus at all costs. He was kidnapped by the organization during the outbreak, so she's spent two years surviving alone in a remote cabin in the Black Hills. Like her father, Catarina is a gene-hacker—in this world people have the ability to rewrite their DNA, downloading and using 'apps' to change their bodies." Regarding the message of the book, Suvada told a writer on the *Regal Critiques* website: "We're hurtling full-speed into a future where we'll be able to alter the DNA of our entire world. Not just our bodies, but our food, our environment, and eventually our society. I think there are a lot of questions that we need to discuss now that this technology is approaching. I really hope readers come away from the book and see that maybe gentech as I've imagined it isn't entirely realistic—but that many facets of the world in *This Mortal Coil* are very real, and grounded in real-world science that's happening right now."

"Suvada's debut novel balances characterization and action with an intensity that readers of dystopian fantasy will find infectious," asserted Tom Malinowski, a reviewer in *Voice of Youth Advocates*. Though *Booklist* critic Debbie Carton described the romance in the book as "predictable," she predicted: "Action and gore fans will delight in the blood and guts throughout." Conversely, Blake Holman, a writer in *School Library Journal*, suggested that the volume features a "nicely developed love triangle." Holman added: "In the crowded field of YA dystopia, this debut stands out with an especially grotesque cause of ruin." A contributor to *Kirkus Reviews* called the book "an original concept but with an ending that requires a suspension of disbelief." Judy Davies, a reviewer on the *Book Bag* website, remarked: "*This Mortal Coil* is the first part of a series and does not disappoint the reader in leaving him wanting more of such a fast paced and intriguing story. The plot introduces us to interesting ideas about what it means to be human and how far we can go before the humanity in us is lost and genetic engineering takes over." "*This Mortal Coil* is a book bursting—as it were—with ideas, and Catarina's voice and perspective are compelling," asserted Amal El-Mohtar at *NPR.org*.

■ Biographical and Critical Sources

PERIODICALS

Booklist, November 1, 2017, Debbie Carton, review of *This Mortal Coil,* p. 66.
Kirkus Reviews, August 15, 2017, review of *This Mortal Coil.*
School Library Journal, October, 2017, Blake Holman, review of *This Mortal Coil,* p. 115.
Voice of Youth Advocates, October, 2017, Tom Malinowski, review of *This Mortal Coil,* p. 78.

ONLINE

Book Bag, http://www.thebookbag.co.uk/ (November 1, 2017), Judy Davies, review of *This Mortal Coil.*
Emily Suvada Website, http://emilysuvada.com (March 24, 2018).
Literary Arts, https://literary-arts.org/ (March 24, 2018), author profile.
NPR.org, https://www.npr.org/ (November 9, 2017), Amal El-Mohtar, review of *This Mortal Coil.*
Readings Website, https://www.readings.com.au/ (October 23, 2017), Kate O'Mara, review of *This Mortal Coil.*
Regal Critiques, http://reading-is-dreaming-with-open-eyes.blogspot.com/ (November 12, 2017), author interview.
Wanderlust Reader, https://wreaderblog.wordpress.com/ (March 24, 2018), author interview.
Write Path, http://dorinewhite.blogspot.com/ (November 10, 2017), Dorine White, author interview.*

Lynn R. Sykes

1937-

■ Personal

Born April 16, 1937, in Pittsburgh, PA; married Kathleen Mahoney. *Education:* Massachusetts Institute of Technology, B.S., 1960, M.S., 1960; Columbia University, Ph.D., 1964.

■ Addresses

Home—NY. *Office*—Lamont-Doherty Earth Observatory, 202D Seismology, 61 Rt. 9W, P.O. Box 1000, Palisades, NY 10964-8000.

■ Career

Scientist and writer. Columbia University, Lamon-Doherty Earth Observatory, New York, NY, Higgins Professor Emeritus.

■ Awards, Honors

Walter H. Bucher Medal, American Geophysical Union, 1975.

■ Writings

Silencing the Bomb: One Scientist's Quest to Halt Nuclear Testing, Columbia University Press (New York, NY), 2017.

■ Sidelights

Lynn R. Sykes is a scientist and writer based in New York. In 1960, he earned both a bachelor's degree and a master's degree from Massachusetts Institute of Technology. He obtained a Ph.D. from Columbia University in 1965. Sykes has devoted his career to researching seismic activity and its connection to nuclear weapons testing. The American Geophysical Union awarded him the Walter H. Bucher medal in 1975.

In 2017, Sykes released a memoir called *Silencing the Bomb: One Scientist's Quest to Halt Nuclear Testing.* In the book, Sykes explains how he helped to develop methods of seismic measuring that would help to detect evidence of nuclear weapons testing. In the early days of his career, he with U.S. government authors to help negotiating the Threshold Nuclear Test Ban Treaty of 1974, which made large underground nuclear testing illegal. Sykes traveled to Moscow for his work on the treaty, where he recalls having been followed by Russian spies. In the more recent past, he was part of the group advocating a law banning all nuclear testing called the Comprehensive Test Ban Treaty.

In an interview with Rachel Becker for the *Verge* website, Sykes explained how history stoked his interest in preventing nuclear weapons testing. He stated: "I came of age during the Cuban Missile Crisis in 1962 as a graduate student. It was work that I thought I could do—as few others could—to develop better methods of identifying underground atomic testing, so that we could eventually have a full ban on nuclear testing. Preventing nuclear war is most the important thing that faces humanity and the United States." In the same interview, Sykes lamented the failure of the Threshold Test Ban to prevent testing: "There were many new weapons that were developed after 1968 including most of the Russian warheads for missiles that carried nuclear warheads that could be independently targeted—a very dangerous development. . . . Also, many other countries like

China went on to develop larger weapons after the Threshold Test Ban was negotiated. So back in 1969, if we'd had a full test ban then, China, India, Pakistan, North Korea could not have developed weapons as easily."

Shervin Taheran, a reviewer in *Arms Control Today*, offered a favorable assessment of Sykes's book. Taheran commented: "This account of his work and his activist role . . . provides a unique historical view." A *Publishers Weekly* critic suggested: "It's mainly a clear, bone-dry rehash of verification science, replete with geological maps, . . . seismic graphs, and details of myriad seismic waves."

■ Biographical and Critical Sources

PERIODICALS

Arms Control Today, January-February, 2018, Shervin Taheran, review of *Silencing the Bomb: One Scientist's Quest to Halt Nuclear Testing*, p. 43.

Publishers Weekly, October 30, 2017, review of *Silencing the Bomb*, p. 73.

ONLINE

Columbia University, Department of Earth & Environmental Sciences Website, http://eesc.columbia.edu/ (March 24, 2018), author faculty profile.

Columbia University, Lamont-Doherty Earth Observatory Website, http://www.ldea.columbia.edu/ (March 24, 2018), author faculty profile.

Penn State, College of Earth and Mineral Sciences Website, http://www.e-education.psu.edu/ (March 24, 2018), author profile.

Verge, https://www.theverge.com/ (March 20, 2018), Rachel Becker, author interview.*

Witold Szablowski

1980-

■ Personal

Born June 27, 1980; married Iza Meyza.

■ Addresses

Home—Warsaw, Poland.

■ Career

Journalist and writer.

■ Awards, Honors

Melchior Wankowicz Award, 2008; Journalism Award, European Parliament, 2010, for "Two Bodies Will Wash Ashore Today."

■ Writings

The Assassin from Apricot City: Reportage from Turkey, translated by Antonia Lloyd-Jones, Stork Press (London, England), 2013.

Dancing Bears: True Stories of People Held Captive to Old Ways of Life in Newly Free Societies, translated by Antonia Lloyd-Jones, Penguin Books (New York, NY), 2018.

■ Sidelights

Witold Szablowski is a writer and journalist from Poland. He has received prizes for his reporting work, including the 2008 Melchior Wankowicz Award and the 2010 European Parliament Journalism Award. Szablowski is best known for his journalistic work focused on Turkey.

The Assassin from Apricot City

The Assassin from Apricot City: Reportage from Turkey, translated from the Polish by Antonia Lloyd-Jones, presents twelve essays on Turkey from Szablowski. He profiles a Turkish terrorist group called All Agca, which was active in the 1980s in the title essay. Another piece focuses on a messianic cult from the seventeenth century led by Sabbatai Zevi. The first essay concerns the current immigrant crisis in Turkey.

Jacob Daniels, a reviewer in *World Literature Today*, suggested: "Sometimes Szablowski makes awkward generalizations. . . . These statements feel lazy and run contrary to his theme of human complexity. But when he tells poignant stories about tangible men and women, a broader picture begins to emerge—baffling as the image may be." Writing on the *Cosmopolitan Reviews* website, Katarzyna Zwolak commented: "There are a lot of colors, flavors, smells and sounds of Turkey in this book, and many incredibly vivid and interesting stories about particular Turkish cities and villages like Adana, Gaziantep or Edirne. As Szablowski uncovers Turkey, his book is like traveling around the country and discovering different places, cultures, environments and very different people that one may meet on his/her Turkish way. And this is the Turkey that Szablowski presents in his collection. If you want to explore such a country, it is a real must-read." A contributor to the *Culture.pl* website remarked: "A good reporter is a catalyst to the story—he removes the gag obstructing people from speaking and makes the story develop according to its own powerful stream that covers more and more areas. And Szablowski has this special ability." Lucy Popescu, a reviewer at the *Huffington Post,* asserted: "For anyone interested in this rich, varied, frustrating country, *The Assassin from Apricot City* is essential reading, seamlessly translated by Antonia Lloyd-Jones. Szablowski's combination of literary reportage and personal reflections are reminiscent of the late Ryszard Kapuscinski's dispatches from foreign parts."

Dancing Bears

In *Dancing Bears: True Stories of People Held Captive to Old Ways of Life in Newly Free Societies,* Szablowski begins by discussing the history of the dancing bears of Bulgaria. The gypsies in the country used inhumane practices to teach the bears to move in a way that resembled dancing. When the bears were released from captivity, it took a significant amount of time for them to regain their natural habits. In an interview with Ari Shapiro at *NPR.org,* Szablowski explained what the meaning of the dancing bears is in context of the book and metaphorically speaking. He stated: "I'm talking about how complicated the freedom is, how painful it might be. They are living in a kind of freedom laboratory where people teach them what freedom is, what freedom means. And when I heard this story for the first time, I realized that actually here in Eastern Europe, in the countries which used to be part of communist world or used to be so-called satellites of Soviet Union, since 1989, we've been living in similar freedom laboratories. And we just try to understand, like the bears in the very first moments, what's going on."

Jodie B. Sloan offered a favorable assessment of *Dancing Bears* on the *AU Review* website. Sloan asserted: "Elegantly pulling together the varied threads, Szablowski combines personal histories, letting his interviewee do the talking, with a unique storytelling device. As a result, *Dancing Bears* is both a compelling social history and a stunning example of literary journalism."

■ Biographical and Critical Sources

PERIODICALS

World Literature Today, March-April, 2014, Jacob Daniels, review of *The Assassin from Apricot City: Reportage from Turkey,* p. 76.

ONLINE

AU Review, http://arts.theaureview.com/ (March 3, 2018), Jodie B. Sloan, review of *Dancing Bears: True Stories of People Held Captive to Old Ways of Life in Newly Free Societies.*

Cosmopolitan Review, http://cosmopolitanreview. com/ (March 30, 2014), Katarzyna Żwolak, review of *The Assassin from Apricot City.*

Culture.pl, http://culture.pl/ (August 10, 2011), review of *The Assassin from Apricot City;* (January 26, 2016), Mikolaj Glinski, review of *Dancing Bears.*

Harpers Online, https://harpers.org/ (February 1, 2018), excerpt from *Dancing Bears.*

Huffington Post, http://www.huffingtonpost.co.uk/ (January 31, 2014), Lucy Popescu, review of *The Assassin from Apricot City.*

NPR.org, https://www.npr.org/ (March 6, 2018), Ari Shapiro, author interview.

Polish Culture, http://www.polishculture.org.uk/ (March 23, 2018), author profile.*

Liara Tamani

■ Personal

Children: one daughter. *Education:* Duke University, B.A.; Vermont College, M.F.A.; attended Harvard Law School. *Hobbies and other interests:* Dancing, yoga, traveling.

■ Addresses

Home—Houston, TX.

■ Career

Writer. Houston Rockets & Comets, TX, former marketing coordinator; production designer for *Girlfriends* television show. Has also worked variously as a yoga instructor, dance teacher, floral designer, and home accessories designer.

■ Writings

Calling My Name, Greenwillow Books (New York, NY), 2017.

■ Sidelights

Liara Tamani is a writer of young adult fiction. She has held a wide variety of jobs, including yoga instructor, dance teacher, floral designer, home accessories designer, television production designer, and marketing coordinator for professional sports teams. She holds degree from Duke University and Vermont College.

In 2017, Tamani released her first book, *Calling My Name.* The novel's protagonist and narrator is an African American teenager named Taja Brown. Taja lives in Houston with her very religious family. The book is structured in short chapters that resemble diary entries. The first of these entries finds Taja skipping church, which involves lying to her family. She deals with her doubts about Christianity, while still maintaining a strong belief in God and communicating with him often. She tries to reconcile her own feelings about spirituality with the Christian beliefs that she was taught throughout her childhood. After Taja enters high school, she begins having romantic relationships and eventually has sex for the first time with her boyfriend, Andre. She feels great shame for what she has done and keeps it a secret from her family. Taja also thinks about her future and daydreams about being a published author one day.

In an interview with Robin Galbraith, a contributor to the *Cynsations* website, Tamani discussed the inspiration behind the book. She stated: "I started writing *Calling My Name* to explore and heal the wounds of my teenage self. Like Taja, the protagonist of *Calling My Name,* I grew up in a very loving and religious family. My family was always in church." Tamani continued: "While *Calling My Name* is not my story, it was definitely born out of my experience. And I wanted to share my truth, to give voice to the struggle of sexual shame and guilt (which a lot of teenagers deal with, especially girls), and to speak to the terrifying experience of departing from one's family and community teachings to find one's own way."

Critics offered favorable assessments of *Calling My Name.* Amanda MacGregor, contributor to the *School Library Journal* website, commented: "This quiet book is beautifully written." MacGregor added: "Taja's story is light on a concrete plot but the very universal question of 'who am I and what do I want?' seems like enough plot to keep readers invested as they watch Taja mature." Writing on the *Lonestar Literary* website, Michelle Newby suggested: "*Calling My Name* is finely wrought young-adult fiction by Houston's Liara Tamani. Her debut novel about an African American girl coming-of-age in the 1980s in Texas is powerfully reminiscent of, and compares favorably with, Judy Blume's seminal *Are You There, God? It's Me, Margaret* (Random House, 1970). *Calling My Name* is a sensory experience, beginning with the beautifully designed jacket." Newby also stated: "Taja's first-person narration is a joy." Anita Lock, a reviewer on the *BookPage* website, remarked: "Tamani manages to seamlessly tie Taja's story together in this witty and thought-provoking coming-of-age novel told from an African American perspective." "An excellent portrayal of African American culture, gorgeous lyrical prose, strong characters, and societal critique make Tamani's debut a must read," asserted Courtney Gilfillian in *Booklist*. A *Kirkus Reviews* critic commented: "It's a slow-build narrative coated in ornate language that may initially distract readers but pays off in the end." The same critic praised Tamani's "stylish prose." A contributor to *Publishers Weekly* suggested: "Tamani's debut novel brims with heart and soul." The contributor continued: "The discussion of religion never feels heavy handed or prescriptive." Suzanne Libra, a writer in *Voice of Youth Advocates*, highlighted "Tamani's poetic language and imagery" and predicted: "Readers who appreciate coming-of-age stories, allowing for deep connection with the main character will enjoy this."

■ Biographical and Critical Sources

PERIODICALS

Booklist, September 1, 2017, Courtney Gilfillian, review of *Calling My Name*, p. 101.

Kirkus Reviews, July 15, 2017, review of *Calling My Name*.

Publishers Weekly, September 11, 2017, review of *Calling My Name*, p. 69.

Voice of Youth Advocates, October, 2017, Suzanne Libra, review of *Calling My Name*, p. 66.

ONLINE

BookPage Online, https://bookpage.com/ (October 31, 2017), Anita Lock, review of *Calling My Name*.

Cynsations, http://cynthialeitichsmith.blogspot. com/ (November 30, 2017), Robin Galbraith, author interview.

HarperCollins Website, https://www.harpercollins. com/ (March 23, 2018), author profile.

Liara Tamani Website, https://www.liaratamani.com (March 23, 2018).

Lonestar Literary, http://www.lonestarliterary.com/ (November 26, 2017), Michelle Newby, review of *Calling My Name*.

School Library Journal Online, http://www. teenlibrariantoolbox.com/ (October 24, 2017), Amanda MacGregor, review of *Calling My Name*.*

Anthony Tambakis

1967-

■ Personal

Born May 22, 1967, in Fairfield, CT.

■ Addresses

Home—Venice, CA.

■ Career

Writer, producer, and actor. Former professor of creative writing in Atlanta, GA.

■ Awards, Honors

Paul Bowles Fellowship for fiction writing.

■ Writings

Swimming with Bridgeport Girls, Simon & Schuster (New York, NY), 2017.

SCREENPLAYS AND TELEPLAYS

(With Gavin O'Connor and others) *Warrior*, Lionsgate, 2011.
(With Renee Zellweger and others) *Cinnamon Girl*, Fox 21, 2013.
(With Cliff Dorfman and others) *Brothers*, Lionsgate, 2015.
(With Brian Buffield) *Jane Got a Gun*, 1821 Productions, 2015.
Sun Dogs, Apartment 3C Productions, 2017.

(With Matthew Stone and others) *Gringo*, Amazon Studios, 2018.
(With Adam Cozad and others) *Suicide Squad 2*, DC Entertainment, 2019.

Also adapter, with Gavin O'Connor, of Walter Tevis's novel *The Hustler* as a stage play.

■ Adaptations

Swimming with Bridgeport Girls is being produced for film by the Gotham Group, with Tambakis adapting his novel for the screen.

■ Sidelights

Anthony Tambakis is best known for his work in film and television. He was the coauthor of the screenplay for the 2011 film *Warrior*, the story of two estranged brothers who come to terms with each other and with their alcoholic father through their participation in a mixed martial arts tournament. He has also been tapped as screenwriter for the DC blockbuster supervillains epic *Suicide Squad 2*. His fiction debut is *Swimming with Bridgeport Girls: A Novel*, a story that draws on his background growing up in Connecticut.

Swimming with Bridgeport Girls tells the tale of a failed ESPN commentator named Ray Parisi who has lost his job, his reputation, and his wife, and has made the decision to get at least one of them back. "As the story opens," wrote a *Publishers Weekly* reviewer, "he is still in love with his recently divorced wife, L, though she is dating another man." Ray's ultimate goal, said Mike Fleming, Jr., in *Deadline Hollywood,* is "to win back his wife, using a faulty recollection of the climax of *The Great Gatsby* as his inspiration." Ray believes that he can win L.'s affections back if he fulfills one of her dreams: to live in a certain southern mansion. Help comes in the form of a 600,000-dollar windfall legacy from his father. Ray decides that he can turn the money into the two million dollars he needs to buy the mansion if he goes to Las Vegas and plays the tables. "Tambakis keeps the humor from getting too broad and Ray from getting too sympathetic," explained a *Kirkus Reviews* contributor, "though the reader usually roots for him anyway."

Critics enjoyed Tambakis's first foray into fiction. "According to a Simon & Schuster press release," recounted Jeanne Muchnick, writing in the *Fairfield Daily Voice*, "'If a Richard Russo protagonist went on a bender in Vegas, the result would be something like this.'" "'It's a fast, fun summer read that's also really about something,' Tambakis said. 'It's humorous and heartbreaking at the same time. I think there's something in it for everyone,'" reported Tara O'Neill at *CTpost*. "He said the story is centered around a love story, but it's a book that manages to be feminine and masculine, appealing to a greater audience." "*Swimming with Bridgeport Girls* [in] no way reads like a thesis," declared Rick Koster in the *Day*. "Instead, it's stunningly comic, with laugh-out-loud lines and descriptions on virtually every page—and yet it's also a tender and desperately sad story of romantic obsession, the shifting sands of a relationship, and the self-delusion embedded in addiction. It's as though Dan Jenkins rewrote *Under the Volcano*—and Parisi,

a former creative writing professor and a recipient of the Paul Bowles Fellowship for fiction, nuances the opposite forces of tragedy and comedy with balletic grace."

■ Biographical and Critical Sources

PERIODICALS

Day (New London, CT), July 9, 2017, Rick Koster, "Anthony Tambakis' Debut Novel Is Hilarious—and Heartbreaking."
Kirkus Reviews, May 1, 2017, review of *Swimming with Bridgeport Girls*.
Publishers Weekly, May 15, 2017, review of *Swimming with Bridgeport Girls*, p. 32.

ONLINE

CTpost, https://www.ctpost.com/ (August 22, 2017), Tara O'Neill, "*Swimming with Bridgeport Girls* Author Grew Up in Fairfield."
Deadline Hollywood, http://deadline.com/ (November 30, 2011), Mike Fleming, Jr., "*Warrior* Cowriter Lands Book Deal."
Fairfield Daily Voice, http://fairfield.dailyvoice.com/ (August 14, 2017), Jeanne Muchnick, "From Fairfield to Hollywood: Writer Pens First Novel with Nod to Bridgeport."
Internet Movie Database, http://www.imdb.com/ (February 21, 2018), author profile.
Simon & Schuster Website, http://www.simonandschuster.com/ (February 21, 2018), author profile.*

Nafkote Tamirat

■ Personal

Born in Boston, MA. *Education:* Columbia University, M.F.A.

■ Addresses

Home—Paris, France.

■ Career

Writer.

■ Writings

The Parking Lot Attendant, Henry Holt & Company (New York, NY), 2018.

Contributor of stories to periodicals and anthologies, including *Best Paris Stories, Anemone Sidecar,* and *Birkensnake.*

■ Sidelights

Nafkote Tamirat is an American writer living in Paris, France. Born in Boston, Massachusetts, she attended Columbia University, from which she obtained an M.F.A. Tamirat has written stories that have appeared in anthologies and periodicals, including *Best Paris Stories, Anemone Sidecar,* and *Birkensnake.*

In 2018, Tamirat released her first book, *The Parking Lot Attendant.* The novel is narrated by an unnamed teenage girl. As the story begins, the narra-

tor is on an island, where she lives with her father, who is originally from Ethiopia. The narrator recalls living in Boston, where she befriended another Ethiopian immigrant named Ayale. Ayale works as a parking lot attendant and is involved in a scheme involving package deliveries. The narrator looks up to Ayale, though it becomes increasingly clear that he may be up to no good. Meanwhile, she deals with resentments she holds for her father.

In an interview with Thu Doan, a contributor to the *Brazos Bookstore* website, Tamirat discussed her writing process: "As I was starting to write this novel, which began as a short story, Ayale and the narrator, who is always unnamed, and set within the Ethiopian community in Boston set itself quite naturally for a mystery-detective novel set up. The first few drafts, the island sections, were much bigger and that element of suspense was taken to a greater degree because part of the mystery was not only what is happening on the island, but the next step as well, and what is the island going to do next." Tamirat continued: "The society of the island, its citizens, and the injustices that they inflict towards the natives. It adds another element to the mystery as well. At one point, it was so overloaded that it was difficult to discern what the story was really about. So it speaks to my profound interest and admiration for the genre as a whole."

The Parking Lot Attendant received favorable assessments from critics. A *Kirkus Reviews* writer asserted: "Tamirat writes blind teenage devotion well." The same writer described the book as "captivating for both its unusual detail and observant take on teenage trust; curious and delightful." "The unsettling conclusion serves as a perfect ending for this riveting coming-of-age story full of murky motives, deep emotion, and memorable characters," asserted a contributor to *Publishers Weekly*. Annie Bostrom, a reviewer on the *Booklist* website, commented: "Tamirat's razor-sharp prose fashions a magnificently dimensional and emotionally resonant narrator, herself a storyteller who frames her own tale with beguiling skill."

■ **Biographical and Critical Sources**

PERIODICALS

Kirkus Reviews, February 15, 2018, review of *The Parking Lot Attendant*.

Publishers Weekly, November 6, 2017, review of *The Parking Lot Attendant*, p. 59.

ONLINE

Booklist Online, https://www.booklistonline.com/ (February 1, 2018), Annie Bostrom, review of *The Parking Lot Attendant*.

Booklist Reader, http://www.booklistreader.com/ (February 9, 2018), review of *The Parking Lot Attendant*.

Brazos Bookstore Website, https://www.brazosbookstore.com/ (March 23, 2018), Thu Doan, author interview.

Macmillan Website, https://us.macmillan.com/ (March 23, 2018), author profile.*

Ann Kidd Taylor

■ **Personal**

Daughter of Sue Monk Kidd; married; children: one son. *Education:* Graduated from Columbia College.

■ **Addresses**

Home—Naples, FL.

■ **Career**

Writer. *Skirt!* magazine, former editorial assistant.

■ **Writings**

(With mother, Sue Monk Kidd) *Traveling with Pomegranates*, Viking (New York, NY), 2009.
The Shark Club, Viking (New York, NY), 2017.

■ **Sidelights**

Ann Kidd Taylor, daughter of famed novelist Sue Monk Kidd, wrote her first book, the memoir *Traveling with Pomegranates*, with her mother in 2009. Taylor then became a novelist in her own right, releasing her debut, *The Shark Club*, in 2017. *The Shark Club* is set in Florida, and it follows shark expert Maeve Donnelly. The heroine's path in life was determined by her childhood; Maeve was bitten by a Black Tip shark when she was twelve years old. The same day of the shark attack, Maeve receives her first kiss. The kiss is delivered by Maeve's childhood sweetheart, Daniel, and the pair eventually plans to wed. Maeve's all-consuming career researching sharks, however, puts a strain on the relationship, and Daniel has an affair. The engagement is called off and the affair results in a child, Hazel. Six years later, Maeve returns to her home town, where she will finally have to reckon with her heartbroken past. From there, as *Booklist* correspondent Melissa Norstedt put it, the story "moves along briskly as Maeve struggles to forgive, let go of past love, and navigate happiness on her own terms."

Taylor shared her path to publication in a *Pat Conroy Literary Center* website interview, in which she told Mindy Lucas: "Writing *Traveling with Pomegranates* definitely prepared me for the writing of *The Shark Club*, even though one is non-fiction and one is fiction. I learned so much about writing, about editing, about re-writing, about structure and just about the kind of internal drive it takes to stay in the chair and do the work." The author added: "Having said that, my son was very young at the time and I think that's why it took so long as it did—to write the book—because I was a young mother, and I had this young baby, and I didn't want to miss a thing. I wanted to do the field trips. And of course if your only hours are during pre-school, you only have half the morning."

Several critics praised Taylor's efforts, and a *Kirkus Reviews* contributor found that "the scenes depicting Maeve's intellectual and emotional ties to sharks are captivating." The contributor went on to call *The Shark Club* "an engaging novel about the loves that define our lives." Connelly Hardaway, writing in the *Charleston City Paper Online*, offered applause as well, asserting: "Taylor has found the formula for a well-balanced beach read. *Shark Club* has the typical love story, but with a strong female lead; the fight between inner and outer demons, featuring realistic, flawed characters; and the quirky qualities of a small town and dreamy beach setting."

■ Biographical and Critical Sources

BOOKS

Taylor, Ann Kidd, and Sue Monk Kidd, *Traveling with Pomegranates*, Viking (New York, NY), 2009.

PERIODICALS

Booklist, April 15, 2017, Melissa Norstedt, review of *The Shark Club*.

Kirkus Reviews, April 1, 2017, review of *The Shark Club*.

Library Journal June 15, 2017, Neal Wyatt, "Well Read for the Summer," p. 110.

Publishers Weekly, April 24, 2017, review of *The Shark Club*.

ONLINE

Ann Kidd Taylor Website, https://www.annkiddtaylor.com (February 22, 2018).

Charleston City Paper Online, https://www.charlestoncitypaper.com (June 28, 2017), Connelly Hardaway, author interview and review of *The Shark Club*.

Pat Conroy Literary Center Website, http://patconroyliterarycenter.org/(February 22, 2018), Mindy Lucas, author interview.

Tampa Bay Times Online, http://www.tampabay.com (May 31, 2017), review of *The Shark Club*.*

Tori Telfer

■ Personal

Female. *Education:* Northwestern University, B.A. (magna cum laude).

■ Addresses

Home—Chicago, IL.

■ Career

Writer and editor. Previously worked in children's publishing and catering.

■ Member

Phi Beta Kappa.

■ Awards, Honors

Edwin L. Shuman Fiction Award, J.G. Nolan Scholarship, Undergraduate Research Symposium Award, Hulda & Maurice Rothschild Endowment award, Edwin L. Shuman Best Senior Honors Thesis Award, all from Northwestern University.

■ Writings

Lady Killers: Deadly Women throughout History, HarperPerennial (New York, NY), 2017.

Also author of the screenplay *Detective in the City of Beautiful Women.* Contributor to periodicals and websites, including *Chicago, Good, Establishment, Hairpin, Awl, Jezebel, Vice,* and *Salon.*

■ Sidelights

Tori Telfer is a writer and editor based in Chicago, Illinois. She holds a bachelor's degree from Northwestern University, from which she received various awards and scholarships. Telfer has written articles that have appeared in publications and websites, including *Chicago, Good, Establishment, Hairpin, Awl, Jezebel, Vice,* and *Salon.* She is also the author of a screenplay called *Detective in the City of Beautiful Women.*

In 2017, Telfer released her first book, *Lady Killers: Deadly Women throughout History.* This nonfiction volume profiles a diverse set of female murderers. Among them is Nannie Doss, whose nickname was the Giggling Grandma. In the 1900s, Doss murdered seven people, all family members of herself and her husband. Alice Kyteler lived during the thirteenth century in Europe and was put on trial for killing her husbands. She was also accused of witchcraft. Telfer calls particular attention to Erzsebet Bathory, a Hungarian woman who lived during the 1500s. Bathory is said to have tortured and murdered young girls. An Irish woman named Lizzie Halliday blamed mental illness when it was discovered that she killed her husband and the people who lived next door. Mary Ann Cotton killed multiple men she married, as well as several of her children. Some accounts say she killed up to eleven of them.

In interviews, Telfer has explained her interest in female killers and why it is important to discuss them. In an interview with Lyz Lenz, a writer on the *Rumpus* website, Telfer stated: "Violent women are violent because they're human. And humans are violent. There are a million reasons for someone to become a serial killer. But they're violent because they're human. They're not violent because she's some special breed of bad woman or the wrong kind of seed was planted in a weird type of soil and that woman spun off. That's a really crazy metaphor." Telfer also remarked: "My current theory on why I like true crimes: There's just something elemental to it, like humans at their most extreme. It's sort of like the most eeriest thing you can do to another person is murder them. It's just so intense and visceral and such an expression of power. It's like a destruction of a creation. I think too, we like to identify monsters because it makes us feel better." Telfer told Suzannah Weiss at the *Broadly* website: "Female serial killers have bursts of publicity when they're apprehended, but people tend to forget about them after they're locked away. I suspect this is because it's too much work to rearrange our conceptions of 'female' to include 'can be a serial killer.' Their crimes reveal that women aren't always the 'gentler sex'—and that's unpleasant or downright scary for people to admit." Telfer also stated: "A lot of the stereotypes about female serial killers hold up under scrutiny: Women tend to use poison, they tend to kill people they know, . . . and they don't use excessive violence."

Reviewers offered favorable assessments of *Lady Killers*. A *Kirkus Reviews* writer asserted: "The book is well-researched and informative, but squeamish readers beware: Telfer doesn't hide the grisly and gruesome details." The same writer described the book as "an illuminating read on a subject that has not received much publicity." "Telfer draws out the tired stereotypes with just enough wit and humor to make the topic of female murderers enjoyable," commented a contributor to *Publishers Weekly*. Of the book, David Pitt, a critic in *Booklist*, noted: "Given its dark subject matter, it's surprisingly lively." Pitt also called it "a welcome addition to serial-killer literature." A reviewer on the *Rebellious* magazine website remarked: "It's important to at least know that these women exist because it's part of the world we live in, even though we all wish it wasn't. . . . And this idea that violence = inherently male is simply false. That being said, this book isn't just for studying human nature. It's also for entertainment." Ximena N. Larkin, a contributor to the *Bitch Media* website, suggested: "It might sound perverse, but seeing women as killers helps us collectively see them as human, capable of being both the executed and the executioner. As progressive as *Lady Killers* is, the 'gender straitjackets' study shows that we are still raising young girls with the harmful belief that they are weaker than boys. *Lady Killers* serves as a warning against underestimating women, and a reminder of what can happen in a society that does. The topic might not be pleasant, but it's a crucial component in the fight for equality." "Telfer not only tells a convincingly creepy story, she gives each case a cultural context, explaining what would drive a woman to this particular kind of madness," asserted Jean Zimmerman on the *National Public Radio* website. Zimmerman added: "As a frequent magazine and web contributor, Telfer knows her way around a pop phrase. Her work is bracingly non-stuffy, with a tone similar to that of Mary Roach's *Stiff*. *Lady Killers* most definitely entertains."

■ Biographical and Critical Sources

PERIODICALS

Booklist, September 1, 2017, David Pitt, review of *Lady Killers: Deadly Women throughout History*, p. 12.

Kirkus Reviews, August 15, 2017, review of *Lady Killers*.

Publishers Weekly, August 7, 2017, review of *Lady Killers*, p. 61.

ONLINE

Bitch Media, https://www.bitchmedia.org/ (December 11, 2017), Ximena N. Larkin, author interview and review of *Lady Killers*.

Broadly, https://broadly.vice.com/ (November 20, 2017), Suzannah Weiss, author interview.

Daily Iowan Online, http://daily-iowan.com/ (November 2, 2017), Salma Rios, review of *Lady Killers*.

National Public Radio Online, https://www.npr.org/ (October 14, 2017), Jean Zimmerman, review of *Lady Killers*.

Rebellious, https://rebelliousmagazine.com/ (February 27, 2018), review of *Lady Killers*.

Rumpus, http://therumpus.net/ (October 16, 2017), Lyz Lenz, author interview.

Tori Telfer Website, https://www.toritelfer.com (March 23, 2018).*

Amy Thielen

■ Personal

Married Aaron Spangler (an artist); children: one son. *Education:* Graduated from Macalester College, 1997.

■ Addresses

Home—Park Rapids, MN.

■ Career

Chef and writer. Food Network, host of *Heartland Table,* c. 2013-14; *Saveur,* contributing editor.

■ Awards, Honors

James Beard Foundation Award for journalism, 2011; James Beard Book Award for American Cooking, 2014, for *The New Midwestern Table: 200 Heartland Recipes.*

■ Writings

The New Midwestern Table: 200 Heartland Recipes, Clarkson Potter (New York, NY), 2013.
Give a Girl a Knife (memoir), Clarkson Potter (New York, NY), 2017.

Contributor to periodicals, including *People, Food Network* magazine, *Country Living, Reuters, Boston Globe, Eater National, Esquire,* and the Minneapolis *Star Tribune.*

■ Sidelights

Amy Thielen is a chef, television host, and writer who has worked as a contributing editor for *Saveur* magazine and as host of the Food Network show *Heartland Table.* She received a prestigious James Beard Foundation Award for journalism, as well as a James Beard Book Award for her cookbook, *The New Midwestern Table: 200 Heartland Recipes.* Thielen grew up in rural Minnesota and later lived on a remote homestead with her husband. The pair then moved to New York City, where Thielen worked with some of the world's most famous chefs, including David Bouley and Daniel Boulud. In her memoir, *Give a Girl a Knife,* Thielen chronicles her journey from Minnesota to New York, as well as her eventual return to her home state. Thielen explains that, after learning all she could in New York, she wanted to return to her roots and focus on her native cuisine. To this end, Thielen explores her Minnesotan food roots, commenting on the dishes and ingredients that have shaped her approach to cooking. The author additionally reflects on her childhood food memories, and she credits her mother as the person who "gave a girl a knife."

Thielen discussed her memoir in a *Journal Sentinel Online* interview with Kristine M. Kierzek, noting: "I think it has three themes that will be universal, and one of those is how to find your motivation. It took me a little while, but I really did find it in cooking. Cooking kind of saved me. . . . I didn't know how to apply myself or have much self-discipline. I'd accomplished some things, but it wasn't until I found cooking that I had discipline. The other thread through the book is about Aaron and I and how we negotiated how to be creative types—he's an artist, I'm a craftsperson—how to live two creative lives and where to do it." The author added: "The book is also about belief and pursuing your dreams. It takes risk."

Margaret Quamme praised *Give a Girl a Knife* in *Booklist*, and she found that "Thielen is as supple and precise a writer as she is a cook." Leah Mirakhor, writing in the *Los Angeles Times Online*, was also impressed, and she announced that "Thielen's ode to living at the crossroads of culinary high and low offers thoughtful insights into the life of the chef, highlighting that when 'you give a girl a knife,' as her mom did when Amy was young, you pass on a legacy: that she will learn how to use it, and someday 'consider that knife an extension of her hand, as wedded to her finger as a nail.'" As Mary Ann Grossmann put it in the online *Twin Cities Pioneer Press*, "If you don't know what 'food memoir' means, you'll understand when you finish reading *Give a Girl a Knife*," which is a "compelling and lyrical account." Another positive assessment was proffered by Kathryn O'Shea-Evans in the online *Los Angeles Review of Books*; she found that "when [Thielen] explains about moving to New York with Spangler to pursue cooking and art, respectively, you can't help but root for them. She's got as much mettle as her homesteading ancestors did moving to Minnesota in the first place, talking her way into an internship by strolling into jackets-required restaurant Bouley and asking to speak with the chef." The critic went on to note: "I love that Thielen brings respect to Midwestern regional dishes, largely ignored on the coasts. . . . And the way Thielen dissects their history? It's the story of immigration in Minnesota itself."

■ Biographical and Critical Sources

BOOKS

Thielen, Amy, *Give a Girl a Knife,* Clarkson Potter (New York, NY), 2017.

PERIODICALS

Booklist, April 1, 2017, Margaret Quamme, review of *Give a Girl a Knife.*
Kirkus Reviews, March 15, 2017, review of *Give a Girl a Knife.*

ONLINE

Amy Thielen Website, http://www.amythielen.com (February 23, 2018).
City Pages Online, http://www.citypages.com/ (April 7, 2017), review of *Give a Girl a Knife.*
Journal Sentinel Online, https://www.jsonline.com/ (February 24, 2018), Kristine M. Kierzek, author interview.
Los Angeles Review of Books, https://lareviewofbooks.org/ (May 20, 2017), Kathryn O'Shea-Evans, review of *Give a Girl a Knife.*
Los Angeles Times Online, http://www.latimes.com/ (June 23, 2017), Leah Mirakhor, review of *Give a Girl a Knife.*
Twin Cities Pioneer Press, https://www.twincities.com (June 4, 2017), Mary Ann Grossmann, review of *Give a Girl a Knife.**

Lesley Thomson

1958-

■ Personal

Born 1958, in London, England. *Education:* Brighton University, B.A., 1981; Sussex University, M.A.

■ Addresses

Home—East Sussex and Gloucestershire, England. *Agent*—Laura Palmer Editorial Director, Head of Zeus, 1st Fl. E., 5-8 Hardwick St., London EC1R 4RG, England.

■ Career

Writer; guest tutor, West Dean M.A. program in creative writing and publishing.

■ Awards, Honors

City Limits top-ten books of the year, 1987, for *Seven Miles from Sydney*; People's Book Prize, 2010, for *A Kind of Vanishing.*

■ Writings

Seven Miles from Sydney, HarperCollins Publishers (London, England), 1987.
A Kind of Vanishing, Myriad Editions (Brighton, England), 2007.

"THE DETECTIVE'S DAUGHTER" SERIES; MYSTERY NOVELS

The Detective's Daughter, Head of Zeus (London, England), 2014.

Ghost Girl, Head of Zeus (London, England), 2014.
The Detective's Secret, Head of Zeus (London, England), 2015.
The House with No Rooms, Head of Zeus (London, England), 2016.
The Dog Walker, Head of Zeus (London, England), 2017.
The Death Chamber, Head of Zeus (London, England), 2018.

Also author of *The Runaway: A Detective's Daughter Short Story,* Head of Zeus (London, England), 2015. Contributor to *Hold onto the Messy Times* by Sue Johnston.

■ Sidelights

Born in London, British writer Lesley Thomson is the best-selling author of acclaimed mystery novels, including her popular "The Detective's Daughter" series. Thomson graduated from Brighton University in 1981 and spent the next several years in Australia, working at odd jobs while she focused on her writing career. She later returned to England, where she continued write fiction and completed an M.A. in English literature at Sussex University. Thomson's first novel, *Seven Miles from Sydney,* was published in 1987. It was named one of the top ten books of the year in *City Limits.*

A Kind of Vanishing

A Kind of Vanishing, a story of a child's unsolved disappearance, received glowing reviews and established Thomson's reputation as mystery writer. In the summer of 1968, two young girls are playing hide-and-seek together when one of them vanishes. Eleanor Ramsay tells police investigators that she has no idea how Alice disappeared or where she might have gone. But as it turns out, Eleanor knows more than she wants to share. Alice, the pampered only child of wealthy parents, had discovered a troubling secret about Eleanor's working-class mother, and she was taunting the Eleanor with this information just before she vanished.

In a parallel narrative set thirty years later, Eleanor's father suddenly dies, and a forty-year-old woman named Alice Kennedy comes to his funeral. No one knows who she is or why she is there. It falls to Alice's teenage daughter Chris to work out the mystery of her mother's past, in the process revealing dark secrets about the Ramsay family. Reviewers expressed great admiration for the novel and commented that Thomson's talent places her among mystery luminaries such as Ian Rankin and Kate Atkinson. *A Kind of Vanishing* won the 2010 People's Book Prize for fiction.

The Detective's Daughter

The legacy of an infamous unsolved murder case sets the context for *The Detective's Daughter*, the first of a series of novels featuring Stella Darnell. Kate Rokesmith's murder in 1981 had made headlines and had become an unhealthy obsession for the police investigator assigned to the case, Detective Terence (Terry) Darnell. The inspector had given everything to the case, neglecting his own young daughter and wrecking his marriage, but had never been able to charge anyone for the crime. Haunted by this failure, Terry had continued working on the case in secret, even after his retirement from the police force.

Thirty years after Rokesmith's murder, Terry suffers a fatal heart attack. When Stella begins clearing out his house she finds his notes on the Rokesmith case, kept meticulously over decades, and they force her to change everything she had come to believe about her father and his work. The man she had seen as a distant and uninvolved father, she discovers, had been a complex man worthy of appreciation and respect. Feeling compelled to honor her father somehow, Stella decides to find out what she can about Rokesmith and her death. In this task, which is ultimately successful, she receives help from Jack Harmon, an enigmatic employee of her cleaning company who is fascinated by patterns and claims to see ghosts. He is also not afraid to get into the mind of psychopathic killers to try to figure out how they think and what they might do next.

Ghost Girl and The Detective's Secret

The series continues with *Ghost Girl*, in which another of Terry's old police files inspires Stella to investigate. The file contains seven photographs showing empty streets, and it is not immediately obvious to Stella why her father had kept them. Looking into the mystery, she learns that one photo was taken in 1966 on the day that a young girl witnessed a traumatic event. In investigating the mystery, Stella and Jack discover a tenuous connection with the infamous Moors murderers, Myra Hindley and Ian Brady, who had sexually assaulted and killed five children near Manchester, England, in the early 1960s. Reviewing the novel in *Booklist*, Karen Keefe said that the story takes time to unspool, but added that Thomson handles the narrative tension well and convinces readers that a "thumping good reveal . . . [is] worth the wait."

In *The Detective's Secret*, a man is found dead beneath a metro London train. His brother believes he was murdered and hires Stella and Jack to investigate the case. But Jack, who works nights as a subway train driver, thinks it more likely that the man committed suicide. As Stella deals with family matters, including the surprise information that she has a brother, Jack moves into a west London water tower that is being renovated and turned into apartments. A decomposed corpse is found in the building, assumed to be the body of a man seen having sex at the water tower in 1987 with a woman who slammed the door behind her afterward, trapping him inside. Clues about the train death point to a connection with the death in the water tower.

The House with No Rooms and The Dog Walker

As Stella works on a new case in *The House with No Rooms*, much of which is set in London's Kew Gardens, she discovers links to an unsolved murder from 1976. In *The Dog Walker*, a frustrated husband asks Stella and Jack to find out what had happened to his wife, Helen Honeysett, who had disappeared on a winter night twenty-nine years earlier while jogging with her dog along the Thames river towpath. The dog returned home, but Helen's body had never been found, and police were unable to offer any answers.

As they begin seeking clues, Stella and Jack discover that no one who lives near that remote section of the towpath is willing to talk. The fact that so much time has elapsed makes matters more difficult. The investigation hinges on who was walking a dog that night, but many pet dogs have come and gone since Helen's disappearance, and it is all but impossible to identify the relevant animal and its walker. A writer for *Publishers Weekly*, describing the book as "busy," observed that the plot and its numerous secondary characters can be difficult to keep track of, but ventured that some readers would appreciate its dark atmospherics.

■ **Biographical and Critical Sources**

PERIODICALS

Booklist, October 15, 2015, Karen Keefe, review of *Ghost Girl*, p. 21.

Bookseller, January 17, 2014, review of *Ghost Girl*, p. 33.

Publishers Weekly, May 15, 2017, review of *The Dog Walker*.

ONLINE

Lesley Thomson Website, https://lesleythomson.co.uk (February 7, 2018).*

Teresa Trent

■ Personal

Born in Chattanooga, TN; children: three.

■ Addresses

Home—Houston, TX.

■ Career

Writer.

■ Writings

"PECAN BAYOU" SERIES

A Dash of Murder, CreateSpace (North Charleston, SC), 2011.

Overdue for Murder, CreateSpace (North Charleston, SC), 2012.

Doggone Dead, CreateSpace (North Charleston, SC), 2013.

Buzzkill, CreateSpace (North Charleston, SC), 2013.

Burnout, CreateSpace (North Charleston, SC), 2014.

Murder for a Rainy Day, CreateSpace (North Charleston, SC), 2014.

Till Dirt Do Us Part, CreateSpace (North Charleston, SC), 2017.

OTHER

Color Me Dead, CreateSpace (North Charleston, SC), 2017.

Murder of a Good Man, Camel Press (Seattle, WA), 2018.

■ Sidelights

Originally from Chattanooga, Tennessee, Teresa Trent is a writer of mystery novels.

A Dash of Murder and *Overdue for Murder*

In 2011, Trent released her first novel, *A Dash of Murder*. The book is also the first installment in her "Pecan Bayou" series. Its protagonist is a young woman named Betsy Livingston, who lives in the small Texas town of Pecan Bayou. Betsy is reluctant to join her Aunt Maggie in a ghost-hunting expedition at a building that once served as a tuberculosis hospital. However, she ultimately relents. While there, she discovers a dead body and feels a strong determination to find out what happened to the person. Betsy's father, a police lieutenant, tries to dissuade her, but Betsy will not be stopped. Meanwhile, she writes a column in the local newspaper called "The Happy Hinter."

Betsy returns in the second book in the "Pecan Bayou" series, *Overdue for Murder*. She has written a book that features household hints and tips and is looking forward to presenting on it to other local writers at the Pecan Bayou Library. A murder ruins their evening. The authorities begin suspecting that Betsy may have been the perpetrator, and she must clear her name before she is put in jail.

Doggone Dead and *Buzzkill*

Doggone Dead, set in the summertime in Pecan Bayou, finds Betsy looking for her lost puppy. During her search, she encounters a corpse on the land of a famous cowboy movie star. Betsy's investigation puts her in contact with townspeople who swear to have seen the deceased cowboy's ghost.

In *Buzzkill*, Betsy is planning her wedding to Leo, a meteorologist. She claims that she wants the wedding to be simple, but complications continue to arise. Betsy's disorganization does not help things go smoothly. Finally, her aunt puts her in touch with a wedding planner named Mr. Andre. Mr. Andre urges her to switch from the florist she chose on her own to a different vendor. The original florist unexpectedly dies, and his death may be linking to Betsy's recipe for homemade calamine lotion, making her a murder suspect once again. She hopes that all will be resolved before her Valentine's Day nuptials. Writing on the *Blackheart* magazine website, Laura Roberts asserted: "All of the characters were fun and well-drawn, even as they played on some typical stereotypes like the rampaging bride, gay wedding planner, and nosey newspaperman. The story itself is engaging (who doesn't love weddings?), and generally well written, despite a couple of small continuity issues (when did Betsy acquire a dog?)." Highlighting an element of the book that worked particularly well, Roberts called out "the concept of a small-town columnist getting tangled up in mysteries, especially with her father as the head of the town's police force."

Burnout and Murder for a Rainy Day

Betsy investigates a fire at the newspaper office and the disappearance of the editor, Rocky, in *Burnout*. Meanwhile, she worries about the attention her new husband is getting from the administrative assistant at his news station.

In *Murder for a Rainy Day*, a pregnant Betsy looks into the disappearance of a town landmark. Later, animals disappear, and a person is murdered. Meanwhile, a hurricane approaches.

Till Dirt Do Us Part

Gossip flies in Pecan Bayou in *Till Dirt Do Us Part*. Betsy fails miserably while taking part in a gardening competition, and rumors circulate about a newly single mother.

In an interview with Terry Ambrose, which appeared on Ambrose's self-titled website, Trent discussed the inspiration for *Till Dirt Do Us Part*, telling Ambrose: "I was inspired by Big Love, the HBO series about a polygamist. I can barely handle one marriage let alone multiple relationships. I was fascinated by what kind of mindset would cause a person to commit their time, love and money to a family setup like that. Of course, in a little town like Pecan Bayou, Texas this sort of thing provides fodder for gossip for years to come."

Color Me Dead and Murder of a Good Man

Trent sets her next series in Henry Park, Colorado. The first novel in the series is *Color Me Dead*. Its protagonist, Gabby Wolfe, is an artist with clairvoyant abilities. She foresees the murder of a young woman named Gigi and tries to stop it from happening. She also deals with her ne'er-do-well brother, Mitch. Paula Mitchell, a reviewer on the *Community Bookstop* website, praised Trent's development of "the relationship between Gabby and Gigi and Gabby and Mitch standing up against their mother who still saw them as lost teenagers who needed to be guided instead of adults who need to decide what they want to do in life." Of the book as a whole, Mitchell asserted: "It draws you in and has you wanting to learn more about the people of Henry Park."

Murder of a Good Man is the first installation in Trent's "Piney Woods" series. In it, grieving daughter Nora finds mystery and danger when she travels to Piney Woods, Texas, to fulfill a promise she made to her late mother. Citing the universality of the story, a contributor to the *Long and Short Reviews* website remarked: "This small town setting with a nice mix of warm people has a lot in common with many other small towns trying to stay alive in today's world." The contributor added: "The story has a few characters that are immediately likeable and each has their own distinct personality." A *Publishers Weekly* writer described the book as a "saccharine series launch" and suggested: "Cozy fans won't mind the rather unlikely solution." Judith Reveal, a critic on the *New York Journal of Books* website, commented: "As cozies go, this is not only a fun read, but it moves along quite well. She has a respectable number of characters—not so many as to confuse the reader but enough to have a growing number of possible perpetrators! This is a keeper." "The first of the 'Piney Woods' mystery series is an entertaining read with a feisty heroine and delightful secondary characters," asserted Keitha Hart on the *RT Book Reviews* website.

Author Comments

Trent told *CA:* "I love a book that has such wonderful characters and settings you don't want to put it down. I wanted to create that kind of a world.

"Authors who have influenced me were Jan Karon, Fannie Flagg, and Phillip Gulley. All of their stories have the stock small-town characters, but they are never flat. There is a lightness to the storytelling and while characters have real problems, the conflict centers on the heart, not violence.

"My writing process changes just a little bit with every book. I do a lot of preliminary work in plotting, character, and theme and then write the first draft quickly, which is usually short and full of holes. I print out, fix errors, and rewrite the book several times until I'm happy with it.

"I'm always surprised when people tell me they've read my books and like them!

"*A Dash of Murder* will always be special to me because it was the book that proved to me that I could do it. My favorite is usually the last book I've written because it is fresh in my mind.

"I hope my readers enjoy the mystery, but also get the feeling of visiting family in a small town full of funny and heartwarming characters."

■ Biographical and Critical Sources

PERIODICALS

Publishers Weekly, November 6, 2017, review of *Murder of a Good Man*, p. 64.

ONLINE

Blackheart, http://blackheartmagazine.com/ (July 27, 2013), Laura Roberts, review of *Buzzkill*.

Community Bookstop, http://communitybookstop. blogspot.com/ (January 24, 2017), Paula Mitchell, review of *Color Me Dead*.

Long and Short Reviews, http://www. longandshortreviews.com/ (October 23, 2017), review of *Murder of a Good Man*.

New York Journal of Books, https://www. nyjournalofbooks.com/ (February 27, 2018), Judith Reveal, review of *Murder of a Good Man*.

RT Book Reviews, https://www.rtbookreviews.com/ (February 27, 2018), Keitha Hart, review of *Murder of a Good Man*.

Teresa Trent Website, http://teresatrent.com (March 22, 2018).

C.J. Tudor

- ## Also Known As

Caroline J. Tudor

- ## Personal

Born in Salisbury, England; children: daughter.

- ## Addresses

Home—Nottingham, England.

- ## Career

Freelance copywriter, scriptwriter, television presenter.

- ## Writings

The Chalk Man, Crown Publishers (New York, NY), 2018.

- ## Sidelights

Born in Salisbury, England, and raised in Nottingham, C.J. Tudor is a British writer of dark and macabre stories. She has worked at various jobs, including freelance copywriter, scriptwriter, voiceover artist, and television presenter. Her first novel, *The Chalk Man*, published in 2018, spans thirty years, offering a psychological thriller of murder and cover up. In 1986 in the English village of Anderbury, twelve-year-old Eddie, Mickey, and their childhood friends cause mayhem and draw chalk stick figures in a secret code known only to them. One day, one of the figures leads them to the mutilated body of a teenage girl. The police believe the killer is teacher Mr. Halloran, who admitted to having sex with the girl and later committed suicide. Thirty years later in 2016, Mickey returns to town, looks up Eddie, and wants to make a documentary film about the murders. But when they encounter chalk figures again, they realize the killer may still be around. Online at *Criminal Element*, Gabino Iglesias said the book "is a riveting and relentlessly compelling psychological suspense debut that weaves a mystery about a childhood game gone dangerously awry and keeps readers guessing right up to the shocking ending."

The story shifts between present and past, offering different perspectives and revelations of plot. "Tudor delivers an assured debut that alternates between 1986 and 2016 with unpredictable twists. . . . Tudor never misses a beat in showing each character as both a child and an adult while also exploring the foreboding environs of a small town," according to a writer in *New York Daily News*. Christine Tran commented in *Booklist* that the book is "an absorbing debut with a well-crafted mystery and a solid dose of *Stand by Me* creepiness." Writing in *Kirkus Reviews*, a contributor deemed the work "a swift, cleverly plotted debut novel that ably captures the insular, slightly sinister feel of a small village. Children of the 1980s will enjoy the nostalgia."

Calling the book a promising debut, a writer in *Publishers Weekly* noted that while Tudor makes some rookie mistakes, "including excessive plot twists seemingly for the sake of surprise, her storytelling prowess is undeniable." *RTE* website reviewer Grace Keane considered the book a must-read thriller that "will have readers glued to every word until the shocking and sinister finale." Keane added: "Although thoroughly enjoyable, the story did flounder a bit towards the end and it was a bit difficult to keep track of all the revelations . . . but nonetheless, she managed to grapple it back for the finale."

■ Biographical and Critical Sources

PERIODICALS

Booklist, December 1, 2107, Christine Tran, review of *The Chalk Man*, p. 31.

Publishers Weekly, October 2, 2017, review of *The Chalk Man*, p. 116.

ONLINE

Criminal Element, https://www.criminalelement.com/ (January 11, 2018), Gabino Iglesias, review of *The Chalk Man*.

Kirkus Reviews, https://www.kirkusreviews.com/ (October 11, 2017), review of *The Chalk Man*.

New York Daily News Online, http://www.nydailynews.com/ (January 8, 2018), review of *The Chalk Man*.

RTE, https://www.rte.ie/ (January 16, 2018), Grace Keane review of *The Chalk Man*.*

Kevin Vallely

■ Personal

Married; wife's name Nicky; children: Caitlin and Arianna. *Education:* McGill University School of Architecture, degree, 1988; Commonwealth Scholarship to Cambridge University.

■ Addresses

Home—British Columbia, Canada. *Office*—Vallely Architecture, North Vancouver, British Columbia, Canada.

■ Career

Architect and adventurer. Vallely Architecture, North Vancouver, British Columbia, Canada, owner.

■ Member

Explorer's Club.

■ Awards, Honors

McGill University, Royal Architectural Institute of Canada medal; Explorer's Club Flag recipient; *Globe and Mail,* named a leading adventurer, 2003.

■ Writings

Rowing the Northwest Passage: Adventure, Fear, and Awe in a Rising Sea, Greystone Books (Berkeley, CA), 2017.

■ Sidelights

Canadian architect, adventurer, and Explorer's Club member Kevin Vallely has traveled around the world including Alaska, Indonesia, and the Klondike. In 2009, he and two teammates broke the world record for the fastest unsupported trek across Antarctica from the Ronne Ice Shelf to the Geographic South Pole. Vallely wrote about his expedition at the other end of the planet in his 2017 book, *Rowing the Northwest Passage: Adventure, Fear, and Awe in a Rising Sea* in which he attempted to be the first to row the passage under human power in a single season. Vallely owns and runs the Vallely Architecture firm and holds a degree from McGill University School of Architecture.

In *Rowing the Northwest Passage,* Vallely and three colleagues describe their 2013 record trek navigating the Northwest Passage connecting the Pacific and Atlantic Oceans in a custom-made, high-tech rowboat, a trip called one of the last "firsts" in adventure expeditions. Sadly, the route was only possible due to global warming in the Arctic that revealed water passages through previously solid ice sheets. The book describes weather and life-threatening storms, wildlife encounters, determination and perseverance, discussions with fascinating people they met along the way, and abuse from climate change deniers.

In an interview with Correne Coetzer online at *Explorers Web,* Vallely explained that the idea to row the passage in one season came from his good friend and champion downriver paddler Jerome Truran. Vallely said it was the symbolism of the endeavor that grabbed him. "This was the Northwest Passage, the iconic crux to the northern sea route from Europe to the Orient, the passage I learned so much about in school, the passage that, through the quest to find it, shaped my country of Canada. I was struck by the idea," said Vallely.

The trip was undertaken to bring awareness to climate change. "The Arctic is melting twice as fast as anywhere on Earth," said Vallely on the *Story Untold* website. "I don't think we realize how profoundly [things] will change. . . . We need to do something about it." When planning the trip in 2013, Vallely said to Scott York online at *Outside:* "To my mind, exploration is about seeking knowledge. . . . Although we're not exploring a new territory, we are certainly seeking knowledge in a changing environment." The book "is as much a history lesson and thrilling travelogue as it is an ecological warning," according to a *Publishers Weekly* reviewer. In *Booklist,* Colleen Mondor remarked that the mix of science and adventure in the Arctic "leave Vallely with a deep respect for local knowledge of the current state of our climate."

■ Biographical and Critical Sources

PERIODICALS

Booklist, September 15, 2017, Colleen Mondor, review of *Rowing the Northwest Passage: Adventure, Fear, and Awe in a Rising Sea,* p. 22.

ONLINE

Explorers Web, http://www.explorersweb.com/ (April 15, 2013), Correne Coetzer, author interview.

Kevin Vallely Website, http://www.kevinvallely.com (April 1, 2018), author profile.

Outside, https://www.outsideonline.com/ (July 10, 2013), Scott Yorko, review of *Rowing the Northwest Passage.*

Publishers Weekly, https://www.publishersweekly.com/ (October 1, 2017), review of *Rowing the Northwest Passage.*

Story Untold, http://storyuntold.blubrry.com/ (January 18, 2018), review of *Rowing the Northwest Passage.**

Glenis Wilson

■ Personal

Born in Radcliffe on Trent, Nottinghamshire, England.

■ Addresses

Home—Radcliffe on Trent, Nottinghamshire, England.

■ Career

Writer.

■ Member

Nottingham Writers' Club, Romantic Novelists' Association, Crime Writers' Association.

■ Awards, Honors

Gladys Bungay Rose Bowl Award, 1988, for *Blood on the Turf;* Writer of the Year Award, 1992, for *Photo Finish;* Gladys Bungay Novel Award, 2001, for *Honey Tree,* 2007, for *Angel Harvest,* 2009, for *Dead Certainty,* and 2011, for *So Wrong—So Right;* Manuscript of the Year, Nottingham Writers' Club (NWC), 2011, for "A Display of Delphiniums," and 2012, for "Freedom"; Gladys Bungay Silver Rose Bowl Award, 2013, for *Dead on Course;* Ena Young Award for Prose, NWC, 2014; Writer of the Year Award, 2014; Manuscript of the Year, NWC, 2015; Gladys Bungay Silver Rose Bowl Award, 2015, for *Dead Reckoning.*

■ Writings

Photo Finish, Darf Publishers (London, England), 1992.
Blood on the Turf, Ulverscroft (Leicester, England), 1993.
So Wrong—So Right, Ulverscroft (Leicester, England), 2015.

"LINFORD ROMANCE SERIES"

Web of Evasion, Linford Romance (Leicester, England), 2005.
Love in Laganus, Linford Romance (Leicester, England), 2007.
The Honey Tree, Linford Romance (Leicester, England), 2009.
Angel Harvest, Linford Romance (Leicester, England), 2010.

"HARRY RADCLIFFE" MYSTERY SERIES

Dead Certainty: A Contemporary Horse Racing Mystery, Severn House (London, England), 2015.
Dead on Course: A Contemporary Horse Racing Mystery, Severn House (London, England), 2016.
Dead Reckoning: A Contemporary Horse Racing Mystery, Severn House (London, England), 2018.

Article contributor to the *Lady.*

■ Sidelights

Glenis Wilson is a short-story writer, article writer, and novelist. Wilson was born in Radcliffe on Trent, Nottinghamshire, England, and began writing at a young age. Wilson writes articles for the *Lady.* Her writing has received numerous awards, including the Gladys Bungay novel award for her books *The Honey Tree, Angel Harvest, Dead Certainty: A Contemporary Horse Racing Mystery,* and *So Wrong—So Right* and the Nottingham Writers' Club Manuscript of the Year award for "A Display of Delphiniums" in 2011 and "Freedom" in 2012.

Wilson is a member of the Nottingham Writers' Club, the Romantic Novelists' Association, and the Crime Writers' Association. She lives in Radcliffe on Trent, Nottinghamshire.

Dead Certainty

Dead Certainty, the first of the "Harry Radcliffe" mystery series, opens with Harry Radcliffe, a champion jockey, recovering from a serious injury following a racing accident. Radcliffe is dejected and hopeless, as his career as a jockey might be over. While waiting for a verdict from his doctor, he receives an offer from Elspeth Maudsley, one of British horse racing's most famous trainers. Maudsley wants Radcliffe to ghostwrite her biography. Radcliffe initially rejects the offer, but recognizing that he needs the money and a distraction, he decides to accept.

Nearly as soon as Radcliffe accepts the job, disasters pop up throughout his life. His house is nearly burned down, someone attempts to drive him off of the road, and someone he knows ends up dead. Radcliffe is certain that someone is trying to silence him, and what he may reveal by writing Maudsley's biography. In addition to writing the biography, he must uncover who is out to silence him. Emily Melton in *Booklist* wrote, "a stunning conclusion make this horsey tale a winner long before it crosses the finish line."

Dead on Course

In *Dead on Course: A Contemporary Horse Racing Mystery,* the second installment of the "Harry Radcliffe" mystery series, Radcliffe has made a full recovery from the riding injury he experienced in *Dead Certainty,* and he is back on the racetrack. After his first win, he is approached by Jake Smith, an ex-con whose sister, Jo-Jo, recently died in a car crash. Smith is convinced that the car crash was a murder, and, privy to Radcliffe's reputation as an amateur detective, he demands Radcliffe's help in the case.

Smith threatens to hurt someone close to Radcliffe if he does not help, so Radcliffe must comply. He begins interviewing the individuals Smith considers to be potential suspects, but does not seem to

find anything useful. Then, while Smith is out of town, another person is found dead. Radcliffe investigates the tragedy and begins to uncover a murder plot that reaches far beyond Jo-Jo's death. Sharon Wheeler in *Crime Review* wrote that the book is "a sprightly adventure, and boasts a decent amount of racecourse action."

Dead Reckoning

Dead Reckoning: A Contemporary Horse Racing Mystery focuses on the previously introduced jockey Harry Radcliffe and hardened ex-con Jake Smith. When Radcliffe makes a visit to street worker Alice, he finds her dead. Alice was a friend of Jo-Jo, Smith's late sister, and Radcliffe is convinced Smith murdered Alice. Radcliffe is surprised when Smith seeks him out, swearing he did not commit the murder and demanding Radcliffe find the real murderer.

As in *Dead on Course,* Smith uses death threats to force Radcliffe to help, this time threatening to kill both Radcliffe and his ex-wife. Though his ex-wife, Annabel, is in a relationships and expecting, Radcliffe is still in love with her, and he agrees to investigate the murder. Unfortunately, Smith is the police force's top suspect, so as Radcliffe is investigating the murder, he must also help hide and protect the man who is threatening his life. Melton in *Booklist* wrote, "Solid writing, a twisty plot, a likable hero, and plenty of horse-racing ambience make for an entertaining read."

■ Biographical and Critical Sources

PERIODICALS

Booklist, May 15, 2017, Emily Melton, review of *Dead Reckoning: A Contemporary Horse Racing Mystery,* p. 20; May 1, 2015, Emily Melton, review of *Dead Certainty: A Contemporary Horse Racing Mystery,* p. 28; October 15, 2015, Emily Melton, review of *Dead on Course: A Contemporary Horse Racing Mystery,* p. 20.

Kirkus Reviews, May 1, 2017, review of *Dead Reckoning.*

Publishers Weekly, May 1, 2017, review of *Dead Reckoning,* p. 40; April 27, 2015, review of *Dead Certainty,* p. 54; October 19, 2015, review of *Dead on Course,* p. 57.

ONLINE

Crime Review, http://crimereview.co.uk/ (June 20, 2015), Sharon Wheeler, review of *Dead Certainty;* (January 2, 2016), Sharon Wheeler, review of *Dead on Course.*

Glenis Wilson Website, http://gleniswilson.co.uk (August 24, 2018).*

Angela Veronica Wong

■ **Personal**

Female.

■ **Addresses**

Home—New York, NY.

■ **Career**

Writer, artist, performance artist, and educator. Performance art has been featured in independent galleries in Buffalo, NY, Toronto, Ontario, Canada, and New York, NY.

■ **Awards, Honors**

New York Chapbook Fellowship, Poetry Society of America, 2011; finalist for Tarpaulin Sky Book Prize, Frost Place Chapbook Contest, Slash Pine Chapbook Contest, and Fordham University Poets Out Loud Prize.

■ **Writings**

How to Survive a Hotel Fire, Coconut Books, 2012.
Elsa: An Unauthorized Autobiography, Black Radish Books, 2017.

Also author of chapbooks.

■ **Sidelights**

Angela Veronica Wong is a New York-based writer, artist, performance artist, and educator. Wong is the author of five chapbooks and was the winner

of the 2011 Poetry Society of America New York Chapbook Fellowship. She has been a finalist for the Tarpaulin Sky Book Prize, the Frost Place Chapbook Contest, Slash Pine Chapbook Contest, and Fordham University Poets Out Loud Prize and a semi-finalist for the Center for Book Arts Chapbook Competition and Akron Poetry Prize. Her creative work has been nominated for several Pushcart Prizes and the Best of the Net.

Wong's performance art has been featured in independent galleries in Buffalo, Toronto, and New York City. She lives in New York City.

How to Survive a Hotel Fire, Wong's first full-length collection of poems, was published by Coconut Books in the spring of 2012. Tony Mancus on the *Diagram* website described the book as "something that will withstand the fire it contains and something that yields more and more of itself upon return readings."

The title of the book introduces the themes repeated in the poems within: those of destruction, struggle, resurrection, and yearning for a sense of home. Destruction, as suggested by a fire, arises throughout the book, as does resurrection. Wong challenges the reader to consider whether one innately leads to the other, or if the two are cyclically related. The narrators' struggles for a sense of home are symbolized in the inclusion of a hotel in the poems. A temporary yet unreliable home, a hotel represents a false or provisional substitute for a real sense of belonging.

The book is divided into six sections, the first and last of which are comprised of a singular poem. In section one, Wong introduces the theme of longing that presents throughout the book. The reader is introduces to an "I," alongside an "other," a person or thing alluded to as a thing absent and valued. The final section reads like a fairytale, one that lacks the charm and magic of a traditional tale. This stylistic choice mirrors themes explored throughout the book; those of loss of innocence and unfulfilled longing.

The other four sections vary in form, ranging from small blocks of text in section two to poems centered on the page in section three. Each poem in section three begin with "in which," and many of the poems include the words "Our Heroine." The resulting effect unifies the poems in this section, while also simulating a feeling of time looping or standing still.

In section four, Wong focuses on the theme of cause and effect. In poems "How to Survive a Hotel Fire" and "How to Start a Hotel Fire" she introduces the tension between the two words, "survive" and "start." The reader is challenged to contemplate the relationship between the two words, considering their opposition and causality. The fourth section is the most violent of the six, depicting the details of a fire alluded to in the title. April Naoko Heck on the *Rumpus* website noted: "The organization is tidy and cohesive, offering a backdrop of stability when language itself turns unstable."

The poems sit alone on the page, surrounded by ample expanses of white. The effect results in a mirroring of the suggested narrator, that of a modern teenager: yearning, lonely, philosophical, and at times giddy. While the narrative perspective shifts from third to first person throughout the sections, a tone of lonesomeness, wistfulness, and contemplative is present throughout. Seth Abramson in *Huffington Post* wrote: "Wong's language is simple, earnest, and unadorned, and her reflections generally brief, to-the-point, and reflective—without the concurrent noodling of reflexive sentimentalism."

■ Biographical and Critical Sources

PERIODICALS

Publishers Weekly, May 15, 2017, review of *Elsa: An Unauthorized Autobiography*.

ONLINE

Coldfront http://coldfrontmag.com/ (July 20, 2012), Steven Karl, author interview.

Diagram http://thediagram.com/ (February 15, 2018), Tony Mancus, review of *How to Survive a Hotel Fire*.

Huffington Post, https://www.huffingtonpost.com/ (July 1, 2012), Seth Abramson, review of *How to Survive a Hotel Fire*.

Rumpus, http://therumpus.net/ (October 17, 2012), April Naoko Heck, review of *How to Survive a Hotel Fire*.

Sink, http://sinkreview.org/ (February 15, 2018), Stephanie Burns, review of *How to Survive a Hotel Fire*.*

Gareth Worthington

1980-

■ Personal

Born 1980, in Plymouth, England. *Education:* B.Sc., Ph.D., BCMAS. *Hobbies and other interests:* Muay Thai martial arts; playing acoustic guitar; studying ancient history; and drawing.

■ Addresses

Home—Zurich, Switzerland.

■ Career

Writer, marine biologist, and pharmaceutical industry executive.

■ Writings

Children of the Fifth Sun, Vesuvian Books (Nashville, TN), 2017.
It Takes Death to Reach a Star, Vesuvian Books (Nashville, TN), 2018.

■ Sidelights

Gareth Worthington is a writer, marine biologist, and pharmaceutical industry executive. He holds a degree in marine biology and a doctorate in comparative endocrinology. He has lived in the United States, Portugal, Netherlands, Singapore, and Switzerland.

Worthington is also an acoustic guitar player and martial arts enthusiast. He has trained in Muay Thai at the Evolve MMA gym in Singapore and in mixed martial arts at Phoenix Sportkampf, Switzerland. Worthington lives in Zurich, Switzerland.

Children of the Fifth Sun opens with protagonist Kelly Graham, a photojournalist with a tortured past, specializing in underwater photography, and his friend and brother-in-law, Chris D'Souza, on assignment in the Amazon. The two are coerced by Freya Nilsson, a U.S. military operative, to help in a super secret mission. A contributor to *Kirkus Reviews* described the book as "an action-packed, globe-hopping science-fiction thriller that questions the validity of humankind's current version of evolutionary history."

The two underwater specialists learn that they are being recruited to retrieve a mysterious underwater orb, a device that will hopefully allow scientists to communicate with the even more mysterious creature named K'in. The K'in, the two discover, is part of an amphibious race that is thought to have evolved alongside humans. In the 1940s, Chinese explorers discovered a frozen corpse of one of these creatures in Siberia. The United States government stole the specimen, and have been conducting experiments on it since. In recent years, scientists were able to successfully clone the DNA of the creature, resulting in a live K'in.

The U.S. government wants desperately to be able to communicate with K'in. Graham and D'Souza are tasked with free diving to find the orb, and quickly, before the equally eager Chinese and Russian military get their hands on it. The plot is complicated when Graham learns that Victoria McKenzie, a scientist and Graham's former rival-cum-friend, will also be helping with the mission.

As the trio prepares to launch the search, information about the creature and the mysterious communication orb is leaked online, resulting in an international race to retrieve both. Tensions rise and time becomes crucial as a sort of World War

III seems imminent. A contributor to *Publishers Weekly* wrote: "Worthington's understanding of the complexities and possibilities of marine biology and endocrinology are evident" in the book.

Worthington told *CA:* "I wrote a lot as a teenager, mainly for school projects and then eventually on my own time during the summer holidays. I loved reading and watching movies and wanted to create my own stories.

"My work is strongly influenced by nonfiction; works on quantum physics, ancient history, predicted future. I like to incorporate as much as possible from facts and theories to make the reader wonder what is real and what is fiction.

"I create an outline, allowing 3,000 words per chapter, aiming for 80,000 words approximately. Then as I write I change things or research something that completely alters the trajectory and so I adjust. So a fluid structure, I'd say!

"The most surprising thing I have learned as a writer is how much one can improve as a writer. Each book I'm learning, and each time I feel I improve. You never finish becoming better.

"*Children of the Fifth Sun* is my first book and will always hold a special place. It's part of a trilogy, and in each book there is a huge chunk of myself poured in reflecting my learnings just being human. Those who know me can see me in the lead characters, especially Kelly.

"While my books are grounded sci-fi, they all have a very strong human element, be it dealing with loss, or crushing self-doubt, or preparing for the very future of our race. I hope people read and see themselves or someone they know, and perhaps reflect a little on why we are the way we are."

■ **Biographical and Critical Sources**

PERIODICALS

Publishers Weekly, May 22, 2017, review of *Children of the Fifth Sun*.

ONLINE

Kirkus Reviews, https://www.kirkusreviews.com/ (May 15, 2017), review of *Children of the Fifth Sun*.

My Life My Books My Escape, https://mylifemybooks myescape.wordpress.com/ (July 25, 2017), author interview.

Miles Young

1954-

■ Personal

Born June, 1954, in Carlisle, Cumbria, England. *Education:* Oxford University, graduated.

■ Addresses

Office—Bedford School, De Parys Ave., Bedford, Bedfordshire MK30 2TU, England.

■ Career

School administrator, former advertising executive, and writer. Lintas, London, England, executive, 1976-79; Allen Brady & Marsh, London, England, executive, 1979-83; Ogilvy & Mather, New York, NY, executive, 1983-90, regional director, 1990-95, head of Asia-Pacific operation, 1996-2009, CEO, 2009-15, chair, 2012-15; New College, Oxford University, England, warden, 2016—. Member of advisory board of Tsinghua University, Beijing; visiting professor at Xiamen University and Wanli Ningbo University. Served as leader of Westminster City Council.

■ Writings

Ogilvy on Advertising in the Digital Age, Bloomsbury USA (New York, NY), 2018.

■ Sidelights

Miles Young is a British former advertising executive best known for having led the esteemed advertising company Ogilvy & Mather. He served as the organization's CEO from 2009 to 2015 and also held the position of chair from 2012 to 2015. Young holds a degree from Oxford University. His first job in the advertising industry was with a London-based company called Lintas. Young left Lintas in 1979 to work for another firm called Allen Brady & Marsh. He joined Ogilvy & Mather in 1983. In 2015, Young announced that he had chosen to step down as CEO and chair in order to become the warden (or chief academic administrator) of his alma mater, Oxford University. He told Andrew McMains and Jesse Oxfeld, contributors to the online version of *Adweek:* "This was a difficult decision, but the attraction of moving to a senior academic position in the UK was very great."

In 2018, Young released *Ogilvy on Advertising in the Digital Age.* The book is a sequel to *Ogilvy on Advertising,* which was written by Ogilvy & Mather cofounder David Ogilvy and published in 1983. In Young's book, he begins by discussing the technological developments that have led to the digital age. He explains how the internet and social media have changed the ways in which people experience products and interact with brands. Young includes six case studies that illustrate how advertising functions in current times. He concludes the volume by offering predictions on how advertising will evolve in the near future. In an interview with Jennifer Risi, a writer on the *Huffington Post* website, Young explained: "I wanted to direct people back to David's book. . . . The point of this book is to say that the screenplay and the script may be different, but the process is very much the same. David believed in big, simple ideas, and one of the challenges of the digital age is that people have confused the medium with the message. In elevating digital platforms as we have, we've forgotten what really matters—what you say to people and how you say it to them."

Ogilvy on Advertising in the Digital Age received favorable assessments. Jennifer Adams, a reviewer in *Booklist*, commented: "This guide is a must-have for those in the advertising profession, including marketers, public-relations experts, [and] entrepreneurs." A *Kirkus Reviews* critic described the book as "a new bible for a new generation of pitchmen and-women." The same critic added: "Young's treatise makes a fine modern marketing 101 textbook—and at far below textbook prices, too."

■ Biographical and Critical Sources

PERIODICALS

Advertising Age, July 28, 2008, Rupal Parekh, "Young's Big Challenge at O&M: Following Legend Lazarus," article about author, p. 1.

Booklist, December 1, 2017, Jennifer Adams, review of *Ogilvy on Advertising in the Digital Age*, p. 11.

Campaign, July 25, 2008, John Tyler, "Young Takes Ogilvy Helm from Lazarus," article about author, p. 1.

Kirkus Reviews, November 1, 2017, review of *Ogilvy on Advertising in the Digital Age*.

Marketing, January 27, 1994, Alyson Cook, "Young, Gifted, and Blue," author interview, p. 39.

ONLINE

Adweek Online, http://www.adweek.com/ (July 28, 2008), Andrew McMains, author interview; (January 26, 2009), Andrew McMains, author interview; (June 17, 2015), Andrew McMains and Jesse Oxfeld, author interview.

Bedford School Website, https://www.bedfordschool.org.uk/ (March 21, 2018), article about author.

Campaign Online, https://www.campaignlive.com/ (October 10, 2016), article by author.

Huffington Post, https://www.huffingtonpost.com/ (November 7, 2017), Jennifer Risi, author interview.*

Manoush Zomorodi

■ Personal

Married Josh Robin (a reporter and anchor); children: two. *Education:* Attended Georgetown University.

■ Career

Writer. *Note to Self*, podcast host; Bored and Brilliant, founder, 2015; Infomagical, founder, 2016; the Privacy Paradox, founder, 2017. Former reporter and producer for BBC News and Thomson Reuters.

■ Awards, Honors

New York Press Club award; Outstanding Host, Alliance for Women in Media, 2014; Best Tech Podcast designation, Academy of Podcasters, 2017, for *Note to Self.*

■ Writings

Bored and Brilliant: How Spacing Out Can Unlock Your Most Productive and Creative Self, St. Martin's Press (New York, NY), 2017.

■ Sidelights

Manoush Zomorodi is a writer and podcast host. She hosts *Note to Self*, a podcast from WNYC Studios, which examines technology in the modern world and how it shapes our lives and identities. *Note to Self* was named Best Tech Podcast by the Academy of Podcasters in 2017.

In 2015, Zomorodi launched Bored and Brilliant, a project intended to help people reconsider the significance of their relationships with their phones and increase productivity. Following Bored and Brilliant, she developed a project called Infomagical, which sought to help people to handle information overload. In 2017 Zomorodi launched the Privacy Paradox, an interactive plan that helps users take control of their digital identity.

Zomorodi grew up in Princeton, New Jersey, and attended Georgetown University. She lives in Brooklyn with her husband, NY1 reporter and anchor Josh Robin, and their two children.

The concept for *Bored and Brilliant: How Spacing Out Can Unlock Your Most Productive and Creative Self* arose out of Zomorodi's 2015 social experiment of the same name. Following Zomorodi's call to listeners to disconnect from their phones for a week, she received 20,000 responses about how the challenge influenced listeners' abilities to be productive and creative. Zomorodi includes this feedback in the book, along with research from social scientists and psychologists regarding boredom. The culminating product is an "illuminating discussion of boredom's history as a concept," wrote a contributor to *Publishers Weekly.*

In the book Zomordi explains how boredom is key to creativity. When we are performing monotonous tasks or are in an non-stimulating environment, our body goes into autopilot mode, a circumstance that encourages our brain's synapses to begin firing in new ways. Contrastingly, according to neuroscientists, when we are constantly switching our attention between numerous devices, not only does our ability to form novel, creative thoughts decrease, but our stress levels increase. Resisting the urge to check our devices is ever more difficult, Zomorodi explains, as the engineers that build the platforms are constantly constructing new ways to engage and divide our attention.

Zomorodi also consults social scientists, who explain that in experiments in which individuals that are forced to do a monotonous task before a creative one are much more creative in their approach than are those who are thrown into the task without the boredom-inciting start. In addition to providing scientific reasoning for her argument, Zomorodi provides a list of six steps readers can take to help them disconnect from distraction and plug into boredom, and thus creativity. Amy Scribner in *BookPage* described the book as "an important reminder that we are not beholden to our devices."

■ Biographical and Critical Sources

PERIODICALS

BookPage, September, 2017, Amy Scribner, review of *Bored and Brilliant: How Spacing Out Can Unlock Your Most Productive and Creative Self.*

Publishers Weekly, May 29, 2017, review of *Bored and Brilliant.*

ONLINE

Dijulius Group, https://thedijuliusgroup.com/ (October 4, 2017), John DiJulius, review of *Bored and Brilliant.*

Forbes, https://www.forbes.com/ (December 30, 2017), Dan Schawbel, "How Boredom Can Actually Make You More Successful," review of *Bored and Brilliant.*

Freedom Matters, https://freedom.to/ (October 6, 2017), Alexandra Dempsey, review of *Bored and Brilliant.*

Ladders, https://www.theladders.com/ (October 3, 2017), Monica Torres "This Is How Boredom Can Make You Brilliant," review of *Bored and Brilliant.*

NPR.org, https://www.npr.org/ (February 2, 2015), Audie Cornish, "It's Time to Get Bored—and Brilliant."

NY Journal of Books, https://www.nyjournalofbooks.com/ (September 4, 2017), Roberta E. Winter, review of *Bored and Brilliant.*

Stacks, http://www.thestacks-books.org/ (September 13, 2017), Emily Thibodeaux, review of *Bored and Brilliant.*

Utah Coalition for Educational Technology, https://www.ucet.org/ (December 11, 2017), Tricia Jackson, review of *Bored and Brilliant.*

Value Walk, http://www.valuewalk.com/ (September 14, 2017), Brenda Jubin, review of *Bored and Brilliant.*

Wired, https://www.wired.com/ (August 30, 2017), Miranda Katz, review of *Bored and Brilliant.**